The Good, Bad, & Ugly

Learning God's Word through Bible Characters

Hunter Sherman

LWG Publications
Springfield, Missouri

ISBN-10: 1-947153-08-0
ISBN-13: 978-1-947153-08-0

Cover Design: Eowyn Riggins
Layout: Rachel Greene

Contents

Foreword

I have known Dr. Hunter Sherman for more than 45 years—and yet he still seems so young. Throughout his career as a preacher, teacher, pastor, and all-around servant of the Lord, he has demonstrated an impressive flair for scholarship while never sacrificing practicality.

In this book, *'THE GOOD, THE BAD, & THE UGLY: Learning God's Word through Biblical Characters,'* Dr. Sherman brings compelling characters—too often seen as one-dimensional—to life. At times we see treasures in jars of clay, at other times we see toxins in similar containers. And all along the way, we learn vital lessons about life, work, spirituality, heaven, hell, community, sin, destruction, joy, and sorrow.

The Bible is primarily a book about God and His dealings with people. We must be ever fascinated with HIM, but it's okay to be curious about the human side of things. Designed with a year-long journey in mind, this book will, I believe, become a vital tool for serious people of faith who seek to live authentic and godly lives before a watching world.

David R. Stokes
Fairfax, Virginia

Introduction

This book began years ago. I have always thought the Bible was best understood by making the people who appeared in the stories real. That is to say they were not "Super Saints" or amazing "Super Heroes." They were real people like you and me. They had good points and bad points, and they are best understood when we consider the culture in which they lived and the advance of the age in which they were participants.

The Bible was not meant to be a theological answer book or a theological textbook. It was meant to tell us the story of salvation and how much God loves humankind created in His very own image. Too often our study of the Bible is merely an academic exercise with little or no practical equivalence or expectation. Theology is derived from the Bible and our interpretation of the Bible must never be derived from our theology.

I have been privileged to teach the Bible for more than 50 years. In that length of time I have seen the biblical literacy of our culture decline. Bible stories which used to be known by everyone are now often unknown and totally mysterious to people—even those in our pews. It was because of this that this series of studies was first contemplated.

When we examine any subject we always look through "lenses." Everything we see and hear is interpreted through these lenses. The most common lenses used in our age are politics, economics, and social impact. Our decisions on what we understand and how we act are regularly filtered through these lenses. The combination of these three lenses creates our mental mindset or worldview.

I propose we must regularly add a fourth lens to our understanding of everything. That lens is the Scripture. We must filter our understanding and actions through the lens of Scripture as well as politics, economics, and social impact. This series was first produced to help amplify our understanding of Scripture so we can use it as the primary "lens" through which we observe and interact with our world.

This study was first produced as a series of monthly expositionally-based Bible character studies with applications. I produced 30 studies per month for one year. The New Testament writers said these things were written for our learning and understanding. Learning without application is useless. If what we know does not affect how we live, the learning process has not been completed.

At the end of each of these character studies I have added questions which are intended to make the reader interact with the Bible and the devotional for that day. For years at Bible College I taught a class on Bible interpretation called "hermeneutics." The course was designed to teach students how to interpret the Bible on their own. In the process of that instruction I tried to

teach them to ask certain basic questions; Who, What, Where, When, and Why. To that very standard list of questions I always encouraged each student to add one final question, "So what?"

It is with that same purpose in mind this series of Bible studies has been produced. It is my hope as each reader works through this book, they will gain a new insight into the stories contained in God's Word and an even greater insight into themselves as they react with God's Word.

I especially want to thank my wife for her support and patience as I wrote this book. She has proofread the entire document several times. I have relied on her questions and understanding to help me realize what she means when she says, "You can't say that, no one will understand." I realize sometimes academicians are too academic. The practicality and applicability of much of this document is a result of her efforts.

The publishing house, "LWG PUBLICATIONS" is an acronym created with letters of her first name and the first names of my children.

Thank you; Louisa, Whitnae and Garrett

Dr. Hunter Sherman
Springfield, Missouri

The Good,
Bad,
& Ugly

Book One

1. Adam: the first man	Genesis 1:26-2:17
2. Adam's responsibility	Genesis 1:26; 2:15
3. Eve: the first woman	Genesis 2:18-3:24
4. Cain: 1st son & 1st murderer	Genesis 4
5. Abel: the 2nd son	Genesis 4:1-18
6. Seth	Genesis 4:25-26
7. Enoch: who walked with God	Genesis 5:18-24
8. Noah: his obedience	Genesis 6:1-9:17
9. Noah: after the flood	Genesis 8, 9
10. Nimrod: the builder	Genesis 10, 11
11. Nimrod: the rebel	Genesis 10, 11
12. Abraham's father: Terah	Genesis 11, 12
13. Lot: Abraham's nephew	Genesis 11-14, 19; 2
14. Lot's last chapter	Genesis 19
15. Abraham: called and chosen	Genesis 15, 17, 22
16. Abraham: obedient and tested	Hebrews 11:8-22
17. Abraham and God	Genesis 12:1-3
18. Abraham's retreat	Genesis 12:10-20
19. Abraham's faith	Genesis 13:8-18
20. Abraham failure at Gerar	Genesis 20
21. Abraham's sacrifice	Genesis 22
22. Abraham: the businessman	Genesis 23
23. Melchizedek: Abraham's friend	Genesis 14
24. Sarah: Abraham's wife	Genesis 16, 18, 21
25. Hagar: Abraham & Hagar	Genesis 16
26. Ishmael	Genesis 16, 17, 25
27. Laban	Genesis 24, 27-30
28. Abraham's servant: Eliezer	Genesis 24
29. Jacob	Genesis 31, 32
30. Leah: the unexpected bride	Genesis 29, 30, 35, 4

Adam the first man — Genesis 1:26-2:17

And the LORD God formed man of the dust of the ground, and breathed into his nostrils the breath of life; and man became a living soul.
Genesis 2:7

The name Adam means "of the ground" or "taken out of the red earth." According to the gospel of Luke 3:38, Adam is the human son of God.

We do not know the exact location of the Garden of Eden. However, two of the rivers which are mentioned in the text, the Tigris and Euphrates, are known today and they are in the Middle East between Iran and Iraq. So, it is a logical assumption this is the area where Adam was created and lived.

Adam is the beginning of all of mankind. He was created directly by God. He was created in "our (God's) image." Being created in the image of God shows Adam was far different from all the rest of God's creation. He is the unique son of God for he was created in God's own image by God Himself.

Adam was created to have fellowship with God; to walk and talk with God on a daily basis. We gather this as fact from the text in Genesis. This is what God and mankind did on a regular basis before sin entered the world. Adam was not some kind of prehistoric caveman! There is no hint of evolution within the Scriptures. Adam was a human created with all the abilities which mankind has ever possessed. He was a perfect creation in every way.

God took a rib from Adam (2:21-25) and created Eve. These two people, the first humans to walk the face of the earth were not the prehistoric creations we see depicted in the illustrations teaching the theory of evolution. They were fully human; their mental capacities were as developed as those of 21st-century mankind. In fact, in many ways they were probably more advanced and more capable than humanity is today. Remember, they were created by God and created in His image; therefore, they were perfect. That is something none of us can claim!

God promised Adam mankind would survive the devastation brought about by sin and continue to exist. To Adam He said, "Because you listened to your wife and ate from the tree about which I commanded you, 'You must not eat of it,' cursed is the ground because of you; through painful toil you will eat of it all the days of your life. It will produce thorns and thistles for you, and you will eat the plants of the field. By the sweat of your brow you will eat your food until you return to the ground, since from it you were taken; for dust you are and to dust you will return." Genesis 3:17-19

There are many questions we cannot answer about Adam. We do not know what he looked like. We do not know what language he spoke. We do know, however, that Adam was fully human and that he was individually and specifically created by God.

He was placed in a perfect environment, the Garden of Eden. One thing the first humans did not possess was the perspective "gained" by having lived elsewhere. As far as they knew the entire universe was as beautiful and perfect as the place where they lived. That, of course, was true! God had created the universe and everything in it and He pronounced that everything was "good"!

God created man with every possibility and opportunity to live in fellowship with Him.

We should praise God! He loves us enough we are created in His very own image.

We should praise God!

He loves us enough He sent His only Son to assure we can have fellowship with Him throughout eternity!

Adam's Responsibility — Genesis 1:26-31; 2:7-15; 3:17-19

Then God said, "Let us make man in our image, in our likeness, and let them rule over the fish of the sea and the birds of the air, over the livestock, over all the earth, and over all the creatures that move along the ground." 1:26

And the LORD God took the man, and put him into the Garden of Eden to dress it and to keep it. 2:15

Who and What

Adam was placed in the Garden of Eden by God and was given the assignment of caring for the garden. He was given "dominion" over all the creatures on the face of the earth. The idea of dominion in the Hebrew language does carry the idea of control and rule, but even more it contains the idea of careful stewardship of what one is in charge to rule over.

Adam was also made the head of the household and he was responsible to lead his family and teach them to obey God. He was given the position of head of the household by God. It was his responsibility to lead and guide his family to obey God.

Why?

All of man's potentialities, all of mankind's tremendous opportunities and all of mankind's capacity for failure were intrinsic in Adam. He was responsible to properly care for everything God had created. He was to instruct his descendants in their responsibilities in relationship to God and His creation. God intended mankind to subordinate all His creation and He also intended for mankind to properly care for His creation. I am sure Adam understood his responsibility quite literally. He was to pass God's creation along to the next generation in as good a condition as he had received it from God.

Adam was not able to fulfill this responsibility because of the fall. Because of the fall and the resulting sin nature there is constant struggle between mankind and his environment. Sin and death entered the world and created turmoil within the relationship between mankind and God. But we often overlook the fact sin has also altered the relationship between mankind and the universe which God created. Man seems to have mastered much of God's creation and in the process, much has been destroyed.

Adam's failure came in eating of the fruit of the tree of the knowledge of good and evil. The apostle Paul makes the point in I Timothy 2; Eve was deceived, and Adam was not. Adam loved his wife and chose her instead of God. As a result, in him, all of mankind fell. What that means is Adam's disobedience brought into his lineage forever what theologians have come to call the sin nature. The image of God in mankind was marred by sin.

Adam had no one to blame but himself! He was in a perfect environment. He had a perfect spouse, created by God especially for him. When given a choice he refused to accept the leadership role God had spelled out for him.

We are all descendants of Adam and we carry on with his responsibilities.

How do you care for the environment in which God has placed you?

What specific responsibilities has God given you to carry out for Him?

The man said, "This is now bone of my bones and flesh of my flesh; she shall be called 'woman,' for she was taken out of man." Genesis 2:23

The name Eve means "life" or "living". Adam named his wife Eve, because she would become the mother of all the living.

What we said about the location of the Garden of Eden applies to Eve as well. They were both created and placed in the garden by God. When they were expelled from the garden after sinning, they probably would not have traveled very far geographically. The time element for Eve is the same as that for Adam.

Woman is the feminine of man. She is not only man's helper, but also his complement and is essential to the completion of his being. Matthew Henry's comment on the creation of Eve is excellent. "If man is the head, she is the crown, a crown to her husband, the crown of visible creation. The man was dust refined, but the woman was double refined, one removed further from the Earth . . . The woman was made of a rib out of the side of Adam; not made out of his head to rule over him, nor out of his feet to be trampled upon by him, but out of his side to be equal with him, under his arm to be protected and near his heart to be loved."

Eve was Adam's second self and differed from him in sex, not in nature. Being first created gave Adam leadership but not superiority. Both man and woman were created with the need for mutual interdependence.

Throughout history, man, through pride, ignorance or moral perversion has treated woman as greatly inferior and has enslaved and degraded her accordingly. Among many groups of people today woman is only property; the burden bearer and the child producer with no rights whatsoever in equality with man.

Eve was the victim of the lies of Satan in the Garden of Eden. Satan enticed her to disobey God by offering her the promise of equality with God.

She saw that the tree was "good for food, pleasant to the eyes and a tree to be desired to make one wise.
Satan used these three avenues to break down her defenses and deceive her. She fell victim to:

- The lust of the eyes; "pleasant to the eyes"
- The lust of the flesh; "good for food."
- The pride of life; "to be desired to make one wise.

Also notice the specific tactic Satan used was a direct frontal assault on God. He attacked.

- God's word; "You will not die."
- God's will; "God knows your eyes will be opened."
- God's wisdom; "You will be like God, knowing good and evil."

We learn from Eve to trust God in everything He says!

His word is the absolute authority for all situations.

His will is always best for us and the world.

His wisdom will sustain us through every situation.

We thank God He has created man and woman interdependent and complementary.

Cain: The first son and the first murderer Genesis 4; Numbers 24:22; Hebrews 11:4; 1 John 3:12; Jude 11

Do not be like Cain, who belonged to the evil one and murdered his brother. And why did he murder him? Because his own actions were evil and his brother's were righteous.

His name means acquisition, fabrication or possessed. When he was born Eve said, "I have gotten a man from the Lord."

We do not know the exact geographic location where Adam and his family lived. We can guess that it was somewhere in the region of Mesopotamia, but we also need to remember geography has changed a great deal since the universal flood in Noah's day.

He was the first person to be born naturally on the Earth. He committed the first murder. He was involved in agriculture as a trade. He did not fear God and appears to have been a very unhappy man.

Cain was jealous of his brother who was accepted by God. His brother was happy in his calling. As a result, Cain's heart was without love for God and he refused to be obedient, his sacrifice was rejected.

According to the writer of the Proverbs, "The LORD detests the sacrifice of the wicked, but the prayer of the upright pleases him" (15:8). Cain was right in his desire to bring an offering, but he was wrong in the way he gave the offering (Genesis 4:3). He wanted to be near to God by virtue of his own labor.

Abel brought the firstborn of the flock, a blood offering. God's acceptance of this offering angered Cain. His anger grew into uncontrolled passion. When he and his brother were in the field together Cain murdered his brother and buried his body. Even though he tried to hide his crime God held him accountable.

God judged Cain by placing a Mark on him. The Scriptures do not tell us what the mark was like, but it was enough to make him feel the anger of God and the hatred of other men. Cain's punishment reveals to us God is holy and must judge sin, but we also see judgment mingled with mercy. Whatever mark God placed on Cain it disgraced him in the eyes of all who saw him, however it also offered protection against those seeking revenge for the murder he had committed.
It was a judgment from God, but it was also a sign of God's compassion.

The first murder was a result of jealousy between brothers.

Cain was the first hard-hearted and unrepentant man.

He went from God's presence with less than the punishment he first feared (4:14), but with resentment and hatred because of the consequences of the deed.

No event is finished in itself; no sin is limited to the time it is committed.

Then, after desire has conceived, it gives birth to sin; and sin, when it is full-grown, gives birth to death. James 1:15

Each act of sin forms a link in a chain, which, unless God breaks it in grace, meshes with eternity.

Abel — Genesis 4:1-18, Hebrews 11:4

By faith Abel offered God a better sacrifice than Cain did. By faith he was commended as a righteous man, when God spoke well of his offerings. And by faith he still speaks, even though he is dead.

Who
His name means "breath" or "brief and transitory". This name was perhaps inspired by God in anticipation of the brevity of his life.

Where?
His life was lived near his parents; in the Middle East somewhere near the Garden of Eden.

When?
Once again, we cannot be specific in fixing a time element in the historical framework for his lifetime. He and his brother were the first children born on the Earth. In his early life experience and the events of his death we have the first account of family life.

What?
Abel was the victim of the first murder. In the conflict between him and his brother we see the result of sin and the impact it has on all of mankind. Cain killed his brother out of envy.

How?
Abel was a shepherd and brought the best of his flock to offer to God. Cain was a farmer and brought the produce of the ground to offer to God. We are told God had respect for the offering of Abel but rejected the offering of his brother.

There are several references to Abel in the New Testament. Jesus refers to him when he is condemning the Pharisees in Matthew 23.

The book of Hebrews lists Abel in the Hall of Fame of Christian heroes in chapter 11. In fact, the writer of Hebrews goes on to say, "You have come to Jesus, the one who mediates the new covenant between God and people, and to the sprinkled blood, which speaks of forgiveness instead of crying out for vengeance like the blood of Abel."

In the Old Testament Abel's death was seen as a cry for vengeance. In the New Testament his death is contrasted to the death of Jesus Christ which speaks of forgiveness and not vengeance.

So what?
The effects of sin; in the account of Cain and Abel we see how quickly and how completely the effects of sin can enter into and destroy family life.

Our nature; we also see how thoroughly sin has penetrated the nature of man. In the first generation after creation Satan can create conflict within the family which results in one family member murdering another.

The character of God; we also see in this account how completely honest God is with His creation. The wages of sin is death and because of the sin of Adam all are under that death sentence.

We see the love of God when He confronted Cain about the death of Abel, He offered salvation and redemption to the first murderer on Earth.

We should be absolutely awestruck by the mercy and love of God!

Seth — Genesis 4:25, 26; 5:3-8; 1 Chronicles 1:1; Luke 3:38

Adam lay with his wife again, and she gave birth to a son and named him Seth, saying, "God has granted e another child in place of Abel, since Cain killed him."

The name Seth means "compensation, appointed or substituted."

We do not know the exact geographic location where Adam and his family lived. We can guess it was somewhere in the region of Mesopotamia, but we also need to remember geography has changed a great deal since the universal flood in Noah's day.

He was the third son of Adam and Eve. He was born after the murder of Abel, when Adam was 130 years old. Seth was seen by his parents as Abel's substitute. He was the father of Enos and died at age 912.

Seth was born sometime after the murder of his brother. We do not know how much time was involved in these early years of life on earth. Cain and Abel had both lived long enough to become full-grown men. We have no record of other children being born to Adam and Eve; therefore, we can imagine the two boys, now grown men, were the only other inhabitants of the earth.

When Abel was murdered it must have devastated Adam and Eve. I am sure the event caused many questions and doubts! We do know by comparing Scripture with Scripture that Adam was 130 years old when Seth was born. We do not know where Cain was living at the time or what his relationship was with his parents.

Seth was seen by his parents as a "replacement" for their firstborn son. For some time, I am sure he was the total focus of their life. It would be interesting to know how Seth was raised, what he was taught and how he was instructed in his relationship with God. We can wonder how careful and protective they were of this new resident.

Why?

Seth represents God keeping His word and moving to fulfill His promise to Adam and Eve. In Genesis 3, when God met with Adam and Eve after the fall, He made a promise. As God confronted a world now infected with sin He spoke first with the serpent, then with Eve and finally with Adam. In speaking with the serpent, He said, *"I will put enmity between you and the woman, and between your offspring and hers; he will crush your head, and you will strike his heel"* (Gen 3:15).

Among Bible students this passage is regarded as the very first promise in the Scriptures of salvation. Christ was crucified and crucifixion is accomplished by nailing the hands and feet of the victim to a cross. One nail is used to pierce both feet; it goes into the top of the first foot and exit the second foot by piercing the heel. Seth was God's provision to complete His promise of salvation.

We see here one of Satan's first attempts to thwart the plan of God. He had tried to destroy Adam and Eve through the sin in the garden.

Throughout the Old Testament we have records of Satan's attempt to short-circuit God's plan of salvation.

We should never doubt today Satan is still doing everything He can to keep God's plan from succeeding!

We should also rejoice in the assurance that God knows the end from the beginning, and He will always bring his plans to completion.

Enoch — Genesis 5:18-24

Enoch walked with God; then he was no more, because God took him away.

Who?
Enoch means "dedicated or teacher". The Bible gives us no information about the location where he lived his life. Most believe it was in the same geographic area of Mesopotamia where the other early biblical characters lived. According to the book of Jude, Enoch lived in the seventh generation after Adam.

Our entire biography of Enoch is given in Genesis 5 in only six verses. We know absolutely nothing of Enoch relating to his profession or his status in life. If it were not for the way Enoch left the earth, he would be most famous for his first son.

Enoch's first son was Methuselah. He had other sons and daughters, but they are minor biblical characters compared to their father and his first son. Enoch was 65 years old when Methuselah was born. Methuselah lived 969 years, which is longer than any other person in recorded history.

Also recorded in the book of Jude is the fact Enoch was a preacher. Therefore, he becomes the first preacher recorded in human history. He is also called a prophet. He warned his listeners of the judgments of God which were coming in the days ahead.

Enoch, the seventh from Adam, prophesied about these men: "See, the Lord is coming with thousands upon thousands of his holy ones to judge everyone, and to convict all the ungodly of all the ungodly acts they have done in the ungodly way, and of all the harsh words ungodly sinners have spoken against him." The judgment spoken of in this passage no doubt came to pass in the great flood of Noah.

Enoch is best known as being one of only two men recorded in the Scriptures who were taken into heaven without experiencing physical death. This is recorded in Genesis and noted in Hebrews 11:5, "By faith Enoch was taken from this life, so that he did not experience death; he could not be found, because God had taken him away. For before he was taken, he was commended as one who pleased God."

According to Genesis 5:22; Enoch walked with God; he lived a life of daily fellowship and communion with God. He also possessed a great faith as noted in the passage in Hebrews. But perhaps the greatest comment on his life was that he "pleased God."

Enoch walked in close communion with God daily. Walking with someone implies a steady growth in relationship between the two who were walking together. Enoch was a man who lived his life in constant companionship with God. He did not attempt to accomplish a relationship with God based on his own works. Only two men in the entire history of mankind have never died; Enoch and Elijah.

Enoch had this testimony; he pleased God. He lived and talked with God enough he was able to prophesy concerning the return of the Lord to the Earth.

What can we learn from this amazing man? It is possible to walk with God daily.

It is possible our words and actions will be remembered long after our time on earth is done.

What kind of a legacy are you leaving for those who follow in your footsteps?

Noah: His Obedience — Genesis 6:1-9:17

Noah means "rest or quiet". He is the son of Lamech and tenth generation from Adam. Beyond the record of his birth the Scriptures tell us nothing of Noah until he was 500 years old.

We are given no specifics as to the location of Noah's birth. The only geographic identification we can use to fix a location is the ark came to rest on Mount Ararat, located in modern-day eastern Turkey.

Noah was given his name because his father had been told by God this child would provide comfort for the world which was suffering from sin (Genesis 6:9). We are told Noah was a righteous and blameless man among the people of his time. He is credited as being a godly man who walked with God.

Because of his faithfulness and love for God Noah was chosen to build the ark which would preserve the world through the flood. The wickedness of humanity had grown to the point where we are told every thought and imagination of mankind was evil.

God gave Noah the plans and the task of building the Ark when he was 480 years old. We are told building of the ark took 120 years (1 Peter 3:20; 2 Peter 2:5). By the age of 500 Noah had three sons; Shem, Ham and Japheth. This tells us these boys never knew a time in their lifetime when Noah was not building the Ark.

It is instructive for us to realize he was such a consistent man of God that despite his strange lifestyle when it came time to go into the ark all his family believed in what he was doing enough to go with him. This fact is often overlooked when we think of Noah. **He was a great father!**

After surviving the flood Noah and his family emerged into what truly would become, for them, a "brave new world." Immediately after leaving the ark Noah and his family built an altar and worshipped God (Genesis 8:20). At this time God gave Noah and his family the sign of the rainbow and the promise as long as the earth remained there would be springtime and harvest, cold and heat, winter and summer, day and night.

Noah's lifestyle and his righteousness are grouped with the lives of Job and Daniel by the prophet Ezekiel (Ezekiel 14:14, 20).

Noah is commended for his fear of God and his faith by the writer of Hebrews (11:7). The writer notes it was his fear of God which caused him to build the ark. He also remarks it was Noah's faith and obedience which saved his own family and condemned the world for its sin.

Jesus referred to Noah as He was teaching His disciples. He told His followers the conditions on the earth would be like the conditions in the days of Noah just before God would destroy the earth with fire (Matthew 24; Luke 17).

"Doing the will of God leaves me no time for disputing about His plans," said George MacDonald. Noah had little time to question the cloudless sky and even less time to be attracted to the carefree and corrupt society around him. He had been told to build. He obeyed. Obedience is the first fruit of trust. This must have been a habitual part of him; it is true obedience is not only performed by the body; it lives in the heart.

Based on the conditions we see in the world today; do you think Jesus is coming soon?

Noah: After the flood — Genesis 8, 9

The ark landed on Mount Ararat which today is in the rugged terrain of northeastern Turkey. The geography of the world had completely changed. Noah and his family had been in the ark for over a year. When they come out of the ark after the flood, they found a very strange and different new world.

"God remembered Noah," says Genesis 8:1. These words are packed with meaning. He and his family had been alone in an unbelievable watery world. The geographic structure they had known was gone. The entire world they had known drowned. All life had been destroyed beneath those waters. These eight survivors undoubtedly experienced anxiety and unbelievable loneliness.

No hint is given in the story of what went on in Noah's mind, but his faith is still apparent. Had God forgotten him? The question could have been a strong insistent one. He released the raven and then the dove, giving us a symbol of peace. God gave him and his family the symbol of the rainbow and the promise of protection.

Faith was the mark of Noah's character, but there were still more problems to endure. In the latter part of this chapter we read of a very strange event in the life of Noah. The man who had earned a place in the honor roll of the faithful is seen drunk on the floor of his tent.

We could have been spared this picture, but the Bible is completely honest in its revelation of the truth about the men and women who are part of God's story. There is much we do not know about the circumstances of these events. Tensions, sadness, joy, we might speculate endlessly concerning what was behind Noah's excess; but we do not know the cause.

We must look at the situation as it is recorded in the biblical record. No amount of speculation or explanation will make the situation any clearer or any better. Here was a good man defeated, in a drunken shameful condition. The situation brought out the crudeness of one of his sons, and the decency and honor of the other two.

Noah had lived through years of tension, while building the ark and his faith had triumphed. Yet he failed and fell, like Elijah, in a moment of victory. Perhaps, the hour of achievement, when the long-borne burden is suddenly lifted, is the time of the most dangerous assault. The mind relaxes from its long guard, and evil finds a new chink in the armor.

The three boys who grew up building the ark with dad and had faith enough to join him on the year-long "cruise" are now faced with a crisis in their own lives. This is a new experience for them; a major failure in the life of their father. One son, Ham, reacts in a way that would shame his father. The other two, Shem and Japheth, remember their teaching and honor their father. As good a father as Noah was one of his sons was still ready to mock him.

It seems the moment of triumph often gives way to the experience of defeat.

Peter warns his readers to always be on guard because the devil is walking about as a roaring lion.

He is looking for any opportunity to destroy someone who trusts God.

It is encouraging to remember that despite this failure Noah is remembered in Hebrews 11 for his faith which saved his family.

Nimrod: The builder — Genesis 10, 11

Cush was the father of Nimrod, who grew to be a mighty warrior on the earth. Genesis 10:8

Nimrod was an amazing man. He was a descendent of Cush, Ham's grandson. Scripture tells us he was a "mighty man in the earth." He was the first of Noah's descendants who became famous for his bold and courageous deeds. Nimrod is only referred to by name three times in the Scripture. With these few mentions it seems strange we assign to him such a great importance. His importance in the Bible comes from his association with Babylon and the area surrounding that great city. The prophet Micah, hundreds of years later, referred to this entire area as the land of Nimrod (Micah 5:6).

We are unable to determine a firm date for the lifetime of Nimrod. It is obvious he lived within a few hundred years of the flood described in Genesis. All the ancient legends of Mesopotamia center on the building at Babylon. Secular history and many ancient traditions tell us Nimrod married a woman named Semrimus. According to several of the legends these two people claimed their son, Tammuz, was the fulfillment of the prophecy given in Genesis 3:15.

It is easy to see how legends would build up early in human history around someone as great and famous as Nimrod. He is referred to as, "a mighty hunter before the Lord." He was a man of "renown." That is to say he was "world famous."

What did Nimrod build? He is associated in all Jewish writing with the building of the tower of Babel. But he built several other things beside this physical structure.

He built his own stature and fame. He used his ability and cunning as a hunter to assure those near him that he would defend them from the wild animals and other danger. He was able to protect them in a very harsh environment as animals continued to multiply on the earth much more rapidly than man.

He was able to build a consensus among those living in the area that they could depend on him as their "defender." His strength and power became proverbial. Scripture also implies with the phrase, "a mighty hunter" that he was known to hunt anyone who opposed him.

Nimrod corrupted the existing patriarchal structure of Genesis by setting up rule based on personality and personal achievement rather than family and social structure.

Nimrod used his fame and the strength of his personality to lead in the building of the tower of Babel. The origin of Babel was the origin of Babylon and all organized rejection of God. The book of Revelation uses the terminology "mystery Babylon the great." In relationship to the destruction of Babylon in the end times the phrase is used "Babylon the great is fallen."

The tower was no doubt spoken of as a refuge and a place of safety in the time of danger, but, was a move away from dependence on God. Nimrod was able to organize the community in such a way that they would work together and make the materials necessary to build such a structure.

This was the first achievement of such community within the history of mankind.

Nimrod built his power upon himself and diminished mankind's allegiance to God.

Nimrod built more than a tower.

Nimrod built more than cities.

He built a mind-set which lacked dependence on God.

Nimrod: The rebel — Genesis 10, 11

He was a mighty hunter before the LORD; that is why it is said, "Like Nimrod, a mighty hunter before the LORD."

The name Nimrod means "let us rebel or rebellion". The Hebrew name was no doubt given to this man by his contemporaries. He must have been one who was always stirring up rebellion. He challenged the existing patriarchal order of society and set himself up in a position of leadership.

Josephus tells us Nimrod persuaded mankind not to attribute their happiness to God, but to think that his own excellence was the source of their prosperity and blessing. He soon changed his rule into one of tyranny. He purposely moved men away from trusting God to trusting him and his power structure.

The Targum of Jonathan says: "from the foundation of the world no one was like Nimrod, powerful in hunting and in rebellious activity against the Lord."

The Jerusalem Targum says: he was powerful in hunting and in wickedness before the Lord, for he was a hunter of the sons of men, and he said to them, "Depart from the judgment of the Lord and adhere to the judgment of Nimrod!" Therefore, it is said; "As Nimrod is the strong one, strong in hunting and in wickedness before the Lord."

There is a Chaldean paraphrase of 1 Chronicles 1:10 which says; "Cush begat Nimrod and he began to prevail in wickedness, for he shed innocent blood and rebelled against Jehovah."

Nimrod was the leader in the building of the tower of Babel and the city of Babylon. He was the founder of the first Babylonian Empire. That Empire adopted the characteristics of its founder and became a great antagonist of God and opponent of God's people.

Nimrod was the first open opponent of God. He told his followers, "Let us make a name and build a tower. The top of which will reach into the heavens." The portion of these directions which is its reassurance in the English translation centers on the use of the word "name."

In particular, the Hebrew word for "name" is "shem." In his charge to begin building the tower of Babel Nimrod is creating a direct confrontation with the God of Shem and his descendants. As we examine the three lines of descendants from Noah's three sons, Shem, Ham and Japheth, the descendants of Shem are described as people who seek God.

Nimrod told his followers let us make us a name like the name of Shem. We no longer need to worship the God of Shem. We can take care of ourselves and there is no need to scatter abroad upon all the face of the earth. We will defend ourselves here and become a mighty empire with this tower.

The tower of Babel was erected in rebellion to God and in direct opposition to his command to spread abroad and repopulate the earth. It represented mankind trying to create a unity, falsely constructed by Nimrod, and take care of all of mankind's needs.

Mankind wanted to be self-sufficient and have no need of God.

Nimrod was undeniably the first rebel to openly organize against God.

The rebellion which he began both politically and religiously has been traced down through the ages and exists in many ways even in the 21st century.

Abraham's Father: Terah
Genesis 11, 12; Joshua 24:1-5

Joshua said to all the people, "This is what the LORD, the God of Israel, says: 'Long ago your forefathers, including Terah the father of Abraham and Nahor, lived beyond the River and worshiped other gods.

The name Terah means "to breathe or to blow." Terah lived in Ur of the Chaldees which was in what today is southwestern Iraq near the confluence of the Tigris and Euphrates rivers.

When

He and his family were prosperous residents of Ur around 2100 B.C. He was the father of Abram (Abraham), Nahor, and Haran. Though Abram is listed first among his sons, it is likely that Abram was not the oldest.

What

According to the book of Joshua, Terah was part of a clan who worshiped strange gods. The picture which emerges is of a patriarchal clan, with major acts of policy still firmly in the hands of the chief, Terah. But Terah seems to have had a great deal of respect and trust for his son, Abraham.

Conviction lays hold of the son, and a call comes to leave Ur and its corruptions. For no other motive, perhaps, than his respect for his son's deep convictions, the head of the family agrees to migrate, but is strongly enough in control to dictate a pause at Haran.

Stephen, in his historic address to the Sanhedrin, says quite clearly that the call to migrate and to begin a people in the wilderness came not to the father, Terah, but to his son, Abraham, while the family still lived at Ur.

Abraham was unwilling, in his father's lifetime, to fully accept the call. He responded with limited obedience to the great call. This points to Terah's own limited understanding and faith. It was only after his father's death that Abraham felt free to move.

In Gen. 12:1 comes the call which Stephen says was clearly given in Ur. When Terah died the call was repeated. There is a renewal of purpose; now the barrier of Terah's weak faith is removed. It is clear a father can muffle his son's call and impede his progress in the work of God.

Terah seems to have been a man of limited vision.

He was lacking in desire to abandon an inadequate life and a corrupt environment.

Without bravery or conviction, he fell short and held his family back with him.

Do you see any of these characteristics in your life?

If you do, what can you do to change your point of view?

Lot: Abraham's Nephew — Genesis 11, 12-14, 19 Luke 17, 2 Peter 2: 7

He rescued Lot, a righteous man, who was distressed by the filthy lives of lawless men

The name Lot means "wrapped up, hidden or covered". He was the son of Haran, the brother of Abraham. He left Ur of the Chaldees with his Uncle Abraham. We do not know how old he was, but he must have been younger than his uncle and in many ways, it appears Abraham raised him through his adolescence and into manhood. He traveled with Abraham, around 2000 BC, into Canaan and later into Egypt and back.

He appears to have gained Abraham's trust and respect. He also gained a great deal of personal wealth while the two were in Egypt. When they returned to the land of Canaan, after Abraham had been confronted with his lie about Sarah, it became apparent the two men had been blessed with such great substance in flocks and herds as well as in servants that they could not coexist long in the barren environment of Canaan.

When a quarrel broke out among the servants, Abraham and Lot met to discuss the situation and it was decided the best alternative would be for the two of them to separate and not try to subsist in the same geographic area.

Abraham offered Lot the choice related to the land he would occupy (Genesis 13). Lot foolishly chose the land to the south and east of Bethel in the natural path to the cities of Sodom and Gomorrah. Soon after these events Lot moved into Sodom. Not long after there was an invasion from the northeast and the cities of the plain were defeated and taken captive. When Abraham heard the news of the invasion of the cities and the capture of his nephew, he brought together a small army of men and pursued after the other armies. In a surprise attack the small army of 318 trained soldiers rescued Lot and the other captives.

Even after this, Lot, having observed Abraham's own long frustration under Terah, thought only in terms of his own personal gain, honor, and advantage. He was not interested in a subordinate post under the patriarch because he felt there was little possibility of personal achievement.

He became a judge in Sodom, and this fact is a glimpse of unexpressed ambitions (Gen. 19:1; to "sit in the gate" was a technical expression for a judge). The city on the plain seemed to offer much to "the lust of the eyes," for it was the old temptation over again, pressing hard on a character who did not look for a "city without foundations." The unseen, which Lot did not consider, was shocking; the corruption beneath the bright surface of Sodom's wealth made sure the judgment of God upon its sin, and upon those who shared its sin. He could not see that a godless, hasty, carnal choice was destined to lead to the death of his wife, the loss of his possessions, the corruption of his family, and the foundation of a pagan posterity. We should beware of what we choose.

We saw two men standing at the place of decision. Such moments, like some persistent whirlpool in a stream, come in life, and determine its texture.

There is a dual tug; the eternal pull of evil, and the eternal pull of God's spirit.

We never know in the flow of life's choices, which will be the final and irreversible choice.

The "great choice" which faced the two men on the hilltop was the founding of a nation for God.

They both chose and the moment passed. So, men choose their destiny.

Lot's Last Chapter — Genesis 19:1-30

Lot and his two daughters left Zoar and settled in the mountains, for he was afraid to stay in Zoar. He and his two daughters lived in a cave.

Lot chose the way which led to Sodom. He pitched his tent toward the city, and like a magnet the city drew him. He became a citizen, and "sat in the gate" as a magistrate. His family was immersed in the wickedness of the dark, luxurious little town as their somber ending shows.

Disaster fell on the valley floor. One science fiction writer has suggested that space visitors exploded surplus atomic fuel there and left a record of supernatural visitors to Sodom and grim retribution. The city's fate needs no such interpretation. Warning certainly came to Sodom, and Lot was urged to flee. He did, reluctantly, as the volcanic fountains broke their bonds, and Sodom rocked under the combined assault of earthquake and volcano. Lot's wife looked back, lingering no doubt in anguish, as the scene of the life she had come to cherish flamed amid the spouting gas. Caught in some red-hot mass flung from the buried seabed of some earlier salt sea, she became a "pillar of salt" and a perennial warning for those who fail to make good a prompt escape when catastrophe threatens a corrupt, disintegrating world.

In the hills, safe on his upland pastures, Abraham looked south, and the smoke of Sodom rose "like the smoke of a furnace." Perhaps some great mushroom cloud arose from the valley, as oil, freed deep in the earth, flared in the volcanic fires. The whole area is burned and scorched even to this day, and the great rift in the earth's surface must bring the living near the beds of fuel which are rich throughout the Middle East.

So ended the "cities of the plain," and with them the land's fertility, its tropical wealth and garden green were gone forever. And like Lot's wife, the towns became a proverb. They became a symbol of the end of the world.

The final chapter of the story is recorded in Genesis 19:30-38. Through incest, Lot became the father of two sons through his daughters. The older daughter named her son Moab. The younger daughter named her son Ben-Ammi. Through the sin of incest and a poor decision standing on a mountaintop years before the nations of Moab and Ammon were born.

Peter says a good word about Lot (2 Pet. 2:7), "He (God) rescued Lot, a righteous man, who was distressed by the filthy lives of lawless men." Even though Lot was "righteous" he had no influence among those with whom he had chosen to link his destiny.

His weakness lost his wife, his daughters, and his place in history.

Much evil can come from weak character, from one poor choice, from one failure to grasp God's opportunity.

It was a vital day when Lot and Abraham stood together on the ridge. The actions of those two men change the history of the world forever.

The subsequent actions of Lot and his weakness of character created two nations that have been at best, a mixed blessing to God's chosen people.

The most famous Moabite in the Bible is Ruth.

The Ammonites were a major enemy of Israel throughout the age of judges and the kingdom age.

Abraham: Chosen & Called Genesis 15, 17, 22; Romans 4:1-5, 9-25

By faith Abraham, when called to go to a place he would later receive as his inheritance, obeyed and went, even though he did not know where he was going. Hebrews 11:8

Abraham's name was changed by God from Abram, meaning "exalted father," to Abraham, meaning "father of a multitude."

Abraham was born and raised in Ur of the Chaldees; a city located in Mesopotamia. This area is in the country of Iraq several hundred miles southeast of Baghdad.

The historical dates for Abraham can be well-established by biblical references which relate to the known history of that geographic area. He was born around the year 2160 BC.

When Abraham was born Ur was the greatest city in the world. He was raised in a rich and powerful culture. The Chaldeans were worshipers of the moon goddess and many other idols. According to Joshua 24:2, before his conversion, Abraham, was a worshiper of idols. According to Acts 7:2 God appeared to Abraham and he became a follower of the one true God.

Abraham was called by God to lead his family from his home and travel to a land which God would show him. Abraham left as God had said, however he took his father and his nephew with him. They traveled as far as the city of Haran, in northwest Mesopotamia; there Abraham's father died. After the burial of his father he resumed his journey as God instructed.

Abraham was 75 years old when God called him to begin his journey. In Genesis 12 God made a covenant with Abraham and promised him and his descendants God would make them a unique people and a blessing to the entire world.

In the next few years Abraham traveled through the land of Canaan, experienced periods of famine and difficulty, traveled down into Egypt and returned to the land of Canaan.

In Egypt, fearful for his life, he lied to the Egyptians about Sarah and told them she was his sister. She was taken into the harem of Pharaoh, but God intervened and saved her from any harm. Despite his disobedience and lack of faith Abraham was greatly blessed materially.

He and his entourage returned to the land of Canaan. They had grown so wealthy in material possessions he and Lot separated because the land could not sustain all of their abundance if they remained together.

Abraham and Sarah struggled with the promise of a child which God had given them. As they grew older, they attempted to help God by adopting one of Abraham's servants. Later Sarah provided a secondary wife to Abraham. The result of that union was Ishmael. Finally, when Abraham was 100 years old and Sarah 90 the long-promised child was born.

When Isaac was a teenager, God presented Abraham with his greatest trial. Abraham was told to go into the land of Moriah and sacrifice his son. Genesis 22-25 gives us a detailed account of God providing for the redemption of this promised child.

Abraham provides us a strong example of the ups and downs, the encouragements and discouragements of serving God.

Abraham: Obedient and Tested Hebrews 11:8-22

By faith Abraham, when called to go to a place he would later receive as his inheritance, obeyed and went, even though he did not know where he was going. By faith he made his home in the promised land like a stranger in a foreign country; he lived in tents, as did Isaac and Jacob, who were heirs with him of the same promise. For he was looking forward to the city with foundations, whose architect and builder is God.

Environment and heredity both play their part in forming the character of a man, and of Abraham's environment we know a great deal. Of his ancestry, and its contribution to the shaping of one of the great men of all time, we know very little. Joshua (Josh. 24:2) described Terah, Abraham's father, as a pagan, and his name seems to be connected with that of the moon goddess, who was worshiped at Ur. This may mean very little, and Ur was no friendly dwelling-place for Terah, or he would not have so readily abandoned it with his son.

The city of Ur and what it signified to its residents is an area of which we have more knowledge. The ruins are not far from the meeting of the two great Mesopotamian Rivers; four millennia of river silt have built a plain which now separates Ur from the water by many miles. Harbor-works are easily identified in the ruins of the town, and in ancient times Ur was obviously the gateway to the Middle East. There were many caravan routes which wound up the Euphrates, curved round what is called the Fertile Crescent to Damascus, then down to the other river valley civilization of Egypt on the Nile. And Egypt's delta looked to the Mediterranean; ships sailed to the Minoan civilization and other cultures of early Europe.

Facing east, Ur faced the sea lanes of the Persian Gulf, where man first learned to sail the high seas. These adventurers coasted eastward to the third river civilization of the Indus Valley, where, in the ruins of the amazingly modern town of Mohenjo-Daro, pottery remains from Ur have been found. The traders doubtless penetrated much farther east even arriving at Ceylon. There they met the junks from China and made contact with all the complex of Far Eastern trade.

Ur lay at the very center of this vast web of human activity. It was a stimulating place for a man of means and intellect. Nowhere, more than at this pivotal point of the ancient world's communications, could a man have gained a greater and more detailed knowledge of the inhabited globe. From Crete, to Egypt, to Syria, and east to the Indian ocean the long chain of Abraham's information stretched.

His departure would prove a mighty challenge.

To give up all of these advantages and the lifestyle they afforded was a major test for Abraham and his family. We have seen the difficulty Terah, his father, had in separating himself from all the advantages of Ur. I am sure this difficulty would extend to the other family members as well.

Truly Abraham's first test was simply leaving this wonderful prosperous land!

A decision such as this had to be undertaken on complete faith. Abraham had no idea where he was going or where his journey would take him.

Have you faced any decisions such as this in your journey with God?

Does the struggle you faced in making the decision give you a greater appreciation for Abraham?

Abraham and God — Genesis 12:1-3; Acts 7:1-8

The LORD had said to Abram, "Leave your country, your people and your father's household and go to the land I will show you.

God always works ahead of our time. He prepares the heart and mind of man for his self-revelation. He also prepares the circumstances and the time.

As God surveyed His world from His vantage point, He must have found one thought obvious. Ur, with its corrupt and idolatrous worship, was no exception. What had been destroyed in the judgment of Noah was reappearing again throughout the entire Earth. From the bull-worship of Crete, to the animal deities of Egypt, from the worship of the Sun-god on the Phoenician coast, to the sadistic and sensual deities of which the sailors who traded to the Indus coast told, it was a world of oppressive corruption.

God must have stirred some longing for something purer and better in the heart of Abraham, because, at his first entrance on the story, he is described as knowing God (12:1). God always meets those who seek Him. He grants His grace to outreaching faith. He speaks to those who listen.

All this must have taken place before Abraham appears in the Bible story. The man knew, as few others in his age knew, the gods of Ur were not gods at all.

The LORD said to Abram, "Leave your country, your people and your father's household and go to the land I will show you. I will make you into a great nation and I will bless you; I will make your name great, and you will be a blessing. I will bless those who bless you, and whoever curses you I will curse; and all peoples on earth will be blessed through you."

God would now move his chosen vessel to begin to return true faith and knowledge of Him to a world which once again was lost and struggling. God knew it would be the beginning of a long journey and so did Abraham. He knew how long it took to ride on camel-back, or sail on shipboard (Paul), to the scattered nations. He knew that no one man could reach them all, and no one generation see their enlightenment.

But he began the process with one man.

Could Abraham begin a nation, away from the corrupt centers of man, in the clean wilderness, a nation dedicated to the One God, and prepared to be the custodian and transmitter of His truth? This was the vision and purpose behind the call of this man.

God had moved in a questing and willing heart. God had prompted and led. Someone had begun seeking, had heard and followed.

This is how the journey began. This is the beginning that led to Moses, David, and ultimately to Christ.

This is how the call came to rise and march. Philip in his defense before the Sanhedrin said, "Brothers and fathers, listen to me! The God of glory appeared to our father Abraham while he was still in Mesopotamia, before he lived in Haran."

What has God been preparing you for in your lifetime?

What are the areas in your life and lifestyle with which you are uncomfortable?

Is God leading you to take a new journey, direction or action?

Abraham's Retreat Genesis 12:10-20

Abram traveled through the land as far as the site of the great tree of Moreh at Shechem. At that time the Canaanites were in the land. From there he went on toward the hills east of Bethel and pitched his tent, with Bethel on the west and Ai on the east. There he built an altar to the LORD and called on the name of the LORD. Then Abram set out and continued toward the Negev.

In Gen. 14:13 there is an odd phrase: "Abram the Hebrew." The word appears to mean "the wanderer", the person who, in the modern world, is called "a man without a country." Abram the Hebrew, the immigrant. He was constantly moving; seeking the place God had prepared for him.

Read again the tribute in Heb. 11. Abraham had left the environment which denied him his life's purpose, but he had left it at some cost. Terah had revealed, and Lot was to repeat the demonstration, attachment to city life was strong in the tribe.

Abraham left his city and those who could not share his faith. And now Haran, like Ur, lay over the rim of the desert. Terah had revealed the attachment to city life was strong in the tribe. These were patriarchal days, and Abraham must have felt alone, and found the load of his responsibility heavy.

Now there was a famine in the land, and Abram went down to Egypt to live there for a while because the famine was severe.
That is why caution overwhelmed faith at the first impact of famine. Abraham withdrew to Egypt, where the regular flooding of the Nile, fed by the vast reservoirs of the interior, protected agriculture, for the most part, from the effects of drought, disastrous in more exposed lands to the north.

Faith in the mind of one who is thoughtful and sensitive is still plagued by doubt. Final victory is not always won in a single fight.
Abraham was not a stranger to doubt and defeat.

He went down to a land as corrupt as the one he had left. He ran head-long into the religious pollution of Egypt. Sarai, his wife, was the first to confront the hazards of the polytheistic world of Egypt. Abraham's half-truth, Sarai was, in fact, a half-sister, reveals the dilemmas into which a man runs when he leaves the circle of God's will.

He lied and ended up being rebuked by a pagan. It was in the course of these events that Sarai acquired Hagar. It was this Egyptian maid, who became part of his household which set in motion a series of events which were to influence Abraham's whole life and heritage.

In truth these events are the foundation for much of the historic turmoil which has plagued the Middle East – even to this very day!

It is impossible, as Macbeth remarked, "with the deed to trammel up the consequences." Abraham was a hinge of history. Great events turned on him.

None of us knows when we may be called to assume such a role. Faith treads bravely and carefully.

Abraham's Faith — Genesis 13:8-18

So Abram said to Lot, "Let's not have any quarreling between you and me, or between your herdsmen and mine, for we are brothers. Is not the whole land before you? Let's part company. If you go to the left, I'll go to the right; if you go to the right, I'll go to the left."

Determined there was to be no strife in the family of God; Abraham gave Lot the choice of dwelling-places.

He had learned a deep lesson of faith in Egypt, and now he left the whole matter in the hands of God, though as the elder patriarch, it was in his right to decide (Phil. 2:5-8). The two men stood on some height on the mountain ridge in the land, from where the entire Jordan valley was visible.

There is a deep rift valley which runs down from Mt. Hermon in the north to the area of the Dead Sea. In its 70-mile length lies the Jordan River, whose wandering path makes the river nearly four times as long as the plain through which it winds.

Lush tropical vegetation filled the land surface at the end of the river. "Lot looked up and saw that the whole plain of the Jordan was well watered, like the garden of the LORD, like the land of Egypt, toward Zoar." (13:10)

Set against this was the scrawny wilderness area of the Judean uplands. From the point of view of material advantage, and human social contact, the choice for a worldly-wise man was quite obviously the Jordan valley. The wilderness held only loneliness, the harsh living of shepherds, the daily search for meager pasture in the more sheltered valleys, and all the stern testing of the adverse environment of which Abraham was as aware as Lot.

Yet Abraham, in quiet and moving faith, allowed Lot to choose. Lot chose and went his way. He "moved his tent as far as Sodom" (12).

Observe now the pattern, setting these 11 verses side by side with those which told of Abraham's descent to Egypt, in search of those same advantages as Lot had chosen, as he moved toward the fertile and comfortable haunts of men.

Moral danger quickly followed Abraham's mistake of moving to the comfort of Egypt. Moral danger quickly followed his nephew's similar error.
Now Abraham had learned his lesson. He chose the wise course and left the outcome in the hands of God.

After Lot had moved toward Sodom, God spoke to Abraham.

The LORD said to Abram after Lot had parted from him, "Lift up your eyes from where you are and look north and south, east and west. All the land that you see I will give to you and your offspring forever.
Genesis 13:14, 15

From the high country of his camp, the length and breadth of the land was visible, from distant Mediterranean, to the blue of the Moab hills, from the Galilee, to the southern haze where the Negev desert lay. This, said the Voice, was to be his land.

Abraham built an altar near Hebron to remind himself of the covenant.

What have you built either physically or spiritually to remind yourself of God's promises?

Abraham's failure at Gerar — Genesis 20

Now Abraham moved on from there into the region of the Negev and lived between Kadesh and Shur. For a while he stayed in Gerar, and there Abraham said of his wife Sarah, "She is my sister." Then Abimelech king of Gerar sent for Sarah and took her. (20:1, 2)

Abraham at this time was now dwelling in the Negev, and his nomadic life was dependent upon water, upon rainfall in a word, and the periodic variations of climate. The coastal plain, agricultural, and commonly the first recipient of the Mediterranean rain belts, was a natural refuge when the hill-country suffered from a spell of drought.

Gerar lay at the foot of the hills; it was controlled by the predecessors of the Philistines, who were probably colonists from Crete. The ruler of the area of Gerar, some tribal prince, is called by a Hebrew term. This term is used here and later in Isaac's time (Gen. 26). Abimelech is probably a Hebrew translation of a royal title, so the ruler who encountered both father and son in similar circumstances is not necessarily the same person.

Abraham, years before in Egypt, had learned the lesson of such duplicity. Now he practices again. It seems the way of humanity to repeat their mistakes.

The patriarch, in a moment of panic, under some stress of testing, again earned the rebuke of an alien. Abimelech asked Abraham, "What was your reason for doing this?" Abraham replied, "I said to myself, 'There is surely no fear of God in this place, and they will kill me because of my wife.'" (20:10, 11)

It takes a long time for any of us to learn the truth, "if God is for us no one can stand against us." Abraham was afraid of what he perceived to be the human consequences of his situation and he forgot he had the protection of God to ensure the completion of his calling.

Curiously enough, he retained for his family the respect of the community he had wronged. This fact is testimony to the completeness and honesty of his repentance which healed the fault. The next chapter shows Abimelech manifesting deep confidence in Abraham and trust in his troubled world (21:22-34).

A lapse of faith can only be remedied, as Abraham had remedied it after his regrettable retreat to Egypt, by a wholehearted return to the position abandoned in fear, doubt, or transient disillusionment.

One of the greatest privileges God ever gave to man; the privilege of repentance. Peter asked Jesus, "How many times must I forgive my brother?" The answer Jesus gave him was, "I tell you, not seven times, but seventy-seven times." Our God is a God of unlimited forgiveness.

This applies to the old, equally with the young. No age is exempt from temptation. Here is another lesson taught in the story of his failure by "the Father of the Faithful."

How can we avoid falling into the sinful patterns others consider good or normal?

God always keeps His word, no matter how often we fail.

Abraham's Sacrifice — Genesis 22:1-19

Sometime later God tested Abraham. He said to him, "Abraham!" "Here I am," he replied. Then God said, "Take your son, your only son, Isaac, whom you love, and go to the region of Moriah. Sacrifice him there as a burnt offering on one of the mountains I will tell you about."

To Abraham, in the grip of his great idea, one common feature bound mankind together, the baseness of a universal polytheism, and the horror of the world's bloody cults. Obeying a Voice within which had become a part of his faith, he had left the busy town and set out to found, as we have seen, in the clean desert, a race dedicated to the service of the One God.

No man pursues a life of faith without his days of doubt, and there came a time when Abraham became obsessed with an awful thought. The voice of God which had so assuredly governed his conscience took on strange tones. Unbelievably, it told him to sacrifice his son, even as he had seen children die in the pagan cities from which he had withdrawn in repugnance. With uncertain steps and many questions, he obeyed God's voice. Abraham, was convinced this terrible pressure on the mind must have a meaning, set out to obey.

Abraham took the wood for the burnt offering and placed it on his son Isaac, and he himself carried the fire and the knife. As the two of them went on together, Isaac spoke up and said to his father Abraham, "Father?" "Yes, my son?" Abraham replied. "The fire and wood are here," Isaac said, "but where is the lamb for the burnt offering?" Abraham answered, "God himself will provide the lamb for the burnt offering, my son." And the two of them went on together. (6-8)

When he arrived at the summit, he set up the altar, he placed the wood, he bound his son...
The book of Hebrews explains his actions. "By faith Abraham, when he was tried, offered up Isaac: and he that had received the promises offered up his only begotten son... Accounting that God was able to raise him up, even from the dead; from whence also he received him in a figure" (Heb. 11:17, 19).

Then, unmistakably, all was clear. There was "a ram caught in a thicket" nearby. The Voice was strong in command. God, even as Abraham had told his son, had provided the sacrifice.

Abraham recognized the Divine provision, performed the expected and found his mind forever freed from the fear that God might indeed demand a parent's ultimate sacrifice. His obedience had been complete.

But the angel of the LORD called out to him from heaven, "Abraham! Abraham!" "Here I am," he replied. "Do not lay a hand on the boy," he said. "Do not do anything to him. Now I know that you fear God, because you have not withheld from me your son, your only son." Abraham looked up and there in a thicket he saw a ram caught by its horns. He went over and took the ram and sacrificed it as a burnt offering instead of his son. So Abraham called that place The LORD Will Provide. And to this day it is said, "On the mountain of the LORD it will be provided."

The race he founded was commanded to record the valuable truth into the law which became their way of life. As we read the Old Testament in the light of the New Testament, another meaning emerges; the substitutionary death of Christ.

Abraham knew nothing of this.

His obedience illustrated the key truth of God's redemptive plan.

God often requires obedience before He grants understanding.

Doing Business God's Way – Respecting Others

Here is a very unexpected lesson. The Bible does not pretend to present a consecutive history of the men and women who made its story. It did not set out to provide the raw materials of history for historians yet to be born. It selected its incidents and families such as Abraham's and preserved the record of events necessary for the guidance of future generations.

The first family burial recorded in the Bible is that of Sarah in the 23rd chapter of Genesis. In this account, there is also the first recorded commercial transaction, in which Abraham paid Ephron "four hundred shekels of silver" for a burial place for Sarah. This is the record of the death of Sarah and the acquisition of a family burial place. Sarah died at Hebron and was buried in the property acquired from a Hittite named Ephron. Abraham was a wealthy man. He had acquired a great deal of wealth as a result of his adventures in Egypt.

Hebron, Beersheba, and Gerar were key points on the caravan routes, and although there is no mention of such business and trade transactions, it seems clear the patriarchal community was engaged in the legitimate commerce of the trade routes of Palestine.

Abraham's wealth allowed him to pay the large amount of silver for one small plot of ground.

By this purchase, Abraham became the owner of a small parcel of the land of Canaan, which was all of Canaan he ever possessed. When he died, "his sons Isaac and Ishmael buried him in the cave of Machpelah" (Genesis 25:9) beside Sarah, his first wife.

To this day the Tomb of the Patriarch's is a holy place near the community of Hebron in Israel. It is venerated by Jews, Moslems and Christians alike. Unfortunately, it is also a place of much sectarian violence.

Observe Abraham's courtesy.

A person's character is sometimes best observed from its reflection in the lives or attitudes of others. In the previous chapter we see the cultured deference of the prince of Gerar toward the man who, on their first encounter, had disappointed and harmed him.

The present scene is also instructive. Abraham knew he was probably being overcharged. That was one reason why he had the document of sale drawn up with elaborate detail (17), and with proper witnesses (18). He judged haggling beneath his dignity, and, in its ancient context, discourteous.

He was a stranger in the land. He had God's word that the land should belong to his descendants.

Until such consummation he recognized the rights of its occupants, observed their laws, and conformed to their courtesies.

A testimony is worth some outlay in cash and it was a testimony that Abraham sought to establish in the alien's land.

There is no outward sign of true courtesy, said Goethe rightly, "which does not rest on a deep moral foundation."

The grace of God is shown in courtesy to others.

Melchizedek: Abraham's friend

Genesis 14:17-20; Hebrews 7:1-10; Ps. 110:4,
Heb. 5:6, 5:10, 6:20, 7:1-17

Then Melchizedek king of Salem brought out bread and wine. He was priest of God Most High, and he blessed Abram, saying, "Blessed be Abram by God Most High, Creator of heaven and earth. And blessed be God Most High, who delivered your enemies into your hand." Then Abram gave him a tenth of everything.

Melchizedek, king of Salem, is an intriguing person. He steps with dignity into half a page of Bible history, and then is gone. His significance, however, is out of all proportion to the amount of space his story fills. He came down from the hills when Abraham returned from his night raid heavy with the spoils of Sodom, then stepped back out of the story, leaving us hungry to know him. His character left a deep impression, for the writer of Psalm 110 and the writer of the Epistle to the Hebrews found him a fascinating picture of Christ.

Psalm 110:4, ***The LORD has sworn and will not change his mind: "You are a priest forever, in the order of Melchizedek."***

This looks forward to one who will combine the offices of king and priest, but a priest apart from the line of Aaron. Occupied as he was with the Old Testament, the writer of Hebrews also finds the mysterious priest of Genesis significant. As the first chapter of the epistle shows (1:3), Ps. 110 was prominent in the authors mind, and in chapters 5-7 he expounds his difficult theme of one who foreshadowed the Lord before Aaron, Aaron's priesthood and the Law.

The passage in Hebrews says that Melchizedek was "without father and mother," which simply means he founded his dynasty. He was also "king of Salem (peace)," who boasts in the famous Tell-el-Amarna letters of 1380 B.C.: "Behold this land, neither my father nor my mother gave it me; the hand of the mighty King gave it me." The words explain the text from Hebrews.

Can you comprehend how significant Melchizedek was!

Scripture describes the patriarch Abraham as a great man and a friend of God, a man God considered righteous because of his faith and obedience. *"And the scripture was fulfilled that says, 'Abraham believed God, and it was credited to him as righteousness,' and he was called God's friend*" (James 2:23). God picked Abraham to be the father of a nation.

As great as Abraham was, Hebrews says to *consider how great this man [Melchizedek] was, because even the patriarch Abraham gave a tenth of the spoils to him.*

Since Melchizedek received a tithe from Abraham, Melchizedek is greater than Abraham (7:7). In this context where the major premise is understood as true, Melchizedek is seen as an awesome person. He is in another class altogether different from the greatest of the patriarchs. Abraham paying tithes to Melchizedek showed he recognized the superiority of Melchizedek.

In the same way, Jesus is in another class altogether different from the prophets, angels, priests, and patriarchs. As is often said of some today, "He is in a class all by himself." In the case of Jesus, this is absolutely and eternally true.

Jesus Christ is the same yesterday and today and forever. **Hebrews 13:1**

Sarah — Genesis 16:1-15, 18:1-15, 21:1-7

Sarah's name was changed from Sarai which meant "quarrelsome," to Sarah, which means "princess." Genesis 17:15-16

When?
She also shares the chronological framework of the life of Abraham.

What?
As the wife of Abraham, Sarah's history is to a large extent the same as Abraham's. She does provide us a window into the life of women in the time in which she and the patriarchs lived. As was the case in that era, she had no status of her own; she was seen either as someone's daughter or someone's wife.

She obviously was a very beautiful woman. On two occasions Abraham feared for his life because he felt someone would kill him in order to obtain Sarah.

She was taken by Pharaoh; however, Pharaoh was warned by God to avoid any physical contact with her. Several years later the scenario played itself out again in amazing detail (Genesis 20). Once again God intervened to protect the wife of Abraham.

How?
It is interesting to speculate on the reason behind her name change. Her original name meant argumentative or combative. This was a name which would be applied to someone who could be whiny or nagging. The new name given to her by God indicates a change in attitude and a much firmer belief in the providence and care of God.

She obviously believed in the promise of God because she made the suggestion Abraham have a child through Hagar. It is clear she knew of God's promise to Abraham of an innumerable posterity. She was merely trying to help her husband along the way.

So what?
In the Old Testament Sarah is seen as being the mother of the nation of Israel. "Listen to me, you who pursue righteousness and who seek the LORD: Look to the rock from which you were cut and to the quarry from which you were hewn; look to Abraham, your father, and to Sarah, who gave you birth. When I called him he was but one and I blessed him and made him many." (Isaiah 51:1-2)

Sarah is referred to on several occasions in the New Testament; she is always used as a positive example for others to be encouraged and to mimic. In Hebrews 11 she is used as an example of the dependability and faithfulness of God.

Paul speaks of her in Romans as an illustration of the power of God and later he uses her to illustrate the sovereignty of God (Romans 4, 9).

Peter uses her as an example and encouragement to show obedience to her husband and her inward true beauty (1 Peter 3:1- 6).

Sarah is a woman who walked with God for many years.

She traveled with her husband from conversion to the completion of Gods plan for their lives.

She should be an example for all believers; even though all does not occur as we expect.

God is faithful and will see us through to the end.

Hagar: Abraham and Hagar Genesis 16

Hagar is a Semitic, not an Egyptian, name and was possibly given to the woman by Abraham when he left Egypt. The name means "flight." Like the Arabic word *hegira*.

Hagar was a servant in Abraham's household, handmaid to Sarah; Abraham probably acquired her during his visit to Egypt.

With the passing years Abraham must have intensely felt the lack of a son and heir. And after the war of the kings described in Genesis 14, with faith he believed God's promise he would have a son. This promise was reaffirmed in Genesis 15:2–6. But as time continued to pass his doubts grew. At Sarah's suggestion they followed a current custom and tried to gain an heir by their own efforts. Following the customary law of the period (shown in tablets from Ur and Nuzi), the childless Sarah urged Abraham to have a son by her servant Hagar.

Here are two applicable provisions of this law, both of which Sarai probably had in mind, "If a man marries a wife, and she has not given him children, if that man marries his concubine and brings her into his house, then that concubine shall not rank with his wife." And again: "If a man has married a wife, and she has given her husband a female slave who bears him children, and afterwards that slave ranks herself with her mistress, because she has borne children, her mistress shall not sell her for silver. The concubine shall be fettered and counted among the slaves." From these provisions it appears in the terms of the secular law, Sarai did not treat Hagar as harshly as she was permitted to do.

After she conceived, Hagar grew to hate the barren Sarah. Hagar went into the desert to get away from Sarah's anger. God met with Hagar at a well and commanded her to return to Sarah and to name her son Ishmael. God also promised her a multitude of descendants. Impressed by this experience with God, Hagar called the well "the well of him who lives and sees me."

After some time, the promised son was born to Sarah. Isaac was the gift of God's supernatural grace. At Isaac's weaning the son of the union between Abraham and Hagar mocked his half-brother. As a result, God then commanded Abraham to expel Hagar and her son, Ishmael.

The line of God's promise was to pass through Isaac.

Why did Abraham resort to secular law when he found himself still without an heir? Sarai was probably as discouraged as her husband. After all, they had staked their entire lives on this venture of faith. They had, at great sacrifice, and at the cost of lonely exile, provided a safe environment for their posterity but what if posterity never came?

It was a failure of a severely tried faith which persuaded Abraham to descend to this legally permitted solution. Abraham was not perfect, and it is important to remember Paul's insistent emphasis on the fact he was not perfect. He was a fallible man, but he believed God, and that was counted to him for righteousness.

No one's faith is perfect!

Faith grows when it overcomes adversity.

Doubt torments our existence and Abraham was no exception. But such mistakes have consequences.

The line of Ishmael still opposes Isaac and continues to multiply the pain one step of faithlessness can cause.

Ishmael Genesis 16:11-16; 17:18-26; 25:9-17; 28:9; 36:3

Ishmael's name was given to his mother Hagar by the Lord before his birth (Gen. 16:11). The name means "God hears". Ishmael was born when Abraham was 86 years old. He was circumcised when he was 13 years of age along with his father and all of their servants.

To understand Ishmael, we must think about his relationship with his parents before the arrival of Isaac. Ishmael was approximately 14 years old when Isaac was born. For all these years Abraham and Sarah lived in the belief that Ishmael, the son of their old age, was the promised son of God's covenant.

They had showered the young man with love and affection, and they were planning on him being the one to continue the lineage of Abraham.

When the announcement was made by the angels to Abraham that Sarah would have a son and this son would be the heir of the covenant all kinds of questions and obstacles came to mind. The immediate question is where does this leave Ishmael? What is the relationship the young man will have to the family of Abraham after the new son is born?

I am sure Ishmael as a young adolescent felt all of these questions and became even unsure of who he was and how his future was to be determined. The result of this was he took the opportunity at the ceremony celebrating the weaning of Isaac to mock the child who was younger.

This earned the wrath of Sarah who asked her husband to have both Ishmael and his mother removed from the family. Abraham prayed to God and was instructed to send Hagar and Ishmael away from his camp (21:11-13).

God had another destiny for Ishmael (Gen. 21:9-14). In the wilderness the fugitive pair soon ran out of water, and Hagar moved away from Ishmael to avoid witnessing his death. God then showed her a well of water. Ishmael grew up in Paran, in the NE Sinai, as a hunter with the bow, and Hagar obtained a wife for him from her Egyptian homeland (Gen. 21:15–21).

The casting out of Ishmael has produced a long lineage of bitterness and hatred in the Middle East. In the Arab world Ishmael is viewed as the chosen one of Abraham. The Muslim Arabs claim descent from Ishmael. Remember Ishmael's mother and wife were Egyptian, which differentiates them from the Hebrews. Arabian tribes springing from Ishmael are scattered throughout the Arabian Peninsula.

Politics in the Middle East

In Genesis the origins of many of Israel's neighbors are explained; Moab and Ammon, 19:30-38, the Ishmaelites 21:17-21; 25:12-18, Midian 25:2 and the Edomites 36:1-43.

In the process at least two points are made. First none of these nations has a valid claim to the land. Some of them are included among the nations which Abraham fathered (Ishmaelites, Midianites, Edomites), while others are counted among those who consider themselves as having been blessed with a family of Abraham (Moab and Ammon).

In Israel's history, these facts were in part responsible for a feeling of superiority on the part of the Israelites. They saw these neighbors as in some way indebted to them and to some degree rejected by God. When one is singled out for a special role, as Israel was, it is easy to start thinking of others as inferior. But beneficiaries of grace have no excuses for assuming an air of superiority.

Historically it seems many times "Christian nations" have seen other nations as inferior.

How can you avoid feelings of superiority toward non-Christians?

Laban — Genesis 24, 27, 28, 29 and 30

The name Laban means "white or glorious". He is a member of Abraham's family; the son of Bethuel and the grandson of Nahor. He is the brother of Rebekah and the father of Rachel and Leah. The elder branch of Abraham's family had remained at Haran in Mesopotamia. It is here we first meet Laban.

The next time Laban appears in the Genesis narrative he is the host of his nephew Jacob at Haran (Genesis 29). Jacob married Rachel and Leah, the two daughters of Laban. Jacob remained with Laban and worked for him 20 years. His extended adventures with Jacob are recounted in detail in chapters 29 through 31 of Genesis. Laban's dishonest and deceiving practices toward his nephew perhaps give us a clue about the source of Jacob's inherited tendency to harsh dealing. Laban is not mentioned again after Jacob left him.

Laban dealt fairly and honestly with the servant of Abraham. He extended hospitality to Abraham's servant and his entire traveling party and he acted honestly in the negotiations for Rebekah to become the bride of his nephew. He seems however to have been very much influenced by the gold and the gifts that were presented to his daughter.

The later adventures of Laban and the grandson of Abraham, Jacob, are detailed for us in Genesis 28 through 30. Jacob agreed to work as a bride payment for Rachel, but seven years later, Laban secretly replaced Rachel with Leah (his older and less attractive daughter) on the wedding night. He then required Jacob to work yet another seven years for Rachel. Laban provided each of his daughters with a maidservant, Zilpah for Leah, and Bilhah for Rachel. He urged Jacob to continue working for him, realizing the hand of God was upon him.

Jacob's decision to return to Canaan is a combination of his awareness of the hostility of Laban toward him and the direction he received from God. As Jacob discussed his plans with Leah and Rachel, he acknowledged his success was attributable to God, despite Laban's continued dishonesty; he also told them of a dream which he had recently received from God that directed him to return to Canaan. Jacob and his entire family took all of their goods and escaped while Laban and his family were away and preoccupied shearing sheep.

In great anger Laban caught up with Jacob in the hill country of Gilead. However, Laban was warned by God in route not to harm Jacob. When Laban caught up with Jacob, he complained to Jacob concerning two matters. Jacob had left without even allowing Laban to say good-bye to his daughters and grandchildren. He also accused Jacob of stealing his household gods. We will discuss this matter in more detail when we examine the life of Rachel.

An uneasy truce was reached between these two powerful and arrogant men. A pile of stones was erected as a memorial to the agreement which was made between Laban and Jacob. The location of the meeting and the commitment was at Mizpah.

I want to make a remark about the "Mizpah Benediction" (31:49). It is not unusual to hear this benediction given by a pastor at the end of a service or even to find it inscribed on the inside of wedding rings. Here we see an obvious misunderstanding and misuse of the words of Scripture. In the Genesis account they express mistrust between Laban and Jacob. A paraphrase might be something like this, "I don't trust you out of my sight and since I will no longer be able to watch you myself, may God hold you accountable for what you do."

This is not the way we would want to close a service or what we would want to express to our spouse.

Do you have an "uneasy truce" with someone?

Is there anything you can do to make the situation better?

Abraham's Servant: Eliezer — Genesis 24: 24:10-61

Genesis 15:2, "the steward of Abram's house, Eliezer of Damascus," literally this is, "the son of business," or "possession of my house". Arriving in Canaan, Abram took with him his chief retainer and adopted him in the absence of a son and heir. He was not "born in Abram's house." This means Abraham had not adopted this dependable servant as an official member of his family.

Yet he faithfully carried out the delicate commission of choosing a wife from his master's relatives for Isaac. His prayer, "Oh Lord God of my master Abraham, I pray thee send Godspeed this day, and show kindness unto my master"; shows us he was looking for a providential guide to help him fulfill the request of his master.

This 24th chapter is often neglected or bypassed in our study of Genesis, yet it gives us an amazing guideline for prayer.

All the preparations for this journey had been properly completed and his trusted servant began the long journey in hopes of completing the task his master had assigned him. In this chapter there is no vision, no apparent intervention from above to disturb the natural course of events. There is not even a "word" from above. God does not intrude on the normal activities of the day. God simply ordered ordinary things to work together with such perfect timing the ordinary becomes extraordinary.

We sometimes must find the door into God's presence and guidance by simply setting out on the way, perhaps by meditating about what the Bible is saying to us, backed up an initial act of obedience.

This servant prayed specifically; asking God for exactly what he wanted down to the very last detail. Much of our prayer is in traditional phraseology and it is hard to tell if we received an answer or not. The central part of prayer is for us to let our requests be made known unto God (Philippians 4:6). We can usually do this effectively if we use the words that come to us naturally; there is no need for a preordained religious vocabulary.

The sheer boldness and innocence of this request causes us to stop and think. It is easy for us to criticize others when we feel they are going above and beyond in their request. We have no right to put limits on the way this man or others pray. We certainly should not imagine putting limits on the answers which come from God.

Everything that happens to this man is now miraculous; God is answering his prayer Rebekah comes with him willingly and an obstinate Guardian Life Laban releases her. It is as if they to sense the presence of God in this moment.

We see here in these events how Abraham has taught his servant. Obviously, his actions on this long extended journey are the result of years of persistent teaching on the part of his master. The servant has watched Abraham for many years and seen how Abraham reacted to threats, trials, joys, disappointment, tragedy and death. He had come to believe the God Who could make such a man out of ordinary stuff would help him as well.

We find God much more often in our everyday activities.

"I am being in the way, the Lord led me." Genesis 24:27

Will you let God lead you in the way?

Jacob was born holding on to his brother's heel (Genesis 25:26). He was given the name Jacob because it means "following after." The noun form of the word came to be used for one who takes the place of another; this is the origin of the often-used definition "supplanter." Jacob would displace his brother, Esau, by stealing his blessing.

Where?
Jacob was born in southern Canaan and moved later in his life to the area of Haran, where he would live for 20 years. After that he returned to Canaan and lived until an old age. As an old man he moved to Egypt to be under the care of his son Joseph; living 17 years in Egypt he died at the age of 147.

When?
Jacob lived around 1900 B.C. He lived when there was no great world power in Mesopotamia and the international power of Egypt was beginning to grow.

What?
Jacob is without a doubt one of the most interesting characters in the Bible. We are given a great many details of his life; his birth, his relationship with his brother, his journey to escape his brother and find a wife, his encounter with God on his journey, the growth of his family and fortune, his return to his homeland, another life-changing encounter with God and the reconciliation with his brother.

In the midst of all these details the birth of 12 sons and one daughter are recorded. We can see his conflict with his in-laws. The strife within his own family is recorded in great detail. As we read these accounts, we are constantly reminded that the hand of God was on this man in an amazing way.

How?
His personal successes and failures are recorded for us in detail. He seems to have inherited the gentle, quiet and retiring character of his father. There also seems to be selfishness and a prudence about him that is calculating.

He constantly manipulated people to achieve his own gain. He was a perfect example of someone who depended totally on himself. Then he met God face to face! Alone, after sending his flock and family ahead to meet Esau, he met God in a prayer session. He wrestled with God all night long and was unable to prevail. God could have destroyed him instantly, but he extended the wrestling match until Jacob himself could not defeat his adversary and he had to ask for His blessing (Genesis 32). As a reminder God injured Jacob's hip in such a way, he limped the rest of his life. God also changed his name from Jacob, the supplanter, to Israel which means, "I wrestled with God."

We will see much more of Jacob later.

He is a perfect example of what happens when we always try to "do it ourselves".

We see the moral consequences of his early sins remain with him throughout his lifetime.

He saw his sin and selfishness cause havoc among his wives and children.

Yet God kept His word and "Jacob" became "Israel" the father of a nation whose descendants would produce the Savior of mankind.

Leah: the unexpected bride — Genesis 29, 30, 35, 49

Because Jacob was Rebekah's son he was related to Leah by marriage. Leah was the elder daughter of Laban who, by deception married her to Jacob, to whom she bore six sons and a daughter. Through her handmaid, Zilpah, Leah added two more sons to her family.

This is a biblical story which never loses its appeal and interest. Jacob arrived at Haran where he met Rachel his cousin drawing water for sheep. It was love at first sight. He went to work for his uncle Laban to earn the right to marry Rachael. At the end of the agreed upon period, however Jacob was deceived by his uncle and the bride given to him was Leah. Whether or not Leah participated in the deceit we have no idea.

This much is very clear; she knew that the love of her husband's heart was not for her; but for her sister. Leah genuinely loved Jacob and was true to him until he buried her in the cave of Machpelah.
God saw Leah was not loved and he gave her many children. The name given to her firstborn, Reuben, means behold "a son" and Leah praised God for His blessing. The name of her second son was Simeon which means "hearing". Leah felt God heard her cry and provided her with another son. The third son named Levi was viewed as one who would unite her to her husband. Judah was the fourth son to be born to Leah and she gave him a name meaning "praise." Perhaps now Jacob would become a little more affectionate and show her more consideration. Leah had two other sons named Issachar and Zebulun and a daughter named Dinah.

It seems Leah was a person of deep-rooted piety and therefore, better suited to become the person chosen to carry out the plans of God rather than her lovely worldly-minded sister. One clear lesson we can learn from the triangle of love is eternal choices should not be based upon external appearances. Rachel was beautiful and the moment Jacob saw her he fell in love. But it was Leah, not Rachel, who bore Judah through whose line Jesus Christ came.

It is possible Leah was unattractive enough she may have repelled others, but God was attracted to her because of an inner beauty. One writer has said, "There is a beauty which God gives at birth and which withers as a flower. And there is a beauty which God grants when by his grace men are born again. That kind of beauty never vanishes but blooms eternally."

Behind many a plain or ugly face there is a lovely person.

God does not look on the outward appearance but upon the heart.

Book Two

Rachel Genesis 29, 30, 31, 33, 35, 46, 48

Rachel was the daughter of Laban and she was the sister of Leah. It is a common characteristic of the Bible to pair certain individuals and force us to compare their lives. Leah and Rachel are two of these people who must be examined in relationship to each other.

The Bible describes Rachel as if she had all the physical loveliness and beauty of her aunt, Rebekah. She is described as beautiful and well favored and this is placed in contrast to her sister Leah who was not nearly as good looking physically.

As the younger daughter it was Rachel's job to go to the well and draw water for her father's sheep. It was not an accident she went the day when Jacob arrived. She could have been ill, there were any number of reasons she may not have been there on that specific day.

The divine guidance of God brought Jacob and Rachel together on that day. We tend to forget often the most seemingly ordinary events in our life are as much a part of the divine plan as the huge events. Jacob and Rachel had no idea God was involved in these events.

We are clearly told Jacob loved Rachel and he was willing to serve seven years as her bride price. The Scripture explains they seemed to him but a few days because of the love he had for her. It has been said that Leah had "the keys to Jacob's house, Rachel had the keys of his heart." Leah seems to have influenced his judgment: Rachel never ceased to hold his love.

We are never told in the Scripture specifically Rachel loved Jacob. She appears to have had somewhat of a mild character. We have no record of any grief she felt or any protest she made when she discovered how Leah had taken the first place in Jacob's life.

Once Rachel became Jacob's second wife, she bore him no children. This caused conflict between her and her sister. There is tremendous unhappiness and anguish in the phrase, "but Rachel was barren."

Rachel probably taunted Leah about the fact Jacob loved her and did not love her sister. Leah then would find revenge in reminding Rachel of the childlessness she had brought into the marriage. Eventually God gave Rachel a child. The grateful mother called the young baby Joseph. Of all the children of Jacob, Joseph became the greatest and most godly.

While Laban was absent caring for his sheep, Jacob gathered all his family, cattle and possessions and left. Preparing for the move Rachel stole the household gods of the family of Laban. These were small images used in prayer, but they also carried with them certain inheritance rights.

This shows Rachel shared some of her father's deceitfulness. It is obvious Rachel did not share her husband's trust in the great God he served. Also, these household divinities show us the laxity of the worship at home. We see how the human heart is quick to forsake the spiritual for the material. **The unseen is not valued as much as the seen!**

Rachel died in childbirth; this is the first record in the Bible of death at childbirth. When Jacob and his family were moving away from Bethel Rachel went into labor and gave birth to Benjamin dying in the process. Jacob buried Rachel on the way to Bethlehem and set up a pillar over her grave.

Rachel's cry was prophetic of the slaughter of the innocents when Christ was born (Matthew 2:16-18). Jeremiah pictures Rachel as rising from the grave to weep over the children being carried away to Babylon never to return (Jeremiah 31:15).

What weaknesses do you see in Rachel? What strengths do you see?

Isaac was the only son of Abraham and Sarah. His name Isaac means "laughter." He was named by Jehovah in commemoration of the child's miraculous birth, and of the *laughing* and joy his birth created. Genesis 17:19

Isaac is the least well-traveled of the patriarchs. We have no record of him ever leaving the area of southern Palestine. He was born when Abraham was 100 and Sarah was 90. This would make the date of his birth 2066 B.C. He lived to be 180 years old. Isaac is the second of the three great patriarchs of Israel: Abraham, Isaac, and Jacob. These three are mentioned together 33 times in the Bible; from Genesis 31 to Acts 7.

Isaac, like his father, had his ups and downs as he followed God. He had enough faith and trust in his father and the God of his father to willingly go with Abraham to mount Moriah. He asked his father where the sacrifice was; they had the wood and the fire but there was no lamb for a sacrifice. When his father replied, God will provide a lamb; Isaac accepted the truth of the fact and continued with his father.

He experienced God's provision of the lamb just as Abraham experienced God's provision. The two men saw God's faithfulness from a much different perspective.

Much later in his life Isaac also imitated the behavior of his father when he lied about his wife and their relationship (Genesis 26-28). Just as God had preserved Sarah; God preserved Rebekah.

God had promised a lineage to Abraham and He renewed that promise to Isaac; these men and women were protected and cared for by God despite their disobedience and lack of faith.

Isaac also experienced waiting for the birth of a child just as his father; but not nearly as long. To Isaac's credit he and Rebekah did not resort to trying to manipulate God's plan through human reason. Isaac and Rebekah had been married for 20 years and they had no children. Genesis 25 records Isaac prayed for his barren wife to produce children. God answered his prayer with "twins."

Later in their married life we see some very typical family relationship problems develop. Isaac and Rebekah had two sons; the boys were very different. Esau was a man of the outdoors and Jacob was a man who preferred to remain around home.

Esau quickly became Isaac's favorite and Jacob became Rebekah's favorite. The friction developed over time and came to a climax with the giving of the family blessing. Rebekah and Jacob schemed against Isaac and Esau to steal the blessing which Isaac intended to give to Esau.

This story provides one of the best examples of the providence of God recorded in the Scriptures. Before the birth of the children Isaac and Rebekah were told the older would serve the younger. Yet Isaac intended to ignore God's providential order and wanted to bless his elder son. Rebekah is willing to deceive her husband in order to secure the blessing for her favored son.

With all four individuals cooperating in the treachery God is still able to achieve His will and purpose.

The life of Isaac assures us God is faithful to His word!

God has always been able to work "all things" together for His purpose!

Isaac: Abraham's son in deceit — Genesis 26

This is a very revealing chapter. Isaac's foolishness in falsely describing Rebekah as his sister is psychologically true to his character in seeking to avoid conflict. Some writers have said this is a retelling of Abraham's action with Sarah in Egypt. However, this is not a mistaken retelling of an old story!

What we have here is an example of; "like father, like son." It illustrates too exactly, and too unhappily, Isaac's imitation of his father, and it shows the unhealthy dominance of a great man over his weaker son.

Abraham had done precisely this, and, in a moment of apprehension and of stress, his son followed the same pattern of deceit and earned the same embarrassing reproof from a pagan.

Isaac was uncertain, and it is not long before the powerful recognize weakness and take advantage of this weakness. These newly arrived settlers from Crete had gained a foothold on the southern coast of Palestine. They were called Philistines. They were a stronger, more developed and cultured people from the west. This area of the Middle East was named after them; it was called Palestine.

There is a perennial hostility between Lowlander and Highlander, and the shepherds of the hills were often at odds with the townsmen of the plain. It is evident from this story of the disputed wells the Philistines from the coastal plains were on the offensive and were actively pushing other people back into their hill country and wilderness surroundings.

This marks one of the first confrontations of Asian (Eastern) and European (Western) cultures.

Isaac, as was his nature, retreated and finally, in the deep desert, found rest. His place of residence came to be called Rehoboth; which means "broad places," or "room."

Today, the Israelis have a dry-farming research center in the city of the same name.

Here Isaac felt he could breathe without any threats. And God demonstrated His care for the man of peace. To move out of an atmosphere of hostility and strife was obviously God's will for this man.

God renewed His covenant with Isaac in this place. Here He blessed him so greatly the foreign enemy now sought his friendship and alliance.

But catch the note of pain at the chapter's end. Esau, demonstrating his lack of sympathy with his family's ideals, married a Hittite, and gave her the Hebrew name of Judith. To give a name does not change a character, and the intruder "made life bitter" for her parents-in-law. There are few sins more contemptible.

To be a good son or daughter to the parents of a husband or wife is not a betrayal of one's own people. It should be a source of satisfaction, a cementing of friendship and a rich reward.

This situation should have been demonstration enough to the head of the clan that Esau was not likely to be a suitable successor.

The truth of this observation is seen in the sequel. Isaac was a simple man, but he was God's man!

Esau — Genesis 25:27-34

The name Esau means "hairy". At birth this is the way the Bible describes Esau, "The first to come out was red, and his whole body was like a hairy garment; so, they named him Esau" (Genesis 25:25). He later acquired the nickname 'Edom', which means red. His geographic parameters are very much the same as his father Isaac. Esau probably traveled farther to the east and the south than Isaac. Esau and Jacob were both born to Isaac when he was 60 years old; about 2000 BC.

Esau is a key link in much of Old Testament history. A great deal of the conflict recorded in the Old Testament is the conflict between the descendants of the two brothers.

We have no account of the early life of Esau. As he grew, he became very skillful in outdoor activity. He enjoyed roaming free and is even termed "a son of the desert." He is also described as "a wild man." He seems to have been impatient with the restraint and responsibilities required to live a more sedentary lifestyle.

The first major event we have recorded in his lifetime is the selling of his birthright. He came home one day tired and worn out after an unsuccessful day of hunting. When he saw his brother Jacob enjoying a meal of stew he asked to share the meal. Jacob replied by offering to sell Esau as much as he wanted, if he would sell his birthright. This was a huge demand; the birthright secured a double portion of the family inheritance. The eldest son also held the position of tribal or clan leadership. This included spiritual as well as a temporal privileges and responsibilities.

Esau displeased his parents by marrying outside of their tribal clan. He married two Hittite girls and later married several Canaanite wives. When he realized how these marriages displeased his parents, he married a daughter of Ishmael. Here again Esau was controlled by his passion and heart and not by the spirit of God.

The story of the stolen blessing further confirms the divisions within the family. After realizing Jacob had stolen the blessing, giving no thought to the fact he had already given the blessing away for a bowl of stew, he vowed to kill his brother.

The enduring results of the disobedience of Esau are amazing!

One of Esau's five sons, Eliphaz, produced a son named Amalek (Genesis 36:12). The Amalekites were constant enemies of Israel. Joshua fought them at Sinai (Exodus 17:8). Ehud fought them at Jericho (Judges 3:13). King Saul died for refusing to kill the King of the Amalekites, Agag (1 Samuel 15, 28). An Agagite, Haman, tried to annihilate the Jews during the Persian captivity (Esther 3-7). Esau also was the father of the Edomites (Genesis 36). Doeg, an Edomite, was a vicious killer in the time of David (1 Samuel 22). King Herod was an Edomite.

The book of Hebrews makes four observations about Esau. Hebrews 12:15-17

- He was sexually immoral.
- He was godless.
- He despised his birthright.
- He tried to have his blessing restored through tears.

In Esau we see the long-term effects of the disobedience of one man!

Judah Genesis 29, 38, 43-46, 49

His name means "praise." He is the founder of the tribe of Israel which bears his name. The Messiah came through the lineage of Judah. He was the fourth son born to Leah when Jacob was in Haran. We catch enough glimpses of his life to understand a great deal more about his character than most of the other sons of Jacob. We will examine his life in three divisions.

It was Judah who urged his nine brothers to sell Joseph into slavery instead of killing him in Genesis 37. When the time came for the family to return to Egypt to buy more food it was Judah who had assumed leadership among the brothers. He spoke with his father and made the case to allow Benjamin to return with them. Judah went to the extreme of guaranteeing the safety of Benjamin with his life (Genesis 43).

It is interesting to note in chapter 44 in all the references to the brothers Judah has the preeminence. He is obviously recognized by them and by Joseph as the leader. When the entire family of Jacob arrived in the land of Egypt it is Judah who was sent ahead to conduct negotiations with Joseph. He has clearly risen to prominence as a leader of the family second only to the aged patriarch Jacob.

The story of Judah and Tamar is one of the most unusual in the entire Old Testament. Sometime after the sale of Joseph into slavery Judah left his brothers and married a Canaanite woman whose name was Shua. Within a very short time she had given birth to three sons; Er, Onan and Shelah. In a very brief summary type statement, we are told that Er married Tamar. The writer in Genesis tells us that Er was wicked in the sight of the Lord and the Lord put him to death. Then according to local custom Judah told Er's brother to raise up a child for his brother. When Onan refused, we are told God put him to death (38:10). Judah had told Tamar to remain in his family and when his youngest son was old enough, he would have him produce a child to continue the lineage.

As time passed Tamar became convinced this was not going to happen and she resorted to a trick. She went to the place where Judah was shearing sheep and posed as a prostitute. Judah saw her as he was traveling and had sex with her. He returned to his home without knowing the prostitute had been Tamar. Later when it became obvious, she was pregnant he called her to account and ordered she be executed. She presented to him evidence, his staff and seal: he was the father of the child she was carrying. He admitted to the family she was more righteous than he. There is no further mention of these events in the Scripture.

What we see in this account is between the selling of Joseph into slavery and the revelation Joseph was alive and well in Egypt. God impacted the conscience of Judah and caused him to rethink his moral actions.

The final words of Jacob spoken to Judah are recorded in Genesis 49:8-12. This is the final blessing passed on by father to son. Jacob is told all his brother's descendants will bow down to him and he shall be their leader. The superiority of the tribe of Judah continues throughout the Old Testament. Judah was first in total population, first in territory, first in marching order, first in strength and first in war.

The most significant portion of this blessing begins in 49:10, "The scepter will not depart from Judah, nor the ruler's staff from between his feet, until he comes to whom it belongs, and the obedience of the nations is his."

This passage is recognized as a prophecy of the Messiah and of the prominence of the Davidic dynasty. This is a clear indication of the emphasis on the blessing of the covenant and on the rise of Judah as the tribe destined for leadership. His tribe will develop the lion of the tribe of Judah.

We see in this story how God is pleased to use imperfect people.

Her name literally means a "rope, noose," as of a woman who ensnares by her beauty. It came to be used of one who flatters someone to achieve an end. She was the daughter of Bethuel, Abraham's nephew (Genesis 22:23).

She was born and raised in Nahor; Abraham's native country and the residence of his family.

She was obviously contemporary in time with Abraham and Isaac so about 2000 BC.

She became the wife of Isaac and the mother of Jacob and Esau. She willingly consented to follow the servant of Abraham home to the land of Canaan and marry Isaac. Her name infers she was beautiful and charming.

Her life with Isaac was a series of emotional highs and lows. She left her family and her homeland and traveled to marry a man she had never met or heard of a few weeks before.

She remained without children for the first 20 years of their marriage. This undoubtedly caused worry and friction between them. Surely Isaac shared the promise God made to his father and the history of his family. Sarah was childless for many years before the birth of Isaac and now it appeared Rebekah was going to have to endure the same sort of trial.

However, after 20 years God answered their prayers and Rebekah became pregnant (Genesis 25). Now her "adventures" really began. We read in Genesis she was pregnant with twins and the babies jostled each other within her, and she said, "Why is this happening to me?" So, she went to inquire of the LORD.

In response to her prayer, God told her, "Two nations are in your womb, and two peoples from within you will be separated; one people will be stronger than the other, and the older will serve the younger."

The babies were born and the conflicts between the two children continued. It was quickly apparent Rebekah favored Jacob and her husband favored Esau. This must have created more distrust and friction.

We read in the next chapter of Genesis that Isaac compromised his relationship with his wife just as his father had done with Sarah. This must have created even more distrust and friction.

Not long after these events we read of Rebekah's role in helping Jacob to cheat Esau out of the blessing his father intended to bestow upon him. As a result of these events Jacob would move away from the land of Canaan and Rebekah would never see him again.

What does all of this mean for us and how can we apply it?

- Early in Rebekah's life we see her willingness to be led by God and submit to His plan.
- We can see and learn a great deal about the stress, dishonesty and deceit can place on a marriage and family relationship.
- We also learn no matter how hard we try we cannot manipulate God or His plan.

Are you willing to be led by God into areas of your life which are completely new and unknown?

Can you be honest and open in your relationship with those around you?

Tamar Genesis 38:6-30; Ruth 4:12; Matthew 1:3

The Bible tells us nothing of her genealogy and background. All we know is that she was a Canaanite who married one of the sons of Judah.

Tamar married Er, the oldest son of Judah. We are not told what her husband did to displease God, but it was sinful enough God killed him. Tamar did not remain a widow very long; she married the next son in the family. According to custom she could continue the lineage of her deceased husband through his brother.

Her new husband's name was Onan. The Bible tells us he purposefully avoided having a child with Tamar. As a result of this incident God killed him as well. Tamar was widowed again and if the normal laws of family life had been followed the next son, Shelah, would have become her husband and it would have been his duty to have a son to continue the lineage of Er.

Her father-in-law Judah, a son of Jacob, promised when his youngest son was old enough this action would take place.

He failed to keep his promise, perhaps he feared his youngest son would die just like the first two men who had married Tamar. After a period of time Judah's wife died. Judah now found himself without his two oldest sons and without his wife.

In all this there is nothing negative said about the character or the action of Tamar.

Later when Judah had gone with his friend Hirah to take care of his flock at sheep shearing time, Tamar decided it was time for her to act. She very carefully set a trap in which she could entangle her father-in-law. She disguised herself as a prostitute and sat in an open place where she could be approached. Judah approached the well, not knowing who the harlot was and they reached a bargain so he could secure her services.

It is interesting to note at this time, in the land of Canaan there seems to be no prejudice whatsoever against nonreligious prostitution.

Several months later when it was apparent Tamar was pregnant, Judah called her to meet him and ordered she be burned to death for sin.

When he learned he was the father of the child he was forced to vindicate Tamar and admit she had been much more righteous than he.

Judah acted in complete sensual lust, but Tamar had acted with more noble motives to become the mother of Judah's tribal representative.

She was pregnant with twins. When sons were born to her they were named Pharez (Perez) and Zerah.

Even though this was an incestuous union and was achieved by deceit, God chose one of these boys (Perez) to be an ancestor of Ruth and ultimately become part of the genealogy given to us in the gospel of Matthew.

Here we see God's grace is enough for the entire world.

This is one of the first specific indications we see in the Bible that all people are welcome in God's house.

The book of Genesis is about the birth of a nation as well as about the birth of the world. God begins to create a people for Himself and for His purposes. Chosen by Him, raised by Him with infinite care, blessed by Him, they are destined to bring to the world's history, and into all human affairs, a revolutionary outlook and direction. Through this "people of God," salvation is to be brought to all people. Its founders are to be Abraham, Isaac, and Jacob.

Our first picture of Abraham came when God called him to go from Haran to Canaan. Now we see him old, well-advanced in years, approaching his deathbed. He has only one more task to accomplish, one final important decision to make. He must find a wife for Isaac. Both Isaac and Jacob are family men. Both have personal encounters with God, and in Jacob's case these moments are especially dramatic and memorable.

The home, as well as the altar, is now seen as the place of destiny. The fortune of the people of God, which in the earlier chapters, has been seen to depend almost entirely on God, is now seen to be brought about no less effectively through the way his people act, react and interact in their lives together at home, through their approach to marriage and the children they have, and through the way they go about their family affairs.

The beginning of family life is shown as all-important. Isaac is "getting on in years" and still unwed. He desperately needs companionship; his mother has just died. Born late in his parents' lives, he has had an unusual and restricted life. Hardly a woman in the world would have been able to understand him. But, far away as distance was then counted, there is one woman as unique as Isaac himself.

Abraham believed he must find for Isaac a woman who will share the same faith as he has in the same God. Without such a basis no marriage can work. He will send his servant to look for her. He felt sure if God has been at work preparing her, she will be willing to come (vv. 5, 8).

Marvelously, Rebekah is ready. She is in no way purchased or compelled by him: "We will call the maiden and ask her . . . will you go?" "She said, I will go." Isaac, too, takes her as freely as she gives herself to him. Their marriage takes place in an atmosphere dominated by a genuine devotion and gratitude to God on the part of both.

The basis, stability and success of the marriage depend on earlier and more basic ingredients, on God's work and on the couples' shared faith in Him, which are there even before the romance begins.

Rebekah was entirely one with Isaac in his purpose of serving Abraham's God. Knowing her interest in the promise given to their Uncle Abraham, her own relatives had pronounced upon her this blessing. "Our sister be the mother of thousands of ten thousands; and may your descendants possess the gate of those who hate them" (Gen. 24:60).

Therefore, of course, it was a shock, and a bitter trial, when the couple began to face the fact Rebekah in the normal course of affairs might be childless: And Isaac prayed to the Lord for his wife, because she was barren (v. 21).

The answer to this prayer is twins; not identical. The third link in the chain is given. The working of God's plan was not as Isaac and Rebekah had expected!

"For my thoughts are not your thoughts, neither are your ways my ways," declares the LORD. Isaiah 55:8 How have God's ways in your life surprised you?

The parents named the two boys. They called the first-born Esau, which meant "red". The boy was born covered with red hair; all his body was like a hairy cloak.

But with the second child it was different. When he was born his hand had taken hold of Esau's heel. They gave him the name Jacob, a name which could mean he takes by the heel. The name can also mean, "He comes from behind!" He takes people unaware! He tricks! Jacob, all his life, until God took him forcibly in hand and radically changed him, was to live up to this name.

His own early personal history was to make the name more uncomplimentary. To be called a "Jacob" was like being called a traitor in our time. In the womb Jacob took his brother by the heel, and in his manhood, he fought with God. As the two boys grew up, contrasting and opposite natural inclinations developed in each which bring them at times into open conflict: Esau was a skillful hunter, a man of the field, while Jacob was a quiet man, dwelling in tents (v. 27).

Here we are reminded a new family of God is now appearing on earth: it is ordinary human nature, unsanctified, transmitted from parent to child, every variety of human nature became incorporated here. God has no favorite types He wants, to set aside and cultivate. He isn't just the God of Abraham, the courageous mystical pioneer; He wants to work with Isaac, ordinary, conservative and retiring; with Esau, was a brash and restless sportsman; and with Jacob, steady and clever, but cunning and manipulative.

We read: "Isaac loved Esau, because he ate of his game; but Rebekah loved Jacob" (v. 28). Mom and Dad do not provide the background of just treatment on which all true unity and family life must be founded.

They each have a favorite; they allow the boys to divide them.

As a result, they further divided the boys and disrupted what they were meant to unite. Isaac is to be blamed for showing his bias for Esau when the boy comes home from hunting with venison.

Jacob grows up to realize nothing he does can please his father as much as Esau does. Rebekah tries to compensate and complicates affairs. In the book of Deuteronomy, the word love is used in the context of family life and is linked with the giving by a parent of the birthright.

Where a family is divided by the personal bias of the father, one side being loved, the other unloved, the father is warned not to allow his love for one side and his dislike for the other to influence his judgement about who should have preference in the passing of the family birthright.

"Isaac loved Esau" tells the reader Isaac is determined to make Esau not only heir to the double portion of his estate, but also the heir to the blessing which will connect him directly with the promise made to Abraham and invest him with the responsibility of passing it on.

So, when we read, "Rebekah loved Jacob" it tells us that Jacob is not just the favorite in her human affections but her candidate to train and rule as being primarily responsible for receiving the promise made to Abraham.

In the end Isaac's determination to give this blessing and the birthright to Esau, despite Rebekah's determination Jacob, and not Esau, should have it, will finally break up the home.

The Family Crisis: Isaac — Genesis 26:34-27:4

When Esau was forty years old, he took to wife Judith the daughter of Beeri the Hittite, and Basemath, the daughter of Elon the Hittite, and they made life bitter for Isaac and Rebekah (26.34).

Abraham had been called by God to sacrifice, and to risk everything in order to create a people who would be free forever from the heathenism of the world of his day. Now two women, deeply committed to paganism, are brought into the heart of the life of the family of Abraham. It must have been a bitter thought to Isaac that this alien, undoubtedly divisive and poisoning influence in his home, was introduced by the willful decision of the favorite son for whom he feels so deeply responsible.

Rebekah on the woman's side of the house comes up against the newcomers even more forcibly than Isaac. They realize she favors Jacob in matters of inheritance and from the start the two are prejudiced against her. Here is a problem facing Isaac in his old age, which is more deeply rooted and complex than any he has had to face before.

This is a reminder to us it is often what happens in the last chapter of our book of life which determines our heritage.

The steps Isaac takes as he tries to face this problem, or rather as he refuses to face it, bring about a crisis in his own relationship with God and the rest of the family become deeply involved, each with his or her own responsibility, in the sad affairs which follow. The situation is still a situation of hope. God is there watching over every detail of these family affairs. Was it time for Isaac to recognize the problem which divided him, and Rebekah had been cleared up?

Esau had disqualified himself beyond recovery.

Rebekah had been right, and he had been wrong?

Within the bitterness and the danger there was opening a new way for him to take; a God-given opportunity for reconciliation with his wife and with the truth.

God is there, waiting for his response so the promises He has made can now be moved on toward fulfilment. But now Isaac totally fails. He is determined to work his own way through the family crisis before the end overtakes him. He will not admit he has been wrong!

In those days the law did not finally determine the son who was physically firstborn should have any priority in the disposition of a family inheritance. There was a recognized practice that a father on his death-bed could name and bless the one he there and then appointed as his successor.

Isaac determined despite Rebekah and Jacob, he will bless Esau finally and officially with the birthright of the elder son, and the blessing which his father Abraham passed on to him will also go along with it. To avoid any danger of conflict he excludes both Rebekah and Jacob from what ought to be the most joyful, meaningful and united affair in the family history; the naming and blessing of the heir to the promise given by God to Abraham.

This plan is deliberately thought out. It is not to be interpreted as the excusable act of one who has become in any way senile. The whole story reveals to us Isaac, though physically blind, has all his natural wits about him.

"Oh! What a tangled web we weave, when first we practice to deceive"

No matter how much Rebekah is to be condemned, she must also be allowed to stand out. In the circumstances in which she finds herself; she is a shining example of how faith must always try to act. Her husband, to whom God had given responsibility for leadership in the family is acting unworthily and is trying to prevent God's will. She feels responsible. She cannot stand by and do nothing.

She seems to believe the fulfilment of the promises of God will be at stake unless she acts. She feels herself called by God to act alone and do something to help God's plan. She is not thinking of herself, but only of God, His Kingdom, her boy, and her husband. Isaac must be rescued from the results of his foolishness.

We should fully recognize the greatness of the thoughts which forced Rebekah into action.

Rebekah's counter plot descends to the level of behavior she despises in her husband. But she feels so righteous in doing it she does not see how unrighteous it is! Her zeal for the Lord seems momentarily to blind her to the issues at stake.

If Isaac is shameful, she becomes for a moment shameless. We should be shocked at her actions which were dominated by only one consideration. If a human life had stood in the way of her aim, I don't think she would have hesitated to sacrifice it.

Her actions darkened the truth with her lie, provoked her husband's anger, set up an uncompromising hatred in Esau's heart and risked Jacob's life. There are no arguments strong enough to justify a mother deliberately launching her son on such a course of deceit. The events and their immediate outcome seem to justify to her the course of action she chose.

Does the end justify the means?

In the end she is clearly condemned for the risks she took. She brings terrible consequences both on herself and on her sons. The words with which she urges Jacob to participate in the plan, offering herself to take the consequences if things go wrong, sound noble when they are spoken. "My son, let the curse fall on me. Just do what I say; go and get them for me."
But these words are empty and foolish. **Jacob himself must pay in full for what he does.**

Yet even in condemning her, we must admit there is a tendency to find ourselves excusing her.

Wasn't Rebekah's activity largely a result and reaction to Isaac's actions? Have you ever heard someone say, "It's not my fault!"?

When God gave Isaac the gift of a wife with such spiritual insight and initiative and willingness for self-sacrifice, wasn't it God's intention he should co-operate and share with her what he had. He was to help to make her wise in spiritual things not frustrate her with strife and deceit.

Perhaps it was because he neglected her that, left on her own, she felt driven to take such a desperate risk!

We must consider the impact our actions will have on others!

To gain what he believes is rightfully his, Jacob copies his brother Esau. He dresses in his clothes and impersonates him. He takes advantage of his father's blindness and weakness to deceive him. Bringing a sacrifice into the presence of God at an altar was regarded as no holier and no more powerful an action than what Jacob was involved in with his father.

Together they called on the Lord to bless what they were doing.

While playing his part in this deception, almost every other phrase Jacob utters is a lie (vv. 19, 20, 24). He defends himself against detection using pious phraseology.

Throughout the incident no aspect of Jacob's behavior is criticized by the writer, by his mother or father, or by God. It almost seems as if God approves of what is happening, because Jacob can succeed. People with Jacob's tendency for self-reliance in the service of God are inclined to see success as a sign of God's approval of their action.

Yet there were aspects of what Jacob did that night which God, even in showing mercy to Jacob, caused to have an extremely painful outcome. God also made sure Jacob, and those who tried to follow in his steps, would know in this case the evil deed brought about the painful consequences.

We can trace the matter through as we read the history

1. Jacob is forced to flee from home.
2. In exile he is brought under the power of Laban.
3. He is tricked exactly as he has tricked his brother.
4. He tries to escape and is degraded and humiliated.
5. He must settle with God face to face.

Jacob must learn that God, for the sake of the honor of His name and the fulfilment of His purpose in this world, expects a far higher standard from people who claim to be His witnesses than from any others.

What God must have hated most in the affair of the blessing was the deception which Jacob introduced into such a solemn act of worship. Jacob was spared immediate condemnation because his heart to some extent was seeking God. But he had to be taught his lesson.

This is the story of a man carried away into deceit and theft by eagerness for God which was not informed or controlled by true understanding of knowledge.

Sometimes today we may be tempted to play a part like Jacob's. Many people are showing an unusual interest in what is religious or mystical, claiming to have taken part in spiritual experiences of great variety.

Sometimes we justify our bold new departures from love, righteousness, and our best traditions with the name of Jesus. We should notice in this story if Jacob had been left to himself, he would have been too afraid of being cursed to have gone ahead.

He was emboldened to proceed by the oath of his mother.

Jesus is the only one who ever had a right to say such a thing as Rebekah said. He took the curse of all our sins.

The New Testament writer who discusses this incident warns us against a superficial judgement. Esau, at the very moment he asks for help, reveals his true self just as he did when he sold his birthright. He was then, now and always an "immoral and irreligious" man. "See that no one is sexually immoral, or is godless like Esau, who for a single meal sold his inheritance rights as the oldest son." (Heb. 12:16).

Esau was rejected by God at this moment, not because God had predetermined to reject him but because of his reaction to what God was doing. When Esau returned from his hunting that day, he confronted an entirely new situation in his home life. God had come to be present, to redirect and renew everyone and everything within the family. Esau, openly and with firm determination, put himself out of the way into which God was now moving affairs. He refused to fit into the new conditions of life with God.

He had always considered himself as set up by God to be dignified as the worthy successor of Abraham. He was so firm in his determination that it should be the case, he would not, and could not, submit to what had taken place. Two modern translations of the phrase, "he found no chance to repent", are revealing: "he was unable to elicit a change of heart", says one (JB); "he found no way open for second thoughts", says another (NEB).

His mind was made up! Don't confuse him with the truth!

Esau illustrates the trouble such a **"root of bitterness"** can cause.

He deliberately chooses the way of bitterness: Now Esau hated Jacob because of the blessing with which his father had blessed him, and Esau said to himself, "The days of mourning for my father are approaching; then I will kill my brother Jacob."

Before the writer passes on to discuss what happened to Jacob, he allows us to see what Esau did when he heard his father forbidding Jacob to take a wife from the heathen women around him.

When Esau saw the Canaanite women did not please Isaac his father, Esau went to his uncle Ishmael and took another wife, besides the two wives he had. He married Mahalath the daughter of Ishmael, Abraham's son (vv. 8-9).

This incident may be told in order to suggest something more. His desire to please his father is emphasized (Gen. 28.8). We can look back and notice the reason he gave for not killing Jacob immediately was a reluctance to hurt his father so long as he was alive (Gen. 27.41).

The writer is suggesting to us there may still be something good in this man. Is he, perhaps, better than we had thought at the time when he made his vow to kill his brother?

The writers of the Bible do not want us to close the books too quickly in order to start counting the number of the damned.

They want to encourage us, today and always, to look at what is worthwhile. In face of people who appear at first to be committed to evil, we are encouraged to go on praying.

He was still Rebekah's boy.

She loved him. She was praying.

For whom are you praying?

Bethel: The Vision

Genesis 28:10-13

The trickery to which Jacob descended in his efforts to obtain both the birthright and the blessing show how unfit he was to have them. But it also indicates his belief he was the one called by God to succeed Abraham and Isaac. He was the one to lead his family toward the great things God had promised.

He knew he must become a man of God. No other interpretation will do justice to the whole account we have of Jacob except one which assumes from the very beginning of his life and steadily throughout it, he wanted the experience, knowledge, and dedication implied in seeking the privilege.

He was a man who wanted God; but he wanted God on his terms. Even at this point in his life the desire was still there, but the fulfilment completely eluded him. Obviously, he did not know the kind of God his fathers had learned to trust in and worship. Jacob, with all the basic desire of his heart, crying out for the living God, was as mixed up in his theology as he was in his psychology.

He was on the first leg of his journey to Haran. He arrived tired and lonely. Probably when he saw the harshness of this spot, he was tempted to give way to gloom and to ask what, really, the future can hold for him. Though the vision is of such short duration, and though he hears only one speech, Jacob is helped by God to see the world in which he now must live has a far more mysterious background and far greater dimension and possibility than he has ever before imagined.

He is led to understand the concerns to which he must now open his mind in thinking about the God of his fathers are far bigger and more urgent than he has ever honestly tried to face. He observes while his family's God, who has spoken to him, is strong enough and exalted enough to cope with such a universe and all its affairs. The vision teaches him about the power and the near presence of the God who loves him. God Almighty appeared to me, he will say later, thinking about the place of this vision.

There was much more in Jacob's vision than Jacob himself grasped at the time he saw it. When God reveals things to any of us through the Bible, He always puts much more into what He gives us than we can grasp at that moment. Our vision is bigger than our thought can comprehend.

We confine God to our understanding and domesticate Him.

He often is not much more to us than a psychological counsellor, family doctor, and mother's help in one small package. He is kind enough to bear with us, and care for us, even though we belittle Him in our thoughts in such a way,

God wants us to grow up!

There is another dimension into which we must move in order to see both God and life properly: the invisible world, the world to come, of which Jacob had his glimpse. This world was there before ours began and will continue to be there hereafter.

Our minds are much too dominated by enlightenment and science, and we are far too afraid of becoming trapped in what we think is outmoded biblical mythology for us ever to enter the Kingdom of heaven!

Therefore, we pay the price. Our world remains too small and God, also, remains small.

How awesome is this place, Jacob said (Gen. 28.16), the gate of heaven!

The God of the Bible concentrates more on what He can achieve by speaking than on what He can communicate through visual imagery. He wants people to believe by hearing His voice. Visions and visible signs, when added, are usually to confirm and illustrate what He is saying in His Word.

Consequently, the voice, at Bethel, and what the voice says, is far more impressive to Jacob, even more than the vision. It is the voice which takes Jacob directly to the heart of what God wants to give him and seeks from him. The vision is the background.

Jacob knows it is the voice of God Himself, the same voice which came to Abraham and to his own father. But never has Jacob heard that voice. He has seen evidence of its having been spoken. He has heard his father witnessing to it. Now the voice comes addressed to him; he hears God, not man. When the voice comes, he knows he is called, confronted, and challenged as he has not been before.

He is invited into a close and warm relationship, but at the same time called to surrender and serve. But he knows he is enabled to serve, for the voice itself brings some measure of God's own vitality, even something of Himself, into Jacob's life. *Then Jacob awoke from his sleep and said, Surely the Lord is in this place; and I did not know it (v. 16).*

At this low period in Jacob's life and fortunes God decided to break into his depression and scatter all the clouds. So, a sinful man was spoken to and commissioned by God. We have them both here together; the thrill and excitement of an overwhelming new discovery, and the confession of the stubbornness which has kept him from discovering it until now.

Often, we are too slow to trust such a thing can happen.

Would we be prepared to admit such an event could happen in our lives? It could come through a visit to a local church or through reading of the Bible.

And Jacob vowed a vow, saying, If God will be with me, and will keep me in this way that I go, and will give me bread to eat, and raiment to put on, so that I come again to my father's house in peace, and Jehovah will be my God, then this stone, which I have set up for a pillar, shall be God's house. And of all that thou shalt give me I will surely give the tenth unto thee.

Jacob is not bargaining. Something transforming in character has begun to happen to him. Jacob took the offered hand and held tightly; he obligated himself by a vow to God. Jacob had difficulty in deciding exactly how best to express his gratitude. He is beginning to try to be a new person. He is trying genuinely to break with the defects which have plagued him.

First, he says very simply: The Lord shall be my God. What more is needed? If we could all say this from the heart, our churches would be renewed. Then he adds he will one day build a temple to God in this very place, and he will pledge a tenth of his income for its upkeep. If we all gave this tenth, our churches would have all the resources they need for spectacular advance.

We must not underestimate what happened at Bethel; we must remember the degree of our human self-commitment to God at any one stage of our life is always imperfect.

There are no degrees in God's commitment to us.

He gives Himself completely and makes Himself known without reserve.

Jacob: The Sweet and the Bitter — Genesis 29:1-30

When Jacob arrived and met Rachel the daughter of Laban, his mother's brother (v. 10), he cried aloud (v. 11). I don't think it was love at first sight which caused this emotion. It was joy after a series of remarkable happenings which had confirmed the vision he had been given at Bethel and the promises of the voice he had heard there. During the long journey Jacob has had time to think over the whole experience and to ask how real it has been. One cannot build one's life only on what happens in a dream! But was it more than a dream?

To prove to himself the whole thing was more than a dream, Jacob wanted some concrete signs to assure him. These events are as surprising as the vision. When he knows he is nearing Laban's neighborhood he comes to a well. There he met people who knew Laban. Then at the same moment as they were speaking of him, Rachel came on the scene: the woman the man had been seeking!

He feels God has led him first to the gate of heaven and is now leading him to the gate of new life on earth as well! Now he dares and achieves something very out of the ordinary. He does it in the energy of his joy. He knows sheep. These sheep around this well, he can see, are suffering greatly for lack of water. He challenges their shepherds about it. But they answer their custom is to wait, even in the heat, until everyone else has come, and then to roll the stone from the mouth of the well together.

When Rachel arrives, he can no longer hold himself back. His desire to do something to show his joy over what God has done breaks through normal wisdom for a moment and he attempts something quite rash. He goes down himself to the mouth of the well and in front of the whole group he tackles the very stone which, they have affirmed, only a crowd of men can move.

And there we see a miracle either of sheer delight or of God! Extraordinary strength is given to him. How changed is Jacob; he is a new man! What has happened to him has taken away all shyness and reserve, has enabled him to cut through the hindering customs and routine of the world around him.

God is going to lead Jacob through a very long, dark, and dangerous valley (Ps. 23.4). His uncle Laban saw people only as financial assets.

Jacob was obviously a good asset and Laban could use his love for Rachel. His coming had enhanced her value enormously. Yet Leah, unwanted by anyone, was Laban's main problem. He thought out a plan to substitute one girl for the other on the wedding night and to trap Jacob into bed with her, so that he would have to take her, as well as Rachel!

After this was successful and Jacob had been irrevocably ensnared Laban put on an innocent air. The moment when Jacob wakes up to find that he has been deceived is almost as decisive as the moment when he awoke at Bethel. For his uncle has done to him exactly what he did to his father and his brother: substituted one person for another by trickery and stealth.

He cannot break with Laban.

He is too closely tied to the man, and Laban still has control of Rachel, whom Jacob will be allowed to marry.

Now his chief task in life can begin: to build his home, to become the father of the people of God. It is not to be as he had hoped. But he still has in his mind the promise: "By you and your descendants shall all the families of the earth bless themselves. Behold, I am with you and will keep you. For I will not leave you until I have done that of which I have spoken to you" (Gen. 28.14-15).

The Building of the House #1 — Genesis 29:31-30:24

Passion, strife, birth, and God!
The later historians of Israel looked on the birth of the twelve sons of Jacob as an important part of the plan which God was very carefully working, even in its details, as He shaped the early life of their nation. The marriage begins, of course, with a rivalry between the two wives. The intensity of the envy grows when the babies come, one after the other for Leah; four of them (29:31-5)!

Poor Rachel! "Give me children, or I shall die!" (30:1) she cries to Jacob. She becomes so jealous her maid is brought in to help her in the situation. The intensity of Rachel's feeling against her sister is revealed in the names she gives to the two children born in this way. She feels vindicated by God when the first arrives. To celebrate the second birth she says, I have wrestled with my sister, and have prevailed, and put the phrase into the baby's name (30:8).

Yet Leah forges ahead, bringing in Zilpah, her maid, who bears two more on her side (30:9-13). One day Leah's son Reuben finds mandrake plants in a field. These were strong-smelling roots which were regarded as having aphrodisiac qualities. The fact a child brought such a thing to his mother makes us realize even he had been led to understand it was only by having babies his mother felt she had any status and use.

The shadow of impoverishment?
What is clearly brought out later is that Jacob, in a few years' time, will discover he has on his hands a deeply divided family of boys. They seem to have failed to grasp with any fullness what it means to serve the God of their father.

Yet this period is Jacob's time of opportunity. God is at work; Jacob too must be at work. God has created a family situation full of entirely new and great possibilities, open and waiting for him to take new leadership.

There are hints in the story that Jacob is more responsible than his wives for falling short. He compares badly even with his own father. Isaac at least prayed with his wife in her distress at her barrenness, but Jacob became angry when Rachel turned to him for support (30:2). Here are the seeds of later tragedies in Jacob's life. When the children were young, some of them in their cradles and some in their infancy, he failed as a father. It is hard to assess the blame for this.

Since God had "opened the womb" for each birth to take place He would surely have opened the mind of each growing child to receive another kind of seed. Jacob should have planted the truth so God could bring about healthy mental and spiritual growth.

Jacob's self-giving to each child around him, as an earthly father, should have reflected something of God's own care, so each child could begin to glimpse what it means to have a heavenly father as well as an earthly one.

Each of his wives appears to be alone before God in her prayers and praises. Did he give them no leadership and was family religion at this stage simply left to become a personal and private matter for each? It is significant that Abraham gave names to both Ishmael and Isaac, but Jacob takes no part in naming any of these eleven boys. The only point at which Jacob seems to exert his influence is to make clear his love for Rachel and his distaste for Leah.

He does not seem to be 'at home' when he is at home.

Those who have families beginning to grow are meant to notice these things.

We must appreciate Leah if we are going to understand Jacob. The more we study her, the more we come to like her and pity Jacob for his own "weak eyes". Externally she is nothing compared to Rachel.

She must be held to blame to some extent for permitting herself to be substituted for Rachel in the first place. Since Laban tricked Jacob, he could have tricked Leah, even more easily, for undoubtedly in contrast to her future husband she was basically naive.

We can only judge her character by the attitude she took in her sufferings and by the prayers she offered to God in her great affliction; *Leah conceived and bore a son, and she called his name Reuben; for she said, 'Because the Lord has looked upon my affliction; surely now my husband will love me.' She conceived again and bore a son, and said, 'Because the Lord has heard that I am hated, he has given me this son also'; and she called his name Simeon. Again she conceived and bore a son, and said, 'Now this time my husband will be joined to me because I have borne him three sons'; therefore his name was called Levi. And she conceived again and bore a son, and said, 'This time I will praise the Lord', therefore she called his name Judah; then she ceased bearing* (29:32-5).

Jacob must become humble enough to see not only has God concealed His blessing in Leah but that he, Jacob, has also to find his future hidden in his relationship with her. No matter in what direction he is inclined by his personal disposition and taste, he was meant to see God has made Leah, rather than Rachel, the leading light of the home.

From Leah came the tribes of Levi and Judah, which shared between them the spiritual and temporal dominion of Israel, providing the two great dominating institutions of the biblical period, the priesthood and the Davidic monarchy.

As we look further to the beginning of the New Testament, we find that it is Judah, Leah's son, who is given a place in the genealogy of Jesus Christ.

Jacob is meant not only to accept her but also to serve, honor and protect her.
There is no way in which he can find peace or a future in bypassing her. She is the stone set there in front of him for him to make both the foundation-stone at the start of his home-building and the headstone of the corner at the end or his life-work will be in vain.

Jacob's attitude to Leah in the home is defined for us in verses 30 and 31. The first observes that he loved Rachel more than Leah; the second says Leah was hated.

When we ask why; the answer is Jacob was too proud. Rachel, he felt, offered him self-fulfillment. She gave him pleasure. Leah demanded self-sacrifice. She stood for the way none of us naturally wants; self-denial.

If we try to analyze the situation psychologically, we see the fact Leah also humbled him because she reminded him of the guilt of his past life. God had made her, on their encounter at the wedding, a symbol of his guilt in the affair of Esau.

For most of us, Leah is a reminder God often places us in a circumstance which is hard for us to accommodate and to deal with adequately.

If Leah, despite all Jacob' prayers and desires is there, she is to be concerned about and cared for!

It was Leah who lived on with Jacob to become his strength and support in the harder days to come.

Simeon

Simeon is rarely mentioned by himself in Scripture. He is almost always associated with his brother Levi. We know very little of his personal history. The first thing recorded in the Scripture about Simeon is he and Levi went on a crusade against the men of Shechem because of the rape of their sister Tamar.

In a gesture of goodwill and an attempt to unite Shechem and Judah in marriage the men of the city had submitted to circumcision. The Scripture says while they were weakened and recovering this operation these two men went into the city and killed all the males.

They were given a "talking-to" by their father, but they rejected any repentance or activity to try to make their sickening crime right. In fact, later, as recorded in Genesis 49:6, Jacob remembered their self-will when he pronounced his final blessing.

The next mention of Simeon occurs in the Joseph story when he is the one kept in prison until Benjamin can be brought back into the land. It looks as if Joseph agreed with his father when he felt Simeon and Levi would be best apart.

Later when the descendants of these brothers lived in the land of Canaan Simeon was such a small and inconsequential tribe, we see very little involving them even in the book of Judges.

It is better if some people are not together.

This tribe is another example of a missed opportunity; they were positioned to be an example to the unbelievers around them - yet they failed.

Issachar

Issachar is the ninth son of Jacob and the fifth by Leah. This name, meaning "hireling" was given to him by his mother because she had allowed Jacob to sleep with her rival. She seems to think this child is God's payment to her for being so open-minded and considerate.

In Jacob's blessing to Issachar he is described as "Issachar is a rawboned donkey lying down between two saddlebags. When he sees how good his resting place is and how pleasant is his land, he will bend his shoulder to the burden and submit to forced labor" (Genesis 49:14, 15).

When the land of Canaan was divided Issachar was allotted most of the Jezreel Valley. This may be what the reference means when it says Issachar is, "lying down between two saddlebags." This Valley passes southward across the land of Israel between the Carmel Ridge and the Gilboa range of hills. This was a valuable inheritance: fertile and it proved to be a part of the main highway between Egypt and Babylon. As a result of the location the descendants of Issachar were forced into slavery by many different foreign foes.

Zebulun

Zebulun was the 10th son of Jacob and the sixth of Leah. Jacob's blessing to Zebulun tells us very little about his son or the descendants of that son. We know nothing of this man individually and we know very little about his descendants. His descendants were a commercial tribe in the north coastal land of Galilee.

All three of these tribes had a tremendous opportunity to show the nations the God of Israel but it appears they were a total failure in this area.

The Sons of Bilhah: Dan and Naphtali

Dan

Dan was the fifth son of Jacob and the first son of Bilhah, Rachael's handmaid. His only full brother was Naphtali. We know nothing about the man personally because nothing is recorded in the Bible to tell us about him. We do, however, know a great deal about the tribe which carries his name.

Jacob's dying blessing pronounced to his son was this, "Dan will provide justice for his people as one of the tribes of Israel. Dan will be a serpent by the roadside, a viper along the path that bites the horse's heels so that its rider tumbles backward." (Genesis 49:16, 17) This prophecy given by the patriarch makes two very different observations about the descendants of this man.

Dan is said to judge his people and no man individually did more to judge and help Israel than Samson. Samson is the most famous Danite recorded in the Bible. The second portion of the prophecy probably has reference to the failure of the tribe of Dan to possess the inheritance it was given in the Promised Land. In the book of Judges their story is recorded in chapter 18. They simply were not able or perhaps willing, as a tribe to militarily possess the land Joshua had given them.

As a result, they sought land which would be much easier and less of a challenge to take militarily. They found that land far to the north in a small city called Laish. They were able to take the land and slaughter its inhabitants. The entire tribe moved north and possessed this stolen land. Throughout the history of Israel, the phrase, "from Dan to Beersheba," has the equivalent meaning of the phrase from "north to south."

One other interesting fact about Dan; when we come to the listing of the 12 tribes in Revelation 7, Dan's name is left out. This omission is absolute and complete. There is no further mention of the tribe. One writer has said that Dan became the Ishmael of Jacob's family.

The Danites were persistent idolaters.

Naphtali

Naphtali was the sixth son of Jacob and the second by Bilhah, Rachael's handmaid. The meaning of his name is "*wrestler.*" Rachel named this baby because she had wrestled in prayer with God for favor and blessing (Genesis 30:8).

The tribe which bears his name inhabited a territory north of the Sea of Galilee extending along the northwest side of the Jordan north of Lake Huleh (Joshua 19:32-39).

Naphtali is praised in the Song of Deborah for placing itself in jeopardy on behalf of Israel (Judges 5:18). The tribe joined with Asher and Manasseh to help drive the Midianites out of the land (7:23).
During the reign of King Solomon, the territory was named a separate district (1 Kings 4:7, 15) and produced Hiram, the king's best brass worker (7:13-14).

The blessing which Jacob gave to Naphtali is recorded in one verse; Genesis 49:21 "Naphtali is a doe set free that bears beautiful fawns".
It is believed by many Bible scholars this is a prediction the descendants of this man would be erratic and need the restraining power of God to be productive.

Many of them were greatly gifted but lacked self-control.

One writer said he will scamper through life aimlessly and be without a goal. Perhaps this is a description of wild extravagance and reckless energy.

Gad

Gad was the seventh son of Jacob; the first born of Zilpah, Leah's maid. Pleased with giving Jacob another son, Leah named the boy Gad, meaning "good fortune" (30:11). Later he moved his family with Jacob to Egypt (Ex 1:4).

When Jacob blessed his sons, he predicted Gad would constantly be troubled by foreign invaders but would withstand them and put them to flight (Gen. 49:19). Gad became the father of seven sons (46:16) and the founder of the Gadites (Num. 2:14), one of the 12 tribes of Israel (Deut. 3:12, 16). The descendants of Gad were cattlemen and had a reputation for being fierce in battle (32:1; Deut. 33:20).

Gad was given a personal name meaning, "good fortune" because his birth was viewed by Leah as a further sign of God's blessing. His mother was Leah's maid, Zilpah. At the conclusion of the period of wilderness wandering, when the Israelites were preparing to occupy Canaan, the tribe of Gad requested permission, along with the tribe of Reuben and half the tribe of Manasseh, to settle east of the Jordan. This was permitted on the condition they would help in the conquest of Canaan (32:20–22; Joshua 1:12–18). Their reason was that they owned large numbers of livestock and the territory east of the Jordan was particularly suitable for raising livestock (Num. 32). This territory became known as Gad (Jer. 49:1). Though the exact limits of Gad's tribal territory are difficult to determine, the Gadites generally occupied land to the northeast of the Dead Sea (Josh. 13:24-28).
I am unaware of any specific descendent of Gad being mentioned in the scripture.

Asher

Asher was the eighth son of Jacob; the second son of Zilpah. His name means happy and is no doubt a response by his mother at his birth. We know nothing else of this son of Jacob individually. In the blessing given to him by his father Jacob he is acceptable to his brothers and as one who is blessed of God with royal foods and bountiful supplies.

Of all the tribes of Israel, Asher appears to have the least eventful history.

After the death of the Israelite judge Ehud, Israel fell into the hands of Jabin, king of Canaan. When the judge Deborah stirred up Barak to lead Israel's forces for battle, God gave their army a great victory and liberated them from their oppressor (Judges 4). After the victory Deborah complained the tribe of Asher had not sent any warriors. "Asher sat still at the coast of the sea, settling down by his landings" (5:17).

The one individual in the Scripture noted to be from the tribe of Asher is Anna. Her story is told in Luke 2:36-38. She was a widow who lived in the Temple at Jerusalem at the time of Jesus' birth. She met Mary, Joseph, and the Christ child in the Temple and proclaimed him as the Messiah.

There also seems to be a promise of endurance in the blessing pronounced by Jacob. "The bolts of your gates will be iron and bronze, and your strength will equal your days. Jacob's blessing said Asher would have rich food that he would give a king (Gen. 49:20), perhaps suggesting a period when the tribe would serve a foreign king. Asher's territorial allotment was in Phoenicia in the far northwest reaching to Tyre and Sidon on the Mediterranean coast (Josh. 19:24-31).

Asher was working for the Canaanites in the ports of the Mediterranean.

After looking at these sons of Jacob we should consider the legacy we will leave for our descendants.

Levi: Jacob's third son by Leah — Genesis 29:34

The name probably means, "to adhere," this no doubt is the hope of his mother his birth would cause her husband to return her affections. "This time my husband will be joined to me, because I have given him three sons" (Gen. 29:34).

Simeon and Levi were responsible for the mass murder at Shechem when all the male inhabitants of the city were ruthlessly murdered. Levi and Simeon committed this atrocity in order to avenge the violation of their sister Dinah by the prince of the city. Jacob condemned the act but did nothing immediately to curb his sons' behavior or to try and make amends for the terrible act they had committed.

Before his death he pronounced a judgment on Levi's behavior: "Simeon and Levi are brothers-- their swords are weapons of violence. Let me not enter their council, let me not join their assembly, for they have killed men in their anger and hamstrung oxen as they pleased. Cursed be their anger, so fierce, and their fury, so cruel! I will scatter them in Jacob and disperse them in Israel. (Gen 49:5-7).

According to these words Levi's descendants were to be dispersed among the tribes. They were to receive no land area in the Promised Land. They were to be scattered throughout the entire country. At first Levi was apparently a "secular" tribe like any other tribe.

The tribe's later position was God's reward for its faithfulness when Israel rebelled against God by constructing and worshipping the golden calf. "So, he [Moses] stood at the entrance to the camp and said, 'Whoever is for the LORD, come to me.' And all the Levites rallied to him. And he said unto them, Thus saith Jehovah, the God of Israel, Put ye every man his sword upon his thigh, and go to and fro from gate to gate throughout the camp, and slay every man his brother, and every man his companion, and every man his neighbor.

The Levites did as Moses commanded, and that day about 3,000 people died" (Exodus 32:26-28).This event began the "covenant with Levi" (Num. 18:19). After this the tribe of Levi would be accepted by God instead of Israel's firstborn sons, who belonged to him by the law of "Firstfruits" (Num. 3:11- 13).

Since Levi, as a tribe, could own no tribal territory, God Himself was their inheritance (Nm 18:20). They were given 48 villages, with their pasturelands, in which to live (Jos 21:1-42). These included the six cities of refuge (Jos 20:1-9). Since a Levite could not accumulate wealth, the tribe was supported by gifts and tithes (Num. 18:21). They were entrusted with the spiritual care of God's people (Deut. 24:29).

The tribe of Levi was composed of the descendants of Levi's three sons: Gershon, Kohath, and Merari. Moses, Aaron, and Miriam traced their genealogy to Kohath (Ex. 6:16). The Levites remained faithful to Jehovah at the occasion of the golden calf by Mt. Horeb. They were rewarded with the right to special service in and around the tabernacle (Ex. 32) and later in the temple.

In the book of Judges, we see the support of the tribe of Levi had fallen on "bad times." This account tells of a Levite traveling from place to place trying to sell his services and make a living. He eventually travels with the tribe of Dan to the north of the Promised Land and becomes the leader as that tribe worships Jehovah along with other idols in the area.

A good beginning does not assure a good ending!

Even this tribe purposely set aside by Moses to serve God was not immune to the idolatry of the people among whom they lived.

This should be a warning to each of us to carefully guard our associations.

Reuben: Eldest son of Jacob — Genesis 29:32; 46:8

As the firstborn son this child brought a great joy to Jacob. His birth marked the beginning of blessings in this foreign land. I am sure his father saw the birth of this child as an answer to prayer and the fulfillment of God's promises to take care of him in this foreign land.

There is an interesting account in Genesis 30 which gives us a window into the development of the family life in Jacob's home. We are told that Leah had stopped bearing children and as a result she gave her servant Zilpah to Jacob to continue producing children and hopefully gain the love of her husband. In the process of what was obviously a very well-known family conflict we are told Reuben goes out into the field (Genesis 30:14) and gatherers some mandrake plants. He brings them as a gift to his mother. In this part of the world these plants were believed to be a very strong aphrodisiac and almost always guaranteed childbirth. So, it is obvious even the children in this family knew about and were involved in the strife which was part of everyday life in Jacob's family.

In almost a side note we are later told in a one verse remark, "While Israel (Jacob) lived in the land, Reuben went in and lay with Bilhah his father's concubine. And Israel heard of it." At this point there is no record of Jacob doing anything about this breach of morality and family respect.

However, it is a major point in his final blessing to Reuben. In the final portion of the father's blessing he said of Reuben, "unstable as water, you shall not have preeminence, because you went up to your father's bed; then you defiled it." (Genesis 49:4)

Here is the example of a sin seemingly ignored, yet a memory is carried throughout the life of the offended Jacob. Because of this sin Jacob tells Reuben he will never have the preeminence of the firstborn within this family.

Reuben does show some maturity and consideration for his father; not to mention his brother Joseph. He objected to the plot to kill Joseph and planned to rescue him from the pit (37:22–35). When the brothers are entrapped by Joseph's plan in Genesis 42 Reuben admonishes them, "Did I not tell you not to sin against the boy? But you did not listen. So now there comes a reckoning for his blood." (Genesis 42:22)

Later, in the wilderness wanderings of the Israelites it was some of Reuben's descendants who were involved in the revolt recorded in Numbers 16. The revolt of Dathan and Abiram, men of the tribe of Reuben, was a challenge against the authority of Moses (16:1). It was also a protest the special position of tribe Levi.

At this point this tribe seems to be claiming the right of the firstborn which had been forfeited by their forefather's sin (Genesis 49:3, 4). The attempt failed, and God's judgment was a lesson (Numbers 16:33).

Reuben was a man of unmatched opportunity: being the firstborn of Jacob he stood in direct line to all the promises given to Abraham and Isaac. Yet his instability and impetuous nature caused him to disregard the spiritual promises which had been made to his father by the angel at Bethel. He was old enough to know and understand the heritage which he possessed. Yet his passion and instability caused him to cast the promises aside for a few moments of sexual gratification.

In this we see the same sort of instability which was demonstrated in the life of his Uncle Esau.

Physical desires often cloud our thoughts and cause us to make very poor decisions.

Many times, the result of these decisions does not become obvious for years.

Benjamin: the 2nd son of Jacob and Rachel — Genesis 35

The only son born in the land of Canaan

Benjamin was the last of Jacob's 12 sons and the only full brother to Joseph. Jacob named him Benjamin ("son of my right hand") after his dying mother Rachel had called him Ben-oni ("son of my sorrow," Genesis 35:18).

After Joseph had been sold into Egypt by his half-brothers, their father, Jacob, assuming Joseph was dead, became very protective of Benjamin. Later, with Joseph controlling the plot, Benjamin was used in the reunion in Egypt of Jacob and his 12 sons (Genesis 42 - 45).

The only events we know from Benjamin's life are those given to us in relationship to Joseph's plan for bringing his father and all his family into Egypt.

When prophesying concerning each of his sons, Jacob spoke of Benjamin's skill as a warrior and prophesied of the military fame of his descendants by saying, "Benjamin is a ravenous wolf, in the morning devouring the prey, and at even dividing the spoil" (Genesis 49:27).

Benjamin was one of the smallest of the 12 tribes of Israel (Numbers 1:36). Though small, the tribe of Benjamin played an important role in Israelite history, particularly in their conduct as great warriors (Judges 20:13–16; 1 Chr. 12:1, 2).

Ehud of Benjamin was the second of the Judges in Canaan. He was called a "savior" of the Israelites. He killed Eglon, king of Moab (Judges 3:15).

Members of the tribe helped Deborah and Barak defeat Sisera (Judges 5:14). The man chosen to be the first King of Israel, Saul, was a Benjamite.

The tribe produced many great men: political leaders, captains in Saul's army and David's army. The Benjamites were extremely skilled archers and overseers in Solomon's labor work.

The tribe displayed disobedience and lack of consistent courage by failing to clear their inheritance of Canaanites (Judges 1:21).

Following the custom of the day, the whole tribe defended the sinful and outlandish treatment and murder of a concubine from another tribe by a few of their members (Judges 19, 20).

These events of gross immorality united the other tribes against them, and the tribe of Benjamin was nearly wiped out in the warfare which followed. To keep the tribe from dying out the other tribes allowed the Benjamites to take captive several hundred women who then became their wives (Judges 21).

Jacob's dying blessing for his youngest son is recorded for us in Genesis 49:27, "Benjamin is a ravenous wolf, in the morning devouring the prey and, in the evening, dividing the spoil." Personal courage and a battle-hardened temperament are characteristics of the Benjamites throughout the Bible.

In the New Testament the apostle Paul was proud of his Benjamite ancestry, twice referring to himself as a Hebrew of Benjamin's tribe (Rom 11:1; Phil 3:5). In his sermon at Antioch of Pisidia, Paul also mentioned Benjamin as the tribe of King Saul, in his brief account of Israel's history (Acts 13:21).

Benjamin is a good example showing just because someone or something is small does not mean they are unimportant.

The tribe also stands out as an example of misplaced loyalty!

Joseph — Genesis 39, 41, 43, 45

His name means "may he add," in reference to Jehovah. He was born while his father, Jacob, was still serving Laban in the area of Haran. Soon after Joseph's birth Jacob and his family moved to Canaan where Joseph lived until he was 17. He was sold by his brothers as a slave. He ended up in Egypt where he lived until his death at 110 years of age. Joseph was born about 1910 BC, he died about 1800 BC.

Joseph is of major importance in the plan of God. He provided the link between Israel as a family and Israel as a nation. He was God's provision for the dysfunctional family of Jacob and their survival in a hostile world.

Joseph was dearly loved by his father because he was the first son born to him by the first love of his life, Rachel. After Rachel's death, Jacob lavished his love on Joseph so much that his brothers hated their younger brother.

Joseph also experienced dreams which indicated to him he would one day rule over his entire family. He unwisely shared these dreams with his brothers. Their hatred for him grew and caused them to come up with a plan to kill him. God intervened in the circumstances and Joseph was sold to a group of Midianite traders who ultimately sold him into slavery in Egypt.

Even as a slave in Egypt, God did not abandon this young man. Even as a slave in Egypt, this young man did not abandon God!

Joseph made the very best of the circumstances in which he found himself. As a slave he determined to serve his master to the very best of his ability.

When given an opportunity to have an affair with his master's wife, Joseph refused. His rejection turned her against him, and he was eventually put into prison by his master. In prison he lived in such a way that soon he became the equivalent of a trustee and was given much responsibility. He later interpreted the dreams of two other prisoners; one was executed and the other was restored to his position.

Several years later when Pharaoh had a dream, the prisoner who had been restored remembered Joseph and his skill in interpreting dreams. Pharaoh sent for the prisoner who could interpret dreams and soon Joseph was promoted to the ancient equivalent of Prime Minister.

In all his suffering and misfortune there is no record of Joseph ever discrediting or disobeying Jehovah. When he rose to a position of authority and importance, his obedience to God continued. By following the direction of God, he was able to preserve the nation of Egypt through a great famine and was able to supply food for his own family who came from Canaan.

This incredible story finishes with Joseph's family living in the land of Goshen and growing prosperous. After Jacob's death Joseph assured his brothers, he bore them no animosity and they could settle down and live out their lives in peace. At the age of 110 Joseph died and was buried in Egypt. Before his death he asked that when the people of Israel return to the Land of Canaan, they carry his bones back and bury them in the land.

The life of Joseph provides us with an incredible story which shows no matter how complicated and confused the circumstances may be God is totally in control and is always planning the best for His people.

We also see how God rewards His followers for constant moral obedience.

We never know who is watching our behavior.

Joseph: the dreamer

After the death of Rachel, Jacob and his family continued to the south and settled in the southern part of the land of Canaan. This story began some years later when Joseph was a teenager. The love Jacob had for Rachel was transferred to her older son. Joseph was given the coat of "many colors" by his father. The exact meaning of this phrase is difficult to interpret, but the coat shows favoritism on the part of Jacob.

It is very apparent from the reaction of his brothers that it gave him special status in the family. One writer has suggested it meant he was in management and not labor. The presenting of the coat to Joseph by his father created a breach between him and his brothers which was to be the source of much grief.

The text tells us Joseph had a dream. Dreams in the ancient world were considered a divine revelation and were taken very seriously. Nearly all people believed dreams to be omens or direction from God. Dreams were often filled with symbolism as we see in detail in the book of Daniel.

Joseph had two dreams. In the first, as he told his brothers, they were all working in a field binding sheaves and his arose and stood upright while all the others bowed down to it. His brothers interpreted this to mean he would control or have sovereignty over them. The Scripture says they hated him even more.

In his second dream he saw the sun, moon and 11 stars bowing down to him. When he told this dream to his father and his brothers his father rebuked him. His brothers became even more jealous of him. The second dream is interesting because it includes the information Joseph's parents will also bow down to him. His sovereignty is not just to touch his brothers, but it is to include the entire family.

Sometime later Joseph was sent to check on his brothers who were tending flocks in the hill country north of where they lived. When his brothers saw him approaching, they made plans to get rid of him.

The chapter ends with a note telling us Joseph is on his way to Egypt. His destination is known, and his faith remains to be decided. His brothers did not just want what Joseph had, his father's love; they wanted to rule him!

What a person who is envious wants is not, first what another person has; an envious person wants the other person not to have it!

Envy is to want someone else's good so strongly you are tempted to steal it; to resent someone else's good so much one is tempted to destroy. Envy carries with it personal resentment; envy resents not only someone else's blessing but also the one who has been blessed. Throughout Christian history envy has been classified as one of the seven deadly sins. In our culture, however, it has gained a certain level of acceptance.

Advertising encourages envy and lust by implying if one is inspired by it in someone else's life then the other person is achieving something that is good.

Our goal should be to learn from and even surpass their success.

We often express our resentment by trying to make a friend or a colleague look badly at every opportunity and in the process, we hope to make ourselves look better by comparison.

Learn to enjoy and praise the accomplishments of others.

When the caravan, which purchased Joseph, arrived in Egypt, Joseph was sold to an important official in the court of Pharaoh. His name was Potiphar, a common name in Egypt. Potiphar is given two different titles in the narrative, "official of Pharaoh" and "Captain of the guard." He appears to have been a high military official in the court of Pharaoh. Joseph's service for this man began with small jobs and we are told Potiphar quickly realized the "Lord was with Joseph." Everything he did turned out well for his owner. He was quickly promoted and soon he was running the entire household for his master. The narrative of the story sounds very much like what happened to Jacob in Haran.

God rewards those who are faithful in his service no matter how inconsequential it may appear.

Soon a new problem appeared for Joseph. His master's wife became captivated with him and tried to seduce him. The account is given in such a way as to make it clear Joseph did not lead Potiphar's wife on or allow himself to enjoy her company at any level. He was placed in danger only by a spiteful and hurtful act of this woman. She accuses him of attempting to rape her.

Potiphar responds with "burning anger" (39:19). Joseph is placed in the King's prison. It is interesting to understand if Potiphar had believed his wife's story at this point Joseph probably would have been executed. The King's prison was a place for political prisoners, and it is surprising a foreign slave is placed in this environment. It is also interesting to observe it is possible this was a prison over which Potiphar was the overseer. The text in 40:3 identifies the prison as "in the house of the captain of the guard." This is the same phrase as the title given to Potiphar and 39:1.

Once again Joseph, through no fault of his own, has been falsely accused and punished.

By combining various references, we can determine Joseph spent 11 years in Potiphar's house and in prison. There is no indication how that time was divided. The people in this prison were high ranking members of Pharaoh's court who had experienced his wrath. These were not "common prisoners." Here Joseph slowly rises to power and is given more and more authority by those in charge of the prison. Very soon two of these prisoners are the recipients of dreams and in the talk within the prison the inmates are trying to decide what these dreams mean. Remember, dreams were thought to communicate information about the future for the recipient. Joseph interprets the dreams of the two inmates; one with a positive result and one with a negative result. His interpretations come to pass exactly as he described the situation.

Two years later Pharaoh had two dreams which could not be interpreted. As these dreams were discussed in the court of Pharaoh, the chief cupbearer, who had been restored after his dream was interpreted by Joseph, remembered Joseph's interpretation and informed Pharaoh of the Hebrew slave who could interpret dreams. Pharaoh quickly sent for Joseph to be brought to him. When Pharaoh presented the problem of the dreams Joseph replied, "It is not in me; God will give Pharaoh a favorable answer." After listening to the retelling of the dreams Joseph was able, with the wisdom granted to him by God, to interpret the dreams. Joseph told Pharaoh the doubling of the dreams meant the thing was fixed and would come to pass.

From this point Joseph moved from interpretation to advice; he suggested to Pharaoh he appoint someone to oversee the collection of crops in the first seven years and the process of distributing what needed to be in the seven years of famine. Pharaoh was so impressed with the suggestion of Joseph; without a doubt this impression was from God. Joseph was appointed as overseer of all the land.

At this point Joseph was 30 years old.

He had been in bondage in one form or another for 13 years.

God's ways are not our ways!

Joseph's Son: Ephraim — Genesis 41:50-52; 48:1-22

Joseph's younger son was born of Asenath before the seven years of famine in Egypt. He was the ancestor of the tribe which bears his name. Later the name came to designate the northern kingdom of Israel.

Ephraim's boyhood overlapped the last 17 years of his grandfather, the patriarch Jacob, who migrated to Egypt during the years of plenty. Therefore, Ephraim could have learned of God's promises and blessings directly from Jacob. Later Jacob obtained a promise from his grandsons Ephraim and Manasseh to bury him in Canaan. After asking them to make this promise and receiving their guarantee they would fulfill his wishes he adopted them. The adoption gave the two brothers position and legal rights equal to Jacob's eldest sons, Reuben and Simeon (Gen. 48:5).

Many Bible commentators think in naming his son Ephraim (Gen 41:52), Joseph was making a play on words based on a Hebrew root meaning "to be fruitful." In support of this theory they note the hill country later assigned to Ephraim's tribe was one of the most fertile areas in Palestine, and at present it is still planted with vines and fruit trees such as pomegranate, olive and carob. Prior to Israelite settlement, the area was wooded (Jos. 17:18).

It is difficult to determine the exact limits of Ephraim's territory, since it is often mentioned with Manasseh's tribe. Ephraim was allotted land in the heart of Canaan, the Promised Land, between the Jordan River and the Mediterranean Sea. One half of Manasseh's allotment formed Ephraim's northern boundary (Jos 16:5-9).

Ephraim became a great tribe, and its members often held prominent positions in the nation of Israel.

The first census taken in the wilderness lists the total of Ephraimite soldiers as 40,500 (Num. 1:33). After the wilderness wanderings the number of warriors dropped to 32,500 (Num. 26:37). In Israel's encampment around the tabernacle, Ephraim was the leader of the western camp, supported by the tribes of Manasseh and Benjamin (Num. 2:18-24).

Joshua, the son of Nun was descended from Ephraim (Num. 13:8). Under Joshua's leadership Ephraim and the other tribes conquered Canaan and received their promised inheritance (Jos 16).

In the days of the judges the Ephraimites felt slighted when they were not called upon to assist others in their battles. They quarreled with Gideon because of his belated invitation to help against the Midianites (Judges 8:1-6). This was the same type of attitude displayed in the judgeship of Jephthah of Gilead, who defeated the Ammonites (Judges 12:1-6).

Judah was Ephraim's main rival and even under David such animosity was evident (2 Sam. 18; 19:41-20:22). Discontent in the north with Solomon's rule (1 Kgs. 11:26-40), combined with a foolish decision by Rehoboam, Solomon's son, brought about the division of the kingdom. The 10 northern tribes (Israel) were then ruled by Jeroboam.

After the northern tribes separated, the capitals of the northern kingdom; Shechem, Tirzah, and Samaria were situated in the territory of Ephraim. The establishment of Samaria by King Omri of Israel gave the Ephraimites more direct access to the great north-south trunk road (Via Maris) through the western plain.

The misplaced pride of the tribe of Ephraim caused much distress and grief.

Their pride eventually caused them to separate from Judah and follow false gods.

Can you see how pride goes before a fall?

Joseph's son: Manasseh — Genesis 41:50-52; 48:1-22

Manasseh was the firstborn son of Joseph and his Egyptian wife, Asenath. Manasseh, along with Ephraim his brother, visited their grandfather Jacob on his deathbed. Jacob announced Manasseh and Ephraim were to be considered his own, not Joseph's, sons (48:5, 6). This explains why Ephraim and Manasseh, in that order, provided their names for two of the 12 tribes of Israel but Joseph did not.

The birth of this son was a highlight of Joseph's happiness after the long bitterness of his experience. In the joy of the moment, the dark years past could be forgotten; therefore, he called the name of the firstborn Manasseh ("causing one to forget"), he said, God has made me to forget all my toil.

When Jacob was near his death, Joseph brought his two sons to his father who blessed them. Jacob preferred Ephraim, the second son of Joseph, to Manasseh his elder brother, thus indicating the relative positions of their descendants (Gen 48). Before Joseph died, he saw the children of Machir the son of Manasseh (Gen 50:23). Machir was born to Manasseh by his concubine, an Ammonitess (1 Ch 7:14). Whether he married her before leaving for Egypt is not said. She was the sister of Huppim and Shuppim. Of Manasseh's personal life no details are recorded in Scripture.

Tribe of Manasseh

Geographically Manasseh was the largest of the 12 tribes of Israel. It was unique because it was the only tribe with two territories, a half tribe in each. Isolated from each other by the Jordan River valley, they developed separately.

The Western Half Tribe

The half tribe west of the Jordan was the more important, both in Old Testament and New Testament times, because it was the main tribe of the northern kingdom of Israel (931–722 BC).

The Eastern Half Tribe

Prominent citizens of the eastern half tribe included the "Judges" Jair and Jephthah (Judges 10:3–5; 11:6– and David's friend Barzillai (2 Sam. 19:31–39). Principal cities were Jabesh-Gilead, a Levitical city, and Ramoth-Gilead, a city of refuge, Jos 20:8; 21:38.

The eastern territory was usually called simply "the half tribe of Manasseh" until David (1000–961 BC) made it an administrative district of his kingdom (1 Chr. 27:21). Under Jeroboam I (930–909 BC), it joined, on equal terms, with eight other tribes and with the western half tribe, to form a confederacy of 10 tribes, the Northern Kingdom of Israel. In 930 B.C. Syria and Assyria both held eastern Manasseh temporarily, in the 9th and 8th centuries B.C.

King Tiglath-Pileser III of Assyria invaded the area, conquered it, deported its people, and scattered them throughout his empire (1 Chr. 5:26) about 10 years before the rest of the northern kingdom fell to the Assyrians in 722 BC.

Most of the people in the western territory were left behind, intermarried with the foreigners, began to worship pagan gods, and became ancestors of the Samaritans (17:24–41). Later, the region was known as Gilead.

Here we have another story of missed opportunity.

A once powerful and influential tribe came to nothing because they left their true God and served the gods of the land.

There is enough detail in Chapter 41 for us to identify the steps taken to raise Joseph to this position throughout all of Egypt. He was given Pharaoh's signet ring, linen robes, and the golden chain. These are marks of installation with power and signify his rank, status, and office. The mention of chariots in relationship to the government would be like our use of limousines today. The men running before the chariots would be like our Secret Service protection.

The meaning of his Egyptian name is uncertain, but it clearly speaks of power and authority. His marriage to a daughter of the priest of On put him into the circle of one of the most powerful priestly families in all of Egypt. It is interesting to speculate on how much these powerful men heard about the God of the Hebrews.

The famine was very severe in the land of Canaan and soon it was necessary for Jacob to send his family into Egypt to try and buy food. Now we see God driving the brothers back into a relationship with their hated brother. We are told Joseph dealt with his brothers harshly and accused them of being spies. Joseph's behavior is to determine whether his brothers have reformed their ways or not. He tests them in specific ways first by keeping Simeon in Egypt and secondly by instructing them to bring Benjamin back when they return. Later in this chapter we see in the 13 years since Joseph's sale into slavery the brothers have experienced guilt and suspicion among themselves over their actions.

When the brothers return home, Judah is finally able to persuade Jacob to allow Benjamin to return to Egypt. If the first visit of these brothers brought guilt and remorse to the surface, this second visit, as set-up by Joseph, seems to have kept them completely off-balance.

This is a test devised by Joseph to see if his brothers are still willing to abandon the sons of Rachel to save themselves. We must remember they have no idea the Egyptian official they are dealing with is their long-lost brother. When the family is ready to return to Canaan, Joseph instructs his servants to place his silver cup in Benjamin's sack of grain. Once the cup has been discovered and the frightened group of Hebrews is returned to the court of Egypt, the plot moves rapidly to a conclusion.

When Joseph is finally convinced his brothers have reformed, he reveals himself to them. His brothers are understandably shocked and speechless and probably very literally scared almost to death.
God had directed all these events in order to accomplish His purposes.

Joseph calms their fears and explains God is in control of the circumstances. Even though the brothers intended everything they did to him for evil, God worked it for good.
Joseph now has a plan for the restoration and salvation of the family.

The family's continued existence literally depends on all of them moving to Egypt. It is clear Joseph has thought this through and has made all the preparations necessary.

Two interesting details can be pointed out.
First, the Joseph story began with favoritism involving a special coat and now as it draws to a close Joseph communicates his favor by giving five sets of clothing to each of his brothers.

Secondly, Joseph warns his brothers not to quarrel on the way back.
What does he mean? He means don't get worked up or agitated about whose fault this was or fear and anxiety will take hold.

God is always in control!

Book Three

1. Moses' Parents	Exodus 1:1-2:10
2. Moses: An Introduction	Exodus, Deuteronomy
3. Moses: The Scholar	Exodus 5-6, 14
4. Moses: The Shepherd	Exodus 3, 4
5. Moses: The Savior #1	Exodus 3
6. Moses: The Savior #2	Exodus 4-6
7. God Changed Moses and His People	Exodus 25-40
8. Miriam	Exodus 15
9. Aaron	Exodus 32
10. Jethro	Exodus 2, 18
11. Nadab & Abihu: Fire from the Lord	Exodus 28; Leviticus 10
12. Korah	Numbers 16, 17
13. Balak	Numbers 22-24
14. Baalam	Numbers 22-24
15. Rahab	Joshua 2, 6
16. Caleb	Joshua 14, 15
17. Joshua: The Servant	Joshua 22-24
18. Joshua: The Leader	Joshua 22-24
19. Othniel	Judges 3
20. Deborah	Judges 4, 5
21. Gideon: Called	Judges 6-8
22. Gideon: in Battle	Judges 6, 7
23. Gideon: Beyond Deliverance	Judges 7:23-8:3
24. Abimelech	Judges 9
25. Jephthah	Judges 11, 12
26. Jephthah's Vow	Judges 11, 12
27. Samson's Parents	Judges 13, 14
28. Sampson: The Plan	Judges 13-16
29. Samson: His Women	Judges 14-16
30. Samson: The End Result	Judges 16

Moses' Parents — Exodus 1:1-2:10

Very little is known concerning the parents of Moses. His father's name was Amram and his mother's name was Jochebed.

The name Amram means "high people." The name Jochebed means "God is honor."

Both people were Hebrew slaves who were born, lived, and died in Egypt. They lived and raised their family around 1400 BC, when Egypt was experiencing one of its most prosperous periods in history.

The importance of these two people is often overlooked when we study the Bible. These were two young Hebrew people born and raised in slavery who loved God and were doing their very best to live according to the principles of God.

When they were thinking of getting married, they were faced with the reality the Egyptian government was severely persecuting all Hebrews. Men were conscripted for physical labor in building projects and were often beaten. Women were pressed into domestic service as maids, cooks, and various other duties. This would have been a major concern and worry as they approached their life together.

They also had to make the decision of whether they would have children. Miriam was probably their firstborn; Aaron probably their second child. It was perhaps after that the Egyptian Pharaoh ordered the death of all male children. I wonder what questions went through their mind as they considered whether to have a third child?

With the birth of Moses, they now faced a major dilemma and challenge to their faith. What would they do with this beautiful baby boy? Clearly, they attempted to hide the child if they could.

There is a very real possibility Moses spent the first three months or so of his life dressed and cared for by his family as though he were a girl. But very soon it became impossible to conceal his gender any longer.

What would they do? We are not given the details or any information relating to the family discussion, but it seems clear Jochebed and Miriam were involved in the plan.

They built a small basket and made it waterproof; the entire family prayed for Gods guidance and protection and then they placed the precious cargo in the Nile River and completely gave Moses over to the care of God.

The Nile was inhabited by crocodiles and hippopotamus; there were many wild and vicious animals which inhabited the reeds along the shore. What would happen if the child were discovered? Would he be killed?

Miriam was sent to watch over her brother and report the results to her family. We know the story and her actions were part of the salvation of Moses.

God used this man and woman to begin the deliverance of the nation of Israel.

They had to act upon their faith and belief in the providence and care of God.

Moses: An Introduction

"*The one drawn out,*" he was taken out of the water. He was saved from certain death to save his people.

Moses' life began in the Nile Delta region of Egypt. He spent 40 years on the "*backside of the desert*" as a shepherd. Then he spent 40 years leading the Israelites through the same desert on the way to the Promised Land. He died on Mount Nebo in the modern-day country of Jordan. He never went into the land of Canaan.

The Exodus took place in 1447 BC; this date can be established in conjunction with II Kings 6:1 and the application of other historical data which is readily available.

The Exodus is the most important event in Jewish history. The Passover, in the spring of the year, is celebrated to memorialize the event which brought Israel from Egypt into the land of Canaan.

God used the 40 years in the wilderness to unify the children of Israel and make them a nation.

In the fall of the year the Israelites celebrate the feast of Tabernacles which memorializes the wilderness wanderings and the hardships of the desert. They were told to explain to their children these events and the importance of each event. God had promised the patriarchs, Abraham, Isaac, and Jacob, that He would give them a land. The deliverance from Egypt and the journey through the wilderness was the first step in the keeping of this promise.

The miraculous events of the Exodus are one of the major highlights in the Bible.

Moses is a man of amazing highs and lows. There is more Scripture devoted to Moses than any other person in the Bible except for Jesus Christ. **Here are some of the unique events in the life of Moses**

- His birth and preservation at birth were miraculous
- He was guilty of murder; yet he saw God
- He performed more miracles than any other person recorded in Scripture
- He was able to lead over two million people out of Egypt to the border of the Promised Land
- He wrote the first five books of the Old Testament
- He was with Jesus and Elijah at the Transfiguration: God did take him to the Promised Land

Moses is referred to by name in the Scriptures 829 times. Abraham is named only 231 times, Isaac 128 times, Jacob 358 times. In the New Testament Peter is named 158 times, John 131 times, Paul 157 times and Jesus 937 times.

This little bit of trivia illustrates how important Moses is in the Bible. The only person of a comparable number of mentions is the Lord Jesus Christ.

Moses shows us God can use anyone! He lost his temper on several occasions. He was constantly frustrated, aggravated, and irritated with the Israelites and their lack of obedience.

He was born a slave and raised as royalty. He lived in the desert as a common and despised shepherd. Shepherds were considered unclean and part of the lowest rung of human society. God moved him from the top to the bottom; from the bottom to the top and left him in the desert.

He was the Prince of Egypt and the shepherd of rebellious people. He was one of the confidants of God and one of the loneliest people on the face of the earth. He never owned a home and as far as we know left nothing to his descendants except his shepherd's staff.

He was God's unique man. In an absolutely unique circumstance!

Moses: The Scholar — Exodus 5:1-6:13, 14:5:31

The life of Moses lends itself to a very easy analysis, he spent one third of his life in three different environments for three different purposes.

- He was a scholar in Egypt becoming learned in all the wisdom of the Egyptians.
- He was a shepherd in the desert learning about the environment and the conditions he would face in the final one third of his life.
- He was a leader and a builder of the nation of Israel as they spent 40 years in the desert.

Moses the scholar was prepared by God in the land of Egypt for the task God had planned for him. He was born to two devout Hebrew parents who faced the opposition of an evil Egyptian Pharaoh. They were able to save the life of their son after the Pharaoh ordered all male children to be killed.

Moses was placed in a basket of bulrushes, waterproofed with an asphalt substance and placed in the Nile River. His older sister Miriam was given the task of watching over her baby brother.

We are told when the basket was seen by the Egyptian princess, she ordered one of her servants to retrieve the basket. When she saw the baby, God moved her heart in such a way she fell in love with the infant. In God's divine guidance she hired Moses' mother to come to the palace and help raise the child. His mother, no doubt, trained him in all the ways of the Hebrews. He was told the stories of the patriarchs Abraham, Isaac, and Jacob, as well as the salvation brought to the Egyptians by his ancestor Joseph.

Later when he became old enough to take part in the Egyptian education process he was educated as an Egyptian Prince.

He would have been well schooled in academics including mathematics, geometry, linguistics, science, and even astronomy.

He also would have been trained in all the physical activities necessary to become a leader in Egypt. He would have received training in the martial arts and warfare.

He would have been educated in the Egyptian culture and Egyptian heritage including a full knowledge of all the Egyptian gods. He would have understood the great building accomplishments and the world leadership of the Egyptian Empire.

In other words, it would be fair to say in the early part of his life he "had it all."

One day however we are told as he was visiting the Hebrews, perhaps feeling a desire to know more about the people who were part of his nationality and Hebrew heritage, he saw an Egyptian beating a Hebrew and he killed the Egyptian. The next day as he was in the same area, he saw two Hebrews fighting and he attempted to stop the fight. One of the men accused him saying, "What, are you going to do kill us like you killed the Egyptian?"

It was obvious others knew what he had done and soon his racial heritage and his rash action would create trouble.

He realized he must flee, and he went into the desert.

He was leaving the comfort of the known for the unknown!

But God prepared Moses' knowledge, skills, and physical training.

At 40 years of age, Moses fled from Egypt, only to spend another 40 years herding sheep in the very land through which he would later shepherd the people of God. Moses went into the land of Midian. He stopped at a well to rest and drink. While he was seated by the well, seven daughters of the priest of Midian came to draw water and fill the watering troughs for their sheep to drink.

Other shepherds soon came along and began to drive the girls away. Moses got up and came to the rescue of the women and watered their flocks himself.

When the girls returned home early in the day their father wanted to know how they had accomplished their task so early in the day. They told him an Egyptian rescued us from the shepherds and even drew water for us. The grateful father invited Moses to come and eat with them. The invitation became a long one as Moses married one of his daughters and learned to care for the flocks himself.

Moses seems to be very much like his ancestor Jacob. Jacob had reacted in anger when he saw a similar event at the well in Haran; Moses reacted in the desert of Midian.

He seems to be a sensitive person: when he saw an injustice, he wanted to do something to correct it. It was this impulse acted on rashly which caused him to kill the Egyptian and made him want to intervene in the quarrel between the two Hebrews.

Leaving Egypt under these conditions allowed God to begin to train him in a new occupation. He has settled down in a very remote location and is learning the life and ways of a desert shepherd.

He has a new family, a new wife and soon two sons. As he spends 40 years in the desert of Midian the years are passing in Egypt as well. Those who wanted revenge on him died and to a large extent he has been forgotten by the Egyptians.

The Israelites' situation in Egypt continued to deteriorate; their labor became more and more difficult and their treatment more and more harsh. But God remembered! He never forgot the nation which He was going to build and the children which He was going to train.

God remembers and blesses at His appointed time.

God was about to change the life of Moses once again! As he was herding his sheep deep in the desert of Sinai, a strange sight caught his eye. He saw a bush which was burning but was not consumed. He stopped to see this unusual phenomenon. When he paused a moment and approached the bush God spoke to him.

In a few verses in chapter 3:6-10 God once again changed the life of this 80-year-old man

1. I am the God of your ancestors (3:6) - the past
2. I have heard (3:7) - the present
3. The rescue (3:8-9) - the future

It was now time to put his training into practice! Leaving the comfort of the known for a new calling.

But God has prepared Moses with new knowledge, skills, and physical training.

Is God calling you today?

Moses: The Savior #1 — Exodus 3

God was about to change Moses' life once again. At the age of 80 he was about to begin a new and surprising adventure.

While caring for his father-in-law's sheep, Moses encountered a bush which was burning, but was not being consumed. He stopped to look, and God spoke to him.

God told him He had heard the continual cries of the Israelites as they were oppressed in Egypt. He was going to rescue them from their misery and Moses was the one He had chosen to do the job.

Moses reaction, not surprisingly, was total unbelief. It was roughly equivalent to today's vernacular expression, "Why me?"

He asked God who he was and how he could possibly do such a thing. God's answer was direct and to the point, "You are nobody, but I will go with you."

Notice God did not attempt to debate the issue. God reminded Moses he was a child of God and because of the presence of the Lord he would be made all he needed to be to face this challenge.

Moses continued with his excuses; "They won't believe me!" After all, why should they; look at my track record. I am a murderer and ran away from Egypt to avoid capture. Moses continued offering excuses, he said, again, they won't believe me.

Moses obviously thought what God was asking was impossible. Once again God did not argue with His chosen deliverer.

God gave Moses two signs to show to the children of Israel. He could throw his staff down and it would become a snake. If he put his hand inside of his cloak it would become leprous; when he put it back inside and took it out once again, it was healed. God told him, if this isn't enough, I will give you more.

Count the "I wills" in Exodus 3.

Moses continued with his excuses and his objections; it is obvious he was aware of his inadequacy in relationship to the task ahead of him.

It is important we face our own limitations and reject trust in our own abilities!

But we can't be too overwhelmed by our own weaknesses to allow God to use us.

For each objection God had a promise, He said "I will" and then He provided His promise.

When Moses said he couldn't speak, God's reply was, "I will send Aaron." Then God added, as a matter of fact, he is on his way to meet you right now.

Moses is leaving the comfort of the known for the unknown!

Leaving the comfort of the known for the unknown is always a dangerous adventure, but God has prepared Moses for everything which lies ahead.

What "I wills" has God given you?

God now begins to put His promise of deliverance into action. He has worked behind the scenes for over 80 years. God will now begin to move Moses to lead Israel from slavery to freedom.

In these chapters we witness the transition of Moses from the shepherd in the Midian wilderness to the leader as the Israelites leave Egypt. After his conversation with God and his understanding of this new mission God had given him, he returned to his father-in-law and explained what God had told him.

Moses was being called to leave his familiar and comfortable way of life and return to the luxury of Egypt. But he knows his life will not be so luxurious, because some will remember his betrayal of what they would see as his Egyptian heritage. He was returning to the land and the culture in which he grew up.

He will face many pressures and fears which had long been forgotten.

After his explanation, Jethro said to Moses, "Go, and I wish you well." The journey had begun! On the way, Moses met Aaron and they began to plan their mission. The first step was to meet with the Israelites and tell them everything God had planned.

Moses and Aaron were able to gain an audience with Pharaoh. Here in front of one of the greatest kings in the world stood an 80-year-old shepherd and an 83-year-old slave. Moses presented his request based on the word of God. They did not begin with meaningless flattery. These two men presented their request for Pharaoh to let Israel go. We know, of course, that Pharaoh refused, and this began the contest of the plagues.

As a result of the appearance of Moses and Aaron before the great King the workload of the slaves was greatly increased. The Israelites reacted with anger and unbelief toward Moses and Aaron. The resulting chaos and confusion caused Moses to return to God and ask, "Why did you send me?"

God answered his questions and overruled his objections. Then He sent him back to Pharaoh! Moses was told, "I will make you like God to Pharaoh, and your brother Aaron will be your prophet. You are to say everything I command you."

The plagues began and escalated until the death of the firstborn. This last plague finally caused the release of God's people from Egypt. There was great excitement as the Jews prepared to leave and enter a totally unknown world.

God did not lead them the way they expected to go. They moved out toward the Red Sea and not toward the coast. They were on the edge of the wilderness and they did not understand why.

God must teach them to be a nation and to rely on Him for their every need. This was not the job Moses had anticipated. I'm sure over and over he and Aaron discussed the problem and expressed the idea, "This isn't at all what I thought it would be like."

What can we learn from the experience of Moses and Aaron?

We need to face our limitations but remember God can expand our limits. We must learn to expect disappointments.

We must learn to use our opportunities as they are presented.

How God Changed Moses and His People — Exodus 25-27, 30-31, 35-40

Let's take special note of God's **"I wills"** of Exodus 19:5-6, 23:20-24, **19:5-6**, *Now* ***if you obey*** *me fully and keep my covenant,* ***then*** *out of all nations* ***you will be*** *my treasured possession. Although the whole earth is mine,* ***you will be*** *for me a kingdom of priests and a holy nation.' These are the words you are to speak to the Israelites."*

Ex. 23:20-24, "*See,* ***I am*** *sending an angel ahead of you to guard you along the way and to bring you to the place I have prepared. Pay attention to him and listen to what he says. Do not rebel against him; he will not forgive your rebellion, since my Name is in him.* ***If you listen*** *carefully to what he says and do all that I say,* ***I will be*** *an enemy to your enemies and will oppose those who oppose you. My angel will go ahead of you and bring you into the land of the Amorites, Hittites, Perizzites, Canaanites, Hivites and Jebusites, and* ***I will*** *wipe them out. Do not bow down before their gods or worship them or follow their practices. You must demolish them and break their sacred stones to pieces.*

The people accept Ex. 24:3-4,
When Moses went and told the people all the LORD's words and laws, they responded with one voice, "***Everything the LORD has said we will do.***" Moses then wrote down everything the LORD had said. He got up early the next morning and built an altar at the foot of the mountain and set up twelve stone pillars representing the twelve tribes of Israel.

What is this "with"?
God said in Exodus 25:8: *"Let them make Me a sanctuary, that I may dwell among them." What does this mean; it is totally different from anything they had experienced in Egypt. God told Abraham He would be a God to him and his descendants. Now he has made an entirely new promise, "You shall be a special treasure to Me above all people . . . A kingdom of priests and a holy nation."* (Exodus 19:5-6). The rest of the Bible is essentially the outworking or fulfillment of Exodus 25:8.

"In" a new promise for this age,
John 16:5-15, *"Now I am going to him who sent me, yet none of you asks me, 'Where are you going?' Because I have said these things, you are filled with grief. But I tell you the truth: It is for your good that I am going away. Unless I go away, the Counselor will not come to you; but if I go, I will send him to you. When he comes, he will convict the world of guilt in regard to sin and righteousness and judgment: in regard to sin, because men do not believe in me; in regard to righteousness, because I am going to the Father, where you can see me no longer; because I am going to the Father, where you can see me no longer; and in regard to judgment, because the prince of this world now stands condemned. "I have much more to say to you, more than you can now bear. But when he, the Spirit of truth, comes, he will guide you into all truth. He will not speak on his own; he will speak only what he hears, and he will tell you what is yet to come. He will bring glory to me by taking from what is mine and making it known to you. All that belongs to the Father is mine. That is why I said the Spirit will take from what is mine and make it known to you."*

"*And the Word became flesh and dwelt among us, and we beheld His glory.*" John 1:14. A literal translation of this passage is, "the Word became flesh and tabernacled among us." When the Old Testament was first translated into Greek (well before the time of Christ), the Greek noun derived from this verb was used to express the Hebrew words for tabernacle. Furthermore, the Hebrew word for tabernacle in Exodus 25:9 is derived from the word dwell in 25:8. "*Then have them make a sanctuary for me, and I will dwell among them.*"

The linguistic ties between Exodus 25:8 and Christ's indwelling of us could not be stronger. This extends even to the book of Revelation 21:2-3, "*I saw the Holy City, the new Jerusalem, coming down out of heaven from God, prepared as a bride beautifully dressed for her husband. And I heard a loud voice from the throne saying, "Now the dwelling of God is with men, and he will live with them. They will be his people, and God himself will be with them and be their God.*"

The coming of Christ is inseparable from Exodus 25:8.

If you want to understand Exodus, you must read your New Testament.

If you want to understand the New Testament you must read the Old Testament.

Miriam — Exodus 15:1-21

Miriam's name is as mysterious as her personality and history. The name probably belongs to a family of words which suggests "*bitterness*". Other names derived from this root would include Mary, Maria and Mariam. The name could mean bitterness or rebellion. It is like the refrain of Naomi when she returned to Bethlehem, "Don't call me Naomi," she told them. "*Call me Mara, because the Almighty has made my life very bitter*." (Ruth 1:20)

Miriam was born in Egypt as a slave; left Egypt with the Israelites led by her brother Moses and died in the wilderness. The time frame for her life was the same as Moses and Aaron. Tradition tells us she was the oldest child of Amram and Jochebed. She was the elder sister of Aaron and Moses. The Hebrew historian Josephus, in his The Antiquities of the Jews, tells us she was the wife of Hur. This would make Bezaleel, one of the major architects and builders of the tabernacle (Exodus 31), her grandson.

She is probably the sister who stood and watched over her baby brother Moses near the Nile. She is the one who convinced the Princess of Egypt to hire a Hebrew woman to nurse the child. The woman she brought to Pharaoh's daughter was Moses' mother. A good guess would be she was probably 10 to 12 years old at that time.

Miriam is mentioned for the first time by name in Exodus 15:20. Here she is called by the title "prophetess." She is also identified as the sister of Aaron.

Both identifications help us understand the position of influence she held among the Israelites. She led the Israelite women in celebrating the victory over the Egyptians with a beautiful song of praise to God.

The Israelites had just passed through the Red Sea on dry ground. They had seen the army of Egypt washed away.

She led the Israelites in celebration as they sang:
I will sing unto the LORD, for he is highly exalted. The horse and its rider he has hurled into the sea. The LORD is my strength and my song; He has become my salvation. He is my God, and I will praise him, He is my father's God, and I will exalt him. The LORD is a warrior; the LORD is His name" (Exodus 15).

Later we see her rebellion and stubbornness revealed. She may have believed she should hold more of a prominent place in leadership since she was the one who "saved" Moses.

She became jealous when Moses married and, in all probability, his new wife ascended in importance to a position somewhat equal to hers.

She and Aaron called Moses' leadership into question (Numbers 12). God judged her with leprosy; her pride and arrogance was destroyed as everyone fled from her.

Aaron and Moses prayed for her and after seven days she was restored to the camp.

We can only wonder what it was like for Miriam in those days outside the camp.

There is a lesson here in the danger of jealousy and the desire for power.

We can also learn how useless it is to attempt to add to our own fame and power.

Aaron — Exodus 32

His name means "enlightenment" or "illuminated." He evidently gained a reputation as an educated, articulate speaker for God allowed Moses to use him when Moses claimed he could not speak for himself. Geographically he was born in Egypt and traveled throughout the wilderness with Moses.
The time and circumstances are identical with those of Miriam and Moses. Aaron was approximately three years older than Moses.

God used Aaron in a pivotal position of leadership to stand alongside his younger brother. Aaron went with Moses on each visit to Pharaoh and he apparently was with Moses on each occasion when Moses addressed the congregation of Israel.

Above all he was Moses' supporter and confidant throughout the wilderness wanderings. Aaron was Moses' supporter at the battle of Rephidim (Exodus 17).

He accompanied Moses to the base of Mount Sinai and saw God's glory from below (Exodus 19, 24).

He became the first high priest of Israel. He was chosen for this position by God Himself. He was anointed with oil, sprinkled with animal blood, specifically dressed in the high priest garments and initiated the office of high priest for the nation of Israel (Exodus 29, 40).

He was the one given the full responsibility of initiating and setting all the precedents for the high priesthood of the nation of Israel. He was the one who initiated the offerings and offered them for the very first time. We cannot help but admire the obedience, innovation, and faithfulness of Aaron. However, his life and conduct were far from perfect.

In our reading passage today, we are told the story of the construction of the golden calf. After Moses had been at the top of Mount Sinai for many days the people became discouraged and began to desire an object of worship.

Aaron gave in to their pressure, murmuring, and complaining, and constructed an idol in the form of a golden calf. The idea for this no doubt came from their history in Egypt; Egyptians worshiped the sacred bull, Apis. When Moses confronted his brother concerning the sin, the eloquence of Aaron disappeared, and he made up a ridiculous lie to try and excuse his behavior.

Later we read Aaron and Miriam criticized Moses' leadership and became jealous of his power and position.

Aaron also faced personal tragedy in his own life when two of his sons, Nadab and Abihu, were killed by God for their disobedience (Leviticus 10). Aaron's two remaining sons Eleazar and Ithamar became the representatives of his family for the high priesthood.

We see in Aaron a very human example of someone in a position of authority, but someone who never attained to the supreme leadership position.

At times he was faithful and supportive of Moses.

At other times he appears critical and jealous. He was subject to the influence of others; especially to the influence of his sister.

One of the most difficult jobs in any type of service is "to play second fiddle."

In the first reference made to Jethro in the Scriptures he is called Reuel (Exodus 2:18). In the next chapter the same man is referred to as Jethro. Another name given to him is Raruel (Numbers 10:29), which is probably another form of Reuel. It was not uncommon then for a man to have more than one name.

Jethro is introduced following Moses' flight from Egypt. When Moses arrived in Midian, he naturally went to the place where men would be most likely to congregate in the dry land: he set down by a well. Soon seven daughters of Jethro came to water their father's flocks. Moses came to their rescue in the difficulty with the other shepherds.

When the daughters told their father of the incident, he sent them to invite Moses to be a guest in his home. That visit was extended to a period of over 40 years. Moses became a member of the family when he married Zipporah, one of Jethro's daughters. Later Moses seems to have taken charge of his father-in-law's flocks. There is evidence a close bond of fellowship grew up between these two men.

He was a son of the desert and as such he was a hearty man. The sparse character of the land would not allow any other type of person to continue long in it. The solitary nature of the Midian desert was reflected in the character of Jethro. He was accustomed to being alone with himself and with his God. He possessed the common sense and wisdom which were born of long years of communion with nature.

Accustomed to thinking and acting for himself, he would not be given to the weakness commonly associated with less independent people. Fearless in the face of the stern realities of existence, he would compare favorably with Elijah or John the Baptist. He had the kindness and tenderness which often marks the strong man who has been called upon to battle alone against the quirks of nature and other evil forces.

When news reached Midian of "*all that God had done for Moses, and for Israel*" as they were delivered from Egyptian bondage, Jethro set out on a visit to Moses taking Zipporah and her two sons with him (Ex 18:1-12). When Moses learned of his father-in-law's arrival at the "*mount of God*," Moses went out to meet him. We are told of the interest Jethro had in all the details of the great deliverance, how he "rejoiced for all the goodness which Jehovah had done to Israel," and how the conviction was formed within him that Jehovah was "greater than all gods" (Ex 18:11).

In this observation there is evidently a reference to the attitude the Egyptians had when they began their pursuit of Israel. There was a religious service in which Jethro and Moses participated. In that service Jethro, as priest, offered a burnt offering. Aaron with all the elders of Israel participated in the sacrificial feast and prominence was given to Jethro over Aaron.

Later Jethro, out of the wisdom he had gained through the years, gave valuable counsel to Moses. During his visit with Moses he noted the heavy load his son-in-law was carrying. These burdens not only sapped Moses' physical strength but also kept him from rendering a greater ministry to God. Jethro came to Moses with good advice (Exodus 18:17-22).

One of most difficult lessons for any man to learn is to delegate responsibility.

Jethro told Moses he was committing three major mistakes:

- He was wearing himself out
- He was hindering the work God had given him to do
- He was neglecting his greater spiritual responsibilities

Are you guilty of trying to do it all by yourself?

Nadab & Abihu: Fire from the Lord — Leviticus 10:1-3

"Aaron's sons Nadab and Abihu took their censers, put fire in them and added incense; and they offered unauthorized fire before the LORD, contrary to His command. So fire came out from the presence of the LORD and consumed them, and they died before the LORD. Moses then said to Aaron, 'This is what the LORD spoke of when He said: "'Among those who approach me I will show myself holy; in the sight of all the people I will be honored.'"

These were the two eldest sons of Aaron. At the introductory sacrifices for the Tabernacle and Priesthood, all five had just been consecrated: Aaron, Nadab, Abihu, Eleazar, and Ithamar. These men had received a privileged instruction and had witnessed God's revelation of Himself to Israel from a special place on Mt. Sinai. They had been among the select group who had approached Mount Sinai when Moses went up to speak with God and receive from Him the tablets of stone which contained the commandments.

Newly authorized, they had spent the previous week in the tabernacle communing with God and preparing for His service. They had seen with their own eyes the fire coming out from the Most Holy Place and consuming the sacrifices on the altar (9:24).

All this made them second only in experience, as well as in importance, to Aaron.

Despite their upbringing, their experience and their training, they *took their censers . . . and they offered unauthorized fire before the LORD, contrary to His command.*

Exactly what made it unauthorized fire is uncertain. We can only speculate based on possible clues scattered about elsewhere. But obviously, Nadab and Abihu were acting in blatant disobedience to God. Their transgression was neither accidental nor unintended. They ignored God's instructions!

In offering "*unholy fire*" (NRSV), they were disregarding what God had commanded, claiming their fire was as good as His, and perhaps seeking to step into their father's sandals. Their motivation may have been pride, ambition, jealousy or impatience, or perhaps even just thinking it wasn't important where the fire originated. But whatever it may have been, they were very far removed from living the life of holiness to which they had so recently been dedicated.

How it ended (10:2-3)
It ended in tragedy as fire came out from the presence of the LORD and consumed both of them. God abruptly put an end to the behavior of Nadab and Abihu. Aaron was stunned into silence.

Why it matters (10:3)
This is of great importance because at this point principles and procedures for worshipping God were being put into place; the honor of God's name and person was involved. It had to be shown no one was exempt; everyone, even the priests, must follow God's rules or face His wrath.

Scripture speaks with a united voice: the closer one is to God, the more careful one must be about God's holiness and honor; the greater the privileges one has received, the more careful one must be to fulfill one's responsibilities.

The fate of Nadab and Abihu has another lesson to teach.

Good intentions are no substitute for exact obedience.

Well-meaning enthusiasm is no substitute for discipline and discretion in worship.

Korah: The Levite who conspired with Dathan and Abiram against Moses

Numbers 16, 17

Korah was the son of Izhar, the brother of Amram, the father of Moses and Aaron, making him cousin to Moses and Aaron (Exodus 6:21; Numbers 16:1-49). About all we know of Korah is in connection with this conspiracy of which he was one of the major leaders. Korah was probably motivated by jealousy because of the high honors and privileges of the priesthood that had been exclusively appropriated by the family of Aaron. Aaron was in the highest position of religious authority and Moses was the supreme authority in civil affairs.

The entire nation seemed to have been taken over by Moses and Aaron. Korah was a near relative and he seemed to think he deserved some power and honor as well. The grievance he took advantage of was the exclusion of all others from the priesthood. This seems to have infuriated Korah and he gained a following among other Levites.

He felt he and his followers were unfairly excluded from the office of priesthood. And those among them who were Levites were being confined to a lower-level of service in the Tabernacle. Having joined to himself Dathan and Abiram and 250 other "*leaders of the congregation*," Korah arrived with them before Moses and Aaron and charged his relatives with taking privileges and offices which rightfully belonged to others. When Moses heard this charge he immediately "*fell on his face*," as if to refer the matter to the Lord (Numbers 16:5) and declared the decision would be left to Jehovah. He told them to appear the next day with their censers and incense.

The next day these rebels presented themselves before the Tabernacle. Along with Moses and Aaron the entire congregation of Israel, encouraged by Korah, gathered to see what would happen.

The Lord appeared and a voice commanded Moses and Aaron to separate themselves from the congregation, so they would not share in the destruction for making common cause with the conspirators. Moses and Aaron prayed the people might be spared and Jehovah would confine His wrath to the leaders of the rebellion.

The congregation, instructed by Moses, withdrew and after Moses had appealed to God for mercy in what was about to happen as a proof of the authority by which he had acted, the earth opened and then closed over the fallen tents of Korah, Dathan, and Abiram.

The other 250 rebels, who were probably in front of the Tabernacle, were then consumed by fire "*from the Lord*." The incense burners of the rebels were made into covers to form an outer coating for the altar, a warning of the just judgment of God (vv. 38-40).

The next morning the whole congregation murmured against Moses and Aaron and charged them with killing the people of Jehovah. It seems some people never understand!

The prayers of Moses and his brother could not avert the burning, wrathful judgment. A plague destroyed 14,700 (vv. 41-50), and the high priesthood of Aaron was vividly confirmed (chap. 17).

Since the descendants of Korah afterward became well-known in the Levitical service, it is obvious his sons were spared. They were probably living in separate tents or had separated themselves from the conspirators at the command of Moses.

In Jude 11 Korah is coupled with Cain and Balaam and is held up as a warning to arrogant and self- seeking teachers.

We must be careful not to assume personal authority; all authority comes from God!

Balak — Numbers 22, 23, 24

Balak, in all probability, is not a proper name. It is more like the title Caesar or Czar. The Hebrew word for King is "Melek," so it is easy to see how a foreign king could be given the designation Balak.

He was the King of Moab and the son of Zippor. After observing the progress of the children of Israel as they made their way north along the Kings Highway through the area of Edom, Balak decided there was very little likelihood he could defeat these people in a military battle. His strategy was to hire a world-renowned prophet to curse the children of Israel. He sent messengers to the prophet's homeland with a substantial fee to pay the prophet to curse these people.

He told his messengers to say this to the prophet, "*a people has come out of Egypt; they cover the face of the land and have settled next to me. Now come and put a curse on these people because they are too powerful for me. Perhaps then I will be able to defeat them and drive them out of the country. For I know that those you bless are blessed and those you curse are cursed.*" Numbers 22:5, 6.

The prophet, following God's directions, refused to return with the men. When the messengers reported to Balak he sent a more impressive delegation with more people and made this offer to the prophet: "*this is what Balak son of Zippor says: do not let anything keep you from coming to me, because I will reward you handsomely and do whatever you say. Come and put a curse on these people now.*"

After some second thoughts, greed won the battle and the prophet decided to return with these men and claim his handsome reward. After his arrival the prophet made three attempts to curse the children of Israel; all of them failed.

After each failure Balak became more and more angry with the prophet. There is no record of any specific fee paid at this time. However, it appears the prophet stayed in the area and gave the king advice on how to spiritually defeat the Israelites.

This King is an example of the superstition of the human mind. He knew he could not defeat this enemy militarily and so he resorted to what he believed was the supernatural magic of curses. Here is a typical world leader who thought supernatural magic would work beyond the length of his sword. He failed to realize the God he was up against.

The failed attempt of Balak to defeat the children of Israel has lived on in the stories of Jewish history; Joshua mentioned Balak during his farewell address to Israel (Joshua 24:9).

Jephthah warned an enemy Ammonite king against attacking Israel, reminding him what God did to Balak (Judges 11:25).

The prophet Micah reminded the nation of Israel God had been faithful as He destroyed the opposition of Balak (Micah 6:3).

Balak is even remembered by the apostle John in Revelation 2:14, "*You have people there who hold to the teaching of Baalam, who taught Balak to entice the Israelites to sin by eating food sacrificed to idols and committing sexual immorality.*"

God does not forget His enemies. God always remembers His friends!

Some trust in chariots and some in horses, but we trust in the name of the LORD our God.
Psalm 20:7

This is the prophet who partnered with King Balak. He lived in the area of Mesopotamia known as Pethor. We know nothing of this man prior to this incident. He does seem to have known about Jehovah and followed Him to some degree.

He was offered a substantial bribe by King Balak of Moab to curse Israel. He refused the first bribe after being warned by God not to receive Balak's money. Balak made a second attempt offering more money and greater honor. Baalam asked the messengers to stay overnight and he asked God for permission to go. What God told him was, "if you want to go - go; but I do not want you to go." He went!

His trip from Mesopotamia to Moab was one of the most unusual ever recorded in history. God sent an unseen, by human eyes, angel to stand in the path. Twice Baalam's donkey saw the angel and refused to go any further along the path.

The second time the donkey moved off the path and the animal crushed Baalam's foot against the wall. I imagine what we see recorded in Numbers 22:31-33 is a prophet losing his temper and beating a poor "dumb" animal. God opened the mouth of the donkey and the animal protested his treatment at the hands of the prophet. One writer on the subject suggested we could title this section "this is the prophet who lost an argument with an ass."

At this point God opened the eyes of Baalam and he saw the angel and he suddenly changed his mind about going. God spoke to him and told him to go but say only what God instructed him to say. Baalam must have known his conduct was displeasing to God and he had been willingly disobedient. When Baalam arrived in Moab he met King Balak who was angry because the prophet had taken so long to arrive. But they settled their differences and began preparation to "curse" Balak's enemies.

Baalam went with great pomp and circumstance to a high place where seven altars were built, and seven oxen and rams were offered. It is clear from the text and the rest of the Old Testament God was not pleased with Baalam's charade. Yet God used Baalam for His own purposes. He put into the prophet's mouth blessings and praises for His people Israel. Baalam seems to have repented of his disobedience and he expressed the desire to die the death of a righteous man, but his death was far from righteous. He died in a general massacre and we have no record of his repentance.

In Baalam we see a man who had a great opportunity to serve God and yet failed miserably:

- **he was self-willed.**
- **he was saved from death by a donkey.**
- **he was double-minded; he pretended to serve God, yet he was seeking money.**
- **he was controlled by his besetting sin of greed.**

Here are some positive observations we can apply after we look at the life of Baalam:

- **The clearest knowledge without grace is worthless.**
- **The presence of any continued sin will ruin your life.**
- **The road to hell can be paved with good intentions.**
- **To die well one must live well.**

They have left the straight way and wandered off to follow the way of Balaam son of Beor, who loved the wages of wickedness. 2 Peter 2:15

Woe to them! They have taken the way of Cain; they have rushed for profit into Balaam's error; they have been destroyed in Korah's rebellion. Jude 1:11

Rahab Joshua 2, 6

The literal translation of her name is "broad" or "wide". Geographically she was a resident of the Canaanite city of Jericho. Archaeologically speaking Jericho is the oldest known city in the world. It sits in a very advantageous position near where the Jordan River enters the Dead Sea. Jericho is known as the city of the palm trees. Later it was the "vacation" home of many of the kings who ruled the area. The Israelites crossed the Jordan River into the Promised Land about the year 1400 BC.

God had chosen the perfect time for the Israelites to come into the land of Canaan. There was no strong central government in Canaan. The small city-states there were ruled by numerous local kings, who were usually in conflict with one another. Since there was no strong international power there was little outside influence or force on the land of Canaan.

God had prepared things perfectly. He was now ready to begin to fulfill His promises to the Jewish patriarchs, Abraham, Isaac and Jacob. The land was open and ready to possess. All Israel needed to do was follow God and Joshua, and then they would take the land.

Rahab's story is unique in the word of God.
Joshua sent spies into the land of Canaan before the Israelites crossed the Jordan. Rahab, "*the harlot,*" lived in the city of Jericho. It was in her home the spies were forced to hide from the soldiers of Jericho who were looking for them.

Rahab hid the spies on the roof of her home, where she had a supply of stalks of flax, probably for the making of linen cloth.

When the soldiers arrived at her home looking for the spies, she told them the spies had already left. Soldiers went off in search of the Israelite spies and later in the evening Rahab helped the spies escape the city of Jericho.

She was given a promise of safety for her entire family. Their lives would be spared if she tied a scarlet thread out the window. She followed the instructions of the spies and Joshua honored their commitment.

When the city of Jericho was destroyed (Joshua 6), she and her family were spared. The gospel of Matthew records for us that Rahab married Salmon. The couple became the father of a baby boy they named Boaz. The story of Boaz and Ruth is recorded in the book of Ruth. So, we find Rahab, the harlot, in the lineage of Jesus Christ.

Rahab is one of the most interesting characters in the entire Old Testament. Because of her place in the lineage of the Messiah we find many Christian and Jewish writers who interpret her occupation as something other than a prostitute. Some have asserted the word could possibly mean innkeeper. This is a big stretch based on the clear reading of the text.

It is best to see this as one of the greatest examples of the saving grace of Jesus Christ.

Some have objected to her use of a lie to protect the spies. They have further pointed out she was disloyal to her own country by concealing their identity.

We cannot approve the use of a lie; God would have preserved the safety of the spies another way.

Regarding her being a traitor; loyalty to her country would have been disloyalty to God!

His name means "old, impetuous," or possibly, "dog". He was the head of a clan in the tribe of Judah. Caleb was born in Egypt and traveled through the wilderness with Moses and the other Israelites. He crossed the Jordan into the land of Canaan. He was one of only two men over the age of 20 when they left Egypt who could enter the Promised Land.

The time frame for Caleb's life falls around the year 1400 B.C. We know he was 85 years old when the events recorded in Joshua 14 occurred. Two major events are recorded in the lifetime of Caleb. First, we see his faithfulness to God as one of the 12 men chosen to spy out the land of Canaan (Numbers 13, 14).

He and 11 other Israelites were chosen to travel throughout the land and bring back a report to the nation of Israel. The spies traveled through the land in groups of two and brought back a report of what they saw and experienced. Caleb's traveling companion was Joshua, who would later become the successor to Moses.

When the spies returned and gave their reports to Moses, they all agreed the land was a good land and very prosperous. However, ten of the spies felt as though the people in the land would be very difficult to defeat. They were very impressed with the cities which had great walls and appeared very strong defensively. They also reported there were "*giants in the land.*" Most of the spies were very near despair because they felt there was no possible way Israel could overcome these people and take the land.

Caleb and Joshua strongly disagreed with the majority report and urged Israel go up and take possession of the land. The reaction of all the people to the information the spies delivered was immediate. Most of the people began to grumble and complain and very nearly stoned Caleb and Joshua.

After meeting with God, Moses announced to the Israelites God would punish the entire multitude for their act of unfaithfulness and disobedience.

Except for Caleb and Joshua, only those under the age of 20 on that day of decision would be allowed to enter the Promised Land. The nation would wander in the wilderness for 40 years and everyone else would die before God would deliver the land to their descendants.

The next mention of Caleb comes about 45 years later when Israel had conquered the land. As the successor of Moses, Joshua fulfills the promise given to Caleb. He was given all the land he and Joshua had explored as an inheritance.

At the age of 85 Caleb gave one of the most tremendous testimonies recorded in the word of God. He gratefully received the promise from Joshua and immediately set out to occupy the land. At 85 years of age he and the warriors who followed and supported him quickly drove out the opposition and secured their inheritance.

Caleb is an incredible example of a man willing to follow God under different circumstances for a long period of time. He supported Joshua when Joshua was appointed successor to Moses.

Unlike Aaron and Miriam, there is no evidence of any jealousy on his part.

He was willing to follow God and accept whatever position and rewards God would supply.

God gave this man the name Joshua! His parents named him "Hoshea," which means salvation. In Numbers 13 God changed his name to Joshua, which means "Jehovah is salvation." He was the leader of the tribe of Ephraim; the spy chosen from the tribe to go search the land. His name change was a reward for his faithfulness to God.
Joshua was born in Egypt and died in the land of Canaan after leading Israel to possess the land. The time frame of his life, like so many others we have examined, centers around the Exodus and the period about 1400 BC.

Joshua's life may be broken up into three specific periods of time;

- With Moses in the wilderness wanderings
- Conquering the land of Canaan
- His life in Canaan

We know nothing of his life before the Exodus. We know he was over 20 years old when he served as a spy. The time period allowed for conquering the land of Canaan was approximately seven years. We know he died in the land of Canaan at the age of 110.

He faced an almost insurmountable task as he tried to replace Moses in the hearts and minds of the Israelites. He had to gain their confidence lead them into battle, take the land, supervise the division of the land, and help the whole nation settle into an entirely new lifestyle.

The great majority of the people who crossed into Canaan had never lived any kind of a settled life in any place. It was Joshua's job to reorient their lifestyle and yet keep them focused and dependent on God. He later had the stressful task of allotting the land to each tribe.

Joshua survived a misunderstanding related to an altar they constructed near the Jordan River before returning to the Eastern side where they would live. Several of the tribes thought the altar was pagan and Joshua calmed everyone down long enough for them to find out it was a memorial to the victory. It was intended to remind everyone that all the tribes of Israel were one people. The matter was settled satisfactorily and a civil war among the 12 tribes was averted. Joshua reminded them of all God had done and of His faithfulness in keeping all His promises. All of God's covenant blessings are summarized in chapter 24.

Joshua is best known for the "battle of Jericho." The first battle fought in the Promised Land was a miraculous victory achieved because of careful obedience to the word of God. This is the event recalled in Hebrews 11. The author reminds his readers, "*by faith the walls of Jericho fell down.*"

Joshua is an encouragement to us because he was a man of no special qualification and yet God used him in an unbelievable way.

We know little of Joshua on a personal basis because the events recorded during his lifetime were of such a spectacular character.

He was a great servant.

He was not a man who insisted on being in the center of everything and receiving all the credit.

His most famous statement came not long before his death, "As for me and my house, we will serve the Lord."

Joshua was commissioned by Moses before his death on Mount Nebo. *"Now Joshua the son of Nun was filled with the spirit of wisdom because Moses had laid his hands on him."* Deuteronomy 34:9. Imagine trying to step into the place of Moses. The leader Joshua was chosen to replace received this eulogy at the end of the book of Deuteronomy. "*Since then, no prophet has risen in Israel like Moses, whom the Lord knew face-to-face, who did all those miraculous signs and wonders the Lord sent him to do in Egypt; to Pharaoh and to all his officials and to his cold land. For no one has ever shown the mighty power or performed the awesome deeds that Moses did in the sight of all Israel.*" (Deut. 34:10- 12).

When Joshua began his work of leadership God instructed him, "*<u>Be strong and courageous</u>, because you will lead these people to inherit the land I swore to their forefathers to give them. <u>Be strong and very courageous</u>, be careful to obey all the laws my servant Moses gave you; do not turn from it to the right or to the left, that you may be successful wherever you go.*" (Joshua 1:6-7).

In one of the most famous verses in the Old Testament Jehovah continued to instruct Joshua, "*Do not let this book of the Law depart from your mouth; meditate on it day and night, so that you may be careful to do everything written in it. Then you will be prosperous and successful.*"

To further encourage Joshua in his new task of leadership the Israelites told him, " *Whatever you have commanded us we will do and wherever you send us we will go. <u>Just as we fully obeyed Moses, so we will obey you</u>.*" Can you imagine how much encouragement it was when you think about the various insurrections and rebellions with which Moses had to deal?

Joshua was born as a slave in the land of Egypt, lived through years of bondage in that nation and survived the wandering in the wilderness as a servant of Moses. He had been the preeminent military leader among the Israelite forces; Exodus 17 records his leadership in the defeat of Amalek. He and Caleb were the only two spies who returned from the land of Canaan with a positive report (Numbers 13:1-16). He faced opposition from the other spies and the mass of the Israelites who refused to believe the positive report. He watched the judgment of God and saw all those who opposed taking the land as God had instructed die in the wilderness.

He was also a magnificent example of unselfish statesmanship. Once the land was conquered and divided, he continued with his task of setting up the tabernacle, appointing the cities of refuge, and arranging the Levitical order and service.

He did all of this with the same order and precision as Moses. Then he retired to his tract of land and lived out his remaining days without seeking any notoriety.

- Joshua was filled with the spirit of God. (Deuteronomy 34:9)
- Joshua enjoyed the presence of God (Joshua 1:5; 6:27)
- Joshua was indwelt by the word of God. (Joshua 1:8)
- Joshua seems to have been careful in his obedience to Jehovah. (Numbers 32:12; Joshua 5:14).

No wonder at his death at the age of 110 years he was deeply mourned, and his tremendous service was universally acknowledged.

There is a brief epitaph recorded at the death of this man; he is simply said to be "*the servant of the Lord.*"

Othniel

Judges 3:5-11

As we move forward in our study of Old Testament history, we will include a look at one of the Judges who is considered a lesser or minor judge in the history of Israel. He is the first Judge mentioned in the book of Judges. We really know very little about him, but his situation tells us a great deal about the conditions in the land and what has happened since the death of Joshua.

The first of the Judges is Othniel. His name means "powerful one" or "lion of God." He is said to be the son of Kenaz, a younger brother of Caleb. He was married to Achsah, the daughter of Caleb. What the book of Judges shows us is how quickly the tribes of Israel forgot the instruction of Moses and Joshua. We are told in Judges 3: 5-7 how much situations had deteriorated in the land of Israel. Othniel was from the tribe of Judah and so the area we are speaking of is probably the south-central part of the land.

The scripture says, "*The Israelites lived among the Canaanites, Hittites, Amorites, Perizzites, Hivites, and Jebusites.*" It is obvious they had already failed in their first duty; they had not driven the inhabitants out of the land. We are also told they intermarried with these other people and served their gods.

They had been specifically instructed not to intermarry with the inhabitants of the land (Deuteronomy 7:3) because this would lead to excessive influence of the Canaanite gods. If this continued, they would soon lose their identity as a unique "*kingdom of priests.*"

Their sin is further described in this manner, "*The Israelites did evil in the eyes of the Lord; they forgot the Lord their God and served the Baals and the Asherahs*" (the female form of Baal). As a result of this sin we are told "*the anger of the Lord burned against Israel so that he sold them into the hands of Cushan-Rishathaim king of Aram.*" The Israelites were in bondage to these foreign oppressors for a period of eight years.

It took eight years of oppression, trial, and tribulation before the Israelites cried out to God for deliverance. When they asked God for help, He sent them a deliverer; Othniel the son of Kenaz.

We are also told the Spirit of the Lord came upon him, so he became Israel's judge and went to war. He overpowered the foreign oppressors and forced them out of the land. As a result, the land had rest (peace) for 40 years until he died.

We are told in the book of James (4:4) friendship with the world often produces trouble and death. James the half-brother of Jesus wrote, "*You adulterous people, don't you know that friendship with the world is hatred toward God? Anyone who chooses to be a friend of the world becomes an enemy of God.*"

David observed in Psalm 119:71, "*It was good for me to be afflicted so that I might learn your decrees.*" It took distress and physical difficulty to bring the Israelites back to God. As always, His mercy was great and sufficient; He raised up for them a deliverer.

Where did he get his commission? He was God called. His contemporaries did not elect him. God set him aside for a very special work. Because he followed his calling, he had excellent success and the land was returned to a state of rest.

Some of the characteristics we see in this man are:

- **He was courageous**
- **He was capable**
- **He was humble**
- **He was a man of God!**

Her name means "bee" or "wasp." She lived in the central part of the land of Israel. She is part of the period in Israel's history when they were ruled by judges, who were called and appointed by God. This would make her lifetime fall in the era 1200 to 1300 BC.

Deborah was a prophetess according to Judges 4:4. We are also told she judged Israel. After Israel crossed the Jordan and conquered the land of Canaan, God appointed judges in different areas of the land. There was no central unified government; the tribes looked to wise men and women to guide them. She met with people under what had become known as the Palm Tree of Deborah. This was in the central portion of the land between the towns of Ramah and Bethel in area of the tribe of Ephraim.

The theme for the book of Judges is repeated four times in the book (17:6, 18:1, 19:1, 21:25). "*In those days Israel had no king; everyone did as he saw fit,*" Judges 21:25. Because of the continuing disobedience by the tribes of Israel, God was forced to judge their sin. He initiated a cycle which we see several times in the book of Judges.

THE FOURFOLD CYCLE IN THE BOOK OF JUDGES

- The Israelites sinned.
- God judged them.
- The Israelites repented.
- God sent deliverance.

Judgment usually came from an outside military power such as the Philistines, the Amalekites, or the Midianites.

In chapter 4 the oppression of the Israelites came at the hands of Jabin, King of Hazor. He was the leader of a confederacy of forces in the northern part of the land. He was able to constantly defeat the Israelites and tax them heavily because he possessed a much-advanced military weapon.

He and his military commander had 900 chariots of iron. They used these to "cruelly" oppress Israel for 20 years.

When Israel finally cried out to the Lord for deliverance, God spoke to Deborah and told her to contact a man named Barak. She gave him instructions to raise a large army of 10,000 men and go to Mount Tabor.

Barak agreed to go, but only if Deborah would accompany him. Deborah agreed to accompany her general but informed him he would not receive the glory for the victory; the glory would go to a woman.

God gave the victory through a miraculous rainstorm which contained large hail and caused the heavy iron chariots to bog down and become immobile in the valley.

Chapter 5 is the song of victory composed and sung by Deborah. It is one of the greatest pieces of Hebrew poetry in the Bible.

In the story of Deborah, we learn that God uses anyone available and willing to follow His direction.

God is not, and never has been, a respecter of wealth, status, ability, or pedigree.

God is always looking for someone who is willing and available.

As far as we know Deborah's greatest quality was availability and willingness to follow God.

Gideon: Called Judges 6-8

His name means "great warrior." Gideon was from the tribe of Manasseh. He lived in the central part of Israel and worked his father's land. He was threshing wheat at a wine press when God first spoke to him.

Israel had once again relapsed into idolatry and God had judged them by placing them under the military control of the Midianites, allies of the Amalekites. The term Amalekite is a general term used to refer to people east of the Jordan River.

Israel had been under this control for over seven years and it was so severe and oppressive we read, "*The Israelites prepared shelters for themselves in mountain clefts, caves, and strongholds.*"

During this time of persecution and oppression God called Gideon to be the deliverer of His people. The Lord appeared to Gideon and spoke to him in the form of an angel. The angel addressed Gideon as a mighty warrior. Gideon's response to the encounter with the angel was to ask him why God had failed to deliver his people. Gideon told the angel he had heard all the stories of the deliverance God provided in the days of Moses and Joshua, but he had seen none of those things happen.

He asked the angel if God had abandoned His people.

The angel responded by telling Gideon to "*go in the strength you have and save Israel.*" Gideon asked for a sign God would be with him and direct him in his deliverance. His request was granted with a miraculous offering and fire from heaven.

Gideon's first step in preparing for the deliverance of Israel was to destroy the pagan altars and build an altar to Jehovah. God led Gideon to destroy the local altar of Baal and use the wood from the altar to offer a sacrifice to the true God.

When the destruction of the pagan altar was discovered in the morning the town people were irate and wanted to kill Gideon. Gideon's father took his son's part in the argument and asked the people if they felt they needed to defend their God. The result of this experience was a second name given to Gideon, Jerubbaal, which means "let us contend."

These two chapters contain many other exciting accounts in the life and adventures of Gideon; there seems to be an "Indiana Jones" type of mystique which surrounds this man.

Here is a summary of the events in these two chapters.

- The sign of the fleece
- The downsizing of Gideon's army
- The defeat of the Midianites
- The conflict with the Ephraimites
- The destruction of Succoth and Penuel
- The refusal to become king

The writer of Hebrews tells us he does not have time to tell all the stories of Gideon.

From Gideon we learn it is all right to ask God for a sign to "confirm" His will.

We also learn a negative lesson as we see the dangers of anger and vengeance.

We also see the continuing value of humility and the difficulty of controlling the arrogance of victory.

Gideon: In Battle

Judges 6, 7

Gideon's story is one of the most unique battle situations in the entire Bible. He had no military experience or training and yet God called him to go out into battle against a large, well-trained military force. God patiently waited until the correct moment and then chose His man. Much like Moses, God carefully prepared him; Gideon was moved to destroy the altar and the idol to Baal in his town.

When Gideon sent out a call to battle his reputation for standing against those who opposed Jehovah allowed him to mobilize a large army. Men came to him from all over Israel, some from a great distance. The distance and difficulty many of these volunteers overcame should have been a great encouragement to this inexperienced military leader.

In this same chapter Gideon made a request of God. "*If you will save Israel by my hand as you have promised, look, I will place a fleece on the threshing floor.*" In this very famous incident Gideon was not seeking God's direction; he already knew what God had told him to do. What he was seeking was assurance and encouragement. God answered his prayer and did exactly what Gideon asked; not once, but twice.

It should be encouraging for each one of us to see how God responded in a very specific and positive way to Gideon and answered his prayer! One writer observed if God can distinguish the fleece from the ground around it, He can surely distinguish Israel from Midian.

In Judges 7 we have the description of the actual battle and it is quite surprising. In fact, to Gideon I'm sure it was shocking! As he was preparing his army for battle, he assessed his strength and he had 32,000 men. God spoke to him and told him he had too many men for God to give him the victory. God wanted to give a victory to Israel in such a way there would be no room for boasting or human credit.

God has been patient; He is now ready to deliver His people.

Gideon, in an example of faith and obedience, told his forces, "*Anyone who trembles with fear may turn back and leave Mount Gilead.*" After this announcement 22,000 of his men left camp. Once again God spoke to Gideon and told him there were still too many men. After another test his army was reduced to 300 men. God told Gideon with these 300 men I will save you and deliver the Midianites into your hand. Again, God moved to reassure Gideon. He was given further assurance when a dream some of the Midianites were discussing which was overheard by some of Gideon's lookouts (7:8-15). In the dream the lookout heard the Midianite soldiers talking about a dream which was interpreted by those discussing it as predicting a victory for Gideon's forces.

After this, Gideon divided his men into three groups and equipped them for battle. He gave each soldier a trumpet and an empty jar with a torch inside. His instructions were watch me and do as I do. Following God's instructions exactly the three groups surrounded the Midianite camp leaving one side open for retreat. They blew the trumpets, shouted, broke their jars and held their torches high.
The Midianites with God's help were thrown into complete panic and began to retreat towards the Jordan River. God had told Gideon to prepare for this and he had men in waiting to destroy the Army.

We learn from Gideon God is willing to help increase our faith.

The nobleman in the Gospels said, "*Lord, I believe, help my unbelief.*" God will always help our unbelief!

We also learn the effectiveness of exact obedience to God's instructions. The battle can be won with few as well as many.

Gideon: Beyond Deliverance — Judges 7:23-8:3

After the initial defeat of the Midianites we are told Gideon recalled those men who had left and were fearful. He needed them to finish the "mopping-up" of the operation. The Midianites were chased to the Jordan River where they crossed into the territory to the East trying to get to a more defensible location.

Later as Gideon was beginning to think about his next move the tribe of Ephraim presented itself and complained they had not been allowed to help in the battle. They had been asked but had sent no one. Gideon gave a classic answer to these complainers! " *What have I accomplished compared to you? Aren't the gleanings of Ephraim's grapes better than the full grape harvest of Abiezer?" A gentle answer turns away wrath, but a harsh word stirs up anger.* (Proverbs 15:1) Gideon pursued the Midianites with very little help from the surrounding Israelite population. He asked for help from the citizens of Succoth and Penuel.

But they were still frightened of the Midianites and they were afraid Gideon and his rag-tag army would lose. They were terrified of a Midianite victory and the punishment they would receive for helping Gideon and his small group of men. Gideon was able to pursue the Midianites; capture and defeat the entire army and execute their leaders. When he returned through the land, he had already passed through he "evened the score" with the men of the two cities who had refused to help his army.

There are lessons to be learned from Gideon and his behavior after this great victory.

- We see Gideon's soft answer turned away the anger of fellow Israelites.
- The importance of persistence in God's work.
- Opposition from friends is a principal source of discouragement; Ephraim - Succoth – Penuel.
- The sin of Succoth and Penuel is self-interest and lack of mutual aid.

Israel's King and Gideon's Ephod - Judges 8:22-32

After this great victory Gideon was offered kingship by the Israelites. This was an honest and sincere offer, however, Gideon turned it down because he understood he had only been following God's orders and it was God who was the great power.

He had performed his deeds as a service and not for his own advancement and glorification. It also shows us he had no visions of glory for his own family in the future.

- Gideon had a correct view of himself: he was a servant not a king.
- Gideon had a correct view of God's order of government. God was the ruler; he was not.
- No good servant can be pleased to receive an honor that is properly due his master.

Gideon attempted to show his reverence for God by collecting the gold ear rings which were part of the spoil from defeating the Midianites. When these pieces of gold were collected the weight was about 42 pounds. With this gold Gideon made an Ephod (a small vest). He hoped the vest would be a reminder of the great victory God had given. The result was not what Gideon anticipated because after his death Israel began to worship the Ephod. Even though it was meant to be a Divine memorial it became a snare and drew the Israelites away from God.

A good man with good intentions led them astray.

One good man's mistaken step can lead many to fail.

Gideon had personal victory over pride.

False doctrine often results from good meaning.

Judges tells us, "*No sooner had Gideon died than the Israelites again began to worship the gods of the land. They made Baal-Berith their God and did not remember the Lord their God who had rescued them from the hands of all their enemies on every side. They also failed to show kindness to the family of Gideon for all the good things he had done for them*."

We see the exact same cycle which has become all too familiar in the book of Judges; sin, judgment, repentance, deliverance. After we read "and the children of Israel did evil again in the sight of the Lord," God once again brings judgment upon His children. The judgment this time is from a unique source. Abimelech was a son of Gideon's born to one of his concubines. She lived in Shechem, not in Ophrah which was Gideon's home. This young man apparently had visions of using the heritage of his father to become the ruler of the entire land.

He presented the men of Shechem, his home town, with a proposition, "*Which is better for you: to have all 70 sons of Gideon rule over you or just one man? Remember, I am your flesh and blood*." He tried to leverage his popularity and his heritage into kingship by driving a wedge between the men of Shechem and the rest of the Israelites in the area. The men of Shechem were impressed enough with his argument to give him 70 shekels of silver from the Temple of Baal-Berith, with this money he hired a mercenary army who are described as, "reckless adventurers."

With his small band of mercenaries Abimelech went to Ophrah, captured and murdered the 70 sons of Gideon. However, the youngest son, Jotham, escaped and went into hiding.

No one would have ever thought of making this man king if he had not advocated it himself.
After the death of the sons of Gideon the men of Shechem crowned Abimelech king. The surviving son of Gideon, Jotham, challenged the men of Shechem to consider the danger in what they were doing as they rejected Jehovah in favor of Abimelech. Later they would pay a great price for their greed and evil.

Jotham spoke a parable to all the men of Shechem comparing Abimelech to a bramble who was offering to allow the people of the city to trust in him for deliverance. He compared this option to resting in the shade of a bramble bush. The point is a bramble is only good for burning; this parable would become prophetic.

Abimelech reigned for three years as the King in this area; notice the absence of the biblical word "judge." Abimelech wanted to be King and enjoy the authority and luxuries of kingship. After three years God began to stir up opposition against this man, the men of Shechem began to reject his leadership and began a rebellion against him. God used an "*evil spirit*" to cause dissension between Abimelech and the citizens of Shechem. God was beginning the process of punishing him for murdering his half-brothers.

Abimelech was plotted against by a disgruntled citizen of Shechem named Gaal (Judges 9:26-38). He led an army of Shechem's citizens against him. Abimelech won the battle, destroyed the city of Shechem, and murdered all its citizens.

Another city, Thebez, had also taken part in the rebellion. Abimelech attacked Thebez and some of the people of Thebez took refuge inside a strong tower of their city. Abimelech and his men surrounded it, planning to burn it.

A woman from the top of the tower dropped a piece of a millstone on his head, which cracked his skull. He then ordered his armor bearer to kill him, so it could not be said a woman killed him.

He was killed with a stone as he had killed his brothers.

***Be not deceived, God is not mocked - whatsoever a man sows that shall he also reap.* —Galatians 6:7**

Jephthah was the son of a harlot, because of this he was considered inferior socially and economically. He had several half-brothers who treated him unjustly because of his birth. He was raised in Gilead, east of the Jordan River, but his brothers later forced him to move away from the family north into the land of "Tob." This is an area in northeastern Syria not far from the region of Galilee.

Here he showed ability and leadership by recruiting a band of unemployed, adventurous men. He molded them into an effective fighting unit. This group has been characterized as "*worthless fellows*," but this may not be justified based on what we know about the later character of Jephthah.

As an army for hire, Jephthah and his men became quite well-known in the area for their successes. When God again judged Israel for their idolatry, the Israelites sent an offer to hire Jephthah and his mercenaries to defend them. Those who made the request are called "*elders of Gilead*" (Judges 11:5) . These men probably made the trip personally in order to influence Jephthah to accept their offer.

Jephthah asked for reassurance he would not be treated as he had been treated by the members of his family. He agreed to become their commander if they would ratify an agreement which would make him their continuing leader, if he were to be successful in his military campaigns.

When this agreement was completed Jephthah began to work on the task he had been assigned. His approach was not what anyone would have expected based on his past military history. Instead he first tried negotiating with the enemy. He went to great lengths to avoid any military confrontations.

He sent a letter explaining the historical background of the settlement in the land of Canaan. He pointed out Israel had peacefully occupied the land for 300 years. He asked why now they felt the land belonged to them. The Ammonites refused any negotiations and began to prepare for war. At this point there are two things to notice. The first is in Judges 11:29, "*Then the Spirit of the Lord came upon Jephthah.*" He was the third judge of whom this statement was made.

This is a prime indication he was God's choice as a deliverer for this series of events.

The second thing to notice is Jephthah now made a tour through the tribal areas of Manasseh and Gilead, which was his home territory. This obviously should be a recruiting trip and it seems he was very successful. Whatever his battle tactics were, he won a complete victory and was able to drive the enemy from the battlefield and chase them far away from his homeland. Israel was delivered from its enemy which had oppressed them for over 18 years.

The area of Ammon was completely humiliated; it did not even have its vital cities for protection and the Scripture states "thus the children of Ammon were subdued before the children of Israel." This was of great importance to the Israelites who lived on the eastern side of the Jordan where Jephthah lived. They were in a very vulnerable position militarily because the eastern side of their homeland was unprotected by any major geographic barrier.

Jephthah served as judge for six years before he died. Here we see the wrong of family exclusion.

It is notable the leaders of Gilead were willing to show humility and approach someone like Jephthah.

Jephthah should also be commended for his attempt at negotiation to settle the problem.

He avoided any attempt to "show off" his military skill.

Before Jephthah began his military campaign, he made a vow which has caused much discussion throughout the years by Bible expositors. As he prepared, he made a promise to God, *"if you give the Ammonites into my hands, whatever comes out of the door of my house to meet me when I return in triumph from the Ammonites will be the Lord's, and I will sacrifice it as a burnt offering."*

God did deliver the Ammonites; Jephthah won a great victory. When he returned home his daughter, who was his only child, was the first to greet him. According to the text (11:34), "*When Jephthah returned to his home in Mizpah, who should come out to meet him but his daughter, dancing to the sound of tambourines! She was an only child. Except for her he had neither son nor daughter.*"

Jephthah told the girl of his vow and told her he had made the vow and could not go back on his promise to God. The young woman must have been a devout and godly person herself, because she agreed with her father. She made only one request of him; that she be allowed before the vow was fulfilled to go to the mountains for three months to grieve over her virginity. Jephthah agreed and allowed her to take this time.

As a result, the biblical text relates, "*She knew no man.*" Then the book of Judges offers as an explanatory comment that this action became a custom throughout the land of Israel, "the daughters of Israel went yearly to lament the daughter of Jephthah the Gileadite four days in the year" (Judges 11:40).

This vow creates many questions. Thousands of pages have been written to explain what happened in this situation. In Hebrews 11 Jephthah is commended as a great example of faith, he is also named in I Samuel 12 as a deliverer God sent. What are we to say about these events? Some facts are clear;

- Jephthah made a vow
- Jephthah kept the vow
- Jephthah is an example of obedience and faith

It seems improbable Jephthah's faithfulness would be held up as an example if he had offered any human being, let alone his only daughter, as a burnt offering. Remember, God stopped Abraham before Abraham could offer Isaac.

The Hebrew prefix used here can be translated *"or."* His words would then read, "*shall be the Lord's, or I will offer it up as a burnt offering*". This is a common usage in Hebrew. In Leviticus 27:28 there is a similar usage.

We know at this period in history there were women who served at the tabernacle. The context seems to imply they were there regularly and performed many of the basic duties necessary for the tabernacle. We know this to be the case because in I Samuel 2:22 these women are specifically mentioned.

Jephthah appears to have been a daring, fearless man, skilled in war, quick to avenge injuries, and ready to defend the helpless as well as to forgive wrong.

He does not seem to have been rash and impetuous, because he did not immediately seek to go to war, but waited and attempted negotiations with the king of the Ammonites which had proved fruitless.

Jephthah didn't offer his daughter as a human sacrifice!

Such an action would be totally contradictory to everything the Bible teaches. He would not be used as an example of faith if he were guilty of such a despicable thing. His daughter went to the tabernacle and served the rest of her life there. As a result, she would never marry and have children. Having a family was the greatest goal of every Hebrew woman and knowing it would never happen would be a disaster.

Hebrews 11 lists Jephthah as a man of faith. He had enough to keep his word to God, even in extreme circumstances. Do you have such faith?

Samson's Parents: The Promise of His Birth — Judges 13:1-25

Judges 13 begins to set the stage for the judgeship of Samson. We are told, "*Again the Israelites did evil in the eyes of the Lord, so the Lord delivered them into the hands of the Philistines for 40 years.*"

Our introduction to Samson begins with a description of the message of his miraculous birth. We are told of a man from the area of Zorah, whose name is Manoah, a member of the tribe of Dan. His wife, whose name is never given, is childless. An angel from the Lord appears to her and announces she is going to have a miraculous son. She is given specific instructions about the birth and how the child should be raised. The boy is to be a Nazarite, living apart for God from the moment of his birth.

The Angel even goes to the extent of reminding this woman of the stipulations involved in the Nazarite vow. She is told, "*See to it that you drink no wine or other strong drink and that you do not eat anything unclean, because you will conceive and give birth to a son. No razor may be used on his head, because the boy is to be a Nazarite, set apart to God from his birth, and he will begin the deliverance of Israel from the hands of the Philistines.*"

She immediately went and told her husband of the encounter and the promise of a son. Manoah prayed to the Lord and asked that the man of God be allowed to return and teach them how to raise him to fulfill this mission.

Then Manoah prayed to the LORD: "*O Lord, I beg you, let the man of God you sent to us come again to teach us how to bring up the boy who is to be born.*" Judges 13:8

God answered the prayer and the angel appeared a second time to the woman.

Once again, she called her husband and we can see the encounter between Manoah and the Angel. Manoah asked the Angel, "*when your words are fulfilled, what is to be the rule for the boy's life and work?*"

The angel told him, he and his wife must follow the orders exactly as they were given. Manoah asked the angel to stay long enough for them to prepare a young goat and offer a sacrifice to the Lord. The angel agreed to their request and the offering was prepared.

When the offering was placed on the rock and they began the process of making the offering, the angel did "*an amazing thing.*" Flame blazed up from the altar toward heaven, and the Angel of the Lord ascended in the flame. At this point Manoah and his wife fell on their faces to the ground and worshiped they realized they had seen the pre-incarnate Christ.

The result of this encounter with the angel was twofold; great fear and great faith.

The child was born, and his parents attempted to raise him exactly as they had been instructed. We can imagine the difficulty in raising a child like Samson. They seem to have made every effort to raise him as they were instructed, but there were many difficulties.

When God grants special favors, we should exercise great care in how we use them.

Our prayer should be, "Lord teach us how to raise our children."

The value of separation is obvious from God's orders to these people.

There is a proper use of separation to bring glory to God.

We should be very careful the separation of our life does not build a wall to keep others from God.

His name has been interpreted several ways. It can mean "distinguished, strong," or "like the sun."

Samson was born in the southwestern portion of Israel. He was from the tribe of Dan. The geographic region known today as the Gaza Strip would be the Philistine territory which Samson visited quite often. Since Samson is usually considered one of the last Judges his time period would be around 1100 B.C. He may have been a contemporary of Eli and Samuel.

We must remember Samson was a miraculous gift from God to the Israelites. His parents were told before his birth he would begin to deliver Israel from the Philistines. His deliverance was to be only the beginning.

The Philistines were finally conquered by David. Samson is a good example of the "local" nature of the judges. He was active only in the southwestern part of the land of Canaan. Remember the key verse for this entire book is, *"In those days there was no king in Israel and every man did that which was wise in his own eyes"!*

Even though Samson and his mission were appointed by God, he is a good example of the above attitude. We only read of two prayers prayed by Samson. Both of those prayers were spoken to God when he was in deep trouble. He does not appear to have asked God what to do or how to deliver Israel. He was given the blessing by God and God honored His promises; even though Samson was disobedient.

It is not clear what characteristic of Samson's life the writer of Hebrews was thinking of when he listed him in Hebrews 11 as an example of great faith. But he is listed in the chapter.

Samson's parents would have told him of the angel's appearance, his miraculous birth and his God- planned mission.

Samson appears to have taken things into his own hands early in his life. He constantly looked for ways to fight with the Philistines. He seems to have planned these events.

- The death of 30 Philistines because of his wedding riddle
- The return to his wife and his revenge in crop destruction
- The slaughter of the Philistines at Etham
- The killing of 1000 Philistines with the jawbone of an ass
- The case of the Philistine harlot
- His misadventures with Delilah
- His death in a Philistine temple

When Samson was finally captured by the Philistines after being betrayed by Delilah, he had violated all three of the provisions in his Nazirite vow.

- He had touched the carcass of a lion (14:8, 9).
- He drank wine at his wedding feast (14:10).
- He had allowed his hair to be cut (16:19).

After the Philistines captured him, they put out his eyes, bound him with brass chains and made him grind grain in the prison house. One writer wrote, **"Samson now learned the high cost of low living."**

Samson is an example of someone who squandered great opportunity and potentiality. Yet, he is also proof God is always true to His word and His promises.

God even granted his final prayer request to help him achieve the mission which God had chosen for him.

If God did not abandon Samson; we can rely on Him to stand with us.

Samson: His Women — Judges 14, 15, 16

The best-known woman in Samson's life was Delilah. Before Delilah, the Bible records his encounters with two other women. We will look, first, at the first two of those women and later devote a full study to Delilah.

The first two women associated with Samson are:

- **The harlot of Gaza, 16:1-3**
- **The woman of Timnah, 14 & 15**
- **The woman of Timnah, Judges 14 & 15**

We are never given the name of this woman; we are only told she lived in the Philistine territory of Timnah, which was not far from Samson's home. We are not told what Samson was doing in Philistine territory, but we are told he saw this young woman and went home and told his parents this was the woman he wanted to marry. They objected and wanted to know why he couldn't marry "a good Jewish girl."

The Scripture has an aside telling us they did not know this was from the Lord and he was seeking an occasion to confront the Philistines. His parents made the arrangements and they went forward with the wedding plans. It was obviously an unusual wedding because normally the wedding is centered at the groom's home and with his family. It is obvious there is more to this wedding.

After an unfortunate riddle and the answer being obtained with pressure and threats made to Samson's wife by the Philistine men, Samson left and killed 30 Philistine men to pay off his debt. In anger he returned home, and his wife was married to one of the Philistines who attended the wedding.

Later Samson returned wanting to "patch things up" with his wife. The details are recorded in Judges 15. These events led to the death of his wife and her entire family and Samson's destruction of the Philistine crops. In retaliation for the death of his wife we are told Samson attacked and viciously slaughtered many of the Philistines. Then he went down and stayed in a cave at the Rock of Etham. The confrontation resulting from this encounter ended with the deaths of 1000 Philistines. We are told after this he led Israel for 20 years.

The harlot of Gaza 16:1-3

There may have been an excuse for taking a Philistine wife, but there is no excuse for this action. There is no indication what business brought Samson to Gath. We are told "he saw a prostitute." His sin began with a look.

Note: The repeated pattern in Scripture – I Saw – I Coveted – I Took

- **Eve - Gen. 3**
- **Achan - Josh. 7**
- **David - II Sam. 11**

The prostitute notified the officials and the gates of the city were locked and guards were placed in position. Samson appeared to be locked in as tight as if he were in prison. He got up at midnight and left.
When he arrived at the city gate, he found it locked and the guards asleep. He broke the lock and carried off the gate; doors, post, bar and all. He carried them up to the top of a hill several miles away.

- **Satan's setups**: whatever Samson's reason for going to Gaza, it was not to do what he did! Satan will always seize on a weakness
- **The Philistine thinking**: there has been a time lapse. Samson's exploits were now 18 years old. Perhaps there was new Philistine leadership. They were aware of Samson, but not as fearful.
- **God's blessing on Samson**: despite his sin, God's blessing was still present. This was the right time for another lesson for the Philistines.

God often uses his servants despite sin in their lives.

He seems to have confessed his sin and made things right with God. This would allow God to restore his strength. Eventually an opportunity arose for Samson to show his restored strength and his loyalty to Jehovah God.

In time there was a celebration for Dagon, the Philistine God. This was the principal deity worshiped by the Philistines and the celebration was held in a great Temple with several thousand in attendance.

Samson was to be the entertainment at the celebration. The Philistines were going to celebrate Samson's and Israel's defeat at the hands of their god Dagon. They were going to make a spectacle of this once mighty man. They had undoubtedly planned to force him to do many humiliating tasks in front of the onlookers. Samson was brought and made to stand between the two supporting pillars of the great Temple. This was the location where he could be seen and mocked by all.

The situation did not turn out as they had planned.

It is interesting to note recently just such a temple has been excavated in one of the Philistine cities and from what the architects can tell of the plan, the entire roof of the building was supported by two pillars close enough together that they could have been touched by one man in the center of the building. It is amazing how archaeology illustrates and confirms details in Scripture.

Samson asked the young man who was guiding him to place one hand on each of the pillars. He asked God, "*Remember me. Oh God, please strengthen me just once more and let me with one blow gain revenge on the Philistines for my two eyes.*" God heard and answered his prayer! He pushed with all his might on the two pillars and the entire building collapsed.

In summary we could say Samson's life was not a great life. But he is named in Hebrews 11, the great Hall of Fame of faith in the New Testament. We need to remember an angel announced to his parents, ***"He would <u>begin</u> to deliver Israel."***

He did not raise an army like the other delivering judges. He seems to have been acting at the direction of God in seeking specific occasions against the Philistines. He was given special strength no other judge possessed. No judge who raised an army to fight Israel's enemies was ever given the power Samson was given.

God's plan seems to have been for Samson to occupy the Philistines so they could not extend their control over Israel. The nation enjoyed a period of beneficial neglect because the Philistines were much more occupied with Samson than with the Israelites in general.

Samson's one great weakness was his lust and passion. This weakness remained with him and showed itself for a long period of time. Perhaps he kept his lust in check much of the time, but he never gained a victory.

It is best to say Samson stands as a negative example of a weak mind and a strong body.

The apostle Paul put it this way, "For physical training is of some value, but godliness has value for all things, holding promise for both the present life and the life to come." 1 Timothy 4:8

Stripped of his strength, Samson was taken away to prison. He was imprisoned in the city of Gaza, the same city where he had first fallen victim to his own lust. Here his eyes were gouged out and he was bound with a chain. He was forced to work for the enemy in the humiliating task of grinding grain at a mill.

In time Samson's hair began to regrow; he probably began to recognize the seriousness of his sin and his own stubbornness as he walked around the circle grinding the grain.

Samson is an example of the truth - God will never His people or His promises!

Book Four

1. Delilah	Judges 16:1-18 Judges 16:1-18, Judges 16:4-20
2. Ruth: deciding	Ruth 1:1-14
3. Ruth: serving	Ruth 1:15 - 2:23
4. Ruth: resting	Ruth 3
5. Ruth: rewarded	Ruth 4
6. Naomi	Ruth 1-4
7. Boaz	Ruth 3, 4
8. Elkanah	I Samuel 1:1-23
9. Peninnah: a very unhappy woman	Proverbs 17:1-5
10. Hannah:	I Samuel 1:2 - 2:11
11. Eli: the priest	I Samuel 2:27 – 4:22
12. Eli: the parent	I Samuel 2:27 – 4:22
13. Samuel: the man	I Samuel 7:3 – 8:22; 12:1-25
14. Samuel's testimony and challenge	I Samuel 12:1-25
15. Saul: opportunity	I Samuel 18, 19
16. Saul: the man	I Samuel 9 - 22
17. Saul's sin and first rejection	I Samuel 13:8-14
18. Saul's period of success	I Samuel 14:47
19. Saul's sin and second rejection	I Samuel 15:10-35
20. David in Saul's court	I Samuel 16:14-23
21. Saul and his son	I Samuel 13, 14
22. Saul and Samuel	I Samuel 15
23. David Anointed King	I Samuel 16
24. David and Goliath	I Samuel 17
25. Saul and David	I Samuel 18
26. Jonathan: the man	I Samuel 13, 14, 20
27. Saul, David and Ahimelech	I Samuel 21, 22; Psalm 52
28. Saul still chasing David	I Samuel 21 - 26
29. David at Gath	I Samuel 27 - 30
30. Saul's Death	I Samuel 28:5-25; 31:1-13

Delilah — Judges 16:1-20

Delilah is a sweet-sounding name which any woman would want, it means "delicate" or "dainty one." Because of the evil deeds of which Delilah was guilty, no other woman in Scripture appears with her name. The record of her deceit and destruction of Samson is recorded in only 18 verses. Yet those 18 verses have given her such a world-renowned reputation there are few who have not heard of her. Scripture records of King Solomon, "*he loved many strange women who turned his heart*" from following God. Samson did not have the opportunity of Solomon, but he had the passion.

Delilah was a woman who used her personal and physical charm to lure a man to his physical destruction. She stands out in the Scripture as one of the lowest, meanest women in the Bible; the female Judas of the Old Testament. This Philistine woman had an unholy persistence and devilish deceit combined with personal charm, mental ability, self-control and nerve; all of which she used for her own purpose: money. One writer has said she, womanly honor and love never met, for behind her beautiful face was a heart as dark as hell, and full of viperous treachery.

Her relationship with Samson was known to the "Lords of the Philistines." These men were the rulers of the five Philistine cities; Gaza, Gath, Ashdod, Ashkelon and Ekron. The involvement of these men shows the level of concern the Philistines felt toward Samson. Each one of these leaders pledged 1100 pieces of silver to Delilah. This would be approximately 30 pounds of silver from each Lord or a total of 150 pounds. It also seems the number of 1100 is a number which is somewhat odd; it probably indicates there was a period of bargaining between these men and Delilah. The risk she was taking was great, but there was a great deal to be gained from the Philistine point of view.

Once she had finished her deal with these leaders she went to work immediately. Her cold heartless efficiency in seeking his secrets makes us wonder why Samson was so lacking in any kind of suspicion. Had he become complacent? Had he forgotten his gift was from God? Was he depending entirely upon his own strength?

She specifically asks where does your great strength lie? How may you be bound? In her first three attempts to extract this information from Samson he seems to have adopted a playful, teasing attitude. It is even possible this period represents six visits: one visit to obtain the information and another visit to try to capture Samson. Delilah effectively applies more and more pressure. She adopted a tone of being hurt. She said to Samson, "you really don't love me, or you would tell me the truth." Finally, Samson relented and told her, "the whole truth and nothing but the truth."

It seems the Philistines had now lost faith and interest in Delilah because she must make a special plea to get them to come back. It is just as evident she had not lost her interest in the reward. And it is obvious Samson had not lost his interest in her.

Two proverbial sayings are applicable here:

- **Hell hath no fury like a woman scorned.**
- **A continual dripping wears away stone.**

She literally wore him down. The Philistines were called; his hair is cut. He is captured and she has earned her money. The power of a woman's wiles - Samson was a giant of physical strength, but he was an absolute weakling in the hands of Delilah.

Physical strength does not assure moral or spiritual strength.

What can you learn from this story about dealing with your own weaknesses and failures?

What does this story teach you about humility and self-esteem?

Ruth: Deciding - between the gods of Moab or The God Ruth 1:1-14

Her name means "friend" or "friendship." She was a Moabite, born on the east side of the Jordan River in the hill country of modern-day Jordan. She became the daughter-in-law of Naomi.

Naomi was married to a man whose name was Elimelech which means "my God is King." The Bible calls these people "Ephrathities." This was an ancient name for the city of Bethlehem. The use of this name in the biblical text indicates that this family was one of the original settlers in the area.

After a long famine Elimelech made the decision to move his family eastward across the Jordan into the country of Moab.

The land which they were leaving was land which had been given to his family by Joshua after the land had been conquered several hundred years before these events.

An original family leaving, a landholder giving up all he owned indicates how terrible the famine was. They went into enemy territory, Moab. They went out seeking prosperity.

Later in the land of Moab the husband died and left Naomi a widow with her two boys. The sons grew and soon married Moabite women. As time passed it seemed events still conspired against Naomi for both of her adult sons died.

Later we are told these three widows received the news the famine had ended in Bethlehem. Naomi made the decision to return to Bethlehem and live out her final days in her home country.

She encouraged her two daughters-in-law to remain in their home country and seek new husbands. The daughters-in-law traveled with her as far as the borders of Moab. One of the young women chose to return to her family and her own land. Ruth chose to remain with Naomi.

She made her choice known in this statement, "Don't urge me to leave you or to turn back from you. Where you go, I will go, and where you stay I will stay. Your people will be my people and your God my God. Where you die, I will die, and there I will be buried. May the LORD deal with me, be it ever so severely, if anything but death separates you and me."

So together, this strange couple returned to Bethlehem.

When they arrived in Bethlehem Naomi asked the people not to call her "Naomi" any longer, but to call her "Mara", which means bitter, for God had dealt very bitterly with her.

Here is the difference in Naomi and Ruth's situation:

- **Naomi left a land of famine to go to worldly prosperity and came back empty.**
- **Ruth left a place of worldly prosperity to come to a land of famine and she became full.**
- **Ruth went up to Judah and gained everything.**
- **She turned her back on the world.**
- **She chose The God instead of gods of Moab.**

In what specific ways can you demonstrate loyalty or devotion to God?

What action can you take today to show your loyalty to a friend or family member?

Write out some of your ideas.

For Ruth, the whole environment must have been extremely strange. There are few things more intimidating than a foreign city where every word spoken reveals by phrase and accent the gulf between the native and the stranger. Every instinct would suggest flight; avoid all contact and confrontation. Naomi told her story, explaining the presence of Ruth to the women of the village and the two widows found a place to live.

The poor were entitled by the Mosaic code of mercy to glean in the harvest fields. The work was very hard and not very rewarding. According to Mosaic legislation, the corners of the fields were not to be harvested. That area and the area nearest the fence row was to be left so the poor could harvest some of the grain for themselves.

This was a difficult situation at best. A Moabite was not welcome in the community of Israel, and it was only the marriage to a Hebrew, and the shield of her mother-in-law, which allowed her to make an attempt at gleaning in this situation.

She was a single woman, unknown in the community, but she was without a doubt the major subject of recent village gossip. She was laboring in a very hostile environment to say the least.

The men who were working nearby were day laborers. They would not be very different in social status from many of our migrant workers. This was really no place for a young unmarried woman.

Nevertheless, the young widow conquered her fears and went out to work to support herself and her mother-in-law as best she could. Ruth had counted the cost and made her choice. And when choice of such sort has been made, it is well to abide by it. Ruth did, and won the reward of faithfulness. She confronted her situation with courage and hard work.

She asked permission from the person in charge of the workers to glean in the field. He gave her permission and she went to work. Later when the owner of the field came to check on the progress of his workers, he noticed this new woman among the leaders. He asked the supervisor who she was, and he was told she was the young woman who had returned with Naomi. Then the supervisor added that she had continued from early morning until then, with only a short rest. She was obviously a hard worker!

At the end of the day, after beating out the chaff from what she had gleaned, she had about 3/5 of a bushel of grain. She returned to Naomi that evening and showed her mother-in-law what she had accomplished.

Her mother-in-law instructed her to return to the same field tomorrow and continue gleaning in the field until the end of harvest.

The chapter concludes by saying Ruth obeyed her mother-in-law and continued to work in the field until the end of barley and wheat harvest.

Have you ever lived in a foreign country?

How does it feel to be a stranger in a foreign country?

What is a step you can take this week toward developing your character?

How could you demonstrate your thankfulness to the Lord for His provision for you?

What can you do in the next few days to help a friend who is struggling to make ends meet?

The owner of the field where Ruth went to work was Boaz. Naomi told Ruth this man was a near kinsman of theirs and she explained to her daughter-in-law there was a possibility he would "redeem" their situation. Perhaps he would restore the inheritance which her family had lost when they moved to Moab. Naomi began very quickly to set in motion a plan to see if this was possible.

She said to Ruth, "My daughter, should I not try to find a home for you, where you will be well provided for? Is not Boaz, with whose servant girls you have been, a kinsman of ours? Tonight, he will be winnowing barley on the threshing floor. Wash and perfume yourself and put on your best clothes. Then go down to the threshing floor, but don't let him know you are there until he has finished eating and drinking. When he lies down, note the place where he is lying. Then go and uncover his feet and lie down. He will tell you what to do." "I will do whatever you say," Ruth answered.

We have little knowledge of the customs common in Israel in this era. The arrangements for marriage recorded in this passage are not mentioned anywhere else in the Bible.

What was to be done where two widows were left on their own? This story gives us an answer as to what might happen, though we have no means of knowing just how common the practice described was.

This was clearly an Israelite and not a Moabite procedure, for Naomi had to explain to Ruth what she must do to show Boaz she was interested in marriage with him. Ruth carried out the plan, but there is no indication she knew anything about the custom until Naomi outlined it.

When Boaz lay down to go to sleep Ruth was instructed to be sure she knew where he was. Later after he was asleep, she was to come and uncover his feet and lie down. The position was also a lowly one and represented Ruth as a petitioner.

This was the completion of Ruth's task, except for her invitation to Boaz to throw his skirt over her, 3:9. The rest was up to Boaz. The context makes it clear this describes a way Ruth signified to Boaz her desire to marry him.

The writer is clear Naomi's plan was not without its dangers. The fact she was prepared to urge this course on Ruth is the measure of her trust in both the participants. This is true because in the Ancient Near East immoral practices at harvest-times were not uncommon.

Boaz is awakened later in the evening and he calls Ruth "a virtuous woman." He then tells her, "I will do for you all that you ask, for my fellow townsmen know that you are a worthy woman."

The following morning, she returns to her mother-in-law and explains the events of the evening.

Naomi replies by saying, "wait, my daughter, until you learn how the matter turns out, for the man will not rest but he will settle the matter today."

Ruth had to wait and trust

- Trust Naomi's advice
- Trust the good character of Boaz
- Most of all, trust the Hebrew God.

How have you seen God's providence at work in your life?

What positive character traits of Ruth stand out?

Is there is an action you can take to benefit from the wisdom and insight of a more mature Christian?

The final chapter of Ruth shows us how, by trusting God, Ruth will receive a reward and God will be honored.

The next morning Boaz went directly to the gate of his city, the equivalent of our courthouse where legal decisions would be made. He gathered a group of 10 "elders" of the city and began the legal process of deciding the inheritance of Naomi.

There was one kinsman who was nearer in his relationship to Naomi than Boaz. Legally this man must be presented with the opportunity of "redeeming the inheritance." According to Deuteronomy 2:5-10, if a man died and had no children, the nearer kinsman was to marry his brother's widow and to produce a child.

The three biblical obligations described in Deuteronomy for a kinsman are:

- to redeem his brother's inheritance
- to avenge his brother's blood
- to raise a successor to continue his brother's lineage

The Hebrew word used to describe a kinsman redeemer is "Goel."

To be a kinsman redeemer the near relative must meet three obligations:

- he must be a blood relative
- he must be able to redeem; that is must have the money to buy the inheritance
- he must be willing to buy back the inheritance and marry the wife of the deceased brother

The nearer kinsman in this case refused to redeem the inheritance because he was already married, had children and did not want to "mar" his inheritance.

In other words, he was more interested in himself and his family then he was in continuing the nation of Israel as God intended.

In the presence of the witnesses the first kinsman took off his sandal and handed it to Boaz. He told Boaz he would not redeem the inheritance and he gave up the right in front of the witnesses to Boaz. At this point in the history of Israel the use of a sandal in such a way was symbolic of taking possession.

Ruth and Boaz were soon married in a public ceremony with great rejoicing.

The same women who had been so skeptical of Naomi's return now praised God and said, "Blessed be the Lord, who has not left you this day without a Redeemer and may his name be renowned in Israel!"

Not long after the wedding a son was born to Ruth. The child was given to Naomi to raise and he was named Obed.

We are told Obed became the father of Jesse, and Jesse the father of David. Ruth, a Gentile, is one of four women named in the genealogy of Christ.

What the law could not do; grace did!

How is this chapter an example of God's providence in our lives?

What does the story of Ruth teach you about God's view of the details in your daily life?

In the next few days, how could you support or help a friend or family member?

Naomi is an example of how God uses seemingly insignificant and unimportant people to make major contributions to His eternal program. The character of Naomi is revealed by the love and devotion she was able to produce in the life of Ruth. With words which have been made a part of the spirit of man, Ruth refuses to go back to Moab, to Chemosh (Moab's god), and the past (1:6ff).

She faces the future confident in another's love. There is a significant picture in her act of facing the unknown, confident the God of Naomi will care for them.

This young woman of Moab knew she would face opposition among the Hebrews, who hated her race. She went with Naomi because she could not be happy apart from the mother she loved. To win Naomi's affection shows the significance of the one who won it.

Naomi returned to Bethlehem and, as so often happens, the old had changed. The place seemed different. She was hardly recognized. The contrast between her present misfortune and her past situation was made more painful and more obvious by the sight of the familiar streets and the crowded houses.

The writer of the later chapters of Judges may have been a man of Bethlehem. That famous little town appears as part of the events recorded in Judges. The Book of Ruth is also a story of Bethlehem and it could be written by the same person.

Both books are vividly written, and it is very possible the same person who told the grim stories which close Judges wrote the book of Ruth. What a contrast when God is honored and obeyed!

Naomi left Bethlehem during a time of famine and moved to Moab. When she took up residence in Moab, she had a husband and two sons.

Sometime later her husband died leaving her with the two boys. Naomi witnessed the marriage of her two sons to Orpah and Ruth.

Within 10 years both of her sons had died. Naomi was now left with her two daughters-in-law and all three were widows. It appears as if she had descended into despair. Then she heard that the famine in Bethlehem had ended and she made the decision to return to her "home."

Both of her daughters-in-law offered to accompany her to Bethlehem, but Naomi discouraged them telling them to remain in Moab. She was sure the hand of the Lord was against her. Orpah took her advice and returned to her home in Moab.

However, Ruth would not be discouraged, and she promised to remain with Naomi. She told her mother-in-law, "do not urge me to leave you or to return from following you. For where you go, I will go where you lodge, I will lodge. Your people shall be my people, and your God my God." The two widows continued their journey across the Jordan River and returned to the village of Bethlehem.

When they arrived in Bethlehem Naomi was a very bitter woman. She told her friends and neighbors to no longer call her by the name of "Naomi", but to refer to her as "Mara", which means "bitter." She felt God had dealt with her very bitterly.

Ruth and Naomi found lodging and began to put together some form of life in the village. Naomi instructed her daughter-in-law in the beliefs of the Hebrews and told her of the Hebrew God. It seems slowly as she taught her daughter-in-law, she regained her faith and began to trust God would indeed provide for them.

How does the relationship between Naomi and Ruth inspire you to relate to loved ones in your own life?

We have met a gracious woman. We now meet a good and generous man. A resident of Bethlehem and kinsman of Elimelech, Naomi's husband, he is described as "a man of position and wealth." He had fields outside the town, and to them Ruth went to glean. It was in these fields he first saw her as she was gleaning. He had heard of her already as a faithful and loving daughter and asked her to remain in his fields.

He not only noticed her, but he extended special kindness and protection to her, asking her to remain with his female workers, and charging the men not to mistreat her. He also gave her some of the reapers' food at mealtime.

It is evident from the book of Judges there was little observance of the Mosaic Law. However, there was some memory of its social provisions and the good provisions of the Law. Boaz had no hesitation in obeying these laws. He was a unique person in this period. This era is characterized in the book of Judges as a time when, "There was no King in Israel and everyone did that which was right in their own eyes."

Boaz appears before us as a man who lived in a time of great immorality and yet contrary to popular practice, he strictly observed the laws which the God of the Hebrews had given through Moses. When Ruth appeared at his feet on the threshing floor during the festive time of harvest, he immediately knew what his responsibility was as a near kinsman.

There were those in the time in which he lived who would have taken advantage of the defenselessness of Ruth, but he had no such intention or thoughts. It is instructive for us to realize, even upon waking from his sleep in the middle of the night, he knew exactly what the Law of Moses required of him as a kinsman.

He did not require any self-examination or discipline, but he immediately promised he would fulfill his obligation as kinsman. He gave Ruth a great deal of grain from the threshing floor to take home and show her mother-in-law.

Do you think this was the equivalent of an engagement ring?

So, the story moved to its happy ending. Ruth and Naomi were rescued from their loneliness and bereavement. The brave, good woman, who had sought her home again after sad and distant wandering, was rewarded by the holding of Ruth's child in her arms.

The girl who had been faithful to a woman who had loved her could now look to the East at the far line of blue mountains with no homesickness, but only joy for the discovery of a God who cared, guided, and planned. The upward path from the floor of Jordan to the hills of Bethlehem had been hard upon the feet, but it was the path of love, decision, and committal; and such paths lead home.

As the book ends, we have met in its pages love, goodness, faith, loyalty, kindness, obedience, generosity, mercy, fulfillment, courtesy – and never a deed or word of evil. And all these qualities and virtues have been shown only where they can be shown – in the persons of two women and a man.

Boaz is a picture of Jesus Christ, the ultimate "Kinsman Redeemer."

- He was qualified to redeem; as Christ became man and was qualified to redeem humanity.
- He had the necessary wealth to redeem; Christ lived a sinless life and was able to redeem us.
- He was willing to redeem; Christ laid down His life for our redemption.

How is Boaz an example of God's providence in our lives?

Elkanah 1 Samuel 1:1-23

Elkanah was a descendant of Levi through Kohath. His name means, "God has created." He lived in the quiet hill country village of Ramathaim-Zophim. Like Bethlehem it was a place of no political or geographic importance. It was far away from the turbulence of the invaders from the eastern desert and the western coastal plains. It was away from much of the evil which haunted the era of the Judges.

The chapter is really a continuation of Ruth's story, with the spotlight of the historian changing from the farm of Boaz to the farm of Elkanah.

He was a quiet and somewhat complacent man, this farmer-father of the last of the judges of Israel, an obscure man made great by his son, or perhaps by the devotion of a good wife, whose prayers gave Samuel to his people.

Elkanah carefully fulfilled with yearly precision the duties of his faith. He made his pilgrimages to the national shrine of Shiloh, where the Ark of the Covenant was kept. He no doubt felt by continuing this meticulous observance of the formalities of religion, all his duty toward God was done. He seems rather methodical and thoughtless in his observance of the Jewish "religion."

This was not a corrupt worship, nor was his view of God a poor and unworthy one, but there was little or no challenge in his faith. There seems to have been little to disturb his genial and somewhat shallow complacency.

Observing his household

Following the precedent of Jacob, he supports two wives; Hannah and Peninnah. Elkanah shows no evidence that he was aware of the strife and division in his household.

Following the example of Jacob, he did nothing to snuff out the venom of the wife who first had children, against her unfortunate partner.

He loved Hannah more than his other wife, Peninnah. He gave her presents. He knew she was distressed. He attempted to comfort her, but he had no understanding of her suffering. She was heartbroken over her inability to bear a child.

Elkanah could not comprehend the pain in Hannah's heart, or the hunger for children of her own. This emptiness could not be satisfied by gifts, by anything, short of the proper fulfilment. There is a faint touch of the absurd in the good man's conviction that the blessing of having him for a husband was all the compensation Hannah should need. He tells the persecuted and distressed woman he is worth more than many sons.

And what if Peninnah was harsh to her? She should not let it get to her. Was he not most abundantly kind and caring? There was no cause for an uproar. When they attended one of the required feasts at Shiloh, he had no word of reproach for Peninnah, who marred the high religious occasion by her malicious attacks on Hannah, the object of her jealousy.

He was a simple man notable for neither good nor evil. He was probably a good neighbor and a reliable friend. He lived a quiet and peaceful life, with small concern for the deeper implications of religion.

Why does competition tend to arise between family members?

What do you think Elkanah should have done in this situation?

Why is it important to take our requests to God?

Elkanah's wife, Peninnah, was an insecure and tormented woman. The divided household reveals all the evils of anything other than monogamy. And, as so often happens in life, justice seemed lacking.

A woman eminently fitted to bring up children, was without offspring. One whose bitter jealousy and hatred unfitted her for the task of motherhood had been entrusted with the rearing of a family.

The children did not make Peninnah gentle and humble. This reveals the degree of evil that was eating her life away.

Of all the passions which afflict humanity, jealousy is the hardest to stand. It exacts the greatest toll and pays the bitterest of wages. It is condemned to watch the success of its enemy.

Perhaps Peninnah was younger, less popular with the village, less beautiful than Hannah. Something took away all the joy she should have had in her children.

Simply seeing Hannah accepted and high in Elkanah's affections, shallow as those affections appear to have been, was an irritation to her spirit.

She was obviously very unsure of her personal worth, and when Elkanah gave his childless wife "a double portion" at the time of religious festival, Peninnah's hatred was stirred to its chaotic depths.

Jealousy is the fear or realization of another's superiority.

Peninnah paid her rival this unsolicited compliment, but in entertaining this deadly guest in her heart, she ruined her peace, and attacked the one she saw as the cause of her discomfort.

Envy, like anger, burns itself in its own fire. It has no other task than that of detracting from another's virtue, and in so doing quenches virtue in its host.

Benjamin Franklin once said: "Whoever feels pain at hearing of the good of his neighbor will feel a pleasure in the reverse. And those who despair to rise in distinction by their virtues, are happy if others can be depressed to a level with themselves."

This was Peninnah's fate and her predicament. This was the poison which spoiled the household of Elkanah, without, as far as the evidence of the story goes, any reaction or attention from that seemingly self-centered man. Peninnah should have been a happy person for she had a home, a family, and all her physical needs were met.

Because she could not have more, first place, she destroyed the unity in the home.

To some extent she merits sympathy as the victim of a society which gave women less than their due.

A quarrelsome wife is like a constant dripping on a rainy day. Proverbs 27:15

A heart at peace gives life to the body, but envy rots the bones. Proverbs 14:30

Why is jealousy such a powerful emotion?

About what do you get jealous?

Hannah 1 Samuel 1:2-2:11

Her name means "grace." Hannah was a godly woman and a good wife. However, she had no children. This was a great burden for any Jewish woman. Girls were taught from childhood, as women, their main duty was to bear children and continue the Jewish nation. They were also taught they were given the possibility of the greatest privilege imaginable; giving birth to the long-promised Messiah and Savior.

When a woman was childless after several years of marriage she was viewed as a failure. Usually gossip circulated among her acquaintances who told stories of some great sin which must have been concealed in her past or present life.

Her husband loved Hannah dearly and showed his loving concern by providing her extra attention and blessing. This no doubt produced discord between the two wives. We read about Peninnah, "And because the LORD had closed her womb (Hannah's), her rival kept provoking her in order to irritate her."

One year when Hannah attended the feast at Shiloh she went into the tabernacle and poured her heart out to God. As she prayed, she made a vow to God: if He would give her a son, she would return him to God for His service. Hannah was in such agony and misery as she prayed and wept before God that Eli the high priest thought she was drunk.

Eli rebuked her for coming into the tabernacle in such a condition. She explained to him the reality of her situation. He then blessed her and said, "Go in peace and may the God of Israel grant you what you have asked of him."

God answered her prayer and Samuel was born. She kept her vow and when he was old enough, she brought the young boy to Eli and explained to him this was the son for whom she had prayed. Samuel lived at the tabernacle and served God. God blessed Hannah with three more sons and two daughters. After she presented Samuel at the tabernacle, she wrote one of the most beautiful songs of praise in the Bible.

As you read this passage of praise notice how many of God's attributes Hannah mentioned. (2:1-10)

- His holiness: "There is none holy as the Lord."
- His omniscience: "The Lord is a God who knows."
- His omnipotence: "The Lord gives poverty and wealth."
- His mercy: "He raises the poor."
- His faithfulness: "He will guard the feet of his saints."
- His justice: "The Lord will judge the ends of the earth."

Hannah was a woman of unemotional faith, strong and quietly decisive with deep commitment. She decided when it was time to go to Shiloh and present Samuel to Eli. She informed her husband of the decision and he made no objection.

***Charm is deceptive, and beauty is fleeting; but a woman who fears the LORD is to be praised.* Proverbs 31:30**

Elkanah shows his easy-going acceptance of his wife in a manner which indicates the strength of character he saw in her. The psalm of praise which Hannah sings in Eli's presence (2:1-10) reveals her understanding of divine things in an age when most people had very little understanding of their God.

It recognizes the power of God and the certainty of ultimate justice. It expresses faith in God's power to keep, and joy at answered prayer. It vibrates with gratitude.

Gratitude was a part of Hannah's character; a quality worthy of our imitation.

What are some things for which you are grateful?

Eli: The Priest — I Samuel 2:27-4:22

His name means "God is high and exalted."

Eli was the high priest and served in the city of Shiloh where the tabernacle was located. Eli served in this capacity at the end of the era of the judges and just before the monarchy began.

When we first meet Eli, he is in the tabernacle and he observes Hannah as she is praying. As she pours out her heart to God with great emotion and tears Eli assumes, she must be drunk.

This says a great deal about the spiritual condition of the nation of Israel.

This is the close of the era of the judges and the book of Judges repeats on several occasions, "In those days there was no king in Israel and everyone did what was right in their own eyes."

Apparently there had been many occasions when, during the partying and revelry of a festival, Eli had seen drunkenness in or near the tabernacle.

Eli had two sons; Hophni and Phinehas. The Bible makes a major point to show their wickedness and their lack of regard for God. They were guilty of misusing the sacrifices offered by the people. They took the meat they wanted and refused the portion assigned to them in the Mosaic Law. This was openly known and was no doubt a reason for the growing disregard of the Tabernacle sacrifices.

It was also true these two men were sexually active with the women who served in the tabernacle.

God soon began to move to judge the sin in Eli's family. God sent a prophet to announce to Eli the judgment of God would fall upon his family.

All his family would die in the prime of their life and before Eli's death he would suffer unbelievable anguish.

God brought Samuel to Eli for Eli to have a proper successor as a prophet and teacher. Eli's sons were in the lineage of Aaron and one would serve as high priest, if God did not intervene.

As Samuel grew and was trained by Eli in the tabernacle service, Eli did not make the same mistakes with Samuel he had made with his own children.

Following the cycle of judgment recorded in the book of Judges, God caused the Philistines to attack Israel. Eli's own two sons carried the Ark of the Covenant into battle, thinking of it as a good luck charm. The loss of the battle resulted in the deaths of Hophni and Phinehas and the loss of the Ark of the Covenant. When Eli received word of the battle, the death of his sons, and the loss of the Ark, he fell from his chair and broke his neck. He died at the age of 98.

Eli is a man of God who served God faithfully all his life.

We have no personal sin attributed to Eli.

His major failure was his lack of discipline for his two children.

It has been said, Eli loved his sons more than he loved God.

Eli was given a second chance to raise a godly young man and he succeeded.

Eli's ancestry can be traced to the youngest son of Aaron. For some reason the older line was passed over in the choice of a priest for Shiloh's shrine. It is probable in his young manhood; Eli was a person of vigor and devotion. We meet him only in his old age. In the first chapter of the book he is shown to be a little imperceptive and impatient with a case of need: Hannah. But he rapidly adjusts to the situation when the real facts are given to him.

In the second chapter he is shown weakly protesting against the dishonorable evils of his sensual sons. In the third chapter he is seen in gentle humility receiving from the lips of a child a somber confirmation of the sentence spoken (2:27-36) to him by "the man of God." There is obviously a great deal about Eli which we do not know.

In these few verses which give us the substance of his biography, or at least the later years of it, Eli appears to be a weak, but pious old man, unable to cope with a mounting wave of evil.

Nonetheless, that evil was of his making. He was passive in days which demanded action, silent in days which called for speech, a weakling in days which cried for strength, and mild when God's name called for passionate defense.

He set his family and their lustful lifestyle above the honor of God, and in his office, there could hardly have been a greater fault.

The unnamed "man of God," declared to Eli, "Therefore the LORD, the God of Israel, declares: 'I promised that your house and your father's house would minister before me forever.' But now the LORD declares: 'Far be it from me! Those who honor me I will honor, but those who despise me will be disdained.'"
I Samuel 2:27-46

In this terrible indictment of the anonymous "man of God," set an immortal verse into the annals of the faith and put into words a promise which millions have discovered in their life experience to be true.

"Those who honor me I will honor, but those who despise me will be disdained."

But the same verse, taken in the context of the grim warning, defines and nails down Eli's sin. He had not honored God. His sons had made themselves vile, and he did not restrain them. He was called to exercise discipline and had failed to exercise it. There was no excuse for his weakness. He was in a place of great responsibility; it seems his work was more important than his family. We should remember God gave Eli a second chance when Hannah brought Samuel to the Tabernacle for Eli to raise.

Eli learned his lesson - too little; too late!

How could Eli have responded differently to reports of his sons' behavior?

In what ways do parents need to take responsibility for their children's behavior?

How do you begin now to teach your family the proper fear of God?

What blessing that you have regarded as a "birthright" can become a reason for humble praise this week?

What blessings have you taken for granted for which you want to praise God?

Samuel: the man — I Samuel 7:3-8:22; 12:1-25

His name means "the hand of God." Another rendition of the name is "asked of God" or "heard by God." Born in the rural farmland of Ephraim, Samuel grew up and served in and around the tabernacle at Shiloh in the central part of the land. As an adult he traveled throughout the central part of Israel and the city of Ramah became his home. He was not the high priest; he was regarded as a prophet and judge.

The time period in which he lived was shortly before 1000 B.C. He is often regarded as a transition person: the last of the judges and the first of the prophets. God used him to set up the monarchy and anoint the first two kings of Israel.

Samuel began life as an answer to prayer! He was dedicated to serve God even before his birth. He was raised by the high priest in the tabernacle.

He saw the godliness of Eli, the wickedness of Eli's children and the nation of Israel as people came to the tabernacle day by day and year by year offering a form of godliness.

His first test in the service of God was to deliver a message of judgment to Eli. Samuel no doubt loved Eli very much and did not want to hurt him or be a source of sorrow and pain, yet he delivered his message truthfully.

He became a faithful man of God. "The LORD was with Samuel as he grew up, and he let none of his words fall to the ground. And all Israel from Dan to Beersheba recognized that Samuel was attested as a prophet of the LORD. The LORD continued to appear at Shiloh, and there he revealed himself to Samuel through his word." 1 Samuel 3:19-21

Samuel served the Lord faithfully all his life. He traveled in a circuit throughout the central part of the land and acted as judge. On a regular basis he traveled from Bethel to Gilgal to Mizpeh.

Apparently, Samuel did not learn from the mistakes of Eli. When he grew older, he appointed his sons, Joel and Abiah, to be judges over Israel. These young men were evil, and their lives of sin were openly known. Because of this and many other reasons the leaders of Israel met with Samuel and asked him to appoint a king to be their ruler.

Samuel was disappointed and openly opposed to the idea of a king. He felt God was the ruler of Israel and no man should usurp His authority. God intervened and told Samuel to grant their request but warned him of the consequences of their choice.

God led Samuel to anoint Saul as the first King of Israel. Samuel went on to warn them of a failure to serve God. When Saul failed as king of Israel, God directed Samuel to choose the next king and he anointed David of Bethlehem, the son of Jesse.

In studying the character of Samuel, it is impossible not to be impressed with his godliness.

His goal was not the possession of power but the welfare of his people. He did not seek place, honor, or power. Yet he possessed all three. When the people, without respect to his gray hair and long service, called upon him to resign his office there was no cry for pity, nor peevish reproach for their ingratitude.

He challenged the people to inspect his character and official life and disputed with Israel on their choice of a king as being an act of disloyalty not against himself, but Jehovah. He warned them of the evils which would come from the establishment of a monarchy. And when Saul was selected as his successor, Samuel received him with the utmost courtesy and even treated him with paternal kindness.

Why is it important to establish personal integrity before becoming a critic of others?

His approach, his almost defiant challenge, his tone of authority and command are patterned on Joshua's last words. *Samuel said to all Israel, "I have listened to everything you said to me and have set a king over you. Now you have a king as your leader. As for me, I am old and gray, and my sons are here with you. I have been your leader from my youth until this day. Here I stand. Testify against me in the presence of the LORD and his anointed. Whose ox have I taken? Whose donkey have I taken? Whom have I cheated? Whom have I oppressed? From whose hand have I accepted a bribe to make me shut my eyes? If I have done any of these, I will make it right." "You have not cheated or oppressed us," they replied. "You have not taken anything from anyone's hand." Samuel said to them, "The LORD is witness against you, and also his anointed is witness this day, that you have not found anything in my hand." "He is witness," they said.* 12:1-5

Samuel appears to have been the only one of the judges who was deeply conscious of his nation's history. It is probable his childhood as the temple-servant at Shiloh had given him access to the stored records of the past. Remember all such records were handwritten and where would they have been more appropriately housed than in the place where Israel's holy relics were kept?

Samuel shows in this encounter with the people a very wide knowledge of Israel's history and its significance. His rapid survey of history from the Exodus on through the troubled story of the nation, to Samson and the day of Saul's victory, shows a sense of the nation's destiny long lacking in the stormy characters who had been in positions of leadership.

The appeal to experience, and the endeavor to root the nation's faith in the realization of God's active hand in their affairs, was a sound and constant preoccupation with Samuel.

He had struck that note when he set up the stone called Ebenezer, between Mizpeh and Shen (I Sam. 7:12). The word means: "'Stone of Help." Help, that is, from God.

Furthermore, Samuel was prompted to the symbolic action by his own knowledge of history. Mizpeh, the name of the Benjamite town (Josh. 18:26), means "watchtower," and had perhaps reminded him this was a name which Jacob had given to a landmark set up as a memorial of the agreement between him and Laban (Gen. 31:45-49). It was a significant memorial.

Not to know what was done in former times is to be always a child. If no use is made of the toil and trouble of past ages, the world must remain forever in the infancy of knowledge. Words of counsel could hardly be nobler than those which Samuel uttered before the assembled multitudes as the conclusion of his speech.

"But be sure to fear the LORD and serve him faithfully with all your heart; consider what great things he has done for you. Yet if you persist in doing evil, both you and your king will be swept away." (I Samuel 12:24, 25)

Here was Israel's religion in brief, as Moses and Joshua might have put it.

The worth of history is shown in these words. A nation which loses contact with its past does so at its own danger.

Why is it important to establish personal integrity before becoming a critic of others?

What is one personal story of God's deliverance which reminds you to "fear the Lord and serve him faithfully with all your heart"?

How can you present your requests to God, so you invite His best in your life?

Saul: Opportunity — I Samuel 18-19

His name means "desired." Saul was from the tribe of Benjamin in the central part of the land of Israel. The time frame for his life is about 1000 BC.

Saul was chosen by Samuel to be the first King of Israel. He was a very impressive young man when he was chosen. He was tall and physically very gifted.

Saul did not seek the office of king; in fact, it seems he did everything he could to avoid taking the position. Samuel called the entire nation of Israel together at Mizpeh. It was here Samuel publicly proclaimed and anointed Saul to be King of the Israelites.

Saul began his kingship with a very humble and forgiving spirit. When informed by Samuel he was God's choice to be king, he told the prophet he did not deserve the honor because he was from the smallest tribe in Israel. Shortly after he was declared King there were those who opposed him, and he displayed a spirit of forgiveness and would not allow his enemies to be executed (1 Sam. 11).

We must remember when Saul became king there was no governmental structure in place, there was no trained military, there were no taxes, there was no palace, and there was no throne to be occupied. He had to begin everything from nothing.

His first challenge came when the Ammonite king, Nahash, surrounded an Israelite city and demanded they surrender and submit to having their right eye gouged out. When Saul heard of this situation, he quickly raised an army, marched all night, and made a surprise attack on Nahash. He won a stunning victory and gained the support of all of Israel.

From this point on in Saul's kingship he became more and more disobedient. He displayed pride and a disregard for Samuel and the word of God. In 1 Samuel 15 God instructed Saul to go to war and destroy the Amalekites because of their past hatred of Israel. Saul led the Israelites to a great victory, but he did not carry out God's instruction. Many of the animals were saved and Saul even spared the Amalekite king. When he was confronted by Samuel with his disobedience, he blamed the people by saying they took the spoil and brought it back. He was going to offer the animals as a sacrifice to God.

He claimed he had been obedient and destroyed everything.

Samuel's rebuke to him included one of the most famous passages in the Bible 1 Samuel 15:22, *"Does the LORD delight in burnt offerings and sacrifices as much as in obeying the voice of the LORD? To obey is better than sacrifice, and to heed is better than the fat of rams."*

Saul moved from humility to jealousy to pride and on to arrogance.

It has been said, "Power corrupts; absolute power corrupts absolutely." Probably no better example of this statement could be found than in Israel's first king. Saul was given one of the greatest opportunities of any man in the Bible and yet he failed miserably.

He consistently refused to accept the responsibility for his own actions.

It was always someone else's fault and never his. His story is one of the saddest recorded in the word of God.

What commands of God can become tests of our character?

Saul is described as a "choice young man, and a goodly," so "there was not among the children of Israel a better person than he." In addition to his handsome appearance, he was a head taller than anyone else.

Saul was a humble man.
Samuel spoke of him in I Samuel 15:17 as having been little in his own eyes when he was made king. Saul gave evidence of this by his reply to Samuel at the time of Samuel's choice of him to be king. Samuel said: "To whom is all the desire of Israel turned, if not to you and all your father's family?" (I Sam. 9:20). And Saul replied, "Am I not a Benjamite, of the smallest of the tribes of Israel, and my family the least of all the families of the tribe of Benjamin? Why then do you speak like this to me?" A proud man would have responded quite differently. Though Benjamin was one of the smaller tribes, the family of Kish may well have been quite prominent considering the indication of wealth noted above.

Saul was a forgiving man.
Saul was also a kindly man, at least at first. Following his victory over the Ammonites at Jabesh-Gilead, when the people were ready to make him king, the cry went up about those who had earlier despised Saul, "The people then said to Samuel, "Who was it that asked, 'Shall Saul reign over us?' Bring these men to us and we will put them to death." But Saul said, "No one shall be put to death today, for this day the LORD has rescued Israel." (I Sam. 11:12, 13). Saul might easily have reacted differently, but he did not. He is to be commended.

Saul was an emotional man.
People vary in respect to emotional stability; some can keep their emotions well in control, while others are either at a high peak of joy or a low spot of despair much of the time. Saul clearly was of the latter group. It was no doubt for this reason that in his latter days, an "evil spirit" could bring him into fear and depression, so the young musician, David, had to be called to play soothing music (I Sam. 16:17- 23).

Later, Saul would fly into a rage at the young player and try to kill him on two different occasions (I Sam. 18 & 19). Later still, in an angry state, he went to Ramah to capture David and fell into a fit of despair and hopelessness when he realized the young man was apparently approved by Samuel.

He was an impatient man.
Being emotional is not necessarily bad, though it proved to be a detriment for Saul, but being impatient is clearly a negative characteristic. And Saul was given to impatience. Saul's impatience became more pronounced as his years of rule passed. Impatience was his undoing at the time of his first rejection. He and Samuel had agreed on a time of sacrifice before engaging in battle with the Philistines; Saul was to wait seven days until Samuel could come. Saul did wait until the seventh day, but when the battle seemed urgent, he went ahead and performed the sacrifice himself. Samuel then came and brought God's severe rebuke to Saul. Saul had simply been impatient, and let this weakness lead him into serious sin.

Saul was an impulsive man.
Again, on the negative side is the fact Saul was impulsive. He could act quickly and rashly, even in respect to serious matters, without due thought or consideration. Saul's actions in trying to take the life of David have already been mentioned. Later, he gave the outrageous order to have 85 priests of Nob killed, simply because the high priest, Ahimelech, had given some aid to David (I Sam. 22). Later he went to see the witch at Endor, whose trade he had earlier outlawed.

Which of the above characteristics might cause people to disrespect a leader?

To what extent is it a problem that "image" matters so much in politics?

Why was Saul particularly vulnerable to the temptation to take matters into his own hands?

Saul's sin and first rejection — I Samuel 13:8-14

Saul's call for an assembly at Gilgal was good, though it resulted in his first rejection as king. Saul arranged with Samuel to meet for the purpose of offering sacrifice. Saul apparently recognized a major battle with the Philistines was inevitable, and he wanted God's blessing when it began.

The agreement with Samuel had specified seven days as the time Saul would wait for the prophet to come to officiate. Saul did wait until the seventh day, but then grew impatient and proceeded to make the sacrifice himself. Then, just as he had finished doing so, Samuel came still within the seven-day period designated.

When he saw what Saul had done, he rebuked him severely. Saul had acted foolishly, because he had not kept God's commandment. Because he had not, Saul's family would not continue to rule, for God would now select another to replace Saul, one who would be after God's own heart. With this severe rebuke and information given, Samuel turned and left.

Reason for the gathering
The full reason for calling the gathering was probably threefold:
First, it provided a way of rallying the people and giving them confidence when they were so very fearful of the dreaded Philistines. No doubt Saul used his seven days of waiting for Samuel to good advantage in attempting to bolster their courage.

Second, the gathering may have served as a way of recruiting more soldiers. Saul now needed more than the 3,000 he had kept with him after the earlier events at Gilgal. This could provide a way of getting them. Saul may have seen the occasion as like the gathering he had called at Bezek (I Sam. 11:8); before the Jabesh-Gilead battle, when 330,000 had come. There was nothing like this response now at Gilgal, however.

And, **third**, it was mainly a time to seek God's favor in the forthcoming battle by offering sacrifice.

Saul's impatience
Patience is a virtue not many people have. Saul became impatient as he waited for Samuel. He decided to offer the sacrifice himself. He thought he had good reason (I Sam. 13:11):

- Because some of the people who had come were leaving, probably in fear that the Philistines might attack
- Because Samuel delayed in coming
- Because the Philistines were gathering at Michmash, Saul was anxious to get on with the actual battle

These reasons, though they may have seemed demanding to Saul at the time, were not enough to demand his sinning as he did. He should have trusted God to take care of such matters and kept his promise with Samuel.

Reason for Samuel being late
The fact Samuel did not come until the last day may well have been at God's direction. It was no doubt a way of testing the new king. Would he demonstrate the kind of faith in God which would keep him from becoming impatient, or would he not? Saul demonstrated he did not have such faith and showed he was unworthy of continuing as Israel's king.

What was Saul's great sin which prompted God's rejection at this time?

Saul failed to demonstrate adequate faith in God to wait for Samuel.

Saul sinned by offering a sacrifice he had no authority to perform.

He directly disobeyed God by doing something only a Levite was permitted to do!

What commands of God can become tests of our character?

Saul's period of success — I Samuel 14:47

It is unusual that one verse only is devoted to telling of the period when Saul enjoyed true success as Israel's king. After Saul had assumed rule over Israel, he fought against their enemies on every side: Moab, the Ammonites, Edom, the kings of Zobah, and the Philistines. Wherever he turned, he inflicted punishment on them.

The thought is Saul now, in view of this victory over the feared Philistines, was able to assume a position of authority not available to him before. People were willing to listen and obey and accept regulations.

The first victory over the Ammonites had led to his crowning; this one led to a higher level of authority in his position as king. It is quite possible, as a result, it was at this time he imposed a stronger taxation program and perhaps made divisions within his country, as is implied in II Samuel 2:9 & 13.

Next the verse gives a list of countries over which Saul in this new position of strength was able to gain victories. They included the formidable powers of Moab and Ammon (both in Transjordan), Edom (to the south), and Zobah (to the far north). The Philistines are also listed, perhaps because they remained a perennial threat, though quiet for a time, or perhaps because some minor battles were fought with them occasionally to keep them in check.

Saul's achievement

Though the indication is brief, Saul's achievement must not be over-looked. He did establish himself as a worthy ruler during the years in view. He won decisive victories over the two main enemies Israel had so feared, the Ammonites and Philistines, and this gave him solid favor with the people. His kingdom became well established at home. And with this firm base in hand, he was able to contend successfully with other powers.

Moab, Ammon, and Edom, all close neighbors, were perennial foes of Israel, and apparently Saul was able to keep them in check. He was not successful to the degree David would be, for these countries were not brought under the control of Israel at this time. They were kept from making raids or taking advantage of Israel, as many enemy groups had done in the days of the judges. This would have enhanced Israel's reputation greatly in the world of the day. This significantly added to Saul's popularity at home.

Duration of this period

What was the length of Saul's successful years? He ruled a total of 40 years (Acts 13:21); how much of this time did Saul's successes cover? The approximate duration can be figured based on David's anointing. David was anointed (I Sam. 16:13) almost immediately after the second rejection of Saul (I Sam. 15). It was this rejection that brought the successful period to a close. So, at what point in Saul's reign was David anointed? The answer is probably about Saul's twenty-fifth year of rule. Saul's successes covered about 25 years, leaving 15 years for his time of decline.

Saul's decline

Following the second and final rejection, Saul's position in Israel declined steadily. His rule was marked by interaction with the young man David, whom God designated as his successor. The account of this second portion of Saul's reign begins with the selection of David by God, still working through the prophet Samuel.

Is it ever good to break a promise?

When is it important to keep a promise, no matter what?

If you had to choose between keeping a bad promise and going back on your word, which would you choose?

Saul's Sin and second Rejection — I Samuel 15:10-35

God appeared to Samuel to tell him of the partial obedience, even before Saul returned. The divine word was Saul was now rejected as head of a royal dynasty because he had "turned back from following" God (15:11).

Saul had outwardly been doing well, and this had pleased the aging Samuel, but now he knew inwardly Saul's heart had been growing more and more rebellious in attitude toward God. This spelled disaster for Saul personally and it meant hardship for the whole country in days ahead.

Samuel now went to meet Saul, who for some reason had returned to Gilgal down in the Jordan Valley, rather than coming back to his capital, Gibeah (15:12). There Samuel first rebuked Saul for sparing the king and the livestock. Saul protested he had really obeyed, and the livestock had been saved by the people for sacrifice, laying the blame on the people. Samuel responded with the well-known statement, "Behold, to obey is better than sacrifice, and to hearken than the fat of rams" (15:22).

Saul did confess he had sinned and asked Samuel to pray for his forgiveness, but Samuel said he would not, for God had rejected Saul "from being king over Israel" (15:24-26). When Samuel turned to leave, Saul grabbed his garment, ripping it, and Samuel then spoke again of the rejection, likening it to the rip Saul had thus made.

Saul now asked Samuel to remain with him long enough to worship the Lord before the elders of the people, and so give a show of solidarity between the two despite the harsh words.

Samuel consented, Saul did worship, and then Samuel commanded that Agag, the Amalekite king, be brought, and Samuel killed him himself.

At this, Samuel left and went to his home in Ramah and Saul returned to Gibeah, never to see each other again while they lived (15:35).

Saul's basic sin–disobedience
The reason God rejected Saul for the second time was his disobedience. God wants His children to obey Him. This was the meaning of Samuel's words when he said God delights in obedience more than in sacrifice. For sacrifice without obedience is meaningless.

So-called sacrifice insults God
The sheep and oxen Saul had spared for the purpose of sacrifice were not suitable for this purpose. God had already claimed these animals; Saul was supposed to have killed them. It was completely paradoxical, therefore, for him to think in terms of giving them to God in sacrifice. One cannot give to God what God has already made His. Saul's action was an insult to God and a repudiation of the command given to him.

Blaming others
Saul only added to his sin by seeking to put the blame for saving the animals on the people. He told Samuel, "I have obeyed, but the people took of the spoil" (15:20, 21). Possibly the people had suggested the idea, but even so, because of God's command Saul had the authority and responsibility to say no.

How can you place a higher value on obedience than on appearances or practical considerations in your life?

How can you avoid rationalizing the next time you are "caught in the act" of something you know is wrong?

David in Saul's Court — I Samuel 16:14-23

After David is said to have had the Spirit of the Lord come upon him, immediately Saul is said to have had the Spirit of the Lord depart from him. The point of I Samuel 16:13, 14 is the person of God's special interest for enablement as king had now changed. From this point forward God's blessing would be on David, not Saul.

Not only did Saul lose the presence of the Holy Spirit to aid him, but he was given the presence of an "evil spirit" to trouble him. These two facts are put side by side in 16:14 to imply so long as the Holy Spirit was with Saul, the evil spirit could not come.

The evil spirit came only when the Holy Spirit had been taken away. Light always drives out darkness!

As a result of the evil spirit Saul suffered periods of terrible depression. Saul's servants suggested a musician be brought to play an instrument and help quiet Saul in these times. Saul approved and David was brought. God obviously directed in this selection as a way of introducing David to court life.

The "evil spirit"

The "evil spirit" which came to influence Saul was permitted by God to influence Saul. Satan, no doubt, had wanted to work against God's plan and he was happy to use Saul, but the Holy Spirit had kept him away. Now, with the enablement of the Holy Spirit withdrawn, the evil spirit could make his play. It is not necessary to believe Saul was indwelt by an evil spirit. This spirit was able to work on Saul's personality. He seems rather to have influenced him by working from the outside, much as Satan with Eve in the Garden of Eden (Gen. 3:1-6).

Periods of terrible depression

The times of trouble the evil spirit brought on Saul were evidently periods of terrible depression, meaning periods of depression characterized especially by fear. The word translated in the King James as "troubled" is used 16 times in the Old Testament, and every time it involves the idea of fear. It no doubt involves fear here, also.

Saul's fear was clearly related to losing his kingdom, having just been informed by Samuel that this would happen (I Sam. 15:28). As a result, he gradually became suspicious of others, especially of the young David, and finally came to the point of trying to kill him (I Sam. 18:10-12).

God's remarkable ways

This story illustrates once more that God accomplishes His will in most unusual and unexpected ways. Saul's times of fearful depression were used to bring into the court and eventually into the public eye the very one who would displace him. Little did Saul know the one brought to help him was the one God had just anointed to succeed him.

The power of music

The story also provides an illustration of the power of music in shaping a person's moods. Soothing music, from David's stringed instrument, could calm a disturbed Saul; harsh music, loud music with a rhythmic beat, can do much to disturb a calm person.

What was good or bad about the way Saul relied on David's music to help him get out of his bad moods?

How do you imagine you would feel if, like Saul, you were first chosen by God and then rejected by God?

Why did Saul have trouble with depression? Could he have asked God for help?

Saul had kept 3,000 of his troops with him, holding 2,000 for himself and 1,000 for Jonathan. Saul kept his men in two places, Michmash and Bethel, and Jonathan kept his in the capital city, Gibeah.

A major battle was precipitated by an early skirmish on the part of Jonathan. Perhaps bolder than his father, he took his 1,000 men and made a raid on a Philistine garrison quartered in Geba, about two-thirds of the way from Gibeah to Michmash.

Jonathan, acting without the knowledge of his father, had the Philistines in flight. The distant noise of battle roused Saul. In his excitement (14:19), he waved aside the priest. He was too busy to pray. It was the same impatience he had shown before (13:8-10).

In his folly Saul swore an oath. "Cursed be any man who eats food before evening comes, before I have avenged myself on my enemies!" (14:24) So none of the troops tasted food; he condemned his army to hunger.

Consider the results.
The victory was incomplete. In the evening the desperate people broke the law (32). Saul remembered his vow and he asked who had broken the vow and eaten during the battle. It was discovered Jonathan was guilty, for he had not heard the vow; he was busy fighting the enemy already. Saul allowed Jonathan to stand oddly condemned. And Saul would have killed Jonathan! A surge of anger through the Hebrew host was all that saved the splendid young warrior.

The contrast between Saul and Jonathan is striking. Saul was a hotheaded and passionate man. This side of his character, properly ordered and controlled, could have led him far. Jonathan was as cool-headed as he was brave. He could assess his father's folly (29), and probably undertook his lonely exploit because he had no confidence in his father's action. Had he been spared his sad ending he would have made an excellent king, but it is part of the tragedy of Saul that he dragged to ruin his fine son.

Such involvement is inseparable from our humanity. The same basic fact worked through to tragedy in Achan's family (Joshua 7). The same truth can be rich and fruitful in joy.

Jonathan's courage and ability
Though Jonathan may have acted somewhat hastily in his attack on the Philistine garrison, he did show remarkable ability and courage in making it. He evidently saw the Philistine garrison as a "open sore" in Israel, and apparently on his own part decided to eliminate it.

The fact he did not consult his father beforehand can be inferred from the fact Saul did not help. Jonathan may not have wanted to consult him for fear his father would forbid the action. Jonathan himself was ready for it and thus displayed courage; that he then won the battle showed ability.

Jonathan attacked and defeated one of the remaining Philistine garrisons. No doubt the number of such garrisons and the degree to which they could exercise control were much less following the battle of Mizpeh, but they did continue in some measure. That they had been greatly reduced, indeed, is evidenced by Saul's ability earlier to assemble his large army to fight the Ammonites at Jabesh-Gilead, apparently without Philistine interference.

Also, during the two years of his rule that had now elapsed, Saul had been able to station his own army at Michmash and Bethel in the very area of the Philistine garrison of Geba and not be molested by them.

Why is a vow not something to be taken lightly?

Our world, confronted with terrorism and bloodshed, may find this chapter, with Samuel's decree of destruction against the Amalekites, unsettling to read.

The Amalekites must first be seen for what they were; a kind of Bedouin tribe, ranging from the eastern borderlands of Israel to the Sinai and northwards, menacing the frontier, raiding, looting, murdering. If peace was to rule in Israel, their defeat was necessary.

The conflict must be seen in the context of wars such as that era had known; where harassed nations with cruelty, aggression and the determination of desperate terrorist groups plaguing their borderlands and damaging all peace.

Saul had the task of making the frontiers peaceful and establishing prosperity to allow growth and normal life to exist. For the new ruler of Israel, this was an absolute necessity if there was to be a "kingdom of Israel." It was a national duty.

Saul had his orders. Samuel said to Saul, *"I am the one the LORD sent to anoint you king over his people Israel; so listen now to the message from the LORD. This is what the LORD Almighty says: 'I will punish the Amalekites for what they did to Israel when they waylaid them as they came up from Egypt. Now go, attack the Amalekites and totally destroy everything that belongs to them. Do not spare them; put to death men and women, children and infants, cattle and sheep, camels and donkeys.'"*

He knew the facts which Ezra was to stress 500 years later (Ezra 9:11, 12). *"But now, O our God, what can we say after this? For we have disregarded the commands you gave through your servants the prophets when you said: 'The land you are entering to possess is a land polluted by the corruption of its peoples. By their detestable practices they have filled it with their impurity from one end to the other.'"*

And Saul, as he usually did, interpreted those orders as he saw fit. It was not because of mercy he spared Agag, the brutal ruler of the desert tribes (33), but for personal satisfaction. He probably envisioned a triumphal procession perhaps with the captive king walking before his chariot. It was an act of royal pride.

He lied to Samuel. He blamed "the people" (21) for what he had himself allowed. He demonstrated once again, and for the last time, his own unreliability. His could not continue as king. Such self-will contained the seeds of his own final defeat. Samuel knew it and grieved for Saul (35), he cared for the man whom his own hands had anointed. He saw his face no more.

Samuel in his stern rebuke shows himself the forerunner of the Major Prophets.

Samuel replied: ***"Does the LORD delight in burnt offerings and sacrifices as much as in obeying the voice of the LORD? To obey is better than sacrifice, and to heed is better than the fat of rams."*** 1 Samuel 15:22

This instruction about obedience and sacrifice should be read in connection with the first call of Isaiah to Israel (Isa. 1:11-20) three centuries later.

This is the old lesson which Israel found so difficult to learn.

Why does God prize obedience more highly than offerings or sacrifices?

What are modern-day equivalents of Israel's offerings and sacrifices?

In what way is rebellion and arrogance toward God like idolatry?

David Anointed King — 1 Samuel 16

It was soon after the day of Saul's rejection when God told Samuel to go to Bethlehem and anoint a son of Jesse as Israel's next king. He also told him to take a young cow for a sacrifice, so Saul would not become suspicious. Samuel did this, arriving in Bethlehem called the men of the city to the place of sacrifice.

After Samuel had offered the sacrifice, he proceeded with the matter of the anointing. He first assumed that Eliab, the oldest son, was the one to be anointed; Eliab had a striking appearance, but God told Samuel not to look on the outward appearance, for Eliab was not God's choice. Then Jesse had the oldest come before Samuel, but God said he was not the chosen one either, and this continued for all seven of Jesse's sons who were present. When none of these was chosen by God, Samuel asked if there was not yet another, and Jesse said there was one, but that he had been left to tend the family's sheep. Samuel had him called. When he arrived, Samuel saw he was *"ruddy and withal of a beautiful countenance."* God now said, *"Arise, anoint him: for this is he"* (16:12). Then Samuel poured anointing oil over David's head, as all the other brothers looked on. Also, and most significantly, at that moment the "Spirit of the LORD came upon David from that day forward."

A problem in truth-telling

The Scriptures are clear that truth-telling is very important in the sight of God (Exod. 20:16; 23:1, 7; Eph. 4:25; Col. 3:9). A problem therefore arises in respect to the pretext God told Samuel to give to Saul for his going to Bethlehem. Samuel had indicated to God that should he tell Saul that he went there to anoint David, Saul would kill him. God then instructed Samuel, *"Take an heifer with thee, and say, I am come to sacrifice to the LORD"* (16:2). Thus, Samuel was to tell Saul part of the truth but not all the truth. The problem is made more pointed by the fact it was God Himself who told Samuel to offer this as the reason for his going. The following remarks are in order.

First, that which God told Samuel to say was indeed true. He was not told to say anything untrue. He was to take an animal with him and offer a sacrifice in Bethlehem, and he did.
Second, that which Samuel was not to tell Saul makes clear that there are certain situations that call for a concealment of truth. Saul had no right to know the full truth because he would have used it wrongly, possibly even to take Samuel's life as Samuel himself indicated.

Today professional people, such as doctors, lawyers, and ministers have the right, indeed the necessity, of concealment of truth as a protection for people who confide in them. They are professionally obligated to keep information confidential, for if people in general would learn of it they might use it wrongly, to the detriment of those concerned.

It should be recognized this right of concealment of truth carries with it a high responsibility for the person employing it. There must be good and adequate reason. It cannot be used simply as a way, for instance, of extricating himself from a difficult situation. It is also important to recognize this right of concealment gives no reason to anyone for speaking an untruth.

Thoughts of the other brothers

The older brothers must have been surprised their youngest brother was chosen in this way over them. It is evident they considered him inferior to themselves.

David visited his three oldest brothers when they were serving in Saul's army against the Philistines and Goliath. When he came to bring them food, Eliab greeted him with unkind words (I Sam. 17:28). After Samuel left the site of David's anointing, therefore, one may believe that the brothers set about giving the young man a difficult time, to remind him of his proper place in the home circle and to keep him from getting any ideas of superiority.

How do you think David's brothers felt about being skipped in favor of David?

Do you think they expressed any dissatisfaction to Jesse or Samuel?

David and Goliath — 1 Samuel 17

Over 20 years had passed, since the first Philistine battle, when Saul was first rejected. The place was the western end of the valley of Elah where this valley runs from the level land of the Philistines northeastward toward Bethlehem. Evidently the Philistines wanted to march up this valley into Judah's territory and Saul met them to stop them.

The two armies faced each other across the valley and one day a champion of the Philistines walked across to challenge any Israelite to fight him. He proposed the outcome of the war be decided by this individual combat. It may be possible the Philistines were remembering Israel's champion, Samson, of some years before. Now they had a powerful man of their own, and they were willing to let their fortunes rest on his shoulders.

The man was Goliath, nine feet six inches tall, covered with armor from head to foot, with a man bearing a protective shield going before him. He was from the city of Gath, his coat of bronze scale armor weighed 125 pounds, His spear shaft was like a weaver's rod and its iron point weighed 15 pounds.

The sight of this powerful man made all Israel's soldiers tremble. Forty days passed, while the giant defied Israel's armies. Finally, young David came to Saul's camp, sent by his father to bring provisions for the three older brothers, who were members of the army, and he saw the humiliating situation. Immediately he volunteered to fight the man, with Saul at first hesitating but then agreeing to the idea. Saul did not believe the young man could possibly defeat Goliath.

Goliath continued to blaspheme God. He demanded Israel send out their champion to meet him in battle. When David appeared, he was incensed. He cursed David by his gods and promised to give his flesh to the birds and beasts (1 Sam. 17:43-44). With only a sling for a weapon, David shot one stone and struck the giant in the forehead, causing the great one to fall. David ran to cut off his head with Goliath's own sword. At this, the Philistines fled, according to the agreement, and the Israelites won the crucial battle. The Israelites chased the Philistines as far as Gath and Ekron, 2 of their 5 main cities.

Saul's reluctance to use David

Saul's hesitation in letting Israel's future hang on the abilities of David is understandable. Saul has been criticized for not going out to meet Goliath himself. He was, after all, the chosen King and he was probably the tallest in his army. He did finally let David go, but only because of the confidence David showed in his God. David seemed to have a source of strength other than physical, and Saul had no one else to send other than himself.

In what sense is there a fine line between bravery and stupidity?

Saul's inquiry regarding David

After David had won the encounter with Goliath, Saul inquired of Abner, his military commander, "*Whose son is this youth?*" This seems strange since David had been with Saul as his personal musician before the Philistine battle. Saul knew who David was, he knew him as a boy musician, but he did not know him in his military role. In addition, Saul had promised the parents of Goliath's conqueror would live tax-free, and this made him wonder who David's parents were. He apparently wanted to know more now, in the light of the remarkable achievement of the young man.

How did David view this as a spiritual battle more than a physical battle?

What were the most important "weapons" in this battle?

David always remembered this moment (Psalm. 27:1-3).

The LORD is my light and my salvation; Whom shall I fear? The LORD is the strength of my life; Of whom shall I be afraid? When the wicked came against me To eat up my flesh, My enemies and foes, They stumbled and fell. Though an army may encamp against me, My heart shall not fear; Though war should rise against me, In this I will be confident.

At first, following the Philistine victory, Saul did not see David as a rival. He seems to have been impressed with what David had done. Saul made David captain of the army, setting "him over the men of war" (18:5). In this capacity, David continued to harass the Philistines with the result the saying rose among the people, *"Saul has slain his thousands, and David his tens of thousands."* As a result, Saul in jealousy turned against David.

The day following one of David's successful raids against the enemy, he was playing his instrument for Saul, who was suffering one of his attacks. Instead of being calmed as before, Saul became more agitated and thrust at David twice with his spear to kill him. It is probable that he only thrust at him, rather than throwing the spear, for it is said David twice avoided him and no mention is made of the spear sticking into the wall as in a later instance (19:10).

Saul was now even more afraid of David. He saw him as a rival for the throne. So, he sent him away from the palace with a lesser number than David had commanded before. Still David *"behaved himself wisely,"* with the result that Saul became more fearful of him, and the people more in favor of him. Saul now tried another way of ridding himself of David. He first offered his older daughter Merab to him as wife. This was intended to fulfill the promise given before David's victory over Goliath (17:25). Later he changed his mind and offered David his younger daughter, Michal, instead.

David at first protested that he was not worthy to be a son-in-law to the king, but finally he did marry Michal, who had fallen in love with him (18:20). As a dowry for Michal, Saul asked *"a hundred foreskins of the Philistines,"* thinking that David would be killed in trying to get them (18:17, 21), but instead David was able to deliver two hundred (18:27). David apparently did not realize Saul had plotted against him in this and when David was not harmed, Saul came to fear him still more, recognizing God's blessing upon him.

David's dual role.
It is quite clear for a time David played a dual role in Saul's kingdom: as Saul's musician and as the new army commander. The two roles differed greatly, and people must have marveled that one who could play so beautifully one day could lead an army so effectively the next. This shows the versatility of the young David and, even more, the blessing of God as the Holy Spirit remained continually upon him for empowerment.

The evil spirit and David.
A change in the evil spirit's reaction to David and his playing is noteworthy here. Earlier, the evil spirit had withdrawn when David played, the evil spirit did not like the soothing music (16:23). Now, the spirit tried to be rid of the hated music by persuading Saul to kill the player (18:10, 11).

Saul had now grown to fear David and to be jealous of him. This change could be used by the evil spirit. He would not have to run away now; he could rather persuade Saul to take the young man's life, and then he would be rid of the music for good.

Saul's problem.
Saul had a problem in respect to fulfilling his promises to the one who defeated Goliath. It concerned the matter of marriage to his daughter. He had promised the marriage, but now he did not want to fulfill his pledge. Marriage to Saul's daughter would give David a legitimate claim to the throne.

How would you describe your feelings about someone you know for whom everything seems to go right?

What concrete step can you take to offset bitterness the next time you find yourself wishing harm on someone near you who is prospering?

Jonathan: the man **I Samuel 13, 14, 20**

Jonathan is one of the great characters of the Old Testament, brave, loyal, gracious, a soldier, and a friend. The story of his adventure at Michmash reveals much about his character. He was made of the same stuff of which commandoes are made. He could inspire the absolute and unquestioning loyalty of his young armor bearer.

We meet Jonathan for the first time in 1 Samuel 13:2. He was second in command to his father Saul. In the encounter described in this passage, Jonathan and his armor bearer attacked a Philistine outpost. The two of them were given a miraculous victory by God. This attack triggered a war between Israel and the Philistines.

Jonathan had a very difficult relationship with his father. As the Israelites pursued the Philistines in the battle Saul issued an order forbidding his troops to eat any food until the battle was over. He did not hear the order because he was already active in the battle when the order was given. As he was pursuing the enemy, he ate some honey. When Saul discovered the fact, his son had violated his order he ordered Jonathan's death. Despite this the Israelites refused to carry out Saul's order.

Later Jonathan came into conflict with his father because of his friendship with David. The more popular David became the more Saul's hatred toward him grew. Jonathan attempted to resolve the dispute and convinced his father David was completely loyal to Saul and all of Israel.

When Jonathan became convinced of his father's plans to kill David, he remained a good friend and informed David of all of Saul's plans. At one-point Jonathan's support for David enraged Saul so much he cursed his son and his son's mother.

Jonathan remained an encouragement for David as long as he could maintain contact with his friend. He met with David and told David he realized God had appointed him to be the next king of Israel. Jonathan asked David to be kind to his family.

Jonathan, along with his two brothers and his father, died in battle with the Philistines. He was fighting side-by-side with his father. Despite the mistrust and hatred, he had experienced within his family he remained fully committed to supporting them.

In this ongoing drama of the relationship between Saul, Jonathan and David we observe two rare personality qualities of Jonathan.

- **Despite the difficulties he was always respectful of his father.**
- **Under all circumstances he remained a true friend to David.**

He was unassuming in his faith and ready to act on it.

Jonathan was troubled and over-shadowed by his fiery father, yet he shows faithfulness and loyalty to God. Jonathan is usually considered the best example of friendship described in the Bible. In a normal situation Jonathan would have succeeded his father as the King of Israel.

What does it say about Jonathan that he chose to remain loyal to David, even to the point of working against his own father's commands?

Despite the personal loss it would mean in his life he supported his friend and God's plan for the nation of Israel.

Jonathan was loyal to God and to David.

His friendship and his loyalty stand as examples for us today.

David's flight took him first to Nob, about two miles southeast of Gibeah. Here was where the tabernacle had been transferred from Shiloh, likely following Israel's defeat at Aphek. Here served the high priest of the day, Ahimelech, son of Ahitub and great-grandson of Eli.

Ahimelech was worried about helping David at first, no doubt knowing the political conflict, and David believed wrongly the situation warranted his telling a lie. He told the high priest he was on a secret errand for the king. He asked for food, and Ahimelech gave him some of the sacred bread from the table of showbread. David also asked for a weapon, and Ahimelech gave him Goliath's sword, which apparently had been brought there following David's victory over the giant. Watching all of this unfold was an Edomite named Doeg. He was a head shepherd for Saul and loyal to him. A few days later, when David had made good his escape, and news of him had reached Saul, the king made accusations in the presence of several of his attendants to the effect no one was on his side in his quarrel with David.

Doeg now returned from Nob, then spoke up concerning what he had seen at Nob, quite clearly as a way of enhancing his position before Saul. Immediately Saul sent for Ahimelech to demand an explanation, and the high priest told him what had happened, making clear he considered David a faithful servant of Saul and he had been completely ignorant of David's reason for coming to him. Saul was not satisfied with the reply, however, and ordered nearby men to "*slay the priests of the LORD*," giving as a reason they had helped David and not reported the matter of his flight to Saul. These men refused this shocking order. Saul then turned to Doeg to order him to do it. He killed 85 priests, including Ahimelech, along with their families, and their livestock. One priest, however, escaped. This was Ahimelech's son, Abiathar. He was able to get away to David, apparently knowing where David was at the time. When Abiathar told David what had happened, David took full blame upon himself, no doubt remembering the lie he had told Ahimelech. Then he told Abiathar to remain with him.

David's lie

We cannot explain away or defend David in his lie to Ahimelech. He apparently thought the end justified the means. The awful results of the untruth are clear in the complete destruction of the priests and their families which resulted.

David's sorrow was great when he learned of the harm he had done, but it was then too late to mend the wrong.

Ahimelech was in a difficult position the day David asked for his assistance. How much he knew of the full story involving Saul and David is not clear, but he had no way of knowing David was now fleeing from Saul. He tried to be careful, but when David lied to him, he thought he was acting properly in giving him help. His later testimony before Saul certainly was innocent and sincere, but still Saul executed him.

Why would God permit such a wrong to be done?

The lesson is a "small lie" may have disastrous results for others.

What was it about David which probably prompted Ahimelech to fulfill his requests?

What sort of person would you be inclined to help, even if he or she were in trouble with the authorities?

How could the story have turned out differently if David had told the priest he was fleeing from Saul?

Often Satan uses people as his tools; sometimes they are innocent and ignorant they are being used.

After leaving and getting help from Ahimelech at Nob, David first tried the foreign alternative. He went to the Philistine city of Gath. He was recognized by the local king and he pretended to be mad to escape harm.

David now tried a different tactic. He returned to his homeland and took up residence in a cave near Adullam. Here he began gathering a protective force of men. Since he was within ten miles of his home at Bethlehem, he was near enough for his father and brothers to visit him.

Somehow David was able to make known, possibly by the help of his family, that he wanted men to join him. A total of 400 came; men described as in distress, in debt, or discontented (I Sam. 22:1, 2). Surprisingly, when the band had been assembled, David again tried the foreign alternative, this time going east to Moab. He took his parents with him this time, no doubt fearing reprisals against them by Saul.

Gad, a prophet who had joined David's band, soon counseled him to leave Moab, and David moved once more back to Judah.

During this time Abiathar, son of Ahimelech, fleeing from Saul, came to David. The time was soon after Saul's terrible slaughter of the priests of Nob, from which Abiathar had escaped. He was high priest now, since his father had been killed. Accordingly, he brought the ephod with him, apparently including the Urim and Thummim for divine inquiry.

Problems David faced

Sometimes David is criticized for seemingly vacillating between alternatives of policy and for moving about so often while a fugitive, as though uncertain and undecided. We must realize, however, he faced enormous problems. A lesser person could easily have wilted beneath them. There was the problem of maintaining safety for himself and his men, when he knew Saul was constantly looking for them.

Also, there was the problem both of persuading enough to join him and of controlling them when they did. It was necessary to feed and provide for this group. This in itself must have been a tremendous challenge. Still further, he had the problem of keeping friends among the populace. He needed to keep their favor, so they would not report his location to Saul, he could not simply seize food wherever he might find it. He had to acquire it by proper means and in a manner, which would keep people sympathetic to him.

David's remarkable success

On all these counts, David clearly did very well. He did continually escape Saul's efforts. He was able to gather a band of men and control them. In fact, he was able to weld them into a unity that has seldom been matched. And as for keeping friends with the populace, few people revealed his location to Saul. And when the time came for him to rule, it was the people of Judah, certainly including the people among whom he moved during these days, who were the first to crown him.

Leadership ability.

David showed remarkable ability in leading his band of men. Men of the kind that gathered to him are the very hardest to lead. Probably most knew of his military ability from days when he led Saul's armies, and this would have helped. But once he had assembled the group, the task of keeping them together and maintaining their loyalty was most challenging. He must have been both fair and firm when disputes arose. His ruling must have been sound, so they recognized they could trust his direction.

Respect for Saul as king

David always showed the highest respect for Saul, since Saul was God's anointed king. This is seen especially in the two times he spared Saul's life, and it is seen also in David's general attitude. Not once is he found speaking ill of Saul, despite Saul's unfair treatment of him. Even when the Ziphites twice reported his position to Saul, David did not retaliate against them. Nor is it recorded he ever spoke derogatory words about them. David's attitude in all this is remarkable and commendable.

David at Ziklag — I Samuel 27-30

Following the second instance of sparing Saul's life, David went again to the foreign area of the Philistines; apparently believing he could not expect always to escape from Saul as he had until that time (27:1). There was probably another reason for this move, suggested by David's request for food from Nabal. David's troops now numbered 600 (27:2) , and though this was reassuring as a protective measure, it meant a major increase in food supplies.

The Philistines, as others of the day, employed mercenary troops, and, if they would accept David's group, the food problem would be solved and there would be remuneration besides. Saul would not follow him there either.

The difficulty with the idea was the Philistines might not accept David and his band, though with this protective group around him David did not have to fear for his life as he had the first time he visited.

David made the move and Achish did accept him. Probably the fact that David had now been a fugitive so long, as well as an apparent need Achish had for such troops, helped in the decision. At David's request (27:5), Achish assigned David to the city of Ziklag, well south of Gath though still in Philistine territory, as a base of operations.

David played a dual role at Ziklag. He pretended to serve Achish as a mercenary. He attacked southern foreign tribes, which had been perennial enemies of Israel, particularly the Geshurites, Gezrites, and Amalekites.

He let Achish believe he was distressing southern Judah, thus maintaining standing with him; all the while, however, he was distributing booty among the cities of southern Judah (30:26-31), thus keeping their favor against the day when he would be their king.

After 16 months of this activity (27:7), the final Philistine battle with Saul drew near, David found himself in a bad spot. He had committed himself to Achish to a degree where he could not remain uninvolved without endangering his own position. But other Philistines objected to his presence and insisted he be sent home to Ziklag.

Disaster met David when he returned to Ziklag. While David and his men were away the Amalekites had destroyed the town and taken David's wives and the wives of all his men, as well as everything of value. As a result, David's men, who to this point had been so loyal to him, came near rebellion. David was quick to act and immediately set out after the captors. David stormed the Amalekite camp and recovered both the wives and the plunder.

David's 16 months at Ziklag probably marked a low point in his spiritual walk with God. He displayed a lack of faith in going there, as though God could not protect him in his own land. He was not honest with Achish after he arrived there, and it was because of God's intervening grace he was spared from having to fight his own people. It was during this time David displayed deceit. He tried to make Achish think he was working in his behalf, while in reality he was working in his own. This is a precarious game to play and is displeasing to God.

God brought David into a very difficult and embarrassing situation. He was nearly made to fight his own people.

God apparently wanted David to see the real harm of his decision to hide among the enemy. God let

David come to the brink of having to fight Israel for the Philistines.

How do you see God's hand at work in the decisions of the people above you in the chain of command?

Saul's Death — I Samuel 28:5-25; 31:1-13

Sad indeed was the end of Israel's first King. He had started well but ended shamefully. His tragic death on mount Gilboa suited the perverted way he had ruled during his last years. Saul is an example of what can happen to a man of promise who does not obey God. He had good potential and even was selected by God for this task. He had an attractive appearance. He had the certainty of God's blessing, if he had only followed God's will.

But his reign proved to be one of continual frustration and lack of accomplishment.

In their initial request, the Israelites wanted one like him to rule so that their country might be strong against enemy attack. But when Saul died, after 40 years of rule, the country had become weaker than when he became King.

Saul was plagued with emotional problems from the beginning. This inborn lack of confidence may have influenced him, for instance, in not imposing strong unifying regulations on the people, a policy which was wise at first, as observed, but should not have been continued.

Saul's main problem, however, was his pride and rebellious spirit toward God. Satan apparently affected him, and he did not control his actions. He forgot God was still head of His people. For this reason, he was rejected by God.

The country was probably as disunited at Saul's death as it was when he became king. Any gains during the early years were likely lost during the later years. Diminishing confidence in Saul as a man would have soon led to loss of confidence in the nation for which he stood.

No doubt, the distrust on the part of the people played a significant role in Saul's final defeat on mount Gilboa. Few men responded to his call to serve in the army and this left him incapable of meeting the Philistine challenge. For this reason, the Philistines won an easy victory; Israel's army was destroyed, and the King killed, leaving the country helpless before the enemy. There is little doubt the Philistines could now move into the land with great strength.

As Saul fell on his sword, he must have realized how he had failed in his attempt to unite and build a nation. He had been promised much when he was young but ended with little. Favored above all in his day, he failed in his great opportunity.

Then the enemy cut off Saul's head and took his armor back to Philistia for propaganda purposes. They fastened his body and those of his sons to the wall of Bethshan, about eight miles east of the site of the battle. The next day, however, men of Jabesh-Gilead, who remembered the deliverance Saul had achieved for them, came and took the bodies back to their city for cremation and burial.

As Saul fell on his sword that day, the remorse he felt in view of all that had happened must have been very great. He had experienced a wonderful opportunity when young, and here he was dying with nothing to show for it. Forty years had passed, and the people were actually worse off than when he had started. Instead of his defeating the Philistines, they had now defeated him and could take over the land.

Now another man would sit on Israel's throne, the man he had wasted recent years in pursuing.

He had lost and David had won. It was an awful way to die.

In your opinion, what circumstances make Saul's desire to die quickly either understandable or cowardly?

Book Five

David the man and his family

David was part of the tribe of Judah, the son of Jesse and great-grandson of Boaz and Ruth (Ruth 4:21, 22). He had seven older brothers, Eliab, Abinadab, Shammah, Nethaneel, Raddai, Ozem, and one unnamed who may have died shortly after David's anointing (I Sam. 16:5-10).

Ruth, Jesse's grandmother, had come from Moab, which was historically allied with Ammon. This tie makes it seem more likely David's mother may once have been related to the king of Ammon. Also, it was to Moab David sent his parents for safety during the days of his flight from Saul (I Sam. 23:3, 4), showing an endurance of the same close tie.

While still young, David was considered the least important in his father's household; he was assigned the family flocks to tend, recognized in those days as a demeaning task. He was not even taken along by the rest of the family to the community time of sacrifice when Samuel came to Bethlehem (I Sam. 16:11).

Also, later when he brought food to his three older brothers in Saul's army, the oldest, Eliab, spoke disdainfully to him (I Sam. 17:28), and this occurred well after the time when David had been anointed. David, however, did not return evil for evil, for after he became king, he appointed Eliab to be leader of the tribe of Judah.

The third brother, Shammah, is also mentioned during the time of David's reign: his son Jonadab was the one who gave wicked advice to Amnon (II Sam. 13:3-5, 32, and 33). Another son of Shammah, Jonathan, killed a giant in Gath (II Sam. 21:21).

David was born and raised in the vicinity of Bethlehem of Judah. Here he learned the beauty of nature, as he cared for the family flocks. Here, too, he learned how to care for himself in the rugged hills of Judah, a lesson which was to help him in later days of fleeing from Saul. He also learned the ways of guiding and disciplining sheep. As a result, he developed the wisdom necessary for governing Israel well.

His appearance

David was not tall like Saul, but he evidently was of fine appearance. When Samuel first saw him, he is said to have been "ruddy" and of "a beautiful countenance, and goodly to look at" (I Sam. 16:12). The term "ruddy" may imply he was a redhead.

Later, Saul's servants described David to the king as "a comely person" (I Sam. 16:18), and later still, Goliath saw David as "ruddy and of a fair countenance" (I Sam. 17:42). These expressions all suggest an appearance which was pleasing and handsome. He was not the warrior type.

At the same time, Saul's servants spoke of David as mighty, valiant, and a man of war. Evidently, they knew of something David had done to show his ability in combat already as a young man. That he indeed had such ability is demonstrated by his later handling of both a lion and bear with his bare hands, catching, as he says, the lion by his beard as the beast revolted against him. Such a feat called for strength, swiftness of movement, and excellent skill. He showed similar dexterity in escaping from Saul's attacks with the spear.

David himself said God gave him feet like "hinds' feet" (feet of a deer) and "hands to war, so that a bow of steel is broken by mine arms" (Ps. 18:33, 34). These details show David was agile, strong, and skilled in combat. Jesse's eighth son was an attractive and capable young man.

David is an example of the old saying "appearances can be deceiving."

Do you know someone of whom this is true?

David's Character

We also want to make some observations about David's character. As we study watch as God develops these tendencies in the man!

He was a man of God.

First and foremost, David was a man of God. In fact, before Samuel went to anoint the young man, God referred to him as a man after His own heart (I Sam. 13:14; quoted in Acts 13:22).

Following his kingship, the degree to which other kings were faithful to God was measured by David's standard (I Kings 3:14; 9:4; 11:4, 6, 33, 38; 14:8; 15:3).

It was because of David's outstanding kingship his posterity would continue to rule and it was for the same reason God would defend Jerusalem (Isa. 37:35) and not take the throne entirely away from Solomon's son, Rehoboam (I Kings 11:12, 13, 32, 36; 15:4).

Much later kings are said to have occupied David's throne (Jer. 22:2, 4, 30; 29:16), and the ruler of the far future is identified as David (Ezek. 37:24, 25; Hos. 3:5).

David is used as the measure of strong men in that future day (Zech. 12:8).

Christ Himself is called the "son of David" many times (Matt. 1:1; 9:27; 12:23; 15:22), and that it was necessary for Christ to be born in Bethlehem because it was the city of David (John 7:42).

David did have his failures, especially in respect to Bathsheba and her husband Uriah (II Sam. 11) and later in calling for a census of the country (II Sam. 24), but the biblical stress is never on David's sin, as with Saul, but on his righteous acts.

The main reason for this exemplary life of David is he was continuously empowered by the Holy Spirit from the day of his anointing forward.

This is the significance of I Samuel 16:13, "*And the Spirit of the LORD came upon David from that day forward.*" During the approximately 15 years before he became king, he was empowered so he would be protected until that time; and he was empowered during the 40 years he ruled.

He recognized this enablement and cherished it highly as is revealed by his prayer at the time of his sin with Bathsheba and Uriah, "*Take not thy holy spirit from me*" (Ps. 51:11).

He remembered the downfall of Saul when the Spirit was removed from him; he did not want the same thing to happen to him. That he knew the Spirit was not removed at that time is shown by his words in his last days, "*The Spirit of the LORD spake by me, and his word was in my tongue*" (II Sam. 23:2).

Saul's servants, who found and described David to Saul as his prospective musician, recognized the young man as unusually able. They said he was "*cunning in playing*" and "*prudent in matters*" (I Sam. 16:18). They of course would not have recommended him at all if he had not been unusually skillful with his stringed instrument. David may have been able to play more than one instrument (II Sam. 6:5) for he is said to have been an inventor of instruments (I Chron. 23:5; II Chron. 7:6; Amos 6:5). Besides playing instruments, David was renowned as a writer of words which could be put to music. For this reason, he is called the "sweet psalmist of Israel" (II Sam. 23:1).

In Hezekiah's time, the Levites were commanded to "*sing praise unto the LORD with the words of David*" (II Chron. 29:30). And the titles to the Psalms indicate David wrote no fewer than 73 of them.

David left a godly heritage. What sort of heritage are you building?

David's Personal Abilities

This is easily seen from his success as a king, and it is demonstrated dramatically by his success with a group of followers during his days as a fugitive. These men were described as those who were "*in distress*," those "*in debt*," and those who were "*discontented*" (I Sam. 22:2). People described in this manner are not normally easy to live with; they have had trouble elsewhere and can be expected to have more in any new situation. David was able to mold them into a unit which stayed with him as an impressive fighting force, not only during his days on the run from Saul, but also during his time as king.

Closely connected with David's ability for leadership was his success as a military man. After he was appointed to be Saul's commander, Israel did not lose a battle with the Philistines. For this reason, the people described his defeated foes as ten thousand and Saul's only as thousands (I Sam. 18:7). He did not lose battles after he became king either, though Joab was the principal commander. It was David himself who defeated the Philistines decisively just after being accepted as king over all Israel.

David was a statesman of great ability
He became Israel's finest king. This was due to God's blessing, but God uses abilities, and the abilities here would have been David's ability in statesmanship. David took a kingdom which was in shambles and built it into an empire. Such an accomplishment does not just happen. The man at the top is all-important. David, in fact, was so important Israel came to be known as David's country rather than David as Israel's king.

David was a man of humility
David, for all his ability, was humble. When chased by Saul through the barren hills of Judah, even though he had been anointed as Saul's successor, he still spoke of himself as a dead dog, a flea, and a partridge (I Sam. 24:14; 26:20). Never did he speak insultingly to Saul, but always respected him as God's anointed. Most men, if anointed to be king, would become boastful and proud. David was still willing to tend sheep.

A likable person
One test of greatness is whether a person is liked by others or not. People whom others admire are liked; those not admired are shunned. David was liked by other people. Jonathan, the logical heir to Saul's throne came to love David as his own brother. This was despite a marked age difference between them and David's replacing him as the heir apparent. But perhaps the most striking example is what David's band of refugee soldiers thought of him. One day when David wished for a drink from his old favorite spring at Bethlehem, three of the leaders broke through the enemy lines of the Philistines to get it for him.

David displayed patience, which is perhaps one of the rarest virtues. We often wonder why he did not flee or take some drastic measure of retaliation against Saul much sooner than he did. Saul had tried to kill him five different times before David was convinced, he would have to leave. Even then, he wanted Jonathan to test Saul once again to see if there was any possibility of reconciliation.

Small people hold grudges; thoughtful people overlook them. David might have held a grudge against his older brother Eliab for belittling him all during his younger days, especially at the scene of the Philistine battle (1 Sam. 17:28). He did not! He later appointed the man as head of the tribe of Judah.

He might also have been vindictive toward Saul, but he was not. He had opportunity twice to take Saul's life, but both times, contrary to the urging of his men, refused to do so (I Sam. 24:3-7; 26:5-11).

Why isn't it wise to take every opportunity we are given for personal advancement and advantage?

How is it possible to make peace with one's enemies without entirely trusting them?

David: The New King — 2 Samuel 1-4

With a report of Saul's death, a new era in David's life begins. The 12 tribes of Israel did not immediately declare David King after the death of Saul. In general, David controlled the South, particularly Judah and its politically important city of Hebron.

Saul's son Ishbosheth became King of the northern tribes, often referred to simply as "Israel." For approximately two years, the two sides were involved in a civil war between the house of Saul and the house of David. In a sense the contrast between Saul and David which was so central in I Samuel 16-31 continues in the form of the Civil War between David and Ishbosheth.

With the news of Saul's death David now began to put together his kingdom. He was no longer a fugitive running for his life; now he must begin to lay the foundation for ruling as King.

The first question he faced was how he would deal with the news of the death of Saul and Jonathan and the defeat of Israel by the Philistines. The news was delivered to the camp of David by an Amalekite who claimed he had killed Saul and brought to David Saul's crown and bracelet as evidence to support his story.

This was enough evidence for David, who had no reason to doubt his testimony. David responded by weeping and fasting for Saul and Jonathan and declaring his admiration for both men.

He had the Amalekite put to death because he had killed the Lord's anointed. David, himself, would have absolutely no part in bringing about the death of Saul.

Remember he had the opportunity on two occasions, and he refused to execute him.

At this time David was much better known in the southern part of the land. His hometown was Bethlehem and most of his activity had been in the southern part of Judah. It made sense at this time for him to set up Hebron as his capital city. He had proven his ability and his leadership in this area for several years. A large majority of people in the area were more than willing to crown him king.

It was here David was anointed for the second time, the first time being at Bethlehem years before by Samuel. Now he is both anointed and crowned as "King of Judah" at the city of Hebron.

Conflict between Judah and Israel was almost inevitable. The conflict first showed itself in a minor incident at Gibeon, six miles northeast of Jerusalem. In this location Abner, who had been Saul's commanding general, met Joab, David's commander in a small but decisive battle. David's forces emerged victorious in this opening battle.

As time passed David and his forces grew stronger and the forces of Abner and Ishbosheth continually lost strength. It was obvious David was increasing and the forces of Ishbosheth in the north were losing territory and influence very quickly.

Abner, realizing he had no possibility of victory, sent a message to David agreeing to end the Civil War and support him as the King of all Israel.

What is the value of remembering the past with all its joy and sorrow?

How should a godly leader step into leadership and strengthen his or her position?

What was the most persuasive argument for the people of Israel to declare David their king?

How can you appeal to our common humanity the next time you are caught between "warring factions"?

David's faith is best seen in the Psalms.

Psalm 27
The LORD is my light and my salvation-- whom shall I fear? The LORD is the stronghold of my life– of whom shall I be afraid?
When evil men advance against me to devour my flesh, when my enemies and my foes attack me, they will stumble and fall.
Though an army besiege me, my heart will not fear; though war break out against me, even then will I be confident.
One thing I ask of the LORD, this is what I seek: that I may dwell in the house of the LORD all the days of my life, to gaze upon the beauty of the LORD and to seek him in his temple. For in the day of trouble he will keep me safe in his dwelling; he will hide me in the shelter of his tabernacle and set me high upon a rock.
Then my head will be exalted above the enemies who surround me; at his tabernacle will I sacrifice with shouts of joy; I will sing and make music to the LORD.
Hear my voice when I call, O LORD; be merciful to me and answer me.
My heart says of you, "Seek his face!" Your face, LORD, I will seek. Do not hide your face from me, do not turn your servant away in anger; you have been my helper. Do not reject me or forsake me, O God my Savior. Though my father and mother forsake me, the LORD will receive me.
Teach me your way, O LORD; lead me in a straight path because of my oppressors. Do not turn me over to the desire of my foes, for false witnesses rise up against me, breathing out violence.
I am still confident of this: I will see the goodness of the LORD in the land of the living. Wait for the LORD; be strong and take heart and wait for the LORD.

Psalm 57 - Written by David when he fled from Saul into the cave.

Have mercy on me, O God, have mercy on me, for in you my soul takes refuge. I will take refuge in the shadow of your wings until the disaster has passed. I cry out to God Most High, to God, who fulfills his purpose for me. He sends from heaven and saves me, rebuking those who hotly pursue me; Selah God sends his love and his faithfulness.
I am in the midst of lions; I lie among ravenous beasts– men whose teeth are spears and arrows, whose tongues are sharp swords. Be exalted, O God, above the heavens; let your glory be over all the earth. They spread a net for my feet-- I was bowed down in distress. They dug a pit in my path– but they have fallen into it themselves. Selah
My heart is steadfast, O God, my heart is steadfast; I will sing and make music. Awake, my soul! Awake, harp and lyre! I will awaken the dawn. I will praise you, O Lord, among the nations; I will sing of you among the peoples. For great is your love, reaching to the heavens; your faithfulness reaches to the skies. Be exalted, O God, above the heavens; let your glory be over all the earth.

What gave David courage while he waited for God's deliverance? (27:13-14)

What did David do in anticipation of God's help? (57:7-11)

What do you think motivated David to praise God? (57:9-11)

How can we follow David's example when we feel threatened?

Her name means "father's joy" or "my father rejoices." She lived in the west central part of Palestine. Later she moved with David to the city of Hebron. The time span of her life is shortly before and shortly after 1000 B.C. When the Bible takes up the story of Abigail, she is married to a wealthy sheep master, Nabal, in the area of Carmel.

David and his band of men had been very kind and protective of the men who worked for her husband. When sheep shearing time arrived David sent some of his young men to meet with Nabal and collect a "present" for their efforts at protecting his men and his flocks.

Nabal met these men and rudely and arrogantly rejected the idea of giving them anything. He said they were nothing more than common bandits. When David's men returned and informed David of these events, he became enraged. He took 400 men and set off to destroy Nabal and his entire flock.
Some of the men who had witnessed the scene at Nabal's camp took word of these events to Abigail. They told her of her husband's insults and the anger of the young men. They told her David would without a doubt bring a reprisal against her husband and their servants.

Abigail had her servants quickly put together an offering of bread, grain and wine. She set off to meet David herself. When she came near to meeting David, she humbled herself before David and all his men.

She bowed to the ground and asked David to forgive her husband. She told David her husband's character was foolish and impetuous, just as his name implies (Nabal means fool). She offered to bear the entire responsibility for the action of her husband. was so impressed by Abigail's attitude and her beauty he ended his mission of destruction. David praised Abigail as a messenger from God who had kept him from committing a great sin.

When Abigail returned home Nabal was giving a great banquet. The Bible describes it as a banquet fit for any King. He was apparently drunk, and she did not tell him anything about her meeting with David until the morning. The next morning when she told her husband the Bible tells us he had a heart attack and about 10 days later he died.

David's response to the news of the death of Nabal was, "Praise God!" He then sent messengers to Abigail with an offer of marriage which she accepted.

In this strange story we see the hand of God preserving his man David from sin. There is no human reason for these events to unfold in this manner. The only explanation is God's care for His chosen one.

David recognized the hand of God was active in his life. He said to Abigail, "*May you be blessed for your good judgment and for keeping me from bloodshed this day and from avenging myself with my own hands. Otherwise, as surely as the LORD, the God of Israel, lives, who has kept me from harming you, if you had not come quickly to meet me, not one male belonging to Nabal would have been left alive by daybreak.*" I Samuel 25:33-34

What were some of Abigail's virtues?

Why did Abigail take responsibility for the insult to David?

In what way did David see God's hand in sending Abigail?

Are you more like Abigail or David?

Are we aware of the ways God is active in our lives?

Nabal was a descendant of Caleb. He was a good business man, but a drunken, bad mannered man with an evil temper.

The success of any rebel movement depends upon the support of the countryside and the goodwill of the population at large. This can be seen from all of history. David and his men had tried to earn the goodwill of the shepherds of this area. After all, they were functioning as a police force against the perennial raiding parties from both the desert and the coastal plain.

David kept Nabal's flocks away from danger; he did not move them into an area where Saul was active. He guided Nabal's men to where supplies were available away from the constant warfare in the center of the land. It was probably at David's suggestion the flocks of this man had moved to the north in Carmel, where also Nabal had property.

David sent his men to the area where Nabal's men were shearing sheep. This was a festive occasion and one of great celebration. When David's men arrived Nabal insulted them and rebuked them for even asking for a protection fee. He was extremely rude and extended his insults to David.

When David's men returned to tell him what the man had said David became extremely angry and swore, he would kill Nabal and everyone associated with him.

When Nabal's wife heard of the visit of David's men and how they had been treated she knew there would be trouble. She quickly prepared an offering of food and other gifts and went to see David.

She was able to arrive and meet him before David could carry out his plan to attack Nabal. She said to David, "*let not my Lord regard this worthless fellow, Nabal, for as his name is, so is he. Nabal is his name and folly is with him.*" With this statement Abigail was able to calm David and prevent a slaughter. She returned home and told her husband nothing of her visit to David until after he awoke from a drunken stupor in the morning. Nabal died of heart failure (36-38). He died as he had lived.

Lack of courtesy is lack of love, and lack of love is lack of God.

Courtesy is a Christian value. It is a gift of our faith to our way of life, and bad-mannered Nabal is a warning and a lesson. The pace of urban living can press hard against the defenses of life; on the congested road, in the packed supermarket, in the perennial line and in the hundred places where man slows down other men and impede and frustrate, we can become frustrated.

Delay, obstruction, incompetence and a seeming unconcern for others try our patience, unravel our temper and put sharpness into our voice and impatience into our action. Courtesy becomes a casualty, because courtesy requires composure and self-command.

A decline of courtesy could have a cause more telling than a deteriorating human environment. The spirit of man betrays a certain weariness. Old standards of conduct, for more than one reason, have been abandoned. The Christian faith is under needless assault. There is a kind of rebellion which finds a perverted satisfaction in damaging old traditions. Sometimes, for all the throwing around of the word "love" in such social contexts, there is little regard for the feelings of others.

The comfort and ease of other men is no concern for men like Nabal.

How important is courtesy in your day-to-day life?

In what situations can foolishness be hazardous to your health?

Abner is one of the most interesting "characters" in the Bible; his name means: "Father of light." It is a name which certainly was not characteristic of his life. We will evaluate Abner not as a central character in any narrative, but in his relationship to four more prominent men; Saul, Ishbosheth, David, and Joab.

Abner and Saul

Abner was related to Saul, being the son of Saul's uncle (1 Sam. 14:50). When Saul became king, he appointed Abner as the director of his Army. When Saul's army was in the field against the Philistines and Goliath, we find Abner, like the rest of Israel, immobilized with fear.

After the victory over the Philistines, Abner found David and introduced him to Saul as the young man who had killed Goliath. He sat at Saul's dinner table next to the king (1 Sam. 20:25). He was witness to all the strife in the dining area between Saul and David. He knew Jonathan well and he knew of Jonathan's friendship with David.

Later when Saul and his army were chasing David, David was able to slip up on the camp of Saul during the night. David silently, with the help of God, crept into the camp unseen by anyone. He could have easily killed Saul, but he did not. Later he rebuked Abner for sleeping on duty and allowing Saul's spear and water jug to be taken (1 Samuel 26:14-16).

Abner and Ishbosheth

After the death of Saul in battle it was Abner who appointed Saul's son Ishbosheth to reign over Israel. He proposed a bloody contest at the pool of Gibeon, pitting 12 warriors of David against 12 of his own. This resulted in the stabbing deaths of all 24 (2 Sam. 2:12-16). His men were then defeated by Joab (captain of David's army) in battle (2 Sam. 2:17).

He was pursued by Asahel (Joab's youngest brother) and was forced to kill him in self-defense (2 Sam. 2:18-23). He was able to temporarily convince Joab of the senselessness of doing battle with each other (2 Sam. 2:26-28).

He was accused by Ishbosheth of sleeping with Rizpah, a former concubine of Saul. Abner angrily denied it and swore to turn the kingdom over to David (2 Samuel 3:16-11).

Abner and David; 2 Samuel 3

Abner sent peace messengers to David's camp. He then urged the elders of Israel to accept David as their king. He followed this by meeting with David and pledged his support to David. David accepted his support and welcomed him into his army as a co-commander with Joab.

Abner and Joab

Joab refused to believe David was "naïve" enough to believe Abner. Joab then pursued Abner, told him a lie in order to get him back to the city of Hebron. There on the outside of the gates of a city of refuge Joab murdered Abner.

With this murder he avenged the death of Asahel his brother and removed a rival for his position. When told of the death of Abner, David went to great lengths to make it clear he had not ordered his death. He publicly blamed Joab.

Abner was always concerned with Joab first and foremost.

David later charged Solomon to punish Joab for killing Abner (1 Kings 2:5-6).

What behavior on your part could convince others of your sincerity better than words?

Abishai 1 Samuel 26; 2 Samuel 2, 3

Abishai was David's nephew, the son of his sister Zeruiah, by an unnamed father, and a brother of Joab and Asahel. He was more impetuous than the shrewd Joab, but equally relentless and cruel.

The first mention of Abishai presents him to us as already one of the most courageous and devoted of David's followers. He volunteers to go down with David to Saul's camp at night and is only prevented by David's reverence for the king's sacred office from killing Saul by smiting him, "*to the earth at one stroke.*"

Later Abishai and Joab pursued Abner because he killed their brother Asahel at Gibeon. Abner had convinced Joab to end the pursuit of the men of Israel by David's army, but this did not end their feud (2 Sam 2:26–8). After Abner had made peace with David, Joab and Abishai killed Abner in revenge for their brother (2 Sam 3:30).

Abishai's character is very clearly shown in the story of David's retreat from Jerusalem. His reaction to the abuse of Shimei is very characteristic of true Eastern vengeance. Abishai is impatient and wants to kill Shimei immediately. Then Abishai said to the king, *"Why should this dead dog curse my lord the king? Please, let me go over and take off his head!"* 2 Samuel 16:9

Later when Shimei humbled himself before David, Abishai would not forgive the man who had cursed the King as he was fleeing Absalom. Abishai said to David, *"Shall not Shimei be put to death for this, because he cursed the LORD's anointed?"* 2 Samuel 19:21

Here are the other references to Abishai;

- Abishai defeated the Arameans while Joab was defeating the Ammonites (2 Sam 10)
- Abishai was assigned one-third of David's army to put down Absalom's rebellion (2 Sam 18:1–18)
- Abishai was one of David's mighty men. He and Joab defeated:
- Sheba (2 Samuel 20:10)
- The Philistines (2 Samuel 21:17; 23:17–18)
- The Edomites (1 Chronicles 18:12–13)
- Abishai killed Ishbi-benob, a descendant of the giants (2 Samuel 21:15–17).

David placed blame on Abishai and Joab for their brutality.

And today, though I am the anointed king, I am weak, and these sons of Zeruiah are too strong for me. May the LORD repay the evildoer according to his evil deeds!" 2 Samuel 3:39

But the king said, "What do you and I have in common, you sons of Zeruiah? If he is cursing because the LORD said to him, 'Curse David,' who can ask, 'Why do you do this?'"
2 Samuel 16:10

David replied, "What do you and I have in common, you sons of Zeruiah? This day you have become my adversaries! Should anyone be put to death in Israel today? Do I not know that today I am king over Israel?"
2 Samuel 19:22

Do you think David was afraid of these men? Why would David work with men like this?

Do you think David sacrificed his integrity by continuing to keep them in positions of authority?

Do you associate with someone you fear?

How can you better handle the situation?

Joab 2 Samuel 26 - 1 Kings 2

Joab is another very thought-provoking man who made a major impact on the life of David. Joab was the commanding general of David's army. Joab was the first person considered in Joab's thoughts. His apparent devotion to David had one objective; he wanted to be placed first in everything. He loved self. He murdered those who stood in the way of his prominence.

He was the son of Zeruiah, David's sister. He was a great general and led David's army to many great victories. He defeated the Ammonites after they refused David's act of kindness and publicly embarrassed the messengers which David had sent to the funeral of the Ammonite King.

His conquests
Shortly after David became king of all Israel, the North and the South, Joab quickly won victories over the Edomites, the city of Rabbah, which is the modern city of Amman, the capital city of today's country of Jordan.

It was Joab who engineered the victory over the city of Jerusalem. He was able to climb up a water tunnel and then inside the city walls, he opened the gates and David's army and conquered the Jebusites.

David made the city of Jerusalem his capital of a United Kingdom of Israel. Therefore, the city of Jerusalem holds such an important place in Jewish history. It was here less than 50 years later that Solomon built the great Temple to God.

His devious nature
Joab arranged at David's command to have Uriah killed in battle so the King would be able to marry Bathsheba. This was done with the knowledge of only David and Joab. There is no doubt Joab used the knowledge of the circumstances of Uriah's death to solidify his place as Commander-in-Chief of the Army. He later arranged for the return of Absalom to Jerusalem. He did this by deceiving the King himself; Absalom had been banished to a foreign land for murdering Amnon, the eldest son of David.

He murdered Abner after deceiving him into coming back to the city of Hebron. Hebron was a city of refuge. Joab met Abner outside the gates, pretended to welcome him with a warm embrace and slipped a knife into his side underneath his fifth rib and into his heart. He then justified the act by saying Abner had killed his younger brother Asahel. This was an out-and-out lie Asahel had been killed in battle.

He killed Absalom in direct defiance of the command of David. He also killed Amasa who was the son of David's sister Abigail and the commander of Absalom's troops.
David expressed his thoughts about Joab shortly after the murder of Abner. He said, "*and I was gentle today though anointed King. These men, the sons of Zeruiah, are more severe than I. The Lord repay the evil doer according to his wickedness!*" (2 Samuel 3:39)

His unsuccessful rebellion
He even joined the plot against Solomon and supported Adonijah against the wishes of David to become the King after David's death. When he realized his plot had failed, he took refuge in the tabernacle, but he was executed by order of King Solomon.

The tragedy of Joab is; despite all his abundant energy, boldness, ability, shrewdness, and common sense, he never manifested any real faith in God.

Full of self-confidence, ambition and selfishness, Joab never got far away from his own interest.

Do you struggle with self-interest against the interests of God?

Ishbosheth 2 Samuel 2:8-4:12

Ishbosheth challenged David for the throne of Israel for a period of seven years. He was the fourth son of Saul (1 Ch 8:34; 9:39). His real name as preserved by the Chronicler was Eshbaal or Ishbaal, but he is better known to us by the name Ishbosheth, "man of the shame."

In this sense the contrast between Saul and David which was so central in 1 Samuel 16-31 continues in the form of the Civil War between David and Ishbosheth. With the death of Saul and his three sons at Mount Gilboa, the text now raises the question of succession. Ishbosheth is still alive and will reign among the northern tribes, we have not yet been told about him.

The contrast in seeking God's will continues to show itself between David and Saul's son. David inquired of the Lord before taking any step, but Ishbosheth becomes King as a result of political intrigues in the North (2:8-11). David is portrayed as relying only on the power and timing of Jehovah, while Ishbosheth will be introduced as a puppet in the hands of human power structures. David patiently inquires of the Lord before he takes any action. This is no "power play" on David's part. Instead, this is "faith play," and the significance of the contrast between David and Ishbosheth will dominate the next few chapters. We are really told little about Ishbosheth himself. The writer draws the ideas about Ishbosheth together with brief summary statements (2:10-11, 17, 30-31; 3:1, 6:36-37; 4:1). These are inserts and they give the unit focus and prepare the reader for the important events to follow in the rest of 2 Samuel.

David's offer to become King in the North (2:4b-7) is of no consequence to the inhabitants of the North. They see Ishbosheth as someone who can continue the dynasty of Saul. Events in the north quickly move against David and his hopes for a peaceful transition of power over a unified Israel are not to be realized. The problem of succession shows the ongoing conflict between the North and the South in Israel. Any union of these two geographic areas is always shaky.

The only time Ishbosheth appears to function as a King, he gives an order to return Michal, the daughter of Saul, his half-sister, to David. In this he was only submitting to the demands of David (3:13-16). Descriptions of his inner life are characterized by fear (3:11; 4:1), and his death is ignominious in the same way his father's was (4:5-12). The text makes it clear Abner was the real power behind the kingship of Ishbosheth. We might call Ishbosheth's rise to power in Israel "an inside job," which has all the trappings of hard-core political intrigue and conspiracy.

At the outset of these two reigns, we learned in Israel there is a right and wrong way to become King. Like the Amalekite of 2 Samuel 1, Abner and Ishbosheth fail to understand how the Israelite monarchy is to be unique from all other kingdoms. Abner and Ishbosheth understand only the wrong way to become King. The brutal murder of Ishbosheth seems inevitable. As long as he had Abner in his camp there was hope. But once he insulted the general's loyalty and drove him into an agreement with David his death was inevitable.

These passages make a final summary statement which emphasizes the reaction of Ishbosheth and his people to the loss of Abner (4:1): "*he lost courage, and all Israel became alarmed.*" Very soon Baanah and Rechab execute Ishbosheth.

Any hint that Ishbosheth's murder was engineered by David could hinder the King's attempt to win the loyalty of the northern tribes. So, David reminds his listeners of the cruel murder of "*an innocent man in his own house and on his own bed.*" (4:9-11)

Why is it better to be given power than to win it in battle?

How can you appeal to our common humanity the next time you are caught between "warring factions"?

What can you do to help a young person cultivate a mature respect for life?

What Was David's View of God?

Practically every psalm David penned gives us insight into his ideas, attitudes and feelings toward God. Consequently, we can only highlight the answer for this first question. The greatest introduction to David as the Psalmist of Israel is the first Psalm:

Blessed is the man who does not walk in the counsel of the wicked or stand in the way of sinners or sit in the seat of mockers. But his delight is in the law of the LORD, and on his law he meditates day and night. He is like a tree planted by streams of water, which yields its fruit in season and whose leaf does not wither. Whatever he does prospers.
Not so the wicked! They are like chaff that the wind blows away. Therefore the wicked will not stand in the judgment, nor sinners in the assembly of the righteous.
For the LORD watches over the way of the righteous, but the way of the wicked will perish.

The Omnipotent Creator

Several of David's psalms focus extensively on God's creative power. David was an outdoorsman, a man who spent many hours, day and night, absorbing the splendor, beauty, and mysteries of nature. At times, inspired by God's Spirit, he put his thoughts on paper.

Psalm 19

This Psalm expresses David's convictions and feelings about the firmament, and particularly the sun in its journey across space:
The heavens are telling of the glory of God;
And the firmament is declaring the work of His hands. Day after day they pour forth speech;
night after night they display knowledge.
There is no speech or language where their voice is not heard. Their voice goes out into all the earth, their words to the ends of the world.
In the heavens he has pitched a tent for the sun, which is like a bridegroom coming forth from his pavilion, like a champion rejoicing to run his course.
It rises at one end of the heavens and makes its circuit to the other; nothing is hidden from its heat.

Psalm 29

David's view of God's creative power in nature often generated praise, thanksgiving, and worship in his heart. While most of us focus on our fears and anxieties amid this kind of natural turbulence, David's heart focused on God. To him the phenomenon he observed, heard and felt reflected the voice of the Lord:
The voice of the LORD is over the waters; the God of glory thunders, the LORD thunders over the mighty waters.
The voice of the LORD is powerful; the voice of the LORD is majestic.
The voice of the LORD breaks the cedars; the LORD breaks in pieces the cedars of Lebanon. He makes Lebanon skip like a calf, Sidon like a young wild ox.
The voice of the LORD strikes with flashes of lightning.
The voice of the LORD shakes the desert; the LORD shakes the Desert of Kadesh.
The voice of the LORD twists the oaks and strips the forests bare. And in his temple all cry, "Glory!"
The LORD sits enthroned over the flood; the LORD is enthroned as King forever.
The LORD gives strength to his people; the LORD blesses his people with peace. 29:3-9

The Omniscient God

David also viewed God as all-knowing. He knew God saw everything about him, every detail of his heart and his actions at any given moment.

Psalm 139: 1-6

O LORD, you have searched me and you know me.
You know when I sit and when I rise; you perceive my thoughts from afar.
You discern my going out and my lying down; you are familiar with all my ways. Before a word is on my tongue you know it completely, O LORD.
You hem me in-- behind and before; you have laid your hand upon me. Such knowledge is too wonderful for me, too lofty for me to attain.

The Omnipresent Spirit

David not only viewed God as omnipotent and omniscient, but also as present everywhere. In other words, there was no place David could go but that God was there to guide, to protect, to comfort and to search out his heart:

Psalm 139: 7-12

Where can I go from Thy Spirit? Or where can I flee from Thy presence? If I ascend to heaven, Thou art there;
If I make my bed in Sheol, behold, Thou art there. If I take the wings of the dawn, If I dwell in the remotest part of the sea, Even there Thy hand will lead me, And Thy right hand will lay hold of me.
If I say, "Surely the darkness will overwhelm me, And the light around me will be night," Even the darkness is not dark to Thee, And the night is as bright as the day. Darkness and light are alike to Thee.

The God of Loving Concern

Seeing God's power in nature led David to appreciate more fully God's loving concern for mankind. The fact the Lord gave human beings a certain degree of authority and control over His natural creation overwhelmed David.

Psalm 8:3-9

When I consider Your heavens, The work of Your fingers, The moon and the stars, which You have made;
What is man, that You have concern for him? And the son of man, that You care for him? Yet You have made him a little lower than God, You crown him with glory and majesty!
You make him to rule over the works of Your hands; You have put all things under his feet, All sheep and oxen,
And also the beasts of the field, The birds of the heavens, and the fish of the sea, Whatever passes through the paths of the seas.
O Lord, our Lord, How majestic is Your name in all the earth!

The God of Lovingkindness, Faithfulness, and Righteousness

The vastness of the universe also reminded David of God's personal attributes.

There are many other psalms which reveal David's view of God. But these few demonstrate dramatically why David was "a man after God's heart."

God anointed David as king of Israel because of David's heart attitude. In some respects, this is an observation which is difficult to understand. God is omniscient and sovereign. He knows the end from the beginning and every detail in between. He is in control of the universe. His perspective is eternal. Yet He instructed Samuel to anoint David because of his spiritual condition as a young man who loved God.

Because of this young shepherd's view of God's attributes, as we have seen in his Psalms, and because of David's own heart which was characterized by faith, thankfulness, honesty, openness, expectancy, humility, dependence, and repentance; because of these qualities, God instructed Samuel to anoint him as the future king of Israel, to eventually replace Saul.

It's clear from David's total life story he was not always this kind of man. There were periods of time when he ceased being a "man after God's own heart." At times he miserably failed God, did his own things and walked directly and deliberately out of the will of God, and indulged in some incredible sins.

The Lord knew, of course, David would fail Him in these areas of his life before He even chose him. In some remarkable way, the sovereign God of the universe anointed David to be king of Israel based upon his spiritual successes in the here and now, not upon his future failures.

How can this be?
From a human perspective there is no satisfactory explanation except God is God and He did it and can do it without violating His knowledge and His wisdom. And the fact is David could have been a "man after God's own heart" all his life and on a consistent basis if he had obeyed God and lived by the same spiritual guidelines he followed as a young dedicated Hebrew.

Saul had this same opportunity, he was anointed by God and promised continual blessing, in fact eternal blessings, if he only walked in the Lord's ways (1 Sam. 12:14). Like David, Saul's failure was not predetermined. In fact, God was terribly distressed when Saul disobeyed Him. Twice we read in 1 Samuel 15, *"The Lord regretted that He had made Saul king over Israel"* (1 Sam. 15:35; also v. 11).

Again, how can this be?
How can a supreme God regret His own decisions when He knows the end from the beginning? We must conclude there is no understandable human explanation. It is beyond our finite mind. The fact is in some remarkable and inexplicable way; God honors man's freedom and makes His decisions accordingly. And part of His decision-making process involves dealing with us at any given period in our life. Because David was a man after God's heart, He anointed David to replace the man who had failed Him.

Saul would not have failed, had he obeyed the Lord, God would have dealt with him according to His promise and all the factors would have fallen naturally into place, including David's role in God's plan.

What about you?
God deals with us based on our current heart attitudes. The fact we have warm sensitive hearts toward God now is no guarantee we will be that kind of person 10, 20, or 30 years from now. The fact God is using us now to achieve His purposes because of our commitment to Him is no guarantee He will use us in the future.
If we, like David, eventually ignore God's will we too will have to pay the natural consequences.

The lesson is clear for each one of us. What we are now, and how God is using us now certainly is no guarantee for the future.

How can you continue to have a soft heart toward God?

Michal: Saul's Daughter 1 Samuel 14, 18, 19

Michal was the younger daughter of Saul. She fell in love with David after his defeat of Goliath. Saul, jealous of David, offered his first daughter, Merab, to David, but David refused, saying he was not worthy to marry a king's daughter. When Michal's love became known to Saul, he renewed his offer of a wife, all he asked was for David to produce evidence of killing 100 Philistines, a condition Saul no doubt felt would lead to David's death.

David met Saul's condition and doubled the quota, he then married Michal. Saul's jealousy was only made greater and he plotted to have David murdered. Michal heard of the plot and assisted in her husband's escape. When Saul heard he had been outwitted, he accused his daughter of disloyalty to her father and was harsh and vindictive as he blamed her.

After this incident Michal's love for David seems to have waned. She saw no future in being the wife of a man who was a fugitive. Saul then arranged a marriage between Michal and Phalti, who was the crown prince of an area known as Gallem. She seems to have felt as the daughter of the king she was entitled to royalty.

Following Saul's death, Abner negotiated peace with David, part of the agreement was the return of Michal to David's household. It does not seem to have required much force to get Michal to leave Phalti. She was more than ready to become David's queen. The closing scene between Michal and David is the most heartbreaking, for what love Michal may have had for David quickly turned to scorn and disdain.

After making Jerusalem his capital, David returned with the ark to Jerusalem. On the day of the Ark's return David was so joyful we are told, "*David danced before the Lord with all his might. And David was wearing a linen Ephod.*" The passage continues to say, *"as the ark of the Lord came into the city of David, Michal the daughter of Saul looked out of the window and saw king David leaping and dancing before the Lord, and she despised him in her heart."*

When David returned to his home his joyful mood was soon shattered. For his wife came out to meet him and said, *"How the King of Israel honored himself today, uncovering himself before the eyes of his servants' female servants, as one of the older fellows shamelessly uncovers himself."*

David's reply was equally sarcastic, *"it was before the Lord, who chose me above your father and above all his house, to appoint me as friends over Israel, the people of the Lord-and I will make merry before the Lord. I will make myself get more contemptible than this, and I will be even more contemptable in your eyes. But by the female servants of whom you have spoken, by them I will be held in honor."*

Michal would remain childless as punishment for her disrespect of God and His servant.

David's overwhelming popularity should not overshadow the courage and passion displayed by Michal as she helped her husband despite her father's plan.

She let her love be known when women rarely took the initiative in courtship.

She saved David's life at the risk of her own. But her life did not end well!

Why was Michal so upset by David's behavior in the procession?

In what ways can we become subtly irreverent in our behavior before God?

How can we combine proper reverence before God with unparalleled joy and celebration?

Gad lived during the time of Saul and David; he is never associated with Saul in the biblical record, but only with David. He is first mentioned when he came to David while David was a fugitive from Saul (I Sam. 22:5), and he apparently stayed with David from that time on.

His work

Gad is called "David's seer," which suggests a major part of his work was serving David. Calling Gad, a seer in this context, rather than a prophet, indicates God used him as a means of divine direction for the king.

The time when he first came to David is not revealed. The first mention of him comes from David's early life as a fugitive when he was in Moab (I Sam. 22:5). He may have joined David when the 400 men came to David at the cave of Adullam. It is also possible Gad had been trained in Samuel's school. David had left Judah and gone to the eastern country of Moab, taking his parents with him. He feared Saul might do them harm. David asked asylum for them from the king of Moab. David went into hiding in a place called *"the hold."* This was probably at the top of one of the mountain peaks of Moab, from where he could see in any direction to know of possible pursuit. It was while David was here Gad brought his first word of advice, counseling David "*abide not in the hold*" but go "into the land of Judah."

Later a contact between Gad and David is recorded in II Samuel 24:11-19. The occasion followed David's sin involving the numbering of Israel. The reason this sin was so serious is not revealed, but it is significant even Joab, harsh as he was in his own personality, did not want to follow this order of David. David insisted, and when the census had been taken, God sent Gad to David to give him a choice of three punishments for his willful sin. One was seven years of famine in the land, another was three months of flight before David's enemies, and the third was three days of plague bringing death to many people. David chose the last, and the result was 70,000 men died (II Sam. 24:15).

The Person

Gad is called *"the king's seer"* (II Chron. 29:25). The title seer must be taken as important because in the same verse Nathan is called *"the prophet."* Gad was thought of as a "seer" while Nathan was more a "prophet." Since "seer" indicates one who receives revelation in distinction from "prophet" indicating one who speaks, this suggests Gad was used in a special way to bring divine messages of direction to the king.

The point to notice is God would not have used someone to hear His direction unless that person was considered spiritually mature and able to receive God's instructions properly. It is evident Gad was a man who was respected by others. For instance, when he advised David while in Moab to move back to Judah, David seems to have done so without hesitation. Then later, when Gad brought the three choices of punishment to David, David again accepted what he said as authoritative. David did argue with the seer but made his selection from the three. When Gad indicated David should buy the threshing floor of Araunah for the purpose of offering sacrifice, David also did this. If David gave this kind of respect to Gad, it follows others did as well.

There is a further clue David respected Gad as a man of judgment. This is found in II Chronicles 29:25, which indicates Gad assisted David in organizing the Levites. Nathan also helped in this, showing that he too was highly regarded. One may imagine David calling in the two when he wanted to do this work and having them offer suggestions and perhaps even formulate guidelines.

David would not have listened to Gad if he had not had a high respect for him.

Would you have had the courage to deliver the message of judgement to David after the census?

Have you ever had to deliver an unpleasant message from God to someone?

Though Gad is depicted as having been with David earlier than was Nathan, more is said regarding Nathan than Gad. There is no way to know when the first contact was made by Nathan with the king, but the first recorded mention is in 2 Samuel 7:2-17.

David brought the ark into Jerusalem and now wanted to build a temple. This was not wrong and Nathan's first response when David spoke of the idea was for David to proceed. That night, however, God revealed to Nathan David should not do this and Nathan then brought God's word to David. The message was, rather than David's building a physical house for God, God was going to build a continuing house for David; a dynasty on Israel's throne. He indicated the matter of building a physical temple would be accomplished by the son of David who would succeed him.

A second major contact with the king was made following the sin of David with Bathsheba, the wife of Uriah. When he later learned she was pregnant, he called Uriah to return from battle so he could be with his wife. Uriah did return but refused to go to his wife; David then had him put in the most dangerous part of the battle so that he would surely be killed. Then David took Bathsheba as his wife.

God then gave Nathan a message of rebuke to bring to David. This was done after the son was born; so, several months had intervened. The point of the message was David had sinned and would be punished. The punishment would involve, first, the death of the child now born and, second, a continuing problem in David's family. History shows this punishment was totally fulfilled, much to David's sorrow.

A third contact of Nathan with David involved one part of this punishment being carried out. It was when Adonijah, fourth son of David, tried to take over the throne for himself. Earlier Absalom, the third son, had tried to do this and had failed. Adonijah now tried to seize the throne. He was able to gain the support of Joab, the head of David's army, and Abiathar, one of the two high priests then living. David had earlier designated Solomon as his successor, but he had not made this generally known. Nathan knew of the designation and now set in motion a plan to stop the attempt of Adonijah. He convinced Bathsheba, the mother of Solomon, to go directly to David and tell him of Adonijah's attempt, and then he, Nathan, went to David.

David was persuaded quick action was necessary, and he directed Solomon be crowned immediately at the pool of Gihon. Nathan directed this with the help of Zadok, the other high priest, and Benaiah, the leader of David's bodyguard. Solomon was made the new king.

Nathan also helped in advising David in the organization of the Levites (II Chron. 29:25). He wrote a book concerning the "Acts of David" (I Chron. 29:29). Apparently, his book was longer, because it included as well the "Acts of Solomon" (II Chron. 9:29).

Like Gad, Nathan showed outstanding courage in bringing his messages to David. All three of his recorded messages were important; this was especially true of the first two. Both were messages which could influence the king in a very adverse manner.

Certainly, it was not easy to tell the king he could not build the temple or that he had sinned seriously in the sight of God.

Nathan could have thought of many other tasks more pleasant to do. Since God had instructed him to bring these messages, however, he did so even though the king was the one being addressed.

Why did Nathan send Bathsheba to David first?

In what ways in your life have you needed courage to do as God directed?

Abiathar: the priest 1 Samuel 21-23; 1 Kings 1

Zadok and Abiathar were high priests. They were put in charge of the bringing of the ark to Jerusalem when David set up the Tabernacle in his new capital city (1 Chronicles 15:11).

Little is known about Abiathar prior to his introduction in 1 Sam 21–23.

Abiathar escaped from the massacre of the priests at Nob, and fled to David, carrying the ephod with him. This was a great achievement and enhanced David's strength and popularity. Public feeling in Israel was outraged by the slaughter of the priests and turned strongly against Saul.

Abiathar was heir of the priesthood, and in his care the holy ephod was now with David. This fact gave great prestige to his cause, and a certain character of legitimacy. David felt terribly because he had been the unwilling cause of the death of Abiathar's relatives, and this made him want to help his new friend. Presumably, also, there was a deep religious agreement between them.

Abiathar seems to have been at once recognized as David's priest. He had brought David the ephod, the means of consultation with Jehovah (1 Samuel 22:20–23; 23:6, 9; 30:7, 8). He was at the head of the priesthood, along with Zadok (1 Chronicles 15:11), when David, after his conquests, brought the ark to Jerusalem.

Due to Abiathar's faithfulness, David chose Abiathar to serve as one of two high priests, the other being Zadok. One writer describes this turn of events, "*Whereas Saul is in this way alienating the priests, David gains possession of one, a 'real' priest, of the house of Eli.*"

In David's flight from Absalom we find Abiathar loyal. He was only prevented by David's instructions from sharing his master's exile. His son Jonathan, with Ahimaaz, was used to transfer information from the priests to David. They gave David secret intelligence of Absalom's plans.

Later when David's health began to fail, Abiathar and Joab anointed David's eldest son, Adonijah, as king (1 Kgs 1:5–7). This was contrary to David's plan to have Solomon take his place on the throne. Bathsheba, at the suggestion of Nathan, went to David to gain his help in bringing her own son, Solomon, to the throne as David had promised. Zadok, Nathan, and Benaiah anointed Solomon as king, while David gave his blessing (1 Kgs 1:30–34).

Though Solomon later executed Adonijah and Joab, he spares Abiathar because of Abiathar's allegiance to King David. But because of his action he was deposed from the priesthood. He continued to be treated with respect because of his early friendship with David (1 K 2:26, 27).

It is possible Abiathar's genealogy also helped spare his life; he may have been a distant relative of David. Solomon exiled him to the Levitical city of Anathoth, located just northeast of Jerusalem.

Particularly apt is the passage in Ps 55:12–14:
If an enemy were insulting me, I could endure it; if a foe were raising himself against me, I could hide from him. But it is you, a man like myself, my companion, my close friend, with whom I once enjoyed sweet fellowship as we walked with the throng at the house of God.

It seems clear even though Abiathar was a man worthy of the friendship of David; he had weaknesses which made him unable to be fully loyal.

Why would it have been unwise for Solomon to leave people like Adonijah, Abiathar, and Joab unrestrained and unpunished?

How can you develop a healthy realism toward the people who ask favors of you?

Zadok: the priest 1 Samuel 22; 1 Kings 1

Zadok was younger than Abiathar, but he is always mentioned first. In the passages in which the two are mentioned together, Zadok is treated as the one who is more responsible and reliable. He was David's priest, probably the most famous and influential of Israel's high priests other than Aaron.

I Chronicles includes Zadok as a member of David's army at Hebron. *"Of the children of Levi four thousand and six hundred. And Jehoiada was the leader of the Aaronites, and with him were three thousand and seven hundred; And Zadok, a young man mighty of valor, and of his father's house twenty and two captains."*

He first appears, as a priest, at the time of Absalom's revolt, when he and his fellow priest, Abiathar, show their loyalty to David by coming to him with the ark, fully prepared to share his exile. They were accompanied by the whole body of the Levites. They went with David across the Kidron, bringing the ark of the Covenant with them. II Samuel 15-17

David sent them back, instructing them to inform him through their sons, Ahimaaz the son of Zadok, and Jonathan the son of Abiathar, of the plans of Absalom.

After Absalom's revolt was crushed, Zadok helped restore the broken union between David and the leaders of Judah. King David sent this message to Zadok and Abiathar, the priests: "Ask the elders of Judah, 'Why should you be the last to bring the king back to his palace, since what is being said throughout Israel has reached the king at his quarters?
You are my brothers, my own flesh and blood. So why should you be the last to bring back the king?' (2 Sam. 19:11, 12).

Years later animosity and competition seem to have developed between Zadok and Abiathar.

When Adonijah attempted to seize the throne, one of his key advisors and helpers was Abiathar. Perhaps Abiathar was jealous of Zadok's close friendship with David.

He may have been influenced by the near success of Absalom. The news of their secret planning session soon came to the attention of Nathan the prophet and Benaiah the leader of David's bodyguards.

Nathan working with Solomon's mother, Bathsheba, took the lead in calling David's attention to the situation (1 Kings 1:11-53). Working together this group was able to convince David to make the long-awaited announcement of his choice as successor.

David's personal bodyguards, as well as Zadok and Nathan the prophet, went with Solomon. He was seated on King David's mule. They conducted Solomon to the spring of Gihon and there Zadok took the horn of oil from the Tabernacle and anointed Solomon as King.

Adonijah, Joab, and Abiathar quickly gave up their attempt to seize the throne!

Zadok was appointed by Solomon as the single high priest, setting aside Abiathar, who had joined Adonijah's revolt. Zadok was also appointed to offer daily sacrifices to God in the Temple Solomon would build.

As a reward for his faithfulness, God promised that Zadok's descendants would serve as priests in the millennial temple (Ezekiel 44:15; 48:11). One of Zadok's descendants was Ezra (Ezra 7:1-2).

Is there a person who has been working against you should you give the benefit of the doubt before you take strong action against him or her?

Mephibosheth 2 Samuel 4, 9, 16, 19

Mephibosheth was the grandson of Saul and son of Jonathan. He was 5 years old when his father and grandfather were killed in battle. He was living in the custody of a nurse, possibly because his mother was dead. News of the disaster at Jezreel and the advance of the Philistines terrified the nurse. She fled with the boy in such a hurry that he was injured in a fall and became disabled for life. His life is a series of disasters, disappointments, and anxieties. The nurse carried him to Lo-debar among the mountains of Gilead, where he was brought up by Machir, son of Ammiel.

When David had settled his own affairs and subdued his enemies, he turned his inquiries to Saul's household to see whether there were any survivors to whom he might show kindness in memory of Jonathon (2 Sam 9:1).

David learned about Mephibosheth and sent for him. His humble behavior was consistent with his broken spirit. In a tribute to Jonathon, David gave the property of Saul to Mephibosheth.

Mephibosheth was also to be a daily guest at David's table (2 Sam 9:11-13). Seventeen years passed and Mephibosheth seems to have lived in Jerusalem. Then came Absalom's rebellion. David was forced to escape because of the actions of his son. He did not want war in the city of Jerusalem.

At the moment of David's flight from Jerusalem, when he was in great depression and need, David was met by Ziba with food, refreshment, and even means for travel. Ziba was the servant of Mephibosheth.

Naturally, the king inquired about Ziba's master. A very deceitful reply was given (2 Sam 16:1-4). Ziba told David Mephibosheth had remained behind for his own purpose, hoping the people would give him, Saul's grandson, and the kingdom.

David believed this and transferred the property he had given to Mephibosheth to Ziba. Not until many days after did the disabled prince get his chance to give David his own version of the story. He met David on his return from defeating Absalom's rebellion and told David the true story.

He had not cared for his feet, trimmed his beard nor washed his clothes since the hour of David's departure (2 Sam 19:24). At David's request Mephibosheth told his story: his servant had deceived him; he wanted to go with David; had even asked for his donkey to be saddled; but Ziba had left him and had slandered him to the king. But he would not plead his cause any more; he said David is *"as an angel of God," whatever he decides will be well!* (2 Sam 19:26, 27).

This was characteristic of this humble man. Even though he was the son of a proud family he graciously accepted his role in life (2 Sam 19:28). David tiredly settled the matter by dividing the property between the prince and his servant; Mephibosheth told David Ziba could have it all as long as David remained friendly (2 Sam 19:29, 30).

David accepted Mephibosheth's explanation and protected him for the rest of his life.

Later when some compensation from Saul's household was considered necessary to turn away the famine sent by an offended God; Mephibosheth was spared when other members of Saul's household were put to death (2 Sam 21:7).

How did David's reaction to Mephibosheth indicate that he wasn't sure whom to believe?

The character of Mephibosheth illustrates the effect of continued disaster, suspicion and treachery upon a sensitive mind.

Mephibosheth also illustrates the salvation of God!

Sheba was an unscrupulous opportunist who maliciously took advantage of the political weakness of David during Absalom's conspiracy. This is the type of rebellion undertaken by deceitful people who rely on secrecy and trickery to acquire power.

The description of him as a "troublemaker" uses the expression "*man of Belial,*" which is the Old Testament Way of describing someone who is at his very best a worthless scoundrel. Some have argued based on etymology the expression refers specifically to someone who is considered "*a man of hell, hell fiend, damnable fellow.*" In any case, Sheba was not seen as a trustworthy person.

After the defeat of Absalom, when David was still on the Eastern side of the Jordan and there was total confusion about who was in charge of the nation. Sheba used this opportunity to try to take advantage of the historical division between the tribes in the north and Judah in the south.

2 Samuel 20:1-2 explains the situation this way, *"Now there happened to be there a worthless man, whose name was Sheba, the son of Bichri, a Benjamite. And he blew the trumpets and said, 'We have no portion in David, and we have no inheritance in the son of Jesse; every man to his tent, O Israel!' So all the men of Israel withdrew from David and followed Sheba the son Bichri. But the men of Judah followed their King steadfastly from the Jordan to Jerusalem."*

Here we can see the continuing division between the north and the south. It has been in existence for years just below the surface ready to be fanned into a flame by anyone with a motive for power. Sheba was just such an opportunist. He saw what he thought was a weakness. David's son had rebelled against him. Joab, against David's orders, had killed Absalom. David's army was in disarray and Jerusalem was on the other side of the Jordan River with no king in residence.

Sheba tried to take advantage of David's distress
Then trouble started. The men of Judah had been the first to arrive to escort the King across the Jordan in his journey back to Jerusalem. Only a very small group of Israel's representatives, from the north, had arrived and jealousies broke out again as the northern tribes thought they saw favoritism on David's part. Heated words were exchanged and finally Sheba, who was particularly vocal, persuaded the northern tribes to break away from David's kingdom and follow him. As it turns out, Sheba's revolt was not serious. After going through "*all the tribes of Israel,*" he was apparently able to gather only a limited number of supporters.

It must have been troubling to David who had just gone through one revolution to have another break out. He stabilized himself and, when he arrived back in Jerusalem, he quickly dispatched Amasa, his newly appointed general, to gather an army from Judah to put down the outbreak (2 Samuel 20:33-22). But Amasa took longer than the three days allotted to him, so David sent another force led by Abishai, Joab's younger brother.

Even though Joab was not in charge, he accompanied the army, and when he encountered Amasa along the way, Joab killed him. The troops quickly caught up with Sheba. They surrounded by David's army in the far north at a city called Abel-Bethmaach. Ironically, in the middle of all this military power and strategy, it is a "*wise woman*" who intervened and delivered the town from destruction. She convinced all the people to cut off the head of Sheba and throw it over the wall of the city.

There are those whose loyalty is unknown, like Ziba and Mephibosheth.

There are those who take the opportunity to make public their hatred for David (Shimei and Sheba).

At every hurdle David passes the test.

Shimei

2 Samuel 16, 19; I Kings 2

As King David approached Bahurim, a man from the same clan as Saul's family came out from there. His name was Shimei, son of Gera, and he cursed as he came out. He pelted David and all the king's officials with stones, though all the troops and the special guard were on David's right and left. As he cursed, Shimei said, "Get out, get out, you man of blood, you scoundrel! The LORD has repaid you for all the blood you shed in the household of Saul, in whose place you ha ve reigned. The LORD has handed the kingdom over to your son Absalom. You have come to ruin because you are a man of blood!" *2 Samuel 16:5-8*

Shimei was a man from the extended family of the house of Saul. He is called son of Gera, which means he was descended from Gera, a son or grandson of Benjamin. The incident so graphically described above should not be seen as an isolated act of rage committed by an individual acting on a momentary impulse. Its true significance is seen when it is taken in connection with the rebellion of Sheba a Benjamite, which occurred very shortly afterwards.

The Benjamites never forgave David for his victory over the house of Saul, who was from the tribe of Benjamin.

When the kingdom divided, the most important of the Benjamite towns, such as Bethel and Jericho, sided against David. David was not directly responsible for the death either of Abner or of Ishbosheth, both of whom were Benjamites, but his involvement in their murders would have been suspected by Saul's supporters. We also should remember; David and his men had earlier formed a part of the Philistine army. It was the Philistine army that killed Saul and his three sons.

Shimei curses David

As related in 2 Samuel, Shimei was a distant relative of King Saul and lived in the town of Bahurim. When David, who was fleeing Jerusalem because of Absalom's rebellion, passed through the town of Bahurim, Shimei threw rocks at him and called him "a man of blood." Shimei had taken the rebellion of David's son as a sign God was avenging Saul, whom David replaced as king. Although David's men wanted to kill Shimei, David told his men God might have inspired Shimei's curses.

David spares Shimei

After Absalom was killed, as David was returning to Jerusalem, Shimei came to David and asked forgiveness. Even though others wanted vengeance and wanted to execute Shimei, David refused to order Shimei's death; probably a decision motivated by political concerns to keep peace with the Benjaminites.

David's conflict with Shimei is not just one man's outburst but reflects the Benjaminite community's hostility toward David's authority.

Solomon kills Shimei

In David's last recorded words, he instructed Solomon to have Shimei executed. Solomon ordered Shimei not to leave Jerusalem, specifically forbidding him from crossing the Kidron, the city's eastern border, along the road to Bahurim. This was likely a move to keep Shimei from instigating a rebellion. After three years, Shimei left Jerusalem to retrieve some runaway slaves, which gives Solomon cause to finally carry out his father's request. After Shimei's execution, the text announces that Solomon's kingdom was established.

In what ways did David think Shimei's behavior might be "understandable"?

How did Abishai think Shimei should be treated now that David was victorious?

Why are greed and the thirst for power such difficult desires to reverse in the life of an individual?

Bathsheba 2 Samuel 11, 12 1 Kings 1, 2

Bathsheba was the daughter of Eliam. He was one of a group of thirty-seven who were some of David's earliest supporters (2 Sam. 23:34). It was in these circumstances Uriah met and married her.

Here's what we know about Bathsheba from the biblical text:

- She was bathing in a location that could be seen from the palace.
- The narrative does not imply David had forced sexual intercourse with her, though he was a king, so not having sexual intercourse with him likely would not have gone well for her.
- David comforts her when the child born of their adultery dies. This suggests David loved her.
- Eliam, Bathsheba's father, was one of David's elite soldiers and the son of Ahithophel, David's trusted counselor.

Who initiated this series of sinful events? It appears from the narrative it was David looking down from his palace roof on the mass of houses and courtyards below. But what was Bathsheba doing? She obviously knew she was visible as she bathed. Did she know David would be on the rooftop patio above? If David could see her; she could see him as well.

From later events in the Biblical narrative it is obvious she was a resourceful and clever woman. David's weakness for women was not unknown. This is a fault of character which cannot long be hidden. Did the young wife construct the situation? There is more than a suspicion she spread the net into which David promptly fell.

Her husband, Uriah, was a fine man. David employed many mercenaries. Men of Phoenician heritage, no doubt mercenaries from the Philistines, followed him when he retreated before Absalom. Based on the evidence of his name Uriah was a convert to the worship of Jehovah. He was one of these strong and trusted men. He was a man of strong discipline and resolution. Observing a prohibition which was probably incorporated in the code of the select bodyguard in which he served the king, Uriah did not yield to the temptation to visit his wife.

The deception by which David tried to cover up his sin failed. Perhaps Uriah had his suspicions. David had made enquiries about Bathsheba and rumor in an ancient city was not likely to spread slower than rumors spread today. David himself should have been with his men. But middle-age brought ease. The flatteries of the city and life in an urban court were weakening his old standards. He grew careless, arrogant, undisciplined, and the Enemy struck at this point when David's defenses where at their weakest. David was either the victim of a scheming woman or of his own backsliding or perhaps both. In either case it was a weak place in his life which provided for the evil which overwhelmed him.

Bathsheba plays a more active role when David is old, and the royal succession is in dispute. She and the prophet Nathan have her son Solomon installed as David's successor. Solomon's half-brother Adonijah was attempting to seize the crown and Bathsheba challenged his action by appealing to David's promise to her that Solomon would be the next king. After David's death, Bathsheba continued to play a prominent role. She told Solomon about Adonijah's request to marry Abishag (David's attendant). Solomon saw Adonijah's request as a bid for the throne and he ordered Adonijah killed. It is likely Bathsheba knew what her son's reaction would be, but the text does not record her feelings.

Eliam, Bathsheba's father, was one of David's elite soldiers (2 Sam 23:34) and the son of Ahithophel,

David's trusted counselor (2 Sam 16:23). Did family jealousy play a part in this saga?

God chose Solomon, her son, to continue the dynasty of David.

No one is sinless and God continually shows He can overcome our sins.

Absalom was David's third son. He was born to Maacah, daughter of Talmai, king of Geshur, a small territory between Mt. Hermon and Bashan. He was born at Hebron and moved at an early age, to Jerusalem, where he spent most of his life.

He was a favorite of his father and of the people as well. His enchanting manner, his personal beauty, his judicious ways, along with his love of pomp and royal pretension, captivated the hearts of the people from the beginning. He lived in great style, drove a magnificent chariot, and had fifty men parade before him. Such magnificence produced the desired effect upon the hearts of the young aristocrats of the royal city. The Scriptures tell us *"In all Israel there was no one as handsome as Absalom."*

The first event recorded in his life is the record of how he avenged the rape of his sister Tamar. She had been raped by his half-brother Amnon, who was David's oldest son. Absalom waited two years after the events described in 2 Samuel 13 and carefully planned his revenge. He gave a large banquet to celebrate sheep shearing. He had previously instructed his servants at a given signal to kill Amnon. After the murder, Absalom fled to Geshur where he spent three years. David's grief over the loss of his son moved Joab to devise Absalom's return to Jerusalem. Joab used a "*wise woman of Tekoa*" to get David to bring Absalom back.

Absalom returned but two years went by without seeing David. After twice appealing to Joab to arrange a meeting with David and receiving no reply, Absalom resorted to burning Joab's field. Joab then communicated Absalom's wish to see David, who then called for Absalom.

Absalom's return to Jerusalem had been brought about through the trickery of Joab. When Absalom returned, David kept a careful watch on him and put many travel restrictions on him. After several years in Jerusalem, Absalom could travel to the city of Hebron, his birthplace. He had given the excuse of wanting to offer sacrifices to God, however he used the journey to plan and stage a revolt against David. At Hebron, Absalom brought together an army and created plans to overthrow his father and become the new king of Israel.

Absalom began a march on the city of Jerusalem and his father, in order to spare the city from battle, left Jerusalem and traveled across the Jordan River. At this time, Absalom was joined by David's old friend and counselor, Ahithophel. Following the advice of this new counselor Absalom publicly took possession of David's harem. This was done to publicly proclaim his disdain for his father and to show the city of Jerusalem he was the new king. There now could be no reconciliation between Absalom and his father.

The war which followed is described in 2 Samuel 17 and 18. Absalom's army was destroyed and thousands of his troops were killed. Absalom himself became entangled in the branches of an oak tree and the mule on which he was riding ran away. When Joab was told of the situation, he took several of his men and made sure Absalom was dead. Absalom was buried in the middle of the forest under a pile of rocks. He had built a tomb for himself in the Kings Valley, but he died in defeat.

Why do you suppose Joab chose to ignore David's plea and killed Absalom himself?

Absalom is an example of what pride, arrogance and entitlement can cause anyone.

Absalom was proud and arrogant and seemingly cared little for others.

Absalom had no appreciation for the struggle his father had gone through to obtain all he had enjoyed for all his life.

Absalom seems to have no acquaintance with God!

Amnon was born at Hebron to David's wife Ahinoam of Jezreel. He was the first son of David. Tamar was the daughter of King David and Maacah. She was a full sister of Absalom. Amnon developed a sensual, erotic love for his half-sister Tamar. A nephew of David named Jonadab suggested to Amnon he pretend to be sick so Tamar might be persuaded to come and look after him, at which time he could force himself upon her.

Amnon did this, persuading the King himself to send Tamar to him. When she came, he did force her to have sex with him. As soon as Amnon had done the deed, he coldly sent her away; this made his sin against her even more reprehensible.

When Absalom learned what Amnon had done, he did everything he could to comfort his sister. He took her into his own home and provided for her. He began to plan his revenge and he would wait as long as necessary for the opportunity. Absalom waited two years, probably thinking by this delay he could put to rest any suspicion Amnon may have had. Then he instituted his plan of action. He called all the sons of David to a feast he held at the time of sheep shearing. The feast was held at a piece of property which he owned.

He instructed his servants to kill Amnon when he became "merry with wine." The servants followed his instructions exactly as they were ordered. Then all the other sons quickly fled for home on their mules. Before they arrived, news reached the King saying Absalom had killed all of David's sons. But Jonadab, the very man who had advised Amnon, assured the King only Amnon was dead. This was shortly confirmed by the arrival of David's other sons. Meanwhile Absalom, knowing David would be enraged, fled northward to Geshur, where Talmai, his grandfather, ruled. He stayed for three years not daring to return to Jerusalem.

The power of sexual attraction

This sad story began as a result of sexual attraction. Amnon's love was not love; it was lust. There was no real love, only sensual desire! When he had gotten what he wanted from Tamar he coldly told her to leave. He had ruined her life because of his lust.

Tamar put ashes on her head and tore the ornamented robe she was wearing. She put her hand on her head and went away, weeping aloud as she went. Her brother Absalom said to her, "Has that Amnon, your brother, been with you? Be quiet now, my sister; he is your brother. Don't take this thing to heart." And Tamar lived in her brother Absalom's house, a desolate woman. Samuel 13:19, 20

Importance of good counsel

Some people give good counsel and others give bad counsel. All too often the latter is followed rather than the former. This was true of Amnon in following the bad advice of Jonadab, who evidently was an evil person. Good counsel would have tried to change Amnon's wicked intentions not to further them, and how much better everything would have been if that had been done.

Warning against taking vengeance

Because of Amnon's sin against Tamar Absalom planned vengeance for two years. This consumed his life; he was intent on bringing vengeance and would not permit himself to be dissuaded. Outwardly he seems to have let others believe everything was all right, but inwardly he raged with bitterness. This is a dangerous frame of mind and can lead only to dire actions.

How would you characterize the advice given to Amnon by his "friend" Jonadab?

In what way was Amnon's sin like the sin of his father David with Bathsheba?

Why is obsession with a person or thing dangerous?

Ahithophel 2 Samuel 14, 15, 17

Ahithophel was a trusted advisor to King David who eventually allied with Absalom in rebellion against David (2 Sam 15–17). 2 Samuel 15:12 introduces Ahithophel as *"Ahithophel the Gilonite, David's counselor, from his city Giloh."* 2 Samuel 16:23 says David and others so highly esteemed Ahithophel's counsel that it was *"as if one consulted the word of God."*

The Talmud describes Ahithophel as a man *"whose great wisdom was not received in humility as a gift from heaven, and so became a stumbling-block to him"*

Role in Absalom's Rebellion
In 2 Samuel, Absalom conspired to rebel against his father. After four years of gaining the trust of the people, Absalom asked David for permission to travel to Hebron to fulfill a vow to Jehovah. While there, Absalom secretly began a movement to seize his father's power and turned to Ahithophel for advice.

There may have been a special reason for this:

- Ahithophel was the father of one of David's mighty men named Eliam (2 Samuel 23:34).
- Bathsheba was the daughter of a man named Eliam (2 Samuel 11:3) who may have been a relative of Ahithophel.
- Since Bathsheba had married another of David's mighty man, Uriah the Hittite (2 Samuel 23:39)
- It is quite possible the same Eliam is in view in both instances, making Ahithophel the grandfather of Bathsheba.

It is possible he held a grudge against David for taking his granddaughter from her husband and saw a way of gaining revenge.

If so, this is another case of an old grudge festering to become an unwise action, which turned out very tragically for the person involved.

When David heard of Absalom's rebellion, he immediately made plans to leave Jerusalem. He wanted to spare Jerusalem and its inhabitants the horrors of becoming a battleground between father and son. When David left Jerusalem, he left 10 of his concubines to care for the palace. (2 Sam 15:16, 17). Ahithophel advised Absalom to have intercourse with his father's wives, whom David had left in Jerusalem. There are three reasons why he would have recommended such an action:

1. It would have cemented Absalom's claim on his father's realm. In the ancient Near East, a new ruler would possess his predecessor's concubines.
2. It would prevent Absalom from ever being reconciled to his father.
3. It would show David's subjects the break was complete, and they needed to pick a side.

Later, Ahithophel advised Absalom to immediately pursue David and his few faithful followers (2 Sam 17:1). However, one of David's other advisers, Hushai, who was secretly loyal to David, advised Absalom to do the opposite (2 Sam 17:7–8). Absalom and the men of Israel judge Hushai's advice superior to Ahithophel's and decided to delay attacking David, which gave David's commander Joab time to regroup. Seeing Absalom had ignored his advice and recognizing reconciliation with David was impossible, Ahithophel returned to his home, set his affairs in order, and hanged himself.

How can we filter the advice we receive to ensure it is according to God's wisdom?

What safeguards should you employ before taking the advice of a widely acknowledged expert?

How do ambitious people manipulate the truth to their own advantage?

Why is it wise to wonder about the motives of people who seem unusually helpful?

Hushai the Archite — 2 Samuel 15:24 - 16:14

This is the narrative of David as he is leaving Jerusalem to avoid Absalom. As he approached the top of the Mount of Olives, he encounters several people; Zadok the priest, then Hushai, Ziba, and Shimei.

We can use this passage of Scripture much like a program to understand these individuals and the context in which they fit into the situation and into David's life. As if David needed more bad news, he learned his trusted counselor, Ahithophel, was among the conspirators (15:31). The subject of this passage seems to be who is loyal to David and who is not.

David's prayer is that Jehovah will turn Ahithophel's counsel, otherwise always dependable, into foolishness. Immediately after receiving the news of Ahithophel's disloyalty David encountered his friend Hushai the Archite, who is at this point an old man.

David said to Hushai, "*If you go with me, you will be a burden to me. But if you return to the city and say to Absalom, 'I will be your servant, O king; I was your father's servant in the past, but now I will be your servant,' then you can help me by frustrating Ahithophel's advice.*"

Hushai returned to Jerusalem prepared to serve as a double agent. He offered his services to Absalom, but his mission was to counter the advice of Ahithophel. David also informed Hushai of the ring of priestly spies prepared to carry the information to the King in the desert. The suspense and intrigue begin to build.

When Absalom and his supporters came to Jerusalem, Absalom seemed assured of success, not only because David is on the run but because Ahithophel is "with them" (16:58). Ahithophel always seemed to be right (16:23). His support of Absalom's rebellion gave it respectability and strength.

When Hushai met Absalom, he repeated the standard loyalty oath (16:16): (Long live the King!) Does Hushai intend to support Absalom or David? By pledging loyalty to "the King," does he mean the young usurper King or the banished King David? The way he carefully used the phrase is judiciously ambiguous.

Absalom may have been suspicious, so he pushed Hushai further about his loyalty to David. *Is this the way Hushai expresses love for his friends* (16:17)? The implication is Absalom can do without Hushai's support if in fact, he is so wavering. Absalom's question put Hushai in a tight spot. He must justify his decision to abandon David and defend his right to advise Absalom, all the while convincing Absalom he is a counselor to be trusted. This is a delicate balancing act, but Hushai can only hope to deceive Absalom later by winning his confidence now. His response is a picture of wisdom and it convinces Absalom Hushai is great in understanding and can be trusted (16:18-19).

Nevertheless, Hushai's task is a difficult one. Ahithophel's counsel is nearly always right as though God Himself had spoken to him.

The conflict between Ahithophel's counsel (16: 20-17:4) and Hushai (17:5-14) is not unlike our own English proverbs: "strike while the iron is hot" and "look before you leap."

Ahithophel advocated striking while David's position is weak. He said to Absalom, *"I would choose twelve thousand men and set out tonight in pursuit of David."*

Hushai argued, *"The advice Ahithophel has given is not good this time. You know your father and his men; they are fighters, and as fierce as a wild bear robbed of her cubs."*

What evidence do we have that intelligence and even wisdom can be used for either good or evil?

Absalom followed the advice of Hushai and David's prayer to defeat the counsel of Ahithophel was answered.

How can we filter the advice we receive to ensure that it is according to God's wisdom?

Ziba 2 Samuel 9, 16, 19

Ziba had been a servant within the household of Saul. The Philistine invasion and the defeat of Israel in which Saul and his family were killed, probably gave him his freedom.

He seems to have been a major steward in the household of the King and with the death of his master's family he was able to leverage some of his power into gaining a degree of Saul's wealth.

Some time had passed since the defeat of Saul by the Philistines. David had now become King of all of Israel and he was now beginning to "settle accounts" and set up his kingdom.

When we first meet Ziba, David has asked him to locate any living descendants of King Saul. This request was made for David to show kindness to the family because of his love and loyalty to Jonathan. Ziba informs King David there is one living relative of which he is aware.

His name is Mephibosheth and he was injured fleeing from the Philistines. He is now living a life of obscurity in Lo-debar.

In order to further make things right and honor Jonathan. David sent for Mephibosheth and brought him into his own house as a permanent guest.

David then restored to Mephibosheth all the estate which had belonged to Saul. Ziba was appointed as Mephibosheth's land steward and director of operations. It is obvious from later developments Ziba feels he has been mistreated by the King and is determined to correct the situation. Ziba's displeasure at his loss of independence is no doubt what motivated him to slander Mephibosheth.

When David was leaving Jerusalem to avoid fighting Absalom in the city, Ziba resourcefully turns Absalom's rebellion and Mephibosheth's physical weakness to his personal advantage.

To display his own loyalty, he brought David a large supply of provisions during the latter's journey across the Mount of Olives, and at the same time, apparently without any grounds, accuses his master of having gone over to the enemy in the hope of obtaining the kingdom of Saul.

For this misrepresentation Ziba was rewarded with a grant of all Mephibosheth's property.

When the rebellion is over, and the king returned to Jerusalem, Mephibosheth was able to refute the false charges made against him by his treacherous servant.

The king might justly have punished Ziba, but in the hour of victory he is in a conciliatory mood.

David seems to feel, if Ziba has not been faithful to his master, he has at any rate been loyal and helpful to his king.

David therefore decided to restore half the property of Saul to Mephibosheth and give Ziba the possession of the other half (2 Samuel 19:24-30).

Why is it not wise to take one person's version of events at face value without hearing the other side?

How is mercy more conducive to building a strong consensus than vengeance?

From a position of power is it more difficult to deal with friends or enemies? Why?

Barzillai 2 Samuel 17:27-29; 19:31-40; 1 Kings 2:7

His name means "made of iron for strength." He was a wealthy Gileadite numbered among the good friends of David listed in 2 Samuel 17. *When David came to Mahanaim, Shobi son of Nahash from Rabbah of the Ammonites, and Makir son of Ammiel from Lo Debar, and Barzillai the Gileadite from Rogelim brought bedding and bowls and articles of pottery. They also brought wheat and barley, flour and roasted grain, beans and lentils, honey and curds, sheep, and cheese from cows' milk for David and his people to eat. For they said, "The people have become hungry and tired and thirsty in the desert." (17:27-29)*

A man of great appeal

Barzillai the Gileadite and his family were remembered for many generations. The dwelling place of his son, Kimham, is found in Bethlehem, the city of David, in the days of the captivity of the land (Jeremiah 41:17). What an amazing charm there is about this lovable old man!

When David greatly needed support at the time of Absalom's rebellion, Barzillai rallied to his side. Like a true man of iron, he offered David strong loyalty. He was not afraid to support his friend. He was willing to face the consequences, if David were to lose the battle with Absalom. Barzillai brought necessities to the hungry, thirsty followers of David.

Are we as loyal to our Heavenly Father as Barzillai was to King David?

Barzillai was drawn to David because of the virtues David showed in his life. Although David, now, was not popular, Barzillai knew the heart and soul of David. He was a man of God's own heart and therefore he was a man worthy of support and honor.

D. L. Moody once said, "Character is what a man is in the dark."

Barzillai knew David was still godly, although a fugitive. He generously provided David with the necessary substance at Manahan (2 Samuel 19:32).

Barzillai is described as a great man, whose possessions were carried with a noble humility (2 Samuel 19:32). He did not squander his wealth on idle privileges nor use them for selfish ends. His position, prestige, and wealth were beneficially used for others.

When David was victorious, he wanted to reward Barzillai, but Barzillai felt his services were trivial and unworthy of any recompense from David. Witness this scene as described in 2 Samuel 19:31-40.

Barzillai the Gileadite also came down from Rogelim to cross the Jordan with the king and to send him on his way from there. Now Barzillai was a very old man, eighty years of age. He had provided for the king during his stay in Mahanaim, for he was a very wealthy man. The king said to Barzillai, "Cross over with me and stay with me in Jerusalem, and I will provide for you." But Barzillai answered the king, "How many more years will I live, that I should go up to Jerusalem with the king? I am now eighty years old. Can I tell the difference between what is good and what is not? Can your servant taste what he eats and drinks? Can I still hear the voices of men and women singers? Why should your servant be an added burden to my lord the king? Your servant will cross over the Jordan with the king for a short distance, but why should the king reward me in this way? Let your servant return, that I may die in my own town near the tomb of my father and mother. But here is your servant Kimham. Let him cross over with my lord the king. Do for him whatever pleases you." The king said, "Kimham shall cross over with me, and I will do for him whatever pleases you. And anything you desire from me I will do for you." So, all the people crossed the Jordan, and then the king crossed over. The king kissed Barzillai and gave him his blessing, and Barzillai returned to his home.

Although not without the infirmities of old age, he retained his charm. At 80 years of age his heart of love was deep and broad.

May we have the grace to grow old gracefully and beautifully!

Adonijah was the fourth son of David. After the death of Absalom, Adonijah, who was next in order of birth, felt he was the rightful successor to the throne. His expectation seems to have been shared by many.

The situation had changed when Bathsheba became a wife of David and Solomon was born. The influence and the ambition of this latest of David's queens made it certain Adonijah would encounter a dangerous rival in his younger brother. It was probably his knowledge of conspiracies against his interests which led to the premature attempt of Adonijah to seize the crown before his father's death.
At first Adonijah's plan seemed likely to succeed. He added to his supporters such important and influential people as Joab, the commander-in-chief, and Abiathar the priest. Adonijah held a great feast at En-Rogel, where the final arrangements were to be made for his coronation.

One person he had not invited to the banquet was destined to bring defeat to the plotters before their plans were matured. Nathan the prophet was one of the closest advisors to King David.

Realizing not a moment was to be lost, Nathan hurried to Bathsheba, whose fears he easily stirred by pointing out the danger to her own life and that of Solomon should the attempt of Adonijah succeed.

Bathsheba had already obtained a promise from David that Solomon would succeed him on the throne. She immediately sought an interview with the aged king and informed him of what was transpiring at En-Rogel. Nathan, as part of the prearranged plan, came in at that moment to confirm her story.

The prophet-counsellor played his part with great skill. He expressed surprise that the king, if he had approved the action of Adonijah, had not taken his friends and counsellors into his confidence.

Listening to the accounts of the queen and the prophet, David renewed his oath to Bathsheba and took prompt measures to secure the accession of Solomon.

At this point the support of David's bodyguards was all-important, and their loyalty was beyond suspicion. Their commander was ordered by David to escort Solomon, mounted upon his father's mule, to Gihon, and to have him anointed king by Zadok the priest and Nathan the prophet. This order was carried out amid the enthusiasm of the people, who split the air with shouts of *"God save King Solomon!"*

The unexpected noise reached the ears of Adonijah's guests at En-Rogel, causing astonishment, which quickly turned into panic when Jonathan the son of Abiathar hurried in with the news David had chosen Solomon to succeed him. The company broke up in confusion, and Adonijah himself was so afraid for his life he fled for protection to the altar in the Tabernacle. Solomon, however, agreed to spare his life on condition of future loyalty.

After the death of his father Adonijah requested Solomon to allow him to marry Abishag the Shunammite, the young woman who had cared for David during his declining years. No one acquainted with the concepts of Eastern courts would be surprised at the resentment of Solomon, or that he took this request as an act of treason. Promptly the order was given and Adonijah was executed.

Why do you think Adonijah had grown up to be rebellious and ambitious?

How can it be useful to ask a question about someone's motives, even if you think it might be safe to assume you know what he or she wants?

It is comforting to realize no matter what people do - God is in control!

Book Six

1. Solomon	I Kings 3; Proverbs 2-4
2. Solomon the Great	Matthew 12:41-42; Luke 12:27-29
3. King Solomon	I Kings 2:10-46
4. Solomon the Wise	I Kings 3; 2 Chronicles 1
5. Solomon the Wealthy	I Kings 4
6. Solomon the Builder	I Kings 5; Acts 7:47-53
7. Solomon and Hiram	I Kings 5, 7
8. Solomon's Wives	I Kings 3; 11:3
9. Solomon the Trader	I Kings9:10-28; 2 Chronicles 8:1-18
10. The Queen of Sheba	I Kings 10; 2 Chronicles 9; Revelation 3
11. Asaph	Psalms 73-83
12. Solomon's Spiritual Decline and Punishment	I Kings 11
13. Ahijah the Prophet	I Kings 11, 14
14. The Rebellion of Jeroboam	I Kings 11:9-25
15. Rehoboam (South)	I Kings 12, 14; 2 Chronicles 10-12
16. "The Man of God"	I Kings 13
17. Jeroboam the son of Nebat (North)	I Kings 12-14
18. War between Rehoboam & Jeroboam	I Kings 14-15; 2 Chronicles 12-13
19. Abijah	I Kings 14-15; 2 Chronicles 12-13
20. Asa	I Kings 15; 2 Chronicles 14-15
21. Nadab and Baasha	I Kings 15:25-16:7
22. Elah & Zimri	I Kings 16
23. Omri	I Kings 16
24. Ahab	I Kings 16, 18, 20-22; 2 Chronicles 18
25. Jezebel	I Kings 16, 20-22; 2 Kings 9-10
26. Ahab & Jezebel - religious error	I Kings16, 20-22
27. Ahab, Naboth, & Elijah	I Kings 21
28. Ahab & Micaiah	I Kings 21-22
29. Ahaziah	I Kings 22:51-53; 2 Kings 1
30. Jehoram	2 Kings 6:8-8:6

Solomon 1 Kings 3; Proverbs 2-4

Solomon's name means "peace." He was also called Jedidiah, meaning "beloved of the Lord" (2 Sam. 12:25). He was the second son of David and Bathsheba; he was born in Jerusalem around 990 B.C. We can calculate this since the kingdom divided in the year 931 B.C. shortly after Solomon's son Rehoboam became king.

There was a marked contrast between the kingship of David and the kingship of Solomon. This contrast was largely caused by the different backgrounds of the two rulers.

David had been raised in open grazing land watching sheep, and later had experienced the harshness of life as a fugitive. Solomon, however, had known only the ease of the palace and all its connected luxuries.

As a result, David was aggressive and efficient. He became a king of action who could personally lead armies to victory. Solomon became a king of peace, happy to stay at home and content merely to retain the land his father had gained.

David's court never grew larger than the requirements of his government, but Solomon's became lavish in the manner of other Near Eastern courts. As a result, Solomon needed greater revenue than David and he raised taxes accordingly. He also engaged more in foreign trade, showing skill and enjoying very great success.

David was a man of the people; Solomon was a man of the court. More significant, David maintained a vibrant faith in God as a "*man after God's own heart*," while Solomon, though beginning well in spiritual devotion, failed to hold his basic relationship before God and fell into sinful ways. He finally came under the judgment of God.

As long as the co-regency between Solomon and David continued things went smoothly between Solomon and those who were opposed to him. When David died this condition changed rapidly. Adonijah, whose claim to the throne was strong enough to win the support of Abiathar and Joab, was a threat to Solomon and would have remained a threat as long as he was allowed to live. He provided Solomon with a reason to have him eliminated and Solomon did just that.

With Adonijah removed as an opponent, Solomon turned to Adonijah's main supporters; Abiathar and Joab. He quickly eliminated any opposition from these two and solidified his position as the only king of the Jews. Shortly after these events Solomon received an unusual token of God's favor. Commendably he recognized the need of God's blessing and sacrificed "*1000 burnt offerings*" at Gibeon where the tabernacle then stood.

While the new king was still present at Gibeon, God showed His pleasure by appearing to him in a dream and inviting him to make a request. Solomon was pleased with this opportunity and requested wisdom to guide him as he ruled. In further approval and blessing God indicated not only this request would be granted, but He promised Solomon "*riches and honor*" to the extent no person of his day would be like him. Solomon's later life gave clear evidence to the fulfillment of these promises.

Can you see how different backgrounds create a different point of view?

Different points of view often create different action.

What practical steps can you take to place a higher value on wisdom?

What can you request from God and be certain He will say yes?

How can you seek God's wisdom as a matter of habit?

Solomon the Great — Matthew 12:41, 42; Luke 12:27-29

Let's pause before turning in greater detail to the life of Solomon to look at the story of his person and his reign. He is a contrast with his father David. He began where David ended. He lived a life of security and peace, not war and conflict. He had the experience of a royal father to guide him. He never knew persecution, injustice, or rejection.

Solomon had enormous advantages.

- He had wisdom from God.
- He had intelligence and insight derived perhaps from his mother, Bathsheba.
- He had, at first, the gift of humility, the fruit perhaps of Nathan's training.
- He had so much wealth the Queen of Sheba was reduced to speechless amazement by his glory.

As men measure earthly kingship in terms of wealth, borders, beauty, and regal pomp, he was Solomon the Great.

What did Solomon do with all these enormous opportunities; opportunities each one of which was a responsibility?

He lived a life of self-indulgence.
His sin was refined and respectable, even within the scope of law and custom which allowed an eastern monarch great latitude. It was sin, nonetheless, unrecognized and unconfessed. It produced no repentance. It was an unproductive life full of spectacle and flaunted sensuality.

His wisdom turned sour in disillusionment.
Ecclesiastes reflects Solomon's later attitude to life. Contrast his cynical and disillusioned piece of worldly pessimism with the heart-revealing psalms of David. Even in the plain wisdom he expressed in the Proverbs, it seems he knew the truth but never could discipline himself to live as he wrote.

Solomon did not seem to be able to apply his wisdom to himself!

The Old Testament is clear about his many relationships and alliances with the world.

- His palace was filled with foreign women, collected in the pursuit of both political and dynastic advantage.
- His trade with Tyre was to open a sequence of events which led straight to Ahab and disaster in another generation.

Solomon's policies were a major contribution to the division of the kingdom and the sufferings of Israel in their captivity. Soon the golden age of Jewish history passed. The day of Solomon's glory turned into clouds and darkness. As he grew older, he began to imitate the heathen ways of his wives and concubines. He did not stop worshipping the God of Israel; he did not stop offering the usual sacrifices in the Temple at the feasts. But his heart was not right with God and his worship became merely formal.

This brought on him divine judgment. His enemies began to prevail against him and one judgment after another fell on the land.

How did the condition of Solomon's heart differ from David's?

Why is it not acceptable to follow God any less than completely?

How old Solomon was when he came to the throne is not known. Josephus says he was 15. He was probably nearer the age of 20.

David had longed for peace. He had named one ill-fated son Absalom, which means "father of peace." Solomon's name means "peaceful." Nathan, who took an interest in Solomon, called him Jedidiah (beloved of God); this was a play on David's own name.

Possibly Nathan had a great hand in raising Solomon. This would account for the old prophet's interest in his succession. It was an orchestrated succession, but with Benaiah, commander of the household troops, standing by, Joab, the only real danger, was neutralized.

There is no doubt Solomon's own personal ability played a part in the first recorded events of the reign which show him in firm control. It must have been a great surprise for Bathsheba when Solomon's deference and courtesy vanished in a flame of anger when she approached him with Adonijah's plea.

Solomon had earlier spared Adonijah, but the request for Abishag in marriage seems to have brought an outburst and the execution which followed. Some have suggested Abishag was the Shulammite of the Song of Solomon and Adonijah's request caused a blaze of jealousy?

It is not good to see the new reign begin in deeds of blood, hatred, and harshness.

Abiathar had been a priest for 40 years and had served the royal house well. For his part in the rebellion he was removed. Shimei was placed under house arrest because he controlled the sympathy of elements hostile to the throne. It was wise to strike him down; Solomon took the action. Joab had often taken up the sword against his enemies. He perished by the sword and he had earned the capital punishment which David felt incompetent to exact.

So, the tale of the kings begins. Samuel long since had predicted as much. (I Sam. 8:10-18). *Samuel told all the words of the LORD to the people who were asking him for a king. He said, "This is what the king who will reign over you will do: He will take your sons and make them serve with his chariots and horses, and they will run in front of his chariots. Some he will assign to be commanders of thousands and commanders of fifties, and others to plow his ground and reap his harvest, and still others to make weapons of war and equipment for his chariots. He will take your daughters to be perfumers and cooks and bakers. He will take the best of your fields and vineyards and olive groves and give them to his attendants. He will take a tenth of your grain and of your vintage and give it to his officials and attendants. Your menservants and maidservants and the best of your cattle and donkeys he will take for his own use. He will take a tenth of your flocks, and you yourselves will become his slaves. When that day comes, you will cry out for relief from the king you have chosen, and the LORD will not answer you in that day."*

The last sentence describes exactly the situation as it occurred at the death of Solomon when the kingdom was divided between Rehoboam and Jeroboam. The Greek writer, Plutarch said, "There is no stronger test of a man's real character than power and authority, exciting every passion and discovering every latent vice." This truth is obvious as we watch Solomon from the beginning to the end of his kingship.

The thought which presents itself is: it is of benefit to all of us to watch with care how we exercise any authority which falls into our hands.

Power corrupts and absolute power corrupts absolutely.

Solomon himself realized this truth perhaps too late in his life to do anything about it.

***"The end of a matter is better than its beginning, and patience is better than pride."* Ecclesiastes 7:8**

Solomon was a very strange and curious mixture of his father (David) and his mother (Bathsheba). His marriage of convenience to the Princess of Egypt was a piece of political wisdom designed to strengthen his southern frontier so he could turn his attention to the exposed and vulnerable borders of his East and North. It is disappointing to observe the mistakes with which the most materially prosperous age of Israel's monarchy opened.

Worship in high places was a feature of the days before the building of the Temple; the writer is setting the stage for the building of the Temple. Worship at the "high place" was not in itself wrong, but it was also a practice of nearby heathen nations and therefore dangerous to religious purity.

The two forces of politics and religion struggled for mastery of Solomon.

The dynastic alliance with Egypt was preached against, but it was a piece of worldly wisdom which one could imagine was a heritage of the cool and calculating Bathsheba. It was not the statesmanship of a man of God.

Solomon's wisdom given by God

One of the most significant times for Solomon took place at Gibeon early in his reign. It was the occasion when the young king was promised wisdom, riches, and even long life if he would follow God as had David. There he was given a dream and heard God tell him to make a request for whatever he desired most.

Solomon responded first by giving praise. God had honored him in making him king and he admitted he was in himself incapable of filling the requirements of the position. Then he said what he wanted most was a wise and understanding heart to judge the people (1 Kings 3:9). In other words, he wanted wisdom for his challenging task. God was pleased with his request and said He would grant not only wisdom, but also wealth, honor, and long life; the entire gift Solomon might have asked for but did not. All of this was dependent on Solomon's obedience.

Solomon's wisdom illustrated

In the record of 1 Kings this account is followed by a story which illustrates the wisdom Solomon received. The story concerns two prostitutes each of whom had a newborn child. One night one of the two lay on her child so that it died. The two women came to Solomon, the one asserting the mother of the dead baby had switched babies during the night, so she could have the live one. The other mother declared this was not so, but the live child was hers.

To determine who was the true mother Solomon called for a sword and commanded the child be divided in two, so each mother could have half. At this, the true mother protested she did not want this to be done, but the false mother accepted the decision. From these two reactions Solomon knew who the true mother was and gave the child to her. News of this wise action spread through the country and caused the people to respect the wisdom of their new king.

The prayer of Solomon is worth careful reading.

There is a large measure of humility and desire to do what is right.

But something is lacking; it is the longing for personal purity and holiness.

He is wise, full of human insight, and altogether lovable.

Here was a man who, had he kept this human touch, might have been one of the great monarchs of all time.

With God's blessing Solomon became very wealthy. His importing and exporting are recorded for us in Scripture. Much of his wealth came through his dealings with other countries and gifts which were brought to him by visitors. The result was he received the incredible income of 666 talents of gold annually. A talent has been estimated at approximately 75 pounds. This would make Solomon's income in gold approximately 50,000 pounds annually. How much would 50,000 pounds of gold be worth? According to my good friend "Siri," this would be $256,643,000 a year and was enough to make "silver in Jerusalem as stones."

From this gold he made many articles. He made 200 large shields of 600 shekels each and 300 smaller shields of 300 shekels each. It is probable these were gold covering the framework of the shield being constructed of wood. Such shields would have been used for state occasions.

Then he made all the drinking vessels of gold, as well as all the vessels of the house of the forest of Lebanon (possibly the name of his own palace). Perhaps most remarkable of all, he made a magnificent throne of ivory and overlaid it with gold. It had six steps, with two carved lions on each step as well as on each side of the seat. The text says that "*there was not the like made in any kingdom.*"

In summary, *"King Solomon passed all the kingdoms of the earth in riches and wisdom"* (I Kings 10:23; II Chronicles 9:22).

Here without a doubt is a spectacle of affluence. Solomon's kingdom was rich and secure. Israel basked in her golden age. The royal figure who presided gloriously over the wealthy nation had nothing to fear from the armed bands of men settled on his borderlands.

The world respected him; most feared him. Men came from far away to tap the deep springs of his wisdom; it is at this point we see Solomon in all his glory.

But in this very situation are seen the seeds of decay.

There is an attraction in ease and prosperity. Hard times harden men, purge their minds of many small, unimportant things. The parable in Deuteronomy 32, 33 had long before expressed, *"Jeshurun (the nation of Israel) waxes fat and kicks, forgetting the pit from which he was lifted, growing proud and hard."*

Thankfulness for the work of other men and the blessing of God, which made Solomon's wealth and greatness, was too easily forgotten. He began to take for granted what others had gained for him; pride and arrogance replaced thankfulness.

The Greeks linked three words, which, with some loss of content, may be translated: "excess," "arrogant behavior," and "disaster."

- The first suggests a lack of morality which comes with ease and prosperity and too great success, and the relaxing of the moral fiber which comes to those favored with fortune.
- The second word speaks of both a loss of moral balance resulting in outrageous confidence, and the conduct which reflects it.
- The third speaks of the catastrophic result which history shows to be inevitable.

This sequence is too obvious in the history of many lands to be much comfort today. We can see its predestined results. The moral law, which is interwoven with the story, is inevitable in its retributions.

This chapter contains no account of sin or calculated wrongdoing. The king is at the moment contemplating a great building for his God.

This is the structure of ease and security into which Solomon is slipping, slipping without consciousness of what is growing weak in his life.

Solomon the Builder I Kings 5; Acts 7:47-53

David wanted to build the Temple but was forbidden by God to construct it. However, he did gather extensive materials for the construction of the Temple, and he gave Solomon the plans which had been revealed to him by the Spirit of God for its construction.

The time was now right to begin the building of God's Temple. The quiet cities of Israel were at ease. The land lived in comfort. Yet there was no wide threat of pagan infiltration. The monarch himself was, at this moment, too close to Jehovah to be tempted to follow the base and degrading superstitions of the pagans of other nations.

Jehovah was honored with splendor and ceremony, but such worship is not a guarantee of spiritual commitment or deep truth of worship. The temple was projected in this spirit. Jehovah was an honored guest, the giver of good things, the architect of all material prosperity.

So, it seems in this spirit the concept of a temple of beauty took shape. Great building programs have, through all history, been a feature of "golden ages," when peace and affluence make available both a workforce and finance.

The actual building of the temple began in the spring of Solomon's fourth year (966 B.C. - I Kings 6:1), and it was completed seven years later in the fall of the year.

Funding was a matter which fell within Solomon's natural ability. We shall look later at his great trading partnership with Hiram of Tyre. This great Phoenician King supplied cedar wood and 10,000 workers per month to assist in cutting and transporting the wood. Cedar was considered the finest wood available for any type of building in this day and age.

Hiram took responsibility for conveying the logs by sea to a Palestinian port of Solomon's choosing. He supplied stonecutters to help prepare the great quantity of stone which was needed (I Kings 5:18).

As expenses mounted, Solomon was not above trading Israelite territory for northern aid. And the provision of labor led Solomon into oppressive organization of the working class of the land. Solomon's weaknesses are beginning to show here.

The temple itself was Solomon's work completely. It had begun first in his father David's mind. It was not specifically ordered by God. It was a praiseworthy project. It seems to have been built, much like the cathedral buildings of the Middle Ages, to show off the skills and wealth of men. God never specifically asked David or Solomon to build the Temple. **It was permitted by God rather than ordered.**

The tabernacle of Moses' day was in quite another category, and it was full of symbolic instruction. The temple was pursued to honor God, and such is a worthy desire.

The testimony of God's people and program is not advanced by the poor and unkempt facilities of worship many times tolerated by Christian congregations.

On the other hand, lavish buildings can become a hollow symbol. It is what is within the shrine which matters, and gorgeous cathedrals have arisen in ages and in places where evangelism, the primary and indispensable task of the church, have not weighed heavily on the conscience of men. Solomon, in pursuing his dream, neglected much which needed to be accomplished nearer to home.

How can you cooperate with and draw on someone else's strengths to serve God more effectively soon?

How can you balance your life between the appreciation of beauty and the practical function of following God's program?

Solomon inherited his father's friendship with Hiram, the great Phoenician king of Tyre. After David had taken the stronghold of Jerusalem, Hiram sent messengers, workmen and materials to build a palace for him at Jerusalem. Josephus informs us, on the authority of ancient writers, Hiram was the son of Abibal, and he had a prosperous reign of 34 years, and died at the age of 53.

He also tells us on the same authority Hiram and Solomon sent difficult problems and riddles to each other to solve. Hiram could not solve one of the problems sent to him by Solomon. As a result, he paid to Solomon a large sum of money, this had been agreed upon before the exchange of these problems began. Later, Hiram did solve the problem and proposed several others Solomon could not explain. Consequently, Solomon was obliged to pay back to Hiram a huge sum of money.

Josephus also tells his readers the correspondence carried on between Solomon and Hiram regarding the building of the Temple was preserved, not only in the records of the Jews, but also in the public records of Tyre. Josephus informs us it was recorded by Phoenician historians that Hiram gave his daughter to Solomon in marriage.

The friendship which flourished between the two kings suited both parties well. Solomon secured the expensive materials and the equally expensive expertise which his building projects demanded.

Hiram furnished the king of Israel with skilled workmen and with cedar trees and fir trees for the building of the Temple. He also furnished algum wood, which was used, together with cedar and pine, in the construction of the Temple, including the crafting of musical instruments for use in the Temple. Likely the wood was brought by the ships of Tarshish, sent from the Red Sea port of Ezion-Giber, from the distant country of Ophir (possibly in India) and was very valuable.

The Phoenicians were trapped in between the Lebanon mountain ranges and the Mediterranean Sea. They were blocked in early years by both Philistines and Egyptians from further growth south and were unable even to grow into Galilee or the fertile Esdraelon plain.

It was the sea in front, and the magnificent cedar forests behind, which led the Phoenicians to their greatness as ship builders and traders. What they lacked in their narrow coastal plain was primarily produce. They needed the produce of the fertile surrounding areas.

The Phoenician ruler secured economic advantages of the first order from Solomon. Apart from what must have been a valuable payment in primary produce, Solomon also traded away frontier areas of his northern province, 20 Galilean villages (9:11-13). There is little doubt Hiram got the best of the bargain. His frontier in the south benefited greatly by gaining territory in Galilee.

There was a surprising result from the exchanging of their timber and craftsmanship for wine and oil (5:11). Ezekiel 27 gives some idea, from four centuries later, of the diversity and magnitude of the trade with Tyre and Sidon. In the days of Ahab, it was an extremely valuable process of financial exchange sealed by the dynastic marriage of the young king and Jezebel, to Israel's ruin.

Solomon seems to have supported the deities of Sidon for his wives' sake (11:4), and women of Sidon were among his wives (11:5). This gives some substance to Josephus statement that a daughter of Hiram was in the king's harem. If so, it set a disturbing precedent later followed by Omri and his son Ahab. Solomon did not anticipate how his example with Hiram would affect his successors in the years to come!

Do you consider the example you are setting for others?

Do you consider the what the result of the example you are setting will be for your children and grandchildren?

Solomon's Wives I Kings 3; I Kings 11:3

Solomon had 700 wives and 300 concubines. The idea of political marriage had been introduced to Solomon early by David. David had made such a marriage for himself when he was only King of Judah. One such marriage was with Maacah, the daughter of Talmai, king of Geshur. The country of Geshur was located on the east side of the Sea of Galilee, in the area of Bashan. A treaty with Geshur at this early time had the advantage for David of placing his rival in the north, Ish-bosheth, between two countries in league with each other. This alliance would also neutralize this important state in David's later struggles with the Armenian countries in the North. David had arranged a marriage for Solomon with Naamah, the Princess of Ammon. This marriage occurred prior to Solomon's succession to the throne. Perhaps this marriage was arranged as a way of giving him standing when the day came for him to assume the throne.

Solomon's most important marriage was with a daughter of the Egyptian Pharaoh. This is shown by the mention of the marriage numerous times. The importance arises from the fact this marriage involves an alliance with a major power of that day, Egypt. All of Solomon's other alliances were with secondary powers such as Moab, Ammon, and Edom. In earlier days Egypt had allowed alliances and marriage only with major powers like Babylon, Hatti, or Mitanni. Even then it was always the case of a daughter from one of these countries coming to marry a prince in Egypt, never an Egyptian daughter going to live on foreign soil. But in the case of Solomon, not only was this alliance formalized by marriage, but the Egyptian Princess came to Solomon. The fact is revealing in two areas: Egypt was significantly reduced in power from former days, and Israel was now considered a major power, possibly even stronger than Egypt.

The date of this marriage was early in Solomon's rule. This is implied by its placement in I Kings 3:1; immediately after the record of Solomon executing Shimei, which was three years after his crowning. There is also a direct indication that the marriage occurred before the building and completion of the Temple, which was in the 11th year of Solomon's reign. The marriage had apparently occurred sometime between Solomon's third and 11th year.

One other early marriage calls for notice: it was with a young lady from Shunem. Described by Solomon in Song of Solomon, the love which Solomon and the Shunammite had for each other suggests these two were still comparatively young. Solomon accompanied the young lady to her house on one occasion; it is not likely Solomon would have done this later in his life. Solomon is also said to have had 60 other wives and 80 concubines, which would indicate a time early in his kingship. It is likely most of his marriages occurred early rather than later in his kingship. This marriage was not a matter of convenience to formalize a treaty with a foreign country; it was made based on true love.

Debasement of marriage

God did not intend for marriages to be plural or for convenience. True marriage is for love and to endure for the life of the partners. More than one marriage is not to be contracted at a time. In Old Testament times God did allow this practice. He surely was not pleased with this but allowed it.

Solomon, however, went far beyond all reason and amassed wives in his endeavor to gain world status and formalize treaties. In this he was very wrong and just as God had warned (Deuteronomy 17:17), the marriages did serve to turn his heart away from God.

The importance of a father's influence

David certainly influenced Solomon in many good ways; however, he did not influence him well regarding marriage. He, himself, married many wives and these marriages served a political end in at least two circumstances. Solomon followed in this pattern and then moved on to increase the wrong of his father many times over. Solomon may have done this without the example of David, but likely he did it in greater degree as a result of his father's example.

Solomon the Trader — I Kings 9:10-28; 2 Chronicles 8:1-18

It seems obvious in terms of trade and frontier adjustment Hiram had the best of the bargain in his dealing with Solomon. But the Hebrews had other things to offer their northern partner besides farm produce and territory. Solomon controlled access to the Gulf of Aqaba, and the Phoenicians were eager for a sea route to the rich commerce of the East.

Solomon developed many other trade relations which also produced considerable revenue. One avenue of trade was through the Red Sea to the South. David's southern conquests had reached to the Gulf of Aqaba making this sea route more accessible.

With the aid of Phoenician experts, Solomon constructed harbors and provided crews for a fleet of ships leaving Ezion-Gerber at the tip of the Gulf (I Kings 9:26-28). The ships went as far as Ophir, the specific identity of this land is unknown, but one of the suggestions is a region on the coast of India. A journey of this magnitude would mean the ships would stop at many ports in route and the trip most likely took three years (I Kings 10:22). The ships almost certainly carried away from Ezion-Gerber a cargo of copper. It is recorded on their return voyages they carried gold, silver, hardwoods, precious stones, ivory and animals.

It is significant Solomon must have been aware of the potential commercial importance of the Gulf of Aqaba. Here he had the better of Hiram. The ships which traded in Southern Arabia (9:28), later were able to navigate all the way to India. Solomon controlled the ships and paid the Phoenician captains well. He hired expert seamen recommended by Hiram. People of this ability and skill were difficult to find and without a doubt they had to be paid well.

An archaeological site to the southwest, not far from the Gulf of Aqaba, was identified by Nelson Glueck as the site of an ancient copper smelting operation. The size of the operation and the size of the "slag heaps" tells us this was a huge center of Solomon's mining activities.

This same site has recently been in the news because an excavation project funded by National Geographic magazine has further solidified the idea of Solomon's involvement in the mining activities. The trading of goods, both to supply the work in the area and to help provide Solomon with his extravagant needs in his court in Jerusalem, has been testified to by these new excavations.

Solomon also carried on trade involving horses and chariots. He not only purchased many for his own use, but he took advantage of his strategic position along the north-south trade routes to buy and sell for others. He bought horses mainly from Egypt and Cilicia and then sold them to the Hittites and the Armenians (I Kings 10:28-29).

As we explore the accounts for Solomon's character in his business dealings, we encounter a man with a very able business understanding. His roving mind had a grip on foreign policy and the international scene. He saw Israel as one of a company of nations, with a part to play, with peace to keep, with wealth to gain. Perhaps his concept of the nation of Israel was like that of modern Israel. The ideal of a new state recently created has begun to fade and now there is involvement in the economics and pressures of international affairs.

The nation would once again face adversity. And the seeds of adversity were sown by the clever, worldly-wise man who was born of Bathsheba.

What behavior does God expect of His people today?

Why is it so horrible to God for His people to turn away from Him and worship other gods?

Why she came

She was moved to visit because the fame of Solomon as the wisest man in the East. The Bible says, "*she came to prove Solomon with hard, or perplexing questions*," and her questions were both numerous and varied. This nameless queen had heard Solomon knew all about "*the name of the Lord*," and it was this which attracted her to Jerusalem. She had not come to see the king's material possessions and wealth, for as a queen she had plenty of this herself. She came to see and hear "*the wisdom of Solomon*," as Jesus said of her. Josephus the Jewish historian says of the queen, "She was inquisitive in philosophy and on that and other accounts also was to be admired." Word had reached her that it was Solomon's God who had made him so remarkably wise, and as a worshiper of other gods she wanted to know about this Jehovah.

What she saw and said

Not only did Solomon's "*wisdom excel the wisdom of the children of the east country*." Although accustomed to grandeur herself, the magnificence which the queen gazed upon in Jerusalem was beyond her conception. What she saw was more remarkable than she had heard; Solomon's gorgeous palace with its retinue of servants and ministers with their beautiful apparel and the most beautiful house of the Lord, in which gold was everywhere. Such external wealth and prosperity overwhelmed her until "*there was no more spirit in her*," implying an almost speechless condition because of all the wonders she had seen. *"The report I which heard in my own country about your deeds and your wisdom is true. But I did not believe these things until I came and saw with my own eyes. Indeed, not even half was told me; in wisdom and wealth you have far exceeded the report I heard. How happy your men must be! How happy your officials, who continually stand before you and hear your wisdom! Praise be to the LORD your God, who has delighted in you and placed you on the throne of Israel."*

What She Gave

After expressing her heartfelt gratitude for all she had seen and heard, she bestowed upon Solomon rare and costly gifts. *"She gave the king an hundred and twenty talents of gold, and of spices very great store, and precious stones. There came no more such abundance of spices as these which the Queen of Sheba gave to King Solomon."*

What She Received

The queen's gifts doubtless were lavish; they were in the nature of tribute for what her ears had heard, and her eyes seen. Solomon loaded her with gifts "*of his royal bounty*." We read that he gave the queen "*all her desire, whatsoever she asked*." But the greatest treasure she took back with her was the knowledge of what God had put into the heart of Solomon.

What Christ Said of Her

As the Queen of Sheba returns to her own country the curtain falls, and we do not know how she acted upon the knowledge of God received from Solomon, or when she died. We hear no more of her until the Lord Jesus Christ came into the world, when, during His public ministry, Jesus said, *The Queen of the South will rise at the judgment with this generation and condemn it; for she came from the ends of the earth to listen to Solomon's wisdom, and now one greater than Solomon is here (*Matthew 12:42).

Who is the most famous or important visitor you have ever entertained?

Why do we often have to "see for ourselves" before we will believe something?

What does a visitor mean when he or she brings a gift to the host?

How can you place a higher value on wisdom among the people you encounter daily?

Asaph Psalms 73-83

His name means "collector" or "gatherer." We know nothing of the place of his birth or death. He served in the city of Jerusalem. He was active during the reigns of both David and Solomon. Asaph was appointed by David as the leader of the Levitical musicians. He was in charge of planning, directing, and overseeing all of the music performed in relationship to the tabernacle during the kingship of David.

He was one of the musicians chosen to participate in the ceremony and the installation of the Ark of the Covenant in the tabernacle in Jerusalem during David's reign. Then Solomon appointed him as the head musician along with several others to organize the music, praise and celebration services associated with the new Temple of Solomon.

We are told he worked closely with Heman, Ethan, and Jeduthun (I Chronicles 15:19; 18:5). We really know very little about the music performed for the tabernacle and the Temple services. It was a great privilege and a tremendous responsibility to be involved and to oversee the music used to worship and glorify Jehovah. Asaph's association of musicians continued to have a role through the reigns of Jehoshaphat, Hezekiah and Josiah. II Chronicles 29:30 suggests a collection of Asaph's Psalms may have existed at the time of Hezekiah.

After the exile, hundreds of years later, members of the Guild he created returned to Temple service (Ezra 2:41) and were involved in the dedication of the second Temple. We know a few other things about this relatively obscure man. He seems to have been multi-talented musically. Interestingly enough the only specific instrument associated with him in his writings are the bronze cymbals (I Chronicles 15:19).

The Ark of God was revered and untouchable; to be near this sacred chest was to be in the very presence of God. He directed a choir consisting of 288 musicians and during the dedication service for Solomon's Temple he led a trumpet corps consisting of 120 priests.

- He had the gift of prophecy according to I Chronicles 25:1-2.
- He helped David collect and edit many of the Psalms.
- He personally wrote Psalm 50 and Psalms 73-83.

What can we learn from such a man as this?

- His service to God was entirely in support of others.
- He was faithful and true to God.
- He does not seem to have worried about personal advancement or glory.

It has been said the hardest instrument of all to play is second fiddle. Asaph was never number one!
He willingly applied his organizational and management talents for the glory of God. He never sought glory for himself! He loyally served two kings who were very different men. David had been raised as a shepherd and had experienced poverty and trials.

Is it difficult for you to "play second fiddle?"

Do you know someone who serves without seeking glory or credit? Encourage that person!

Often people who are not "well-known" have a very lasting impact for Christ!

Solomon was a very good administrator. Israel continued strong and outwardly prosperous during his rule. The people never had such a good life as during the reigns of both David and Solomon, even though taxes continued to rise, which produced dissatisfaction by the close of Solomon's rule. Religiously Solomon brought the disgrace of God upon himself. He had started well. Divine approval had been shown by Jehovah's promise of wisdom, riches, and honor. Solomon did not remain faithful to his early religious commitments. He compromised the convictions he had expressed in his prayer at the temple dedication. When he experienced this spiritual decline himself, his country was influenced as well.

A principal reason for this depressing development is found in Solomon's international affairs and the resulting effect upon him. He permitted the thinking and customs of other nations to influence his decisions and manner of living. This situation developed especially as a result of his marriages to foreign women. At the start these marriages, as we have observed, were symbolic of the establishment of foreign alliances. However, they became far more for Solomon; his wives "*turned away his head from his God.*" The extent of his defection is indicated by the notice he built "*a high place*" to "*Chemosh the detestable God of the Moabites,*" and to "*Molech the detestable God of the Ammonites,*" and apparently also to the false gods of "*all his foreign wives*" (I Kings 11:7-8).

It is not clear at what point in Solomon's reign this defection began to show itself. No signs of it are evident at the completion of the Temple, 11 years after his coronation. The defection from worship of Jehovah may have come gradually after the midpoint of his reign, when the influence of the foreign wives had had time to work.

Commendably, however, prior to his death Solomon seems to have realized what had happened and turned back to God, as is evidenced in his final book, Ecclesiastes, where he concludes that the "*whole duty of man*" is to "*fear God and keep his commandments*" (12:13).

The punishment; I Kings 11:9-43
Early in Solomon's reign God warned him against such defection. His failure in this area brought an evitable judgment; God told him most of his kingdom would not be ruled by his son. In the latter years of his reign God's punishment came through three men.

- **Jeroboam; I Kings 11:26-40**
- The first was Jeroboam, he became the first King of the northern kingdom of Israel. We will discuss him later.
- **Hadad of Edom; I Kings 11:14-22**
- This man reduced Solomon's control over the empire in the south. He was the sole survivor of the royal family of Edom. Joab had slaughter them during David's reign.
- **Rezon of Damascus; I Kings 11:23-25**
- His power was in the region of Damascus. Rezon also had escaped an attack by Joab during the reign of David. Rezon's main success was his ability to control Damascus and harass others in the area. It may be the control by Solomon in both Edom and the Damascus region was all but lost by the time of his death.

Solomon the king; Closing thoughts
Solomon's reigned for 40 years as had his father before him. It was a rule of prosperity and peace; a time of genuine accomplishment. As a result of extensive building, trading and international relations, Israel became known throughout the entire Near East. Beside this, the arts, particularly music and literature were advanced. The true worship of God at the Temple assumed a form of dignity in keeping with the regulations of the Mosaic Law. All of this can be said to Solomon's credit. He stands as one of Israel's most significant rulers.

Solomon failed to meet God's standard. He did not remain faithful to God's will. Consequently, this great potential for Israel was not realized; instead there came a gradual diminishing of world power in Solomon's last years. In fact, he had to be informed before his death only a small part of his realm would be passed on to his son.

Ahijah the prophet — I Kings 11, 14

Ahijah was from the town of Shiloh. Several events are described regarding him and his contact with Jeroboam. There are clues he ministered during the reign of Solomon and may have had contact with him.

His work

Ahijah's first contact with Jeroboam, the future king of the Northern Kingdom, came during the reign of Solomon. At the time Jeroboam was serving as manager of a work project Solomon was carrying on in the city. Ahijah found Jeroboam one day when Solomon was away from the city. The prophet took a new garment and tore it into 12 parts. He took 10 of the parts and gave them to Jeroboam with the words, *"Take ten pieces for yourself, for this is what the LORD, the God of Israel, says: See, I am going to tear the kingdom out of Solomon's hand and give you ten tribes."*

He told Jeroboam the full kingdom would not be taken from Solomon because of God's promise to David. He also told him if he would follow God, God would give him a lasting household as He had promised David.

The second main episode involving Ahijah concerned a message of rejection he gave to Jeroboam toward the close of Jeroboam's reign. Over 22 years has passed since Ahijah's first encounter with Jeroboam. This situation involved a time when Jeroboam was worried about his son Abijah who was ill. He told his wife to go to Ahijah and ask if the boy would get well. By this time the prophet was an old man and could not see.

Jeroboam told his wife to disguise herself so Ahijah would not recognize who she was. God, however, revealed to Ahijah who was coming. Therefore, Ahijah greeted her as the wife of Jeroboam.

Giving God's message to her, he spoke of the evil ways Jeroboam had followed since becoming King, saying God would bring evil on him as a result. Then he said when Jeroboam's wife returned to her home city the child would die. He further warned her God would raise up a king to destroy and replace Jeroboam's line. Jeroboam's wife returned to the capital city and as she approached the palace the child died.

Ahijah's work both times was the same; he served as a prophet in bringing God's message. In contrast to the first time, however, the second message was a very unhappy one. In the first instance, he announced that Jeroboam would reign, but now he indicated his reign would be taken away and his entire house destroyed by a succeeding king.

Spiritual status

The great spiritual status of Ahijah is evidenced by the importance of the messages God entrusted to him. The first message really involved two significant facts regarding the nation of Israel.

- First, Solomon's family was rejected as the continuing line to rule the entire country.
- Second, Jeroboam was God's selection to be the first king of the new northern division.

Courage

Both messages given by Ahijah show he was a man of courage. When he gave the first message, he must have recognized Solomon would be very angry. The same must be said regarding his second message. This message was displeasing to Jeroboam and he faced the fact Jeroboam may have wanted to take his life.

Command of respect

As was true of both Gad and Nathan, Ahijah commanded respect when he spoke. He did the first time in speaking to Jeroboam directly. This is not evidenced so much in that Jeroboam received his message, but that Solomon was impressed. Solomon did not challenge Ahijah, nor did he disbelieve what Ahijah said.

Why do you think Jeroboam tried to question the prophet anonymously?

Why do we try to "fool" God when we know it's not possible?

How can you avoid calling on God only when you are afraid or in great need?

The Rebellion of Jeroboam (North) — I Kings 11:9-25

Because of Solomon's sin, it is remarkable God showed great grace toward him.

- First, he was allowed to live out his days as the ruler of a United Kingdom.
- Second, his son would be permitted to rule over part of the kingdom instead of losing it all. This promise of grace was God's way of honoring the Davidic Covenant of II Samuel 7.

It is fascinating to watch God preparing for the day the kingdom would be divided long before Solomon's spiritual defection! For example, Hadad the Edomite fled to Egypt (I Kings 11) and Rezon of Syria rose to power even before David died. Jeroboam's rebellion was the climax of a very long and extensive series of events in Israel's history.

Jeroboam's tribe, Ephraim, was a very proud tribe.

Joshua, the conqueror of Canaan, was an Ephraimite. The tabernacle was first located at Shiloh within their tribal boundaries; and, one of the very first places where Abram built an altar in the Promised Land was at Bethel, within their territory. It was apparently for such reasons as these the Ephraimites reproached Joshua about the small size of their territorial allotment: *"Why have you given us only one allotment and one portion for an inheritance? We are a numerous people and the LORD has blessed us abundantly."* (Josh. 17:14).

With a kind answer Gideon avoided a civil war. But the Ephraimites did not fare so well later, when they denounced Jephthah of Gilead for not calling them to lead the battle against Ammon. A rugged frontiersman of illegitimate birth, Jephthah challenged their intolerable pride and cut off their retreat across Jordan by demanding the "Shibboleth" password and slaughtering 42,000 of them in the bloodiest civil strife in centuries. Thus subdued, the Ephraimites submitted to the Philistine conquest and to the reign of Saul of Benjamin and David of Judah.

But in the process of time the pride of Ephraim raised its head again. The colossal burdens of taxation and forced labor which Solomon imposed on all the tribes for building programs, which were centered largely in Jerusalem (I Kings 9:15), proved too much for Ephraim and the other northern tribes. Although they were awed by the wisdom and glory of Solomon, smoldering resentment was present according to their later complaint to King Rehoboam: *"Your father put a heavy yoke on us."*

Jeroboam's Plot

It was against this background that Jeroboam came to the lead. Ambitious and highly competent, he was soon placed by Solomon over the Ephraimite work crews which labored in Jerusalem. In consultation with his fellow workers, an assassination plot was hatched, and Jeroboam went back to Ephraim to rally support. Ahijah the Shilonite met him on the way and confronted him with God's proposal. If he would stop this murderous plot and honor the Davidic kings and the priests in Jerusalem, God would give him 10 tribes and a perpetual dynasty in the North. This was a magnificent and gracious offer, but Jeroboam, like Ahaz two centuries later (Isaiah 7:11-12), was not content with God's plan and provision. And this brought about his ultimate ruin. As it turned out, his plot was a failure and he barely escaped with his life and fled to Egypt.

Why is it pointless to try to oppose something that is ordained by God?

In what relationship do you need to resist using force and intimidation?

What made Jeroboam a "natural" for leading the protest and then the rebellion?

How has God prepared you for His service?

Rehoboam (South) — I Kings 12, 14; 2 Chronicles 10-12

It is probable Rehoboam's mother was a worshipper of the heathen deity Molech, since she was an Ammonitess (I Kings 14:21; cf. 11:7). Not only so, but she had to compete with 700 other "wives" for the affections of an apostate king (I Kings 11:3). This was the "home life" and the "spiritual environment" in which Rehoboam grew to manhood. Is it any wonder, then "*He did evil because he had not set his heart on seeking the LORD.*"? (2 Chron. 12:14)

Immediately after he assumed his responsibilities as the king, Rehoboam revealed his total incompetence for this high office. He rejected the wise counsel of the older men who had served his father concerning the demands of the northern tribes. He then followed the proud and immature ideas of "*the young men who had grown up with him and were serving him.*" (I Kings 12:8).

The result was open rebellion and a permanent split in the kingdom, exactly as God had prophesied through Ahijah (I Kings 12:15; 11:30-35). Barely escaping from Shechem with his life, Rehoboam planned to involve Judah and Benjamin in great civil war which was avoided only because God intervened. Speaking to the king through Shemaiah the prophet, the Lord explained the split in the kingdom was neither a chance occurrence, nor a mere human scheme, nor was it accomplished by Satan's power – *"This is what the LORD says: 'Do not go up to fight against your brothers, the Israelites. Go home, every one of you, for this is my doing.'"* (I Kings 12:24).

Not until the nation experiences its great renewal will God re-unite the two kingdoms into one (Ezek. 37:15-23).

Somewhat humbled by this information, Rehoboam followed Jehovah for about three years. It was at this time the remnant of true believers in the northern tribes began to follow the priests and Levites in the permanent abandonment of their homes and move to Jerusalem because of Jeroboam's religious revolution (II Chron. 11:13-15; 13:9).

This arrival of spiritually-minded Israelites "*strengthened the kingdom of Judah and supported Rehoboam son of Solomon three years, walking in the ways of David and Solomon during this time.*" (II Chron. 11:17) They were able to modify God's otherwise negative evaluation of his entire reign: "*in Judah there were good things found*" (II Chron. 12:12). In a vain and ridiculous attempt to match the glory of Solomon, Rehoboam took 18 wives (including granddaughters of Jesse, David, and Absalom) and 60 concubines, and fathered 88 children (II Chron. 11:18-23).

Proud of his harem, building projects, and great prosperity, Rehoboam abandoned the Lord. This time God's instrument of chastening and humiliation was Shishak, king of Egypt, equipped with 1,200 chariots, 60,000 horsemen, and countless soldiers (II Chron. 12: 14).

Because of timely repentance caused by the preaching of Shemaiah the prophet (I Chron. 12:5; I Kings 12:22), Rehoboam and the kingdom were spared the tragedy of total defeat and subjugation at the hands of the Egyptians.

See how much the situation had changed since the early days of Solomon when the pharaoh was happy to give his daughter to the king of Israel!

Stripping the temple of all its golden vessels and ornaments symbolized the fact the glory had already begun to depart.

The continuance of the southern kingdom for 300 years is a stunning tribute to the longsuffering of God! What older, more mature Christians do you have access to when you need advice?

"The Man of God" I Kings 13

This "man of God" was sent north from Judah to the false altar which Jeroboam had built at Bethel. King Jeroboam was there himself on the day the prophet arrived. The prophet did not hesitate because of the monarch's presence but prophesied against the altar, *"Oh altar, altar, this is what the Lord says: behold, a child shall be born under the house of David, Josiah by name; and upon you shall he offer the priests of the high places that burn incense upon them and men's bones shall be burnt upon you"* (13:2). Jeroboam, standing by the altar, was infuriated at these words and stretched out his hand toward the prophet. He directed those nearby to "*lay hold on him.*" At that, Jeroboam's hand was "*dried up, so that he could not pull it in again to him*" (13:4) and the altar was broken so the ashes poured out, keeping further the words of the man of God.

With these two supernatural events having taken place, Jeroboam became completely changed in attitude and asked the prophet's help in respect to his hand. "*Then the king said to the man of God, 'Intercede with the LORD your God and pray for me that my hand may be restored.' So the man of God interceded with the LORD, and the king's hand was restored and became as it was before.*" The king asked the "man of God" to come to his palace for a meal. The man of God replied, *"If you will give me half of your house, I will not go with you neither will I eat bread nor drink water in this place"* (13:8). He said God had commanded him to return immediately to Judah. He started his return.

Until this point the prophet had acted very well, but now there came a change. An "*old prophet in Bethel*" had learned of his visit and followed him. He caught up with the younger man as he was resting under a tree. The old prophet told him he also was a prophet and he was instructed by God to bring the young man to his home. He lied, but the younger man did not know this. In disobedience to the word of God the younger man returned to Bethel. Then as the two sat eating together the old prophet rebuked the young man for returning and told him, when he left and started home, he would be killed (13:22). The young man laughed, but as he was on his way a lion met him and killed him and his body was left by the roadside where later the old prophet found it and gave it an appropriate burial.

Indication of his spiritual maturity is the fact God gave a prediction and worked a miracle through him. The prediction was a remarkable one that Josiah (who lived approximately 300 years later) would one day offer the bones of the priests of the altar upon that very altar. He even gave Josiah's name, making this one of the more remarkable predictions in Scripture. He also stated the altar would be broken and its ashes poured out and this happened even while he was there. The miracle was completed with the restoration of Jeroboam's hand. When the prophet prayed, the hand was restored.

It should also be observed in the young man's favor at first, he obeyed God and began returning home without eating or drinking in the town of Bethel. There would have been an attraction in being invited to dine with the King. The man must be credited for having refused.

The one factor to the man's discredit was his disobedience of God after he started home. When the old prophet in Bethel caught up with him and told him the lie, the young man was too easily convinced and went directly against God's instruction. This indicates he did not realize God never contradicts Himself. The old prophet's deception was wrong, but it gave no excuse for the younger man to do as he did. The result of the disobedience was the punishment of being killed.

This took real courage, but courage coupled with obedience is what God is seeking.

How do we know God's clear instructions are not meant to be corrected or amended?

Why is it easier to resist temptation that comes from an enemy than from a friend?

Jeroboam the son of Nebat (North) — I Kings 12-14

Jeroboam was ingenious and industrious; he used the skills he had developed under Solomon. He established two capitals: in the south, Shechem, *near* the border of Ephraim and Manasseh near Mount Ebal and Mount Gerizim where Joshua had first dedicated the Promised Land to God. He also established Penuel across the Jordan.

Jeroboam's New Religion

The greatest challenge which confronted Jeroboam was Jewish faith was centered in Jerusalem. Three times a year the nation went to Jerusalem to worship. There the Levites would educate the people concerning the significance of the sacrifices, they would also take occasion to refer to Rehoboam as the legitimate Davidic king who reigned in Jerusalem. Before long, the people from northern tribes could easily begin to draw certain conclusions concerning Jeroboam, he was both illegal and unnecessary.

Jeroboam adopted measures to bring these influences to an end. He revolutionized the religion of Israel by changing (1) the symbols of religion, (2) the centers of worship, (3) the priesthood, and (4) the religious calendar.

First, he changed the symbols of Israel's religion. In the place of cherubim above the ark, Jeroboam substituted two golden calves. Calves or bulls were sacred to the Egyptians, and during his stay in Egypt Jeroboam had become captivated by the popularity of this cult. He was able to find a precedent for using a golden calf; Aaron had used a calf as a symbol of Jehovah.

Jeroboam was determined to satisfy the desire of the average Israelite for a spectacular symbol of God. He assured the people these calves were historical symbols intended only to point to Jehovah. This was nothing new but was an extension of the form of Israel's wilderness religion.

Jeroboam assumed the position of high priest himself, and by a mixture of popular pagan idolatry with the name Jehovah, created a compromise religion more dangerous for the nation than out-and-out paganism. Twenty-one times after this, Old Testament writers refer to Jeroboam as the one who "***made Israel to sin.***"

Next, Jeroboam created two new worship centers at Bethel and Dan. These were excellent choices, for Bethel had been Jacob's worship center where Jehovah had spoken to him twice. Dan was also significant because Jonathan, a grandson of Moses, had a worship center and a dynasty of priests for the tribe of Dan during years the tabernacle was at Shiloh. Why bother to go all the way to Jerusalem to worship Jehovah when these God-honored places, newly equipped with Aaron-style calves, were already at hand?

Third, a new religion needed a new priesthood. It would be futile to attempt to persuade Levites to function in such a context, so Jeroboam opened priestly privileges to the highest bidders. Completely disgusted with this drastic departure from divinely revealed tradition, most priests and Levites fled southward to Judah, taking with them the remnant of true believers from the northern tribes and leaving behind a situation of near-total apostasy.

Finally, Jeroboam changed the religious calendar. To have no religious calendar at all would have been as foolish as to have no symbols, worship centers, or priests. A substitute religion has always been Satan's supreme goal. The seventh month, with the Feast of Trumpets, Day of Atonement and Feast of Tabernacles was the climax of the religious year. So, Jeroboam shifted the calendar one month to the eighth month, "*a month of his own choosing.*" The ceremonies were even more spectacular than those in Jerusalem.

What are the pros and cons of finding a more convenient way of doing things?

In our own day religious movements which have the least Biblical truth often have the most elaborate ceremonies and the most impressive worship centers.

Should our own desires and convenience never dictate the terms of our worship of God?

War between Rehoboam (Judah) & Jeroboam (Israel) — 1 Kings 14-15; 2 Chronicles 12-13

Judah's history paralleled Israel's but ran over a century longer. The nation left with Rehoboam, following the secession of the northern tribes, consisted primarily of the tribe of Judah. Rehoboam held basically the same area David did when he was first made king at Hebron. When Ahijah, the prophet, first spoke to Jeroboam concerning the division, he mentioned only one tribe as remaining loyal to Solomon's descendant.

At the time, however, he gave Jeroboam only 10 of the 12 pieces of the torn garment as a symbol of the tribes he would rule, implying another tribe would be added to Judah. Benjamin was the added tribe. Historically, the tribe of Benjamin had always aligned with the northern group, but now came to follow Rehoboam and was soon referred to regularly as part of the southern nation.

Rehoboam probably brought pressure on the leaders to switch loyalty, employing threats and/or attractive bribes. Jerusalem, after all, lay directly on the Benjamite border, and a buffer zone was really needed between Judah and the new northern kingdom.

Rehoboam became king at age 41 and ruled for 17 years. He was an evil king and did not follow the pattern of his grandfather, David.

He was influenced too much by the religious failures of Solomon's latter days. Rehoboam built high places, images and Asherah poles, and he also permitted male prostitutes in the land (1 Kings 14:23-24).

Rehoboam had military encounters with two main enemies, Jeroboam of Israel and Shishak of Egypt. With Jeroboam he was generally successful.

With Egypt he suffered tragic losses as God's punishment for the religious defection.

We are told Rehoboam had frequent struggles with Jeroboam (1 Kings 14:30). There is no indication this was all in violent, open warfare, however. In fact, violent conflict had been directly forbidden by God. When Rehoboam arrived in Jerusalem, he gathered the house of Judah and Benjamin; 180,000 fighting men to make war against Israel and to regain the kingdom. But this word of the LORD came to Shemaiah, the man of God and instructed him: "*Say to Rehoboam son of Solomon king of Judah and to all the Israelites in Judah and Benjamin, 'This is what the LORD says: Do not go up to fight against your brothers. Go home, every one of you, for this is my doing.'" So they obeyed the words of the LORD and turned back from marching against Jeroboam*.

The friction was centered in border disputes, especially involving the Benjamite area. Rehoboam felt he needed Benjamin as a buffer zone, and Jeroboam naturally would have wanted it too. Benjamin seems to have sided with Judah. It makes sense Rehoboam won in these disputes more often than Jeroboam. The victories would have involved military clashes at the border. Rehoboam needed the land and the good will of the people. A logical result of Rehoboam's success in Benjaminite territory is his endeavors in building the defenses of his nation. Rehoboam demonstrated an aggressive spirit in fortifying no less than 15 cities located in Judah and Benjamin.

How were the sins of Jeroboam and Rehoboam similar although they were enemies?

How can you work toward consulting God first when you face difficulties before you assess your own options?

Abijah (Abijam) 1 Kings 14-15; 2 Chronicles 12-13
2nd King of Judah

The author of Kings dismisses Abijah with very few words, none of them encouraging.

But in II Chronicles 13 we learn of a great victory God gave to him against Jeroboam of Israel. The victory was unique, not only because of the vast number of Israelites killed (500,000), but also because of the special appeal he made to the northern enemy and their deceitful king (II Chron. 13:4-12).

With surprising skill and bitter sarcasm, Abijah exposed the rottenness of Jeroboam's administration which was built upon *"worthless scoundrels"* (II Chron. 13:7), and the irrationality of his man-made religion, propped up by "*the golden calves which Jeroboam made you for gods*" (II Chron. 13:8) with the sacred offices being staffed by any non-Levite who could pay the price Jeroboam asked: "*But didn't you drive out the priests of the LORD, the sons of Aaron, and the Levites, and make priests of your own as the peoples of other lands do? Whoever comes to consecrate himself with a young bull and seven rams may become a priest of what are not gods.*" (II Chron. 13:9)

In contrast to this empty fabrication, Abijah said we Judeans have the true God, Jehovah. We have legitimate Aaronic priests who offer genuine atoning sacrifices. We have the original table of showbread and the golden candlestick.

These pointed reminders of happier days and God's ways must have stung the conscience of many northerners!

Furthermore, the bold young king declared we have the ultimate weapon. His superb challenging speech ended with a nostalgic appeal: "*God is with us; he is our leader. His priests with their trumpets will sound the battle cry against you. Men of Israel, do not fight against the LORD, the God of your fathers, for you will not succeed.*" 2 Chronicles 13:12

But even while he pretended to listen at this "summit meeting" discourse, Jeroboam was plotting the destruction of his enemies by means of an ambush. God, however, had the final word; for through the passionate prayers of godly Judeans and their Jericho- like trumpet blasts and expectant shouts, He brought an unparalleled destruction to Jeroboam's army from which he never recovered (II Chron. 13:20).

Jeroboam did not regain power during the time of Abijah. And the LORD struck him down and he died.

We could conclude from all this Abijam, or Abijah as the Chronicler calls him, was one of the greatest of the southern kings.

However, the last verses of this chapter tend to modify our praise and to help us recognize Abijam was capable, like his father, of occasional acts of faith in a life of general disobedience to the revealed will of God.

What false gods do some religious leaders offer to people nowadays?

What does it mean to rely on the Lord when the opposition is greater than your abilities or resources?

In what ways does praying change a situation or a person?

How does our allegiance to the Lord affect the outcome of our life's battles and struggles?

Asa — 1 Kings 15; 2 Chronicles 14-15

3rd King of Judah

Rehoboam and Abijah, two wicked but occasionally obedient kings, were followed by Asa and Jehoshaphat, two righteous but occasionally disobedient kings. One great problem, shared by the first three southern kings, was Maacah, the granddaughter of the self-centered and ambitious Absalom.

She was Rehoboam's wife, Abijah's mother, and the "Queen Dowager" who controlled the power in the early days of Asa's kingship. Asa's own mother had died when he was a child.

The reader is surprised at the boldness of young Asa in deposing Maacah; "*He even deposed his grandmother Maacah from her position as queen mother, because she had made a repulsive Asherah pole. Asa cut the pole down and burned it in the Kidron Valley.*" (I Kings 15:13).

He not only cut down her Asherah pole; but burned it in the Kidron valley!

This was part of a great revival, which probably occurred during the Feast of Tabernacles, in Asa's fifteenth year. These sweeping changes were significant for their intensity and zeal. Not only did Judah renew their covenant promises "*with a loud voice and with shouting and with trumpets and with cornets,*" but they determined to kill any man or woman who refused to be revived!

Two important points must be observed here.

In the first place, Israel was the only nation in history which God ruled through royal **and** priestly mediators. Therefore, "church and state" were almost always a unity, and a religious offense was also a crime against the state!

The worship of any other god was to be dealt with by public execution (Exod. 22:20); even close relatives were responsible for exposing the offender and taking the leading part in his execution (Deut. 13:6-11).

Secondly, the very fact people who did not worship Jehovah were executed proves regeneration was not the condition for "revival" in ancient Israel. Those who conformed to the religious regulations of the nation and avoided the worship of other deities were accepted as legitimate citizens of the theocracy and were exempt from the penalties of the law. In the New Testament times false worship is never dealt with by physical punishment (I Cor. 5:12-13), and "revival" can only occur in the hearts of regenerated people.

Having made this distinction, we must also recognize God's desire for Israel was always individual regeneration first (Ezek. 36:27).

Thus, Isaiah (1:10-20), Micah (6:6-8), and Hosea (6:6) all denounced outward conformity to ceremonial requirements without a corresponding revival of the heart.

Examine yourselves to see whether you are in the faith; test yourselves. Do you not realize that Christ Jesus is in you– unless, of course, you fail the test? 2 Corinthians 13:5

What sinful practices and idols do Christians often fail to remove from their lives?

What standard can you use to determine whether any idols, loyalties that take God's place, exist in your life today?

Examine yourself!

Nadab and Baasha — I Kings 15:25-16:7

Nadab the 2nd King of the Northern Kingdom

He ruled for two years and was assassinated by one of the soldiers of his military. Jeroboam's lifestyle and example lived on in his son and successor. Nadab followed his father's evil example. The constantly recurring phrase, "*made Israel to sin,*" displays stubbornness in the hateful idolatries of Jeroboam's reign.

The second King of Israel occupies only a brief space in the records of Scripture. He and all Israel began a siege against Gibbethon which was probably a Philistine garrison.

Nadab was plotted against and assassinated by Baasha. The death of Nadab completed the destruction of the family of Jeroboam, as foretold by Ahijah (1 Kings 14).

Such a murder was to be common throughout the entire history of the Northern Kingdom, which was one of revolution and counter-revolution.

Baasha — the 3rd King of the Northern Kingdom

2nd Dynasty

Apart from his attack on Judah and its failure, we know little of Baasha who reigned 24 years in Israel. Scripture tells us he was of common birth (1 Kings 16:2) and he came from an obscure tribe, undistinguished in its history. He built a type of "Berlin Wall" against Asa to prevent anyone from leaving or entering the territory of Judah (1 Kings 15:16-17). He was finally distracted from his opposition to Judah by an alliance between Asa and Syria (1 Kings 15:18-21). He murdered Nadab, Northern Israel's second king, and then killed all the royal family (1 Kings 15:27, 29).

One writer comments, "Baasha is the first of many military chiefs who by violence or assassination seized upon the throne of Israel." The constant succession of short-lived dynasties is in striking contrast to the unchanged royalty of the house of David in the south. True to his name which means "wicked," Baasha was an extremely immoral king, who continued in the sins which he used to destroy the house of Jeroboam.

To make his throne more secure, he massacred all the relatives of his predecessor and by his cruel actions fulfilled the prophecy made against Jeroboam (1 Kings 14:1).

Baasha carried on a continued warfare against Asa, King of Judah. He was prevented by Ben-Hadad, King of Syria, from building the town of Ramah as a buffer between the north and the south. Baasha then sent a bribe, hoping to gain the help of the Syrian king, but Ben-Hadad continued to fight against Baasha and drove him back to his capital city. Asa in the south then marched on Ramah, the new buffer city and demolished it.

The prophet Jehu warned Baasha because of his sinful reign he would suffer the same fate as Jeroboam. (2 Kings 9:9). Judgment came in the form of total and utter destruction as the complete family of Baasha was destroyed.

Why do you think the writer makes a point to tell the reader Baasha's house was going to come to the same end as Jeroboam's?

Evil works which accomplish God's purpose are still sin!

The end does not justify the means!

***The LORD's curse is on the house of the wicked, but he blesses the home of the righteous.* Proverbs 3:33**

Elah & Zimri — 1 Kings 16

Elah: 4th King of the Northern Kingdom

This son of Baasha was a useless, bungling and worthless person. The biblical writer believed a few lines were more than enough to record the evil history of this drunken king known as Elah. He was Israel's fourth king and he reigned for two years.

His reign was far from happy; his unlimited self-indulgence brought about his fall, even as it did in the case of another royal drunkard, Belshazzar.

This son of Baasha was as bad a king as he was a debauched drunkard. The Scripture says while he was "*drinking himself drunk,*" he was conspired against and killed by Zimri.
Zimri was one of the military commanders of Israel's army. This assassination fulfilled the prophecy given earlier about the extermination of the house of Baasha.

One writer says this dynasty had its origin in murder and it ended in murder. The government had no stability! These continued revolutions illustrate the truth, "they who live by the sword shall die by the sword."

The short-lived reign of Elah also reminds us of the observation recorded in Proverbs, ***"As the whirlwind passes, so the wicked is no more."*** **Proverbs 10:25**

When Zimri attacked Elah, the king was so drunk he never knew what was happening to him.

Writing about the curse of drunkenness Solomon says, ***"In the end it bites like a snake and poisons like a viper."*** **(Proverbs 23:32).**

Zimri, 5th King of the Northern Kingdom 3rd Dynasty

He was captain of the chariots under Elah. Zimri used his position to plot against the king and was therefore a traitor and a usurper. The biblical record makes special mention of the treason he committed. A proverb has it, "The King is not King by reigning, but by ruling according to law." Zimri recognized no law. A kingdom founded on treason and murder cannot possibly stand.

Zimri assumed the rule of Israel after his murder of Elah. This crime and conspiracy lacked the support of the people, but as soon as the news of the events reached Gibbethon, the army raised Omri to the throne. In one short week this wicked king destroyed the house of Baasha. The phrase, "*sins which he sinned,*" covers Zimri's entire life, not merely his seven-day reign.

Commenting on the constantly recurring phrase, "*walking in the way of Jeroboam,*" one writer observes this indicates the historian's sense of the curse lying on the whole kingdom for its idolatry. Zimri did not renounce Israel's idolatry and as a result he was doomed to failure. He tried to hide his conspiracy with a righteous zeal in fulfilling the prophecy of Jehu. After the executions he threw off this religious pretense.

In despair, Zimri set fire to his palace and died in the flames which he, himself, had kindled. The humiliating end of Zimri's one-week reign remained as a blot even on the bloodstained record of the northern kingdom. The name of Zimri passed into a proverb signifying unusual treachery.

Why did kings after Jeroboam feel that the "sin of Jeroboam" would be a good practice?

What "idols" do some of today's world rulers prefer that we serve rather than the living God?

Why does God take it so seriously when a person leads others into sin?

Omri

6th King of the Northern Kingdom

1 Kings 16

4th Dynasty

Omri was founder of the fourth dynasty in the Kingdom of Israel. Jeroboam and Baasha were founders of the first two dynasties, but they were each followed by sons who reigned only two years. The third dynasty hardly deserves the title, for it only lasted a week! Zimri, who had murdered Baasha's son, died in a siege seven days later when Omri, captain of the army, attacked him in the capital city of Tirzah. Within five years, Omri crushed a rival to the throne (Tibni) and greatly strengthened the kingdom by purchasing a strategic hill called Samaria and building a new, well-fortified capital there. This move was so important from an international standpoint that for over 100 years the Assyrians called Israel "the land of Omri."

Omri's other claim to fame was the finalizing of an alliance with Phoenicia through the marriage of his son Ahab to Jezebel, daughter of Ethbaal, King of the Sidonians. To make Jezebel feel at home, a temple was erected for Baal in Samaria. This was an act officially abandoning the compromise calf-cult of Jeroboam. Possibly an appeal was made to the example of Solomon who had encouraged his foreign wives by erecting pagan shrines for them around Jerusalem (I Kings 11:7).

With Omri, the political situation in Israel became stabilized again. Omri represented the third ruling family within a short span of three years. The civil war between Omri and Tibni had been disturbing and costly to the nation, but with this settled Omri began a dynasty that lasted three generations.

This calming came none too soon because the Armenian (Syrian) state in the North, with its capital at Damascus was a rapidly growing power. In addition to the potential threat of Damascus a greater danger was growing further in the East. Assyria, which had been striving to become a world power for a few decades, was now breaking out and taking control of the region.

Omri was a strong ruler. He was easily the most capable and aggressive king Israel had yet known. There is a great testimony of this provided by an unexpected source. Assyrian rulers, living over a century later still referred to Israel as the land of Omri.

Even though the biblical record says very little about him, his power and strength must have been remarkable to impress the rulers of this strong state to the east.

There are three major events in his reign that are worthy of comment.

The first is the establishment of the new capital at Samaria. After the defeat of his rival, Tibni, he purchased a new site, the hill of Samaria, and there he built an entirely new city. A decisive move of this kind tells us he was a man of vision and courage. The city became such a strong site that the kingdom took its name later from that capital city and became the country of Samaria.

A second accomplishment is known to us from archaeology and the Moabite stone. This was a Memorial Stone found near the Arnon River in 1898. Part of the text tells us "Omri, King of Israel," had conquered the Kingdom of Moab.

The third accomplishment of Omri is perhaps the one with the most lasting effect on his people and the people of the region of Samaria. He married his son, Ahab, to the Phoenician Princess, Jezebel. This was a political alliance which would have had benefits for both participants.

The lasting effect of the alliance and the marriage came when Jezebel brought her Baal worship with her into Israel.

Is this an example of how a bad marriage can bring trouble for generations?

Ahab — 1 Kings16, 18, 20-22; 2 Chronicles 18

7th King of the Northern Kingdom

His name means "my brother." We know nothing of his birth place. However, he was the king of Israel and lived in the central portion of the land.

Ahab is one of the most interesting and well-known characters in the Old Testament. His wife is even more widely known; her name was Jezebel. Diplomatically and politically he was one of the most successful kings of the northern kingdom. As the seventh king he was the most wicked king to rule up to that time.

In an attempt to establish a political alliance, he married the daughter of the Phoenician king. She was beautiful, wicked and a worshiper of Baal.

In a military way and administratively Ahab was able to expand the economic influence of Israel to a great extent. He defeated the Syrians in several battles and made the country of Moab pay tribute to his kingdom. He even created a defensive alliance with the southern kingdom of Judah.

God spoke often to Ahab, but He was ignored.

There was a three-year drought followed by the slaughter of 450 prophets of Baal at the hand of Elijah. Soon another disaster loomed over the horizon in the person of Ben-Hadad, King of Syria (I Kings 20:1), who laid siege to Samaria. Realizing he had overextended his supply lines, Benhadad tried to make a bargain with Ahab: "*Your silver and gold are mine, and the best of your wives and children are mine*" (I Kings 20:3).

When Ahab quickly accepted these terms, including the loss of Jezebel, Ben-Hadad demanded even more. To Ben-Hadad's next ridiculous demands, Ahab replied with calm dignity, "*One who puts on his armor should not boast like one who takes it off.*" (I Kings 20:11).

Despite his spiritual blindness, Ahab remained king of Israel. God honored him by speaking encouraging words to him through a prophet on different three occasions.

Ahab made the fatal mistake of assuming, in the hour of Ben-Hadad's humiliation, that he, not Jehovah, could dictate the terms. Instead of executing God's enemy, Ahab, like Saul before him (I Sam. 15:9), decided to spare the captive king and accomplish his own purposes through him. Apparently, he wanted a strong kingdom in Damascus to serve as a buffer between Israel and Assyria instead of trusting Jehovah to be his wall of defense (Isa. 26:1).

Ahab's life is seen more by the people he was involved with than by his own actions.

- Ahab and Elijah
- Ahab and Jezebel
- Ahab and Ben-Hadad, the king of Syria
- Ahab and Naboth
- Ahab and Jehoshaphat
- Ahab and Micaiah

As we look at the list of these people Ahab encountered, there are several things worth noting.

He was in constant conflict with God and chose to act in opposition to God's prophets and servants. He was even willing to put them to death to eliminate opposition to his power.

He allowed Jezebel to influence his life in such a way he turned from any loyalty he had to Jehovah and followed his Phoenician wife as she led him and the entire nation into worshipping Baal and Asherah.

He was willing to lie and steal and even murder in order to obtain his own goals.

He was willing to make political deals with anyone he felt would help him realize his political and economic goals.

Jezebel 1 Kings 16, 20-22; 2 Kings 9, 10

She was the daughter of Ethbaal, king of the Phoenicians. These people were one the great maritime people of the ancient world, but they were idolaters who regarded Jehovah as only a local deity, "the god of the land." Their gods were Baal and Ashtoreth or Astarte.

Ahab was captivated by Jezebel and "*took her to wife, and went and served Baal and worshipped him*." All the other sins of Ahab were insignificant compared with his marriage with Jezebel and the serving of Baal. Jezebel was not an ordinary woman and she attracted immediate attention. While the Bible does not analyze or even portray her character; it simply sets forth the events in which she played a prominent part. As we read between the lines, we see her as a woman with great force of intellect and will. Aggressive and relentless, this strong-minded woman carried out her evil schemes. She used all her gifts for the expansion of evil; her misdirected talents became a curse.

She Was a Dominating Wife
Ahab was like a puppet in the hands of his overpowering wife. Because he was weak, Jezebel found it easy to achieve her evil purposes. How could worthless and spineless Ahab withstand the evil scheming of his unscrupulous partner? He couldn't and didn't!

Her children continued in the sin in which they grew up.

Jezebel's evil influence was continued in her daughter Athaliah, who married Jehoram of Judea. Her evil character reappears in her eldest son, Ahaziah, who, like his idolatrous mother, was a worshipper of Baal. It was her second son, Joram (also called Jehoram), who would face Jehu who was called by God to destroy the dynasty of Ahab. Jehu told Joram there would be no peace in Israel, "*How can there be peace," Jehu replied, "as long as all the idolatry and witchcraft of your mother Jezebel abound?"* (II Kings 9:22).

She Was a Dangerous Schemer
The tragedy of Naboth and his vineyard reveals what a loathsome woman Jezebel was. Life was cheap to such a person. Her father, Ethbaal, murdered his predecessor. Brought up in a home political and economic plotting what else could we expect from her? Jezebel was prepared to murder as she moved toward any sought-after objective. Her actions in relationship to Naboath and his vineyard display this.

King Ahab knew of this fruitful vineyard and inquired as to its owner. Learning it belonged to Naboth, Ahab called him to the palace and offered to buy the vineyard. But it was not for sale. It had belonged to Naboth's forefathers and had become precious to Naboth, and as an Israelite Ahab understood his desire to retain it. He was upset he could not have what he wanted. Like a child, he pouted and in depression took to his bed and refused food. When Jezebel discovered what had happened, she revealed herself as a strong and evil woman. She "comforted" Ahab by saying. *"Is this how you act as king over Israel? Get up and eat! Cheer up. I'll get you the vineyard of Naboth the Jezreelite."*

Jezebel ordered an assembly of the people of Jezreel to try the godly Naboth for blasphemies against God and the king. Naboth was arrested, tried, and condemned on the testimony of false witnesses secured by Jezebel. Found guilty, Naboth was stoned and Ahab took possession of the much-coveted vineyard.

Have you ever known a girl named Jezebel? Why?

How do you react when you fail to "get you way"?

How can you turn an unfulfilled desire into an occasion for humility before God rather than a cause of bitterness?

Baal had no follower more dedicated than Jezebel. No one could match her zeal for the worship of Ashtoreth, the famous goddess of the Zidonians. She was enthusiastic and generous in her care of hundreds of idolatrous priests of Baal.

Not being satisfied with the idol worship of her home country, she began to pursue the conversion of all Israel to Baal worship. Two Baal sanctuaries were built; one in Samaria with its 450 priests, and the other in Jezreel with its 400 priests.

In cruel and ruthless ways Jezebel began to drive out the true followers and prophets of Jehovah from the land. From her father, a high priest of Ashtoreth, she inherited her fanatical religious enthusiasm which inspired her to seek to exterminate the worship of the true and living God. She almost succeeded in the attempt.

As she seemed to be succeeding in her attempt to destroy the worship of the true God, God brought upon the scene a new leader of His prophets, Elijah.

Elijah appeared suddenly before Ahab and predicted three years of extreme drought. Three years later at the end of the period he unexpectedly appeared again and challenged the prophets of Baal to a supreme test of power on the top of Mount Carmel.

In language of unbelievable fearlessness Elijah ridiculed these false prophets with the weakness of their deities, and the contest ended in the complete victory of Jehovah. The people seized the priests of Baal and slaughtered them; Ahab was completely defeated and frightened. Jezebel was not!

The triumphant Elijah, who had stood firm before Ahab still had to deal with Ahab's queen, Jezebel. When she heard from Ahab about the slaughter of all her well-fed priests, she swore an to destroy Elijah "*by tomorrow this time.*"

Elijah was now faced with a truly evil and terrifying opponent! Although he had defied the king and stood out alone against the multitude of the priests and worshippers of Baal, he felt the fury of a murderous woman was more than he could face and fled for his life south across the kingdom of Judah.

He left the arrogant and conceited queen, for the time being, in undisputed possession of the stage.

Baal worship was to plague both the Northern and Southern Kingdoms for many years. Many people abandoned the worship of the true God altogether. God finally judged both kingdoms!

In the end, evil, craft, and godlessness bring their own reward, and the wicked reap what they sow.

Retribution overtook Jezebel when her body was thrown out of the window to be torn and mangled and then eaten by dogs.

How can you pray so you will be ready to represent God's Word even when it is unpopular with those around you?

Why does God take it so seriously when a person leads others into sin?

When we break the commands of God, how can we know whether we have led anyone else into sin?

Who is likely to follow your example?

Ahab wanted a field which would show his power in Jezreel. Such seizures of property were not uncommon. Samuel had earlier warned this would happen if Israel chose a king like the other nations. Naboth's refusal to give up his ancestral property was in the spirit of each family retaining its heritage in Israel. For Naboth the family heritage was worth more than any monetary compensation. Ahab reacted like a spoiled child, but he apparently did not intend to try to overcome Naboth's opposition. Jezebel seeing Ahab's response as weakness exercised royal authority in his name to acquire the property (v. 7). She wrote letters and signed them in the name of the king. In this we see in Israel the corruption of authority had even extended to supervising leaders who had the power to exercise judicial authority.

Naboth appears to have been the head of an influential local family, since he was given a place of honor at a banquet. His refusal to cooperate with the royal request made him a rival to the supporters of the king. It was an offense to curse a ruler of the people (Ex. 22:28), so it was not difficult for dishonest witnesses to bring a sentence of death against Naboth. The ease with which such a plot was accomplished demonstrates the widespread corruption of Ahab's reign. Once Jezebel received word of the execution, she informed her husband the vineyard was now his for the taking.

Ahab and Jezebel could escape legal consequences for murder and commandeering of property by acting through corrupt judges, but they could not escape the judgment of God who gave the land to Israel.

Jehovah commissioned Elijah to confront Ahab in Naboth's vineyard. Ahab had gone from Samaria to Jezreel to inspect his property (21:16, 18b). Elijah was to confront Ahab at the scene of the crime. The judgment pronounced against Ahab, by Elijah, was the dogs would lick up his blood just as they did Naboth's (21:19). The dogs did lick up the blood of Ahab in Samaria, but later when the chariot in which he died was washed (22:38). Later the dogs licked up the blood of his son in the vineyard of Naboth when the body was thrown there.

This human wrong is followed by divine judgment in a double sense. Ahab will die in battle and his dynasty will end with the death of his son. The judgment against Ahab was not that every male will be prevented from ruling, but all his descendants will be exterminated. His death and Jezebel's are described in the terms of Jeroboam and Baasha (21:23-24; 14:10-11, 16:4). The fire of divine judgment will pursue his sons (21:21) until the last of the royal descendants dies.

Ahab's response to Elijah betrays knowledge of his own guilt: *"So you have found me, my enemy!"* (21:20). Elijah is Ahab's enemy because Ahab has violated his responsibility as a king. Elijah describes Ahab's guilt: *"You have sold yourself to do evil"* (v. 20). Greed had led Ahab into the sin of murder and theft, so there is no one who can be compared to him (v. 25). Though Jezebel is an accomplice in his crime, Ahab is still guilty as he agreed with her actions. The end of the narrative offers a surprising turn on the character of Ahab. One would not expect a king described as more abominable in his deeds than the Amorites (vv. 25-26) to have a change of heart at the proclamation of judgment. Ahab shows his repentance by wearing sackcloth, fasting, sleeping in sackcloth, and conducting his affairs with gentleness.

God noticed Ahab's change of heart, *"Have you noticed how Ahab has humbled himself before me? Because he has humbled himself, I will not bring this disaster in his day, but I will bring it on his house in the days of his son."* 1 Kings 21:29

God showed mercy and patience toward Ahab!

There is no one beyond the reach of God's mercy!

Ahab & Micaiah 1 Kings 21, 22

Jehoshaphat, the good king of Judah, had come north to Israel to visit Ahab. While he was there, Ahab, remembering the earlier victory over Ben-Hadad, suggested the two of them go together in an offensive battle to recover the city of Ramoth-gilead and its surrounding area from control by the Aramaeans.

Jehoshaphat was willing but he wanted to inquire as to the will of God. Ahab called his 400 prophets together to ask their counsel, and they agreed he should go ahead with his plans. Jehoshaphat realized the kind of prophets these were and asked, *"Is there not a prophet of the LORD here whom we can inquire of?"* Ahab said there was, namely, Micaiah, but he didn't like him since the man never prophesied good things concerning him. Jehoshaphat insisted Micaiah be called.

When Micaiah first arrived, he pretended to speak as he knew the king desired, but immediately Ahab recognized insincerity on his part and told him to say, "*nothing but that which is true in the name of the LORD"* (22:16). Micaiah then replied, *"I saw all Israel scattered upon the hills, as sheep that have not a shepherd"* (22:17), indicating Ahab would be defeated and killed if he carried out his plan.

He continued by telling Ahab how he knew this was God's true word. He said he saw God in heaven ask the host of heaven, *"Who shall persuade Ahab that he may go up and fall at Ramoth-gilead?"* (22:20). He said further he saw a spirit come and say he would be "*a lying spirit in the mouth of all his prophets.*" God approved this suggestion.

"Then Zedekiah son of Kenaanah went up and slapped Micaiah in the face. 'Which way did the spirit from the LORD go when he went from me to speak to you?' he asked." (22:24). With this statement he indicated his anger at Micaiah's words.

Ahab also was angry and directed Micaiah should be taken away and placed in prison until Ahab came home safely from the battle. To this Micaiah replied, "'*If you ever return safely, the LORD has not spoken through me.' Then he added, 'Mark my words, all you people!'"* (22:28). Ahab and Jehoshaphat then went to battle, with the result that Jehoshaphat was nearly killed, and Ahab did suffer a fatal wound.

When Jehoshaphat asked if there was not another prophet they might look to, Ahab readily knew of Micaiah and of the type of message Micaiah would give. Apparently, the messenger sent for Micaiah also knew of him because the messenger tried to persuade him ahead of time to speak favorably, rather than the way he knew Micaiah normally spoke. We should think of Micaiah, then, as a prophet who was ready to give God's true word to Ahab whenever asked, and who did so on several occasions.

Micaiah was a man of courage.
He had gained his reputation for courage with Ahab for being a prophet who did not speak well concerning him; he continued in this manner in the account here.

Though 400 prophets had spoken a message which was pleasing to the king, and though Micaiah knew Ahab wanted to hear a similar message from him, Micaiah still gave the true contrasting word God desired. Micaiah's courage was enough not only to give the message but also to suffer imprisonment for speaking the truth should this be necessary, as it proved to be.

When have you been asked for an opinion and you knew what answer the questioner wanted to hear?

Why would someone totally ignore God's revealed will and do what he or she wants anyway?

What are the pros and cons of trusting someone who has demonstrated scorn for God's wisdom?

How can we live our lives, so we are not expecting God to "rubber stamp" all our goals and desires?

Ahaziah

1 Kings 22:51-53; 2 Kings 1

8th King of the Northern Kingdom

The brief and inglorious reign of Ahab's son lasted less than two years. He is one of the most mysterious figures in the entire list of kings. He turned his back on the true God. "*And he did evil in the sight of the LORD, and walked in the way of his father, and in the way of his mother, and in the way of Jeroboam the son of Nebat, who made Israel to sin: for he served Baal, and worshipped him, and provoked to anger the LORD God of Israel, according to all that his father had done.*"

Israel was in a short period of peace after the battle in which Ahab died, but the land was exhausted. For this reason, Moab, which had been in subjection since the conquest of David, took the opportunity to rebel, and assert its independence. The famous Moabite Stone, discovered in 1868, records the successful revolt from the point of view of Mesha, King of Moab, who devotedly ascribes his victory to Chemosh, his god. It was a deep humiliation for Ahaziah.

As the story continues in 2 Kings there is hopelessness about Ahaziah. Ahab must have retained enough faith in Israel's God to put the divine name into the name of his heir, but Ahaziah, which means "the Lord takes hold," contradicted the name. He followed the idolatry of his wicked and powerful mother Jezebel, as the event which forms the chief theme of the chapter shows.

Ahaziah had a terrible accident. Coming down from some rooftop chamber of his palace at Samaria, he fell through a railing or an open window and was critically injured. His superstitious reaction was to send a deputation to consult Baalzebub, the god of flies, whom the Philistines worshiped at Ekron. Tormented, no doubt, in the heat of the Middle Eastern summer by the flies which added misery to the pain of a broken back, Ahaziah turned to misconceptions inherited from the princess of Tyre.

On their way the messengers from Ahaziah met an awe-inspiring presence, Elijah. *But the angel of the LORD said to Elijah the Tishbite, "Go up and meet the messengers of the king of Samaria and ask them, 'Is it because there is no God in Israel that you are going off to consult Baal-Zebub, the god of Ekron?'"*

Ahaziah became furious at Elijah, who rebuked him for looking to Baal instead of God to heal him. The king sent out 150 soldiers in three separate groups of 50 to arrest Elijah. Elijah promptly called down fire from heaven, which destroyed the first two groups. The captain of the third group asked for and received mercy from Elijah.

Elijah gave this message to the captain. The angel of the LORD said to Elijah, *"Go down with him; do not be afraid of him." So Elijah got up and went down with him to the king. He told the king, "This is what the LORD says: Is it because there is no God in Israel for you to consult that you have sent messengers to consult Baal-Zebub, the god of Ekron? Because you have done this, you will never leave the bed you are lying on. You will certainly die!" So he died, according to the word of the LORD that Elijah had spoken.* (2 Kings1:15-17).

Ahab's experience with the prophet was repeated. Stern and terrible as he was four years before in Naboth's vineyard, Elijah appeared from some hideout on Carmel and told of Ahaziah's coming doom.

Jezebel had done her work well upon her son. Ahab was not without blame, from Ahab Ahaziah probably inherited his strain of weakness.

In what ways are modern believers tempted to consult false gods?

To honor God in the giving of a favorable name is not enough.

To honor god demands work, principle, and above all example, if our children are to walk the way of faith.

Jehoram (Joram) — 2 Kings 6:8-8:6

9th King of the Northern Kingdom

This long passage tells some very unusual stories.

- The blinded Syrians,
- The Famine in Samaria,
- Elijah's prediction
- The siege abandoned
- The city surrounded by 4 lepers
- Their revelation to the city

It is recorded for our reading because some clear-cut facets of human character are revealed from the story. Jehoram reigned for 12 years. He was an evil king, but not as bad as was his father Ahab. He at least destroyed the sacred image of Baal which Ahab had made. He did, however, continue worshiping other idols as Jeroboam, Northern Israel's first king, had done. On one occasion he mobilized an army against Moab, who had rebelled against him, persuading both Jehoshaphat, king of Judah, and the king of Edom to join him in the attack.

In this episode the king of Israel stands out with some clarity. He was respectful toward Elisha. At this time the prophet was a man of tremendous prestige, but the king's faith in the prophet would soon face a demanding test. He had shown kindness in allowing the Syrian task force, which had been led into his fortifications, to go home unharmed. He had followed Elisha's advice.

Later, because of some thoughtless marching, his army became stranded in the burning desert without water. The prophet Elisha, who had been traveling unnoticed with the army, agreed to supernaturally provide water. The text makes clear this was done only for the sake of godly King Jehoshaphat.

Then Ben-Hadad invaded again. This shows us the anxiety under which Jehoram continually lived. Samaria itself was a hilltop town, a fortress of impregnable solidity, but Israel's manpower was insufficient to keep the country's borders secure. Samaria was besieged by an exasperated Ben-Hadad, who could, for all intents and purposes invade and subdue Israel's territory any time he wanted. He could loot and raid for slaves, but he was unable to enforce subjugation or an effective conquest. This was a condition of stressful stalemate.

Samaria was hard-pressed, surrounded and impoverished. The people were forced to eat the bulbs of Chiryonim (Dove's Dung) whose flowers (Star of Bethlehem) are seen in abundance in the spring. Dried and pounded into flour, the bulbs are still eaten in parts of Italy.

The harassed king deserves some sympathy. He was Ahab's and Jezebel's son; poorly grounded in the worship of Jehovah. It was natural enough for his faith to stagger under the terrible strain of the siege. He showed his distress when he wore sackcloth against his skin; the people saw this with shock (6:30) when he tore his clothes in anguish for his city's degradation.

The siege came to an end suddenly and dramatically. On several occasions in the historical books, outbursts of panic among mixed military armies have been noted; Midianites, Philistines, Moabites had been subject to this same God-given fear which sent the Syrians running for the Jordan. Jehoram handled the situation well. He was not a vicious man, and in the beginning of chapter 8 he shows concern as he seeks information about the prophet. There is something sad about this king.

What was good and bad about the king's reactions to the hardships of his subjects?

What associations or friendships in your life should you examine to make sure they are not subtly drawing you away from God?

Book Seven

1. Elijah	1 Kings 17, 18
2. Elijah: running from God	1 Kings 19
3. Elijah: a new ministry	1 Kings 19
4. Elijah: an evaluation	1 Kings 17-19
5. Elisha	2 Kings 2-4
6. Elisha: His miracles	2 Kings 2-13
7. Naaman of Syria	2 Kings 5:1-9
8. Gehazi	2 Kings 5, 6
9. Jehu	2 Kings 9-10
10. Jehoahaz, Jehoash	2 Kings 13-14
11. Jeroboam II	2 Kings 14
12. Zechariah, Shallum	2 Kings 15:8-15
13. Menahem, Pekahiah	2 Kings 15:16-26
14. Pekah	2 Kings 15:27-31
15. Hoshea	2 Kings 17
16. Asa	1 Kings 15; 2 Chronicles 14-16
17. Jehoshaphat	1 Kings 22:41-50; 2 Chronicles 17-20
18. Jehoram, Ahaziah	2 Kings 8-9; 2 Chronicles 21-22
19. Athaliah	2 Kings 11; 2 Chronicles 22-23
20. Joash	2 Kings 11-12; 2 Chronicles 23-24
21. Amaziah	2 Kings 14; 2 Chronicles 25
22. Uzziah	2 Kings 14-15; 2 Chronicles 26
23. Jotham	2 Kings 15; 2 Chronicles 27
24. Ahaz	2 Kings 16; 2 Chronicles 28
25. Hezekiah: Approved of God	2 Kings 18-20; 2 Chronicles 29-32; Isaiah 36:37
26. Hezekiah and the Assyrians	2 Kings 18-20
27. Hezekiah's illness and fame	2 Kings 18-20
28. Manasseh, Ammon	2 Chronicles 33:1-20
29. Josiah	2 Kings 22, 23; 2 Chronicles 34-35
30. Josiah; Huldah's Prophecy	2 Kings 22, 23; 2 Chronicles 34-35
31. Josiah; His Death	2 Kings 22, 23; 2 Chronicles 34-35

Elijah: an overview 1 Kings 17, 18

His name means "My God is Jehovah." Elijah was from the small rural town of Tishbe in Gilead. He lived and ministered as a contemporary of King Ahab of Israel. He is a prophet of God, but we possess nothing he wrote! He is well-known for his miracles, his courage, his prayer and his dramatic struggles with the emotional ups and downs of his life. As a man of God, his life was centered on his work with and for others.

When we first encounter Elijah he stands in direct opposition to King Ahab of Israel in relationship to the worship of Baal. He told the king the truth, all his problems were a result of his disobedience to Jehovah. He told Ahab it would not rain until he, Elijah, prayed to God and asked for rain. Afterward, Elijah went into hiding for over three years. God then sent Elijah back to Ahab to once again confront the king with his sin. Ahab again refused to repent. He was no doubt strengthened in his resolve by Jezebel.

When the three-and-a-half years of famine were ending, God told Elijah to go back to Israel. To arrange a contest to end the lesson God had been intending by the famine. Through the hesitant assistance of one of Ahab's servants (18:7-16), Elijah contacted the king and the contest was arranged (18:17-20). He asked the king to have the 450 prophets of Baal present on Mount Carmel, along with the 400 prophets of Asherah who ate at Jezebel's table. He also wanted the king to gather together people from all Israel to the mountain, so they would see what the contest would reveal. It was necessary for Ahab to give this invitation to the Israelites, because the leaders would not have dared come otherwise.

Ahab did as the prophet requested; the reason was he wanted rain to be sent as much as Elijah did. His nation was starving. The idea of the contest was to provide a way to prove before the people who was Israel's true God. In this connection it is well to notice another contest had been in progress since the time that the famine had started. Baal was supposed to be the god of storm and rainfall, the announcement by one of God's prophets that it would not rain had amounted to a challenge to the priests of Baal to make it rain by the power of Baal. When three-and-a-half years had gone by and it had not rained, this meant to the people Baal was not living up to what he was supposed to do. It would have become increasingly apparent Baal was not all Jezebel said he was. Ahab did as Elijah desired, so on the day of the contest both the people and the prophets of Baal were on hand.

When all were present, Elijah began to speak and outline the way the contest was to be held. The prophets of Baal were to call upon their god to miraculously light a fire on an altar of Baal, and later Elijah would do the same in respect to an altar to the God of Israel. The God who answered by fire would be proven the true God. Elijah also told the prophets of Baal they could select the animal they wanted to sacrifice and proceed first. The prophets of Baal sacrificed their animal and began to call upon Baal to send fire. They continued to call throughout the morning hours until noon, and then in the afternoon. When Elijah mocked them, they called still louder and cut themselves with knives to bring blood on their bodies. All this show produced nothing as the afternoon wore on; Baal did not answer. Late in the day Elijah called the people over to a place where there had once been a small altar to Jehovah. He repaired it, using twelve stones, one representing each of the tribes of Israel.

This was an insignificant altar to look at in comparison with the large altar the Baal worshippers had used. Elijah also dug a trench around his altar and then called for a total of twelve containers of water to be poured over it. This drenched the altar completely, proving there could not possibly be any fire secretly hidden underneath. Elijah offered a brief prayer, recorded in only two verses (18:36, 37), and God answered with the fire. The fire which fell was so intense it consumed the wood and the offering, the stones of the altar, and even licked up the water in the surrounding trench.

The result was the people immediately cried out, "The LORD, he is the God; the LORD, he is the God" (18:39). The demonstration had been unmistakably convincing, and the people were ready to acknowledge it. They had been prepared through the prior three-and-a-half years by the contest for rain, and now they were persuaded by this contest for fire.

How can we be confident of the power of God yet humble about our ability to dictate anything to Him?

What "god" could the Lord use you to unmask before a friend or acquaintance?

Elijah - running from God 1 Kings 19

After the victory on Mt. Carmel, when Elijah arrived at his own home in Jezreel, he received an intimidating message from Jezebel. She had learned from her husband what had happened at Mount Carmel. Her message read, "*May the gods deal with me, be it ever so severely, if by this time tomorrow I do not make your life like that of one of them.*" Elijah, who was so strong at Mount Carmel, now showed weakness as he ran that very night in fear of Jezebel. He evidently did not stop to eat or drink as he ran to get away from the danger of this wicked woman. Then, leaving his servant in Beersheba, at the far south of the land, he went on alone and, sitting down under a juniper tree, asked God to take his life, saying, "*Oh LORD, take away my life; for I am not better than my fathers*" (19:4).

God did not fulfill Elijah's request, but sent His angel to minister to the prophet. The angel awakened Elijah from his sleep and told him to eat and drink of food there before him, a jug of water and cakes freshly baked on a fire. Elijah did eat and drink and then lay down to sleep again. After a time, the angel once more woke him and directed him to eat and drink, and Elijah did. Then Elijah made his way further south through the Sinai Desert until he came to Mount Horeb, where the Law had been given to the Israelites many centuries before. Finding a cave in which to stop on Mount Horeb, Elijah soon was contacted by God with the words, "*What are you doing here, Elijah?*" (19:9). This question must have been very disturbing. In effect God was asking Elijah why he was down here at Mount Horeb when the contest had been arranged up in Israel, where there had been such success in turning key people to God that memorable afternoon. **Elijah had fled when he had not needed to, and now he was not where God wanted him to be.**

Elijah tried to defend himself by indicating he had been jealous for God and had done his best to maintain God's word, but it had been impossible, and he had just managed to save his life under difficult conditions. God told him to go out of the cave and watch what was about to happen. God then caused three object lessons to take place. The first was a strong wind which blew hard enough to cause rocks of the mountain to break in pieces. Then God stirred up an earthquake that shook the entire mountain. Thirdly, God kindled a fire in front of where the prophet stood which apparently blazed with fierceness parallel to the wind and earthquake. When these displays were completed, God caused Elijah to hear a still small voice, which came in complete contrast to the terrible devastating actions of the earlier demonstration. God had not been "in" the three mighty actions. He was in the still small voice.

Elijah did not need to run from Jezebel because God could stir up such things as a great wind, a strong earthquake, or a burning fire to destroy her completely so she could not touch God's prophet. Elijah had shown a lack of faith in not recognizing the ability of God to protect him.

God's method to deal with Jezebel was not to be such destructive measures as these. As Elijah had moved south through the desert, his thinking had probably been the only way to solve the problem in Israel was for Jezebel to be destroyed, and he may have tried to think of ways in which this could be done. Now, God showed him three ways it might be done. As successively the wind blew, the earthquake rocked, and the fire burned, Elijah may well have thought each time, "Yes, Lord, this will do very nicely." God, however, was saying, "No, Elijah, this is not the way we will do it. We will not destroy her either by wind, earthquake, or fire, but we will work by a still small voice."

Elijah should know God's way of carrying on His work was not by sensational methods but rather by simple hard work, symbolized by the still small voice. Until this point Elijah had worked with the big and dramatic and had thought this was the only way. When the big contest had not worked out in total victory Elijah had believed all was fruitless and the only thing left for him was to die. God was now saying all was not over, the battle had not been lost, and Elijah did not need to die because thus far he had tried only the unusual methods. What was left was the more normal activity.

In what discouraging circumstances can you remind yourself God is in control?

Elijah – a new ministry 1 Kings 19

How soon these three lessons registered in Elijah's mind is hard to say. He was to do three things: anoint Hazael as king over Syria, anoint Jehu as king over Israel, anoint Elisha as a prophet to serve in his own place. The first two matters were not possible for Elijah personally to carry out, but later Elisha would act in his place (II Kings 8:7-13; 9:1-10). The third direction, however, Elijah could carry out and he did as soon as he returned to the land.

The call of Elisha

Elisha lived at Abel-meholah, located in the Jordan valley a few miles south of the Sea of Galilee. Elijah came to him and cast his mantle upon him. Elisha evidently realized the significance of the action, for he quickly ran after Elijah and asked permission first to say farewell to his parents before following the prophet. Elijah granted the permission, and Elisha made a feast using the oxen he had been plowing with for the meat and the plow and equipment for the firewood. Then at the feast he said farewell to his parents and friends and went after Elijah. The two apparently ministered together until the day of Elijah's departure, probably a period of about 10 years.

Hazael 2 Kings 8:7-29

With strange ease Elisha seems to have been able to cross the embattled frontiers at will. He appears in Damascus and is soon the object of a deputation from Ben-Hadad, who was lying old and sick in his palace. Pretentiously a present was distributed on 40 camels. This was sent to persuade the prophet to speak. It was led by the army commander, Hazael.

The story of the interview must be read carefully. 8:9-12
Hazael went to meet Elisha, taking with him as a gift forty camel-loads of all the finest wares of Damascus. He went in and stood before him, and said, "Your son Ben-Hadad king of Aram has sent me to ask, 'Will I recover from this illness?'" Elisha answered, "Go and say to him, 'You will certainly recover'; but the LORD has revealed to me that he will in fact die." He stared at him with a fixed gaze until Hazael felt ashamed. Then the man of God began to weep. "Why is my lord weeping?" asked Hazael. "Because I know the harm you will do to the Israelites," was Elisha's reply.

Elisha did not lie (10); he merely set out the facts. Ben-Hadad was not going to die from his illness. But he would soon be murdered. Elisha understood the cruel, ambitious man who stood before him. Hazael was Syria's Macbeth. He was already planning to murder his king, and the prophet knew it. Therefore, the penetrating glance, and then the tears. Hazael's reply is ambiguous and deceptive. The knowledge he was to be ruler of Syria was already in Hazael's mind. Hazael found the goal which he had long held was now within his reach. Elisha wanted to make it clear he was not responsible for Hazael's actions. The Lord told Judas, who had already yielded irrevocably to evil: "What you are going to do, do quickly." And in this case Hazael's mind was already made up.

Jehu Anointed King of Israel 2 Kings 9:1-13

Elisha had personally fulfilled the commission God had given to Elijah to anoint Hazael king of Syria (I Kings 19:15; II Kings 8:8-15); but he delegated to one of the "sons of the prophets" the task of finding and anointing Jehu to be king of Israel. Perhaps Elisha wanted to avoid giving the impression he was responsible for, or in favor of the policies of Jehu.

The rush and confusion of Jehu's anointing seemed to be prophetic of the entire career of this mad warmonger. As Jehu and his captains were seated in a council of war in Ramoth-Gilead near the battlefront, a wild-eyed young prophet burst upon the scene, invited Jehu into a nearby house, anointed him as king of Israel with the primary commission of annihilating the dynasty of Omri and Ahab, and then the prophet fled. When the captains found out what had happened, they made a throne, placed their garments under him as an act of homage, blew the trumpet and shouted, "Jehu is king."

Do you ever have trouble understanding what God is doing?

His prayer life

It has been noted he prayed God would send famine because of the sin in the land, and God responded by turning off the rain for three-and-a-half years. What Elijah asked for was no small thing, but God still answered. Elijah was a man of prayer, who knew what it was to ask big things from God and receive them. The same was true later when he asked God to send fire as the crowd of people watched on Mount Carmel, and then as he asked for rain while alone on the same mountain top.

James used Elijah as an example of the power of prayer (James 5:17-18).

- Pointing out he was a man, just like us
- That he prayed earnestly that it would not rain
- That it did not rain for 3 1/2 years
- That he then prayed for rain, resulting in a downpour

A man of faith

Elijah demonstrated faith in many ways. He showed it in his prayer God would send the famine, believing clearly God could and would do so, and God as a result did that very thing. He showed it in telling Ahab, the king there would be no dew nor rain until Elijah gave the word. This took great faith because there is nothing more impossible for man to do than to control the elements of nature. Yet Elijah believed God would work through him to stop rainfall, until Elijah gave the word for it to rain again. He showed it, thirdly, in his belief that the son of the widow of Zarephath would live again. This is the first recorded occasion of resurrection in the Bible, so Elijah had no prior event on which to base this faith. Elijah had to believe God would do this because he was certain God would not bring further problem and harm upon the widow of Zarephath. Great faith was demonstrated by Elijah later when he called on God to send fire upon the altar on Mount Carmel as all the people looked on.

Courage

Elijah demonstrated courage on many occasions. He did so in coming to Ahab the first time. He must have known Ahab would not like to hear a message famine was coming to his land. Kings feared few things more than famines, because they meant terrible suffering for the people. It took courage for Elijah to bring this kind of message, but he brought it. It took courage to come to Ahab later when he rebuked Ahab for taking Naboth's vineyard. Elijah, having been instructed by God, did go and give the message despite the danger. Courage was involved in Elijah's going to King Ahaziah, the son of Ahab. Ahaziah had sent messengers to Baal-zebub of the Philistines. Elijah, however, had intercepted them and sent back word to the king which again was a word of rebuke. Certainly, Ahaziah was in no mood to receive such a communication, and Elijah would have known this. But Elijah sent it and finally went himself.

Obedience

Elijah was an obedient person, showing this on numerous occasions. One was the time when he went to Ahab with the message regarding the famine. He had already prayed for the famine. God evidently had told him He would agree to the request and then instructed Elijah to go and tell Ahab it was to happen. That Elijah did this, despite possible anger on Ahab's part, shows he was obedient to God. Obedience was remarkably demonstrated when Elijah moved from the brook Cherith to Zarephath. Elijah probably had been at the brook Cherith about one year at the time, and all the while he had been completely hidden from people. Now the instruction came to go where people would be, even to a city called Zarephath.

There he was to dwell with a widow in this time of famine. Elijah knew widows suffered more during times of famine than did others, since there was no breadwinner to provide food for the table. He must have wondered at these instructions from God and could well have asked God to explain them before moving to obey. We do not read he hesitated, however, but simply that he "arose and went to Zarephath (I Kings 17:10).

How quickly do you obey God?

Elisha **2 Kings 2-4**

His name means "God is Savior." He lived and served in the central part of the land of Israel. Most of his ministry was conducted in the geographic area between Galilee and Judea. The time period of his ministry probably falls sometime shortly before 880 BC. Elisha was the assistant to Elijah. He was called at the instruction of God to help and encourage Elijah. While Elijah was alone with God on Mount Horeb, God instructed him where to find and call Elisha to serve as his successor. Elisha's work was basically the same as that of Elijah; resistance to the worship of Baal. Elisha may have come from a rather wealthy family, since he was plowing with a team of oxen in a field where 12 other teams preceded him at the time of his call. If so, he contrasted in this way with his master, Elijah, who had been raised in the poor area of Gilead near the desert. Elisha's decision to follow Elijah was final and decisive. He killed his own oxen to prepare a farewell feast for relatives and friends, and he used the wood from his tools as fuel for the fire (I Kings 19:2 1).

Though having the same objectives in service as Elijah, Elisha's manner in reaching them was somewhat different. In keeping with his contrasting background, he was more at home in cities and was often in the company of kings. Also, whereas Elijah had been more a man of moods, either strongly courageous or despairing to the point of death, Elisha was self-controlled and even-tempered. Elisha never staged dramatic contests nor sulked in a desert. It may be, too, that Elisha was more interested in the needs of people, for many of his miracles were for the purpose of aiding and giving relief to persons in difficulty. As indicated, the stories from Elisha's life come almost entirely from the reign of Jehoram. No doubt, similar stories could have been included from the reigns of Jehu, Jehoahaz, and Jehoash. Those given are undoubtedly intended to be representative. It is probable; too, that many more could have been included from the reign of Jehoram, and so one may believe those recorded are specifically chosen to show us how God used this man.

Elisha was present with Elijah when God took him to heaven in a whirlwind. Elisha received a double portion of the spirit of Elijah, as promised by the prophet, because he had seen him when he was taken into heaven. As he, Elisha, retraced his steps and returned to the land of Israel he began his supernatural ministry as the leader of his people.

He continued the training ministry of the "sons of the prophets" which had been begun by Elijah. Several of his miracles were performed to help these young potential prophets in their training. In 2 Kings 4 we have a record of his caring for a family who had befriended and provided for him. He predicted a child would be born to this barren woman and the following year she gave birth. Years later the child became sick and died. The grief-stricken mother went to the prophet seeking his help. Elisha returned home with her and raised her son from the dead.

Elisha performed miracles under different circumstances. He healed a Syrian military commander, Naaman, of leprosy. He seems to have been very involved in the international affairs of the northern kingdom. He predicted the defeat of the Syrians on several occasions and gave instructions on how to defeat the Moabites. He was declared an enemy by the Syrian king who sent an entire division of soldiers to arrest him. After Elisha's prayer God blinded the Syrian army and led them into the city of Samaria (2 Kings 5).

Elisha stands in great contrast to his master Elijah. Elijah was a man of the desert; Elisha was a man of the population centers. He was close to kings and generals, he was involved with men and women, he supplied the needs of rich and poor; he truly was a man for all seasons.

He was not enticed by the availability of power. He was not drawn to the luxuries of money.

He does not seem to have been afflicted with the emotional ups and downs of his mentor.

He represents one of the most consistent servants of God in all of Scripture.

Elisha: His miracles — 2 Kings 2-13

1.	Dividing the Jordan	2 Kings 2:13, 14
2.	Purifying the spring of Jericho	2 Kings 2:19-22
3.	Cursing the teenagers	2 Kings 2:23, 24
4.	Supplying water for the three kings	2 Kings 3:1-27
5.	Oil for a widow	2 Kings 4:1-7
6.	The Shunammite's son	2 Kings 4:8-37
7.	Poisonous food	2 Kings 4:38-41
8.	Multiplying the loaves and grain	2 Kings 4:42-44
9.	Healing of Naaman	2 Kings 5:1-27
10.	Saving a lost axe-head	2 Kings 6:1-7
11.	Aiding Jehoram	2 Kings 6:8-12
12.	Episode at Dothan	2 Kings 6:13-23
13.	Starvation and food in Samaria	2 Kings 6:24-7:20
14.	Return of the Shunammite's property	2 Kings 8:1-6
15.	Elisha and Hazael	2 Kings 8:7-15
16.	The anointing of Jehu	2 Kings 9:1-3;
17.	Elisha and Jehoash	2 Kings 13:14-19
18.	The raising of a dead man	2 Kings 13:20-21

Why did God cause Elisha, and Elijah before him, to perform these wonders? The answer is this was a time which was very crucial in Israel's history. Baal worship had been brought in by Jezebel and the land had very few believing people and hardly any God-fearing prophets. These miracles stood as their credentials.

Think about some of the characteristics which stand out in the life of Elisha Indifference to wealth
Most people are very impressed by wealth. Because of the love of money, they act in ways and do things which are not commendable; Elisha was not like this. Elisha very quickly left his affluent home and followed Elijah when he was called. To go with Elijah meant leaving all the wealth and security of his family and submitting to the meager life of the prophet. It is possible when Elijah asked Elisha what he could do for him before he was taken home to heaven, had in mind to offer Elisha the opportunity of returning to his home. When Elisha responded he wished a double portion of the Elijah's spirit, he not only indicated he knew he needed this empowerment, but he did not wish the material things which others of his family knew. He had watched his master and he was totally surrendered to the God Elijah served.

Energy
He was active in doing many things and going many places. He was involved not only in the geographic area of his home, but he could be found in northern Israel at Mount Carmel, staying at the home of the woman in Shunem or confronting Kings as far South as the southern region of Moab. Several of his miracles involved the students at the prophetic schools, indicating he apparently traveled continually from Gilgal to Bethel to Jericho. He seems to have taken on the responsibility of seeing that the schools continue to operate properly and had adequate provisions for the students. This is a good indication he was a man with a high energy level as we know how much work it is to keep up with college students. Everywhere he went we can be sure he gave out God's word. He preached urging people to repent and turn to God; to turn away from their idols. The fact his dead bones were used by God to give life to a man is probably representative of the work of Elisha throughout his ministry.

What benefits do you see in humbling yourself to do what God requires of you?

What can you do to serve someone else without payment?

Naaman of Syria 2 Kings 5:1-9

The root of Naaman's name means "charm" or "loveliness," and, although this name was given at birth, the man's character may have formed under its influence. Perhaps here is the secret of the little slave girl's devotion. He seems also to have been held in high esteem by Ben-Hadad of Syria. It seems Naaman, with all his prestige, needed a deep lesson in humility. Elisha was not impressed by the importance of his visitor, he merely sent a message to the visiting notables standing at his door, and the message contained a strange direction. "Go, wash yourself seven times in the Jordan, and your flesh will be restored, and you will be cleansed.

But Naaman was offended and said, *"I thought that he would surely come out to me and stand and call on the name of the LORD his God, wave his hand over the spot and cure me of my leprosy. Are not Abana and Pharpar, the rivers of Damascus, better than any of the waters of Israel? Couldn't I wash in them and be cleansed?"* So, he turned and went off in a rage. Naaman was correct about the Jordan. It is not one of the majestic rivers of the world. Its twisted course runs through a plain built of its own silt-laden waters. The beautiful streams of Damascus were certainly a more inviting bathing place. It was also a long way, as a map will show, to the river from Samaria, and it is a downhill, rough, and heat- ridden road from the height of this place to the deep trench, far below sea level, where the Jordan wound toward the Dead Sea.

Naaman's servants reflected their master's quality. They were not "yes-men," accustomed to abrupt orders and instant obedience. They cared for their master and felt free to speak with him and were able to convince him to follow the prophet's directions.

So Naaman did as he was instructed, and he was healed!
Unlike some who take the blessings of the Lord as if they were a personal right and not of grace, he returned all the grueling uphill way to Samaria to give thanks for the blessing he had received. Elisha, more concerned for the spiritual benefit of his noble visitor, refused any reward.

The next verses convey an interesting insight into the view of God held by many Old Testament people. *"If you will not," (receive my gift) said Naaman, "please let me, your servant, be given as much earth as a pair of mules can carry, for your servant will never again make burnt offerings and sacrifices to any other god but the LORD.*

Old Testament gods were viewed as local and geographic; the ground of a nation belonged to the god of that nation. Naaman wanted "*as much earth as a pair of mules can carry"* to create his own personal place to worship Jehovah. In Damascus there was to be a small part of a foreign land on which, as though it was embassy property, Jehovah could be worshiped.

In this situation Elisha gave a slightly ironic approval of this new convert's plea to be allowed an outward conformity with the worship of the god Rimmon. Life may have been impossible for Ben-Hadad's right- hand man without this permission. Naaman no doubt was conflicted with his new understanding of the true God as well as with his official duty. Yet he wanted to worship the true God he had now come to believe was all-powerful. Jesus used the story of Naaman's healing during a sermon preached in His hometown synagogue of Nazareth to illustrate the faith of the Gentiles and the faithlessness of Israel. He said: *"And many lepers were in Israel in the time of Elisha, the prophet; and none of them was cleansed, but only Naaman, the Syrian"* (Luke 4:27). Naaman became the only man in the entire Old Testament to be healed of leprosy.

If an unnamed young girl had not been taken captive by the army from Damascus in an earlier raid, none of these events would have taken place! God really does see the end from the beginning, and we don't. God can and does make all things, good and evil, work for His purpose!

Naaman said, "I thought." How often do we hinder God's work because we think God is going about His work all wrong?

As hard as it often is – obedience is always best!

His name means "Denier or Diminisher." We know nothing of Gehazi's background or his birth. We are not told anything of his family. Perhaps he was one of the "sons of the prophets." He was chosen to serve and train with the hope he would one day continue the ministry of Elisha. A bright future lay ahead of Gehazi. He was the natural successor of Elisha, as Elisha had been of Elijah. He ruined all possibility of such usefulness by one act of greed. To accomplish that end, he lied to Naaman, and in the process ruined the testimony of Elisha in the foreigner's mind and lied to Elisha to cover up his earlier.

Gehazi was privileged to walk side-by-side with Elisha, to work under his direction, to carry his messages and to provide for his daily needs. If these things took place in the 21st century we would say that Elisha was mentoring Gehazi. He was privileged to listen to his master tell him of all the miracles and experiences his master had experienced as he walked with Elijah.

In 2 Kings 6 he awoke one morning in the city of Dothan to find that the King of Syria had sent an army of troops to arrest him and Elisha. He quickly awakened his master with the question, "What are we going to do?" Elisha's answer is recorded for us, "Fear not for those with us are more than those with them." I am sure Gehazi thought his master had not yet fully awakened because he was sure there was no one else outside other than the Syrian army. Elisha prayed and asked God to open the eyes of his servant. When Gehazi looked he saw there were horses and chariots of fire protecting them.

After the healing of Naaman, Elisha refused any payment from the Syrian general. Later Gehazi took the opportunity to follow the Syrian and receive some of the reward his master had refused. When Gehazi returned Elisha asked him where have you been and what have you been doing. The prophet received an answer most of us have heard from our children many times. "I went nowhere and did nothing." As a result of his disobedience Gehazi suffered the leprosy of Naaman until his death.

Does this sound familiar? – What are you doing? Nothing.

Here is a man who had the remarkable opportunity to observe and serve with one of the greatest men of the Bible. He was unable to withstand the temptations which came with the privilege.

We are not told Gehazi's motives. Such wrong doing always involves deceit, and the judgment on deceit is the deceiver first deceives himself. It is clear the activities of the "schools of the prophets" were expanding, and in need of money. So Gehazi could persuade himself, "this is needed for God's work." He thought of his master as an impractical dreamer, somewhat out of touch with contemporary life.

Perhaps, considering the refusal of Abraham for Sodom's gifts, in a quite different situation, Gehazi thought his master was unwisely imitating Abraham's example. Reflecting that Abraham himself, as good a businessman as he was, had at least brought himself to accept a refund of actual expenses, Gehazi had perhaps found "scriptural" justification for his act of covetousness.

It is astounding how people can justify, on the most sacred grounds, what they want to do.

Thus, through an unsurrendered corner of a life, Satan broke in to destroy and to corrupt. In this same way men destroy their usefulness, ruin the plan of God for their lives, and construct the habitation of their own unhappiness. "Love of money," says Paul, "lies at the root of every sort of evil." It can inspire, in other words, every other kind of wrongdoing, being a basic sin like pride.

How did Gehazi underestimate Elisha's relationship with God?

Do you think Gehazi could have been Elisha's successor if he had not failed this test?

Jehu — 2 Kings 9-10

10th King of the Northern Kingdom

The two strongest ruling families of Israel reigned consecutively: first, the family of Omri, and second, that of Jehu. Jehu's dynasty ruled longer than Omri's. It included five generations (Jehu, Jehoahaz, Jehoash, Jeroboam II, and Zechariah), in comparison with Omri's three. Jehu's dynasty was not as strong as Omri's, for during its time Israel experienced heavy losses to both the armies from Damascus and the Assyrians. Religiously, each dynasty was deficient, but at least Jehu did not foster Baal worship as Omri's had.

Jehu's destruction of the house of Omri (2 Kings 9:11-10:28)
Jehu, first king of the 5th dynasty, is best known for his slaughter of the family of Omri. Before this time, God had prophesied through Elijah such a time of punishment would come to this family. With the urging of Elijah and Elisha, Omri's family had been given opportunity to repent of its sin in Baal worship and needless destruction of life.

Elisha himself ignited the situation, which Jehu then fueled. Elisha sent one of the "company of the prophets" to anoint Jehu as king in place of Jehoram and to instruct Jehu regarding the purging (2 Kings 9:1-10). Jehu, Jehoram's military captain, was still at Ramoth-gilead, the place of the last battle, and he quickly accepted the honor. His men were pleased as well and moved across the Jordan to Jezreel to carry out their purpose. King Jehoram of Israel was recovering from wounds. He was killed before he could recover. Ahaziah, Judah's king who was visiting, ran for his life from Jezreel, but was later killed by the men sent by Jehu.

Jehu rode into Jezreel and ordered the servants of Jezebel to throw her from an upper window. They eagerly complied, and dogs ate her flesh as Elijah had predicted long before (1 Kings 21:23). Later at Jehu's insistence, Ahab's 70 sons were then killed by Samaria's leaders. Jehu arrived at the capital and killed all the officials there as well. Lastly, he called all the prophets and priests of Baal to their temple in Samaria, as if to extend favor to them, but then he sent 80 of his men into the temple to kill them all. Seldom has history witnessed a more thorough blood purge of a previous royal family and privileged religious order.

Jehu as king (841-814; 2 Kings 10:29-36)
Jehu's zeal to rid the land of Omri's house was not matched by his capacity to rule. His 28 years as king were marked by unrest and turmoil, with serious social and economic abuses common among the people. Religiously, Jehu received God's approval at the beginning because of obedience destroying the house of Omri, but then he failed to follow the path he had started. God gave His approval of the purge; even though Jehu certainly killed more than divinely intended. This was the punishment which had been decreed against the family years before, and it dealt a shattering blow to the cult of Baal. God promised four generations of Jehu's family would succeed him on the throne. Jehu, however, then chose to perpetuate Jeroboam's worship centers at Dan and Bethel (2 Kings 10:29) and so forfeited the divine approval and consequently experienced difficult times.

Secrecy, rapid action and fierce cruelty were marks of Jehu's personality. He was Jehoram's general, a tough and competent soldier, who was left in command of the siege operations at Ramoth-gilead, when his royal master retired to Jezreel to be healed of a combat injury. Ambition came easily with troops at his disposal, some of dissatisfaction to exploit, and popularity to work upon. He acted. Before it ends, Jehoram is dead with an arrow between his shoulders from Jehu's bow. Ahaziah, Jehoram's royal guest and nephew, king of neighboring Judah, was shot down as he fled, and the notorious Jezebel, tossed from an upper window, was eaten by dogs in the alleys of Jezreel, while Jehu dined.

How can you free yourself from people who want to control you with shared guilt?

What responsibility do we have to stand for God, as Jehu did?

Jehoahaz 2 Kings 13

11th King of the Northern Kingdom (814-798; 2 Kings 13:1-9)

Jehoahaz succeeded Jehu, his father, and reigned 17 years. Little is said of his rule, apart from a further level of subjection to Hazael of Damascus. The only thing stated in addition is he sought help from God against Hazael and was given a "deliverer" (2 Kings 15:5). This "deliverer," in a strange turn of fate, must have been the Assyrian emperor, who would later destroy this same kingdom.

The Assyrians did serve as "deliverer" to Israel because they attacked and crushed Damascus in 803 BC, thus bringing relief to Israel from Syrian opposition. The result was Israel, along with Tyre, Sidon, Edom and Philistia, was forced to pay tribute, but it did not undergo the devastation brought upon the Syrians of Damascus. The Syrian state was hurt enough that Israel was now able to start on a long road toward a new position of strength.

Jehoash 2 Kings 13, 14

12th King of the Northern Kingdom (798-782; 2 Kings 13:10-25; 14:15-16)

At Jehoahaz's death, his son Jehoash assumed the throne. During his rule, Israel made rapid strides in regaining military and economic strength. Soon after assuming office, Jehoash was promised resurgence in military strength by Elisha. An old man now, he called the new king to him and predicted victory over Damascus. He instructed Jehoash to smite the ground with arrows. The king did so, but only three times; Elisha chided him for not smiting it more. The old prophet explained Israel would have defeated Damascus a corresponding number of times. He would, however, still be victorious on three occasions.

The succeeding years saw Jehoash experiencing the fulfillment of this prediction, enabling him to recover all the cities Damascus had earlier taken from Israel (2 Kings 13:25). Jehoash also became strong enough to withstand an attack by Amaziah, king of Judah (2 Kings 14:8-14). Later he became strong enough to enter an alliance with the king of Judah. This alliance was an attempt to gain control of lucrative trade routes; the cooperation ended in sharp disagreement.

Border warfare was probably the reason for Amaziah seeking some type of negotiation with Judah's king, Jehoash (2 Kings 4:8). Jehoash's response tells us these "negotiations" were put into effect with a threat of military force. The King of Judah seriously overestimated his military capability after his defeat of Edom. Jehoash was not intimidated by the southern king's bragging and in a carefully planned attack Jehoash captured Beth Shemesh, a Judean city on the southwest border of Judah, near the connection of the Sorek Valley and the road leading to Jerusalem.

With this decisive victory; Jehoash was able to take the southern king prisoner. Then he marched unhindered to Jerusalem, broke down part of its walls and plundered a large part of the city. The hostages who were taken were probably nobility or members of the royal family. They were kept under guard or held for ransom. Another item of significance is Jehoash appointed his son as co-ruler. This was usually done before a battle since the King could not be certain he would not be killed. In this way the King would establish the certainty of his succession. Jeroboam II became co-regent when Jehoash had ruled only five of his 16 years.

What act of praise and thanksgiving can express your gratitude for your political freedom?

What do you need to remember the next time you are feeling particularly successful?

How can you respond the next time someone tries to goad you into a confrontation through an attack on your self-respect?

Jeroboam II — 2 Kings 14

13th King of the Northern Kingdom (793-753; 2 Kings 14:23-29)

Jeroboam II was the third successive descendant of Jehu to occupy the throne, and he proved to be one of Israel's most capable rulers. Under him Israel rose to a position of remarkable influence. No description of Jeroboam's battles is given, but the result of his kingship is made clear: He was able to establish approximately the same boundaries on the east and north which had existed in the empires of David and Solomon. It is said he placed Israel's northern limit at the "entering of Hamath." This is the same phrase which describes Solomon's northern boundary (1 Kings 8:65).

It is also said, "He recovered for Israel both Damascus and Hamath that had belonged to Judah" (2 Kings 14:28), the last phrase is no doubt a reference to David and Solomon's time, since these cities had not belonged to either Judah or Israel since that time. This reference allows us to draw the conclusion Jeroboam was able to restore control of this area and create the same general relationship between the cities of Israel and the cities in the land to the north. By gaining control of Damascus he recovered all the land and influence which Hazael had seized earlier. With these historic boundaries once again under his control, Israel was the largest and most influential country in the world of the Eastern Mediterranean.

There were three factors which contributed to the historic change in the status of Israel in the region. The first, Damascus, which had been a long-time enemy of Israel, had now been weakened by successive attacks from Assyria. The second, Jehoash, the King of Judah and Jeroboam II were both very capable rulers. They each managed their assets well and worked with their strengths in such a way that they could control their kingdoms and make them grow. The third, Syria, which might have been able to interfere in the international and domestic affairs of these two kingdoms, was now suffering through a period of decline. They were invaded from the north and had to move their military powers in that direction.

Hosea 6 and 14

The prophet Hosea wrote during this time period. He says little of Jeroboam II directly. But he does show the land's deep departure from its ancient faith, and this thought is obvious in the mind of the historian as he writes his accounting in Kings and Chronicles. However, measured by the common standards of man, Jeroboam was a strong and vigorous monarch. He was the ablest of the kings of Israel, and a map will reveal he restored the borders of the land almost to where they were in the imperial days of David long before. The Northern Kingdom was not far from destruction.

Amos and Hosea saw the greatness of a land does not rest upon temporary military success but upon the quality of life lived by the men and women who form its population.

Had Jeroboam been perceptive, and we know little of what went on in his mind, he would have seen much of the success which was experienced in his wide-ranging military endeavor was due, in fact, to the pressure of the rising power of Assyria on the old rivals. Hosea warned no nation could safely rely upon the chance swing of a balance of power for ultimate salvation (12:1; 14:1), or upon entangling alliances, certain to be transitory, with pagan powers such as Assyria and Egypt. What played into Jeroboam's hands was the destruction of Syria by Nineveh. Syria, the old persecutor of Israel, acted for a generation as a buffer against the cruel aggressor of the north. It was a time of false peace, a lull before the storm, a breathing space in which a whole-hearted return to God might have brought salvation. Amos and Hosea knew this and preached the truth concerning the need for repentance. The prophet Jonah also was on the scene at this time in history, but we know very little of his ministry within the land of Israel.

Jeroboam II was a man well-endowed with ability to guide his people in human affairs.

He was not equipped to lead them back to God.

Political and economic action must always be filtered through the lens of the word of God.

Zechariah 2 Kings 15:8-12

14th King of the Northern Kingdom - 753

Zachariah, or Zechariah, the son and successor of Jeroboam II, was last in dynasty of Jehu. At his death, the House of Jehu became extinct as foretold. The king lived just long enough to fulfill God's promise to Jehu (II Kings 10:30). R. K. Harrison says, "With the death of Zachariah, the dynasty of Jehu came to an end and ushered in a period of civil unrest and strife, similar to that which marked the beginning of the House of Jehu." Zachariah, who reigned for only six months, received a wonderful inheritance, not only to the kingdom of the Ten Tribes, but of the Syrian state of Damascus which his father had conquered. Unfortunately, the unusual wealth and power of his position led to his failure.

Not many people are strong enough to balance wealth, power and prestige.

The days of Zachariah must have been overshadowed by the memory of the prophecy concerning the end of the dynasty of Jehu. He was the fourth generation of that dynasty and it had been prophesied the dynasty of Jehu would last only for four generations. After six very confused and disastrous months Zachariah was assassinated by Shallum. The people evidently were angry at Zachariah and supported Shallum's attempt to seize the throne. It is a sad commentary on the state of the nation that its citizens sympathized with the crime. It shows a very rapid increase in the corruption of morals and lifestyle in the northern kingdom. In his brief reign as king, Zachariah continued to support the false worship of the golden calves which Jeroboam I had instituted. He is another bad king in the lineage of the history of Israel.

Shallum 2 Kings15:13-15

15th King of the Northern Kingdom – 752

Shallum, who took the throne by conspiracy and murder, was himself assassinated. All we know of Shallum is he was a son of a man named Jabesh and he (and his dynasty – the 6th) ruled for a month. When he murdered Zachariah and seized the kingdom, he fulfilled the prophecy that Jehu's dynasty should last only to the fourth generation. Shallum was killed by Menahem, a general of Zachariah's army, who was stationed near Samaria.

Again, we see the terrible carnage of the history of Israel, with its successive reigns founded on bloodshed!

What prophecy was fulfilled when Shallum assassinated Zechariah and took over as king?

What judgment is repeated about the kings of Israel?

What's wrong with the thinking that ruthlessness is necessary for success in leadership?

Menahem 2 Kings 15:16-22

16th King of the Northern Kingdom – 752 – 742

Menahem was another wicked ruler. He was also terribly cruel. This son of Gadi was the 16th king of Israel, reigned for 10 years, and was a strong and determined ruler who, with a firm hand, enforced his seizure of the throne. Whatever military ambitions he might have entertained were crushed by a resurgence of Assyrian power. Menahem thought it wise to become a vassal to Tiglath-Pileser III, in whose annals his victory is described, "As for Menahem, terror overwhelmed him . . . he fled and submitted to me. Silver, colored woolen garments, linen garments I received as his tribute." Menahem was guilty of savage cruelty, for he ripped open pregnant women, copying the unscrupulous cruelty of the Syrian Hazael. In religion he did not depart not from the sins of Jeroboam I. He attempted no reform in religion.

Like predecessors he followed the worship of the golden calves, and like them incurred the heavy censure of the writer.

Pekahiah 2 Kings 15:23-26

17th King of the Northern Kingdom – 742 - 740

Within two years of his accession, Pekahiah, son and successor of Menahem, was murdered by a military group. Thus, he became the seventh king of Israel to meet death by violence. The others were Nadab, Elah, Tibni, Jehoram, Zachariah and Shallum. Pekahiah was unable to appease the Assyrians as his father had done. When he came to the throne, he was surrounded by the danger which accompanies the successor of an exceptionally strong ruler. It is possible Pekahiah preferred his father's policy of tributary vassalage to resistance to the power of Assyria, but he was unable to control the internal opposition to Assyria. In the brief record of Pekahiah's short reign nothing is said of his personal character apart from the fact that, like his predecessors, he adhered to the system of false worship introduced by Jeroboam I.

The chief plotter against Pekahiah was Pekah, his assistant, who, with 50 Gileadites penetrated the palace and murdered the king and his bodyguards. This act of treachery and violence agrees with all the prophet Hosea tells us of the internal condition of Israel at that time. "They devour their judges; all their kings are fallen" (7:7).

For what leaders of your country or the world do you feel moved to pray this week?

In what role of leadership in your life can you ask God to temper your ambition with concern for those you lead?

What do you suppose God would have liked to see the threat of foreign invasion inspire in the leaders and people of Israel?

Pekah — 2 Kings 15:27 - 31

18th King of the Northern Kingdom - 740 - 732

Menahem's "dynasty" lasted only two years beyond his own death, for his son Pekahiah was assassinated by one of his generals, Pekah the son of Remaliah. Additionally, it appears Pekah had already established himself as a rival for the throne and a leader of the anti-Assyrian party especially in the trans-Jordan region of Gilead (II Kings 15:25), for he counted the beginning of his reign retroactively to the beginning of Menahem's.

It was only a year after Pekah took the throne that King Uzziah of Judah died as a leper, and Isaiah saw the vision of Jehovah on the throne of heaven (Isa. 6:1). With the powerful Uzziah now dead, Pekah began to exert great pressure upon Judah to join his western confederacy of anti-Assyrian states. But when Ahaz, in the south, became co-regent with his politically weak father, Judah refused to join the anti-Assyrian alliance.

As a result, Pekah of Israel and Rezin of Syria invaded the southern kingdom, killed 120,000 soldiers and took 200,000 captives, who were soon released because of the threat of divine judgment (II Chron. 28:5- 15). A few months later Pekah and Rezin, of Damascus, plotted to replace Ahaz with a Phoenician puppet named Tabeel (Isa. 7:6). They invaded Judah again and "went up to Jerusalem to war against it but could not prevail against it" (Isa. 7:1; II Kings 16:5). Ahaz had, in the meantime, succeeded in bribing Tiglath- Pileser III to attack Damascus and northern Israel (II Kings 15:29; 16:7-9; II Chron. 28:20).

"When Ahaz son of Jotham, the son of Uzziah, was king of Judah, King Rezin of Aram and Pekah, son of Remaliah, king of Israel marched up to fight against Jerusalem, but they could not overpower it. Now the house of David was told, "Aram has allied itself with Ephraim"; so, the hearts of Ahaz and his people were shaken, as the trees of the forest are shaken by the wind.

Then the LORD said to Isaiah, "Go out, you and your son Shear-Jashub, to meet Ahaz at the end of the aqueduct of the Upper Pool, on the road to the Washerman's Field. Say to him, 'Be careful, keep calm, and don't be afraid. Do not lose heart because of these two smoldering stubs of firewood– because of the fierce anger of Rezin and Aram and of the son of Remaliah." According to Isaiah 7:1-4, Pekah and Rezin now amounted to nothing more than "tails of smoking firebrands" (Isa. 7:4) because Jehovah was not their leader (Isa, 7:7-9).

So, the great darkness of Assyrian deportation fell first upon the northern land of Galilee (Isa, 9:1). Absolutely terrified by the prospect of total collapse under the iron fist of Tiglath-Pileser III, the majority of Israelites now backed Hoshea's plot to remove Pekah and to come to terms with Assyria. Pekah, unpopular with his subjects, was humbled but still defiant. A plot was formed and carried out to assassinate Pekah. Hoshea, whom Tiglath-Pileser had made a vassal, was the person chosen to slay Pekah (II Kings 15:30). All the schemes of this son of Remaliah, who reigned for 8 years (20 by his retroactive reckoning), ended in total disaster.

The following interesting record is found in the Assyrian annals; "Paqaha (Pekah) their king I deposed, and I placed Ausi (Hoshea) over them as king . . . talents of silver as tribute I received from them." A noticeable absence from the biography of Pekah is any reference to the religious conduct of the king. Evidently, he followed the wicked course of previous kings and the historian felt Pekah's influence was beneath notice.

Isaiah, who ministered during the reign of Pekah, has several references to him (7:1-10:4).

What's wrong with the thinking ruthlessness is necessary for success in leadership?

How do you suppose the average citizen of Israel was affected by this succession of selfish and violent kings?

Hoshea — 2 Kings 17

19th King of the Northern Kingdom – 732 - 722

Having killed Pekah, Hoshea assumed rule, thus establishing Israel's ninth and last royal family. The nation, at the time of Hoshea's rise to power was no longer large. The Assyrians had taken both the north (Galilee) and Transjordan, incorporating these areas as Assyrian provinces, leaving Hoshea only the hill country west of the Jordan.

Hoshea himself was nothing more than a feudal lord, a vassal, controlled by the Assyrian king. Little of the glory which had been Israel's under Jeroboam II remained. Even so, Hoshea soon turned to revolt once more against the hated Assyrians, to whom he had submitted only for the sake of expediency. The rebellion came soon after Tiglath-Pileser was succeeded by his son Shalmaneser V (727- 722).

Hoshea foolishly made a pact with Egypt, now weak, divided, and therefore unable to give the assistance Hoshea needed. Trusting in this alliance he refused to pay the annual tribute to Assyria. In 724 B.C., Shalmaneser V marched on Israel (2 Kings 17:3-6). Hoshea went to meet him, now bringing his overdue tribute, but this no longer satisfied the Assyrian monarch. Hoshea was immediately taken captive and Shalmaneser moved on to Samaria, placing the capital under siege.

He expected it to fall quite readily, no doubt, since the king had already been imprisoned; but it stubbornly resisted. The siege lasted from 724 to 722. Finally, the inevitable happened and Samaria fell, bringing the days of Israel (the Northern Kingdom) as a sovereign nation to a close.

ISRAEL UNDER ASSYRIAN CONTROL

After Samaria's fall, an Assyrian governor was instituted in place of the Jewish leaders over the land, thus incorporating all the Northern Kingdom into Assyria's provincial system. Many Israelites were taken captive by Assyria, either prior to the final collapse or at that time, and in place of these a foreign upper class of people was brought into the land.

This policy of mixing populations had also been instituted by Tiglath-Pileser III. It was a way to assure there was less chance of renewed rebellion on the part of the newly conquered people. It seems to have worked well in Israel, but it also brought about religious chaos. The foreigners brought with them their own native ideas of deity and of approach to worship. This practice resulted in a combination of many different religious observances. False deities and Jehovah were worshiped side-by-side. (2 Kings 17:29-41). This mixing of the population also resulted in intermarriage between the Israelites who were left in the land, of which there were many and the new foreign people, who were fewer in number.

The descendants of these marriages came to be called Samaritans.

Israel lasted as a nation for just over two centuries, 931 to 722 B.C. Nineteen kings reigned, representing nine ruling families. Eight kings were either assassinated or committed suicide. Not one of the 19 was considered a good king by God. Each followed either the substitute worship at the golden-calf centers or the more evil cult of Baal. For this reason, God's blessing was withheld.

Through Elijah and Elisha, warning was given to the house of Omri concerning the excessive sin of turning to Baal. When no change came about, punishment was handed out, first in the destruction of the family of Omri by Jehu and then in the complete humiliation of all Israel before the Syrians of Damascus. Once again warning came through Amos and Hosea to the house of Jehu during the prosperous days of Jeroboam II. During this time there was gross wickedness related to the material affluence then existent. Nevertheless, again the people would not hear.

Israel had been given opportunity to repent but would not. God's judgment fell upon her.

What warning from your parents or teachers do you wish you had heeded?

Asa

1 Kings 15:9-15; 2 Chronicles 14-16

3th King of Judah - 911-870

We now return to a discussion of the kingdom of Judah. We will begin with a discussion of Asa, the third king. We are going back in time nearly two centuries. Asa was the godly son of a godless father. Asa's heart was "perfect with the Lord all his days." The first years of his rule were occupied in abolishing idolatry and in religious reforms.

Asa was no respecter of persons, including his own family. Relying upon God, he served Jehovah with much zeal, breaking down all altars and images. His covenant with God is worthy of copying.

His spiritual leadership included removing all the shrine prostitutes from the land of Judah and eliminating all the idols his father had erected. He even deposed his own grandmother, Maachah, as Queen Mother because she had set up an idol. He had it burned by the brook Kidron (1 Kings 15:13).
One thing he did not do, however, was to remove the old Canaanite high places.

In his 15th year, following a victory over an Egyptian army and encouragement by the prophet Azariah (2 Chron. 15:1-7), he called for an assembly of people from Judah and Benjamin, also including Israelites from the tribes of Ephraim, Manasseh, and Simeon, to renew their covenant promises with God.

Sacrifices were offered of the 700 oxen and 7,000 sheep taken as spoil in the recent conflict. He also added some newly dedicated furnishings to the temple and in some way renewed the altar of God. Many people from the kingdom of Israel came to these ceremonies, believing God was with Asa (2 Chron. 15). Later he began a war with Baasha, king of Israel, who fortified Ramah to prevent his subjects from turning to Asa.

The first ten years of his reign the kingdom enjoyed peace, which Asa spent in fortifying his frontier cities and raising an army of over 500,000 men. On one occasion when he was threatened by an overwhelming force from Ethiopia, he cried out to God for help and God miraculously answered his prayer. In the latter days of his life, sad to say, Asa did not do as well in God's sight. He seems to have become proud and self-reliant.

This is evidenced by Asa's imprisonment of Hanani, a prophet, for a rebuke Asa deserved. It may also be indicated by his trust in physicians rather than God when he became diseased in his feet. "In the thirty- ninth year of his reign Asa was afflicted with a disease in his feet. Though his disease was severe, even in his illness he did not seek help from the LORD, but only from the physicians." (2 Chron. 16:12). The physicians he consulted almost certainly practiced a combination of very primitive medicine and magic, in which case the criticism implied in the text would have been directed at the magical elements of their craft.

The prophet Azariah had met Asa when he returned from the Battle described in 2 Chronicles 14 and encouraged him and the people to continue their trust in Jehovah. Asa continued to carry on his reforms; a meeting of the people was held at Jerusalem, sacrifices were offered, and a covenant was made with Jehovah.

The good king then committed the great error of his life. He resorted to an alliance with Ben-Hadad king of Damascus. He created this alliance by purchasing his assistance with material riches from the Temple and the king's house. Ben-Hadad created a military diversion in Asa's favor by invading northern Israel. This caused Baasha, Israel's king, to move his troops from the war with Asa to the North to defend himself against Ben-Hadad. Asa took all the material abandoned by Baasha and built the cities of Geba and Mizpeh.

Asa's lack of faith was rebuked by the seer Hanani, who told him he had lost the honor of conquering the Syrians because of this alliance, and prophesied war for the rest of his days. Asa, angered by the prophecy of Hanani, put him in prison and oppressed many of the people at the same time.

Why was Asa so active in removing the idols and false gods from the towns around his nation?

Jehoshaphat

4th King of Judah - 870-848

1 Kings 22:41-50; 2 Chronicles 17-20

Religiously, Jehoshaphat was the second good king of Judah. He followed in his father's footsteps by further eliminating the much Baal's cultic influence. He gave special orders to Levites and others to teach the "Book of the Law" throughout all Judah. Jehoshaphat correctly recognized if the people were to obey God's Law, they needed first to be instructed in it.

An example of Jehoshaphat's faith in God is seen in an attack made against him by a coalition of Moab, Ammon, and Edom. When he learned of the invasion, Jehoshaphat did not panic, but called for a time of fasting and prayer in Jerusalem. God responded to the prayer spoken by the king himself and promised victory. When Jehoshaphat's troops, led by singing Levites, came to where the enemy was located, they found an inter-army rivalry had led to armed conflict between their enemies. The only task of the Judean army was to collect the spoil from the dead.

We should not think Jehoshaphat was a weak ruler with a weak army. He had, in fact, a strong army consisting of five divisions, three from Judah and two from Benjamin. Jehoshaphat also gave attention to strengthening the defenses of his country, building both fortresses and supply cities. His might became known abroad, and other countries feared to make war against him, perhaps accounting for the three-nation structure of the invading enemy referred to above. Both the Philistines and Arabians wanted to maintain his good will by bringing valuable presents.

He also took steps to improve juridical procedures in the land. Jehoshaphat called for the divinely ordained regulations to be reinstated. He appointed judges in important cities, thus making more local courts (legally prescribed by Moses: (Deut. 16:18; 19:12; 21:18-19; 22:13-14), and he urged those appointed be fair in all decisions. He appointed certain priests, Levites, and leaders to serve in a court in Jerusalem. When the matter to be considered at this court involved religion, Amariah, the high priest, was to act as chairman; when it involved a civic question, Zebadiah, a civic leader, was to officiate.
In this he recognized the separation of church and state. 2 Chronicles 19:11, records his declaration for us.

The major flaw we see in the life and reign of Jehoshaphat was his tendency to rely on military alliances for protection. He did not to continue to rely on God. He had a continuing political relationship with Ahab which almost cost him his life.

Other problems arose from this alliance. These resulted from the three specific times that Jehoshaphat aided Israelite kings.

- He helped Ahab in his battle at Ramoth-Gilead and was nearly killed for his trouble.
- He joined Ahab's son in shipbuilding on the Gulf of Aqaba, and every vessel was destroyed before its maiden voyage.
- He allied himself with Ahab's second son, Jehoram, in a military offensive against Moab to coerce tribute-paying to Israel. He nearly died, along with the related armies, for lack of water (2 Kings 3:4-27).

We will see the results for the nation when he allowed his son to marry the daughter of Ahab and Jezebel. Prophets of God were involved each time:

- Micaiah warned the Ramoth-Gilead battle would be lost.
- Eliezer warned Jehoshaphat's ships would be broken due to God's displeasure at the alliance.
- Elisha revealed God's way of deliverance for the allied kings in their need for water.

Jehoshaphat should have learned a lesson the first time, but he did not.

In Jehoshaphat we see a man who loved God and instituted the first nationwide Bible study.

Yet we see someone who had difficulty putting everything he knew into consistent practice.

His practice of teaching the Word of God lived on after his death.

Jehoram

2 Kings 8:16-24; 2 Chronicles 21

5th King of Judah – 853- 841

Jehoshaphat, following the pattern of his father, appointed his son Jehoram as co-regent for the last four years of his reign. During the years of co-regency, Jehoram should have learned from his godly father; and perhaps he did in secular matters, but it is certainly not evident in religious matters.

Jehoshaphat had been one of Judah's best kings in God's sight, but now Jehoram is characterized as one who did evil. A contributing reason was his marriage to the wicked Athaliah. He ruled alone for eight years after his father's death and five unhappy events marked the time. The first was his slaughter of his own six brothers, all of whom their father Jehoshaphat had previously given gifts of gold, valuable articles, and fortified cities (2 Chron. 21:2-4). Jehoram's purpose must have been to insure his own rule against rivals, a procedure which was common throughout the ancient world but was without precedent in Judah.

The second and third unhappy events concerned two successful instances of revolt against his rule. One was by the country of Edom, who earlier had helped Jehoram and Jehoshaphat against Moab. The submission of Edom to Judah likely dated from Jehoshaphat's earlier triumph over a coalition that had included Edom. Jehoram fought to put down the revolt at this time but was not successful. The other revolt was by the city of Libnah. This one was successful, for no indication is recorded Jehoram even tried to retaliate.

The fourth was an invasion of his country by Philistines and Arabians, in which Judah suffered substantial loss. Material goods were seized, and all Jehoram's own wives and sons (except for Ahaziah, the youngest) were captured. Little could be more tragic and humiliating for a king than this. The fifth was the gruesome death of Jehoram himself. He died of a fearful disease of the intestines, in accordance with a warning given by Elijah (2 Chron. 21:12-15, 18-20). In all, one must say Jehoram's reign was disastrous politically, militarily and religiously.

Ahaziah

2 Kings 8, 9; 2 Chronicles 22

6th King of Judah - 841

It was a deplorable mistake of the good king of Judah, Jehoshaphat, to ally his son Jehoram with the wicked daughter of Jezebel. Jehoram succeeded to the throne of the southern kingdom upon his father's death and held it for eight dreadful years. He was, like Ahab, completely dominated by his wife and her aged mother Jezebel, with predictable results. The fundamental weakness of his character is exposed by this fact. The chronicler (21:11) tells of the Phoenician atrocities which the feeble king introduced into Jerusalem at the bidding of the two evil women who dominated his life. Murder (21:4) and paganism marked his eight dark years. Ahaziah his son, whose death at Jehu's hands had already been prophesied, succeeded to the throne at the age of 22 and survived for one ill-fated year. Athaliah, his mother, was supreme. She "was his counselor in doing wickedly" (22:3). It was well for Judah the reign was short. The southern kingdom reproduced over the next few years the events which happened in Samaria.

We should pause at this point to consider the confusion of evil which mars the record of Scripture. Where have all the good men gone? It is well to remember the great age of the literary prophets had already begun. The first great movement of the prophetic spirit, developing through Samuel to Elijah and Elisha, was closing. It was time for the Old Testament to take its final shape. Recording scribes like those who put the Chronicles together, were watching the flow of the nation's history and drawing the spiritual lessons from it which later ages were to note.

There were good priests like the man whom we shall meet in the story of Joash.

Events, too, center in the city. And the city, as David found, was no nursery for true religion.

Is the situation any different today?

Athaliah

2 Kings 11, 2 Chronicles 22, 23

Usurper - 841-835

She was born in Samaria. She married into the royal family of Judea then lived and died near the city of Jerusalem. She ruled for approximately five years around the time of 840 BC. Athaliah was the daughter of Ahab and Jezebel; she was the granddaughter of Omri.

These are the final consequences of the fateful marriage between Ahab and the princess of Tyre, which brought pain and bloodshed to the northern kingdom, and then, like some terrible plague, infected the land of Judah. Athaliah was Jezebel's true daughter. Her mother is the woman who threatened to kill Elijah and caused him to run for his life into the Negev desert. With a family lineage such as this, she was not likely to end up a biblical heroine.

In a marriage arranged for political purposes she became the wife of King Jehoram of Judah. It is said of this Judean king, "He walked in the way of the Kings of Israel, just as the house of Ahab did." This was undoubtedly due to the influence of Athaliah and her worship of the pagan deities she had learned from her mother. After the death of her husband, Athaliah's son became King. He continued to lead politically and religiously by following the example of the Northern Kingdom. He was king for only one year and was assassinated by Jehu, who was carrying out the prophetic words of the prophet Elisha.

With her son dead, she saw the path to her ambition open. Her husband, Jehoram had murdered his six younger brothers. Earlier an Arab and Philistine raiding party had stripped the palace of all heirs except Ahaziah. They must have been babies and infants, since the king died at Jehu's hand when he was only 23 years of age. With all her sons dead, Athaliah committed an even worse crime. She had Ahaziah's children (her own grandchildren) slaughtered so she might herself seize the throne. Human decency, apart from a normal grandmother's love, called for her to go into mourning and seek to comfort and care for her son's offspring, but this was not Athaliah's way. She had them all killed; all of her grandchildren, except Joash, who, thanks to a woman's daring, was overlooked. His nurse and Ahaziah's half-sister Jehosheba, the wife of Jehoiada the priest, hid the child.

Athaliah began this bloody purge to destroy the entire royal line of the house of David. She was successful in having all the male members of the house of David executed except for one small infant; Joash. God had promised the line of David would continue and Athaliah failed in her attempt to destroy God's chosen lineage!

We see a window into her soul and the reality of her relationship with her "gods" when we realize she had her own grandchildren executed. In this we can see some of what she learned growing up in the house of Ahab and Jezebel. After this Athaliah ruled for six years.

The fact Jehu had dealt a serious blow to the cult in Israel by his well-known blood purge probably motivated her to do even more in Judah, but it may also have contributed to greater opposition against her. Seven years later, Jehoiada decided to produce the young prince; arrangements had been made for defense in case of necessity. The young boy, Joash was declared king. Athaliah, who was probably worshiping in the house of Baal, heard the shouts of the people and went to the Temple, where her cry of "treason" only produced her own arrest. She was taken beyond the confines of the Temple and put to death. The only other recorded victim of this revolution was Mattan, the priest of Baal.

In Athaliah we see a woman who was molded for evil by her own family.

In Athaliah we see the effects of power and privilege when they are passed down from generation to generation with no knowledge of responsibility which comes with such power.

Her addiction to using power and privilege to always have her own way should be a warning to all of us.

Joash

2 Kings 11, 12; 2 Chronicles 23, 24

7th King of Judah - 835-796

Joash became king at the age of seven and ruled 40 years. The young king needed an advisor; and the aged, godly high priest, Jehoiada, who had already protected and anointed him, served in this capacity. To Jehoiada must go most of the credit for the fine record of Joash's early years.

The training Joash received under Jehoiada was like that of the boy Samuel, who spent the formative years of early childhood in the quiet precincts of the Temple, absorbing the meaning of its sacred rituals.

Years later, when Joash had come to an age to act for himself, he gave orders for the temple to be repaired of damage done to it by Athaliah's sons (2 Chron. 24:7). He set out to restore the ancient temple and found himself frustrated by the apathy of the priests who were content to pursue the formal exercises of their religion, and resistant to work and change.

This is often a widespread fault of those engaged in the service of God. They become content with the situation and conform to the fashions of the day in lethargy or shyness.

Joash, in this 23rd year suggested a new method of raising the necessary money. A box was placed at the side of the altar for people to give when they came with their sacrifices. Workers were hired and the required repairs made, with money enough left over to provide new furnishings.

Jehoiada was growing old. It is likely he was grooming his son, Zechariah, for the office of high priest. The accounts, in Kings and Chronicles, are too brief for us to unravel motives and explain some puzzling actions. But it is not impossible Joash earned the resentment of the priestly hierarchy by his firm takeover of the finances for the repair of the Temple. So long as Jehoiada continued as high priest, Joash ruled as a God-fearing king; but when Jehoiada died, the king changed. This development came sometime after Joash's 23rd year, for it was then he gave the order relative to offerings for temple repair just noted, but how long after is not indicated.

Jehoiada died at the age of 130, which was sometime in the latter part of Joash's reign. Following the great man's death, the king began to listen to new advisors who were more sympathetic to the cult of Baal. He was so influenced he had Jehoiada's own son, Zechariah, stoned to death for rebuking him. At the end of the year in which Zechariah was stoned came great loss for Joash at the hands of Hazael, king of Damascus. Having brought a severe defeat on Israel, Hazael marched south as far as Gath in Philistia and seized it. Then he turned toward Jerusalem. He brought destruction throughout Judah and took many lives, including those of several princes. Only by paying Hazael tribute did Joash succeed in persuading him to not destroy Jerusalem (2 Kings 12:17-18). Joash was assassinated by conspirators. Even his own servants took part, prompted by their disapproval of his reversal in policy after Jehoiada's death. Death in this way was a bitter end to a life which had begun with great promise. It is sad to see a reign, which had begun so well, end in such failure. Brought up in seclusion, Joash was no man of war. Rather than fight he compromised with the ever-present bandit of Damascus, Hazael, who was bought off by sacred treasure. Perhaps his compromise with paganism, promoted by the apostate princes despite warning (24:19), was made in consciousness of growing hostility from Jehoiada's successors in the hierarchy. We cannot tell.

The impression remains of a good man, deeply tried, who broke under testing.

How do we try to silence God's voice in our lives when we are living in disobedience?

How was Joash's death related to what he had done in his life?

How were Joash's reforms and accomplishments tarnished by his choices later in life?

Amaziah

2 Kings 14; 2 Chronicles 25

8th King of Judah – 796-767

Amaziah succeeded his father. The assassination did not bring an end to the dynastic line. He ruled 29 years, though the last 24 were in co-regency with his son, Uzziah. Amaziah stood approved of God in life and reigned like his father, but also like him, he did not remove all the high places. One of Amaziah's first actions was to punish his father's assassins by having them all killed (2 Kings 14:1-6).

Two major battles were fought by Amaziah, the first of which was with Edom and ended in complete victory. Edom revolted against Jehoram and lost in the resulting battle. Edom continued was attractive to Judah because of the southern trade routes and the revenue to which it gave access. Amaziah made ambitious plans to strengthen control there, even hiring soldiers from Israel, the Northern Kingdom.

He was rebuked by a "man of God" for securing them. After listening to the rebuke, he sent the men back home, much to their displeasure. He killed 10,000 of the enemy and took another 10,000 captives, only to kill them by throwing them from the top of a high rock. Following this victory, he displeased God by bringing images of Edom's false gods back to Judah and worshiping them.

An unnamed prophet brought the king a rebuke from God by pointedly asking, "Why do you consult this people's gods, which could not save their own people from your hand?"

The second battle was with Israel. Amaziah, made proud and self-confident by his Edomite victory, challenged Jehoash of Israel. Israel recently had suffered several defeats at the hands of Hazael of Damascus, but by now she was experiencing a recovery, which Amaziah apparently did not realize. Jehoash, the ruler of Israel, tried to discourage the Judean ruler; but Amaziah insisted and war came near Beth-Shemesh, west of Jerusalem. Judah was defeated, and Jehoash then continued to Jerusalem, destroying some 600 feet of city wall, a sign of total subjugation, and seizing substantial booty and many captives. It is likely, among these captives was Amaziah himself (2 Kings 14:13), which, if so, was a humiliation of the harshest kind. The writer in Chronicles states all this came in punishment for Amaziah having "sought the gods of Edom" (2 Chron. 25:20).

If Amaziah was taken captive, which fits with the beginning of his son's co-regency, he likely was kept in Israel as long as Jehoash of Israel lived (2 Kings 14:17) and was then allowed to return to the rule of Judah.

Death

No information is given regarding Amaziah's rule after he returned except the unhappy note that he, too, as his father, saw a conspiracy formed against him. He tried to escape death by fleeing to Lachish but was followed and killed there. His body was returned to Jerusalem for burial.

What advantages and disadvantages do you see in a government ruled by one person who is succeeded by his son from generation to generation?

How would you handle a child who says he or she loves you but continues to disobey what you instruct him or her to do?

Why do you think Azariah is credited with the accomplishments of his reign although the Scripture records that his son was the "power behind the throne"?

How does it feel to have someone else get the credit when you have done most of the work?

Why would Ahaziah be described as someone who did what was right, but not wholeheartedly?

How did pride contribute to Ahaziah's problems?

Uzziah 2 Kings 14, 15; 2 Chronicles 26

9th King of Judah - 790-740

Amaziah's son and successor is called by two names, Uzziah and Azariah, names closely associated in meaning and perhaps used interchangeably. Uzziah was one of Judah's most capable rulers. For the most part he followed the positive life-patterns of his two predecessors. God, in approval, used his inborn ability to restore a high status for Judah in the world. This improvement in Judah's position came at approximately the same time as Israel's growth under the able Jeroboam II. Between the two men, the total land-area finally controlled came to rival even that of the days of David and Solomon.

Uzziah ruled longer than any prior king of either Judah or Israel; 52 years (2 Kings 15:2; 2 Chron. 26:3). The first 24 were in co-regency with his father, and the last 12 were similarly served with his son Jotham, leaving only 16 years of individual rule. Uzziah would have been 16 years of age at the time of his father's captivity by Jehoash of Israel. He would have ruled the nine years his father was captive, then in a secondary capacity in the period when his father resumed his reign. The reason for his son Jotham's co- regency, spanning Uzziah's last 12 years is Uzziah becoming a leper at the beginning of this period. The disease was imposed as punishment from God for intruding into the priest's office (2 Chron. 26:16-21).

It was following the death of Jeroboam II, Uzziah reached his best moments. By 743 B.C., the year of the first western campaign of Tiglath-Pileser III of Assyria, Uzziah had become the strongest ruler along the Mediterranean coast.

Syrian states north of Damascus had long been kept weak by continued Assyrian aggression and could not lead in resisting Tiglath-Pileser. Consequently, Uzziah, who had become known because of his success in the south, was now recognized by these others and given leadership of a coalition to withstand the coming Assyrian conqueror. Tiglath-Pileser himself gives record of this coalition and encounter, indicating it was led by one "Azriau of Yaudi," which can only mean Azariah (Uzziah) of Judah. Uzziah was no longer young at the time, for this was the 48th year of his rule, when he was 65. It would have been a memorable occasion to find himself thus honored by fellow rulers.

He was outstanding as a builder. He reinforced the walls of Jerusalem. He made the gates and the towers stronger to reinforce the safety of the city against enemy attack. He continued his strengthening of the nation by building towers and digging wells throughout the southern part of the country. He had great success in many different areas. He was able to build and maintain a large army. He placed defensive "machines" in the towers defending Jerusalem. He maintained a large ranching program with cattle and sheep in the foothills near Jerusalem and was able to expand the ability of the people of Judah to grow and produce their own crops.

His great weakness is revealed to us in 2 Chronicles 26:16, "*But after Uzziah became powerful, his pride led to his downfall. He was unfaithful to the LORD his God and entered the temple of the LORD to burn incense on the altar of incense.*" The Law of God specifically forbids anyone other than a qualified priest to burn incense within the Temple. This sin is not unlike the pride of King Saul who refused to wait on the prophet Samuel and offered his own sacrifice when he had been told to wait for the proper authority.

Immediately after this action Uzziah was challenged and denounced by the high priest Azariah. In order to show the seriousness of this violation of the Word of God Azariah brought with him 80 other priests to stand before the king of Judah. Uzziah became furious these priests had the boldness to confront the priest. He was the king; how could they charge him with sin? His pride had clouded his judgment and caused him to act against the direct instruction of God. He became angry and enraged at the priests for their lack of respect for who he was. God intervened at that very moment and struck him with leprosy. The king was removed from the Temple and forced to live the rest of his life in a separate house.

In Uzziah we see a man who was greatly blessed by God and who encouraged many others to follow God; yet we see a man whose success clouded his judgment.

In his success he lost humility and perspective. He thought he had been successful through his own efforts and he forgot the source of everything he had achieved with his obedience to God.

Jotham

2 Kings 15; 2 Chronicles 27

10th King of Judah – 750-731

Jotham succeeded his father, Uzziah, and reigned 20 years, however the first 12 were as co-regent with his father. Since his father was able to lead in creating a northern alliance, it seems he was not seriously incapacitated by his leprosy during these early years. Jotham may have been installed co-ruler mainly as a "front" man, to meet people and convey orders worked out and given by the capable Uzziah.

Jotham later installed his son Ahaz as his co-regent. Biblical cross-references show this was done about 12 years before Jotham died, which means surprisingly there were co-regencies which overlapped. Jotham made his son, Ahaz, his co-regent while he was still co-regent with his father, Uzziah.

For four years, Judah had Uzziah as chief ruler, Jotham as his co-regent, and Ahaz as Jotham's co-regent.

Sometimes we think our government is confusing. Political intrigue is not limited to our day and age!

The year of Ahaz's accession as Jotham's co-ruler was 743 BC., the same year Uzziah went north to lead the northern coalition. This is most likely the explanation for this unusual situation. Jotham, now left alone in Jerusalem and was fearful of the consequences for his father in this battle. He was probably thinking Tiglath-Pileser would bring vengeance on Uzziah's own country if he won victory over the coalition. This caused him to try to strengthen his home base by making Ahaz co-ruler with him. He may have doubted seriously that his father would return.

Jotham was not a great leader and was motivated often by fear for his own position.

Jotham was the fourth successive God-approved king of Judah. Consequently, he continued to experience blessing in his reign and was able to maintain his country's strong position. Only one military engagement is mentioned, that with the Ammonites; he won the battle. As a result, Israel received tribute payment from Ammon for three years.

Jotham also carried on extensive construction activity. In Jerusalem he built an important temple gate and added to the "wall of Ophel." Elsewhere he enlarged cities and erected "forts and towers" as means of fortification.

But prosperity often leads to religious neglect, and it did here in Judah. This is evidenced by the words of the prophet Isaiah, who began to serve at this time. Isaiah speaks much of the sin of the nation which had become proud and selfish through comfort.

He warns punishment would come if changes were not made.

This punishment was already at hand at the time of Jotham's death. Pekah, king of Israel, and Rezin, king of Damascus, were at the gate of Jerusalem, laying siege to force Judah to cooperate in a revolt against Assyria (2 Kings 15:37). Ahaz had this distressing situation to face as he took over as chief ruler.

To what extent can a ruler influence the spirituality of the people he or she governs?

What would do you think Jotham would say was his secret of success in life?

What measures of success in life should be secondary to our focus on loving and serving God?

What lessons have you learned about following the Lord by watching other people and their faith?

What is one change you can make in your plans for the near future to reflect your commitment to God?

Ahaz — 2 Kings 16; 2 Chronicles 28

11th King of Judah - 735-715

The might of Assyria now made itself felt in Judah much more directly than at any previous time. Until this period, Damascus and Israel had served as terminating points for Assyrian campaigns. Judah was next in line. From the beginning of his reign, Ahaz was pro-Assyrian in his policies. There is reason to believe he was able to assume power over his father while Jotham yet lived. The reason must be the Jerusalem nobles believed they were better off in submitting to Tiglath-Pileser than resisting him, and accordingly supported the sympathetic Ahaz in seizing the throne.

The Siege by Pekah and Rezin

Because of the pro-Assyrian feeling in Jerusalem, Pekah, king of Israel, and Rezin, king of Damascus, had joined as allies to besiege Jerusalem and force Judah to support a revolt against Assyria. The siege came in Jotham's closing years, but since Ahaz had already assumed leadership, the task of resistance was mainly his. Recognizing his inability to meet the combined foe in combat and wishing to keep in the good favor of Assyria, he requested help from Tiglath-Pileser III. Ahaz asked Assyria to enter the region and attack both Damascus and Israel, thus forcing the two to lift the siege and return home.

The Rise of Assyrian Influence

Ahaz gave the Assyrian king a substantial payment of gold and silver as a bribe. Ahaz's plan worked, for Tiglath-Pileser did attack and Pekah and Rezin were forced to return to their respective countries. Before they did so, however, they produced extensive damage in Judah, killing 120,000 people and taking 200,000 captives. These captives were permitted to return home to Judah almost immediately as a result of a caution by one of God's prophets.

Ahaz, himself, received a rebuke from God for his way of finding relief from the siege. Isaiah brought a warning from God at the time Ahaz was considering sending his letter and gift to Tiglath-Pileser (Isa. 7-8). The prophet told Ahaz his real enemy was not these smaller, neighboring kings, but the mighty Assyrian power whose help he was about to seek. The truth of Isaiah's statement is borne out by the destruction Tiglath-Pileser then inflicted in the region during the next three years.

Religiously, Ahaz ended the tradition of godly rule established by the four kings who had preceded him. He made images of Baal, practiced infant sacrifice in the Valley of Hinnom, and worshiped in the high places. While meeting with Tiglath-Pileser in Damascus, at the close of the conqueror's brutal campaign, Ahaz saw and admired a pagan altar and sent a plan of it home to Uriah the priest to copy for Jerusalem. When he later returned, he established this altar as the official place of sacrifice at the temple, in place of the brazen altar prescribed in the Mosaic Law. He intentionally damaged several of the sacred vessels of the temple and even closed the doors of the temple.

Military Reverses

The first came at the hands of Edom, who once again revolted, even carrying captives from Judah, reversing Amaziah's earlier treatment of Edom. The important port of Elath on the Gulf of Aqaba was once again lost to Judah, when it was seized by Rezin of Damascus for his country (2 Kings 16:6).

Ahaz and God

In his time of trouble King Ahaz became even more unfaithful to the LORD. He offered sacrifices to the gods of Damascus, who had defeated him; for he thought, "Since the gods of the kings of Aram have helped them, I will sacrifice to them so they will help me." But they were his downfall and the downfall of all Israel. 2 Chronicles 28:22-23

In what way do you think our problems and difficulties are God's way of getting our attention?

Why didn't all his troubles turn Ahaz's heart back to God?

Hezekiah: Approved of God — 2 Kings 18-20; 2 Chronicles 29-32; Isaiah 36-37

12th King of Judah - 715-686

As we look at the line of Jewish kings it seems as if heredity does not always operate. Sometimes children depart from the ways in which they were trained (Proverbs 22:6). Wicked Ahaz, one of the most dreadful characters recorded in Scripture, was the son of a godly father and the father of a godly son.

Godly Hezekiah in turn, was the son of a wicked father and the father of a wicked son.

King Hezekiah, who reigned for 29 years, is more completely commended than any other king of Judah. The history and literature of his reign occupy 17 chapters of the Bible. At the time of his accession to the throne, Judah was reduced to a low state. Through the wickedness of Ahaz, true religion had vanished, and the people were guilty of the grossest idolatry. Then the strength of the kingdom had been exhausted by the tribulations and captivities it suffered during the reign of Ahaz.

God, however, did not give His people up to utter desolation. He did not forget His promise, "Here I will make a horn grow for David and set up a lamp for my anointed one." (Psalm 132:17).

Under Hezekiah, God made the people of Judah the inheritors of His unique mercy. We see whenever God's people need help, His chosen instrument is at hand. According to the general laws of heredity no good could have been expected of the son and immediate successor of godless Ahaz, but Hezekiah appeared. Hezekiah succeeded his father, ruling for 42 years, though the first 13 were as co- regent.

There is reason to believe Hezekiah assumed chief rule four years before his father died, likely at the insistence of a growing anti-Assyrian party objecting to further pro-Assyrian actions by Ahaz. It is likely his accession as co-ruler had been at the insistence of this group, even though Ahaz was still permitted to keep the top position. Hezekiah was one of Judah's finest kings in the sight of God. He is given the high accolade of having acted as David, his father, and of being the peer of all Judah's kings in trusting God (2 Kings 18:5).

After the deliberate idolatry of Ahaz, drastic reform was necessary, and Hezekiah accomplished it.
The doors of the temple were again opened, and the priests and Levites were instructed to remove all foreign cult objects. Then they were to clean and restore all the proper items so true worship might be reinstated. A magnificent time of sacrificing and celebrations marked the return to the true Mosaic ceremonies. Further, Hezekiah ordered the Passover to be observed once more. This had been neglected for many years, even before the rule of Ahaz. Hezekiah invited Israelites from Beersheba to Dan to take part in the festive occasion. Many responded, and a time of feasting and worshiping followed such as had not occurred since the reign of Solomon (2 Chron. 30:26).

This in turn led to a cleansing of the land generally; soon the high places, images, Asherah poles, false altars, and even the brazen serpent which Moses had made in the wilderness centuries before were destroyed. Even further, Hezekiah retrained and revitalized the organization of priests and Levites. The new king also strengthened their support by the tithes of the people (2 Chron. 31:1-21).

Why was David always the standard of comparison for the kings of Israel and Judah?

How did Hezekiah's leadership change the direction of the nation?

What priorities did Hezekiah set when he became king of Judah?

How important was Hezekiah's example in bringing about the revival of the nation?

How is it possible for symbols of Christian faith and history to become idols to us?

Hezekiah and the Assyrians — 2 Kings 18-20; 2 Chronicles 29-32; Isaiah 36-37

12th King of Judah - 715-686

Hezekiah was anti-Assyrian, in contrast to his father. He did not, however, openly rebel against the eastern power as long as Sargon II was ruling. When Sargon's son, Sennacherib (705-681), came to the throne, Hezekiah joined an anti-Assyrian alliance. A change in kings was always seen as a favorable time for rebellion, as subject people tested the strength of the new ruler. This new alliance was composed of more members than an earlier alliance, with Tyre the leading city and a new Egyptian king, who gave promise of providing more support, having come to the throne.

Hezekiah made thorough preparations for an expected retaliation by Sennacherib. He constructed further fortifications, made new weapons, and reinforced his military strength. He gave special attention to stopping the water supplies the enemy might use. At the same time, he provided a more convenient access to water for his own people by digging the famous Hezekiah's Tunnel from the Spring of Gihon, through the hill of Ophel to a place within the city lower than the starting point; a truly remarkable piece of engineering.

Sennacherib's invasion

During Sennacherib's first four years of rule, he was occupied with maintaining Assyrian control over Babylon; but in 701 B.C., he came to put down this revolt in the west. He dealt first with Tyre, the leading city, by crushing resistance there, and Tyre's king fled to Cyprus.

At this point many of the coalition's less enthusiastic members surrendered, including the kings of Byblos, Arvad, Moab, Edom, and Ammon. Then Sennacherib moved south along the Mediterranean and punished another leading city, Ashkelon, deporting her king to Assyria. It was probably at this point, with the coastline in his control Sennacherib moved inland toward the city of Jerusalem. Hezekiah foolishly tried to buy off the Assyrian king by stripping all the gold and silver from the Royal Palace and Temple (2 Kings 18). The king refused the offer and continued to move toward Jerusalem finally surrounding the city and beginning the process of the siege.

Sennacherib sent three lieutenants and a large force of men to pursue psychological warfare against Hezekiah and his people (2 Kings 18:17-37; 2 Chron. 32:9-16; Isa. 36:1-21). Their threats were effective in causing the people to fear and in causing Hezekiah to consult with Isaiah, from whom the king received a comforting word from God. At this juncture, Sennacherib heard Egypt's army was coming to the aid of the coalition and turned to meet it rather than continuing immediately to Jerusalem.

He sent a letter to Hezekiah at the time in which he restated the threats already made by the lieutenants. With this letter in hand, Hezekiah and Isaiah bowed before God and asked for God's deliverance. The prophet told the king that Sennacherib would not capture Jerusalem, nor even come near it. **That night the angel of the Lord moved through the camp of the Assyrians and 185,000 soldiers died.**

From Sennacherib's report, we learn he did encounter an Egyptian force and defeat it. He also speaks of capturing many nearby cities. Sennacherib further states he conquered a total of 46 strong cities of Hezekiah, numerous villages, and seized over 200,000 prisoners. Of the death of 185,000 men Sennacherib says nothing, as one might expect. His account, however, indirectly corroborates the fact, because he does not claim to have captured Jerusalem, which would be most unusual otherwise, since Jerusalem was certainly one of his prime objectives from the first. His own words speak only of shutting Hezekiah in Jerusalem "like a bird in a cage." The Assyrian king quickly returned home and shortly after his return to Nineveh he was assassinated by two of his own sons.

Why is it better to pray for God to avenge His own name rather than that He will avenge us?

Hezekiah's illness and fame 2 Kings 18-20; 2 Chronicles 29-32; Isaiah 36-37

12th King of Judah - 715-686

Two other episodes in Hezekiah's life, both related to this Assyrian campaign, are recorded. The first one concerns a time of severe illness from which the king recovered only because of God's hand of healing. The time was during, or just prior to, Sennacherib's invasion of the land. We will reproduce the text which describes his illness so we can get a feel for the miraculous nature of these events.

In those days Hezekiah became ill and was at the point of death. The prophet Isaiah son of Amoz went to him and said, "This is what the LORD says: Put your house in order, because you are going to die; you will not recover." Hezekiah turned his face to the wall and prayed to the LORD, "Remember, O LORD, how I have walked before you faithfully and with complete devotion and have done what is good in your eyes." And Hezekiah wept bitterly. Before Isaiah had left the middle court, the word of the LORD came to him: "Go back and tell Hezekiah, the leader of my people, 'This is what the LORD, the God of your father David, says: I have heard your prayer and seen your tears; I will heal you. On the third day from now you will go up to the temple of the LORD. I will add fifteen years to your life. And I will deliver you and this city from the hand of the king of Assyria. I will defend this city for my sake and for the sake of my servant David.'" Then Isaiah said, "Prepare a poultice of figs." They did so and applied it to the boil, and he recovered. 2 Kings 20:1-7

In consideration of his emotional distress, God gave Hezekiah a remarkable sign as evidence the promise would be fulfilled: the return of the sundial shadow ten degrees.

Messengers from Babylon

The second episode concerns the visit to Jerusalem by messengers from king of Babylon. They arrived soon after the king's recovery from his illness (Isa. 39:1). Hezekiah yielded to the conceit of his own importance. He felt he was worthy of the special favor God had given him. On account of the divine and human favors received the Scripture says, "His heart was lifted up." The king of Babylon, eager to gain favor, sent many presents and a letter of congratulation on his extraordinary restoration from fatal sickness.

Carried away with pride, Hezekiah responded by displaying the magnificence of his palace and treasures before the pagan monarch. "God left him to try him, that he might know all that was in his heart" and Hezekiah quickly learned the depravity of his heart! Hezekiah's pride did not go unpunished. Isaiah came to him with a serious reprimand and threat of captivity and of confiscation of his boasted treasures by the very man to whom he had paid court. The Babylonians, Isaiah said, would one day come to Jerusalem and carry off to Babylon all they had seen. The king humbled himself before God and was given a delay. He was assured the judgment would not come in his time. From then on, he was fully surrendered to God and tried to lead the nation of Judah to follow God as well. As a result of his faithfulness God increased his power, riches, and honor.

Extraordinary prosperity completed the 29 years of Hezekiah's reign. The writer of Chronicles says, "The other events of Hezekiah's reign and his acts of devotion are written in the vision of the prophet Isaiah son of Amoz in the book of the kings of Judah and Israel. Hezekiah rested with his fathers and was buried on the hill where the tombs of David's descendants are. All Judah and the people of Jerusalem honored him when he died." 2 Chronicles 32:32-33 The final 15 years of his life produced a son by the name of Manasseh who had the longest and most evil kingship of all the monarchs of Judah.

In what sense might it have been better for Judah if Hezekiah had died at the earlier date?

From God's perspective why do you think our heart's desire is or is not always best for us?

What is unwise about boasting and showcasing our possessions?

What drives us to try to impress our peers?

Manasseh
2 Chronicles 33:1-20

13th King of Judah - 695-642

His name means "Causing forgetfulness." This was the name chosen by Joseph for his first son in Egypt because the blessing caused him to forget all his trial and pain. This Manasseh was born after Hezekiah petitioned God and God extended his life for 15 years. Perhaps this is the reason the name was chosen because his birth allowed Hezekiah to forget the pain and disease that almost caused him death.

Manasseh may well be the most unique king ever to rule Israel or Judah. He had the longest reign of any king recorded in the Bible. He reversed the trend of many kings which we have studied. He began his rule as an extremely evil and disobedient person, but he repented and died serving God. Manasseh began to rule when he was 12 years old and he immediately began to work to undo all the religious reforms of his father. He rebuilt the high places which his father Hezekiah had destroyed. He erected new altars to Baal and Asherah. Black arts flourished and all forms of wickedness were allowed. The prophetic voice of truth condemning all vile worship went unheeded. The king turned a deaf ear to God who was calling him. The long-lived monarch despite divine and human warnings persisted in his evil ways.

But amid all national wickedness, the godly remnant continued, grew, and was purified. They were inspired by the influence of Isaiah. Manasseh persecuted the prophets and their followers, and he shed much innocent blood. Tradition tells us he killed Isaiah by placing him inside a hollow tree and sawing him in half. This belief relates to the passage in Hebrews 11:37.

He worshiped the stars and observed the signs of the zodiac. He even built pagan altars in the very temple of God. The Scriptures also tell us he offered his sons as burnt offerings to the pagan deities in the Valley of Hinnom. The writer of Chronicles tells us, "He did more evil than the Canaanites had done." He persecuted anyone who continued to serve Jehovah. He practiced sorcery, divination, and witchcraft. For direction he consulted mediums and fortune tellers instead of the prophets of God.

God judged him by allowing the Assyrians to defeat him in battle and take him prisoner. He was led away in shackles and put in prison. During this time of confinement Manasseh turned to the God he had learned of in his childhood, prayed and asked forgiveness. God heard his prayer and restored him to his position as King of Judah. He immediately began to attempt to undo all the evil he had done, but for the most part this was unsuccessful. He had caused an entire generation to turn away from God.

It is impossible to sink so deeply into sin God would not be willing to lift a person up and restore him.

God is true to His word; anyone who calls upon Him will not be turned away.

Amon
2 Kings 21; 2 Chronicles 33

14th King of Judah - 642-640

Amon succeeded his father but ruled only two years. Only a few verses are used to explain Amon, whose brief reign was a weaker continuation of the regime of his wicked father. Amon's name was associated with the Egyptian local sun-god, Amon, and was given him when his father was immersed in his idolatrous practices. It indicates Jehovah had no more claim to worship than heathen deities.

Moral and religious intemperance went hand in hand. Amon "trespassed more and more." Amon copied all his father's sins but not his sorrow over his sins.

He rejected the grace shown to Manasseh. As a young man he probably thought life was before him and he could have his fling in all that was licentious and then, in later life, repent like his father. But such a day of repentance never came.

Josiah

2 Kings 22, 23; 2 Chronicles 34-35

15th King of Judah - 640-609

The three decades of Josiah's reign were among the happiest in Judah's experience. They were characterized by peace, prosperity, and reform. No outside enemies made war on the nation; the people could concentrate on constructive activity. Josiah himself sought to please God by reinstituting obedience to the regulations commanded in the Mosaic Law.

Josiah was made king when he was only a boy of eight. Religious idolatry was widespread as a result of Amon having reverted to Manasseh's earlier practices. But apparently the boy had God-fearing advisors who offset any influence of his father, for Josiah returned to following the way of Jehovah.

At the age of 16, he began "to seek the God of his father David" (2 Chron. 34:3). At the age of 20 he began to cleanse Jerusalem and Judah of the idolatrous objects his father and grandfather had brought into the land (2 Chron. 34:3-7).

Successful in his own land, he even pursued similar activity to the north in Israel, where Assyria now held nominal control, removing altars and images of false deities.

Finding the Book of the Law (II Kings 22:8-13)

In the process of cleansing the Temple of the loads of rubbish which had accumulated during the reigns of Manasseh and Amon were removed. The high priest Hilkiah discovered a copy of "the book of the law" (II Kings 22:8). The Priest gave it to Shaphan the scribe to read, who in turn brought it to the king.

Shaphan first told the king the Temple repairs were proceeding according to schedule; then he told the king about the newly discovered book. After listening to portions of the book read by the scribe which described Jehovah's neglected warnings of national judgment, King Josiah was completely overwhelmed when he heard God's description of apostasy and its consequences echoing through the centuries from the time of Moses. He feared it might already be too late to bring the nation to repentance.

What was "the book of the law" that Hilkiah discovered?

Some Bible students believe it was the entire Pentateuch, while others claim it was either the Book of Deuteronomy or just certain sections like Leviticus 26 and Deuteronomy 28 which list the judgment God would bring upon His people if they continued to defy His Word. It is difficult to imagine a king descended from David could be unaware of such a significant portion of Scripture, especially when God had so clearly commanded each king must "*write him a copy of this law in a book, out of that which is before the priests and Levites: and it shall be with him, and he shall read therein all the days of his life*" (Deut. 17:18).

It appears, at this time in the history of Judah, even the priests and Levites did not have copies of the Law. They were living by oral tradition! We must remember Manasseh had wiped out almost every trace of the true religion of Israel during a period of 50 years.

Thus, whatever copies of the sacred scrolls survived this period were probably hidden in caves much like those near the Dead Sea where so many priceless manuscripts have been discovered.

What does it indicate about the spiritual condition of Judah that the Book of the Law had been missing for a long time?

What is commendable about the way Josiah responded when he heard the Book of the Law read?

What conclusions can we draw from the fact Josiah was the son and grandson of wicked kings?

Do you think we take the Bible for granted?

Josiah: Huldah's Prophecy

2 Kings 22, 23; 2 Chronicles 34-35

15th King of Judah - 640-609

Five years before this, Jeremiah had begun his prophetic ministry in Judah; Zephaniah was also proclaiming the word of the Lord. But apparently neither of these men were in Jerusalem at this time. So, Josiah's official representatives went to a prophetess in Jerusalem named Huldah, who was probably an aunt of Jeremiah (II Kings 22:14; cf. Jer. 32:7).
Despite Josiah's well-meaning efforts, the reformation was superficial; almost everyone involved in this great "revival" was insincere except the king and a tiny remnant of true believers. Jeremiah seems to suggest this problem when he said in one of his earlier sermons: "Judah did not return to me with all her heart, but only in pretense," declares the LORD." (Jer. 3:10). As has been true in many "revival meetings" since then, God was "near in their mouth, and far from their heart" (Jer. 12:2).

Because of this the judgment of God, though postponed, would be certain. Apostasy and paganism were too deeply entrenched in the hearts of the people to be rooted out by mere decrees emanating from the royal palace. But God would spare Josiah from seeing the coming national catastrophe, even as he had spared Hezekiah three generations earlier, "Because your heart was responsive and you humbled yourself before the LORD when you heard what I have spoken against this place and its people, that they would become accursed and laid waste, and because you tore your robes and wept in my presence, I have heard you, declares the LORD." II Kings 22:19

The Great Passover (II Kings 23:21-23; cf. II Chron. 35:1-19)
Full details of Josiah's great Passover celebration in 622 B.C. are provided for us in II Chronicles 35.

Three points of special interest should be noted in this account.
First, it appears conditions had deteriorated so badly in the Temple since the days of Hezekiah that faithful Levites had removed and hidden the Ark of God! Josiah ordered it to be returned, "Put the sacred ark in the temple that Solomon son of David king of Israel built." There could be no proper observance of the Passover without it.

Second, the Levites showed extraordinary zeal in preparing Passover lambs, not only for themselves, but also for the priests, the singers, and the porters.

Third, this was the greatest Passover in 500 years. "The Passover had not been observed like this in Israel since the days of the prophet Samuel; and none of the kings of Israel had ever celebrated such a Passover as did Josiah, with the priests, the Levites, and all Judah and Israel who were there with the people of Jerusalem.

Imagine a Passover greater than Solomon's
It was great because of the obstacles which had to be overcome and because it was done with such great zeal and according to the Law. Hezekiah's Passover had to be held on the second month because so many people were ceremonially defiled. Josiah was not content to bring about this reform merely in Judah. He gave orders about the north as well, taking advantage of Assyria's period of general weakness. A place of interest was Bethel, long the center of golden-calf worship. According to a prophecy given over 300 years before, Josiah burned the bones of the false priests; he did this on the altar that Jeroboam I had erected, and then he destroyed the altar and its high place.

By the word of the LORD a man of God came from Judah to Bethel, as Jeroboam was standing by the altar to make an offering. He cried out against the altar by the word of the LORD: "O altar, altar! This is what the LORD says: 'A son named Josiah will be born to the house of David. On you he will sacrifice the priests of the high places who now make offerings here, and human bones will be burned on you.'" That same day the man of God gave a sign: "This is the sign the LORD has declared: The altar will be split apart and the ashes on it will be poured out." I Kings 13:1-3

Josiah's Death

2 Kings 22, 23; 2 Chronicles 34-35

15th King of Judah - 640-609

Josiah was an able king. The sweeping reforms he instituted could not have been brought about by a weak leader. A public celebration of the Passover, on a scale unheard of since the time of the Judges, was observed. This was 100 years after the destruction of Samaria. Judah's king consistently pursued righteousness as his nation prospered. Some 13 years after his great work of revival, Josiah blundered.

He attempted to stop a northward march of Pharaoh Necho II of Egypt in 609 B.C. Necho was moving to the aid of the Assyrians who were attempting to stop Babylonia from becoming the new world leader. Assyria's two main cities, Assur and Nineveh, had to attacks by the Medes and Babylonians. In 610 B.C. Haran was taken by the king of Babylon, which all but finished the Assyrians.

Necho, who had just become king of Egypt, wanted Egypt to regain world prominence instead of Babylon. He was marching northward to help Assyria's few remaining forces. Josiah, in order to show favor toward Babylon, attempted to stop the Egyptians at strategic Megiddo and he was killed in the effort. His body was returned to Jerusalem and was buried there. It seems as if God removed Josiah in mercy so he would not see the coming desolation of Judah.

In this undertaking, Josiah revealed a lack of stability in his character. He was criticized for beginning such an expedition which probably was undertaken without due deliberation or consultation with the Lord and His prophets. God sometimes allows godly men to follow foolish and evil counsel to punish those with whom they are connected. Josiah's death was a great national calamity. In his untimely death the hopes of the godly remnant received a setback. His passing was widely lamented.

Josiah's monumental reforms were only superficial. After his death the people went back to their idolatries!

Josiah's day was one of outstanding prophets; perhaps three or four writing prophets. **Jeremiah** began to minister in Josiah's 13th year and continued after Jerusalem's fall to Babylonia in 586 B.C. **Zephaniah** also dates his book to Josiah's reign (1:1) and likely began his ministry about the time Jeremiah did, at least prior to Josiah's reforms, for he speaks of foreign cults yet existing in the land (1:4). **Nahum** does not date his book to the reign of a king but is best placed in Josiah's time. His main theme concerns the fall of Nineveh, which came in 612 B.C., three years before Josiah's death. **Habakkuk's** prophecy as well can be located either at the close of Josiah's rule or during the succeeding reign of Jehoiakim, for he speaks of the Babylonian invasion being near at hand (1:5-6).

At no other time in the history of either Israel or Judah was there such a concentration of writing prophets. The significance must be that God was giving Judah one last intensive warning of impending punishment. No doubt, too, much of the credit for the reform Josiah achieved must go to these stalwart men.

Jeremiah, for instance, speaks harshly of the inexcusable idolatry filling the land (2:5-13), warning of punishment if repentance were not forthcoming (3:1-5, 19-25). Zephaniah predicts severe punishment for Judah's sin (2:4-3:7). Nahum's warning was more indirect, telling of Nineveh's corning destruction; but the message that God brings punishment on all who do wickedly could not have been missed. Habakkuk again speaks directly of the Babylonians coming against Judah.

Why do you think Josiah persisted in making war against Pharaoh Necho?

When have you gotten a message about God's will for you from an unexpected source?

How has failing to listen to the Lord led to trouble in your life?

Book Eight

1. Hilkiah	2 Chronicles 34:14-33
2. Jehoahaz, Jehoiakim	2 Kings 23;
3. Jehoiachin	2 Kings 24;
4. Zedekiah	2 Kings24, 25;
5. Obadiah	Obadiah
6. Joel	Joel
7. Amos	Amos
8. Hosea	Hosea
9. Hosea & Gomer	Hosea
10. Jonah	Jonah
11. Micah	Micah
12. Nahum	Nahum
13. Zephaniah	Zephaniah
14. Habakkuk	Habakkuk
15. Zerubbabel	Ezra 1-6
16. Ezra	Ezra 7-9
17. Ezra: The Helper	Ezra 7-9
18. Nehemiah	Nehemiah 1-2, 4
19. Nehemiah: The Leader	Nehemiah
20. Esther	Esther 2, 4-5, 7-8
21. Esther: The Book	Esther
22. Mordecai	Esther 2-9
23. Job	Job
24. Isaiah: An Introduction	Isaiah 6, 40, 53
25. Isaiah: Work Summarized	Isaiah 6, 7, 36-37
26. Isaiah: The Person	Isaiah
27. Jeremiah: An Introduction	Jeremiah 1, 8, 32
28. Jeremiah: His Life	Jeremiah
39. Baruch	Jeremiah 36, 43, 45

Hilkiah

2 Chronicles 34:14-33

641-609 BC

He was the high priest in Jerusalem during the reign of King Josiah. He was the High Priest who was responsible for following the directions of King Josiah which led to the greatest revival the kingdom had ever experienced.

He was also in charge of a special fund Josiah set up for the people of Israel to contribute to in order to cleanse and repair the Temple of God. He was also responsible for the administration of these funds. He directed the renovation of the Temple which had fallen into disrepair and ruin during the kingship of Manasseh and Amon.

Ordered by Josiah to complete the work of cleansing the entire land he led in the removal of all the idols from the Temple in Jerusalem. He organized and set up a place to burn them outside the city of Jerusalem in the Kidron Valley just east of the city of Jerusalem. He then carried the ashes to the city of Bethel, north of Jerusalem where Jeroboam had erected the first pagan altars in the land.

He did away with all the pagan priests and prostitutes and destroyed their living quarters. He removed any evidence they had ever been in the city of Jerusalem.

We know little of his ancestry other than he was a Levite in the lineage of Aaron.

The event for which he is best known, and which was the direct cause of the great revival was the discovery of a copy of the Law of Moses buried in the rubble of the Temple. We should remember at this time all the copies of the Hebrew Scriptures which existed were produced by hand and were often destroyed by the pagan priests in order to advance their false religious beliefs.

It is very possible this was the first and only copy of the Law of Moses which the King, the priests and the people of Israel had ever seen. When it was read its contents were shocking. The King of Judah repented in sackcloth and ashes and was fearful the judgment of God would fall upon the entire nation.

The king ordered the cleansing and restoration of the Temple, the removal of all paganism, and the destruction of all the false priests. With that accomplished they began cleansing in preparation for the greatest Passover celebration the nation of Israel had experienced in hundreds of years.

Think of the consequences of this find! What if he had overlooked the old scroll? What if he had chosen not to make it known to the king for fear of his position?

We see in Hilkiah a man who chose to serve God even though he was not sure of the consequences. He was vulnerable in his position and in his relationship to the King. We can be encouraged by God's proven faithfulness when his followers are willing to make difficult choices.

We also see two other people mentioned who were willing to stand with Hilkah: Shaphan, the secretary to Josiah, and Huldah, the prophetess.

As Elijah discovered, we are never alone when we serve God.

What surprising "finds" have you made while cleaning your attic, closets or garage?

When have you been surprised by support you received for an unpopular decision?

How can reading or not reading the Bible influence the way you live?

Jehoahaz 2 Kings 23; 2 Chronicles 36

16th King of Judah - 609

The career of Josiah's successor was too short to make any marked impression on the history of Judah. At 23 Jehoahaz came to the throne, but his reign only lasted for three months. It was as brief as it was bad, and its end was bitter.

Jehoahaz, son of Josiah, is called Shallum, which might have been his name before the untimely death of his father brought him to the throne.

Jehoiakim, an older brother of Jehoahaz, was in direct line for kingship, but was passed over by the people of the land, doubtless because oppressive tendencies had shown themselves in him.

Jehoahaz, the fourth son of Josiah, was chosen king probably because the people felt they had in him a more capable ruler for the emergencies of the time. Jeremiah's account of him shows that their estimate was mistaken (Jeremiah 22:11).

In his three-month reign, Jehoahaz persisted in the abominations of his forebears, Amon and Manasseh. "He did evil in the sight of the Lord." In Ezekiel's lamentation for the princes of Judah, Jehoahaz is called a young lion that "devoured man," alluding to his oppressive rapacity and shameless abuse of power.

After Josiah's good reign, Judah began a sad change for the worst. The Egyptian Pharaoh felt it unsafe to leave the nation that had meddled in his plans unpunished.

Judah was conquered, made a tributary province and heavily taxed. Jehoahaz was deposed and carried captive to Egypt where he died as foretold by Jeremiah (22:11, 12; 27:10-12).

Jehoiakim I Kings 23:35-24:7; II Chronicles 36:5-8; Jeremiah 22:18-21; 25-27; 38

17th King of Judah - 609-597

Jehoiakim was raised to the throne of Judah by Pharaoh Necho and made a vassal king in the place of his younger half-brother Jehoahaz and reigned for 11 years. His original name was Eliakim, but the Pharaoh changed it to Jehoiakim to assert his authority.

Put on the throne by the king of Egypt, Jehoiakim was removed by Babylonian king, Nebuchadnezzar, whose name first occurs here in Scripture. Jehoiakim was carried captive to Babylon along with Daniel.

Jehoiakim's miserable death was foretold by Jeremiah, "buried with the burial of an ass," meaning, he had no burial, for asses had no burial. Dragged in chains to captivity, probably he died on the journey and his corpse was left behind, unburied, as the army marched on.

When Jeremiah, the prophet, came to the king with the divinely inspired prophecy of the king's and his nation's coming catastrophe, the roll of parchment containing the prophecy was read to the king and his advisers in one of his palaces.

Exposing his contempt for God and the prophet, Jehoiakim took a scribe's knife, cut the roll in pieces, flung them into the fire and watched them until they were reduced to white ashes. But while the king destroyed that roll, he did not get rid of the solemn truths it contained; they were added to and re- written.

Nothing good is recorded of this godless sovereign who pampered himself in the erection of costly royal palaces by enforced and unpaid labor.

What could any of Judah's last kings have done to save the nation and the people?

Jehoiachin — II Kings 24:8-16; II Chronicles 36:9, 10; Jeremiah 22:24-30

18th King of Judah - *597*

The son and successor of Jehoiakim reigned alone for only three months and 10 days, not long enough for his evil ways to make much of an impression upon the life of the nation. He is also spoken of as Coniah and Jeconiah.

Jehoiachin's brief span as a free king was more of a historic landmark than a reign. The first extensive deportation of Jewish captives to Babylon took place in Jehoiakin's time, with the king himself being taken captive along with most of the royal household and the court.

Jehoiachin's resistance to Nebuchadnezzar's siege of Jerusalem proved to be unsuccessful and with his surrender to the King of Babylon, 10,000 captives, including "*all the better and sturdier elements of the people from prince to craftsman*," were taken.

The most valuable treasures of the Temple and the royal palace were taken as loot. The wicked King Jehoiachin remained a captive for 37 years.

When Nebuchadnezzar first attacked Jerusalem in the reign of Jehoiakim, a company of hostages was carried away, including Daniel and his three friends.

The second attack, in Jehoiachin's reign, saw Ezekiel and Mordecai taken prisoner. Jeremiah evaded capture and urged the exiles in Babylon to make themselves at home and to be good citizens (29:1-10).

Jeremiah predicted that Jehoiachin would never have a descendant on David's throne. He died "childless" as to the throne. Not one of his seven sons succeeded him as king (I Chronicles 3:17, 18).

In him, the scepter departed from Judah. Zedekiah, who succeeded Jehoiachin, perished before him (Jeremiah 52:31). The scribes, keeping the royal register, named Jehoiachin as the last of his line.

After Jehoiachin's long captivity in Babylon, a strange thing occurred.

In the first year of the reign of Nebuchadnezzar's successor, Jehoiachin was released and raised to the dignity of king and ended his life in royal fashion still living in Babylon (II Kings 25:27-30; Jeremiah 52:31-34).

The writer evidently dwells with pleasure on this shadowy gleam of light amid the darkness of the exile. It was a kind of prefiguring of the pity which afterwards was to be extended to the captive people, when the divine purpose had been achieved, and the exile had done its work of chastisement and purification (Psalm 106:46; Ezra 9:9; Nehemiah 2:2). We have no account of Jehoiachin's death and burial.

What was the primary cause of the total destruction of Judah?

What could any of Judah's last kings have done to save the nation and the people?

What did all the last kings of Judah fail to do?

How many chances did Judah have to respond to God's call to return to Him?

What makes us resistant to hearing God's warnings?

Zedekiah

II Kings 24, 25; Jeremiah 52

19th King of Judah - *597-586*

Judah's last king broke his oath to Nebuchadnezzar and refused to listen to the faithful testimony of Jeremiah and consequently reaped a terrible harvest. Zedekiah rebelled against the King of Babylon even though he was bound by an oath which he took when he was made vassal-king of Judah. He had to swear loyalty by the God of his fathers.

The prophet Ezekiel makes this a point of a prophecy against Zedekiah and his dignitaries, "My oath that he hath despised" (Ezekiel 17: 11-21). Jeremiah also exhorted the king to conform strictly to his oath, in opposition to all those lying teachers, who, with their false divinations, encouraged Zedekiah to throw off the yoke of subjection (Jeremiah 27, 28).

Jeremiah told the king it would be vain, as well as sinful, to resist the Babylonian monarch, and that, upon their rebellion against him, they would be given up to complete devastation. Zedekiah, however, persisted in his determination to take the advice of his flattering counselors, and by his treachery provoked Nebuchadnezzar to invade the land and surround the city.

Indecisive Zedekiah (Jeremiah 38:19, 20) was totally unable to stand against the invading army. When Nebuchadnezzar took the best of the people, men of influence and character, under Jehoiachin, he left behind a people broken in resources and spirit so they would not be moved to rebellion (Ezekiel 17:14). In his distress the king sent for Jeremiah, a prophet for whom he had respect, and asked his prayers on his behalf (32:1), but Zedekiah was too weak and timid to follow the prophetic counsel of Jeremiah in defiance of his princes who were intriguing with Egypt.

It seems as if Zedekiah hoped for some miraculous deliverance like Hezekiah's deliverance from Sennacherib, but there was no deliverance to come. Judah was carried away into captivity and ended the kingdom as Jeremiah had predicted (20:4).

Feeling the end was near and God had forsaken the land (Ezekiel 8), Zedekiah had turned the nation into a pool of idolatry and of vulgar temple rites. Zedekiah, whose name was changed from Mattaniah, was the third son of Josiah and the full brother of Jehoahaz. Jehoiakim was childless at the time of his captivity. Zedekiah, after reigning for 11 years, was brought before the king of Babylon at Riblah and had the anguish of seeing his sons and the nobles of Judah slain before his eyes. Zedekiah's own eyes were then gouged out. How long Zedekiah remained in captivity and when he died, we are not told. Jeremiah had prophesied he would die in peace and have a state mourning (34:4, 5).

A remarkable illustration of how the obscurity and apparent contradiction of unfulfilled prophecy is removed by this event is seen in comparing the prophecies of Jeremiah and Ezekiel concerning Zedekiah. Jeremiah had foretold that Zedekiah should behold the king of Babylon and go to Babylon (34:3); Ezekiel foretold that Zedekiah should not see Babylon (12:13).

Josephus tells us these prophecies are contradictory. But both were exactly fulfilled. Zedekiah did see the King of Babylon, not at Babylon, but at Riblah, where his eyes were put out. He was taken to Babylon, which he never saw and died there, and Judean royalty ended.

What happened to the first king of Judah, who obeyed God and surrendered to the Babylonians?

What made Zedekiah's punishment much worse than that of the first king of Judah, Jehoiachin, who had surrendered to Babylon?

How did God use the motives of evil men to fulfill His Word and drive the people of Judah from His presence?

Obadiah
About 840 BC

We now move back in time about over two hundred years. This age was a time of great turmoil. Jehoram the king of Judah was the son of Jehoshaphat, a good king, but he had married Jehoram to Athaliah, daughter of Ahab and Jezebel, probably the result of a formal alliance between Judah and Israel.

This marriage worked to the disadvantage of Jehoram and Judah, much as the marriage of Ahab to Jezebel had worked to the detriment of Ahab and Israel. No longer were the godly ways of Jehoshaphat followed; instead, Jehoram allowed Baal worship in all its degradation to enter the land.

Jehoram had killed all his brothers to safeguard his throne, probably as a result of the influence of Athaliah. He was the only king in either Judah or Israel to take such a drastic step. The time in Jehoram's reign when Obadiah wrote his book is best placed shortly after the destruction carried out by the Arabians and Philistines. This would account for the prominent place Obadiah gives to this disastrous occasion. His general ministry would have both preceded and followed the time of this writing.

The theme of Obadiah's book relates to a coming punishment of Edom by God. He makes clear the reason for this punishment was Edom's violence against her brother Jacob, God's chosen people. God was going to defend His own honor, because His own people had been attacked. God would bring destruction upon Edom as Edom had brought destruction upon Jerusalem (v. 15).

In contrast, writes Obadiah, there would be rescue and holiness for Zion, as the house of Jacob would possess all her possessions (v. 17).

Obadiah was knowledgeable of the world of his day. He knew of Edom, he knew what Edom had done, and he was interested in what God was going to do to this southern neighbor in return. His world was larger than only Jerusalem and Judah.

Obadiah, though living during a wicked time in his own land, did not write of the sins being committed at home. He could have done so, in the spirit of Hosea or Amos a century later, but as inspired of God, he saw fit to direct his statements to Edom in the south.

The reason is not apparent! We do not know why God so guided His servant. One can say only God saw need for such a book of warning to Edom and chose Obadiah to write it.

One may be sure, however, since the times were so distressing and sin so serious, Obadiah was very active in voicing protest in an oral way. He doubtless preached frequently in the gates of the city and contacted specific individuals, urging conformance to God's will. It would be interesting to know details concerning this oral ministry but for some reason the Scriptures do not include them.

The Edomites and the Israelites shared an old and negative family history.

How do longtime family problems affect the spiritual health of believers?

Does your church show pride and self-confidence?

If we treat others poorly, how should we expect God to treat us?

Based on God's dealings with the Edomites, how can we expect Him to judge nations today that rebel against Him, dominate others, or trust in their own strength and possessions?

Joel

About 840 BC

Though Joel does not mention the terrible sins of Athaliah's time in his book, we may be sure a man like Joel would have been highly interested and actively opposed in every way possible.

Later, he no doubt did all he could to further the reforms instituted by Joash under the leadership of Jehoiada. He probably was still living when Zechariah suffered his shameful death by stoning and no doubt felt great sorrow. According to II Chronicles 24:19, prophets were sent at this general time to bring reprimand and warning to the king and his advisors, and it may be Joel was among this number.

Very little is known of Joel's personal life. His father was named Pethuel, apparently a man of godly character, for the name he gave his son means "Jehovah is God." Nothing is said as to Joel's birthplace or conditions under which he was raised. In his early days he evidently witnessed a terrible plague of locusts, for Joel makes such an invasion the theme of his opening chapter. As God had punished the land by this terrible scourge, so in days to come He would bring a similar punishment when a nation would come upon the land from the north.

In view of his prediction about the future, we believe Joel was given to thinking about God's judgment as a result of sin. Warnings regarding the future constitute the general theme of the book. Joel speaks of the coming Day of Judgment because the people had offended God in their shameful sin. God's honor had to be avenged. There was need on the part of the people for prayer, fasting, and repentance in order to avert this divine judgment.

The principal point of the book concerns a coming day of judgment, called "the day of the LORD." God would bring this day as a punishment for Judah's sin and later would bring deliverance from it.

To stress and illustrate this overwhelming occasion, the locust invasion is described (1:1-20). The people are depicted in repentance as a result of this time of devastation of their land (1:8-20), and Joel then describes the coming day of the Lord itself, saying it will result in weeping by the people (2:1-17).

Because the language used by Joel in describing this day is like language used in other passages which predict the time of great tribulation of the future, we see the Spirit of God inspiring the prophet in his visions.

In 2:1-40, the assembling of a vast Gentile army is described, and this seems to be the army brought together by the Antichrist in the latter days of the great tribulation. Then 2:11 speaks of the destruction of this army, which would correspond to Christ's destruction of Antichrist's army at the climax of that period.

Joel 2:10 speaks of the heavens trembling and the sun and moon becoming dark with the stars withdrawing their shining, something which did not happen in the time of Sennacherib.

Peter quoted 2:28, 29, dealing with the outpouring of the Spirit, as being fulfilled in part at Pentecost; Acts 2:16-20. Some of the matters here were partially fulfilled at Christ's first coming.

Joel is often called the "Prophet of Pentecost."

When natural disasters strike people and places throughout the world, what bothers you most?

If Joel were to preach a threatening sermon about the coming Day of the Lord, how would your congregation likely respond to his words?

Amos
About 740 BC

Amos dates his prophetic work much in the way Hosea does his. He says it occurred during the reigns of Jeroboam II, king of Israel, and Uzziah, king of Judah.

Amos also dates his ministry as having been "two years before the earthquake" (1:1), but this is of little help because there is no way to know just when this earthquake occurred. It must have been very severe, however, for it is mentioned also by the writer Zechariah (14:5-7), who lived following the Babylonian exile well over two centuries later. It should be noted, since Amos mentions this earthquake, he must have written his book after it occurred.

Like Hosea, Amos carried on his ministry in the northern nation of Israel, but unlike Hosea his home was in Judah to the south. He was called by God while he was living in Judah and instructed to go to Israel and there prophesy in the name of the Lord. When Amos ministered in Israel, then, it was a day of prosperity and luxury, which led to a life of indulgence and sin.

Person and work

Amos gives more information concerning himself than do many of the other prophets. For one thing he names his home town as Tekoa (1:1), located about five miles southeast of Bethlehem. He describes his profession as "a herdsman, and a gatherer of sycamore fruit" (7:14).

The word herdman is best taken in reference to a person who tended cattle and sheep. Since he also describes himself as a gatherer of sycamore fruit, we can presume we was not wealthy because he had two jobs.

Amos differed from Hosea and from most other prophets in that he was not full-time in this work.

One great value of the Book of Amos is that it provides, along with Hosea, a fruitful source of information regarding conditions in the northern kingdom during the reign of Jeroboam II.

As indicated, it was a day of national strength, when trade and commerce flourished, and people were prosperous. But it was also a day of moral and religious decay. Bribery of officialdom was common, and it became difficult for ordinary people to receive justice in the courts of the land. The result was a large gap developed between rich and poor, with the latter often being sold into bondage by their masters for trivial matters (Amos 2:6).

In this situation, Amos' message was that people should leave their sinful ways and return to seeking God and His will. They should heed the regulations laid down in the Mosaic Law given long before. If they did not, there would be a day of punishment from God. This would be a day of darkness rather than light, one of punishment and sorrow rather than reward and gladness.

How do you think Amos felt about presenting God's message to the northern kingdom of Israel?

Who, in your view, speaks out for the Lord in our society?

From your perspective, which group or nation today needs an extra measure of the Lord's mercy and grace?

What does the term "Sovereign Lord" mean?

In what areas of your life do you want to ask the Holy Spirit to refresh or restore you?

Hosea
About 750

Hosea, unlike Obadiah and Joel, dates himself exactly. He ministered during the reigns of Uzziah, Jotham, Ahaz, and Hezekiah, kings of Judah, and in the days of Jeroboam II, king of Israel (1:1).

Though Hosea would have enjoyed living in a time of prosperity and influence, still there was a sobering factor. The era was characterized by wealth and luxurious living which led to sinful conditions. It is not prosperity which normally brings about righteous conduct, but hardship and difficulty. When conditions are good people tend to be self-confident and self-sufficient, forgetting their dependence on almighty God.

It is for this reason both Hosea and Amos have so much to say concerning the sin they found around themselves. They saw the land was producing abundantly and many people were enjoying riches. Building activity was flourishing (Hos. 8:14), and this led to a widespread feeling of pride (Isa. 9:10; Amos 3:15; 5:11). Social and moral conditions were developing which were wrong and degrading.

Side by side with the wealth, extreme poverty was growing. Through dishonest gain and false balances, the strong were taking advantage of the weak (Isa. 5:8; Hos. 12:7; Amos 8:5, 6). Those who had wealth felt quite free to oppress orphans and widows and even to buy and sell the destitute on the public market (Amos 8:4, 8). Justice was at a premium and the courts apparently were doing little to change the situation.

We can see five basic themes running through the Book of Hosea.

First and foremost is the fact God had made a covenant with Israel and Israel continued to break it by severe sin.

Second is the broken marriage of Hosea and Gomer and the parallel made between it and this broken covenant.

Third is God's love and patience with Israel through all this time of breaking the covenant. We can see this, for instance, in 11:1-4 where God is depicted as having loved Israel from the time of being a child and as drawing the people with bands of love; and in 14:1-9 where, speaking of a future day, God says, "I will heal their backsliding, I will love them freely: for mine anger is turned away from him."

Fourth is a note of solemn warning of severe punishment upon the people for breaking God's covenant. This is seen, for instance, in 5:1-15 where general statements regarding this punishment are set forth; in 8:1-14 where, because of the false calf worship, God says, "They have sown the wind, and they shall reap the whirlwind," and in 10:5-8 by a direct indication that the people would be carried captive to Assyria.

The fifth is a glory note of future restoration, when Israel would again enjoy gracious benefits at God's hand.

How has God shown fatherly love to you?

How have you responded to God's love?

When has God's discipline been a blessing in your life?

What does facing the Lord's anger mean to you?

What good things happen in your life when you consistently walk in the ways of the Lord?

Hosea & Gomer
About 750

The marriage of Hosea and Gomer
In view of Hosea's obedience to God as he married Gomer, it is clear he was a man who was carefully obedient to the will of God no matter where it led. Nothing proves the devotion of man to God more than such obedience.

Little is known of Hosea's history beyond what we find in his writings. He has been called the first prophet of Grace, and Israel's earliest evangelist. He was a native of the Northern Kingdom, the iniquities and idolatries of which he obviously hated. He had the same name as of the last king of Israel (II Kings 15:30).

The home tragedy overtaking him earned him the title of "The Prophet of a Sorrowful Heart." Through the wrongs he suffered he came to understand the sins committed by Israel against God, and the long history of unfaithfulness to Him. The accounts of Hosea's marriage, the births of his children, and his wife's unfaithfulness and restoration make sad reading. Hosea was called to express God's message and to demonstrate His character.

Gomer, his wife, was immoral; hence the word of the Lord came to him amid much personal suffering; his home life was destroyed. Society was corrupt, God's law was spurned, and Hosea came to see in his own suffering a reflection of what the sorrow of God must be, when Israel proved totally unfaithful.

Three children were born to Hosea and Gomer:
Jezreel, recalling the deed of blood (II Kings 10) and by it a toll was rung in the ears of Jeroboam. The name of this child was an omen of coming judgment. God would scatter the kingdom.

Lo-ruhamah, meaning, "one who never knew a father's love." This expressive name pointed to a time when, no more pitied by Jehovah, Israel would be given over to her enemies.

Lo-ammi, suggests "one not belonging to me." Israel had turned from a father's love and deserved not to belong to God. Thus, this third child's name prophesied the driving out of the children of Israel from their land to exile.

Gomer, the cheating wife, is received back (Hos. 3:1, 2), the price of her redemption was paid by Hosea. So, the prophet was not only God's messenger of grace - he reflected God's character and foreshadowed ultimate redemption through the Messiah and Israel's re-establishment as a nation.

The four lessons we learn from the broken heart and the Book of Hose:

- Distress accelerates anxiety.
- Sin inspires moral outrage.
- Suffering teaches sympathy.
- God's character purifies human behavior.

What do you expect from God when you "betray" Him repeatedly?

How do you tend to deal with a loved one who has wronged you in some way?

How should Christians deal with people in the church who commit adultery?

How is God's faithfulness to us an example of the way we should treat others?

About 750BC

Most people know the story of Jonah and the "whale." We need to begin by pointing out the word used in Hebrew is "*dag.*" This is the word used to describe any type of extremely large or threatening sea creature.
The Philistines worshiped a god called Dagon, which was represented by a figure which was half man and half fish. The translation "whale" was no doubt derived simply because a whale was the largest sea creature known to the translators.

In Matthew 12:40 Jesus used Jonah as an illustration to teach the truth of His death, burial, and *resurrection. "For as Jonah was three days and three nights in the belly of a huge fish, so the Son of Man will be three days and three nights in the heart of the earth."* The word used in this context is also a word to describe "huge fish" as translated in the New International Version.

Jonah was called by God to preach to people whom he hated. Jonah knew the nation of Assyria would destroy his people. Nineveh was the capitol of the hated nation. Jonah told God he did not want to preach to them because he knew God was a God of mercy.

This is one of the greatest lessons in the book of Jonah. God is a God who loves the world; John 3:16 *"For God so loved the world that he gave his one and only Son, that whoever believes in him shall not perish but have eternal life."*

God even loves the people we hate.

We are told other people will know we are followers of Jesus because of our love. This was a hard lesson for Jonah to learn, but he learned the lesson; he wrote the book.

We can also see God's love and care for his rebellious prophet.

In this short book we see God prepared four things to direct His prophet to a proper understanding of the love of God.

- A great fish
- A gourd plant
- A worm
- A strong wind

Jonah was thankful for the shade provided by the gourd, but he became angry when God took the shade away.

God used this to teach him a lesson relating to priorities; What was more important; Jonah's gourd or the people of Nineveh?

What are some temporary things in our life on which we probably place too much value?

Has God prepared some unusual things to help you understand His priorities in your life?

Jonah wanted Nineveh, Israel's enemy, destroyed. When have you wanted revenge rather than restoration in a relationship?

What hard lesson have you had to learn from God?

How can you express thanks to the Lord this week for all the love and mercy He has given to you and others?

Micah

About720 BC

Micah was a contemporary of Isaiah, possibly a few years younger. He dates his ministry to the reigns of Jotham, Ahaz, and Hezekiah (1:1). Perhaps the years 735-710 B.C. are likely for his time.

Work and person

Micah gives a few clues in his book as to his work and person, but he does not include any historical episodes as does Isaiah, nor is he mentioned in any of the historical books of the Old Testament.

He identifies his home town as Moresheth (1:1), which is no doubt to be identified with Moresheth-gath (1:14), located in the western lowlands of Judah about 20 miles southwest of Jerusalem. Since Moresheth was a small rural city, Micah had contact with rural people, who were for the most part poor people, and his book reflects a serious concern for the poor of his day.

The city also was located near the international highway leading north and south for caravan travel, and this may account for his acquaintance with international affairs. He shows interest in and knowledge of Israel to the north. In this interest, he may have been influenced by Amos who had ministered at Bethel only about 25 years earlier. He may also have been influenced by Amos' writing, as indicated by a comparison of Micah 2:6 with Amos 2:12 and 7:10-16. It should be realized that Tekoa, the home of Amos, was only 20 miles from Moresheth. There could well have been contact between the two men

That Micah did move about and not stay merely in the area of Moresheth is indicated by implied contacts with Jerusalem and people there. For instance, he was familiar with false prophets, whose center was the capital city, saying that they made God's people err (3:5-7).

Micah was well known because Jeremiah mentions him. Since the prophets did not ordinarily mention each other and especially since Jeremiah lived a century after Micah, this reference to Micah is very unusual. It implies that Micah made a strong impression in his day, and this indicates he must have ministered frequently in and around Jerusalem, the place where a lasting impression would have been made.

Furthermore, the manner of reference by Jeremiah is significant for it shows Hezekiah, king during Micah's later ministry, not only knew Micah but held him in high respect.

The Book of Micah is made up of three sections, each beginning with the imperative "Hear" (1:2; 3:1; 6:1).

In bringing together a variety of thoughts in this way, taken from different times of his ministry, Micah shows a parallel with Isaiah, for Isaiah does the same thing. Micah also shows similarity to Isaiah in many of the thoughts he brings and the way he brings them, even including at one time a passage which is nearly identical with one in Isaiah (Mic. 4:1-3; cf. Isa. 2:2-4).

Some matters to note from the content of the book are;

- a definite reference to the fall of Samaria (1:5-7);
- urging about the oppression of the poor (2:1-3:4);
- prediction of the Messiah; His first and second advents (4:1-8; 5:2-8; 7:7-20).

He has showed you, O man, what is good. And what does the LORD require of you? To act justly and to love mercy and to walk humbly with your God. - Micah 6:8

What steps can you take to act justly, show mercy, or be humble toward your co-workers? Your family?

Nahum
About 640 BC

Nahum does not date his ministry to the reign of one or more kings, as do the eighth-century prophets, so his time must be determined by internal evidence from his book.

Two matters give help. One is a reference to the destruction of the city of "No" in Egypt. This was the city Thebes, which was destroyed in 663 B.C. by the Assyrian Ashurbanipal. The event is spoken of as past, and therefore Nahum must have prophesied after it happened (3:8-10). The other clue is the fall of Nineveh is indicated as still future. The theme of the book is the predicted destruction of this city. The prophesied destruction came in 612 B.C., and so Nahum's ministry is somewhere between these dates.

Little is known regarding the work and person of Nahum. He gives no historical information regarding himself in his book and he is not mentioned elsewhere in the Old Testament.

Nahum was probably born in a rural area as was Micah; he also must have had considerable contact with larger cities where world events would have been discussed.

His writing speaks of the world political situation; he must have been familiar with Assyria's recent history. He would have known of the fall of Israel to the Assyrians in 722 B.C. and he would have been greatly concerned about the danger this foreshadowed for Judah.

He would have been familiar with the campaign of Sennacherib in the time of Hezekiah and the extensive destruction he brought upon the country. He also would have been very familiar with the reign of Ashurbanipal.

Ashurbanipal's reign had been a period of glory for Assyria, when the empire reached its highest point of power, and this fact would have dominated Nahum's thinking as he wrote of the destruction of the great capital city of Assyria.

Even though Nahum did his writing specifically regarding Nineveh, we should not think he was silent to his own people in his preaching ministry. He may be likened in this respect to Obadiah, who wrote only of Edom but was active in preaching to his countrymen.

Being thus familiar with Assyria, Nahum would have known of Manasseh's captivity there and doubtless used this fact as a word of warning to people generally. Knowing also of the destruction of Thebes in Egypt (3:8-10), he warned against any dependence on Egypt, like Isaiah a century earlier.

Being thus aware of the world at large, he certainly had contact with the king of his own country, Josiah, and no doubt along with Zephaniah and Jeremiah, had much to do with encouraging the king in making his reforms.

The Book of Nahum

- Nahum begins his book with a psalm of triumph, in which he praises God and announces God's punishment on the wicked and blessing of goodness on those who trust Him.
- In chapter two he foresees scenes from Nineveh's destruction, using forceful and vivid language.
- Then in chapter three, using vivid language still, Nahum gives the reasons for this destruction.

How do the sins of our nation compare with Nineveh's pride, cruelty, selfishness, and lies?

The name Nahum means comfort.

How can we be a comfort to others in disturbing circumstances?

How has God cared for you?

Zephaniah
About 630 BC

Zephaniah (1:1) dates his ministry in the reign of King Josiah (640-609 B.C.).

Nothing further really needs to be said as background history for Zephaniah, the world of Zephaniah was the same as the world of Nahum.

It is good to see God's plan for the coming of Zephaniah and the three other seventh-century prophets in a group. Together they were to sound a forceful eleventh-hour warning to Judah.

Hosea and **Amos** had sounded such a final message to Israel just prior to her fall to Assyria, and now these four, **Nahum, Zephaniah, Habakkuk,** and **Jeremiah**, were to do the same in respect to Judah's fall.

Zephaniah is unusual in tracing his lineage over four generations. Since he is the only prophet who does this, there must be a reason; the reason apparently lies in the identity of the fourth person mentioned. The name is Hezekiah. This may be King Hezekiah. The length of time since Hezekiah lived fits this identification. If this is correct, Zephaniah was a descendant of the royal line.

If you like to study genealogies, you will like this! The lineage he gives is Hezekiah, Amariah, Gedaliah, Cushi, and Zephaniah. Comparing this with the line of Judah's kings yields the following results:

- King Manasseh and Amariah were brothers,
- King Amon and Gedaliah were first cousins,
- King Josiah and Cushi were second cousins,
- The three sons of Josiah, all of whom ruled (Jehoahaz, Jehoiakim, and Zedekiah), were third cousins of Zephaniah.

If this relationship did exist, Zephaniah had an access to the royal court not available to other prophets. In the early part of his ministry, using the easy access to the royal court, he no doubt visited Josiah many times and urged the institution of reforms. Sometime during those years, he wrote his book.

The Book of Zephaniah is first a theme of warning and then of promise.

The warning relates to the coming day of the Lord. A double fulfillment seems to be in reference. The first is the captivity to Babylon. The second is the great tribulation of the last days.

This aspect of the fulfillment is evidenced both by the description of the day of the Lord and by a reference in the last of the book to the coming millennial age which will follow the great tribulation.

The theme of promise is presented in the last two-thirds of chapter three and concerns the future day of millennial blessing Israel will experience. It will be a day when "the King of Israel, even the LORD," will be in the midst of Israel and the people will not see evil any more.

In what way do you tend to be a pessimist or an optimist?

What future event are you either dreading or anticipating?

When have you experienced restoration and rejoicing after a period of rebellion?

What in your life brings you the most joy?

Habakkuk

About 600 BC

Once again, with Habakkuk the time of the prophet's ministry must be established upon the basis of internal evidence from the book he wrote. Habakkuk does not mention the reign of any king. Evidence available points to the rule of Jehoiakim (609-598 B.C.) as the period during which he wrote his book, the approximate time of Nebuchadnezzar's first invasion of Jerusalem in 605 B.C.

Habakkuk gives no history regarding himself nor is he mentioned in other places of Scripture. In view of the historical conditions we may conclude certain things. He would have been active in attempting to counteract the wicked practices of Jehoiakim. He would have known of the influence Nahum and Zephaniah had been able to bring on Josiah. He would have wanted to do all he could to the same end. Nahum and Zephaniah were likely now dead, Jeremiah was still alive, and it may be Habakkuk teamed up with Jeremiah.

The Book of Habakkuk is extremely unique in form. It is unlike any other prophetic book. Rather than setting forth a series of prophetic statements or addresses warning people of sin and punishment, Habakkuk presents his first two chapters in the form of a dialogue between God and himself. The prophet first shows his concern that sin in the land seemed to go unchecked on the part of God. He then tells of God's response there will be punishment, and this will come in an invasion by the Babylonians.

This quickly raises a question in the prophet's mind, for he wonders how God can use a nation which is more evil than the people of Judah to punish God's people. He says, for instance, "Your eyes are too pure to look on evil; you cannot tolerate wrong. Why then do you tolerate the treacherous? Why are you silent while the wicked swallow up those more righteous than themselves?" (1:13). God answers, "See, he is puffed up; his desires are not upright, but the righteous will live by faith." (2:4).

The thought is those who are proud, like the Babylonians, have no faith and therefore will in the end stand condemned before God. Those who will live at that time are those who have faith and who live by this faith. In other words, the punishment God will bring by means of the Babylonians will give the Babylonians ascendancy only for a time, just long enough to bring the punishment to Judah. But eventually they will experience their own punishment and it will be far more severe than that of Judah.

The third chapter of Habakkuk is different in that it is a prayer offered by Habakkuk. It shows his settled faith in God and unshakable trust that all is well when God is in charge.

When people suffer because of violence and injustice, how do you feel?

How does God speak to Christians through the actions of pagans today?

When have you been perplexed about why God allowed something to happen?

When has God given you an answer to prayer that surprised you?

What sins of your nation are disgraceful to you?

What "woes" might Habakkuk pronounce on our culture today?

If your earthly sources of satisfaction and security were stripped away, how would you continue to hope in the Lord?

Zerubbabel

The Book of Ezra

About 520 BC

There were three separate returns from captivity.

- The first came shortly after the Persian conquest of Babylon (538 B.C.; Ezra 1:1), led by Zerubbabel.
- The second came 80 years later, in the time of Artaxerxes Longimanus (458 B.C.; Ezra 7:7), led by Ezra.
- The third came 13 years later, in the 20th year of Artaxerxes Longimanus (444 B.C.; Neh. 2:1), led by Nehemiah.

In the first year of Cyrus, Zerubbabel was living in Babylon. He was known as a prince of Judah in the captivity. He was probably in the king's service, as he had received an Aramaic name (Sheshbazzar) and was entrusted by Cyrus with the office of governor of Judea. Zerubbabel led the first gathering of captives to Jerusalem, accompanied by Jeshua the high priest, many priests, Levites, and heads of houses of Judah and Benjamin. Arriving at Jerusalem, their first task was to build the altar on its old site and to restore the daily sacrifice (Ezra 2; 3:1-3), about 536 B.C.

The great work of Zerubbabel was the rebuilding of the Temple. Aided by a grant of material and money from the Persian King, Zerubbabel was able to lay the foundation in the second month of the second year of their return. This was done with great dignity, with the trumpet blasts of the priests, the music of the Levites, and the loud songs of thanksgiving of the people (Ezra 3:8-13).

Hindrances

The work had not advanced far before the mixed settlers in Samaria offered to take part in it as well. Zerubbabel and his companions declined the offer; then the Samaritans attempted to obstruct its completion. They "frightened them from building" and hired lawyers to misrepresent them at the court. The result was, no more progress was made during the remaining years of the reign of Cyrus and the eight years of Cambyses who followed Cyrus on the Persian throne (Ezra 4:1-24). Zerubbabel does not appear completely faultless for this long delay. The difficulties in the way of building the Temple were not great enough to have stopped the work. And during this long suspension of 16 years Zerubbabel and the rest of the people had been busy in building costly houses for themselves.

Moved by the preaching of the prophets **Haggai** and **Zechariah**, Zerubbabel, once again, threw himself energetically into the work. He was enthusiastically supported by Jeshua and all the people. This was in the second year of the reign of Darius Hystaspes. This king commanded the Samaritans to assist the Jews at the king's expense with whatever they needed.

The work advanced so rapidly that on the third day of the month Adar, in the sixth year of Darius, the Temple was finished. It was then dedicated with much pomp and rejoicing (Ezra 5:1-6:22), 516 B.C. The only other works of Zerubbabel mentioned in Scripture are the restoration of the divisions of priests and Levites, and of the provision for their maintenance, according to the method instituted by David; the registration of the returned captives according to their genealogies; and the keeping of the Passover in the seventh year of Darius.

What comes to your mind as an example of an offer that seemed "too good to be true"?

Why did Israel refuse their neighbors' help?

In what ways has your faith ever come under attack, been tested, or opposed?

What opposition have you experienced in your Christian walk?

Ezra
About 530 BC

His name means "help" or "helper." He was born in Persia and died in Jerusalem.

Ezra is one of the most unique people in the Bible. He was a priest descended from Aaron and Zadok. He was also a prophet, a scribe and an excellent teacher of the Law. He apparently was also somewhat musical because Nehemiah 12 records he led the musical celebration following the completion of the wall around Jerusalem.
He wrote the history of the first return from exile to Jerusalem. This return took place in 538 B.C. He was the leader of the second return from exile to Jerusalem. This return took place 80 years later in 458 B.C. His book is devoted to describing the return and activity or these first two journeys.

In the first return led by Zerubbabel nearly 50,000 people left Babylon and returned to Jerusalem. The return led by Ezra was a mission to complete much of the work that had begun in the earlier return.

When Ezra arrived in Jerusalem, 80 years after the first return, he soon learned the Jews had compromised their testimony and had begun practicing heathen customs and religion. They even had begun to intermarry and were losing their Jewish distinctiveness.

His reaction to this was to move into immediate prayer. His prayer is recorded in chapter 9; we can learn much from his approach to God in this prayer.

- He confessed and acknowledged the former sins of the nation of Israel. (6-7)
- He confessed and acknowledged the present sins of Israel. (10-15)
- He acknowledged and asked for an expression of the grace of God. (8-9)

Ezra's ministry was one of a kind. He began his ministry living in Babylon under Persian control working for King Artaxerxes.

He was a priest and took his responsibilities seriously. He was a gifted Bible teacher and went to great efforts to teach the *word of God* to everyone in Jerusalem. Nehemiah 8:18 records Ezra stood alone and read the word of God in public hearing for seven full days.

Ezra is an example of what one man can do when he is totally committed to be obedient to the word of God. He was born in captivity after the first return to Jerusalem had left for Israel. He was impressed with the prophecies in the word of God relating to the return. He was able to research and write the history of the first return.

It is probably this research led to his vision to return to the city of Jerusalem.

How do you explain Ezra's great success?

What character traits of Ezra would you like to have?

What blessings has the Lord bestowed on you?

What can we learn from Ezra's response to success?

How can you change your spiritual habits to become more devoted to God?

Why do you think God grants power and financial security only to some people?

Ezra: The Helper

Ezra 7-9

About 530 BC

Like Zerubbabel 80 years before, Ezra, received great benefits from the Persian king.

These privileges included;

- The authority to take as many of his countrymen who wanted to return;
- To receive gold and silver for the Jerusalem temple;
- To draw upon the royal treasury for needs that might arise;
- To purchase animals for sacrifice at the temple;
- To exempt temple personnel from Persian taxation;
- To appoint civil magistrates in the land of Judah to enforce the laws of Jehovah.

Ezra's interest and his task was not to build the country materially, as it had been with the first return and would be again with the third, he was to build the people socially and spiritually.

Reform was needed so the people might live more as God had instructed.

Ezra assembled those who wanted to return at a river near Babylon. The size of the group is shown by the number of men, 1,500, a number much smaller than the first return. When no Levites were found in the group, Ezra delayed while 38 Levites were persuaded to join, and they were accompanied by 220 helpers. Departure occurred the twelfth day of the first month (458 B.C.) and arrival in Jerusalem the first day of the fifth month (Ezra 7:9; 8:31), a journey of just over three and one-half months.

The main area of reform which confronted Ezra was the intermarriage of several Jews with surrounding peoples. Jewish people had permitted their sons to marry heathen daughters of neighboring nations, and even the priests, Levites, and civil leaders were involved.

Ezra was told of this defection from the Law soon after his arrival and reacted with remorse. He tore his clothing, pulled hair from his head, and sat confounded until the evening. Then he offered a prayer of confession.

When he finished, those standing by were deeply moved and expressed their conviction the marriages should be dissolved. Ezra agreed and solicited approval from some of the more sympathetic religious and civil authorities as well. Details were worked out to accomplish this difficult and grievous task.

Decision was made that each case be judged separately. To insure justice, it was determined judgments should be passed by the elders and the appointed judges from the villages of the respective parties. They would know the situations better than someone who was unacquainted with the facts. Judging began as soon as arrangements could be made and was completed within three months. Since intermarriage had occurred so soon after the return from captivity, the situation could soon lead to serious consequences. Ezra recognized the fact and took the unpleasant but appropriate action.

How much influence do you think your family has on you?

How much influence do you think your friends have on you?

Why do you think peer pressure is so powerful?

What would you say are the most important relationships in your life?

In what way can you give credit to God at this point for any successes you've enjoyed?

His name means "Jehovah is great." He was born in Persia and traveled to and from Jerusalem. He died in Jerusalem. He was a contemporary of Ezra and led the final return to Jerusalem in 444 BC.

Nehemiah was younger than Ezra. Ezra was a priest and Bible teacher and his primary concern was teaching the people of Israel to obey God. Nehemiah was a politician and a builder. He was primarily concerned with providing for the safety and defense of the people of Israel.

The book of Nehemiah is autobiographical. This book marks the end of the historical progression of chronology in the Old Testament.

The first two chapters of this book set the stage and introduce the narrative for the remainder of the book.

The first chapter tells us of the news arriving relating to the condition of the walls of Jerusalem. With the use of other historical information, we can place this time period as December of 446 B.C.

The terrible condition of the walls of Jerusalem was related to Nehemiah by his brother on a visit to Susa. Nehemiah was heart-broken by the news relating to the condition of the city of Jerusalem. He wept and prayed God would soften the heart of the king so he might be able to travel to Jerusalem and try to correct the problem.

Chapter 2 tells us of his request to the king. It is important to note this request took place four months after he had received the news concerning the condition of the city. Nehemiah had spent four months in prayer and fasting.

He asked the King to send him to Jerusalem with the authority and means to rebuild the city because it was the home of the God of his fathers.

We see his efforts to rebuild and restore the city were met by many different forms of opposition. The book records at least nine different kinds of opposition.

- Ridicule (4:1-3)
- Discouragement (4:10)
- Conspiracy (4:7-8, 11)
- Laziness (3:5)
- Internal opposition (5:1-5)
- Compromise (6:1-4)
- Slander (6:5-9)
- Treachery (6:10-14)
- Fear (6:9, 14)

There are many other highlights in the book of Nehemiah. One of the greatest of these highlights is his public prayer recorded in 9:6-38.

The book ends on a note of rejoicing. When God's work is done in God's way, joy will follow. At the celebration with the completion of the work, people sent presents to one another and praised God.

Nehemiah was willing to leave his position in the royal palace of Persia where he served the king on a daily basis and return to the rubble of Jerusalem.

How far are you willing to go to serve God?

How far away can your joy in Christ be heard and seen?

Nehemiah served as the official cupbearer of the Persian king Artaxerxes; a position of great importance and influence in ancient Near Eastern courts.

Personal Character

Although Nehemiah is never called a prophet, nor is his work placed among the prophetic writings, his ministry nevertheless resembles that of the prophets:

- He declares to the people what God has revealed to him.
- He intercedes for his people and calls on them to return in faithfulness to the Mosaic covenant.
- He calls down imprecations on his enemies.
- He addresses social issues with the same vigor as the great eighth-century prophets.
- He illustrates his message with a symbolic act.
- Like many Old Testament prophets, he was harassed by the deceitful message of a false prophet.
- Nehemiah is often regarded as a perfect servant-leader.
- The following list of attributes is an analysis of Nehemiah. Nehemiah was a man of:
- Service–demonstrated by his exalted position as the king's cupbearer;
- Responsibility–demonstrated by his appointment to the position of governor of Judah;
- Faith–demonstrated by his wholehearted devotion to and utter trust in his God;
- Preparation–demonstrated by his practice of planning before acting;
- Prayer–demonstrated by his consistent prayer life;
- Action–demonstrated by his realization of what needed to be done and his willingness to do whatever it takes to see the mission accomplished;
- Cooperation–demonstrated by his willingness to work with others;
- Discretion–demonstrated by his inspection of the walls of the city at night;
- Delegation–demonstrated by his willingness to delegate authority to those under him;
- Determination–demonstrated by his unwillingness to let opposition deter him from fulfilling his objectives;
- Confidence–demonstrated by his conviction that he was doing God's will;
- Compassion–demonstrated by his heart for his people;
- Unselfishness–demonstrated by his refusal to accept the governor's portion;
- Triumph–demonstrated by his success over both physical adversaries (the opposition group) and material adversaries (walls of Jerusalem);
- Confrontation–demonstrated by his earnestness in confronting sin and wrongdoing;
- Motivation–demonstrated by his desire to serve God;
- Convictions–demonstrated by his unwillingness to tolerate evil around him;
- Inspiration–demonstrated by his ability to motivate others to serve God;
- Vision–demonstrated by his focus on God's expectations rather than on people's limitations;
- Perseverance–demonstrated by his ability to finish the task at hand.

Which of these attributes do you see as the greatest?

Which of these attributes do you see in yourself?

Which of these attributes would you like to work on increasing in your life?

Which of these attributes do you think is the hardest for a leader to exhibit?

How can we develop integrity so that God can use us as leaders?

Esther — Esther 2:1-23, 4:1-5:8. 7:1-8:8

Esther was also called Hadassah; her Hebrew name. Hadassah means "myrtle" which is a five-pointed star shaped flower. The name Esther is a name of Persian derivation and means "star." She was born in Shushan, Persia. She later became the queen of Persia. She married King Ahasuerus, who is also known as Xerxes. He ruled Persia 486-464.

Esther saved her people from a plan to destroy the entire Hebrew nation. She risked her life in order to preserve the Jewish nation. She was raised in the city of Shushan by her cousin Mordechai. She was from the tribe of Benjamin. Since her parents are never mentioned we assume they were dead, and Mordechai took her to raise.

The unfolding of events in the book of Esther is one of the most interesting stories in the Bible. She is often compared to Ruth. Ruth was a Gentile woman who married a Jewish man and became the great grandmother of King David. Esther is a Jewish woman who married a Gentile king and saved the entire Jewish nation. These two women show us how God is willing to use people who are faithful and obedient to His law. We never really know what God will do with us until we are simply obedient.

Here is a biblical account of how God can move and work in the highest levels of world government. Esther was not a prominent person by any stretch of the imagination and yet God chose her and honored her obedience.

Esther is a key element in the way God has kept the promises He made to Abraham, Isaac, and Jacob. God promised King David there would be someone to sit on his throne forever.

Mordechai warned Esther of the plot to exterminate the Jews which had been put into place because of Haman. The King had acted on the advice of this man and allowed a law to be passed to eliminate the "enemies of the kingdom."

Esther prevented this attempt by Satan to destroy the Jewish nation and wipe out the plan of God. The Jews were allowed to defend themselves and in the providence of God they emerged victorious on the day Satan had planned to wipe them out.

To remember this victory and the faithfulness of God, Mordechai and Esther instituted a memorial feast called Purim. This is one of the greatest Jewish holidays and events observed with a celebration of joy, the giving of presents, and feasting. It is celebrated in the early spring.

Are you surprised God could use a "nobody" to save His entire plan of redemption?

What family traditions are most important to you?

What traditions in your family have spiritual significance to you?

Do you feel we undervalue many of our national and religious traditions?

How can we help remember what God has done in our lives and pass it on to the next generation?

In your service to God are you more like Mordecai or Esther?

The story of Esther is filled with palace intrigue, personal adventure, and anti-Semitic drama. Hill and Walton write, "It would be difficult to find a more riveting, dramatic, and suspenseful plot in the pre-Hellenistic world than the book of Esther."

The cast of characters alone would make it a best-seller in today's world: the powerful king, the defiant queen, the diabolical villain, and the courageous Esther.

The anti-Semitic thread of Gentile animosity runs through nearly every chapter as does the providential hand of the unnamed God of the Jews.

Despite the book's popularity, critics have questioned, criticized, debated, and sometimes excluded Esther as an inspired canonical book.

It is the only Old Testament book missing among the documents and fragments of the Dead Sea Scrolls. Esther is also the only Old Testament book in which the name of God does not appear.

Yet the religious practice of fasting by Esther, Mordecai, and the Jews certainly indicates a dependence on God's divine intervention (4:16). Despite these challenges Esther has remained a message of hope over the centuries for Jewish and Christian readers alike.

The title of the book is derived from its central character, an obscure Jewish girl who became one of the queens of Persia. Esther's Hebrew name, Hadassah (2:7), means "myrtle," but it was changed to the pagan name, Ester, derived from the Persian word for "star" (stara). Esther's name was a form of the Babylonian goddess Ishtar or Ashtar.

The book of Esther is one of the five books the Jews called the Megilioth or "Rolls." The other four books are Canticles, Ruth, Lamentations, and Ecclesiastes. These books are read at Israel's various feasts. The book of Esther is read at the Feast of Purim, celebrating the deliverance and preservation of the Jews during the Persian period.

The story of Esther is one of the greatest accounts of a strong-minded woman in ancient history. From her life and character here are some of the lessons we can learn:

- To seek divine guidance in all times of difficulty (4:15-17);
- When there is a necessity, to be ready to surrender self and exert ourselves for the good of others;
- To value and seek the cooperation of fellow-believers.

Looking at the deliverance and safety of the Jews which Esther secured, we learn;

- To have complete confidence in God's control and not to undervalue small things;
- To acknowledge God as the source of all blessing and mercy.

Thinking of the reversal of fortune of Haman, which Esther brought about, we should learn:

- There is such a thing as righteous retribution. Haman himself received what he had proposed for others;
- The fleeting nature of earthly magnificence and the end of all dishonest earthly power and possessions.

What sacrifices would you be willing to make for the people you love?

For what cause or person would you be willing to risk your life?

How can we use family traditions to celebrate and share God's goodness?

Mordechai was from the tribe of Benjamin. He had been taken into exile from Jerusalem by Nebuchadnezzar. He had raised his cousin named Esther when her parents had died. After a nationwide beauty contest to find a new queen Esther was chosen and she became Queen of Persia.

Mordechai advised her not to reveal her nationality or background (2:10). He felt it would be dangerous for her to admit she were Jewish and not Persian. The Jews were still considered an inferior race and slaves in the land.

Mordechai discovered and reported to Esther there was a plot on the part of two royal gatekeepers to assassinate King Ahasuerus. The plotters were quickly arrested and executed (2:23).

Time passed and Mordechai received no rewards or acknowledgment for his action. Later he refused to bow and pay honor to Haman, Persia's wicked and arrogant prime minister appointed by the king.

Haman observed this refusal and plotted to kill not only Mordecai, but all the Jews in the entire kingdom (3:3-15). Haman was able to influence the king in such a way that he signed an edict allowing the destruction of the Jewish race in Persia.

Learning of these events and plans, Mordecai went into deep mourning. After much prayer Mordecai sent the information relating to Haman's death decree to Esther.

Mordecai gave her the following advice (4:13-14):

- Don't think you will escape the fate of your people simply because you live in the palace.
- If you keep quiet, the Jews will be delivered some other way and you will die.
- You have probably been brought to the kingdom for such a time as this.

At Esther's request, he gathered the Jewish leaders in Susa for a three-day fast as the queen prepared to approach, uninvited, her husband the king.

Shortly after this, in the foresight of God, two totally unexpected events occurred.

- The king learned Mordecai had once saved his life and determined to reward him (6:1-3).
- Haman was forced by the king to arrange an honor parade for Mordecai (6:10-11).

Haman was eventually hanged upon the very gallows he had built for Mordecai. After Haman's death, Mordecai was appointed over the wicked prime minister's estate.

At the king's command, Mordecai wrote a new royal edict, letting the Jews defend themselves against their enemies. Mordecai took Haman's place as Prime Minister.

Following the victory over their enemies, the Jewish leaders received a letter from Mordecai commanding them to celebrate the newly established Feast of Purim (9:20-32).

Imagine Mordecai standing erect in a throng of prostrate palace officials. Do you think you would have this courage?

He refused to bow down, and it could have cost him his life! He feared God more than man; do you?

His name means "Where is the father?" He lived in the land of Uz. We are not sure of the location of this place. Bible scholars believe this was somewhere in the area of Edom.

There is no specific date given for Job and there is very little internal information which can help us establish a good time frame. Since there is no mention of the Law, it is generally believed he lived in the days of the biblical patriarchs or perhaps even before their lifetime.

The Bible tells us Job was a godly man. He feared the Lord and lived his life to glorify God. We know he was a man with a large family. He had seven sons and three daughters. He was also a very wealthy man. He had a great deal of livestock and had many servants.

He was well known and very well respected in his community and was considered a man of some social importance.

The book of Job is an account of the events in his life when Satan set out to test him and tried to make him turn from following God.

Satan attacked Job in the following ways;

- **His wealth: he lost all of his livestock and his servants were killed.**
- **His family: his children were killed, and his wife mocked his faith in God.**
- **His physical health: Satan struck him with painful boils which caused him to despair of his life.**
- **His friends: these people presumed some secret sin in his life and that God was punishing him.**

Most of the book is an account of the conversations between Job and his friends. They attempted to convince him God was punishing him for his disobedience.

Job defended both himself and God to these "friends."

In the end of the account, God personally intervenes and confronts these false accusers. He defends Job and praises his obedience. We have no record Job was ever told of the conversation between Satan and God.

Job is almost always associated with the word patience. James makes the observation in his book, *"As you know, we consider blessed those who have persevered. You have heard of Job's perseverance and have seen what the Lord finally brought about. The Lord is full of compassion and mercy" (James 5:11).*

God restored all Job had lost and blessed him even more. His friends admitted their errors and his health was restored.

There are several things we can learn from the book of Job.

- **God is proud of His children.**
- **God sets limits on what Satan can do to his children.**
- **This book explains the error of thinking suffering is always caused by personal sin.**
- **We can see how important our lives are to God and Satan.**
- **It is amazing to think we might be the subject of conversations in heaven.**

What event, thing, or person has had the biggest impact on your life?

When have you ever had to take back something you said?

Why do people often associate material prosperity with God's blessing?

His name means "God is salvation." Isaiah was a prophet during the reigns of Uzziah, Jotham, Ahaz, Hezekiah and Manasseh kings of Judah. He was probably martyred by Manasseh. We know nothing of the place of his birth. It is believed he began his prophetic ministry "*in the year that king Uzziah died.*" Uzziah died about 750 BC.

Isaiah is generally believed to be the greatest of the Old Testament prophets. The book of Isaiah is sometimes called the fifth gospel because of its many prophecies about Jesus Christ.

Within the structure of the book of Isaiah there are some interesting characteristics when compared to the rest of Bible.

- The book of Isaiah is divided into two parts; chapters 1-39, chapters 40-66. The Bible is divided into the Old and New Testament; the Old Testament contains 39 books; the New Testament contains 27 books.
- The first half of the book of Isaiah deals with the judgment of Israel because of their failure to consistently follow the law of God. This bears a close similarity to the content of the Old Testament.
- The second half of the book of Isaiah begins with the message of comfort from God to his people. Isaiah 53 prophesies the crucifixion of the Messiah and portrays the information very much as the Gospels portray it.

The book of Isaiah concludes with the prophecy of the new heavens and the new earth; the book of Revelation concludes the New Testament with an account of the coming of the new heavens and the new earth.

Isaiah gives a many-sided, much like a diamond, picture of the coming Messiah, the Son of God

He describes Him as the Lamb.

- His incarnation (7:14-15; 9:6)
- His lowliness and youth (7:15; 11:1-2; 53:2)
- His relationship to the Father (42:1; 50:4-5)
- His specific ministry to the Gentiles (9:1-2)
- His gracious ministry to all (42:2-3)
- His miracles (35:5-6)
- His message (61:1-2)
- His suffering and death (50:6; 52:14; 53:1-10)

He also describes Him as the Lion of God.

- His resurrection (53:10-12)
- His millennial reign (9:7; 32:1; 33:22)

One of the most interesting references to Isaiah in the New Testament occurs in Acts 8:26-35. This is the account of Philip and the Ethiopian eunuch. The eunuch was reading this passage of Scripture: "*He was led like a sheep to the slaughter and as a lamb before the shearer is silent, so he did not open his mouth. In his humiliation he was deprived of justice. Who can speak of his descendants? For his life was taken from the earth.*" The Ethiopian asked Philip to explain this passage of Scripture. We read in verse 35, "*Then Philip began with that very passage of Scripture and told him the good news about Jesus.*"

In the synagogue in Nazareth Jesus read from the scroll of Isaiah as He taught the Scripture lesson. He read from Isaiah 61:1-2; then He said unto them today this scripture is fulfilled in your ears.

Isaiah saw the glory of the Lord and he continued to speak of Him for the rest of his life.

Do you talk about Jesus?

Isaiah talked about God's glory; what do you talk about?

There are three specific events recorded which stand out in the prophecies of Isaiah.

The first major event is his call

Isaiah tells us, *"In the year that King Uzziah died I saw the Lord, high and lifted up."* In this vision he describes God seated upon a throne lifted in the Temple. Around him were six angels called seraphim, having six wings each. They cried to each other, *"Holy, holy, holy, is the LORD of hosts; the whole earth is full of his glory"* (Isa. 6:3). Isaiah felt a strong sense of personal sinfulness, and he cried out, "Woe is me." One of the angels flew to him to place a coal on his mouth and to cleanse it, and then Isaiah heard the voice of God saying, "Whom shall I send, and who will go for us?" Isaiah responded, "Here am I; send me" (6:8). God told Isaiah, the people would hear him but not understand, and they would see but not perceive. In other words, Isaiah should indeed answer God's call, but he should also be aware ahead of time that there would be few results coming from his efforts.

This occasion may have constituted Isaiah's initial call to service, or it may have been merely a call to a special aspect of work.

A second episode is recorded in Isaiah

It took place in the reign of Ahaz (Judah) and concerned the time of the siege of Pekah (Israel) and Rezin (Syria). The siege was in progress when God told Isaiah to go to Ahaz and encourage him in his difficult situation, and to instruct him to ask for a sign from the Lord that deliverance would come. Ahaz's response was, *"I will not ask, neither will I tempt the LORD"* (7:12), accordingly in false piety refusing to do as God and Isaiah directed. Isaiah gave Ahaz a sign anyway, which was the well-known messianic indication; *"Behold, a virgin shall conceive, and bear a son, and shall call his name Immanuel"* (7:14). Isaiah went on to say that before this child would know the difference between good and evil, Ahaz would be delivered from the two surrounding kings.

But instead of listening to Isaiah's promise or depending on God to bring the deliverance indicated, Ahaz in his wickedness sent to the emperor of Assyria, to come and invade the northern countries so that Pekah and Rezin would have to go home to protect their own interests. In doing this, Ahaz showed his pro-Assyrian preferences. He also showed a lack of recognition of the fact his greatest enemy really was Assyria rather than Israel or Syria. Isaiah now informed him of this fact in definite terms, though apparently the king paid no attention.

The third episode is recorded in Isaiah 36 and 37

These events occurred during the reign of King Hezekiah. Isaiah was involved on two occasions. **The first** came after a visit to Jerusalem by three envoys from the king of Assyria. Hezekiah sent a messenger to Isaiah to inform him of what had happened and to urge him to beseech God for help. Isaiah sent a response saying Hezekiah should not fear, for God would work in such a way Sennacherib would return to his own land without harming Jerusalem.

The second contact came after Hezekiah received a letter from Sennacherib, threatening to destroy the city of Jerusalem. Hezekiah prayed for help to God and God sent a message of encouragement through Isaiah. The message was of some length but had one main point: the king of Assyria would not come near Jerusalem but would be made to return to his own city.

It is obvious these episodes are only a small part of Isaiah's total ministry.

What is one thing you might expect God to do about pagan challenges to His Lordship?

In what new way could you pray about a situation in which you've been awaiting God's help?

He was the son of Amoz, this was not Amos the prophet, who was his contemporary. He was married to a "prophetess" (8:3), and they had two sons, Shear-jashub (7:3) and Maher-shalal-hashbaz. His is the longest name recorded in the Bible. (8:4).

Prince of prophets
Isaiah is often called the "prince of prophets." The term is appropriate and for two reasons. The first is the ability and work of Isaiah. He was a man of great ability, who possessed a wide knowledge of the world as well as a huge capacity for work. Few prophets and perhaps few people in the land could have matched him.

Also, his ministry contains some of the Old Testament's clearest messianic prophecy. It seems fair to say God told him more regarding the Messiah than He did to any other man of the Old Testament. This was certainly a great honor and privilege.

Ease at the royal court
Probably none of the prophets exhibited greater ease than did Isaiah in visiting the royal court. He came to Ahaz and not only had courage to bring a stern rebuke but spoke at considerable length on the danger Ahaz faced from Assyria.

Later it was to Isaiah that Hezekiah sent for help when Sennacherib was invading the country. This showed Hezekiah's high respect for Isaiah as a prophet and friend. Soon after, God sent Isaiah to tell the ailing Hezekiah God would make him well and extend his life for 15 years (Isa. 38:5).

This ease of royal contact may have been due to a blood relationship Isaiah held to the royal line. Jewish tradition tells us Isaiah's father, Amoz, was a brother of King Amaziah, the father of Uzziah, thus making Isaiah a cousin of King Uzziah. The ease of contact was probably due also to Isaiah's own knowledge and ability, which were apparent in his day. Kings liked to have people of Isaiah's caliber on whom they could call, and they gave him respect and honor accordingly.

Intellectual ability
Isaiah clearly was one of the intellectuals of his day. He was a man of broad knowledge of the world. No less than 11 chapters of his book (13-23) are allotted to prophecies of judgment God would bring on surrounding nations. These nations were not only those near to Judah but included Babylonia and Assyria far to the east and Egypt and Ethiopia far to the southwest. To write in as much detail as he does shows he was informed regarding these lands. He must have read widely and made a point to speak with caravan travelers and visiting foreigners.

Courage
We must also see Isaiah as a prophet of outstanding courage. The evidence is clear. It took courage to go to Ahaz with words of denouncement and rebuke. Ahaz was the king and might retaliate with severe punishment, but this apparently made no difference to Isaiah. It took courage to speak as he did in the day of Hezekiah. He warned repeatedly concerning the danger of foreign alliance and especially dependence upon Egypt. This was an unpopular message, for people were interested in any measure that would be anti-Assyrian. Isaiah was not in favor of Assyria either, but he knew the folly of trusting in Egypt and local alliances. He, therefore, gave the warning whether popular or not.

What can we learn about God from the fact that He gave a sign that wasn't even requested?

What fear do you need to surrender to God in order not to be controlled by it?

For what recent act of concern and faithfulness can you thank God today?

Jeremiah: An Introduction — Jeremiah 1, 8, 32

His name means "Jehovah is high." Jeremiah was born in Anathoth, about three miles north of Jerusalem. He died as an exile in Egypt. His ministry extended nearly 50 years, 627-580 B.C.

Jeremiah is known as the "weeping prophet." From a human point of view the career of Jeremiah was a failure. He was called by God to be a prophet; he was the son of a priest, but from what we can tell never served in any priestly function.

When he was called, he protested to God he was too young to serve in such an important position. God encouraged the young man by telling him He would put the words in his mouth, and He would stand beside him.

Jeremiah's message was extremely unpopular. He was instructed to announce the judgment of God upon his nation. As a result, he faced much opposition. He was persecuted and mistreated by many different groups. He faced opposition from his own family, his hometown, the religious establishment, and was actively persecuted by the political establishment.

His own brothers turned against him and were involved in a plot to put him to death (12). He was arrested and put into stocks to be ridiculed (20). He was nearly murdered by a mob of priests and false prophets after one of his messages (26). He was bullied by King Jehoiakim, arrested and accused of treason.

He experienced frustration and oppression. He tried to resign as a prophet; he even told God he would no longer speak His name or prophesy.

He prayed one of the most discouraging and despondent prayers recorded in the entire Bible. It begins with the words, "*Cursed be the day when I was born*" (20).

Despite all his trials and tribulations Jeremiah remained faithful to God and His word. Jeremiah continued to prophesy; telling the remnant living in Babylon the captivity would last 70 years and after 70 years Israel would be returned to her home (29). This prophesy is referred to by three other Old Testament writers. It is mentioned in 2 Chronicles 36. Ezra speaks of it in the first chapter of his book. It is the prophecy which encouraged Daniel to pray for the return of his people.

There is so much more we could say about Jeremiah. It is difficult to properly introduce his service to God in such a short space.

There is one other aspect of his prophecies we cannot leave out of this introduction. He is the prophet of God who introduced the New Covenant (31:31-34). This is the prophecy which tells of the promise of God to change the heart of His people. He will give them "a new heart."

This promise is one of the three great unconditional covenants of the Old Testament.

- The Abrahamic Covenant (Genesis 12)
- The Davidic Covenant (2 Samuel 7)
- The New Covenant (Jeremiah 31)

These promises of God assure Israel of a land, a people and a Savior. They were promised the Messiah will one day sit on the throne of David.

When have you been chosen for a task for which you felt totally unqualified?

What difference can it make to know that God knew us and set us apart even before our birth?

What reservations do you have about your ability to serve God according to His call?

Jeremiah was a man with a deeply emotional temperament.
He may have seemed hardhearted to people as he preached his message regarding the coming defeat at the hands of the Babylonians, but in his own heart he cried out with pain. For instance, in 9:1 he writes, "*Oh that my head were waters, and mine eyes a fountain of tears, that I might weep day and night for the slain of the daughter of my people!"*

Again in 13:17 he says, *"But if ye will not hear it, my soul shall weep in secret places for your pride; and mine eye shall weep sore, and run down with tears, because the LORD'S flock is carried away captive." Still again in 14:17 he states, "Therefore thou shalt say this word unto them; Let mine eyes run down with tears night and day, and let them not cease: for the virgin daughter of my people is broken with a great breach, with a very grievous blow."* Thus, he was a man to whom tears were not strange, as he contemplated the fate of his people.

At the same time Jeremiah could rise to heights of exaltation as he expressed joy and confidence that God was with him to provide in all ways. For instance, he writes of his joy in 15:16, *"Thy words were found, and I did eat them; and thy word was unto me the joy and rejoicing of mine heart: for I am called by thy name, 0 LORD God of hosts."*

He was also a man of great courage.
We might think otherwise in view of times of his despondency and discouragement (15:10; 20:14-18), but those times came only in reaction to the severe opposition he faced. He was only human after all, and when one encounters almost continual conflict, one can hardly help but break occasionally.

But overall Jeremiah demonstrated remarkable courage. He stood up day after day and proclaimed a message that others believed to be not only wrong but traitorous. His message was one of capitulation when others spoke of victory. Jeremiah by nature certainly wanted victory too, but God had given him this contrary message, and he was willing to stand and proclaim it before people and king alike.

His book
The book Jeremiah wrote is one of the great prophetic documents of the Old Testament, ranking probably second only to Isaiah in its force and significance. Like other prophetic books, it is composed of numerous messages by the prophet that were written at different periods of his life. Part of it is in poetry and part in prose, both exhibiting a wide range of literary figures and types. Though it does not show quite the literary excellence of Isaiah, it displays an excellent style which rates high among the other prophetical books. One matter that is particularly noteworthy is that the book contains so much historical material, a great portion of which is autobiographical in that various episodes and situations from the life of Jeremiah are set forth.

A natural question concerns the relation of this book with the material Jeremiah dictated to Baruch. It has been observed that in the time of Jehoiakim God came to Jeremiah and told him to record in a book all the things God had revealed to him, and Jeremiah did so (36:1, 2). Later, after this book had been burned by the foolish king, Jeremiah rewrote it and added to it (36:27-32). The present book of Jeremiah, however, could not be that work because much of what is recorded concerns history and revelation following that time. Possibly Jeremiah continued to add to what he wrote then, or it may be that the final work was a new one based on the earlier one as far as that went historically.

What person of faith could you study in the coming weeks in order to learn how to take a stand for God's righteousness while maintaining compassion for sinners?

What is your favorite story, true or fictional, of a total reversal of fortunes?

What do we learn about Jeremiah's character and motives from the fact he chose to stay with his people rather than receive honor in Babylon?

In what area of your life could it be helpful to ponder the truth that nothing is too hard for God?

Baruch — Jeremiah 36, 43, 45

Baruch was Jeremiah's scribe. He physically wrote Jeremiah's words as the prophet dictated to him. It is difficult to comprehend how long this would have taken. It would have been a long and tiring process for both men. We have difficulty making time to read the entire book of Jeremiah.

The early copies of the Bible were all hand copied; this process was long and arduous but imagine the added difficulty of writing down what someone was saying. The creation of the original book of Jeremiah written on a scroll must have taken years.

Seldom does archaeology come face to face with people mentioned in the Bible, but just such an event has happened with Baruch. A cache of clay seals which was found in the middle 1980's contained not only a seal impression of Baruch, son of Neriah, but also one from King Jehoiakim's son Yerah\me'el, who was sent on the unsuccessful mission to arrest Baruch and Jeremiah.

Baruch's seal impression reads as follows:
(Belonging to) Berakhyahu son of Neriyahu
the scribe

In 1996, a second clay bulla emerged with an identical inscription; presumably stamped with the same seal. In addition, this bulla also was imprinted with a fingerprint; Hershel Shanks, among others, speculated that the fingerprint might be that of Baruch himself.

Baruch's full name was apparently Berekhyahu, a fact not previously known. The common suffix *-yahu* in ancient Hebrew names, especially in Judah, is a form of Yahweh. Baruch means "the blessed." Berekhyahu means "blessed of Yahweh."

When Baruch finished writing all Jeremiah had said, he was told by the prophet to take the scroll to the Temple and read it publicly (36:5-8). Probably Jeremiah did not intend for Baruch to read the entire scroll, but that may have been exactly what happened.

This original scroll was burned by King Jehoiakim (36:22-23, 27). After this God ordered Jeremiah to reproduce his book with all the oral sermons, he had preached the past 23 years included (36:1-2).

Baruch became so discouraged and despondent he was ready to quit. God gave Jeremiah a message to be delivered to his scribe. "*This is what the LORD, the God of Israel, says to you, Baruch: You said, 'Woe to me! The LORD has added sorrow to my pain; I am worn out with groaning and find no rest.'" The LORD said, "Say this to him: 'This is what the LORD says: I will overthrow what I have built and uproot what I have planted, throughout the land. Should you then seek great things for yourself? Seek them not. For I will bring disaster on all people, declares the LORD, but wherever you go I will let you escape with your life.'*" (45:2-5).

Baruch was accused of treason by those angry at the messages which he delivered (43:3). He suffered much persecution because of his friendship and loyalty to Jeremiah. Along with Jeremiah, he was forced by his own countrymen to leave Judah and live in Egypt (43:7).

Baruch is an excellent example of someone dedicated enough to God he was willing to serve his entire life in a position of lesser importance. He could have earned a good living as a scribe and lived a quiet "normal life." He was willing to endure the ridicule and shame because he believed in his master and the God his master served.

He is one of the best examples of loyalty in the Bible.

When could a routine duty suddenly require courage to do the right thing?

Book Nine

The Inter-Testamental Period

Daniel — Daniel 1-2, 6

His name means "God is judge." Daniel was born in Judah and died in exile in Babylon.

He was a teenager in 605 B.C. when he was taken into Babylon. He served as advisor to several Babylonian kings, until the time of Cyrus in 530 B.C. He was given the Babylonian name of Belteshazzar.

Daniel is an example of what God can do with someone who is willing to trust Him totally. Daniel and his three friends wanted to follow the traditional Jewish diet instead of the diet Nebuchadnezzar ordered.

Daniel proposed a test suggesting the four be allowed to follow their Jewish diet for 10 days and then their superintendent could make the decision regarding their diet.

God rewarded their faithfulness and they could continue eating their unique diet. At the end of their training, they were said to be 10 times smarter than any of the other students in their class. At the direction of King Nebuchadnezzar, Daniel was appointed as a leader in his kingdom.

Daniel is best known for his visions and the interpretation of those visions. The first of these visions is recorded in chapter two. Daniel interpreted the dream of the King, who saw a great statue composed of gold, silver, brass, iron and clay. Daniel told the king what this dream represented:

- The gold was the Babylonian Empire
- The silver was the Persian Empire
- The brass was the Grecian Empire
- The iron was the Final Empire

The iron mixed with clay was the final world power which would be destroyed at the end of the age.

One of the first stories most children learn in the Bible is the story of Daniel and the lion's den. God preserved His faithful prophet and created a lasting testimony of His greatness in the Babylonian Empire.

According to the prophet Ezekiel (14, 28), Daniel was the equal to Noah and Job as an illustration of the virtues of righteousness and wisdom.

Daniel was able to serve three Babylonian kings, Nebuchadnezzar, Belshazzar and Darius without any compromise in his faith and practice. He served these men faithfully and loyally, yet he also served his God.

Daniel himself is unique in the word of God because he was ministered to by both archangels; Gabriel (8, 9) and Michael (10, 12).

Daniel was so highly thought of in heaven that on two occasions the pre-incarnate Christ appeared to him; in the lion's den (6) and later by the Tigris River (10).

Daniel is an encouragement to us to serve God faithfully. I am sure Daniel did not understand why God allowed him and his friends to be taken away from Jerusalem to Babylon. I am sure there were times when he felt discouraged and abandoned, yet he never stopped trusting and serving God.

When have you taken a Christian stand in a non-Christian setting?

Are there things in your life you do not understand?

Do you think God could use these events to show His power?

Daniel stands out as one of God's greatest servants. One indication of Daniel's maturity is God's revelation to him of four great visions. Also, Daniel was not shy about passing on rebuke and divine communications even to kings in Babylon. Another indication comes from the God-centeredness of Daniel's thinking when he interpreted Nebuchadnezzar's dream in chapter two. He could have claimed credit for himself at the time, but he went out of his way to tell the king the interpretation was completely from God.

Integrity
Closely connected to Daniel's spiritual maturity is the integrity he demonstrated throughout his life. His integrity is shown in chapter one. There was great appeal for Daniel and his friends to accept the menu the king gave. For one thing, it came in the form of an order from the king. Also, there could be severe punishment if the order was not observed. It must have seemed to turn the menu down would be to forsake all possibility of getting ahead in the training program. Yet, despite these benefits, Daniel and his friends did request the menu be changed because they knew this was the right thing to do.

Courage
Daniel's courage appears again and again in the stories regarding him. In the first chapter as Daniel and his friends made the decision to refuse the menu order by the king, Daniel made this decision despite the danger it created and the advantages of doing otherwise.

In chapter two, Daniel showed courage in the way he encountered the executioner of the king. Many would have reacted in fright and pleaded for mercy, but Daniel asked the man why the order had been given by the king to kill all wise men.

In chapter four Daniel showed courage as he told the king the shocking and unpleasant news the great Emperor would become insane. One can hardly think of a more unpleasant message to convey, but Daniel did so.

Capability
After graduation, Daniel and his three friends were given high positions of honor as a result of their good work. Daniel was made chief of the wise men. It is one thing to receive such an important position and another to keep it.

Daniel apparently had no trouble keeping this position, for Nebuchadnezzar toward the close of his rule referred to Daniel with the words, "Oh Belteshazzar, master of the magicians" (4:9). This means Daniel must have been capable both as an administrator and as a speaker.

Another indication comes from Daniel's remarkable situation when Darius became king of Babylon following the change of government. In chapter six Daniel was then made one of three leading administrators over 120 princes. Not only this, but the king was planning to make him the head of these three. The granting of such a high position would not have come except for demonstrated ability.

In chapter two, after Daniel had given the interpretation of Nebuchadnezzar's dream and the king had bestowed high honor on Daniel, Daniel immediately thought of his three friends who did not have such positions. As a result, the last verse of the chapter reads, "Then Daniel requested of the king, and he set Shadrach, Meshach, and Abednego over the affairs of the province of Babylon."

Sometimes people forget their friends when they themselves have been honored, but not Daniel.

Do you have friends you can encourage and help?

The Fiery Furnace: Shadrach, Meshach, Abednego — Daniel 3

These are the Babylonian names given to these Jewish teenagers in exile

- To Hananiah: Shadrach, which means "Command of Aku, the moon god."
- To Mishael: Meshach, which means "Who is like Aku, the moon god."
- To Azariah: Abednego, which means "servant of Nego."

These three young men were taken captive along with Daniel in 605 B.C. by King Nebuchadnezzar. They lived their adult lives and died in Babylon. We know nothing more of their service than the events recorded in the first three chapters of Daniel.

These three young men stood with Daniel and refused to defile themselves by eating the food prepared and designed for the Babylonians. This was a diet which included many items forbidden to the Jews to eat.

Along with Daniel they requested and were given permission to eat a special simple diet for 10 days. After the 10-day test period, it was determined that the four young men were healthier physically and mentally than the remaining portion of the class with whom they were studying.

At the end of a three-year course of study they were examined by the king's teachers and found to be far superior in their understanding and learning than all the rest of the young man in their classes.

In chapter two, Nebuchadnezzar had a dream he could not remember or understand. He asked all the wise men of Babylon to tell him his dream and interpret it. When the wise men told the king this was impossible, he gave orders all the wise men in the kingdom should be executed. Daniel and his three friends met together to pray and ask for God's instruction in the matter. God answered their request and Daniel was able to recall and recount the dream for the king.

In Daniel three we are given the account of the fiery furnace. These three men refused to bow down to a Golden statue which Nebuchadnezzar had erected. The King gave them another opportunity to follow his decree. When they refused, he ordered them thrown into a huge fiery furnace.

They were bound hand and foot and cast into the furnace. When King Nebuchadnezzar looked into the furnace, he saw four men unharmed by the fire walking about talking to each other. The fourth man was the pre-incarnate Christ Himself who appeared to protect His servants. The three men were promoted and prospered greatly during Nebuchadnezzar's kingdom.

From these three men we learn the rewards of obedience to the eternal God.
God protected them from the fiery furnace, and He provided them wisdom to prosper and be great examples of Jehovah to the men they worked with.

From these several things we can learn:

- **Obedience is not always easy**
- **God's ways often seem difficult**
- **God is always faithful to His promises**
- **Even though we don't understand the circumstances, obedience is always best**

How are we tempted to glorify national symbols?

How do you distinguish God's authority from those in authority around you?

If someone in authority over you told you to do something wrong, how would you respond?

What are you willing to risk in order to obey God's clear commands?

Nebuchadnezzar **Daniel 4:1-27**

His name is Babylonian for "Nabu protects." He was the son of Nabopolassar, who is mentioned prominently in the Bible as an enemy of the Jews. He was raised under the influence of this king and practiced everything he was taught by his father.

Nebuchadnezzar was king of Babylon from 605-562 B.C. He led and planned the battle for the Babylonian army when the Egyptians were defeated at the battle of Carchemish near the Euphrates River in 605 B.C. This battle changed the balance of power in the ancient near East for over a century. He became the Emperor of the empire that year when his father Nabopolassar died.

He led the armies which surrounded Jerusalem on three occasions (605 BC, 597 BC, and 586 BC). On the third occasion he ordered the city of Jerusalem and the great Temple destroyed.

There are two great dreams of Nebuchadnezzar described in the book of Daniel. In Daniel chapter two he had the vision of the great image composed of four metals. This vision was an overview from the time of Nebuchadnezzar to the second coming of Jesus Christ. Daniel was able to interpret the vision when no one else could and he was given a great promotion with power and authority.

Nebuchadnezzar had a second dream recorded in Daniel four. In this dream he saw a large very healthy tree which increased in size until it reached into heaven and filled the entire earth. The birds and the animals were benefited by its fruit and shade and the entire world was glad for its fruit supply.

As the dream continued a figure appeared and ordered the tree to be cut down; only the stump was left. Daniel told the Emperor that he was the tree, and he would be cut down. Daniel also told Nebuchadnezzar he would remain in this condition for seven years.

These events occurred exactly as Daniel had prophesied. The king was filled with pride. Chapter three shows us the pride of this man when he erected a statue 90 feet high and required everyone to worship the statue. It was this event which led to the three Hebrew men being thrown into the fiery furnace. Then in chapter four, Daniel records in great detail how God struck Nebuchadnezzar with a form of madness and he spent seven years living like an animal in the wild. God had to deal with him on a very personal basis.

Nebuchadnezzar issued a decree following these events making it a crime punishable by death to blaspheme the God of Israel.

The greatest lesson we can learn from Nebuchadnezzar is the danger of pride! The Bible is full of warnings about pride.

- **Psalm 10:4,** ***In his pride the wicked does not seek him; in all his thoughts there is no room for God***
- **Proverbs 8:13,** ***To fear the LORD is to hate evil; I hate pride and arrogance, evil behavior and perverse speech.***
- **Proverbs 11:2,** ***When pride comes, then comes disgrace, but with humility comes wisdom.***
- **Proverbs 16:18,** ***Pride goes before destruction, a haughty spirit before a fall.***

When was the last time you talked about your faith with an unbelieving neighbor or coworker?

In what area of your life do you have to battle pride?

Nebuchadnezzar; Disciplined by God — Daniel 4:28-37

Few men have held greater power than Nebuchadnezzar of Babylon. It was no idle boast he made one evening on his palace roof when he looked across the greatest city of the ancient world and cried: "*Is not this the great Babylon I have built as the royal residence, by my mighty power and for the glory of my majesty*?" (4:29, 30)

It is an archaeological fact that half the bricks in the ruins by the Euphrates are stamped with his name. He had a building mania similar to many other tyrants and despots through the ages. And from the summit of his pride and self-exaltation he tumbled and touched the very bedrock of despair.

Nebuchadnezzar had been warned by Daniel after his second dream described in chapter four. "*Therefore, O king, be pleased to accept my advice: Renounce your sins by doing what is right, and your wickedness by being kind to the oppressed. It may be that then your prosperity will continue.*" (4:27)

Nebuchadnezzar ignored the advice of Daniel and we read of the following events one year later in 4:31-33. *The words were still on his lips when a voice came from heaven, "This is what is decreed for you, King Nebuchadnezzar: Your royal authority has been taken from you. You will be driven away from people and will live with the wild animals; you will eat grass like cattle. Seven times will pass by for you until you acknowledge that the Most High is sovereign over the kingdoms of men and gives them to anyone he wishes." Immediately what had been said about Nebuchadnezzar was fulfilled. He was driven away from people and ate grass like cattle. His body was drenched with the dew of heaven until his hair grew like the feathers of an eagle and his nails like the claws of a bird.*

This great conqueror and megalomaniac, demanding divine honors, had been brought down to nothing. God later restored sensibility to Nebuchadnezzar and he realized his wild self-exaltation had dethroned his reason.

At the end of that time, I, Nebuchadnezzar, raised my eyes toward heaven, and my sanity was restored. Then I praised the Most High; I honored and glorified him who lives forever. His dominion is an eternal dominion; his kingdom endures from generation to generation. All the peoples of the earth are regarded as nothing. He does as he pleases with the powers of heaven and the peoples of the earth. No one can hold back his hand or say to him: "What have you done?"
(4:34-35)

The throne was waiting for the restored king, protected during his madness by the awe which was always attached to those who were mentally deranged in ancient times.

Are you amazed at the patience of God?

When have you ignored what you felt was a warning from God about specific sinful behavior?

What recent insight about God has given your faith a boost?

How is God blessing you right now?

What area of your life do you need to start giving over to God's power and control?

His name means "Bel is leader." He was the son of the Babylonian King Nabonidus. Having been born in Babylon as the son of the king, his every desire and whim were accommodated. He had no appreciation of what it took to run an empire or what it had taken to achieve the greatness that was Babylon.

He served his father Nabonidus as regent in the city of Babylon for 10 years. He died in 539 BC.

Everything we know of Belshazzar is recorded in Daniel five. He is mentioned in one verse in Daniel 8:1 helping us to establish a date for a vision which Daniel received.

The account in Daniel five is the story of what is known as "the handwriting on the wall." This event is legendary in history and it has come to be a euphemism for being able to see negative events in the future.

An interesting archaeological fact about Nabonidus and Belshazzar is we have several different Babylonian king lists which have been recovered from archaeological digs. These king lists give the last three kings of the Babylonian Empire as Nabopolassar, Nebuchadnezzar and Nabonidus. There is absolutely no mention in any of this material of a king whose name was Belshazzar.

The lack of his name in these lists caused many people to think the Bible was in error at this point. As archaeologists explored the Middle East an oasis in the Arabian Desert named Tema was excavated. This site proved to be military headquarters for the Babylonian army. In these records there were many references to Belshazzar. He was the son of Nabonidus, and these records indicate he had been left in charge of the city of Babylon.

The book of Daniel was not in error in representing Belshazzar as the last king of Babylon, as negative criticism once believed, nor can it be said to be wrong in calling Belshazzar the son of Nebuchadnezzar. He was a grandson.

This also accurately explains why this prideful "King" only offered to promote Daniel to third in the kingdom. The reality of the situation was he, himself, was only number two.

The handwriting on the wall revealed the demise of Belshazzar and the Babylonian Empire.

a. *Mene:* "God has numbered your kingdom, and finished it"
b. *Tekel:* "You are weighed in the balances, and found lacking"
c. *Peres:* "Your kingdom is divided, and given to the Medes and Persians"

Some Lessons we should learn:

- Belshazzar, like his grandfather, is a warning of the sin of pride.
- In Belshazzar we also see the sin of perversion. He perverted the truth of Jehovah and used the holy vessels from the Temple in Jerusalem as a part of the drunken feast.
- This should also serve as a warning relating to how we raise and educate our children. Belshazzar had no concept of what it took to build the Babylonian Empire. He only understood the privilege in which he had been raised

Why was Belshazzar proud?

What makes people proud nowadays? What makes you fearful and anxious?

How does God and His judgment affect you?

How have you benefited from the lessons learned by others' life experiences?

If you were struggling with a difficult personal problem, whose counsel would you seek? Why?

The Book of Daniel - Summarized

The Book of Daniel divides itself into two parts of equal length. The first part is formed by the first six chapters, which are primarily historical. The second division is made up of the last six chapters; these tell of the four visions God gave to His prophet.

Chapter seven presents the first vision as it tells of four great beasts which appeared before Daniel. These represent four empires which either had already arisen (Babylon) or were to arise in the future. The vision also refers to events of the last days.

Chapter eight presents the second vision which describes two other beasts. These symbolize the Medo-Persian and Grecian empires. A goat with one horn appears and destroys a ram with two horns; this symbolizes the defeat of the Persian Empire by Alexander the Great.

Chapter nine gives the third vision. This is the well-known vision of the 70 weeks. These are weeks of years rather than weeks of days, meaning they represent 490 years total. The 70th week or final period of seven years represents the great tribulation period of the future.

Chapters 10, 11, and 12 give the fourth vision. Chapter 10 tells of the glorious heavenly messenger who brought the vision to Daniel and chapters 11 and 12 present the vision proper. It concerns especially Antiochus Epiphanes and the one he typified, the Antichrist.

The Book of Daniel is written in two languages: Aramaic, extending from 2:4 to 7:28, and Hebrew, covering the other parts of the book. The reason for the use of the two languages is directly related to the subject matter.

Aramaic was the language of the Gentile world. The chapters written in Aramaic have little to do with the Jews. Therefore, God inspired Daniel to write in Aramaic. This was more suitable to record those matters than was Hebrew, which was distinctly Jewish. The Hebrew section relates directly to Jewish matters.

Chapters six and seven give material pertaining to Gentile history. The second and seventh chapters are parallel in content, setting forth the overall scope of Gentile history following the time of Daniel.

The second chapter does this through the symbolism of Nebuchadnezzar's dream, and the seventh chapter is Daniel's vision relating to the scope of Gentile history.

These four chapters (3-6) fall into two pairs. The third and sixth chapters set forth Gentile power as God's people, the Jews, are persecuted.

The fourth and fifth chapters relate revelations given to Gentile kings, and in each case, Daniel is the only one who can interpret the revelation.

Chapter four concerns Nebuchadnezzar's second dream which remained a mystery for him until Daniel came to give the meaning. This chapter is followed by the account of the handwriting on the palace wall of Belshazzar which was interpreted by Daniel.

The first pair of chapters illustrate the fact the world has long brought persecution on the people of God and God has granted gracious protection for those faithful to Him.

The second pair pictures the dependence of the world upon God, and the need for the children of God to tell the people of the world about God's truth.

What kind of a vision do you think God would give today to explain His working in history?

His name means "God is strong." Ezekiel was born in the Kingdom of Judah and died in exile in the land of Babylon. He was active in his ministry in exile in the land of Babylon from 593-570 B.C. Ezekiel was a priest and a prophet.

Let's review some background for this period. There were three invasions by Babylon which led to the destruction of Jerusalem.

- In 605 B.C. - Daniel and others of noble birth were carried away (Dan. 1, 2 Chron. 36:6- 7).
- In 597 B.C. - King Jehoiachin and Ezekiel and many others were taken into Babylon (2 Kings 24).
- In 586 B.C. - Judah's last king, Zedekiah, was carried away, the walls of Jerusalem were destroyed, the Temple and the city were burned (2 Kings 25:1-7).

The events recorded in chapters 4-24 took place between the second and third invasion of Jerusalem by Babylon. The other portions of the book of Ezekiel contain primarily accounts of his visions and messages.

We have chosen to highlight the first three chapters of his book which describe his dedication and preparation for service.

In chapter one Ezekiel records for us a vision of four living creatures, which are later identified as cherubim. In chapters two and three Ezekiel heard the voice of God speak directly to him. Ezekiel recorded God spoke to him on at least 90 occasions, more than any other biblical writer. On each of these occasions, God referred to Ezekiel as "son of man."

Ezekiel was given a specific commission from God in this passage:

- He was to become a watchman for God
- He was to feed upon the Word of God
- He was anointed by the Spirit of God
- He was allowed to see the glory of God

Ezekiel gives us more detail in his descriptions of the glory of God than any other biblical writer. Chapters 40 - 48 describe in detail the appearance of the glory of God in the future Temple of God.

In many ways Ezekiel was also used as a symbolic prophet. His own wife often became an object lesson which God used to proclaim a message to his people.

There are 13 symbolic acts recorded in the book which Ezekiel performed to help him deliver his message. His message was one of judgment; there are 12 specific messages of judgment recorded in his book. His book also contains six parables or allegories which God used to convey the message to his people in exile.

Ezekiel records an extended vision in chapters 8-11 of the Temple in Jerusalem. In this vision God revealed to His prophet the sinfulness of the people and the priesthood in Jerusalem. He also showed Ezekiel the process of the removal of God's glory from the Temple in Jerusalem. Ezekiel had a unique relationship with God; recording far more occasions where God spoke directly to him than to any other biblical writer.

What experience can you say has left you awestruck?

Ezekiel was given a vision of the glory of God which no other biblical writers saw.

Can you set aside something from the material blessings God has given to honor and thank Him?

To understand the work Ezekiel performed, it helps to see him in relation to Daniel both chronologically and socially.

As we have said, Daniel had been taken captive eight years earlier than Ezekiel. By the time of Ezekiel's arrival Daniel's three years of training were over and he already had experienced five years in his work as a leader of the wise men in Babylon.

In terms of social position, there was a great contrast between them. By this time, Daniel had been head of the wise men for five years, meaning he was very prominent in the land. Ezekiel, on the other hand, was simply a newly arriving captive. It seems logical on arrival he would have soon taken steps to learn about his fellow countrymen who were high up in the Babylonian court.

Doing so and being the kind of capable person, he was in his own right, he would have then made careful inquiry. He would have wanted to know what sort of a person Daniel was and what events had transpired which resulted in Daniel attaining his high position. An actual meeting between the two probably occurred before long, and a close friendship may have been established in spite of their different positions in life.

Ezekiel by birth was a priest, a son of Buzi (1:3). He probably served as a priest in whatever ways priests were able to carry on their work in the foreign land, until the time God called him. In the fifth year of his captivity God commissioned him as a prophet, and then he took up his new calling.

There may have been others among the 10,000 captives who were also prophets, but God especially called Ezekiel.

From this time on Ezekiel pursued his prophetic ministry: preaching to the people, urging obedience to the will of God, and conducting pastoral work as he counseled and extended comfort.

He lived by the river Chebar, probably the great canal which flowed near Babylon. This canal was an important part of the irrigation system of Babylonia. Ezekiel's home was located somewhere near the city Tel-abib, which he visited at least one time.

He and other Jews were able to move about freely, for he received elders of the Jews in his home apparently for the purposes of fellowship and consultation (8:1; 20:1). Ezekiel was married but his wife died in the ninth year of his captivity (24:1, 15-18). Ezekiel continued his prophetic ministry at least until the 27th year of captivity or until an age of 52.

There was a marked difference between the respective ministries of Daniel and Ezekiel. Daniel served in the palace court in an administrative capacity. Here he had the important tasks of maintaining the honor of God and of watching out for the welfare of the Jewish people.

He was not occupied in going about the land preaching or in a pastoral-type ministry. Ezekiel, on the other hand, did have this kind of work. His time was spent in proclaiming God's word, visiting people, and doing the work of a prophet. He was not connected with the palace, nor did he have any administrative position.

Both men were important in their own place. The tasks of both were crucial to God's program for the captivity.

What task have you had to perform even though it seemed unlikely to produce results?

In the lives of these two prophets we see God can use people who are very different in skills and in their position in life to help accomplish His purpose.

Ezekiel was controlled and guided by the Holy Spirit in a very unusual way. No less than seven times Ezekiel spoke of the Spirit transporting him from one place to another.

He was taken to the city of Tel-abib, where he stayed for a period of seven days (3:15). He was even transported to Jerusalem, though this may have been a vision and not a physical transporting. (8:3).

Ezekiel speaks of the Holy Spirit eight other times (1:12, 20, 21; 10:17; 36:26, 27; 37:14; 39:29). For instance, in chapter one the Spirit is presented as controlling a vision given to Ezekiel. In chapter 10 the Spirit is seen directing a vision of a similar nature.

In chapter 36 God promises to put His Spirit within His people in a day still in the future when they will have a new heart and attitude towards Him.

Spirit-awareness of this kind is a clear indication the person concerned was fully committed to knowing and doing the will of God.

Ezekiel also appears to have continued his priestly work while he was involved in his prophetic ministry. As an example, in 22:25 he speaks of false prophets and their deceitful ways, in 22:26 he speaks also of priests who had violated God's Law and profaned His holy things, putting no difference between the holy and profane. Very clear evidence of his priestly interests comes from his treatment of the future temple of Israel (40- 48). That God would inspire Ezekiel to write regarding this temple indicates His recognition of Ezekiel's natural interest in these things.

Ezekiel was a giving and caring person.
This is shown in a general way by his unselfish manner in giving himself for ministry among his captive people. It is shown in a remarkable passage of his book (14:14-20). In this paragraph he speaks of Daniel. Ezekiel would have investigated what kind of person Daniel was. At first might have thought unkind things about him; he may have thought Daniel was someone who catered to Babylonian ways. It would have been natural, too, for Ezekiel to have felt a little jealous.

In this paragraph Ezekiel shows he was not jealous at all. In fact, he had come to admire Daniel a great deal. The passage talks of the great sin of Jerusalem and says, *"Though these three men, Noah, Daniel, and Job were in it (Jerusalem), they should deliver but their own souls by their righteousness, saith the LORD God"* (14:14). Ezekiel picked out three very righteous men and said, even if these people were living in Jerusalem at the time, the sin of Jerusalem was so great their righteousness could not deliver the city from destruction.

Certainly, Ezekiel had thought about Daniel many times and in many ways. It would have been natural for him to be critical of Daniel's success. Still it is clear Ezekiel had found nothing to criticize but only to admire. Daniel had not compromised his position or done anything wrong to achieve the high place.

A more significant indication of the righteous life of a person is hard to imagine.

Like many other prophets, Ezekiel was knowledgeable of the world in which he lived. Normally people of the day were concerned with their own affairs, and their world was about as large as the local community in which they lived.

What nagging area of rebellion can you ask God to change in you this week?

For what rebellious or unbelieving friend or neighbor can you begin to pray, looking for an opportunity to warn him or her of God's righteous judgment and tell him or her of God's mercy?

The Book of Ezekiel divides itself into four parts:

- First, there is the announcement of the approaching fall of Jerusalem, written between the time of Ezekiel's call and the time when Jerusalem proper fell in 586 BC (1-24)
- Second, there are prophecies against foreign nations (25-32)
- Third, there are prophecies of Israel's future restoration (33-39)
- Fourth, there is a description of the millennial Temple and sacrifices (40-48)

Unbelieving scholars have spoken of Ezekiel as a prophet who was mentally unbalanced. They say this particularly because of his many references to the Holy Spirit and his description of the millennial temple.

When Ezekiel's book is carefully examined, we find no indication of a mind which was unbalanced. The book actually conveys a very orderly arrangement, and Ezekiel dates many of his prophecies in careful chronological sequence.

The basis for this dating is a reference always to the captivity of the Jewish king Jehoiachin. For instance, in 1:2 he states his own call to the prophetic ministry came in the "fifth year of King Jehoiachin's captivity."

In the first section of his book which was written prior to Jerusalem's destruction in 586 BC, Ezekiel speaks strongly against the sin of the people, he speaks of those still living in Judah and those already in captivity.

The sins named are largely the same as those referred to by Jeremiah, for Jeremiah was writing from Jerusalem at the same time Ezekiel was writing from Babylon.

Ezekiel vigorously denounced false prophets of the time, who were leading the people on in false hopes of peace.

Ezekiel pictured the people of Jerusalem as a worthless vine, suitable only as fuel for fire, and the people in Babylonian captivity as a "rebellious house," "briars and thorns," and "scorpions." He felt all these people were continuing in the ways of their fathers, seeking sin and enjoying their rebellious actions.

In the last division Ezekiel gives a message of hope and anticipation of a glorious future.

The people who were now captive could look forward to a day of deliverance when their disgrace and suffering would be over, and the long-separated kingdoms of Judah and Israel would be united.

Their enemies would all be defeated, and a grand new temple and manner of worship would be restored in the land.

From the first to the last chapter of Ezekiel one supreme thought runs throughout, the sovereignty and glory of God.

He is sovereign in Israel and in the affairs of the nations of the entire world.

This is true even though the loud and boisterous claims of men seem to have drowned out His truth.

It is God's purpose for us to glorify Him in life and witness to the ends of the earth.

Why are you glad that you worship a God who is not the product of human hands?

Zechariah: An Overview

About 520 BC

Zechariah was contemporary with Haggai. He dates three of his revelations very precisely.

- The first came in the eighth month of Darius' second year, 520 B.C. (1:1)
- The second three months later in the 11th month of Darius' second year, 520 B.C. (1:7)
- The third about two years later in the ninth month of Darius' fourth year, 518 B.C. (7:1)

A fourth message begins at 9:1 but is undated. It is commonly placed several years later, possibly after 480 BC, it contains a reference to Greece (9:13), and Greece became much more prominent after that time.

Zechariah was probably a much younger man than Haggai and he could have lived until after 480 BC, while his older prophet friend may have died soon after Zechariah's ministry began in 520 B.C.

Zechariah's ministry probably did not begin very much before the date of 520 BC; thus, the two overlapped briefly in their service.

Background and history

Because Zechariah and Haggai were contemporaries, the same background history applies to each. The work of rebuilding the Temple had ceased about 16 years earlier and needed to be started again.

God considered this need as crucial enough to use two men in a special way to inspire people to resume the task. He spoke to Haggai in the sixth month and two months later to Zechariah.

It is likely Zechariah lived many years after 520 BC, because of this it is appropriate to say a little about later history. The people began to rebuild the temple in 520 B.C. as a result of the preaching of these prophets; and the structure was completed in March, 515 B.C.

Darius continued to rule over Persia until 486 BC, when he was followed by Xerxes until 465 B.C. During the rule of Xerxes, the history of Esther took place.

Politically during these years, Judah was a part of the large Persian providence, which included all the land southwest of the Euphrates to the border of Egypt. In this large unit, Judah composed one province over which a governor, called a Tirshatha, meaning "He who is to be feared" (Ezra 2:63; Neh. 8:9; 10:1), ruled.

Little information is known regarding life in Judah during these years, but three clues give some help. From Haggai's condemnation of the people in his first message (1:3-11), it is obvious they were building comfortable houses and farming their land.

From the fact Nehemiah found it necessary much later (445 BC) to come from Persia and build Jerusalem's walls, it is evident little was being done in reconstructing the capital city apart from erecting private homes. Ezra's confession of the people's sin concerning their intermarriage with surrounding pagans (Ezra 9:1- 15), makes it obvious the Jews were not acting properly with their neighboring peoples, which led to wrong religious practices.

In what way do you tend to be a pessimist or an optimist?

What future event are you either dreading or anticipating?

What in your life brings you the most joy?

Do you see any parallels in this time period to the day in which we live?

Zechariah: The Man Zechariah 1-14

About 520 BC

Zechariah tells us his father was named Berechiah and his grandfather, Iddo (1:1). When these names and their meanings are combined, they give an excellent summary of the book of Zechariah. God remembers (Zechariah) and blesses (Berechiah) at the appointed time (Iddo). God selected Zechariah along with Haggai, to renew a desire in the residents of Jerusalem to rebuild the temple.

We can think of Haggai as having been selected for this purpose at the close of his life and Zechariah at the beginning of his, thus they complemented each other as a team. Haggai would have had more appeal to older folk to inspire their participation and Zechariah to younger. An important factor showing the spiritual maturity of Zechariah is God gave several revelations to him. He received eight very mysterious visions. Often an angel served as the host introducing these stations and sometimes explaining them to Zechariah.

It is likely Zechariah was a forceful speaker. God would have wanted a prophet who could inspire people to action and be forceful in his presentation for the work on the temple to be started and done properly. We can also think of Zechariah as a person with a natural inclination to ponder the future. It was through him God gave some of the more specific information in the Old Testament regarding the last days. In many ways the work of Zechariah was parallel to the work of Haggai. The temple needed to be rebuilt and both prophets were called for the purpose of instilling a desire in the people to get busy at the task.

The approach God wished each prophet to take was different. Haggai's assignment basically was to create action. The people were simply to get busy and do what they should have done long before. Zechariah's sermons were directed more at the manner and attitude of the people as they worked. Zechariah's interest was that the people have right attitude of heart, showing true dependence on God for His blessing. **For this purpose, he was given a series of night visions, recorded in chapters 1-6; these centered in symbolism around this factor of approach and attitude.**

The Red-horse Rider among the Myrtles	1:7-17	God's anger against nations & blessing on restored Israel
The Four Horns and the Four Craftsmen	1:18-21	God's judgment on the nations that afflict Israel
The Surveyor with a Measuring Line	Chapter 2	God's future blessing on restored Israel
The Cleansing and Crowning of Joshua the High Priest	Chapter 3	Israel's future cleansing from sin & return as a nation
The Golden Lampstand and 2 Olive Trees	Chapter 4	Israel as the light to the nations under Messiah, the King-Priest
The Flying Scroll	5:1-4	The totality of divine judgment on individual Israelites
The Woman in the Ephah	5:5-11	The removal of Israel's sin of rebellion against God
The Four Chariots	6:1-5	Divine judgment on Gentile nations

Because Zechariah continued his ministry following the beginning of the rebuilding activity, it follows God had other work for him to do as well. One of his first tasks was answering the practical questions which were on the minds of people, one of which was whether God wanted them to fast. Zechariah's reply was that God desired obedience more than merely outward fasting (8:19). Another area related to the future. Evidently the people were wondering what the future held, now that they were back in the land with their temple rebuilt. What was going to happen now? God's answer to them through the prophet concerned the far future. The prophet told them of a coming glorious time in the messianic kingdom awaiting them.

What do we have to look forward to in God's kingdom today?

Zechariah: His Book

About 520 BC

Zechariah's book divides itself into four sections, based on both logical and chronological considerations. The first division forms a general call to the people to repent before God. It was given in the eighth month of 520 B.C.

In the second division, the eight visions which have been mentioned, have as their central message instructions regarding the rebuilding of the temple, and they also contain overtones of eschatological significance. They were given in the 11th month of 520 B.C.

The third section (7:18:23) was a message given in the ninth month of 518 B.C. and considers two matters. One concerns whether or not God desired the people to fast, and the other the fact that God held in store a grand day of blessing for His people in the far future.
The fourth section (9:1-14:21) is undated and likely was given much later. It also divides itself into two parts, each beginning with the phrase, "*The burden of the word of the LORD.*"

The two parts deal with the same subject matter: the overthrow of world powers and the final supremacy of the nation of Israel. The first part is more general in its presentation and stresses the overthrow of the powers; the second is more specific and stresses Israel's final purification and supremacy.

The first eight chapters concern matters which relate largely to the time of Zechariah, but the last chapters are mainly eschatological. For one man to have written both sections, he must have experienced extraordinary spiritual growth and understanding from the beginning to the end of his ministry.

F. F. Bruce writes in The Shepherd King that Jesus saw His own role as the Messiah and quoted from the book of Zechariah often. The passages from Zechariah which are listed below give a striking example of God's revelation relating to the future which was given to Zechariah.

13:7-9 The smitten Shepherd and the scattered sheep
9:16 The thankless flock
9:9-10 Behold, your King
14:4 The Day of the Lord
11:12 The pieces of silver
12:10 The pierced One
14:21 The expulsion of the traders from the Temple

In the book of Zechariah one writer notes there are four elements for our reflection:

- Triumph,
- Transformation,
- Worship,
- Holiness.

Bruce also says, "The triumph of God comes in the conquest of evil. The transformation of nature points to a transformed world in which there will be universal worship of the Lord and holiness will be universal."

How does God warn His people today? How is the Lord bringing peace to your life?

What can you expect from God when you are spiritually renewed?

How do you celebrate God's goodness to you?

Haggai: The Man

Haggai 1-2

About 520 BC

His name means "festive." Haggai was born in Babylonian exile, returned to Jerusalem and died there. Haggai lived at the same time as Zechariah and, as an older man, worked with the younger man to encourage the returned Babylonian exiles to finish rebuilding the Temple. In his book we have three prophetic messages which can be dated between August and December 520. After the return from the Babylonian exile Haggai is the first of the three prophets who encouraged and exhorted the Jews to finish the work started on the city of Jerusalem and the Temple.

The first of his messages which we have recorded was delivered in August 520 B.C. Encouraged by the words and actions of these three prophets, Haggai, Zechariah and Malachi, the people diligently went about their work and the Temple was completed and dedicated in 516 BC.

In many ways Haggai's book is the story of three Temples:

- The first temple, built by Solomon (2:3)
- The second temple, being built at Haggai's encouragement (1:7, 14)
- The third temple, to be built by Christ Himself (2:6-9)

Haggai was probably one of very few people who returned from exile who could remember seeing the Temple of Solomon before its destruction in 586 B.C. He would have been one of the oldest people present in Jerusalem when the new Temple was dedicated.

One of the major themes in this book can be summed up in the word "consider." This word is used in each one of Haggai's messages to the people of Jerusalem.

The theme of his book can be simply summarized in the phrase **"Consider your ways."**

- Now this is what the LORD Almighty says: Give careful thought to your ways. (1:5)
- This is what the LORD Almighty says: Give careful thought to your ways. (1:7)
- Now give careful thought to this from this day on; consider how things were before one stone was laid on another in the LORD's temple. (2:15)
- From this day on, from this twenty-fourth day of the ninth month, give careful thought to the day when the foundation of the LORD's temple was laid. Give careful thought (2:18)

As a part of Haggai's last message there is a little-noticed promise to these residents of Jerusalem. They have decided to rebuild the Temple and they have begun their work. In 2:19 Haggai asked them, "*Is there yet any seed left in the barn?*"

He goes on to tell them until now, the vine and the fig tree, the pomegranate and the olive tree have not borne fruit. But announces from this day forward since they have begun the work on the house of God they will be blessed. "*From this day on I will bless you*" is the message he delivered to them directly from God.

When do you procrastinate?

When do you tend to own up to your mistakes, and when do you find it easier to make excuses for yourself?

God always keeps His promises!

God always keeps His promises on His schedule!

We are never too old or too young for God to use us.

Haggai: His Work

Haggai 1-2

About 520 BC

Haggai, like Ezekiel, dates the time of his prophecy precisely. He says the word of the Lord came to him for the first time in the second year of Darius in the sixth month on the first day of the month. He gives similar precise dating for three other times of revelation, all falling still in Darius' second year.

The material Haggai records in his book all came to him from God within a space of four months in the year 520 B.C. He had been active as a prophet for some time before this and continued for a few years following.

The period when his ministry was the most significant was probably the time indicated in his book. Haggai ministered less than 20 years after the death of Daniel. Even more years had intervened since the time of Ezekiel for Ezekiel died several years prior to Daniel.

The first return of Israel came shortly after the Persian conquest of Babylon occurred in 538/537 BC, led by Sheshbazzar. Cyrus, king of Persia, gave permission to the Jews to return to Judah in the first year of his reign following the fall of Babylon.

The decree he issued in permitting this return was unusual and is recorded twice in Scripture: Ezra 1:2-4 and 6:3-5. The edict is remarkable because it gave orders for the Jerusalem Temple to be rebuilt and the cost would be paid from Cyrus' own treasury.

Do you think Daniel had something to do with its origin and possibly its writing?

The people who came back at this time are listed in Ezra 2; their number is indicated as 42,360 besides 7,337 servants (Ezra 2:64, 65). This was only a small portion of the Jews who were living under Persian domination. Just over a half-century later, in the time of Esther, enough Jews still lived in Persia they were able to kill 75,000 enemy opponents in two days of fighting (Esther 9:16).

Jews had achieved surprisingly satisfying conditions in the east and obviously many did not want to leave when given the opportunity.

Those who did return to Jerusalem properly recognized the first order of business concerned the rebuilding of the Jerusalem Temple. Construction began soon after arrival in the land. The first task was to build an altar and reinstate prescribed sacrifices.

In the second month of the second year, the work on the temple buildings began. The first step was to lay the foundation, which seems to have been accomplished rather quickly. When it was completed the people celebrated.

At this point, however, trouble began. Opposition was experienced from Samaritans to the north (Ezra 4:1-5), and the Jews themselves working on the temple began to use more of their time for building their own houses and farming their own lands (Hag. 1:3-11).

It was not long before all work stopped. The result was the temple was little more than a foundation until the second year of Darius, the time of Haggai's prophecy, a total period of about 16 years.

It was the need for the restarting the building activity that called for the ministries of Haggai and Zechariah.

What steps do you need to take to stop procrastinating and get involved in ministry for the Lord?

What do you want to remember the next time you are rightly confronted with a need to change?

Haggai: His Book

About 520 BC

Haggai 1-2

Because the Book of Haggai concerns only the four messages given to the prophet in the fall of 520 BC, it is likely he wrote the book shortly after this, perhaps about the time the rebuilding of the temple got under way.

His book is second only to Obadiah for brevity, comprised of merely two chapters, a total of 38 verses. Though it is brief, it still contains four divisions corresponding to the four messages God revealed.

The first was given on the first day of the sixth month, 520 BC, and concerns a general advocating to the people to get busy and rebuild the temple. The people were reminded since they had stopped building 16 years before, they had not been as prosperous as they had thought they would be.

They had sown crops but had not enough to eat, and prices were high because food was scarce. The reason was God's blessing had been withheld since they had not been doing His will.

The solution to the problem was that they should go to the mountain, bring wood, and start building the temple again; God would send rain from heaven so that crops would grow, and the people would once more prosper. When Haggai had brought this message, the people obeyed and on the 24th of the month work began as he urged.

The second message came on the 21st day of the seventh month of this year. It was to give encouragement to Zerubbabel, the governmental leader, and Joshua the religious leader. The people were encouraged to continue the work they had begun.

The people were to be strong and believe God would enable them to accomplish what seemed to be a very large task. They were not to fear since God was in control of the entire world. He would supply the silver and the gold and all the materials necessary for building, as promised. When the building was complete God would fill the house with His glory.

The third message came on the 24th day of the ninth month. It was to warn the people God wanted more than merely the building of a temple or even the offering of sacrifices.

He wanted the people to be in a right relationship to Him. God did want the temple rebuilt, but even more He wanted an obedient people who were dedicated to doing His will.

The fourth message came on the same day as the third one. It was different from the others for it spoke of a day still in the future when God would overthrow the kingdoms of the world and establish His own glorious kingdom.

What effect would a luxurious life-style have on your spirituality?

What excuses do you make for not doing the will of God?

How has God's discipline influenced your life?

On what future blessings of the Lord do you depend?

Malachi

Malachi 1-4

About 430 B.C.

Malachi, the last of the Hebrew prophets, does not date his ministry. Clues as to his time must be found in his book, but there are several.

First, a Persian governor was in authority (1:8), which locates the time as following the return from captivity when Judah was under Persian governors.
Second, religious ceremonies evidently conducted at the temple were in evidence (1:7-10; 3:8), placing the **date after 515 B.C., when the temple was finally completed.**
Third, the sins of the people about which Malachi speaks are not those condemned by Haggai and Zechariah, who were interested especially in laxity and improprieties in respect to rebuilding the temple. The message of Malachi is like Ezra and Nehemiah during the middle of the following century.
Fourth, neither Ezra nor Nehemiah mentions Malachi, so it is not likely he ministered at or near the time they wrote.

Nehemiah, who came after Ezra, wrote his book around 430 BC, following his return to Jerusalem after having gone back to Babylon for a few years. A date shortly after this return seems as likely as any for the time Malachi wrote.

Malachi makes no references to his personal life or work, and he is not mentioned elsewhere in the Old Testament. Therefore, the nature of his work must be inferred from material he wrote. His writing shows him to have been a dedicated prophet, who was used effectively to warn people of sin and urge them to conduct their lives in a manner pleasing to God.

The main sins with which he was concerned were intermarriage with foreign people, failure to pay tithes, and offering of imperfect sacrifices. Probably the most outstanding fact regarding him was God granted him the privilege of bringing the distinguished and notable line of writing prophets to a close. He was the last of the Old Testament prophets. Malachi gives no information about himself, not even the name of his father or of the city in which he was born. His name means "my angel" or "my messenger," and some have suggested it should be understood as a designation of an office rather than a proper name.

Because this man was selected to be the leading prophet in the closing days of the Old Testament, we believe God saw him as a spiritually outstanding person. No doubt, there were other prophets living, but he was chosen to write the final prophetic book of the Old Testament. He spoke plainly concerning sin and urged people to put their sin away.

We can think of him working in this way side by side with Nehemiah, after Nehemiah returned from the Persian capital. How long each lived, or which one lived longer, there is no way to know. We think they knew each other well and labored together in furthering God's work.

The Book of Malachi is composed of four divisions:

1. A statement of God's great love for His people Israel.
2. A rebuke of the sins of priests, as they were negligent in carrying out the Mosaic ceremonies.
3. A rebuke for the sins of people generally, among which were intermarriage with foreigners, neglect of paying tithes, and deficiency in offering sacrifices
4. Warnings to keep God's Law and wait for the return of Christ.

What attitudes or actions can you change to show honor to the Lord?

What would it take for you to start giving God your best in your worship, your finances, and your time?

Starting today, how can you encourage one other Christian to remain faithful to the Lord?

Malachi to Matthew: What Next?

The Old Testament narrative stops suddenly with the prophet Malachi. It is resumed four hundred years later in the New Testament. These 400 "missing years" are known as the intertestamental period. They were full of activity and events which created the world into which Jesus was born. This world is confusing if the events and changes which took place between the Testaments are ignored.

In four centuries many things change. At the conclusion of the Old Testament there were no Pharisees or Sadducees and the Jewish institution of the synagogue is never mentioned in the Old Testament. In the time of Malachi, the Jewish nation was controlled by the Persian Empire. When the New Testament era began the Jews were dominated by the Romans.

If we are to understand the New Testament and the cultural background in which Jesus lived and in which the church was born, it is necessary to understand some of what went on in the intertestamental era.

The Old Testament period ended with the Jews under control of Persia. In the New Testament, Rome is in command. In the years in between, a series of Greek rulers fought for power. Alexander the Great defeated the declining Persian Empire. But he died a little more than a decade later, and one of his generals, Ptolemy, assumed the throne of Egypt and Palestine. After a century of confusion and battles the Ptolemies gave way to the Seleucids, who were descendants of another of Alexander's generals.

These Greek leaders began a policy of imposing Greek culture on Israel. This imposition eventually led to the Maccabean revolt.

As a result of this revolt a family of native Israelites took the throne. Their dynasty, the Hasmonean, was ended by the Roman general Pompey, who took the Near East and Israel with it, for the Roman Senate.

Internal politics among the Jews during these years were often violent and bitter. A variety of groups developed in response to an increasingly complex set of forces within Judaism. The three most noteworthy groups which developed were the Sadducees, the Pharisees, and the Essenes.

The Pharisees and the Sadducees appear often in the Gospels and represent much of the opposition to Jesus. The Essenes, who are not mentioned in the New Testament narrative, were nevertheless important.

Their monastic retreat at Qumran, on the shores of the Dead Sea, produced some of the most important documents to survive to the present; the Dead Sea Scrolls.

The intellectual world of the intertestamental period was very productive. The clash between Greek and Jewish culture over different worldviews, the continual frustration of the Jews who had come to anticipate a miraculous military victory over the forces of the gentile world, all produced a rich literary tradition.

Of greatest interest for the Christian reader are the Apocrypha, the apocalyptic writings, and the Dead Sea Scrolls. The development of the oral law, which would later become the Talmud, began with this movement, which ultimately became the religion of the Rabbis.

It is obvious that, while Old Testament canonical history concludes with Malachi, the history of Israel continues its vigorous course well beyond that prophet's time.

How could anyone understand culture without knowledge of the last 400 years?

The Persians 539-331 B.C.

When the Book of Malachi was written, Judah was a part of the Persian Empire.

The Old Testament writers take us just past the work of Nehemiah and there the story ends. Both biblical and secular histories are all but silent about the affairs of the Jews and their land during the two centuries which follow.

The main period of Persian history began when they captured Babylon in 539 B.C. The fall of the city of Babylon is described in Daniel 5. The Bible tells us after Cyrus gained control of the Empire, he made a proclamation permitting the people of Judah who had been deported by the Babylonians to go back to Palestine and rebuild the temple. Cyrus reversed the policy of deportation which had been used by the Assyrian conquerors, as well as by the Babylonian king, Nebuchadnezzar.

Archaeology gives us an interesting commentary and confirmation on this event. The Cyrus Cylinder, a small clay cylinder approximately 9” x 4”, was found in 1879 in the ruins of Babylon. The cylinder tells of Cyrus’ taking the city of Babylon without violence and, later, of allowing captive peoples to return to their former dwellings.

With the permission of Darius, who succeeded Cyrus, the Jews could resume the rebuilding of the temple at Jerusalem, which was finished in 515.

The events of the book of Esther took place during the reign of Xerxes (Ahasuerus of the book of Esther, 485-465).

The next Persian king, Artaxerxes I (Longimanus, 464-424), allowed Ezra to return to Palestine and gave permission for Nehemiah to return in 444 to supervise the rebuilding of the walls of Jerusalem. When Artaxerxes died, there was a struggle for the throne among three of his sons.

During this period Egypt was a part of the Empire. The Persian ruler of Egypt left Egypt to make a report to the new king in the year 411. In his absence the Jewish colony on the island of Elephantine was attacked.

This colony had been established when Jeremiah and many other Jews fled to Egypt after the assassination of the Babylonian governor in Judea. These Jews had built a Jewish temple on the small island. During this attack this Temple was destroyed; later the Jews wrote to the Persian governor in Jerusalem, to enlist his aid in urging the chief Persian authorities to give them permission to rebuild their temple.

At the beginning of the 20th century, a fascinating discovery which relates to these events was made on the island of Elephantine. Evidence of papyrus documents had been found on the island by native diggers and in 1904 excavations uncovered many papyri, including documents written in the Aramaic language by the colony of Jews. One of the documents was a letter written to the Persian governor of Jerusalem in the year 407 or 408, asking for permission to rebuild the temple on the island of Elephantine.

These letters even mention biblical characters such as Sanballat, the opponent of Nehemiah.

Archaeology does not prove the Bible; but it is encouraging to see the Bible record verified over and over.

This is another example of how archaeology illuminates the biblical text.

The appearance of Alexander began one of the stormiest periods in Israel's history. Alexander was an ideological conqueror. He was raised under the teaching of Aristotle and dedicated himself to the establishment of a world unified by the influence of Greek culture.

Had it not been for his policy of establishing Greek cities as centers for Greek culture, the military conquests of Alexander would have had little more impact on Israel than those of the Assyrians, the Babylonians, or the Persians.

Because of the challenge of Greek culture (Hellenism) the faith of the Jews was put to a difficult test. This change in culture was as dangerous as the cult of Baal had been in the days of Elijah and Elisha.

It was actually even more treacherous because much of the Greek way of life was attractive, sophisticated, and economically appealing.

The military acquisition of Palestine came quickly, easily, and without much historical notice. Alexander's defeat of the Persian army at Issus (333 BC) left the way open for the control of Persia's holdings in Syria and Palestine.

The only opposition came from the Phoenician city of Tyre and the southern city of Gaza. Alexander moved through Palestine on his way to Egypt, where he was welcomed as a liberator and immediately made Pharaoh.

The acquisition of Egypt completed the conquest of the western portion of the Persian Empire. Alexander went on to claim the rest of Persia's holdings, pushing as far east as India before he died of fever in the city of Babylon at age 33. As impressive as Alexander's military conquests were, they were merely a prelude to events which would shake the world of Judaism.

Following Alexander's death, his generals began a series of wars and conspiracies. They eventually divided his conquests among themselves. After approximately 40 years of struggle, the families of two of the generals had acquired control of most of the Fertile Crescent.

Ptolemy, I took and held Egypt, founding the Ptolemaic dynasty, which would be the last dynasty to rule over Egypt. Farther to the north, Seleucus I controlled Syria, Mesopotamia and Asia Minor.

Palestine, however, would remain a point of conflict between the Ptolemies and the Seleucids. This resulted in armies from the two generals meeting often in battles in the area of Palestine. Between 320 B.C. and 301 B.C. Ptolemy invaded and controlled Palestine and Phoenicia three times.

The conflict between these two dynasties continued for just over 100 years (301-198 B.C.). These two dynasties waged war intermittently throughout the period, but the Ptolemies remained in control of Palestine.

Antiochus the Great finally established Seleucid rule in 223 B.C. This dynasty controlled Jewish life for over 100 years and began dramatically trying to change Jewish culture.

The upper classes among the Jews rapidly assimilated the Hellenistic culture and values.

We see much of this influence in Jewish society at the beginning of the New Testament.

How do current social views cause problems today?

The term "Maccabees" refers to the group of Jewish rebel warriors who took control of Judea. They founded the Hasmonean dynasty, which fought for control of Judea from 164 B.C. to 63 B.C. They reasserted the Jewish religion, partly by forced conversion, expanded the boundaries of Judea by conquest and reduced the influence of Hellenism and Hellenistic Judaism.

In 174 B.C., political rivals for the high priesthood challenged the loyalty of the newly appointed high priest. The Syrians deposed him and appointed a replacement.

This intervention by a "foreign" power began the period when the hereditary nature of the high priesthood was set aside, and the Seleucid, and later Roman rulers, saw it as their right to appoint high priests.

For the next seven years the Syrians were engaged not only in war with Egypt, but they were desperately trying to keep order in Palestine. Finally, the Syrian ruler sent a representative to Jerusalem to punish the Jews for their rebellion. The government representative committed the ultimate blasphemy when he erected a statue of Zeus in the Temple and 10 days later offered a pig as a sacrifice in the Temple area.

The enraged Jews reacted by killing the Syrian officers. They also killed any Hellenistic Jews who participated in the sacrifice. This action changed the Jewish resistance from passive to militant. The pagan altar was dismantled, and their rebellion began.

The goals of this coalition were rather limited at first. Operating as a guerrilla army, they brought destruction on apostate Jews, destroying pagan altars and forcing circumcision on any uncircumcised males they found.
Within a year the elderly Jewish leader died of old age and the rigors of the fugitive existence. Judas took command of the rebellion. He later came to be called Maccabeus (the Hammer).

The early phase of the rebellion under Judas seems to have been primarily religious. His allies, the Hasidim, had no interest in political power or objectives other than the reestablishment of orthodox worship and the expulsion of the radical Hellenizers who controlled Jerusalem.

Judas' coalition was strong only so long as the threat to orthodoxy existed. After centuries of foreign domination, most Jews had changed allegiance from the nation to the temple and were willing to die for their faith, but not for their state.

In 142 B.C. the Seleucids recognized Jewish autonomy. The Seleucid kings kept a formal authority, which the Hasmoneans acknowledged.

This began a period of population growth and religious, cultural, and social development. This included the conquest of the areas of the Transjordan, Samaria, Galilee, and Edom.

Here we see the entanglements and confusion caused when politics becomes involved with religion.

Hanukkah

Hanukkah is celebrated for eight days and nights, starting on the 25th of Kislev on the Hebrew. In Hebrew, the word "Hanukkah" means "dedication." This date corresponds approximately to December in the Western calendar.

The celebration is also known as the Feast of Lights, Feast of Dedication, and Feast of the Maccabees. Hanukkah commemorates the rededication of the Temple of Jerusalem by Judas Maccabee in 165 B.C. after the Temple had been profaned by Antiochus IV Epiphanes, king of Syria and overlord of Palestine.

The History of Hanukkah

In 168 B.C. the Jews' holy Temple was seized and was changed into a Temple dedicated to the worship of Zeus.

Some Jews were afraid of the Greek soldiers and obeyed them, but most were angry and decided to fight back.

The fighting began in Modin, a village not far from Jerusalem. A Greek officer and his soldiers assembled the villagers, asking them to bow to an idol and eat the flesh of a pig, activities forbidden to Jews.

The officer asked Mattathias, a Jewish High Priest, to take part in the ceremony. He refused, and another villager stepped forward and offered to do it instead. Mattathias became outraged, took out his sword and killed the man, then killed the officer.

His five sons and the other villagers then attacked and killed the soldiers. Mattathias' family went into hiding in the nearby mountains, where many other Jews who wanted to fight the Greeks joined them. They attacked the Greek soldiers whenever possible.

Judas Maccabee and his soldiers went to the holy Temple and were amazed at the things they saw in the holy place.

Many things were missing or broken, including the golden menorah. They cleaned and repaired the Temple, and when they were finished, they felt they needed to purify and rededicate the sacred place.

For the celebration, the Maccabees wanted to light the menorah. They looked everywhere for oil and found a small flask that contained only enough oil to light the menorah for one day. The legend tells that miraculously, the oil lasted for eight days. This gave them enough time to obtain new oil to keep the menorah lit. Today Jews celebrate Hanukkah for eight days by lighting candles in a menorah every night, thus commemorating the eight-day miracle. The observance takes place near Christmas time.

Never be afraid to stand up for what's right.

Judah Maccabee and his band faced daunting odds, but that didn't stop them. With a prayer on their lips and faith in their heart, they entered the battle of their lives, and won. We can do the same.

Always increase in matters of goodness. Sure, a single flame was good enough for yesterday, but today needs to be even better.

A little light goes a long way. The Hanukah candles are lit when dusk is falling. Perched in the doorway, they serve as a beacon for the darkening streets.

No matter how dark it is outside, a candle of goodness can transform the darkness itself into light.

Diaspora Judaism

A letter from around 590 B.C. refers to Jewish mercenaries in the army of the Egyptian Pharaoh. Other correspondence shows there were Jewish mercenaries serving in Egypt for the next two centuries.

Contingents of Jewish soldiers could be found throughout the Greek-speaking world. From this it is reasonable to believe Jewish fighting men had started taking positions with foreign powers even before the Exile.

This movement away from Judea was accelerated because of the exile. A large proportion the population of Judah was carried to Babylon, and most of the remaining people of importance sought refuge in Egypt after the murder of Gedaliah.

These Jewish communities on foreign soil continued to exist after the exile, flourishing as pockets of Judaism. Josephus tells us the Jews beyond the Euphrates were "countless myriads whose numbers cannot be ascertained."

By the first century the Jewish colony at Alexandria was estimated at between a half million and one million. This was nearly two-fifths of the population of the city. It is likely by the time of Christ there were more Jews outside Palestine than in it; estimates of their numbers run high as ten percent of the total population of the Roman Empire.

The effects of this wide dispersion were mixed. While it was all but impossible to find a city in the Empire without some Jewish population, Jews of the diaspora frequently became objects of anti-Semitism. A significant body of anti-Semitic literature flourished toward the end of the Hellenistic era. Jews, who rejected all pagan gods, were attacked as atheists or slandered with stories designed to make them appear either sinister or ridiculous.

On the other hand, religiously sensitive pagans frequently found themselves drawn to Judaism, which, with its high ethical standards and monotheistic faith, stood in sharp contrast to other religions. This popularity caused, of course, further hostility.

Another product of this period was a great deal of writing both defending and attacking the Jewish population of the Empire.

The adoption of a Hellenistic veneer on the part of these dispersed Jews might indicate the Judaism of the diaspora was of an inferior sort, but current scholarship has been uncovering evidence of the general homogeneity of early Judaism.

It was the dispersion of the Jews throughout the Roman Empire which allowed the gospel to spread much more rapidly.

The combination of the good Roman road system and the presence of Jewish synagogues throughout the empire provided a connecting point for the apostle Paul and any other Jewish person, such as Barnabas, to preach the gospel by proclaiming Jesus as the fulfillment of all the Jewish messianic prophecies. Many of the early converts to Christianity were the Gentiles who were attending the Jewish synagogues.

The apostle Peter begins his first epistle with these words, "*Peter, an apostle of Jesus Christ, to the elect who are sojourners of the Dispersion in Pontus, Galatia, Cappadocia, Asia, and Bithynia.*"

The dispersion of the Jews throughout the empire was part of God's plan for spreading the gospel.

The Synagogue

The origin of the synagogue is difficult to define. The beginning probably goes back to the time of Ezra. He was a scribe who made it his mission to teach the Scriptures to the Jews who had returned from Babylon. The Old Testament mentions earlier places that were called "the meeting places of God" in the Psalms.

Some scholars are of the opinion the synagogue may have originated in Ezekiel's messages to the Babylonian exiles. Such gatherings in the prophet's house (Ezekiel 8:1; 20:1) could have been the forerunners of the synagogue gatherings. In the time of Christ "teaching in the synagogue on the Sabbath day" was already an established custom.

Since only a small proportion of the people could become skilled in the study of the law under the scribes, and as it was necessary for all people to have at least a basic acquaintance with the Torah, the custom grew in postexilic times of reading the Scriptures on the Sabbath in the synagogue.

It must be understood the main object of these Sabbath day meetings in the synagogues was not public worship but religious instruction.

Thus, Josephus writes, "Not once or twice or more frequently did our lawgiver command us to hear the law, but to come together weekly, with the cessation of other work, to hear the law and to learn it accurately."

Philo called the synagogues "houses of instruction," in which "the native philosophy" was studied and every kind of virtue taught. In the New Testament the teaching always figures as the chief function of the synagogue.

Over a period of time, therefore, the synagogue became the local Jewish religious center. Simple as this may seem today, the shift from a priestly to a popular religious center was radical. It was a first step toward the decentralization of Judaism.

The synagogue became the means of preserving Jewish faith and worship. Jews all over the world continued to maintain their distinctive faith.

These synagogues became the seedbed for Christian faith as missionaries took the message of Christ to new places. Nearly everywhere the missionaries went they found a Jewish synagogue.

The first-century synagogue worshipers believed in the one true God, studied the Scriptures, and looked for the coming Messiah. What better place for Paul and others to go first with the message of Jesus Christ!

Wherever Jews went, ten men could gather and form a synagogue. Judaism was freed from the geographical restrictions of temple and land.

It is unlikely Judaism outside of Palestine would have survived without the synagogue.

The Jewish Council in Acts 15:21 stated the fact, "*Moses from ancient generations has in every city those who preach him, since he is read in the synagogues every Sabbath.*"

***"In the fullness of time God sent his son,"* the synagogue was also part of God's preparation for spreading the good news throughout the world.**

The Pharisees

The name Pharisee means "separated one." We are not sure of the exact origin of the name; many think it goes back to the time of Ezra. He challenged the Jews who had returned from captivity in the Persian Empire to give up their uncleanness and separate from their ungodly habits and neighbors. Their adversaries soon were calling them "the separatists."

The Pharisees as a party spring from the Hasidim of the Maccabean period. They are first mentioned in Josephus' account of their fall from favor under Hyrcanus.

The continuation of the Pharisaic movement is explained by the ability of the Pharisees to adapt themselves to the changing situations of later eras. This accommodation was made possible by the Pharisaic doctrine of oral law; what the New Testament refers to as "your own tradition."

Since the written law was fixed and nothing could be done to alter it, some of the more specific laws applied to the agrarian world of Moses and seemed irrelevant in the multicultural world of the intertestamental period. More importantly, many situations had arisen for which there was no specific biblical teaching.

To deal with this, the Rabbis taught God had given both a written law and an oral law to Moses on Mount Sinai. The oral law formed the core of the Talmud. This remained oral until a century after Christ.

The oft-quoted statement from rabbinic tradition states a "hedge" should be made for the Torah. Since many situations were not covered specifically in the written law and one could therefore break the law without realizing it, the oral law applied the precepts of the written law to situations not specifically covered in the latter.

By keeping the ordinances of the oral law, the Jews could be sure to avoid breaking the written law. This desire to make the law relevant to a new age and to avoid the past disasters sent by God in punishment for previous transgression lies at the root of the Pharisaic enterprise.

Whatever their motives, the Pharisees became a party with considerable popular influence. Josephus describes them as having the ability to sway the masses, even against kings or the high priest. This power no doubt derived from the fact the temple was becoming more and more removed from the private lives of Jewish worshipers as it became increasingly political and aristocratic.

The Pharisees were the party of the synagogue, deriving authority from the interpretation of Scripture and the rigor of their adherence to that interpretation.

We cannot overestimate the importance of the Pharisees, of their association with the synagogue, and of their emphasis on the study of Torah.

The Pharisees became the spiritual forerunners of modern Judaism. The synagogue became the prototype of the early church. The Christian emphasis on Scripture as the Word of God, although in a somewhat different form, has antecedents in the writings of the Rabbis.

They remained in existence for approximately 500 years. They were active in Judea and remained a major force in the Jewish religion until the destruction of Jerusalem.

After 70 A.D., with no Temple and no city of Jerusalem they slowly lost their power and identity.

Their separation became more important than their godliness or humanity toward other men.

The Sadducees

There is a great deal of confusion relating to the origin of the name Sadducee. The name is originally thought to have conveyed the idea of righteousness. They were aristocratic and usually wealthy.

The Sadducees are of less enduring interest than the Pharisees, primarily because they were connected inseparably to the temple. Their party came to an end in A.D. 70 when the temple was destroyed.

They were aristocratic, drawing their base of support from the upper class and the priesthood. The Sadducees were the dominant political force in Palestine prior to A.D. 70.

In some ways, the Sadducees were actually more traditional than the Pharisees. They rejected the additions of the oral law; they accepted only the Pentateuch as canonical and interpreted it literally.

The religious sensibilities of the Sadducees, tied as they were to the uninterrupted operation of the temple, were not offended by accommodation with Hasmoneans or Romans, which makes them seem more liberal than the Pharisees to the modern reader.

Their origins probably go back into the third century B.C. They cooperated with the Romans and supported many of the Roman reforms.

Josephus says they were a political group who only allowed the rich and politically influential in their membership. They were wealthy, aristocratic, and controlled the high priesthood with the help of the Romans.

The Sadducees did not believe in the resurrection of the body, or in judgment in the future life. They also did not believe in any kind of continuity of the individual throughout eternity. Today they would probably be considered annihilationist.

With no life after death, this physical life was all there was to live for, therefore, they sought to acquire as much wealth, power, and influence as was possible.

The Sadducees also denied the existence of angels or spirits. They felt God was the only spiritual reality.

The ultimate difference between the Pharisees and the Sadducees seems to amount to their view of God's sovereignty and man's free will. Pharisees emphasized God's pre-ordination and permitted only slim human influence on what happened in life. It was the job of man to cooperate with the will of the divine.

The Sadducees, since they did not believe in "spirits" or other powers, emphasized to an extreme the freedom of humanity. With this strong influence of human freedom there came a decreasing stress upon religious motives and religious practices. The choice of man to do good or evil was entirely dependent on his own inclination.

The beliefs of the Sadducees and their cooperation with the Roman government brought Jesus into constant conflict with their teaching. The key elements of conflict were the denial of the resurrection and the denial of the power of God in the everyday aspect of men's lives.

We could say that the Sadducees were the "secularist" of Jesus' day. They lived a very materialistic life, cloaked with religious verbiage.

Their strongest point was politics; they were wealthy power seekers who tried to manipulate the Romans for their own purposes.

The Essenes

The Sadducees tied themselves to the political status quo. The Pharisees withdrew from the political arena to mark out a unique religious approach to accommodate to life in this world.

The Essenes withdrew completely from society to prepare for an apocalyptic conclusion to history.

Much more is known about the Essenes now than before the discovery of the Dead Sea Scrolls and the excavation of the Qumran monastery, but there are still large gaps in our understanding.

Today it is generally accepted the residents of Qumran were the Essenes known from Josephus and other sources.

The Essenes, like the Pharisees, stressed personal piety and a separation from life's impurities. The Essenes, however, took the notion of separation to far greater lengths than did the Pharisees.

Because of what they considered to be the religious corruption of main line Judaism, they withdrew, refusing to participate in the sacrificial system.

What distinguished the Essenes from other Jewish sects was their conviction they alone represented the true remnant of Israel and, therefore, only their understanding of Scripture was valid.

The apocalyptic elements in Essene theology are evident in the documents of Qumran. The War Scroll in particular describes an apocalyptic Armageddon in which the Sons of Light would fight for God against the Sons of Darkness.

The attitude of the residents of Qumran toward the rest of Judaism was extremely negative; they considered all those outside their sect, and especially the Jerusalem priesthood, to be the Sons of Darkness. They looked forward to the coming of two Messiahs; one kingly, another priestly.

Their strictness was excessive, even when compared with the Pharisees. The Manual of Discipline prescribes severe punishments for seemingly trivial offenses.

Like the Sadducees, they appear to have connected their existence to a particular situation, namely, the impending apocalyptic end of history, and, like the Sadducees, they did not survive the destruction of Israel that took place in A.D. 70.

The Essenes, particularly the Qumran Essenes, are important for the firsthand evidence they provide of the importance of apocalyptic thought for early Judaism.

They are also the only sect of Judaism to leave extensive contemporaneous writings about themselves, thus providing important background for both the study of intertestamental Judaism and the New Testament.

Finally, their library, preserved in the caves around the Dead Sea, provides Old Testament scholarship with the most ancient manuscripts of biblical texts known to be in existence.

The Essenes are not mentioned in the Bible and there is no evidence Jesus had contact with any of them. Some have tried to associate John the Baptist with this group but there is no evidence to support this identification.

Their contribution to history and our understanding of Scripture is the preservation of the Dead Sea Scrolls.

The Dead Sea Scrolls

The initial discovery of scrolls in 1947 and the later excavations in the caves in the Judean desert are one of the major document finds in archaeological history.

W.F. Albright called it "the greatest manuscript discovery of modern times." The discovery captured the thoughts of the public in a way that few discoveries have. The result of this interest was the publication of a flood of books: technical, semi-technical, and popular.

The early writing about the scrolls was often based on misinformation and sometimes on particular biases. This tended to be sensational and, in many cases, misleading.

With the publication of the text scrolls and the deeper examination which followed, all but a few extremists have adopted a much more sober stance toward the scrolls.

What we know about them today is they represent the library of a Jewish sect dating from the Maccabean period through the fall of Jerusalem in A.D. 70. The scrolls were stored in jars in caves to protect them from the anticipated destruction of the monastery at Qumran during the first Jewish revolt.

Excavations, conducted under extremely difficult and sometimes dangerous conditions, uncovered scrolls and scroll fragments in more than eleven caves. In 2016 more new scroll fragments were discovered.

Some of the most spectacular of the finds came from cave 1 where two Isaiah scrolls, the Manual of Discipline scroll, the Habakkuk scroll, the Genesis Apocrypha scroll, the War Scroll, and the Thanksgiving Hymns were found.

Two copper scrolls were found in cave 3. They record the hiding places of 60 treasure hoards. If they are true and the ancient landmarks could be found, these scrolls would lead searchers to over 200 tons of gold and silver! Explorers and adventure seekers have been trying to find the treasure ever since the publication of these scrolls, to no avail. The treasure must still be out there somewhere!

The scrolls and fragments of biblical books are probably of greatest interest to students of the Bible for their impact on the study of the biblical text. Every book of the Old Testament with the exception of Esther is among them. The Isaiah scroll is a complete text of the book of Isaiah. It measures 24 feet in length and is the oldest extant biblical book in the world.

Such ancient copies of the books of the Old Testament prove the reliability of their transmission over the nearly 1000 years between their transcription at Qumran, beginning in the second century B.C. and the standardization of the Masoretic text in the eighth and ninth centuries A.D.

Because the sectarian documents illuminate the life and beliefs of the Qumran residents in greater detail than is available for any of their contemporaries, they are of importance for the study of intertestamental Judaism.

Their commentaries on biblical books help to clarify some obscure biblical readings and provide helpful examples of the hermeneutical methods of at least one segment of early Judaism.

This is a superb witness to God's care of His words.

Jesus reminded His listeners, *"I tell you the truth, until heaven and earth disappear, not the smallest letter, not the least stroke of a pen, will by any means disappear from the Law until everything is accomplished."* Matthew 5:18

The Septuagint (LXX)

The Septuagint owes its origins to the conquests of Alexander the Great and the resulting spread of Greek language and culture throughout most of the ancient world. Even after the exile, Jewish people remained for centuries in Greek-speaking areas. Alexandria, Egypt, for instance, had a sizable community of Jewish people who had, for the most part, lost their homeland's native language. The need for an Old Testament in Greek led to the Septuagint.

According to the Letter of Aristeas, the Old Testament was translated into Greek during the reign of Ptolemy Philadelphus (283-245 BC). The story describes Ptolemy's desire to acquire a copy of the Jewish law, in Greek, for the library at Alexandria. Seventy-two scholars, six from each of the twelve tribes, were called to Alexandria, where, isolated on the Island Pharos, they produced the translation in 72 days. Philo asserts all of the translators were inspired and they miraculously produced identical translations. The name "Septuagint" which means "seventy," derives from this legend. The Roman numeral for seventy, LXX, is used as its abbreviation.

The LXX became the Bible of the Diaspora. The LXX soon become the Bible of the church, and it was this adoption by the Christian community which preserved the translation.

The importance of the LXX from every angle cannot be overestimated. Religiously and spiritually the LXX gave the great truths concerning creation, redemption, sin, and salvation to the world. It released these from the narrow isolation of the Hebrew language and gave them to the Greco-Roman world through the divinely prepared instrument of the Greek language, the common language of the age.

The LXX was a major factor in the preparation for the coming of Christianity and the New Testament revelation. In making the Old Testament available in the same universal language in which the New Testament was destined to appear, it foreshadowed the giving of the Holy Scriptures in one international and universal language of the period.

The LXX was the Bible of early Christianity before the New Testament was written. After the New Testament Scriptures came on the scene, they were added to the LXX to form the completed Scriptures of Christianity. Besides this momentous ministry, the LXX met the religious requirements of Jews living in Alexandria, Egypt. This was the center of culture and learning of ancient Judaism. It also met the needs of Jewish proselytes in the Greco-Roman world in the pre-Christian era, and it was a vital force in both Alexandrian Judaism and philosophy and in the philosophy of the Jewish Diaspora.

Historically as well as religiously and spiritually, the LXX is of immense importance. As the first translation of the Hebrew Old Testament into a foreign language, the LXX gained great fame. The very fact it was put into the language of culture and education of the day made its use wide.

Philo of Alexandria used the LXX extensively. Josephus depended upon it. Jesus and the New Testament writers quoted from it as well as from the Hebrew. The Jews of the Diaspora used it. With the dawn of Christianity, the LXX became the Scripture of Christians. It was venerated and quoted and used in controversy.

What would it be like if you did not have the Bible available in your language?

Book Ten

1. Zachariah	Luke 1
2. Elizabeth	Luke 1
3. Gabriel: The Archangel	Luke 1
4. Mary	Luke 1
5. Joseph	Matthew1, 2
6. The Shepherds	Luke 2
7. Simon and Anna	Luke 2
8. The Magi	Matthew 2
9. Herod the Great	Matthew 2
10. John the Baptist	Mark 1, 6
11. Nathanael/Bartholomew	John 1, 21
12. Andrew	John 1, 6
13. Simon Peter	Matthew 26
14. Simon Peter: Denial & Restoration	John 18, 21
15. Simon Peter: The Apostle	Acts 15
16. James and John	Matt. 20
17. Nicodemus	John 3
18. The Woman at the Well	John 4
19. The Nobleman	John 4
20. Matthew Matthew	2; Luke 5
21. The Pharisees	Matthew 12
22. The Gentile Woman	Mark 7
23. The Rich Young Man	Mark 10
24. Bartimaeus Matthew	10; Luke 18
25. The Poor Widow	Mark 12; Luke 21
26. Mary Magdalene	Luke 8, 24; John 20
27. Mary and Martha	Luke 10; John 11
28. Lazarus	John 11

Zachariah (Zacharias) — Luke 1:5-25, 57-80

His name means "God remembers." Zacharias lived in a small town near Jerusalem. He was old before the birth of John the Baptist.

Zacharias and his wife Elizabeth lived in Judea. He was a priest serving in the division of Abijah. He and his wife are both said to be *"righteous before God, walking in all the commandments and ordinances of the Lord blameless."*

The fact this godly elderly couple had no children was a source of rumor and gossip around town. It was the Jewish view when a couple remained childless it showed there was a secret sin they were hiding in their lives. They were surely the topic of gossip and innuendo. When it was Zacharias time to go to Jerusalem and function in the Temple, as he was serving and preparing incense for the altar, an Angel appeared to him.

The Angel told Zacharias his prayers had been heard. The prophecy actually contained five parts:

- He and his wife would have a son
- His name would be John
- He would become a Spirit-filled Nazarite
- He would prepare the way for the Messiah
- His style would be similar to Elijah

Zachariah asked the angel, *"How shall I know this will happen? I am an old man and my wife is beyond the age of childbearing."*

Probably Zacharias thought he would receive some miraculous sign to confirm his faith. He was given exactly what he asked for! A miraculous sign! He was struck "dumb," he would be unable to speak until after the birth of John.

He returned home; soon his wife became pregnant and in the course of time she delivered a son. When the parents were asked the name of the boy; they replied, "his name is John." After the birth of John, Zacharias was filled with the Holy Spirit and gave a beautiful poetic prophecy.

Zacharias and Elizabeth are examples of people God placed here on earth and used in His program for one specific purpose. They were to be the servants of God and faithful children of God, as any other good Jew should have been. There was nothing special, unique or miraculous to draw attention to these two people. They were faithful, consistent and unspectacular. They were probably considered boring by many people in their village.

Yet they had a major part in the program of God! They were chosen to give birth and raise the forerunner of the Messiah.

When have you doubted the reality of God's provision for you?

We do not know the plans God has for us!

All he expects of us is faithfulness and consistency.

"Who knows if we have been placed here for such a time as this?"

Elizabeth — Luke 1:24, 25, 39-45, 57-63

She is the mother of John the Baptist, the wife of Zechariah, and a relative of Mary, mother of Jesus. The story of her miraculous pregnancy is recorded in the opening chapter of Luke.

Background

The Gospel of Luke identifies Elizabeth, whose name means "oath of God," as the wife of Zechariah, "of the division of Abijah." Both Elizabeth and Zechariah were descended from Aaron. The couple lived in "a town in the hill country of Judea."

Priestly divisions were established in 1 Chr. 24:11-19 so no single group would have the task of ministering at the temple. The divisions were to serve in a sequence for one week at a time. Abijah was the eighth division, indicating Zechariah was serving in the eighth week of the year. This gives an approximate time marker for Elizabeth's narrative.

Birth Narrative of John the Baptist

Luke 1:6-7 records Elizabeth and Zechariah were old, righteous, and lived in obedience to God's commands. The Bible emphasizes the human impossibility of the events which are about to occur by telling us Elizabeth was barren and they were both "advanced in years."

In ancient patriarchal society, childlessness carried a social stigma and often meant an unstable future and the end of the family line. Elizabeth's life would have been particularly difficult, as barrenness was usually believed to be the fault of the woman.

One writer believes Zechariah displayed righteousness by standing by his wife rather than leaving her in favor of someone who could give him an heir.

In Luke's narrative, an angel informs Zechariah while he is serving in the temple that God has heard his prayers and Elizabeth will give birth to a son, despite her age and barrenness. Zechariah doubts the angel's words and is struck mute.

Luke goes on to record Elizabeth conceives, but she keeps her pregnancy a secret for five months (Luke 1:24-25) . When Gabriel later tells Mary, she will give birth to the Messiah, the angel tells her of Elizabeth's pregnancy as proof that "nothing will be impossible with God."

Mary then traveled to visit Elizabeth in Judea, and when Elizabeth heard Mary's greeting, the baby leaped in her womb.

Filled with the Holy Spirit, Elizabeth blessed Mary as "the mother of my Lord" and then exclaimed, "Blessed is she who has believed that the Lord would fulfill his promises to her."

In this way, Elizabeth and her child are the first persons in the Bible to praise Jesus.

Luke 1:57-66 records Elizabeth gave birth to her son, whom Zechariah insisted be named John in accordance with the angel's announcement. Upon naming the child, Zechariah regained the ability to speak (Luke 1:63–64).

What can we learn from Zechariah and Elizabeth which can help us handle long-term problems?

When have you doubted the reality of God's provision for you?

Gabriel: The Archangel

Gabriel is one of two angels named in the Bible, the other being Michael. Gabriel interpreted Daniel's vision (Dan 8:16), gave Daniel the prophecy of 70 weeks (Dan 9:21), and announced the births of John the Baptist (Luke 1:19) and Jesus (Luke 1:26).

Gabriel in the Old Testament
Gabriel first appears in Dan 8:16 when "a man's voice" commands him to interpret Daniel's vision. In Daniel 9:21–27 Gabriel explains the vision of 70 weeks to Daniel. The unnamed angel in Dan 7:16 and Dan 10:5 is likely Gabriel as well.

Gabriel in Second Temple Literature
The Jewish literature of the Second Temple period, from the end of the Old Testament to the destruction of the Temple in 70 A.D., developed a more detailed theological doctrine of angels than the Old Testament.

Much of the understanding of angels in this literature is undoubtedly taken for granted by the New Testament writers. The concept of four archangels appears during this time; the number four may have originated from the four living creatures of Ezekiel 1–2.

Throughout the book of 1 Enoch, written during the Inter-Testamental period, Gabriel is part of a group of four prominent archangels:

1. Michael
2. Gabriel
3. Raphael
4. Sariel/Uriel/Phanuel (the fourth archangel varies).

1 Enoch 20:7 tells readers Gabriel is "over Paradise and the serpents and the Cherubim." Elsewhere in 1 Enoch, Gabriel is sent out to judge the children born to the "Watchers" mentioned in Genesis 6:4.

In the Dead Sea Scrolls, we are told the names of the four archangels (Michael, Gabriel, Sariel, and Raphael) are written on the shields of the elite soldiers described in the War Scroll. The New Testament and later writings assume the existence of this higher order of "archangels" (1 Thess 4:16, Jude 9).

Gabriel in the Gospels
Gabriel is best known for his role in the birth narratives of the Gospel of Luke, where he announces the birth of John the Baptist to Zechariah (Luke 1:11-20). Here, Gabriel identifies himself as one who stands in the presence of God (Luke 1:19).

Six months after he made this announcement, Gabriel announced the coming birth of the Messiah to Mary.

The church father Cyprian suggested Gabriel is also the angel who spoke to Joseph in the Gospel of Matthew, though the text does not specifically name him.

Gabriel in Rabbinic Tradition
There is an abundance of material about Gabriel in the non-canonical writings of the Jews. In the books of Enoch, he is pictured as one of the four chief angels, along with Michael, Raphael, and Uriel.

He is one of the holy angels who looks down from heaven and is a principal intercessor. He is to destroy the wicked and cast them into the furnace and is set over all powers.

Michael sits at God's right hand and Gabriel sits on the left. Michael, as guardian angel of Israel (Dan. 12:1) is more occupied with affairs in heaven.

Gabriel is God's messenger who comes from heaven to execute God's will on earth.

Mary **Luke 1:26-58; 2:1-7**

The name Mary means "bitter." We do not know where Mary was born. Some feel she was born in Bethlehem and later moved to Nazareth with her parents. We do know she traveled to Egypt with Joseph and Jesus. Tradition tells us later she traveled to the city of Ephesus with the apostle John. There is a site near the ancient city of Ephesus which is venerated as the tomb of Mary.

The Gospels of Luke and Matthew provide the following information about Mary and the events surrounding Jesus' birth and childhood:

- They refer to Mary as a "virgin."
- They specify Mary and Joseph were Jesus' parents, and that they were betrothed but not living together.
- They list Jesus as a descendant of David.
- They record an angel declaring Mary's pregnancy.
- They record Mary became pregnant through divine conception, without Joseph's involvement.
- They explicitly mention the Holy Spirit's role in the conception of Jesus.
- They record God calling for the baby to be named Jesus.
- They specify Jesus is the "savior."
- They record Joseph assisted Mary prior to Jesus' birth.
- They record Mary gave birth to Jesus during the time of Herod the Great.
- They record Mary gave birth to Jesus in Bethlehem of Judah.
- They record that Jesus grew up in Nazareth.

Most people know the story of Mary and the birth of Jesus well. It is repeated in some detail every Christmas season. The message to Mary from the angel Gabriel came when she was engaged to marry Joseph. Using Jewish tradition as a guide this engagement could have taken place while Mary was in her early to middle teens.

Her faith shines through this experience in an amazing way! She was willing to accept the choice of God; her reply to the Angel was, *"I am the servant of the Lord, let this happen according to your word."*

She trusted God to work out the details.

Later she visited her relative Elizabeth who had become pregnant in her old age. The two women rejoiced in the blessings of God and looked forward to what God was going to do for their people.

Mary and Joseph raised Jesus following what they knew of God's plan and law. The Scripture tells us Mary had four other sons; James, Joseph, Simon and Judas (Luke 2:7). Matthew 13:56 also indicates she had several daughters whose names we are not given.

Imagine the difficulty involved in raising the Son of God! Every Jewish mother thinks her son is perfect! Mary's was!

Imagine what it was like to grow up with Jesus as a big brother.

Mary's humble acceptance of the plan of God for her life shows us how we should accept God's plans and follow His principles explained in the Scriptures.

There is no indication in Scripture Mary was ever to be worshipped or the object of prayer.

His name means "increaser or may God add."

He probably was born sometime around 30 B.C. and died the beginning of Christ's ministry around 30 A.D.

Joseph was chosen by God to raise His Son. He was engaged to Mary and was faced with a major dilemma when he found she was pregnant. Joseph was "a just man." His actions reveal him as caring, honorable, and godly. He loved Mary deeply and wanted to do what was right. As he prayed about his options God spoke to him in a dream.

Many people miss the fact God spoke to Joseph at least four times through dreams.

- His first message from God related to Mary and his actions toward her.
- His second dream came after the visit of the wise men and instructed him to take his family and move to Egypt.
- The next dream, sent from God, told him Herod was dead and he could return to the land of Israel.
- Matthew 2:22-23 records a fourth dream warning him not to return to the land of Judea. As a result, the new family settled in Nazareth.

Most of our decisions will not be overruled by angels, but that's no reason for lack of confidence. To make good decisions, we must pray.

We should also evaluate all the options, talk with trusted friends and then act in faith. Remember what Habakkuk said, " *The just shall live by faith.* **"**

Joseph faced a dilemma nearly all of us face at some point in our lives. **"But What Will Everyone Think?"**

He changed his plans quickly after learning about God's plan for his life from the angel. He obeyed God and continued with the marriage plans.

Without a doubt many people disapproved of his action. Many of his own family were probably worried about the family reputation. However, Joseph went ahead with what he knew was right.

Sometimes we avoid doing what is right because of what others might think. Like Joseph, we must choose to obey God rather than seek the approval of others.

Do you often consider what others think and make your plans in order to make them think more of you?

How hard do you think it was for Joseph to tell his family he had decided to marry Mary?

What do you think Mary's family thought of Joseph's decision?

Have you ever done something you knew God wanted you to do when others were telling you it was foolish?

The Shepherds   Luke 2:8-20

This is not a person but a group of people. I know of no ancient tradition attaching any names to these people.

They were watching their flocks in the hills around Bethlehem. This is probably an indication it was fall or winter. If the weather had been warmer and more consistent, they would have been farther out into the countryside.

There were numerous caves in the area near Bethlehem where they could sleep, and the sheep could be protected if the weather turned sour.

The routine shepherd's duties were: In the morning he led his flock from the fold, which he did by going ahead of them and calling them. Arriving at the place of pasture, he watched the flock with the assistance of dogs.

If any sheep strayed, he had to search until he found it. He supplied them with water. In evening he brought them back to the fold and checked to see that none were missing by passing them "under the rod" as they entered the door, checking each sheep as it passed.

He watched the entrance of the fold through the night, acting as gatekeeper. The shepherd's office required great watchfulness, particularly at night. It also required tenderness toward the young and feeble, particularly in leading them to and from the pasturage.

Shepherds were not held in high esteem by most people because of their nomadic lifestyle. In New Testament times they were considered uncultured and undesirable. They were not even allowed to give testimony in court.

In God's choice of announcing the birth of His Son to people such as this we see His habit of doing things differently than we would. Most people would have expected God to announce the birth of His Son with a great miraculous event.

We would have expected Jesus to be born in one of the great cosmopolitan centers of the world; not in the small village of Bethlehem.

Telling All You Know

These shepherds told everyone who would listen all they had heard and seen. Often people who try to tell all they know are politely avoided.

But in the shepherds' case, people listened, because:

- Shepherds were not supposed to know much, and these shepherds had astonishing information.
- The message was revolutionary, breathtaking, and transformative. It changed listeners' lives.
- The shepherds spoke from the heart, and their words connected to the deepest needs of others.

When we tell about Jesus, we should start with what we know best: our life experience.

Tell the story of God in your life.

We don't need to exaggerate, but don't hold back either.

Our words will change many, and God will use us to change the world.

Simon and Anna

Luke 2:21-39

Simon's name means "hearing." Anna's name means "grace."

The only time these two people are mentioned in Scripture is when Mary and Joseph brought Jesus to the Temple to have him circumcised. This was the eighth day after the birth of Christ.

When Mary and Joseph brought Jesus to the Temple to fulfill the Jewish requirement of circumcision, they encountered these two very unique people: Simon and Anna.

Every Jewish boy was circumcised and named on the eighth day. This was a symbol of the Jews' unique relationship with God. When the presentation of the firstborn son in the Temple took place, a special offering was given as a memorial of the Passover in Egypt and God's redemption of the firstborn.

When Mary and Joseph met Simon, he was an old man who had served God all of his life. He had been looking for *"the consolation of Israel ."* This phrase is another way of saying he had been looking for the Messiah. God had promised him that he would see the Messiah before his death. This was Simon's hope.

He apparently came into the Temple each day waiting and looking to see if God would show him the answer to his prayers. This day was the day he had been waiting for literally all of his life.

He was able to convince the new parents to let him hold the baby. He took Jesus in his arms and praised God. We are told Mary and Joseph marveled at the words this old man spoke.

Anna is called a prophetess. She had been given special words from God for Mary and Joseph. She was very old and had lived most of her life as a widow. The phrase *"she never left the Temple "* means she made it her life practice to be in the Temple every day, all day.

Her lifestyle of worship, prayer, and fasting shows a woman of great faith and devotion to her God.

These two people show us how God can and does use "common people." These two were neither rich nor famous. They simply loved God and made it their practice obey and worship Him. Another lesson we learn from these two people is they never lost their hope. They were older, but they were faithful to God and He rewarded their faithfulness.

Today's society tends to glorify youth over wisdom and potential contribution over past successes.

Older people should be encouraged by the testimony of these two to share their life and experiences with younger people.

As we grow older, we need to offer our friendship and help.

We can share life experiences with younger people and perhaps make the lessons they must learn a little bit easier.

How important is it to introduce our children to faith in God as early and consistently as possible?

Who is one of your most interesting elderly friends?

What wisdom have you gained from elderly friends or relatives?

The word Magi is taken from the Greek word used in Matthew. It is a direct transliteration of the Greek letters. Most Bible versions translate the word "wise man."

The only thing we know for sure about the origin of these men is they were from the "East." The term "Magi" was used as the name for priests and wise men among the Medes, Persians and Babylonians.

They arrived in Jerusalem some time before Jesus was two years old. We arrive at this conclusion by realizing Herod killed all the babies two years old and under.

These men came to Jerusalem and asked, "Where is he that is born King of the Jews?" Herod was paranoid about his grip on power and he immediately became terrified someone was planning to destroy him. Herod called together all the Jewish leaders and asked them about any prophecy relating to the birth of a King. Their reply was the Scriptures spoke of a Jewish king being born in Bethlehem.

The King met privately with the wise men and tried to find out everything they knew about this new baby. He then told them to report to him when they had found the child. He indicated to the wise men that he also wanted to worship the child. We know, of course, he had other plans in mind.

When the wise men arrived in Bethlehem, Mary and Joseph were living in a home. Joseph was supporting his new family working as a carpenter in Bethlehem. They worshiped the small child and presented their gifts. God warned them they should not return to Herod but returned to their own home another way.

The account of the wise men teaches us the Jewish Scriptures were well known in the East. This was a result of the faithfulness and service of such people as Daniel, Esther, Ezra and Nehemiah. These Old Testament people had left their mark on the wise men of the East.

The Scriptures tell us the heavens declare the glory of God. The account of the wise man is an example of exactly what that Psalm means.

Often, we feel we are the only ones who know the true God. The Jews were guilty of that misunderstanding. In fact, they gloried in the fact the Gentile world knew nothing of Jehovah.

The Wise men are testimony God moves in mysterious ways.

We may think we know exactly how God is going to handle a specific situation. The Jews believed God was going to send a mighty soldier to destroy the Roman world and set up a Jewish kingdom to rule the world with an iron hand.

Instead God sent His Son as a servant to die on a Roman cross to provide eternal redemption, not for just the Jews, but for all of mankind.

How would you define worship?

What sort of activities does worship involve?

What are some various "presents" we might give to Christ?

What star-like, shining deed can you do today to point a non-Christian friend to Christ?

Herod the Great — Matthew 2

Josephus referred to Herod as Herod "the great." This term probably referred primarily to the fact he was the oldest son of Antipater.

A shrewd politician, Herod was also great as a soldier, an orator, and a builder. Aside from his appearance in Matthew's nativity narrative, Herod's building projects serve as the backdrop for many New Testament events.

The three time periods of Herod's reign include:

- 37–27 B.C.: Consolidation. Herod impressed Rome with his ability to pacify the Jews whose homeland he occupied. Herod was capable at collecting taxes and quelling uprisings.
- 27–13 B.C.: Peace and prosperity. Herod rebuilt forts, instituted the games, and began rebuilding the Jerusalem temple.
- 13–4 B.C.: This period was marked by Herod's increasing instability. He was plagued by problems with his 10 wives and his children.

Herod was born in the 70s. His family was Idumaean, an Edomite. After his father's assassination, Herod fled the land. He returned to Rome and was officially crowned king of Judaea.

Herod became a paranoid tyrant, worried he would lose his kingdom. The fortresses he built reflect this; they provided refuge when he felt threatened.

Herod married 10 women and fathered 15 children by them. According to Josephus, Herod was so protective of his favorite wife, Mariamme, he instructed his soldiers to kill her if anything were to happen to him while he was traveling abroad.

Herod's motives for marrying the young Hasmonean Jewess were partly to gain approval with the Jews. Later Herod had both of her parents killed. Later still, the arguments he had with her and the wishes of his sister caused him to have her tried and executed.

After her death, Herod was terribly distraught and became ill. Josephus tells that Herod later ordered the killing of two of his sons with Mariamme, Alexander and Aristobulus, over suspicion they were jockeying for his position as ruler of the kingdom.

At the end of his life, Herod suffered from a severe illness. Josephus described Herod's symptoms: "For a fire glowed in him slowly, which did not so much appear to the touch outwardly as it augmented his pains inwardly; for it brought upon him a vehement appetite to eating ... His entrails were also ulcerated, and the chief violence of his pain lay on his colon; an aqueous and transparent liquor also settled itself about his feet, and a like matter afflicted him at the bottom of his belly."

What is it about competition that makes us feel so threatened?

What is the best response to "rivals" or "opponents"?

How can Christians serve those who are the victims of senseless violence?

John the Baptist — Mark1:1-11, 2:18-22, 6:14-29

His name means "Jehovah is a gracious giver." John was born in a small town not far from Jerusalem and was executed in prison by Herod Antipas. He was born about six months before Jesus and died during the ministry of Jesus.

Jesus told his followers, "I tell you the truth: Among those born of women there has not risen anyone greater than John the Baptist; yet he who is least in the kingdom of heaven is greater than he" (Matthew 11:11).

John's birth to Zacharias and Elizabeth was a miracle. Both of his parents were old and well beyond child bearing years. God spoke to Zacharias as he was ministering in the Temple and told him the news, he and his wife were going to have a child. The child was going to be the miraculous forerunner of the Messiah.

The ministry of John the Baptist was prophesied by Isaiah (40) and by Malachi (3). God sent this man to announce the coming of His Son. He was the voice crying in the wilderness: prepare the way for the Lord, make his pathway straight.

John was called "the baptizer" because his preaching called people to repent and submit to baptism to show everyone their true commitment to change their way of living. He confronted the Pharisees and the Sadducees by calling them "a generation of vipers." He warned them to flee for the wrath of God was coming upon them.

John confronted everyone who listened to him the challenge of repenting from their sin and following God.

He challenged the tax collectors to be honest and upright in their collection of taxes and repent from their sins (Luke 3). To the soldiers he said, "Do violence to no man" and "be content with your wages" (Luke 3).

It was John's direct method of preaching which led to his martyrdom. John had openly proclaimed to Herod, "It is not lawful for you to have your brother's wife." Herod's wife hated John because of the public proclamation of this message. She wanted her husband to have John executed, but Herod feared the people and their reaction.

John was put into prison and executed by Herod after he made a promise at his birthday party.

John lived a simple lifestyle in the desert. He had no money, no power and no property, yet his preaching of righteousness was so powerful it shook the entire Jewish world.

Many, at first, thought he was the promised Messiah. However, he was direct and consistent in his testimony, he was not the Messiah. The Messiah was coming soon; he was his forerunner.

John is another biblical example of the fact God rarely does anything the way we expect. Who could have imagined the creator of the universe would send someone like John the Baptist to announce the coming of His Son.

Why was John the Baptist so harsh with the religious leaders of his day?

When we are confronted with a call to repent, why do we tend to accept or reject the invitation strongly?

Nathaniel/Bartholomew John 1:43-2:11; 21:1-13

Nathaniel means "gift of God." Bartholomew means "son of Tolmai."

We know nothing of the geography connected with Nathaniel's early life. He apparently was in the area listening to John the Baptist preach. There are no reliable traditions relating to his birthplace or parentage.

Nathaniel's name occurs only in the Gospel of John. He appears to be referred to as Bartholomew in the Synoptic Gospels. He was a friend of Philip and when Philip found out about Jesus, he immediately found Nathaniel and told him of his discovery.

John gives us the account of Nathaniel being introduced to Jesus. When Philip mentioned the city of Nazareth Nathaniel's reply was, *"Can anything good come out of Nazareth?"*

We are not sure why Nathaniel felt this way. Some have speculated that Nazareth was so small and insignificant he felt nothing could possibly come from that village which would have any value.

This reveals the danger of prejudging someone based on from where they have come.

Phillip's answer was a masterpiece of logic and tact. Rather than arguing about Nathaniel's prejudice; he challenged him, *"Come and see."*

This phrase, *"Come and see"* is the key phrase for the entire Gospel of John. To Nathaniel's credit he was willing to go with Philip and evaluate Jesus based on what he saw and heard.

When Jesus saw Nathaniel approaching, he said, *"Here is a true Israelite, in whom there is nothing false."* This figure of speech is translated elsewhere, *"Here comes an honest man."*

Nathaniel was totally surprised at Jesus' recognition of him in this manner. When he asked Jesus, *"how do you know me?"* His reply was even more startling; Jesus told him I saw you while you were sitting under the tree before Philip found you.

Having "seen Jesus" he immediately accepted Him as *"The son of God - the King of Israel!"*

As little as we do know about Nathaniel, we can make several very important observations.

He was a man who studied the Scriptures and wanted to know truth.

He was a man of complete sincerity.

He was a man who was prepared to listen to what others had to say.

He was a man of prayer.

He was a man who once convinced was totally committed.

He was a man with staying power.

He was still there with the apostles after the death of Jesus on the cross.

Andrew — John 1:35-42; 6:1-13; 12:20-36

His name means "manly" or "a man."

Andrew was born in the city of Bethsaida in northern Galilee. He was the brother of Simon Peter.

Andrew and Peter were fishermen. Their father owned a fishing business that operated on the Sea of Galilee.

Andrew was a follower of John the Baptist. It was John who pointed Andrew to Jesus. When John saw Jesus he said, "*Look, the Lamb of God!" When the two disciples heard him say this, they followed Jesus. Turning around, Jesus saw them following and asked, "What do you want?" They said, "Rabbi, "where are you staying?" "Come," he replied, "and you will see." So, they went and saw where he was staying, and spent the day with Him. It was about the tenth hour. Andrew, Simon Peter's brother, was one of the two who heard what John had said and who had followed Jesus.* (John 1:36-40)

The first thing Andrew did was to find his brother and begin to tell him about the teacher he had found. He told Peter, " *We have found the Messiah.*" He convinced Peter to come with him and introduced him to Jesus.

Andrew is remembered for his ability to reach others and bring them to Jesus.

Later, after Peter and Andrew had returned to Galilee, they resumed their lives as fishermen. Jesus returned to Galilee and began to preach throughout the region.

No doubt there were many times when the two brothers were able to listen to His preaching and teaching.

Later as Jesus was walking along the shore of Galilee, He saw the two men working as fishermen; they were casting the small nets into the Sea of Galilee and drawing them in hoping for a catch of fish.

Jesus drew near the edge of the seashore and spoke to them with a loud voice shouting, "*follow me and I will make you fishers of men.*" The Scriptures tell us the two brothers left their fishing tools and immediately follow Jesus.

I am sure this was not the first time they had thought about Jesus and it was not the first time they had encountered Jesus in Galilee. This call probably was a result of many conversations.

Tradition tells us after the resurrection of Jesus, Andrew preached in Greece and was martyred because of his rebuke to a King. Tradition also tells us he was crucified on an X-shaped cross. This shape is still called, "St. Andrew's cross."

Find your gift and serve God with what you were given.

Andrew apparently had the ability to talk with others and to share his knowledge. He brought the boy to Jesus with five barley loaves and two small fish; as a result, the entire multitude was fed.

What are your abilities?

Are you willing to let God use them and you?

Simon Peter

Matthew 26:20-75; I Peter 1-2

An Introduction and Overview

Simon means "hearing." Peter is Greek for "rock." He is also called Cephas, which is Aramaic for "rock." Peter was a fisherman born and raised in Bethsaida in Galilee. Tradition tells us he was martyred by crucifixion, crucified upside down, near Rome.

Peter was one of the "big three" among the apostles, one of the best known of the twelve. His brother was Andrew and they were partners in a fishing business with James and John. We know he was married and was brought to Christ by his brother Andrew.

He wrote the two New Testament books which bear his name. He was the leader in the early church until the rise of Paul. Peter was impetuous and outspoken. He often spoke before he thought, and it appears from the biblical text he often acted before he thought.

He was a willing and enthusiastic follower of Jesus from the beginning. At Caesarea Philippi (Matthew 16) it was Peter who answered the question of Jesus, "Whom do men say I am?" His reply is classic theology and a tremendous summary of what we need to know about Jesus Christ. Peter replied, "You are the Christ, the son of the living God."

Peter was one of the three disciples present on the Mount of Transfiguration when Moses and Elijah appeared to speak with Jesus about his upcoming death and resurrection.

Peter was the apostle who walked on the water during the storm described in Matthew 14. He is often faulted for his lack of faith, but the fact remains he was the only one of the twelve willing to get out of the boat.

It was also Peter who denied Christ on three occasions after Jesus had been arrested by the Romans. He fell short of living up to his promise that he would never deny Jesus. But he was one of only two disciples to follow Jesus to see what was going to happen. He was also forgiven and restored completely by Jesus as recorded in John 21.

Peter is a tremendous lesson; a role model for those of us who seem to have very high emotional points and later suffer from very low and depressing moods. We would have to say Peter had his ups and downs, but there was no doubt he loved the Lord.

After the ascension of Christ, Peter was willing to go to places no other Jew would have considered going. God used him to open salvation to the Gentiles when he went to the home of Cornelius.

Peter is an example of how God can change and use someone. He and Andrew, his brother, were from the tiny village of Bethsaida in Galilee. Philip was also from this town. This little village no doubt had only a few hundred residents and yet God chose three men from this community to become his chosen apostles.

No one is too small; no place is too unimportant!

God uses Peter to tell us he doesn't call the qualified; he qualifies the called.

God used Peter in many unique ways even though he was not by any means perfect.

This should be an encouragement for each one of us!

Simon Peter: Denial and Restoration

When it was time to arrange for the Last Supper Jesus sent Peter and John to make the preparations and secure the room where He and His disciples would meet. Once they arrived for this meal, Jesus began to wash the disciples' feet, but when He came to Peter, he declared, "You shall never wash my feet." To the statement Jesus replied, "If I do not wash you, you have no part with me." When Jesus spoke these words Peter reconsidered and replied, "In that case, wash not only my feet but my hands and my head as well."

When Jesus told the disciples one of them would betray Him, Peter gestured to John that he should ask of who He was talking about. Later, Peter asserted under no circumstances would he ever leave his Jesus, to which Jesus replied by saying, "Simon, Simon, behold, Satan has demanded permission to sift you like wheat," and told him of his speedy denial.

At Gethsemane

Peter, James, and John accompanied Jesus to his place of prayer, Gethsemane (Matthew 26:36-37; Mark 14:32-33), and when Judas came with his company to seize Jesus, Peter drew his sword and cut off the right ear of Malchus, a servant of the high priest, for which he was promptly rebuked (Matthew 26:51-52; John 18:10-11).

Denial

When Jesus was arrested, Peter, along with John, followed Him at a distance to the palace of Caiaphas and entered his court. While he was there a slave girl said to him, "You are not also one of this man's disciples, are you?" Peter answered, "I am not" (John 18:15-17; Matthew 26:58, 69-70; Mark 14:66- 68; Luke 22:55-57). Peter's *second* denial occurred on the porch, to which he had withdrawn. Another servant girl declared to those who were standing about, "This man was with Jesus of Nazareth." Peter, with an oath, denied even an acquaintance with Jesus (Matthew 26:71-72; Mark 14:69-70; Luke 22:58, where the accuser was a man; John 18:25). His *third* denial was uttered after a while (Luke says *an hour*) and was in reply to some who charged him with being one of the disciples of Jesus, saying, "The way you talk gives you away." Peter probably made some remark in his Galilean dialect. He cursed and swore, then declared, "I do not know the man!" The crowing of the cock and the look of our Lord awakened Peter to a sense of his guilt, "and he went out and wept bitterly" (Matthew 26:73-75; Mark 14:70-72; Luke 22:59-62; John 18:26-27).

Restoration

"We are told in Luke and later by Paul that Christ appeared to Peter first among the apostles. It is important to note on that occasion he is called by his original name, Simon, not Peter. The name which Jesus had given him was not used in the gospel accounts again, until he had been publicly reinstated, so to speak, by his Master.

This restoration took place at the Sea of Galilee. After fishing all night as Peter and some of the disciples approached shore, they saw Jesus with a fire of coals. John was the first to recognize Jesus; Peter was the first to reach him: he brought the net to land.

After eating breakfast as Jesus and Peter were talking Jesus asked him three times if Peter really loved him. These three questions were obviously meant to remind Peter of his three-part denial. He was restored and forgiven.

If Peter, who was closer to the Lord than any of the other disciples, could have weak moments of faith and be restored we should be encouraged, our weaknesses are forgivable.

Have you ever restored a broken relationship? When? How?

How did Peter feel after Jesus had asked him the same question three times?

Simon Peter: The Apostle

Prominence as an Apostle

Sometimes Peter spoke in the name of the twelve and sometimes he answered when questions were asked of them all; sometimes Jesus addressed him in place of all the apostles.

His importance among the apostles probably depended on the fact he was the first chosen and partly on his own unique traits. This position became more obvious after the ascension of Jesus and may have been as a result of the events described in John 21:15-19. The early church regarded him as the representative of the apostolic body.

After the Ascension

After this Peter stands out as the recognized leader of the apostles, although it is clear he did not exercise or claim any authority apart from them, much less over them.

First Miracle

Peter and John went up to the Temple to pray, and as they were about to enter, a lame man, who was lying at the entrance of the gate called Beautiful, spoke to them, asking alms. Peter said to him, "Look at us! I do not possess silver and gold, but what I do have I give to you: In the name of Jesus Christ the Nazarene, Walk!"

When a crowd ran to Solomon's porch to see what was happening, Peter preached Jesus to them. For this the apostles were imprisoned, and the next day they were brought before the Sanhedrin to answer the question, "By what power, or in what name, have you done this?"
Peter replied with boldness, and they were freed and told not to cause any more disturbances.

Miraculous Deliverance

Sometime later, Herod, having found the execution of James pleased the Jews, arrested Peter and put him in prison. He was kept under the care of four squads of soldiers. Two were stationed at the gate, while the other two were attached to Peter by chains. Despite these precautions, an angel delivered the apostle, who went to the house of Mary, the mother of John Mark, where many of the church was gathered praying for his safety.

Salvation Extended to the Gentiles

God used Peter to extend salvation to the Gentiles. While Peter was in Joppa, he saw a vision of a large sheet let down from heaven. In this sheet were all kinds of animals, some of which the Jews were allowed to eat and some of which they were to consider unclean. This vision was repeated two more times.

The vision caused Peter to accept an invitation to the home of Cornelius, a Roman centurion and a Gentile. He told them about Jesus and the entire family became followers of Jesus. Because of this experience Peter came to understand God intended salvation for the entire world and it was not reserved only for the Jews.

Peter took the lead in the discussion described in Acts, contending salvation comes through grace, which is received through faith, and all distinction between believers is removed (15:7-11).

In these events God used Peter to move salvation from a "Jewish only experience" to being available to the entire world. This opened the door for Paul's ministry to the Gentiles.

Once again, we see God uses unexpected people to accomplish his purposes.

No one would have imagined a Jewish fisherman extending salvation to the Gentiles.

Has God used you in unexpected ways?

James and John

James was the son of Zebedee and Salome, and the elder brother of John. James appears first in the biblical narrative as a fisherman, he and his brother were partners with Simon Peter (Luke 5:10).

When called by Jesus to be His followers in the spring or summer of 27 AD. James and his brother responded immediately which makes them models of obedience.

These brothers and Peter seemed for some reason to be especially fitted to live in close relationship with Jesus and were with Him on several very important occasions.

They alone were present

- at the transfiguration
- at the raising of Jairus's daughter
- at the Garden while Jesus prayed

Along with Andrew they listened to the Lord's private message on the fall of Jerusalem (Mark 13:3).

Because of faulty views of the Messiah's kingdom and an ambition to share in its glory, they joined in the request made to Jesus by their mother (Matthew 20:20-23; Mark 10:35-40).

James was the first of the apostles to be martyred. He was beheaded at the command of Herod (Acts 12:2).

From the desire to punish the inhabitants of a village in Samaria because they refused to receive Jesus (Luke 9:52-54), we understand James and John were warm and impetuous in temperament. They were called by Jesus (Mark 3:17) "Boanerges"–*sons of thunder*–probably because of their boldness and energy in discharging their apostleship.

John

John was the younger brother of James. The reference to the "hired servants" and his acquaintance with Caiaphas the high priest (John 18:15) implies a position of at least considerable influence and means.

The incident recorded in John 1:35-39 indicates John had first become a disciple of John the Baptist. John was probably among the disciples who followed their new Teacher to Galilee (John 1:43), were with Him at the marriage feast of Cana (John 2:2), journeyed with Him to Capernaum and thence to Jerusalem (John 2:12, 23), and came back through Samaria (John 4:5). He then returned to his former occupation.

When the betrayal occurred, Peter and John followed from a distance and through an acquaintance gained admittance into the palace. John was the only disciple present at the crucifixion. He was chosen by Jesus to care for Mary.

Friendship for Peter

- Together they witnessed the ascension
- Together they went into the Temple as worshipers
- Together they were imprisoned, and protested the threats of the Sanhedrin,
- They were also sent together to preach to the Samaritans.

During the persecution under Herod Agrippa he lost his brother, James, by martyrdom, while his friend Peter sought safety in flight (Acts 12:18-19). Fifteen years after Paul's first visit he was still at Jerusalem.

He was one of the "pillars" of the church and took part in settling the controversy between the Jewish and Gentile Christians (Acts 15:6-13; Galatians 2:9).

Nicodemus — John 3

His name means "Victor over the people." This probably indicates his aristocratic upbringing and family lifestyle. His family is unknown; some recognize him as Nicodemus Ben Gorion, the brother of Josephus the historian. This Nicodemus was a member of the Sanhedrin and was believed to be one of the three richest men in Jerusalem.

But it was said he became poor, and his daughter was seen gathering barley for food from under the horses' feet. Some have conjectured this was the result of the persecutions he received for having accepted Christianity.

Nicodemus is known as the man who came to Jesus at night. Some have conjectured he came to Jesus at night because he was afraid of what others would say if they saw him speaking to this controversial Rabbi. He has been called a coward and been charged with deceit for not openly proclaiming his faith in Christ. I think it is much more logical to assume he went to see Jesus at night because it was the best time for both Jesus and he to have a quiet, uninterrupted conversation about spiritual matters. Nicodemus had probably been occupied throughout the day with his teaching duties. Jesus had been active teaching and ministering to the people in the city of Jerusalem.

In the evening life slowed down in the great city of Jerusalem. The two would have been free to meet, probably on the rooftop of the place where Jesus was staying. The evening would have been cool and refreshing and it would've provided an excellent opportunity for Jesus to use the wind as an illustration in His conversation with Nicodemus.

Nicodemus began his conversation with Jesus by acknowledging Him as a "*teacher come from God.*" He also referred to the many "things" Jesus had done.

No doubt Nicodemus had heard Jesus speak and was aware of His miracles. He may even have interviewed some of the people who had been cleansed or healed by Jesus. He was willing to approach Jesus personally and to ask Him directly to explain His teaching. Nicodemus, unlike Nathaniel, did not immediately grasp the reality of what Jesus was teaching. We know he considered everything Jesus said and later became a committed follower.

What do we know of Nicodemus?

- He came to Christ
- He defended Christ in the Sanhedrin
- He honored Christ by helping Joseph of Arimathea prepare the body for burial

Nicodemus was a fair-minded, honest man, but he appears to have been timid and afraid of peer pressure. In the end he was able to overcome his fear and stand with a friend in recognizing Jesus as his Savior.

When would you say you were born again?

How would you describe what it means to be born again to someone?

What were the circumstances which led you to Jesus?

What were some of the things which caused you to believe that Jesus is the Son of God?

We do not know this woman's name and there is no tradition of a name associated with her.

These events took place in the central part of the land of Palestine. The New Testament city Sychar was located near the Old Testament city of Samaria.

As Jesus was leaving the region of Judea, He chose to go through the region of Samaria. This was a very unusual decision for a Jewish rabbi. The Jews and the Samaritans hated each other. The Jews viewed the Samaritans as half breeds who had originated after the return from exile. Those returning from Babylon had intermarried with the foreigners living in the area; the result was the people called Samaritans. The Jews looked down on these people because they were a product of not only intermarriage but a mixture of Jewish religion and other local religions.

The result was a hatred which caused both groups to despise each other. A "good Jew" would never travel through the land of Samaria. He would travel east from Jerusalem to the Jordan River Valley and North to the region of Galilee. This would allow him to go from the North to the South in the land of Israel without passing through Samaria. I am sure the disciples were wondering what their Master was thinking to follow such a course on His journey. They were concerned with what the other religious leaders would say.

Stopping about midday near the well the disciples went into town to buy food and Jesus remained near the well by Himself. This woman came to draw water around noontime. This was unusual and it indicates she was not welcome in the company of most of the "good" women of the area because they would have come to the well early in the morning or later in the evening.

When Jesus met the woman, He broke many social prohibitions by speaking with her. Men did not directly speak with women in public. He was a Jew; she was a Samaritan. For a Jew and a Samaritan to engage in conversation was taboo.

Jesus asked the woman for a drink. She was astonished He even had spoken to her and she began to question Him concerning His disregard for conventional social wisdom. Jesus quickly directed the conversation toward God. She tried to divert His attention by engaging in a "theological" discussion about where God should be worshiped. Jesus quickly brought the subject back to her personal relationship with God.

He directly approached a Samaritan woman and spoke to her about her need for salvation. When His disciples returned, they were astonished He had spoken to this woman.

This account shows us the disregard Jesus had for meaningless tradition.

What groups of people do you feel uncomfortable being around? Why?

His conversation and His willingness to reach out to one individual caused the salvation of many.

What if Jesus had been more concerned about what people thought than He was about what people needed?

How is Jesus' gift of salvation different from what the world offers?

The Nobleman John 4:43-53

In the latter part of the fourth chapter of John's Gospel we meet an unnamed governmental officer from the court of Herod in Capernaum. When this His man heard about Jesus and His miraculous teachings and miracles, he made the journey from Capernaum to Cana in Galilee. This was a journey of 16 miles.

His willingness to make this journey was created by an extended illness his son was suffering. His son had gradually begun to decline in health and now he had taken a sudden turn for the worse. He felt his son was about to die. He no doubt had tried every method possible to heal his son and all had failed. Now in a desperate attempt he turned to Jesus.

When he found Jesus in Cana, he asked this new teacher to come with him to Capernaum and heal his son. This man appears to have been persistent and even though he possessed a high social status he was willing to beg the new teacher to come with him.

When Jesus heard this request, He replied to the man, loud enough for the assembled crowd to hear, "Unless you see signs and wonders you will not believe." The interesting part of this statement comes in the pronoun "you." In the original language the pronoun is plural. Jesus is using the request of this man to make a point with the entire crowd.

Why have you come to see me, He is asking them. He is trying to bring to their attention the fact they are here only because they believe in the signs and wonders he has performed. They were looking at the externals. They were looking to get something "from" Jesus. This seems to be a very severe answer to the worried father but is necessary to make a much larger point to the crowd.

The governmental official immediately replies to Jesus, "Sir, come down before my child dies." The man freely admits he is seeking a miracle. He certainly had no idea that Jesus could deal with the problem from miles away. He wanted the physical touch of this healer upon his son. He came desperately seeking help from Jesus. Jesus reply is immediate and totally unexpected. Jesus said to him, "Go. Your son will live." This grieving and agonized father is now faced with another decision. What should he do? Will he take Jesus at his word? He has no material assurance anything is changed. He has only the word of this strange teacher.

If he refused to take the word of Jesus, he risked insulting the one he had asked for help. This would risk everything that he had come to accomplish. Jesus' reply forced the man to decide. Without any kind of a sign he must believe the word of the teacher. We read in John 4:50, "The man believed the word that Jesus spoke to him and went on his way." He began his journey home; it was a long walk and he had much time to think. On the road home some of his servants came to meet him and brought him word that his son was recovering. He asked them what time the child had begun to get better. They told him yesterday, shortly after the noon hour. John tells us, "The father knew that was the time when Jesus said to him, "your son will live."

The key words are "the father knew!"

His earlier faith came from the fact there was no other solution than Jesus. Notice the phrase says, "He believed."

There is no reference whatsoever to "what" he believed. He simply believed - he believed Jesus!

Here we see the progression of faith

- **First Faith** — **He came**
- **Further Faith** — **He asked**
- **Full Faith** — **He believed and acted on his belief**

Can you see a progression in your faith?

How do you "act" on your faith?

Matthew had two names; this was not uncommon in the Roman world. His Jewish name was "Levi," it means "one who joins." His Roman name is Matthew, it means "gift of God."

Based on where Matthew lived many people feel he was born in the Galilean city of Capernaum. Tradition tells us he preached in Ethiopia and was martyred there.

Matthew lived in the city of Capernaum and he was a "publican." This was a person who was a tax collector for the Roman government. There was a large population living around the cities near the Sea of Galilee. There were many businesses in the area related to fishing.

The Sea of Galilee provided a livelihood for the majority of people living in the area. Rome had established several custom collection points near the cities around the Sea. The people who were in charge of these collection booths were usually Romans.

Often, they "subcontracted" the actual work of collecting the tolls to Jews who were willing to work for them. Matthew was one of these "subcontractors." The Jews who were willing to work for the Romans were hated by nearly all other Jews.

Matthew was sitting at such a toll booth when Jesus came to him and said, "Follow me." Matthew probably had already heard Jesus speak on several occasions.

It is probable he had had previous conversations with Jesus and some of his followers. Collecting "taxes" in the area makes me feel he surely knew Peter.

Shortly after he began to follow Jesus, he gave a large banquet at his home. Matthew 9 tells us there were many tax collectors and sinners at the banquet. We may surmise this banquet was a farewell reception given to honor many of his associates. He probably offered Jesus a chance to speak to these people.

Matthew wrote the gospel which bears his name. It is written with a very "Jewish emphasis." He presents Jesus as the Jewish Messiah, the Lion of the tribe of Judah, and the King of the Jews.

Many times, in his gospel we read phrases such as, "These things happened that the Scriptures might be fulfilled." Tradition tells us that after the ascension of Jesus, Matthew preached 12 to 15 years in the land of Israel. After that he traveled to North Africa.

Matthew shows us Jesus was willing to reach out to all men and women. The Jews hated anyone who worked with the Roman tax collectors so much they refused to take any money from them. They even refused their money to support the synagogue.

There are many legends and traditions relating to Matthew's faithfulness and total dedication to Jesus. He never "got over" his amazement that the Son of God reached out to him.

How do you feel about taxes?

Would you like to be seen as a tax collector?

What jobs do you think present the greatest temptation to do wrong? Why?

Have you ever felt resentment because of your occupation?

Again, the name Pharisee means "separated." Many think it goes back to the time of Ezra. If so, they originated shortly before 400 B.C. and over the course of the next four centuries they remained in the land of Palestine until shortly after the destruction of Jerusalem and the Temple.

The Pharisees were the religious conservatives of Jesus' day. They believed in the immortality of the soul and eternal rewards based on the life that one lived here on earth. They believed in angels and spirits. They felt there was a constant war of good versus evil. In this they very much reflected the views of the common Jewish man in the first century.

According to the Jewish historian, Josephus, they made "everything depends on faith and on God and taught that the doing of good is indeed chiefly the affair of man, but they also cooperate in every transaction" (Josephus Wars 2. 8. 14).

Politically the Pharisees were almost always opposed to any Roman influence on Jewish life. They were truly a "religious" party. Their goal was to enforce the law of God to absolute perfection. As a result, they engaged in long discourses related to what one could or could not do and still follow the law of God.

As far as possible a good Pharisee would avoid any contact with any non-Jewish person. To contact such a person would render him unclean and in such a condition he could not offer the proper sacrifices to maintain his proper relationship with God.

There are many comparisons that can be made between the Pharisees and the teachings of Jesus.

The Pharisees viewed the law as something that must be kept in absolute minute detail. Jesus taught it was the spirit of the law that was important and not the minutiae.

The Pharisees thought keeping the law of God was an end in itself. Jesus sought to call man to God.

Jesus taught men true godliness did not consist in "form," but in "substance." It was the inner reality of a man's life that was important. The Pharisees thought godliness was in the smallest observance of details.

Jesus taught compassion was to be shown to all people.

The Pharisees avoided anyone they saw as beneath their status in life.

What kinds of lawful behavior are Christians often quick to condemn in others?

What are some ways we trample over the feelings of others in our quest to be righteous?

How do you use God to justify wrong attitudes such as snobbery, jealousy, prejudice, or selfishness?

The Gentile Woman Mark 7:24-30

Jesus traveled about 30 miles northwest from Galilee to the vicinity of Tyre and then went to Sidon. These were port cities on the Mediterranean Sea north of Israel. Both cities had flourishing trade and were very wealthy. They were proud, historic Canaanite cities.

The word of Jesus' arrival spread from village to village. One woman had heard about Jesus' miracle-working power and how He cast out demons, so she came and fell at His feet asking Jesus to help her little girl who was possessed by an evil spirit.

Mark calls this woman a Gentile, a Syrophoenician; Matthew calls her a woman of Canaan. Mark's designation referred to her political background. His Roman audience would easily identify her by the part of the empire which was her home. She begged Jesus to cast the demon out of her daughter. The woman wasted no time. As she fell at Jesus' feet, she made her request: would Jesus cast the demon out of her little girl?

Jesus said to her, "Let the children be fed first, for it is not fair to take the children's food and throw it to the dogs." Jesus used a word referring to a little dog, a household pet. The parable showed the children at the table are fed before the pets; it would not be right to take the children's food and give it to the dogs.

But she answered him, "Sir, even the dogs under the table eat the children's crumbs." Unlike many of Jesus' Jewish listeners, this woman understood His parable. Her answer was wise, for she replied to Jesus, by extending His parable, the children who love the pets often drop morsels of food to them. Not all the Jews accepted Jesus, while some Gentiles chose to follow Him.

Why couldn't she have some of those "leftovers" which the Jews didn't "eat"? She skillfully pointed out such "dogs" ate with, not after, the children. She did not ask for the entire meal, just for a few crumbs; or one crumb in particular, one miracle of healing for her daughter.

The woman knew what she wanted; she believed Jesus could provide; she persevered; she seized the opportunity. We could learn from this woman's singular purpose and optimistic resilience

Jesus told her, "For such a reply, you may go; the demon has left your daughter." Jesus was pleased by the faith of the woman. He granted her request because of her humility and persistence. Her request had been made in faith that Jesus could perform the healing. His words had been meant to test her and she had passed the test.

She understood Christ's lordship and as a Gentile she had no right to request mercy from Jesus. She also willingly accepted His conditions.

She went home, found the child lying on the bed, and the demon gone. The woman knew her request had been granted.

She did not beg Jesus to come with her; she took Him at His word that her child was healed.

In Jesus there is hope for all of us. The woman was a Gentile; Jesus crossed the barrier to reach out to her.

He crossed many barriers: nationality, religion, and tradition.

No barrier can keep Jesus from reaching us.

What barriers to sharing the gospel have you faced?

The Rich Young Man — Mark 10:17-31

We do not know this young man's name. This was probably in Judea on the way to Jerusalem.

On the way to Jerusalem Jesus was met by this young man. He asked Jesus the following question, "*Good Teacher, what must I do to inherit eternal life?*" This question revealed a misunderstanding on his part. Jesus' reply was short and to the point, "*Why do you call me good?*"

Jesus was teaching a truth we all need to understand, "*Only God is truly good.*" The word good is capable of a "good" many meanings. Synonyms given for this word are: well-behaved, suitable, decent, effective, high-quality, enjoyable, skillful, nice, to name a few. All of these words are adjectives, they modify another word.

Jesus' reply taught the fact; only God possesses the quality of goodness. Only God is good. Was this young man attributing the quality of goodness to Jesus because he felt Jesus was God? I doubt it very much.

Another misunderstanding revealed in his question was his idea he could earn "eternal life." Jesus listed five of the Ten Commandments in reply to his question. Jesus did not list the first commandment or the last. These two commandments relate to the love of God and the treatment of neighbors; both of these this man was guilty of breaking. Jesus wanted him to figure this out himself.

Another misunderstanding is seen in the young man's answer to Jesus' listing of the Commandments. He said, "I have obeyed all the Commandments since I was young." He missed the point; it is not the letter of the law but the spirit.

Jesus told the young man there is one more thing, "*Go and sell all your possessions and give the money to the poor.*" The Scripture says the young man went away sorrowful and with a heavy heart because he was very rich.

Jesus used this opportunity to teach His disciples. "*How hard it is for the rich to enter the kingdom of God.*" We all tend to trust our own ability whether it is physical or financial.

In the 21st century I am afraid we trust much more in our credit cards then we do in Jesus.

The disciples were amazed at His analogy of the camel and their reply revealed their amazement. How was it possible for anyone to be saved?

Jesus' answer is the ultimate in brevity and clarity, "*Humanly speaking, it is impossible. But not with God. Everything is possible with God.*"

What are the advantages and disadvantages of being wealthy?

In what ways can money stop us from doing what God wants?

How can wealth interfere with a person's Christian faith?

How do you think God wants you to use the material wealth He has given you?

What practical steps can you take to insure you place value on eternal things and not merely on material things?

Bartimaeus — Mark 10, Matt. 20, Luke 18

His name means "son of Timaeus."

The location of these events is Jericho. There is an interesting mystery in the Bible accounts of this event:

- Mark 10:46 - Then they came to Jericho
- Matthew 20:29 - As Jesus and his disciples were leaving Jericho
- Luke 18:35 - As Jesus approached Jericho

The question is, "Are they coming or going?" This "discrepancy" has been pointed out by unbelievers. They use this passage to say, "Look there are errors in your Bible." How can we answer such an observation?

There is an answer and archaeology provides that answer. Today there are three Jerichos: Old Testament Jericho, New Testament Jericho, and modern Jericho.

In the days of Christ there were two Jerichos: the Old Testament city, which was mostly rundown and to some extent uninhabited, and the New Testament city - the place where all the activity was located.

Jesus and His disciples would have come to the Old Testament city first and then gone on to the New Testament city. Bartimaeus, a blind beggar, was located between the two cities where he could encounter the most people. Archaeology has consistently provided answers to seeming difficulties in the Bible.

Bartimaeus was blind, a disabled person. He was not able to work or provide for himself. He was a beggar. A beggar was someone who went to public places and depended upon the Jewish practice of "alms giving."

New Testament Judaism taught one of the major responsibilities of a godly Jew was giving to the poor. As Bartimaeus was sitting by the roadside he heard a crowd coming and inquired concerning the cause of the noise. He was told that the great Rabbi from Nazareth was coming. When he heard this, he began shouting and trying to get the attention of Jesus.

Many in the crowd tried to silence him, probably out of the fear of embarrassing themselves and their city in front of so important a person. It is easy to imagine a few of the disciples had gone ahead to make sure everything was in order and they probably had tried to "secure the area" so there would be no distractions or problems.

Bartimaeus refused to be silenced and continued crying out. Jesus heard him and commanded those around him to bring the man to Him. Jesus asked him very simply, "What do you want?" Bartimaeus wanted to see and that is exactly what Jesus did for him. Jesus told him, "*Go your way; your faith has made you whole.*" How much faith did Bartimaeus have? He had enough faith to be willing to create a disturbance in order to take advantage of his one opportunity to meet this man.

When has persistence paid off for you?

Why do you think the people rebuked the blind man?

Why do you think Jesus singled out Bartimaeus for healing among the many needy people He must have encountered along the way?

Do you have persistent faith?

The Poor Widow — Mark 12:41-44; Luke 21:1-4

We have no idea who this woman was; her act of generosity challenges us every time we read this story.

This occurred in the Temple Courts of Jerusalem during Passover week. Hundreds of thousands of people came to the city this week and gave offerings and sacrifices. Along the outer walls of the Temple Courts were offering boxes for people to give their gifts. Some of the richer Jews hired people to go before them and announce how much they were giving. Others like this woman would not be noticed.

Jesus was in Jerusalem to celebrate His final Passover meal. He would soon be arrested and crucified.

Jesus was in the Temple area, probably teaching and answering questions. We may conjecture His disciples were watching those who came by to give their offering. They were probably very impressed with some of the large offerings.

This woman, poor, anonymous, and unnoticed, walked by one of the chests and dropped in her two small copper coins. These coins were the smallest Jewish coin in circulation in Palestine. Each coin was called a *lepton*. Two *lepta* amounted to one-sixty-fourth of a denarius, which was considered a day's wage for a laborer. The NIV translates them for us as amounting to merely *a fraction of a penny.* Her small gift was a sacrifice, but she gave it willingly.

Herbert Lockyer in his book, All the Women of the Bible, says this widow would have known the story of Hagar. Hagar was comforted by the knowledge God saw and watched over her (Genesis 16:13). She gave her tiny offering that day feeling no one would notice or care, except God.

She did not know the one sitting near the offering box was the Son of God. He knew all about her and He knew the sacrificial nature of her gift.

The Bible does not tell us whether Jesus spoke to her or not. I personally think He must have laid His hand on her shoulder and encouraged her to continue following her heavenly Father.

Because of her poverty she would remain unnoticed by the great "powers" of Judaism. But the omnipotent power of the entire universe took notice of her action.

The widow gave all she had, and she gave it gladly.

She is a great example of someone who gave out of love.

She surrendered all she had to God willingly; she had not been coerced or manipulated into giving. She loved God and wanted to show Him her love and devotion the best way she could.

What does it mean to be poor?

How does God evaluate a person's giving?

Why does God want us to give sacrificially?

How does God judge our gifts?

Why do you think the widow gave all she had to live on?

"The eyes of the Lord are in every place; he sees the evil and the good" (Proverbs 15:3).

Mary Magdalene — Luke 8:2; 24:10; John 20

Her name means "bitter." The name "Magdalene" is usually taken as a designation of the town Magdala. This was a small town on the western shore of Galilee.

Mary is introduced in the gospel narrative, with other women, as ministering to Jesus "*out of their private means*" (Luke 8:2-3); all of them were motivated by gratitude for their deliverance from "*evil spirits and sicknesses.*" Of Mary it is said that "seven demons had gone out" of her (Luke 8:2; Mark 16:9).

Most of what we know about Mary comes from the events recorded after the crucifixion and resurrection. She was among the first group of women to come to the tomb on that Easter morning.

When the three women found the tomb was empty, the other two ran back to tell the apostles the tomb was empty. Mary seems to have been so moved that she remained behind and wept. When she stooped and looked into the tomb, she saw the angels and they asked her why she was weeping. She replied to them, *"They have taken away my Lord and I do not know where they have placed him."*

As a result of her choice she became the first person to see the risen Lord. When she turned away from the tomb, still in tears, she saw Jesus standing nearby. Jesus spoke her name and she immediately recognized Him. He told her to go and tell "my brethren" that He had risen from the dead.

Mary Magdalene has been identified, in popular tradition, as the woman in Luke 7 who anointed Jesus feet at the banquet of Simon the Pharisee. She is not mentioned by name until 8:2 and there is nothing to connect her to the events of the preceding chapter.

This idea was recently popularized in several fictional books, such as The da Vinci Code. There is no historical evidence to connect her to the woman in Luke. The earliest form of this idea comes from the Talmudic writers who said her name "Magdalene" meant, "Mariam with the braided locks." It was a later writer who said this phrase meant "the woman who was a sinner" in Luke 7.

More than anything else the attachment of the word Magdalene to her name seems to be chosen to distinguish her from the several other Marys named in the Gospels.

What we see in Mary is a woman who was so grateful for what Jesus had done in her life she was willing to contribute to His ministry. She contributed financially.

She contributed by helping others as she traveled among His disciples. She was there at the cross because of her love for Him.

Why do you think the resurrected Jesus appeared first to Mary Magdalene?

How would you respond if you met someone you had presumed to be dead?

What would you do if you saw an angel?

If you had been one of the disciples who had heard Mary's exciting news, how do you think you would have reacted?

When have you been exceptionally thrilled about your relationship with Christ?

Mary and Martha — Luke 10:38-42: John 11

Mary: Meaning of her name: "Bitter." Martha: Meaning of her name: "Lady, mistress."

Mary and Martha were from the town of Bethany. This is a village located on the other side of the Mount of Olives from the city of Jerusalem. This was their ancestral home because they had a family tomb in the area.

The passage we have chosen to highlight in Luke shows the differences in these two women. The two women are hosting Jesus and His disciples in their home.

We are told by Luke that Mary was sitting and listening to Jesus as He taught. Martha, on the other hand, was very busy with all of the preparations necessary for the extra people and the meal to be served. Martha went to Jesus and asked him, *"Lord, don't you care that my sister has left me to do the work by myself? Tell her to help me!"*

Martha had the gift of hospitality and was doing all in her power to make Jesus and His followers comfortable. She had become overwhelmed with all she needed to do. The more she worked, the more she thought, the angrier she became at her sister for not helping.

The reply Jesus gave can be a little confusing. He told Martha, *"You are worried and upset about many things, but only one thing is needed. Mary has chosen what is better, and it will not be taken away from her."*

Jesus is not rebuking Martha. He is trying to show her the difference between the eternal and the temporary.

The meal would be eaten, the remains would be cleaned up. They would sleep that night and soon go on their way. The truth Jesus was teaching was eternal and it would have lasting value.

Temporary things are just that: temporary! It is not that they are unimportant, it is not that they do not need to be done; it is that they are temporary. We sometimes speak of the "urgent" taking priority over the "important." This is the lesson Jesus was explaining to Martha. She was a servant and hostess, but she was too involved in the details to see the reality of the events surrounding her.

In John 11 Jesus brings this teaching back to this house on another occasion. Mary and Martha's brother, Lazarus, had died. The sisters sent for Jesus. Jesus raised him from the dead and restored him to his family.

If you had been Martha in this situation, how would you have reacted to your sister's choice?

Do you struggle with busyness?

How can you begin to properly prioritize your schedule?

Do you struggle with the overwhelming nature of material concerns?

What can you do to slow down and worship God?

His name means "whom God helps." Lazarus lived in the village of Bethany on the east side of the Mt. of Olives, with his sisters Mary and Martha. He was a contemporary of Jesus. The events described in these chapters occurred near the end of Jesus' ministry.

Jesus and this family had apparently been friends for several years. Mary and Martha are mentioned earlier in the gospel narratives. It is possible that on many occasions when Jesus was in Jerusalem preaching and teaching, He spent the night with these friends in this village which was only a short distance from Jerusalem.

Lazarus is the last of three persons Jesus raised from the dead in His three-and-a-half-year ministry. The other two people, whose names are not given, had only been dead a very brief period of time. Lazarus, on the other hand, had been dead for three days. This length of time removes any doubt about his death.

Jesus' relationship with this family is emphasized when He is told of Lazarus's illness. The sisters sent word to Jesus, *"Lord, the one you love is sick."* Jesus waited three days before He made the trip to Bethany and then He raised Lazarus from the dead. This story is well-known so I want us to think about the lessons we can learn and the applications we can make in our own lives because of these events.

There are several lessons we can learn from this account. The first of these is the way in which Jesus used this event to teach His disciples. He told them, *"Lazarus is dead and for your sake I am glad I was not there, so that you may believe. But let us go to him."*

The observation I want to make here is that Jesus used nearly every event recorded in the Gospels when the disciples were present as a teaching tool. He did everything possible to build their belief.

Another observation is on His arrival, when He met Mary and Martha, He did not rebuke them for their sorrow. Many think He should have told them, "Don't cry I'm going to raise him." But He participated in their sorrow and was deeply moved to the point of tears when He came to the tomb.

When Jesus prayed at the tomb His prayer is not what we would expect. He said, *"Father, I thank you that you have heard me. I knew that you always hear me, but I said this for the benefit of the people standing here, that they may believe that you sent me."* Because of Jesus' constant interaction with His Father, we can infer He had been praying about Lazarus for some time.

Once again, the motivation is not to draw attention to Himself or even to alleviate the sorrow of Mary and Martha as rapidly as possible. He is trying to create and build belief in those who are present.

Sometimes God's response is not immediate.

Sometimes God's response is not what we anticipate.

Our prayers are misguided if we assume *how* God will answer.

Our prayers are confident if we understand God listens.

Book Eleven

1. Herod Antipas	Matt 14; Mark 6; Luke 3; 8; 9; 23; Acts 4; 13
2. Herodias	Matthew 14:1-14; Galatians 6:7-8
3. Salome	Matthew 14:6-11; Mark 6: 22-28
4. The Crippled Man	John 5:1-29
5. The Adulterous Woman	John 8
6. The Good Samaritan	Luke 10:25-37
7. The Man Born Blind	John 9:1-41
8. The Rich Fool	Luke 12:13-34
9. Three Parables	Luke 15
10. The Younger Son	Luke 15
11. The Father	Luke 15
12. The Older Brother	Luke 15
13. Zacchaeus	Luke 19:1-10
14. Pontius Pilate	John 18-19
15. Joseph of Arimathea	Matthew 27:32-61
16. Judas Iscariot	Mark 3:19, 14:3-11, 43-49
17. The Dying Thief	Luke 23:26-43
18. Cleopas	Luke 24
19. Thomas	John 20
20. Ananias and Sapphira	Acts 4, 5
21. Stephen	Acts 6, 7
22. Philip the Evangelist	Acts 8
23. Simon the Sorcerer	Acts 8
24. Ananias	Acts 9
25. Cornelius	Acts 10, 11
26. Barnabas	Acts 9, 11, 13
27. John Mark	Acts 13:1-13
28. Lydia	Acts 16:11-15
29. Do the Wicked Prosper?	

Herod Antipas Matthew 14; Mark 6; Luke 3; 8; 9; 23; Acts 4; 13

Antipas appears in the New Testament more frequently than any other member of the Herodian dynasty; his rule coincided with the ministries of John the Baptist and Jesus. This Herod plays a major role in three New Testament narratives.

Death of John the Baptist

Antipas was directly involved in the death of John the Baptist. When John rebuked Antipas for marrying Herodias, Antipas imprisoned him. According to Mark and Matthew, when Herodias's daughter danced at Antipas's birthday party, Antipas was so pleased he offered to give her anything she desired. Her request, at her mother's prompting, was John's head on a platter. Antipas reluctantly granted her request.

Crucifixion of Jesus

Jesus appeared before Antipas during the proceedings prior to His crucifixion. After being interrogated by Pilate, who learned Jesus was Galilean and under the jurisdiction of Antipas, Pilate sent Jesus to appear before Antipas. At first, Antipas was glad to see Jesus and hoped He would perform a miracle. However, after questioning Him and receiving no response, Antipas and his soldiers mocked Jesus and sent Him back to Pilate, concluding He was innocent. Though Antipas' role in the trial and death of Jesus was limited, Luke later records the early church implicated Antipas in Jesus' death along with Pilate, the Gentiles, and the people of Israel (Acts 4).

Reference by Jesus

In Luke 13:31–35, several Pharisees warned Jesus to leave the area because Antipas wished to kill Him. Jesus responded with a message for Antipas, labeling him a "fox." This depiction is fitting given his political shrewdness, his execution of John the Baptist, and his eventual involvement in Jesus' trial.

This descendant of Herod the Great was from Galilee and was a Sadducee. As such he denied a moral law and life after death. Sadducees were also distinguished for their ferocity and inhumanity in their legal roles. This fact makes the remarks of Antipas concerning John the Baptist, whom he beheaded, a remarkable instance of the power of conscience struggling against a man's will and the power of infidelity.

Antipas had a historical profile far from commendable. He was superstitious, inquisitive about truth without loving it, crafty, incestuous and wholly immoral, foxlike in his cunning. John the Baptist, who openly rebuked him for his gross immorality and defiance of the Mosaic Law, paid for his courage with his life.

He was a perfect example of an all-powerful eastern ruler. He was sensual, capricious, yet he seemed to have a sense of honor and had some respect for piety in others; but like Ahab he was too weak to resist a bad woman's influence, under which false moral integrity outweighed true conscientiousness. He ended up, like his father, burdened by superstitious terrors.

Herod wanted to see Jesus, and he managed to do so only during his trial. There he showed he was not really interested in having a personal encounter with Jesus, but rather in meeting a celebrity.

Jesus once thanked the Father for showing the little ones who he really was and hiding it from the wise and the proud.

How can position and family pride keep someone from knowing Jesus?

Can we be small enough to desire a personal encounter with Jesus?

Why do you think pride keeps people form coming to Jesus?

Herodias Matthew 14:1-14; Galatians 6:7-8

Herodias was the daughter of Aristobulus, son of Herod the Great. Her first husband was Philip I, son of Herod the Great, so she married her own uncle, by whom she had a daughter, Salome, whom she used to destroy John the Baptist.

When Herod Antipas visited Rome, he was lodged by Philip and Herodias. Herod stole his royal brother's wife. Herod's current wife, an Arabian princess, was a barrier to the marriage, so he divorced her, and Herodias became queen. The immorality of Herod's family shows itself in this marriage with his brother's wife and the insult to Jewish sensibilities.

There was one man who had no fear of the Herods: John the Baptist. But Herod "feared" John and regarded him as "a just man" and one "he heard gladly."

Antipas was interested in John's message until he was called out by Herodias. John reprimanded the king by saying of Herodias, "It is not lawful for you to have her." But such a warning was to be the key to John's doom. For his faithful rebuke of Herod's sin, John was cast into prison, and the evil, scheming mind of Herodias began to work.

She was stung by the charge from this strange man from the desert. She hated him for exposing her sin. "For Herodias's sake," he was imprisoned and so the greatest of the prophets was to be sacrificed for her evil lifestyle. Herodias, her conscience in turmoil, planned to silence John. She did not want Herod to listen too closely to John's forceful preaching. She feared her new husband might repent and her position as queen could be endangered.

Herodias knew her husband very well. He easily yielded to sensual excitement, and as his birthday drew near her plan emerged. At his birthday party Herodias used her own daughter to inflame Herod's passions. Herod was overcome by Salome's beauty. He was influenced by the act of the dancing girl and made a rash and foolish oath to give her whatever she asked, even to half of his kingdom. Approaching her mother, Salome said, "What shall I ask?" Without hesitation Herodias, replied, "Ask for the head of John the Baptist."

Because of his oath Herod ordered the execution of John. No wonder he was later struck with fear when he heard of the fame of Jesus, thinking it was John the Baptist risen from the dead to torment his conscience.

Herodias has been likened to Jezebel. What Herodias was to Herod, Jezebel was to Ahab! Both Ahab and Herod were wicked, and in both cases the woman was more wicked. Both Jezebel and Herodias fostered hate which became deadly against a prophet of God.

Jezebel hated Elijah and tried to kill him; Herodias hated John the Baptist and succeeded in his murder.

What was the end of Herodias? She was the source of Herod's sin and she became the source of his shame. According to Josephus, Herodias's ambition was the ruin of Herod. Jealous of the power of Agrippa her brother, she prodded Herod to demand the title of king.

Agrippa saw to it that this demand was refused, and Herod was banished and ended his days in shame and exile.

The pride of Herodias forced her to live in shame with her husband in the disgrace and misfortune she herself had caused.

Do you see the similarities between Herodias and Jezebel?

Salome Matthew 14:6-11; Mark 6:22-28

Salome is the feminine form of Solomon and is the Greek form in shalom meaning "peace."

The New Testament does not give her name. It is Josephus the Jewish historian who identifies her as Salome.

She was the daughter of Herodias by her first husband, Herod Philip, a son of Herod the Great. Josephus tells us Salome was married first to Philip the tetrarch, and afterward to Aristobulus, king of Chalcis, the grandson of Herod, and brother of Agrippa.

Mention has already been made of the part Salome played at the birthday of Herod and how, because of her sensual dancing, John the Baptist was beheaded, and ultimately Herod lost his kingdom.

The evil heart of Herodias planned the seduction of Salome's dance.

The daughter of Herodias is mentioned, but not named, in the Gospels (Matt. 14:3–11; Mark 6:17–28). She danced in front of many guests at this banquet given by her uncle and stepfather Herod Antipas. He was so enamored by the young woman and her dance that he offered to give her anything she desired.

At the instigation of her mother, she requested the head of John the Baptist on a platter. Josephus, who does not recount this incident, gives the location of John's imprisonment and death as the Herodian fortress of Machaerus; he also gives Salome's name and says she later married her uncle Herod Philip the tetrarch.

The story of her dance before Herod, the beheading of John the Baptist, and the presentation of his head on a silver platter led medieval Christian artists to depict her as the personification of the sexually erotic woman, a temptress who lures men away from God.

Christian traditions also portray her as the image of the dangerous female because of her seductiveness. This was notably true in regard to the dance mentioned in the New Testament, which is thought to have had an erotic effect on Antipas. In later transformations her dance has become legendary as the Dance of the Seven Veils.

Other elements of Christian tradition concentrate on her lighthearted and cold foolishness. A similar theme was struck by Oscar Wilde in his story *Salome*, in which she plays the role of femme fatale. This parallel representation of the Christian tradition has been made even more memorable by Richard Strauss' opera based on Wilde's work.

According to the Roman Jewish historian, Salome lived long enough to marry twice and raise several children. Few literary accounts elaborate the biographical data given by Josephus.

Despite Josephus' account, she was not consistently called Salome until the 19th century when Gustave Flaubert, following Josephus, referred to her as "Salome" in his short story "Herodias."

How can sin control people? Is there a sin you struggle with?

What can we learn from the negative example of these people about preventing sin from getting out of control?

The Crippled Man by the Pool of Bethesda — John 5:1-29

This nameless man appears near the pool of Bethesda at one of the great Jewish feasts. Because of this great Jewish festival there are many thousands of visitors present in the city. Gathered around this pool were many hopeless people wanting to be cured by the appearance of an angel at the pool.

One writer describes these people as ill-kept, foul-smelling, and pathetic. Many of the visitors in the city because of the feast would have regarded this scene with great irritation. For the Jerusalem city officials, it was probably regarded with embarrassment.

During this unpleasant situation, Jesus' attitude was far different from the others. He was moved with compassion toward the huge crowd and His attention was drawn to this particular man who had lain helpless in the area for 38 years.

Jesus approached the man and asked him, "Do you want to be healed?" When asked this question the man began to answer with excuses. There was no one to help him! He could not do it himself! Of course, he wanted to be healed. But he could see no way this could happen in his situation. He was completely preoccupied with his own problems and had no idea with whom he was speaking.

Jesus told the man, "Get up, take up your bed, and walk." This was entirely impossible, and the invalid knew it. Nevertheless, we are told the man obeyed Jesus, picked up his mat, and began to walk. We do not know when he became aware of the restoration of his body; this is not revealed to us in the text.

What we do see is faith is always the condition of divine blessing and here, as usual, it requires a demonstration of obedience by action. John tells us the man had no idea with whom he was speaking. Yet he was obedient, and God honored his obedience.

The newly-healed man soon encountered the religious kill-joys in the area. He was told it was the Sabbath day and he was not allowed to carry his mat. The healed man replied to his accusers, "The man who healed me, that man said to me, 'Take up your bed and walk.'"

These religious hypocrites asked him who the man was who had healed him and had ordered him to break the Sabbath. The man told them he did not know the man's name. As John completes his account, he tells us Jesus later found the man in the Temple. The verb used for "found" is a word which indicates Jesus was looking for the man. In the course of His conversation with the newly healed man, He told him who He was.

This unnamed man, full of joy, went searching for those who had asked who had healed him. He told them it was Jesus.

There are some who acquire a preference for ill health. They have a satisfaction in their own suffering. This man could have abandoned hope after nearly four decades of waiting.

He was ready to embrace what the Lord gave him.

The basic problem of Sabbath observation in Jesus' day was an exaggerated emphasis on legalism which blinded many to the need for the relief of suffering. The Pharisees considered only the external legal aspects.

Jesus considered the motive.

They were concerned with an institution.

Jesus was concerned with the man.

he Adulterous Woman — John 8

We do not know this woman's name and there is no tradition of a name associated with her. These events took place in the city of Jerusalem during the feast of Tabernacles in the fall of the year. This was one of the great celebrations of Judaism. The people built small shelters or "booths" and lived in them to remember the time of the wilderness wanderings.

The events described here occurred during one of the most festive occasions of Judaism. All Jewish men were required by the law to attend the three great feasts each year. These were the feasts of Passover (in the spring), Weeks (summer), and Tabernacles (fall).

When the Feast of Tabernacles was observed, people lived in small, temporary shelters they built around Jerusalem to remember their ancestral journeying through the wilderness. Tens of thousands gathered around Jerusalem in what was a very festive atmosphere. In this type of situation women such as the one described in this account made their living.

The Scribes and Pharisees used this convergence of circumstances to try and embarrass Jesus. He had a reputation as a teacher of love and forgiveness. If He condemned the woman, He would soon lose His following among the common people and if He failed to condemn the woman, they would charge Him with ignoring the Law of Moses. They felt they had created the "perfect trap." They brought the woman to Jesus and asked Him what should be done. *In the Law, Moses commanded us to stone such women. Now what do you say?"*

This scene occurred in one of the outer courts of the Temple. During this feast there were thousands of people in these areas. I am sure the Pharisees created quite a scene as they pulled this woman through the outer court of Temple area to Jesus. A crowd quickly gathered to see what was going on. John tells us, "*They were using this question as a trap, in order to have a basis for accusing him. But Jesus bent down and started to write on the ground with his finger.*"

The longer Jesus spent writing on the ground the more loudly her accusers demanded an answer from Jesus. Finally, Jesus stood up, looked at them and said, "*All right, stone her. But let those who have never sinned throw the first stones!*"

When the Scribes and Pharisees who had brought the accusation heard His statement they slowly began to slip away into the crowd. Jesus looked at the woman and asked her, "*Where are your accusers? Didn't even one of them condemn you?*" Jesus told her He would not condemn her either. She should go and stop living a life of sin.

How quickly and self-righteously we bring before Jesus the sins of others while overlooking and denying our own sins. These hypocrites were guilty of sin in their own lives and were unwilling to face it. They claimed concern for truth and justice but were arrogantly using the woman who had fallen into their hands.

How would you react if a dirty, unkept person came to you in public and acted as if you were a friend?

Do you know someone who only uses people?

Do you use people?

In their anger at Jesus they made her life cheap.

How should we treat people who have sinned?

About what do you tend to be self-righteous?

The Good Samaritan Luke 10:25-37

In our three preceding studies we have examined people who were not given names. In this study we will look at a man who not only is not named, but in all probability, did not exist. He was part of a parable which Jesus created in order to make a point. In a discussion Jesus was having with a lawyer He had been asked the question, "Who is my neighbor?" This story is told in response to that question.

The story features four people. There is a traveler who was going to Jericho. On the way he was robbed, beaten, and left for dead. As Jesus told the story the man was encountered by a priest and a Levite. Both of these "models" of society passed the needy man and did nothing. Soon afterward, a Samaritan came upon the injured person.

When the Samaritan saw the man in need he stopped and helped him. We are told he anointed his wounds, bound them, set him on his own animal, and took him to an inn to be cared for.

When they arrived at the inn the Samaritan instructed the innkeeper to "Take care of him and whatever more you spend I will repay you when I come back."

Having finished the story, Jesus questioned the expert in the law, asking him who had been a neighbor to the wounded man. Basically, Jesus was forcing the legal expert to answer his own question, "Who is my neighbor?"

Which of these three, the priest, the Levite, or the Samaritan, had kept the law?

The priest and Levite were obliged by the law to help the victim, but the law also told them not to touch a dead body. They chose religious purity over service to a man in desperate need.

They loved themselves more than their neighbor; they loved keeping the letter of the law over loving a person in need. In so doing, they broke the law.

The Samaritan, unrestricted by concerns over religious purity, was free to serve and he did so. The legal expert had no choice but to admit the man who was a neighbor to the wounded man was the one who showed him mercy: the Samaritan.

The Samaritan traveler and the injured Jewish man were far apart in distance and spiritual heritage, but the Samaritan had loved his neighbor far better than the wounded man's own religious leaders.
Jesus said the legal expert answered correctly and told him he should go and do the same. Jesus taught love is shown by action, it should never be limited by its object.

In this story, the Samaritan was extremely generous, and Jesus highlighted his helpful actions. Generosity inspired by God does more than

- cook the meal; it lights the candles
- say grace; it prays God's blessing on each one present
- pass the food; it draws people into friendly conversation
- clear the table; it washes the dishes.

When you see a job to do, go overboard.

Do it to show just an ounce of what God's care for you is like.

Do it with all the joy God has put in your heart.

The Man Born Blind John 9:1-41

One day as Jesus was walking in Jerusalem, He saw a man who had been blind from birth. Jesus and the disciples recognized the condition of this man. The disciples began to discuss the possible reasons for his blindness. As they discussed among themselves, they raised various theological questions: was this condition the result of sin in his parents' life, or could it be a result of sin in his past life? They were puzzled by the injustice of his situation, but it just seemed to them an abstract problem. They showed no concern for the man himself.

Jesus saw the man in an entirely different way; this man was a person with a deep need. The situation called for action not debate. He told the disciples neither of the situations they were discussing was the reason this man was blind. The man's condition was an opportunity for God to be glorified.

An interesting aspect of the situation to consider is the blind man was sitting there by the side of the road and listening to this discussion. Surely as he listened it was painful and discouraging for him. As always, he was being treated as an object and not as a person.

Jesus now acted. He spit on the ground, made clay, and smeared it on the man's eyes. He told him to go and wash in the pool of Siloam. The blind man did exactly as he was told. He washed and was able to see.

Why would Jesus even consider performing this miracle when He knew the problems it would create for Him and the disciples? He could not benefit personally, and He would be creating a great deal of trouble and opposition for Himself. It was, after all, the Sabbath day!

He knew He would be challenged and knew the blind man who had been healed would be harassed as well. The healing did cause great controversy and a great deal of debate.

The religious leaders called his parents and spoke with them. His parents were afraid of these men and their power; they answered, "This is our son who was born blind, but we do not know what has happened to him." The religious leaders went to the man who had been healed and asked him what had happened and how he had been cured. He told them exactly what Jesus had done.

He did not know who had healed him, but he was sure this man was from God. No one since the beginning of creation had been able to accomplish anything like this. He faced harassment and he was expelled from the synagogue. But he refused to yield to their criticism.

Jesus later found him and spoke with him to encourage his faith. Jesus asked the man do you believe on the Son of God. The man's reply was "Who is he that I may believe on him?" Further emphasizing the completeness of the miracle, Jesus answered, "You have seen him and is he who speaks to you at this moment." The Bible tells us the man worshiped him!

In this account there are several lessons for us to observe.
Who are you more like?

- The disciples who were seeking a theological discussion
- The neighbors - who were just indifferent
- The Pharisees - who lost the light they once had and lapsed into complete spiritual darkness
- The blind man - who gained physical and spiritual light through faith

Would you rather talk theology or tell people about Jesus?

Why are people indifferent to the difficulties of others?

The Rich Fool Luke 12:13-34

In His teaching Jesus emphasized the need to act with honor and justice. Someone in the crowd asked Jesus to resolve a dispute about an inheritance. Jesus told this story to expose the motives of greed and self-interest. God's perspective on the desire for material things is that it is absolutely and totally foolish.

All of Jesus' teaching gives us a glimpse into God's perspective of our daily lives. This parable probably gives us the clearest picture of God's point of view in relationship to human greed.

The rich man in this story had everything he would ever need for the rest of his earthly life. He decided what he would do was pull down his barns and build bigger barns. He would become a "hoarder." He would collect everything he possibly could and keep it to himself.

Literally translated, the text says, he "dialogued with himself." This is a very sad scene. In the Middle East, village people make decisions about important topics after long discussions with their friends. Families, communities, and villages are tightly knit together. Everybody's business is everybody else's business. Even trivial decisions are made after hours of discussion with family and friends. But this man appears to have no friends. He lives in isolation from the human family around him, and with an important decision to make the only person with whom he can have a dialogue is himself.

Some well-known responses to surpluses include:

- Hide them
- Flaunt them
- Spend them on expensive vacations
- Upgrade one's lifestyle

God said to him in no uncertain terms, "*You are a fool! Tonight, you will die and what good will all of your 'stuff' be?"* This man thought he was going to live for many years and enjoy his "stuff," but it didn't work that way. Jesus warned against greed for possessions. Greed keeps track of every tool borrowed, every dime shared, every overtime minute worked, every check to charity grudgingly written. Jesus leads the way to generosity, a rare trait today.

As you move closer to God you will hold on to what you own less and share more of what you have been given. Pension plans and life insurance are synonymous with wise stewardship. Everyone should provide for older age and family survivors. At the same time and with the same resolve we must realize life is more than money.

God wants us to share generously today with those who are poor. And, should wealth accumulate, never, never put your hope and pride in real estate, insurance, or mutual funds. God should be your security and joy. The rich fool failed to account for his mortality. He failed in securing both his life and his possessions. Human life is on loan from God. It is a gift, not a right. The rich man assumed he owned his own soul. He discovered his mistake when God suddenly asked for the loan of his life to be returned.

Trust in the Lord with all your heart and do not lean to your own understanding. In all your ways acknowledge him and he will direct your path. **Proverbs 3:5-6**

What signs of greed can show up in a person's life?

On what basis would you like your life to be judged?

With what parts of the parable can you identify?

What parts of the parable make you uncomfortable?

Three Parables **Luke 15:1-31**

The first two parables in this chapter build to the climax, the parable of the lost son, a parable which is unique to Luke. Through these parables Jesus presents a vivid illustration of God and His mercy for repentant sinners.

Jesus taught these parables in His ministry in Galilee. This was near the midpoint of His three-year ministry. This entire chapter can be viewed as one extended parable with three specific and separate parts. This teaching came in response to the grumbling of the Pharisees and teachers of the law about Jesus associating with "sinners."

Jesus told three separate stories:

- The story of the lost sheep
- The story of the lost coin
- The story of the lost son

As you read these stories notice a common denominator in each account which is often overlooked. In each case, finding what was lost resulted in rejoicing (5, 9, 24).

There is another fact in these stories which is worth examining. There is a decreasing ratio regarding what was lost:

- The story of the lost sheep 1 in a 100
- The story of the lost coin 1 in 10
- The story of the lost son 1 in 2

Jesus constantly emphasizes the rejoicing in heaven when the lost "one" is found. No matter how large the crowd the one will be sought. In the final story there are three major points of emphasis in this story:

- The lost son
- The father
- The elder son

Each of these has a lesson to teach us.

The younger son was rebellious and foolish. He wasted everything his father had given him.

The father had been seeking his son every day. He was willing to receive him home unconditionally. When his son appeared and confessed the error of his ways, he quickly restored him to his position with no reservation.

The elder brother became jealous and angry. He felt all he had been doing was unappreciated. Even when his father explained the joy of having his son back, he seems to have remained unreconciled to his brother.

These three stories show us the love of God and His willingness to seek one person.

They also illustrate the unconditional nature of God's love.

They show us the joy in heaven over a sinner who comes back to God.

They also show us the emptiness of self-righteousness.

The Younger Son Luke 15:1-31

Normally the son would have received his inheritance at his father's death. Fathers sometimes chose to divide up their inheritance early and retire from managing their estates. What is unusual is the younger son initiated the division of the estate. This showed arrogant disregard for his father's authority as head of the family.

After he received his inheritance the younger son was on his way, indicating this had been his plan when he had asked for his inheritance in the first place.

He packed all his belongings and got as far away from his family as possible. He traveled to a "distant land" where he was not dominated by Jewish law.

The young man apparently wanted to live his own way, be his own master, get out from under the rules of his home and his father. Money was his ticket out, so he took it and ran. In this distant land, he wasted all his money on wild living.

So, he lived on the wild side for a while, spending freely on whatever he chose. But then his money ran out.

Young people need to plan for the future while they're still young. Two more years of school now, painful as it may appear, could mean a career they would not otherwise have. Plan for the unexpected even when your immediate needs seem immense. The young son in this story wasted his money just before a famine.

Thinking ahead is a Christian's duty, yet many treat it as a useless hindrance to moving on. Wild living may offer short-term thrills, but it's all a waste. Your treasure and time are God's gifts. Use them for Him.

The young man became so desperate he hired himself out to work feeding pigs. For a Jew to stoop to feeding pigs would have been a great humiliation, and even beyond this, this young man's life fell to the point where he wanted to eat the food being given to the pigs. He was degraded beyond belief.

Sitting among pigs which were better fed than he was, he reflected on life back home. He realized at home even the hired men had more than enough food.

With no money, no dignity, and, so he thought, no claim to sonship in his father's household, he decided to go home, confess his sin, and ask to be taken on as a hired man. At least there he would not go hungry.

While his motivation at first seems to have been his hunger, he could have saved his pride by never going back. Instead, this young man chose to go home. His understanding is revealed in the words that he planned to say to his father: "I have sinned against both heaven and you."

It often takes great sorrow and tragedy to cause people to look to the only one who can help them.

Youth loves freedom and needs a growing portion of it. Youth needs family, friends, and community to provide the solid base of identity and support.

Are you trying to live your own way, selfishly pushing aside any responsibility or commitment that gets in your way? Stop and look before you hit bottom. You will save yourself and your family much grief.

In what way did you and your siblings compete with each other?

How do you feel when other people get rewards greater than they deserve?

The Father Luke 15:1-31

The son returned home to his father, not knowing what to expect. The best he could possibly anticipate was a cold shoulder, a halfhearted welcome, but in hopes of being hired to work for his father he returned.

The father, however, seems to have watched the horizon daily since his son had left. He was hoping one day to see him returning. Finally, his father saw him coming even while he was far away. The father ran, embraced, and kissed his son. He was filled with love and compassion at the sight of his son who had come home. For the patriarch of the family to run was to lose all caution and dignity. The father went beyond normal forgiveness and showed incredible love. The son began to give his father the speech he had prepared (15:19), but he didn't even get to the part about asking to be hired, for the father wanted to welcome his son back into his home with a grand celebration.

In the two preceding stories, the seeker actively looked for the sheep and the coin, which could not return by themselves. In this story, the father watched and waited. He was dealing with a human being with a will, but he was ready to greet his son if he returned.

In the same way, God's love is constant and patient and welcoming. He will search and give people opportunities to respond, but He will not force them to come to Him.

Like the father in this story, God waits patiently for people to come to their senses.

This father's love and compassion picture the love God has always shown to his wayward people. The psalmist wrote: *"As a father has compassion on his children, so the Lord has compassion on those who fear him."* (Psalm 103:13)

Jeremiah the prophet wrote: *"So there is hope for your future,"* declares the Lord. *"Your children will return to their own land. I have surely heard Ephraim's moaning: 'You disciplined me like an unruly calf, and I have been disciplined. Restore me, and I will return, because you are the Lord my God. After I strayed, I repented; after I came to understand, I beat my breast. I was ashamed and humiliated because I bore the disgrace of my youth.' Is not Ephraim my dear son, the child in whom I delight? Though I often speak against him, I still remember him. Therefore, my heart yearns for him; I have great compassion for him," declares the Lord.* (Jeremiah 31:17-20)

God's love reaches out to sinners who, repenting of their sin, come to Him for forgiveness. They can be assured of a warm welcome from the one who has been watching for them to come.

In the first century a father would typically wait until a son showed some sign of respect before addressing him, here the father threw all social conventions aside.

He couldn't wait to see his son. He started running toward him. With open arms, he hugged his son, pulling him tightly to himself.

God is like this loving father.

He wants to welcome sinners back home with open arms. This parable is a picture of God's grace. Thank Him for showing this type of compassion to you.

How does the forgiving love of the father in this story God's love and forgiveness to us?

How have you been like the prodigal son in this story?

What can you do to thank God for His amazing love for you?

The older brother, according to tradition, would have received a double inheritance. While he would inherit it, this would not take place until his father's death. So, he was in the fields working, "being responsible" to do the work he should do, patiently following the typical plan for passing on the family inheritance.

Imagine this older brother's surprise at returning from a day of hard work to the sound of a grand celebration going on in the house. Naturally he wondered what was going on. He asked a servant, who told him: the sinful brother has returned, the calf has been killed, the feast has been prepared, and everyone is celebrating the brother's safe return. The older brother became angry and refused to join the celebration.

In this parable the father's response is contrasted with the older brother's

- The father forgave because he was filled with love
- The son refused to forgive because he was bitter about what he saw as injustice

The older son's resentment made him just as lost to the father's love as his younger brother had been. The older son was quite reasonable in his list of complaints.

The father could have pacified his older son with more gifts and rewards. But relationships prosper on love, not on fairness! When relationships need love, we often must let fairness take a back seat.

The key to understanding this story is found in the context of 15:1-2. The younger son stands for the tax collectors and sinners, the waiting father is God, and the older brother represents the religious leaders.

The younger son had lived as a sinner, so the brother wanted nothing to do with him. The father, who had gone out to meet his younger son, also went out to plead with his older one. Instead of acknowledging his father's words, the older son let out a torrent of pent-up anger and frustration, telling how he had been slaving away for his father, never getting any special favors.

He did not take time to understand he would inherit everything he was working for and he was dearly loved by his father. He only felt anger because his father was celebrating "your son's" (not "my brother's") return. Why should he celebrate for an irresponsible person, when the model son got nothing comparable?

The religious leaders always claimed how hard they "slaved" for God. They were attempting to keep all the rules and regulations, many of which God never even demanded. They had the Father's love but had chosen to reject it in favor of hard work and self-denial. When God eagerly welcomed the sinful, common people into the kingdom, the religious leaders refused to join the celebration. But God rejoiced when these sinful people came home, and He invited these religious leaders to join the party. But they reacted with anger and resentment.

People who repent after leading sinful lives are often viewed with suspicion.

Instead, we should rejoice like the angels in heaven when an unbeliever repents and turns to God.

Like the father in the parable, accept repentant sinners truly and give them the support and encouragement they need to grow in Christ.

How can you guard yourself against feeling resentment when God shows mercy to people you think don't deserve it?

How can you show acceptance to someone who doesn't seem to deserve it? When?

Zacchaeus Luke 19:1-10

We are told Jesus "was passing through." He chose not to accept the hospitality of the community. He was on His way to Jerusalem and did not intend to stay the night in Jericho. No doubt the public is deeply upset.

Zacchaeus is identified as the town tax collector and a rich man. The system of taxation in place was called "tax farming." The local person who acquired the right to collect taxes for Rome was expected to turn over a specific amount at the end of the year. The "collector" could collect any amount he could. The man was despised, he and his entire family were considered unclean. The system created corruption and economic injustice. It was bad enough Zacchaeus was a tax collector, but he had become rich in the process. In the vocabulary of the day "tax collectors" and "sinners" were often paired. The town hated its chief Roman collaborator.

Zacchaeus wanted to see Jesus but was unable to do so "because of the crowd." His problem was he was short and hated. Were he respected, the crowd would naturally have "made way" for such a rich and powerful person. But Zacchaeus was the "collector" collaborator and despised. He could not ask the crowd to make way for him and doubtless was afraid even to mix with them.

Collaborators did not mix in crowds. They were always careful about "their backs." This problem was greatly intensified since he was short. What would happen to him if he dared push his way into the crowd? The quick flash of a knife, a stifled cry, and it would all be over. Only after the crowd moved on would the body be found and by then the culprits would be gone. Yet Zacchaeus wanted to see Jesus. To accomplish this, he carried out two highly unusual acts: he ran, and he climbed a tree.

Despite Zacchaeus' hope of remaining unseen, he was spotted. We know this because when Jesus reached the tree, He looked up and called out Zacchaeus' name. If Jesus can see Zacchaeus, so can the crowd. But how did Jesus learn Zacchaeus' name?

The natural explanation for Jesus' awareness of Zacchaeus' name and history is all this information is heard by Jesus from the crowd which was insulting the humiliated man caught up a tree. The crowd was hurling all the insults they had wanted to use for years. One insult kindled others, quickly darkening the atmosphere and likely producing a whiff of anticipated violence.

Jesus perceptively sized up the tensions of the scene and decided to intervene. Zacchaeus was rescued. The tax collector hosted a banquet for Jesus and those travelling with Him that evening. Zacchaeus felt he should honor the courageous man who had "crossed the picket line" and entered his house as his guest for the night and by so doing has taken upon Himself the hostility of an entire town.

Zacchaeus responds with acceptance and belief of Jesus' message. He says he will pay back fourfold anyone he has cheated.

Zacchaeus is the recipient of costly love. Perhaps for the first time in years he has experienced unqualified acceptance and love.

How has gossip affected you in the past?

Why do people pay attention to tabloids?

Why do you think people pay attention to gossip and rumors?

How does a person's reputation affect our opinion of them?

God's love is a powerful life-changing force.

Pontius Pilate John 18-19

Pontius, his family name, indicates he was connected by descent or adoption to the family of Ponti. We have no knowledge of this family. Pilate's surname is typically Roman. It is modeled on Greek and Roman mythology. The meaning is, "Pikeman, someone armed with a javelin."

The early history of Pilate is unknown except for a few unreliable legends. He repeatedly angered the Jews with his disregard for their Jewish faith. On two occasions he caused confrontations with the Jews which nearly led to rebellion. He was appointed governor of Judea by Tiberius in 26.

Pilate is primarily known because of his interaction with Jesus during the trial that led to the crucifixion of Jesus.

Jesus actually appeared before Pilate in two "trials." The first trial began when Jesus was brought to the judgment hall of Caiaphas. Jesus was charged with treason against Rome by claiming to be the Messiah of the Jews and the King.

When Pilate examined Jesus on this charge Jesus replied His kingdom was not a kingdom of this world. After further examination Pilate stood before the Jewish accusers of Jesus and told them he could find no fault in this man and there was no reason to spend further time on the case.

After Pilate found Jesus was from Galilee, he sent Jesus to Herod who was the ruler of the region. After questioning Jesus, Herod returned Him to Pilate for final judgment.

Once again Pilate examined Jesus and was unable to find any guilt in His actions or His comments. Pilate wanted to release Jesus, but he was afraid of the political influence of the Jewish leaders.

He ordered Jesus to be beaten in the hope that would placate the anger of the Jewish mob. When he announced his decision that the prisoner would be beaten and released the Jewish leaders were able to whip the crowd into a rage; they continued to demand the death of Jesus.

There was a custom during the Passover for a prisoner to be released. Pilate even attempted to use this custom to free Jesus, but this tactic failed as well.

He ultimately gave in to the crowd and ordered the crucifixion of Jesus.

Even though this man was an important political leader he was manipulated by his fear of losing power. He knew Jesus was guilty of no crime; yet he ordered Him put to death.

What a different story this would have been if Pilate had followed his own conscience and declared Jesus not guilty.

The application for us is clear; we must be careful not to allow our desires and circumstances to control our actions when it comes to decisions of right and wrong.

How could a politician rationalize bending the rules in order to please a group of concerned citizens?

When have you been tempted to do what works rather than what's right?

Why is it easier to observe religious traditions than to love other people?

Pilate was a weak man controlled by his passion and desire to be powerful and important.

Joseph means "may God increase" or "may God add." He is called "Joseph of Arimathea." Arimathea was a small village northwest of Jerusalem.

Even though he came from a small and insignificant village in Judea, he was a respected member of the Jewish Sanhedrin Council. The fact he had a private tomb and was able to provide the linen as a wrapping for the body of Jesus is evidence of his ample wealth.

Luke describes him as a good and upright man (Luke 23:50). John describes him as "a disciple of Jesus, but secretly, because he feared the Jews" (John 19:38).

The crucifixion of Jesus seems to have made him much bolder. As a member of the Sanhedrin Council, he was informed about the discussion and planning of the events relating to the crucifixion of Jesus.

We can speculate he was frustrated and angry over the outcome of that evening. He used his position and standing in the Jewish community to go to Pilate and asked for permission to take the body of Jesus down from the cross (Mark 15:43-46).

This implies Joseph himself took the body of Jesus down from the cross. With the assistance of Nicodemus, he wound it in the fine linen and spices he had brought to the tomb.

The Scripture says they, Joseph and Nicodemus, laid him in the tomb. This would have been a very unusual activity for a person of his stature and wealth. I think it shows the character and devotion Jesus' death created in this man.

There are a number of legends which tell stories of Joseph. According to "The Gospel of Peter," an apocryphal book written in the middle of the second century, Joseph was "the friend of Pilate and the Lord." He was present at the trial of Jesus and immediately upon its conclusion asked Pilate for the body.

Legends of a later origin record Joseph was sent by Philip from Gaul to England with the "Holy Grail." He was also supposed to have been instrumental in the building of a church at Glastonbury. There is also another legend that it was he, Joseph, who freed Ireland from snakes, not Saint Patrick.

What can we make of the available information we have about this man? The crucifixion of Jesus seems to have given him a new strength and boldness. Before the crucifixion he had been a secret disciple; after the crucifixion he was willing to face the Roman governor and ask for the body of Jesus.

After the ascension he seems to have become a preacher of the gospel of Jesus and traveled wherever the Holy Spirit led him!

In what ways are you a secret disciple of Christ, afraid to publicly follow Him?

How would your reputation suffer if you let it be known your main desire in life is to love and serve Jesus Christ?

When, if ever, is it inappropriate to use your power and position to support Christ and His work?

What new possessions would you be willing to part with for the sake of Christ?

Judas Iscariot — Mark 3:19, 14:3-11, 43-49

His name means "praise." The word *Iscariot* literally means "the man from Kerioth." Kerioth was a town in southern Judea. Thus, Judas was the only non-Galilean among the twelve apostles.

Judas was a thief!
John tells of Mary anointing the feet of Jesus in his gospel. When Mary performed this act of worship Judas was only concerned with the value of the oil she used. The oil was expensive and was often given as part of a girl's dowry. It could be worth as much as a year's wage.

John adds this comment in 12:6; "*Judas said this not because he cared for the poor but because he was a thief. He was the treasurer for the apostles and often helped himself to the money in the bag.*"

Judas was a traitor!
The New Testament speaks of the sin of Judas at least 16 times. The Scriptures make it clear Satan was behind the behavior of this man. Jesus referred to Judas as "the son of perdition" (John 17:12).

Judas was surrendered to following Satan from the very beginning of Christ's ministry. Jesus said, "*I have chosen you twelve and one of you is the devil.*"

The Gospels tell us Satan entered Judas twice:

- Luke 22:3 - Before the events recorded in the upper room the night of Jesus arrest: "*Satan entered into Judas.*"

- John 13:27 - in the upper room, during the Last Supper: "*After the bread, Satan entered into him. Jesus said to him, what you are going to do, do quickly.*"

Judas sold out Jesus for 30 pieces of silver. These 30 silver shekels were equal to 120 denarii, less than $25, then the current price of a slave. There was no doubt contempt for Jesus in the minds of both the Sanhedrin and Judas in this bargain.

When Judas saw the result of his treacherous bargain, he tried to give the money back, however, the religious authorities refused to accept the money because it was blood money. In agony over his deed, Judas threw the money onto the Temple pavement and hanged himself (Matthew 27:5)

A few verses later Matthew makes this observation, "*Then what was spoken by Jeremiah the prophet was fulfilled: "They took the thirty silver coins, the price set on him by the people of Israel, then they used them to buy the potter's field, as the Lord commanded me* " (27:7-8).

Judas was led by "the father of lies." He became a thief and a traitor.

Judas is a graphic example of the lies Satan tells and the results of following his lies.

Why did Jesus' disciples desert Him?

When are you most tempted to compromise your commitment to Christ?

How can we prepare for those times?

The Dying Thief — Luke 23:26-43

Have you ever heard two people describe the same thing from totally different perspectives, a football game, a movie or a television program? Their descriptions could sound so different you may wonder if they are talking about the same event.

Luke recorded something similar in our text for today. Two convicted criminals were dying the same horrifying death, on opposite sides of the cross of Jesus. One saw another failed opportunity to get himself off the hook; the other saw and understood the way of salvation was opening for himself and the whole world.

The first thief said, "*Aren't you the Christ? Save yourself and us!*" Both thieves ridiculed Jesus. They "*hurled insults*" at Him. The religious leaders were vigorously and openly berating Jesus. No doubt the thieves were emboldened by the hatred of the religious folks.

One of the thieves had a change of heart! Our text says one of the condemned men "*rebuked*" the other. They deserved their punishment; Jesus had done absolutely nothing wrong.

It is possible this thief had heard Jesus speak or even viewed some of His miracles. Hanging on the cross, next to the creator of the universe, this man came face to face with his sin, the reality of the perfection of God and the need for reconciliation with God. He reached out to Jesus in belief and asked for salvation.

He said, "*Jesus, remember me when you come into your Kingdom.*" What kingdom was he thinking about? They were physically dying, there was no hope of physical salvation!

The dying criminal had more faith than all of Jesus' followers put together. Although the disciples continued to love Jesus, their hopes for the kingdom had been lost. Most of them had gone into hiding. As one of his followers would sadly say two days later, "*We had hoped that He was the one who was going to redeem Israel*"

Jesus answered the thief and told him, "*Today you will be with me in paradise.*" This man who had lived a sinful, dissolute life which resulted in the sentence of death was saved by turning to Jesus and asking for His help. The first man died in his sins; the second received the gift of forgiveness and eternal life. Perspective makes all the difference.

Ask God to help you get or maintain proper perspective in your walk with Him. We must all remember we are, "*Only sinners saved by grace.*"

We must do all we can to maintain that perspective. As children of God we understand we should not think of ourselves more highly than we think of others. It is never too late to turn to God. Even in His own misery and pain, Jesus had mercy on this criminal who decided to believe in Him.

People's lives are more useful and fulfilling if they turn to God early, but even those who repent at the very last moment will be with God in paradise.

What can you learn from the actions of the repentant criminal?

Why didn't both criminals plead for mercy from Jesus?

What prevents many people from turning to Jesus?

How can we help others see "today" is the time of opportunity?

His name means "the whole or all of the glory." The only place we meet this man is on a road outside of Jerusalem traveling to the village of Emmaus. The events described in this chapter occurred a couple of days after the crucifixion.

Cleopas is only mentioned in this account in Luke 24. He may be the same person who is named in John 19:25. "*Near the cross of Jesus stood his mother, his mother's sister, Mary the wife of Clopas, and Mary Magdalene.*" Clopas is a variant spelling of Cleopas.

He was one of the followers of Jesus. He was able to share some of the discussion he had been part of in Jerusalem relating to the events of the crucifixion. Jesus asked him what he and his companion had been discussing as they were walking along the road. Cleopas told this stranger of the hopes he and others had *of the coming of the Jewish kingdom. He said they had been talking* "about Jesus of Nazareth." "He was a prophet, powerful in word and deed before God and all the people. The chief priests and our rulers handed him over to be sentenced to death, and they crucified him; but we had hoped that he was the one who was going to redeem Israel. And what is more, it is the third day since all this took place."

His hopes and dreams had been shattered. He and his friend were struggling with discouragement and depression. Even in his disheartened condition Cleopas had not lost his ability to act as a good host. He invited Jesus to stay with them that evening. As they ate the evening meal together Jesus was able to give them new hope.

Jesus very carefully opened the Scriptures to them as they talked. He explained the meaning of the Old Testament prophecies relating to the death of the Messiah. Without harshly rebuking them he explained to them their misunderstanding of the kingdom. This was not the time for Jesus to establish the physical kingdom, Jesus was establishing His spiritual kingdom.

They suddenly realized who was teaching them when He prayed, and they began to eat. "*Their eyes were opened and they knew him.*" Then He disappeared from their sight.

They immediately got up and began their return journey to the city of Jerusalem. They knew where to go to find the 11 disciples of Jesus. They met with them and explained that Jesus had appeared to them and they were informed Jesus had also appeared to Simon Peter.

What if Cleopas had refused to answer the question of Jesus? What if he had replied, "Oh nothing, I don't want to talk about it"?

Have you thought about how tired these two must have been after the events of the crucifixion and their journey along the dusty road home? Yet they were willing to leave the comfort of their home in order to tell other people the good news of the resurrection.

How long has it been since you inconvenienced yourself to tell someone about Jesus Christ?

Take a moment now and thank God for the one who told you about Jesus.

When have you ever suddenly understood a truth that had earlier confused you?

What is it like to have an event turn out differently than you had expected?

Thomas means "twin" (Greek); Didymus also means "twin" (Aramaic). Several of the early Christian writers attempted to identify his twin. But it is likely the twin is not even mentioned in the New Testament, making such identification impossible

Thomas is said to have been born in Antioch, but he is also considered by some a native of Galilee, like most of the other apostles (John 21:2).

In the first three gospels there is an account of his call to apostleship (Matthew 10:3; Mark 3:18; Luke 6:15). The rest we know of him is derived from the gospel of John. When Jesus declared His intention of going to Bethany after Lazarus' death, Thomas, apprehensive of danger, said to the other disciples, "*Let us also go, that we may die with Him*" (John 11:16).

At the Last Supper, as Jesus was speaking of His death, Thomas said to Him, "*Lord, we do not know where You are going, how do we know the way*?" (14:5).

Thomas is most famous for the events recorded in this chapter of the Gospel of John. When Jesus appeared to his followers on the day of His resurrection Thomas was not present. Later when he was told of the appearance of Jesus his reply was, "*Unless I see these things for myself I will not believe.*"

A week later Jesus again appeared to the group of disciples; this time Thomas was present. Turning to Thomas He said, "*Put your finger here, see my hands. Reach out your hand and put it into my side. Stop doubting and believe.*"

The effect upon Thomas was immediate. Doubt was removed, and his faith was restored. The words in which he expressed his belief give a wonderful description of the true nature of Jesus Christ: Thomas said to Him, "*My Lord and my God!*"

The answer Jesus gave to Thomas can be used as a summation of the truth of this entire incident. Jesus said to him, "*Because you have seen Me, have you believed? Blessed are they who did not see, and yet believed.*"

After this we hear of Thomas on only two occasions: near the Sea of Galilee with six other disciples (John 21:2), and later with the apostles after the ascension of Jesus (Acts 1:13).

Early traditions, as believed in the fourth century, represent him as preaching in Parthia, or Persia, and as finally being buried in Edessa. Later traditions say he was a missionary to India. His martyrdom is said to have been by arrows as he was praying.

Thomas is an example to each of us in the area of doubt. Jesus was not harsh with His disciple; He met with Thomas and took away all of his doubts.

It is all right to express our doubts to Jesus! We need to remember He walked this earth just as we do. He knows and understands our difficulties and He has faced the same trials.

When have you had doubts about your faith? How should we deal with our doubts?

On what evidence do you rely for your belief Jesus rose from the dead?

Now faith is being sure of what we hope for and certain of what we do not see.
Hebrews 11:1

Summary of Acts 5:1-11

Ananias and Sapphira were a married couple in the early church at Jerusalem. After selling a piece of property, Ananias brings some of the proceeds to the apostles as a donation for the church community, but he secretly withholds the rest of the money. The text makes it clear that Sapphira is aware of the deception (Acts 5:1–2). Peter rebukes Ananias, who falls dead and is quickly buried (Acts 5:3–6). Sapphira arrives several hours later, and Peter inquiries about the property sale. After she lies about the price, Peter rebukes her, and she too falls dead and is buried with her husband (Acts 5:7–10). Their deaths generate fear within the church and the community (Acts 5:11).

This story's placement in Acts suggests a contrast with Acts 4:32–37, which describes the believers holding all things in common and donating real estate profits to the church.

Barnabas had been introduced in the previous chapter because he would be a major player in the immediate future of the church and an example of a generous giver. Many believe the positive response of the church to gifts from people like Barnabas became a source of envy for Ananias and Sapphira. Desiring that same esteem from others, *Ananias, together with his wife Sapphira, also sold a piece of property,* to give money to the apostles for the needy.

They could have given any amount of the selling price, but because they apparently desired the esteem Barnabas had received, they pretended to give all the money they had received for the field. Instead, however, they *kept back part of the money.* That would have been their prerogative. The problem was they were representing what they gave to the apostles as the total selling price. Their initial sin was lying and misrepresenting themselves to the apostles and the believers. They were hypocrites, boasting in a gift when they deceptively held back some for themselves. They also sinned in being selfish. They were serving themselves, not others, by their cover-up

Peter confronted Ananias with his sin and Ananias immediately dropped dead. Shortly after Sapphira arrived at the church meeting place, Peter asked her if what Ananias said was true and had he really given the entire purchase price for the church. When she replied that was correct, she also was instantly killed by God. Immediately fear fell on the entire church and people began to discuss the situation and talk to one another about what had happened.

The story of Sapphira and her husband forms parallels with several Old Testament accounts, most notably the story of Achan. In Joshua 7:1, Achan held back what was devoted to Jehovah at Jericho, a sin which resulted in death for him and his family (Josh 7:25–26). In Acts 5:2, Luke uses the same word for "kept back" as the Greek translation of Josh 7:1, suggesting he might have been thinking of Achan.

Other similarities may be found in the Old Testament stories of:

- Nadab and Abihu in Lev 10:1–2
- Gehazi in 2 Kings 5:26–27

Here is an example of how much God values truth and honesty in our service for Him.

The result of these events was great fear and "awe" of God.

Another point to notice here is no one seemed to think Peter, or the apostles had the power to make these events happen. All the credit was given to God!

When was a time you kept a gift that you had planned to give away?

In what ways do we sometimes try to gain undue credit or recognition?

Stephen

Acts 6-7

As the early church grew at Jerusalem there was more work to do than the apostles could do alone. A group of seven men were chosen to help meet the physical needs of the growing congregation. These men were to do the common daily tasks necessary to maintain the unity of the growing congregation. Stephen was one of the men chosen for this task. The Scriptures say he was a man who was full of faith and the Holy Spirit.

As he matured and grew in his relationship to Jesus, he was given great power. The Scriptures say he did many "wonders and miracles."

Stephen was so outspoken in his testimony for Jesus that soon many of the prominent Jewish authorities began to speak evil about him. They debated him publicly and were unable to answer his wisdom.

As he continued to preach and teach about Jesus their opposition grew more and more heated and soon, they began to attempt to remove him anyway possible.

They were unable to discredit his preaching, so they had him arrested and brought him before the Sanhedrin Council. This group of "godly religious leaders" hired men to give false testimony against Stephen. He was accused and convicted of blasphemy against the Temple and the Law.

Stephen was allowed to give a defense for himself. He was asked by the high priest, "Are these charges true?" We have a record of his answer in Acts 7.

Stephen began his defense by reviewing Jewish history from the time of Abraham until he arrived in his narrative at the time of the second Temple. He was attempting to show those who were listening that God was a God who could not be contained or limited to the land of Israel or the Temple in Jerusalem.

He illustrated his point by showing historically how often the Jews had strayed away from following God. He was bringing his narrative to a conclusion by showing how the Jewish "fathers" had persecuted the ancient prophets. He reminded them many of these prophets had been killed by their forefathers. He concluded by charging it was this group itself that had put Jesus to death.

The effect of this message was great conviction and anguish upon his listeners. They reacted in rage, seized him, and pulled him outside of the nearby gate in the wall of Jerusalem and stoned him to death. As these events were happening God granted Stephen peace and a vision of the glory of God with Jesus seated to the right of His throne. He prayed for the forgiveness of those throwing the stones as he died.

The story of Stephen's conflict with other Jews, his speech before the Sanhedrin, and martyrdom indicate he was one of the first believers to fully grasp the radically inclusive vision of Jesus. He may have integrated his cultural openness to Gentiles with Jesus' offer of grace. Stephen understood God and His presence was not defined by the prejudices of first-century Judaism or confined to the area of the temple. True spiritual union with the Father could occur in any place and at any time. Stephen didn't open the door to the Gentile mission; he provided the key. His successors, like Philip, stepped through the door and embarked on full-fledged Gentile mission.

If Stephen were alive today, how would other religious groups oppose him?

What qualities of Stephen would you like to see in your own life?

Faced with the violent mob, Stephen seemed fearless; how was he able to face this danger?

What would make it possible for you to be calm and sure in the middle of extreme danger?

He was a resident of Jerusalem during the earliest days of the church. He is later mentioned as preaching in Samaria and Gaza. Later in his life he lived in the city of Caesarea.

Philip was one of the seven men chosen as deacons in Acts 6. Of the seven men who are named (Acts 6:5) Stephen and Philip are the only two spoken of elsewhere in Scripture.

Philip is first mentioned when he is chosen as a "deacon" by the early church. These men were to care for the distribution of food and other daily tasks of the early congregation to allow the apostles more time for prayer and study of the word of God. The description of these seven men is they are to be men *"who are known to be full of the Spirit and wisdom."*

After the death of Stephen, the church began to face great persecution. Philip went to the area of Samaria and began to preach the gospel of Jesus Christ. Many people were saved, and Scripture records great joy filled the city.

As Philip was preaching and teaching in Samaria the Holy Spirit spoke to him and told him to go to the South; on the road leading from Jerusalem to Gaza. On his way Philip met an Ethiopian who had traveled to Jerusalem to worship. He was the treasurer of the government of Candace, queen of Ethiopia. The man was reading from Isaiah. Philip asked him if he understood what he was reading. His reply was no, he needed someone to help him understand. Philip began to explain the prophecy of Isaiah and its relationship to Jesus Christ.

The Holy Spirit helped the Ethiopian man and soon he understood the truth of Jesus as the Savior of the world. As they traveled, no doubt Philip explained more and more to him from the word of God. Soon they passed near a body of water and the Ethiopian asked Philip, *"Look here is water. Why shouldn't I be baptized?"* They stopped and Philip baptized him. When they came up out of the water the Holy Spirit suddenly took Philip away and the Scripture says the man **"went on his way rejoicing."**

Later Philip is found in Ashdod, one of the five ancient cities in the Gaza Strip. Here he preached the gospel in all the entire area and later settled in the city of Caesarea. Philip was still living in this city and serving God when the apostle Paul visited him in Acts 21.

We only know a few highlights in the life of Philip, but they are very instructive. He was a man God used greatly to open the gospel to many. He was willing to move into unchartered territory speaking to the Samaritans, who were considered half breeds by the Jews. Later, he spoke to the Ethiopian and to the Gentiles who lived in the area of Gaza and Caesarea.

He is not a man who was well known!

He is a man who was willing to follow God no matter the difficulty!

What can you do to be sensitive to the Holy Spirit's leading each day?

What is one thing you can do this week to overcome fear in witnessing?

If you could give all your effort to a single occupation and be among the best in the world at it, what occupation would you choose?

What one talent or gift would you really like to have?

Simon the Sorcerer Acts 8

The first time we meet this man he is a well-known celebrity in the city of Samaria. He was known for his miraculous great powers. He was a miracle worker and was the center of attention among all the people of the area. The people said of him, "*This man is the divine power known as the Great Power.*" He was amazingly popular and had a huge following because of his magic. He had been practicing his "miracle working" for a long period of time in the area.

He heard Philip preach and was amazed by the miraculous signs he saw Philip perform. He became a disciple of Philip and tried to learn all he could about the power Philip so openly displayed as he preached and worked among the people.

When the apostles in Jerusalem received word of the miracles and the reception of the gospel in Samaria, they sent Peter and John to the area to see what was happening.

When the apostles arrived, they met with Philip and listened to his account of how God had been working among the Samaritans. They met with the new converts and prayed with them.

One of the important things to remember as we think about these events is this is very early in the expansion of the church and the preaching of the gospel. These people in Samaria are the first to receive the gospel publicly outside of the city of Jerusalem.

There was no understanding about the indwelling of the Holy Spirit, or the power God gave to these new converts. The apostles came from Jerusalem to Samaria to ensure the unity and the cohesiveness of this new religious "movement." When the apostles prayed and laid hands on these new believers, they received the Holy Spirit.

When Simon saw the Holy Spirit was given with the laying on of hands by the apostles, he offered to give them money. He said, "*Give me also this ability so that everyone on whom I lay my hands may receive the Holy Spirit.*"

Peter quickly replied, "*May your money perish with you!*"

Simon asked the apostles to pray for him. We know nothing of him after this account. Possibly he was able to overcome his greed and serve God.

There are two major points in this passage.

- **The danger of associating money with the power of God is always present.**
- **The importance of maintaining unity in the work of God is primary!**

How are some religious leaders today like Simon?

How are some religious leaders today like Peter and John?

When is it most tempting to brag?

What are some of the trappings of money?

Most Samaritans and Jews didn't get along; why then did early Jewish Christians tell Samaritans about Christ?

What can help us change our prejudices against people groups?

In what way do some people try to "buy" God's favor?

His name means "God has been gracious." Ananias was a resident of Damascus. The time period was between 30 and 40 AD.

Ananias was an early Christian who had probably left Jerusalem and moved to Damascus because of the persecution that began after the death of Stephen. We need to remember at this point in the history of the early church nearly all of the members were Jews who had accepted Jesus as their Messiah.

The persecution which began after the death of Stephen was sponsored by the Sanhedrin Council of Jerusalem. They were acting in a way they thought was best to protect Judaism.

The mastermind behind this persecution was a man named Saul. The Christians of Damascus had heard Saul was on his way to Damascus to begin persecuting the new group of Christians who lived in that city.

As Saul was traveling to Damascus he was suddenly and miraculously converted when Jesus appeared to him in a light from heaven.

As a result of this experience Saul was blind. He had been brought to Damascus and was lodged in a house on Straight Street. We have no information about what other arrangements had been made to take care of Saul.

Whatever the arrangements were, God had other plans for him. Those plans involved Ananias.

God spoke to Ananias in a vision and told him about Saul. Ananias was instructed to go immediately to the house were Saul was lodged. He was further instructed that when he arrived at the house, God would tell him what to do.

The reaction of Ananias was immediate and predictable. He objected! The entire Christian community had heard many reports of the terror and persecution Saul had led in the city of Jerusalem. Why would God want him to go and see this man? What would happen if he did? I am sure all of these thoughts entered his mind. In all probability he presented all these objections to God. God gave Ananias a very simple and direct reply, "Go!" God did explain to Ananias, "*This man is my chosen instrument to carry my name before the Gentiles and their King and before the people of Israel. I will show him how much he must suffer for my name.*"

Ananias obeyed. He found the house. He found Saul. In probably the most difficult words this disciple would ever speak he said, "*Brother, Saul.*"

Imagine the fear Ananias felt as he approached the house. Imagine the excuses he could have come up with not to make the visit. But he obeyed God!

Because of this little-known believer's obedience, the man who wrote over half of the New Testament was brought into the fellowship of the church at Damascus.

We never know with whom we are dealing!

We never know how God will use an individual!

What do older, more mature Christians have to offer younger, less mature Christians?

How can you be a guide and help to younger Christians in your church?

Cornelius   Acts 10-11

These events took place near the Mediterranean Sea in the coastal area of Israel. Cornelius was a Roman military commander stationed at the military center in Caesarea. Cornelius was a Centurion, which means he was the commander of at least 100 men. He was part of a small group of Roman military officers assigned to the center of Roman authority in the area.

There are several interesting aspects to this account. One is the contrast between the two cities involved: Joppa and Caesarea. Joppa was one of the oldest cities in the area. It was viewed by the Romans as old, rundown, and not desirable. On the other hand, Caesarea was a beautiful new Roman city, with entertainment and attractions of the Roman world.

Another interesting observation is that Cornelius was obviously a Roman, but he was an observer of much of the Jewish law and morality. He and his family were devout and "God-fearing." He was a good moral man, but he did not know Jesus as his Savior.

God saw him and listened to his prayers, "*Your prayers and gifts to the poor have come up as a memorial offering before God.*" God sees and hears all men and He honors those who seek Him.

In a vision Cornelius was told to send someone to Joppa to the house of Simon and bring a man named Peter back to his home in Caesarea.

Cornelius sent messengers. They found Peter and he was brought to Caesarea. Cornelius had gathered together his family and many friends expecting the arrival of Peter.

Peter explained he had been told in a vision to expect the message from Cornelius. Cornelius, then, told Peter of the vision he had received and why he had sent messengers to bring him. Peter explained the gospel to those present and all who heard him were saved. The Holy Spirit was given to them and they were baptized. Peter stayed with them a few days and continued to teach them the things of Jesus.

This account is full of very important information about the expansion of the early church.

- We see Peter's struggle with the idea of Gentiles being accepted on an equal basis with the Jews.
- We see God's careful planning to assure the unity of His new church. God carefully teaching the continuation of many of the rules of Judaism would not be necessary under the "New Covenant."
- We see God in His love and kindness honoring those who seek Him; no matter their race or ethnic background.
- We see how important it was for God to maintain the unity in His new church.

Do you have neighbors and friends who remind you of Cornelius?

If a family from another country moved in next door, how could you welcome them to the neighborhood?

How do cultural and religious barriers hinder growth in our faith?

How do you know when God is speaking to you?

When do you act on what God tells you to do?

How can you be more open to God taking command of your life?

Barnabas: The Encourager — Acts 9, 11, 13

Barnabas was born on the island of Cyprus. He traveled through much of the Middle East and Asia Minor.

Barnabas is first mentioned in the New Testament because of his generous giving in Acts 4. He had relatives who lived in Jerusalem and was a cousin of John Mark. It may have been at the home of one of these relatives where the early church met.

He was the first to befriend Saul and believe his story of conversion on the road to Damascus. He brought Saul into the church at Jerusalem and guaranteed his truthfulness.

He was later sent by the church at Jerusalem to verify the reports of the remarkable growth of the Gentile church in Antioch. When he saw the reception, the gospel was receiving in this Gentile community, he brought a very encouraging report back to the Jewish Christians in Jerusalem.

He returned to the area and became a teaching pastor and later went to search for Saul of Tarsus, soon to be known as Paul. He wanted him to be a fellow teacher with him in Antioch.

After returning to Antioch and teaching for over a year Saul/Paul and Barnabas were commissioned to begin a missionary outreach to Barnabas's native island of Cyprus.

This missionary journey would grow in vision to include the area of Asia Minor just North of Cyprus. Churches were founded in Pisidian Antioch, Iconium, Derbe, and Lystra. Barnabas and Paul returned and gave a report of their success in spreading the gospel to the Gentiles.

Later Barnabas and Paul would separate and form two separate missionary traveling teams. The book of Acts follows the journeys of Paul and tells us nothing of the later work of Barnabas.

Consider these observations about Barnabas:

- Barnabas was a man on a mission for God. He was willing to go and do whatever God wanted him to accomplish.
- Barnabas was a man with a message from God. When he saw the results of the grace of God in the lives of the Gentiles, he quickly accepted their salvation and encouraged others to do so as well.
- Barnabas was a man of God. Scripture tells us he was a good man and full of the Holy Spirit.
- Barnabas was a man who was not bound by tradition. He was the first of the Jewish Christians to willingly accept Gentiles into the family of God.
- Barnabas was a man of passion. He believed in the salvation of the Gentiles enough to confront those who disagreed with him in Jerusalem and win their support.
- Barnabas was a man unimpressed by wealth. He sold what he had and gave his life to serve God.

If you and a coworker of your choice were transferred to jobs overseas, whom would you want to go along with you?

How could someone like Barnabas help heal wounds in a church group?

When should you give up your rights, your position, or your point of view for the sake of peace with another person?

How can God use the strengths and weaknesses of your personality to get His work done?

John Mark — Acts 13:1-13

He was the son of Mary, an apparently wealthy Christian, probably a widow, whose house was used by the Jerusalem church as a meeting place (Acts 12:12). He later traveled with Paul and Barnabas through Asia Minor. Legend tells us he was martyred in Alexandria Egypt by being dragged through the streets with a rope around his neck.

Mark was a cousin of Barnabas. Barnabas brought him to Antioch to help with the Gentile church in Acts 12. In the following chapter he accompanied Saul and Barnabas as they began their missionary journey traveling to the island of Cyprus.

We read early in this first missionary journey that Mark left the missionary team and returned to his home in Jerusalem. In Acts 15 when Paul and Barnabas were preparing for the second missionary journey, Barnabas wanted John Mark to accompany them and Paul refused. The dispute became so contentious the two missionaries separated and created two different missionary teams. Paul took Silas and returned to Asia Minor. Barnabas took John Mark and they returned to the island of Cyprus.

Although we are told nothing further regarding the success of the mission Barnabas and John Mark undertook, it is probable that Mark had matured enough to meet the difficulties of mission work.

The growth of his maturity is testified to by the fact that Paul mentions him in Colossians and Philemon as a companion and servant during Paul's first Roman imprisonment.

Later Paul wrote to Timothy and asked that Mark be brought to him during his imprisonment in Rome. He told Timothy that Mark was profitable to him for the ministry.

Mark also seems to have been a close friend of Peter. In 1 Peter 5:13 Peter refers to him as his son, perhaps because Peter was the one who had led Mark to Christ.

Mark is also the author of the gospel that bears his name. That gospel is the shortest of the four Gospels and it is the gospel of action. In this gospel Jesus is presented as a servant of God. Mark records many of the miracles and events in the life of Christ and gives special attention to all Jesus was doing.

What can we learn from this young man?

He did not get off to a very good start with the apostle Paul! Yet later in Paul's ministry Mark had served the Lord consistently enough he had gained Paul's faith and confidence.

We can also see how valuable family is in our relationship to Jesus. It was Mark's family which brought about his connection to Jesus and His disciples. His mother was a relative of Barnabas. It was to her house Peter went when he was released from prison by the Angel.

All of these "coincidences" show us how valuable our family ties can be.

What kind of an influence do you have on your family?

Lydia

Acts 16:11-15

Philippi did not have the required 10 Jewish men necessary to organize a synagogue. In cases such as this there usually was a place outside of town where Jews gathered to pray. Paul and his companions went to this place and there they found several women who had gathered. Lydia was one of these women and she responded to the gospel.

It is not clear if Lydia was Jewish or not. What is clear is that she was a woman impressed with Judaism and the morality of those who follow that religion. She is the type of person who was referred to in the book of Acts as a "God-fearer." In the book of Luke this term is often used to refer to Gentiles who attended the synagogues. There was no synagogue in Philippi, yet she came to here to pray.

Lydia was a business woman, apparently single, and very prosperous. Business people are often absorbed in their affairs and have no time for religion. But Lydia, despite all her secular obligations, found time to worship according to the Jewish faith. She made her way to the riverside where prayer was made. She knew in order to successfully meet the stiff competition of the Philippian traders, she needed grace as well as knowledge. At the riverside prayer meeting, perhaps, she met Jewish merchants, and with them eagerly listened to the words of Paul and his companions. As evidence of her surrender to the claims of Christ she was baptized. Her conversion was stated by a public confession and in her enthusiasm, she told her household what happened; all of them also believed.

Lydia was Paul's first convert in Europe. She was the first of many who would accept Jesus as the result of Paul's preaching. Becoming a Christian did not make her less of a successful business woman. Now she had Christ as her senior partner and with Him we can imagine trade remained good and much of her profit was used to assist His servants in the work of the gospel.

When Paul wrote his letter to the Philippians, we can be sure Lydia was included in all the saints at Philippi to whom he sent his salutations (Philippians 1:1-7); and was also on his mind as one of those women who labored with him in the Gospel (Philippians 4:3). When Paul wrote his exhortation - "Not slothful in business, fervent in spirit, serving the Lord" (Romans 12:11), he may have had Lydia, in mind.

"Not slothful in business"
If your business is moral and you work at it, we have the pledge if we honor Him in all transactions, He will honor us. God gives no reward for idleness or laziness.

"Fervent in spirit"
Moffatt's translation is good here. He expresses it as, "Maintain the spiritual glow," which, by God's grace Lydia was able to do as she cared for her business interests and pursuits, which were no hindrance to her spirituality. Too often, we can allow the secular world to rob us of our glow.

"Serving the Lord"
Lydia not only sold her dyes; she served her Savior. She stayed in business and used the money to help God's servants in their ministry. Her generous care of Paul and Silas, and of others, must have encouraged their hearts. Lydia was a devoted woman, and a conscientious business woman.

What is your idea of hospitality?

Why should we extend hospitality to others?

How can we have fellowship with other Christians when we are away from home?

What responsibility do you feel to witness to others wherever you happen to be?

Do the Wicked Prosper?

The senseless man does not know, fools do not understand, that though the wicked spring up like grass and all evildoers flourish, they will be forever destroyed. (Psalm 92:6-7)

It is deeply distressing to see abusive and reckless persons placed in positions of power and influence and to witness liars, cheats, crooks, and charlatans reveling in their success and enjoying the spoils of their dishonest behavior. For those of us who believe in a God of justice the prosperity of the wicked poses a serious challenge to our worldview. How can evil flourish if the universe is governed by a completely good and all-powerful deity?

For Judaism in Christ's day this problem was very real. The return from exile and the rebuilding of the Temple implied the punishment for their sins in the days of the Israelite monarchy had been paid in full

But the Jewish people continued to be subject to Gentile kingdoms whose rulers were guilty of idolatry, bloodshed, sexual transgressions, and every sort of wickedness. Jewish people lived in a world which daily challenged their view of riches: that power, happiness, and success are proof of God's blessing and approval.

It seemed those who worked with Israel's oppressors were awarded riches and honor, whether it was King Herod and his sons or the high priestly families who were infamous for their abuses. It was the godly who suffered shame and the faithful who suffered for their loyalty to God.

The resolution to this contradiction offered by the Psalmist, the temporary good fortune of evildoers ultimately leads to their destruction, was developed in ancient Judaism and is also reflected in the New Testament.

In the Israel Museum in Jerusalem are displayed, within a few feet of each other, the casket of **Herod the Great** and the ossuary of **Caiaphas** the high priest. Each of these men attempted to take Jesus' life, Herod failing when Jesus was an infant, Caiaphas succeeding with the help of the Roman governor, Pontius Pilate.

Each of these men enjoyed lavish lifestyles, exercised power, and boasted of success in their lifetimes. They received their reward in full. But now their bones have crumbled into dust and their success, their wealth, and their power are meaningless.

What will you leave behind?

Book Twelve

1. The Epicureans	Acts 17:18
2. The Stoics	Acts 17:18
3. Gallio	Acts 18:12-17
4. Paul in Corinth	Acts 18:1-18
5. Priscilla and Aquila	Acts 18
6. Apollos	Acts 18
7. Felix	Acts 22-24
8. Festus	Acts 24, 25
9. Herod Agrippa II	Acts 25, 26
10. Saul of Tarsus	Acts 8:1-3
11. Saul's Persecution	Acts 8:1-2; 9:1-25
12. Paul: Waiting on the Lord	Acts 9, 11
13. First Missionary Journey	Acts 13, 14
14. The Council in Jerusalem	Acts 15
15. Second Missionary Journey	Acts 15-18
16. Third Missionary Journey	Acts 18-21
17. Rome and Beyond	Acts 22-28
18. The Letters of Paul	Galatians
19. The Letters of Paul	I & II Thessalonians
20. The Letters of Paul	I & II Corinthians
21. The Letters of Paul	Romans
22. Prison Epistles	Philemon & Colossians
23. Prison Epistles	Ephesians & Philippians
24. The Pastoral Letters	I & II Timothy & Titus
25. Epaphroditus	Philippians 1-2
26. Timothy	Acts 14, I & II Timothy
27. Philemon	Philemon
28. Luke	Luke 1, Acts 1
29. Titus	Titus
30. James, half-brother of Christ	James
21. John	I John 1-2, Revelation 1

The Epicureans

"A group of Epicurean and Stoic philosophers began to dispute with him. Some of them asked, 'What is this babbler trying to say?' Others remarked, 'He seems to be advocating foreign gods.' They said this because Paul was preaching the good news about Jesus and the resurrection."

The Epicureans were a group of philosophers who followed the teaching of Epicurus. He founded a school of philosophy in Athens in 307 B.C. Three centuries later Paul met some of his philosophical descendants still following and studying his teaching.

The Epicureans relied upon sense experience for knowledge. This put them in opposition to those who chose to make statements about the world on the basis of reason alone, distrusting or rejecting the data of the senses. Epicureans were concerned with natural evidence and with practicalities, thus showing a somewhat scientific character.

The Epicureans judged the value of an action or thing in terms of the pleasure or pain it brought; a position called hedonism. It was egoistic hedonism because the person pursued his own pleasure rather than the pleasure of others. This description can bring to mind the image of an irresponsible glutton or lover of wild parties, but the image, encouraged by the modern sense of the word "epicurean," is misleading. Epicurus rejected just such behavior.

He realized temporary pleasure can lead to enduring pain and some pain can be beneficial. He viewed pleasure more as a quality of life than a series of thrills.

What he sought is better called happiness.

Basing his counsel on experience, he urged moderation, calm, friendship, a simple life. He avoided feasting, sexual passion, and strife.

The pleasure of tranquility, of peace, could be found in the absence of pain, and this was his aim. To ensure tranquility, a man must tend to his stomach; he must also attend to his mind, directing it toward wisdom.

Epicurus saw belief in gods as a serious threat to tranquility. Gods were generally viewed as emotional, meddling, and powerful beings who terrified ordinary mortals and created insecurity, not peace and happiness.

Epicurus taught we, and everything in our world, are made up of atoms of different qualities. For example, the atoms of the human soul are smooth and round. Although atomic theories often lead to the conviction that all human actions are determined by the laws that rule the motion of atoms, Epicurus' theory did not. He allowed for human freedom by claiming some atoms spontaneously leave their straight paths, thus setting off an unpredictable chain of collisions. Man's behavior is then free and not machine-like.

In spite of his freedom, man is still a collection of atoms, and when the atoms separate, the man ceases to exist; he is not immortal. Epicurus saw this as reason no longer to fear death, for after death all experience ceases. There will be no pain, and so there is no cause for anxiety.

In opposition to this thought: Paul taught about a God who is intimately involved in the world, the immortality of man's soul, and the truth that genuine happiness depends upon communion with and service to God. (Rom 8:6; Phil 4:6-7).

How do you see this philosophy expressed in today's society?

"A group of Epicurean and Stoic philosophers began to dispute with him. Some of them asked, 'What is this babbler trying to say?' Others remarked, 'He seems to be advocating foreign gods.' They said this because Paul was preaching the good news about Jesus and the resurrection."

Paul was familiar with the Stoic philosophy. It was very popular in his home town of Tarsus. It had begun in Athens around 300 BC, with Zeno's teaching in the "stoa" (porches) of public buildings and had spread throughout the Greco-Roman world.

The earliest Stoics were primarily concerned with the study of nature's origin and its laws. They were materialists, who believe all things come from the one basic element of fire and will eventually be burned up in a vast cosmic conflagration.

They had a cyclical view of cosmic history; one universe after another arises and is destroyed. Both the orderliness of things as we know them, and this cyclical pattern of history, were ascribed to the organizing and sustaining power of a universal force known as the *Logos* which was sometimes regarded as divine.

Its laws were the laws of nature to which all creatures must conform. It gives to all things their essential nature and so gives life and reason to men. In fact, the *Logos* is in man, taking the form of the human soul. Therefore, to live according to reason is to live according to the natural order of things, and this is good.

Zeno taught conscious obedience to natural law liberates a man from fear and concern about external.

The good life, then, is one in which reason, not passion, rules, and peace of mind and harmony with nature consequently prevail.

Stoic ideas proved attractive to Christians because of apparent similarities between the Stoic logos and the Logos of John 1:1–18, and between the idea of natural law and the Law of God.

Perhaps more significant is Paul's apparent agreement that the natural order of things embodies moral law, as in his verdict that homosexual behavior is contrary to nature (Rom 1:26, 27). For the Bible teaches the moral universe governed by divine providence: God's Law is written into the created nature of man.

Paul's address at Athens should be understood against this background. He preached a God who made the world, gave it order, and gives men life; a God who is Lord over all nations of men so they must live within the framework of his Law, but a God also who is both Judge and Savior.

The Stoics could not altogether agree with this last idea for, while they might regard whatever happened as the work of providence, their cyclical view of history conflicted with Paul's claim that all history is moving in linear fashion towards its culmination.

The last straw for these philosophers was Paul's mention of the resurrection. They were materialists whose god was an organizing force within nature rather than a transcendent personal being acting in ways forbidden by nature's orderly cycle of life and death. For them, death was a rationally inevitable fate to be accepted with equanimity, though ultimately without hope.

How do you see this philosophy expressed in today's society?

Gallio Acts 18:12-17

While Gallio was proconsul of Achaia, the Jews made a united attack on Paul and brought him into court. "This man," they charged, "is persuading the people to worship God in ways contrary to the law." Just as Paul was about to speak, Gallio said to the Jews, "If you Jews were making a complaint about some misdeed or serious crime, it would be reasonable for me to listen to you. But since it involves questions about words and names and your own law; settle the matter yourselves. I will not be a judge of such things." So he had them ejected from the court. Then they all turned on Sosthenes the synagogue ruler and beat him in front of the court. But Gallio showed no concern whatever.

Gallio was the brother of Seneca, who was the teacher and advisor of the Roman Emperor Nero. His name would have been well known throughout the Roman world. This may be the reason Luke chooses to tell us who the proconsul was in the case of Paul's hearing in Corinth.

The Roman government allowed the Jews to worship their God. When the residents of Alexandria, Antioch, and cities of Asia Minor sought to persecute the Jews because of their religion, Roman authorities always upheld the religious freedom of the Jews, as long as they did not forfeit these rights through revolutionary action.

To Gallio, the accusation the Jews leveled at one of their own countrymen must have seemed absurd. If they were unable to prove Paul was a threat to the security of Rome, he would dismiss the case. Further, the wording of the accusation referred to one God, namely, Israel's God, and not to pagan deities. In short, the Jews defeated their own purpose by their choice of words.

When the Jews appeared before Roman authorities, they usually wanted legal protection. For example, if the Jews had complained the civic officials in Corinth prevented them from worshipping on the Sabbath, Gallio would have to defend the Jews or face Caesar's wrath. But now the Jews came as accusers. Gallio understood they were talking not about Roman law, but about internal matters related to their own religion.

Gallio did not even give Paul a chance to defend himself before his accusers, because to him the matter had nothing to do with Roman law but with the details of Jewish religion. He told Paul's accusers. "If you were bringing to my attention information about a misdeed or a serious crime (but you are not doing so), I would have been justified in listening to your accusation (but now I won't have to do so)."

He concluded by telling the Jews he would not be party to their religious squabble. We can't gauge Gallio's tone of voice, but it seems his words were full of disdain and scorn: "I am unwilling to be a judge of these matters."

The Jew's case was dismissed and a group of the Greeks who had been watching the events turned on the ruler of the synagogue and beat him.

This decision gained some protection for Paul as he continued to preach in the city of Corinth. It is also worthy of note that there was tremendous hatred for the Jews in the Roman world.

Is there hatred of the Jewish race today?

Why is there hatred of the Jewish race today?

Do we see this sort of confusion in the 21st century Christians when we argue with each other about theology?

In these verses there are several other people mentioned by name: Priscilla and Aquila, v. 2; Silas and Timothy, v. 5; Titus Justus, v. 7; Crispus, v. 8; and Sosthenes, v. 17.

Paul seems to have remained in constant contact with the church in Philippi by sending people back and forth with information. The church in return sent messengers. The church even sent Paul an offering to help with all his expenses in Corinth.

Priscilla and Aquila received Paul into their home and allowed him to work with them in their profession of leather-working and tent making. We will discuss them in another study.

Silas and Timothy were traveling companions of Paul on the second missionary journey. We remember Timothy had joined the traveling group in Asia Minor, and Luke had traveled with Paul from Troas to Philippi.

Silas, of course, was with Paul in the Philippian prison at the time of the earthquake and the salvation of the Philippian jailer.

These two men, Silas and Timothy, are probably the source of information for the material we read in the book of Acts, for they filled Luke in on the details of what was happening in Corinth.

Titus Justus, v. 7, is probably also known as Gaius Titus Justus. He was a convert to Paul's preaching here in Corinth and was baptized by Paul himself. He is mentioned in Romans 16:23 and I Corinthians 1:14. He allowed Paul to center his preaching in Corinth in his home.

These last two names provide an interesting narrative about Paul's work in the church at Corinth.

After Paul moved into the home of Titus Justus, we are told that Crispus, the synagogue ruler, and his entire household believed on the Lord and many of the Corinthians who heard him believed and were baptized.

It was the synagogue which usually provided Paul with a preaching place and eventually his opposition. In an unusual turn of events, the president of the synagogue believed and became a follower of Christ.

The opposition then became so furious because of Paul's preaching that God appeared to him in a vision and told him no one would harm him. Therefore, Paul continued his preaching for a year and a half.

The next event we have recorded at Corinth is Paul's accusation by the Jews and his appearance before Gallo. The final verse of this scene tells us the Greeks present at the court turned on the Jewish leader of the synagogue and beat him. His name is recorded as Sosthenes. He had been chosen to replace Crispus.

When Paul later wrote to the church at Corinth, he mentions Sosthenes and calls him "our brother." Apparently after Sosthenes was beaten in the presence of Roman officials and they did not interfere, the other Jews present fled the scene and left Sosthenes beaten and wounded on the pavement. In all probability, Paul and the other Christians ministered to the man and as a result he was converted and became a believer.

Why would Paul have welcomed an encouraging word from the Lord?

Christianity throughout the Roman world was known for its love and concern for others, even its enemies!

How do Christians take for granted their freedom to practice their faith?

Priscilla and Aquila — Acts 18

Priscilla is a Roman name meaning "ancient" or "little old woman." Aquila is a Roman name meaning "eagle."

They were born in Pontus, a large geographic district in northern Asia Minor. They were living in Rome when the Emperor Claudius issued a decree requiring all Jews to leave the city.

The decree which caused Aquila and Priscilla to leave Rome was issued by Claudius in 49 A.D.

We do not know when this Jewish couple became Christians. When Paul arrived in the city of Corinth after leaving Athens, he met them because they were of the same occupation. He apparently became part of their business establishment and for a period lived with them.

We do not know if they were Christians before they left Rome, but we do know they worked with Paul very closely in establishing the church at Corinth. So, if they were not Christians when they arrived in Corinth, very soon after meeting Paul they became believers.

It is probable the early church in Corinth met in their home. We can also determine from the background material the three of them, Paul, Aquila, and Priscilla, were involved in the synagogue at Corinth.

Later they traveled with Paul to Ephesus and helped establish the church in that city as well.

In Ephesus we are told they remained behind when Paul returned to Jerusalem after the second missionary journey. While Paul was in Jerusalem a Jew named Apollos came to the church at Ephesus and began teaching. This man's knowledge of Jesus Christ and the Holy Spirit was incomplete and when Aquila and Priscilla heard him preach, they understood he needed more instruction.

He was an excellent teacher but at this stage in the early church he did not have all the information about the coming of the Holy Spirit. Because of this Aquila and Priscilla took him into their home and very carefully began to teach him the complete truth of the indwelling of the Holy Spirit.

This shows us something of the sensitivity of this couple. They did not confront him publicly or create a negative situation. They instructed and cared for him and as a result he became one of the great teachers in the early church.

From the letter to the Romans we learn that Aquila and Priscilla later moved back to Rome and were active in the church in that city.

When we stop and think about this couple, we should be amazed at the impact they had on the early church and the spread of the gospel throughout the Roman world.

They played a major part in the churches of Corinth, Ephesus, and Rome.

This is a couple, though not widely recognized, who played a major part in the development of the early church and the writing of the New Testament.

What could Priscilla and Aquila do to help your church?

What methods did Priscilla and Aquila use to encourage and teach other Christians?

What means has God given us for communicating encouragement to one another?

They were not theologians; they were not apostles: they were common people.

Acts 18:24 introduces Apollos as a Jew and a native of Alexandria in Egypt. Since Alexandria was the cultural and educational center of the Hellenistic world, Apollos would have been raised in a context of both Greek and Jewish scholarship. Luke goes on to describe Apollos as learned in the scriptures.

Ministry in Ephesus and Corinth (Acts 18:23–19:1)
Luke records Apollos had been "instructed in the way of the Lord" and he displayed a "burning zeal" in his speaking and teaching. However, he possessed a limited knowledge of things pertaining to Jesus and was acquainted only with the work of John the Baptist. When Priscilla and Aquila heard Apollos speaking "boldly" in the synagogue in Ephesus, "they took him aside and explained the way of God more accurately."

Apollos then left Ephesus for Corinth, having received letters of recommendation from the Ephesian believers. According to Acts 18:28, his ministry in Corinth was highly effective. He "greatly helped those who through grace had believed, for he powerfully refuted the Jews in public, showing by the Scriptures that the Christ was Jesus." Apparently, the negative reception Paul had received earlier (Acts 18:5–17) did not discourage Apollos from directly confronting the Jews in public debate, perhaps in the very synagogue which had given Paul trouble.

Familiarity with John the Baptist
Acts 19:1 record when Paul arrived in Ephesus, he encountered some disciples who, like Apollos, had only known the baptism of John and had not heard of the Holy Spirit. The clearest explanation is that while he lived in Alexandria (or, less likely, Jerusalem), Apollos learned of the earthly life and teachings of Jesus from the disciples of John, who continued spreading John's teaching after his death. This means that Apollos and the disciples in Acts 19:1 had not yet heard of Christian baptism and the coming of the Holy Spirit on the day of Pentecost. Acts 19:5 records Paul baptized the disciples familiar with John the Baptist "in the name of Lord Jesus."

Paul and Apollos in 1 Corinthians
In his reprimand of the Corinthians for their devotion to various Christian leaders, Paul mentions Apollos as one of the church's influential leaders, along with himself, Cephas, and especially Christ. Apparently, Apollos' teaching in Corinth had led to the formation of a group of disciples who aligned themselves under him. Apollos's highly effective ministry had incited jealousy and strife among them (1 Cor 3:3).

Apollos in the book of Titus
In Titus 3:13, Paul writes to his disciple Titus, "Do your best to speed Zenas the lawyer and Apollos on their way; see that they lack nothing" (Titus 3:13). The text implies Zenas and Apollos had been given the responsibility of carrying Paul's letter to Titus, which tells us Apollos had remained in association with Paul throughout his ministry.

Apollos and Hebrews
Apollos has emerged in scholarly circles as a candidate for the authorship of the anonymous book of Hebrews. Reasons that Apollos has been proposed include:

- His Alexandrian background
- His knowledge of Scripture
- His rhetorical gifts

How did Apollos put his gifts and knowledge to good use?

What approach did Apollos use in defending the Christian faith?

How effective would Apollos be in your church evangelism ministry?

Felix: The Man Who Procrastinated Acts 22-24

As Paul discoursed on righteousness, self-control, and the judgment to come, Felix was afraid and said, "That's enough for now! You may leave. When I find it convenient, I will send for you." Acts 24:25

Felix played an important role in the life of Paul as the judge to whom Paul was sent when his life was threatened by a group of religious leaders (Acts 23–24). Paul was brought before Felix, who was to decide whether Paul had committed a crime. Paul's appearance before him gave Paul the opportunity to share his faith in Christ with Felix, who was already familiar with "the way" (Acts 24:22–25); Paul was imprisoned for nearly two years (Acts 24:27), during which time Felix requested to meet with him frequently, apparently in hope that he would receive a bribe (Acts 24:26). Consequently, Felix's greed gave Paul repeated opportunities to share Christ with him.

Felix was married three times, but the names of only two of his wives are known. One was the granddaughter of Marc Antony and Cleopatra. His second wife, Drusilla, was the daughter of Agrippa I. His third wife remains unknown.

Rise to Power

Felix was assigned as the fourth procurator of Judaea by the emperor. Claudius appointed Felix at the request of the high priest Jonathan, who was in Rome protesting Felix's predecessor Cumanus' mishandling of Jewish uprisings. Approximately 30,000 Jews died during the Jewish riots while Cumanus was procurator. The rioting and Cumanus' reluctance to punish a Samaritan who murdered a Jew in Galilee, led to his removal.

Felix was a favorite in the household of the Emperor Claudius, so he was an obvious choice as the new procurator.

Reign in Judaea

Felix was a brutal and firm-handed governor over the province of Judaea. Although he was sent to bring the appearance of peace, his reign was marked by great violence and uprisings. He was forced to address problems which his predecessor had failed to handle.

Felix was serving as governor when the apostle Paul was brought before him in Caesarea to answer charges against him after the riot in Jerusalem (Acts 23:24–24:27).

After a five-day delay, Tertullus, spokesman for the Jews, and others arrived to state their charges. Felix put off a decision until he could hear from Lysias, the military captain.

In the meantime, Paul was placed in custody. Felix hoped to obtain bribe money for his release. As a result, Paul was detained for two years, during which time he and Felix often conversed.

The apostle's message of "justice, self-control, and future judgment" alarmed Felix greatly (24:25).

Why do you think most people do not trust or like public officials?

How was Paul "caught in the system"?

Why would Felix, known as a mean-spirited and selfish leader, show restraint in dealing with Paul?

Why do you think Felix rejected Christ even though he showed interest in Paul's teaching?

How can you show patience with the changes for which you are still waiting?

In what way is the gospel difficult to accept?

Felix, seeking to gain favor with the Jews, left Paul in prison, thinking that the Jews would compensate him for such a favor. But the Jewish complaints against Felix led to his recall by Nero, so Paul passed into the hands of Festus, Felix's successor.

As the trial in Caesarea progressed, Festus, like his predecessor Felix, appears more interested in appeasing the Jews than in providing a fair hearing, even though Paul insists on his innocence and the charges against him cannot be proved.

Festus, wanting to do the Jews a favor, asked Paul if he is willing to go to Jerusalem for trial. At this point, Paul was in danger of being attacked in Jerusalem, and he faced an unjust trial in Caesarea.

Paul appealed for a trial before Caesar, and Festus agreed to send him to Rome. As a Roman citizen, Paul had a legal right to appeal to Caesar. This plan also suited Festus, because sending Paul to Rome saved him from having to release a man whom the Jews wanted dead.

Festus recognized the case against Paul had more to do with religious disputes than with any violation of Roman law. In order to determine a charge, Festus had Paul testify again in a fact-finding inquiry, this time before King Agrippa, who was more knowledgeable on Jewish matters.

Rather than giving a legal defense, Paul takes the opportunity to proclaim the gospel.

Festus, unable to comprehend either a crucified Messiah or a physical resurrection from the dead, thinks Paul is out of his mind: "Your great learning is driving you insane."

Despite this reaction, Agrippa agreed with Festus that Paul had broken no Roman laws, saying, "This man could have been set free if he had not appealed to Caesar."

The material in Acts shows Festus to be an astute politician, seeking favor with the Jews, while at the same time trying to avoid a distortion of justice.

Festus's own account of Paul's trial (Acts 25:13–21) has "dashes of self-serving interpretation" in which he is careful to portray himself in the best possible light.

It is unclear what Festus might have done to appease the Jewish leaders if Paul had not appealed to Caesar, but he does appear concerned to give Paul a fair trial.

Paul's imprisonment under Felix and Festus was marked by politics and corruption, yet it was pivotal in sending Paul to Rome to preach the gospel.

One writer has said "What looks like a legal can of worms tainted with the odor of corruption is the unfolding of God's plan"

Why was opposition to Paul by the Jewish leaders still strong, even though Paul had been under house arrest for two years?

Why do we tend to hold on to past grievances?

How do you express yourself when you are on the defensive?

What does Paul's example of self-defense have to teach us?

Herod Agrippa II — Acts 25, 26

He was brought up in Rome with Claudius who would later become the Emperor. He was a descendent of Herod the Great, the Roman ruler of Israel at the time of the birth of Christ. He ruled Palestine from A.D. 50-70. When Herod Agrippa I died in A.D. 44, Agrippa II was only 17 years old. He was living in Rome and was a close friend of Claudius Caesar. At first Caesar contemplated making Agrippa ruler of all of Palestine, but he decided on a smaller geographic area for the time being.

Four years later at the age of 21, Agrippa II was appointed to be governor of the entire area. At the same time, he was made the director of the Temple at Jerusalem and the manager of its treasury. He had full power to remove the high priest from office at any time. This was a power both he and his father exercised regularly. These frequent changes in the Jewish priesthood for purely political reasons made Herod Agrippa II extremely unpopular with the Jews.

When we are introduced to Agrippa II in Acts 25, he had come to Caesarea on the Palestine seacoast to greet and honor the new governor, Festus. The Apostle Paul had been left in prison in Caesarea by the preceding governor. Festus asked Agrippa II to help him decide what to do with Paul. Agrippa II was viewed by the Romans as an expert on Jewish religion and customs. Festus had little training in these areas and was seeking the wisdom of an expert.

Luke gives a detailed account of the presentation Paul is allowed to give before these two Roman officials. Luke emphasizes the spectacle of the appearance by Herod Agrippa II and his wife Bernice. Paul was allowed to speak for himself in order to answer the charges being brought against him by the Jewish officials. When Paul addressed Agrippa II, he said, *"I consider myself fortunate to stand before you today as I make my defense against all the accusations of the Jews, and especially so because you are well acquainted with all the Jewish customs and controversies. Therefore, I beg you to listen to me patiently"* (Acts 26:2, 3).

Festus understood very little about Judaism and as Paul began to make his explanation Festus quickly became lost in the argument. At one point, Festus interrupted Paul and said to him, "*You are out of your mind; your great learning is driving you insane*." But Agrippa II was able to follow everything Paul was saying. Paul replied to Festus, "*What I am saying is true and reasonable. The King understands these things*." Paul asked Agrippa, do you believe the prophets? Without waiting for Paul told the King, "*I know you do.*"

After hearing everything Paul had to say, Agrippa II said Paul had done nothing worthy of being arrested. However, since Paul had appealed to Caesar their hands were tied and he must be sent to appear before Caesar in Rome.

How are some Christians like Agrippa and Bernice?

How did Festus use Paul to placate the Jews?

How did Agrippa's background and experience help Festus deal with Paul?

When you need the right kind of help, how do you go about getting it?

Why do you think Festus brought Paul's case before Agrippa and Bernice?

What was Paul's primary goal in his speech?

Agrippa was a man who knew with his head but denied the truth with his heart.

In all probability, his politics and position caused him to reject the truth of Jesus Christ.

Saul of Tarsus Acts 8:1-3

We are first introduced to Paul when he was Saul of Tarsus. He was standing over the first Christian martyr, Stephen, looking on as Stephen was stoned to death. From this gruesome introduction to the completion of his missionary journeys Paul became, except for Jesus, the most important person in the New Testament.

Before becoming the great missionary, Paul was known as Saul of Tarsus. As a devout Jew, Saul tried to stop the growing movement of men and women who followed Jesus Christ. He had permission from the High Priest to persecute those found worshiping Jesus (Acts 9:1, 2).

Saul was born in the city of Cilicia, in modern day southeastern Turkey. He was raised by a devout Jewish family, circumcised on the eighth day, and given the name Saul.

He inherited Roman citizenship from his father and was probably also given the Roman name of Paul. In good Jewish tradition he was taught the trade of leatherworking and became a "tent maker."

He received an excellent education, indicating his family was of some substance. He was taught all the Old Testament ideals of Judaism.

It is obvious from his letters that he was an excellent student. Sometime between the age of 10 and 15 he was sent to Jerusalem to study with the famous Rabbi Gamaliel.

Here he quickly moved to the head of his class and gained the confidence of his mentor by showing absolute dedication to the Jewish faith.

It is obvious from his early reaction to Christianity he saw the early Christians and their belief in Jesus as the promised Messiah as a threat to Judaism and everything he had been taught.

He was present when Stephen was on trial and heard his sermon relating the Old Testament prophecies of Jesus. He seems to have listened very intently and thought on these things.

Perhaps we see a conscience which has been stirred because he became a vehement opponent of what came to be called "the new way."

He was active in persecution and by his own testimony gave his support in trials in which early Christians were sentenced to death. Acts 8:3 tells us, "Saul began to destroy the church. Going from house to house, he dragged off men and women and put them in prison."

He was so totally consumed with his hatred of the early church that he devised a plan to take the persecution to cities beyond Jerusalem.

As a result of the persecution which arose in Jerusalem, we are told the church was scattered into many cities away from Jerusalem.

It is not overstating the case to say this persecution was in many ways fueled and maintained by the anger and hatred of this man Saul.

In what ways are Christians under attack today?

How can you respond whenever others attack or reject you for your Christian identity, views, or life-style?

At this point in his history it would be beyond imagination to think that someday people would name their dogs Nero and their sons Paul.

Saul's Persecution — Acts 8:1-2; 9:1-25

The stoning of Stephen was the starting point for a great persecution against the early church in the city of Jerusalem. Saul seems to have been the major impulse for this persecution. He proceeded from an inward impulse to murdering these people he saw as heretics. It is easy for us to miscalculate the ferocity with which Paul tracked down and destroyed these people.

The book of Acts uses a term in 8:3 which is used in secular Greek to describe a wild boar uprooting and destroying a vineyard. The translation most often used to describe this action is, "laid waste."

Much of our information comes from Saul himself as he writes describing his past actions when he is giving the testimony of his salvation.

Listen as he describes his own actions

- *For I am the least of the apostles and do not even deserve to be called an apostle, because I persecuted the church of God.* 1 Corinthians 15:9
- *Even though I was once a blasphemer and a persecutor and a violent man, I was shown mercy because I acted in ignorance and unbelief.* I Timothy 1:13
- *I persecuted the followers of this Way to their death, arresting both men and women and throwing them into prison.* Acts 22:4
- *And that is just what I did in Jerusalem. On the authority of the chief priests I put many of the saints in prison, and when they were put to death, I cast my vote against them.* Acts 26:10

He was on his way to continue this persecution in the city of Damascus when he met God personally.

As he and his companions were traveling along the road to Damascus suddenly an unbelievably bright light focused directly on this man. He fell to the ground and met Jesus personally.

As a result of this encounter he became blind and had to be led into the city of Damascus. Jesus told him, "Arise, go to Damascus; and there it shall be told you all things which are appointed for you to do."

Paul stayed in the home of a man whose name was Judas on the street called Straight.

God had already been working in preparation for the arrival of his newly chosen follower. God spoke to a man by the name of Ananias and instructed him to go and meet Saul, pray with him, and baptize him.

After this meeting Paul stayed with the Christians in Damascus for some time and later went into the desert that the Bible calls "Arabia." Paul sets the time of his return to Jerusalem as three years after his arrival in Damascus.

Paul makes several references to being taught by Jesus personally. These events seem to have been what was going on in his time in the desert for he was given individual instruction in a one-on-one classroom session with his new Savior.

Why do unbelievers sometimes oppose those who tell others about Christ?

Why do Christians sometimes get angry at preachers?

When your conscience is pricked, how do you tend to react?

What is the difference between opposition to our faith and opposition to our personality?

Paul was forced to escape Damascus by going over the wall at night. His preaching had stirred up such opposition in the city that the other Christians felt it would be better for him to leave.

He went back to Jerusalem and, not surprisingly, had difficulty finding anyone who would accept him. The Jews had heard stories of his conversion and he was considered a heretic. He found himself hunted down by the very establishment he had been helping.

The Christians, on the other hand, were not sure of his conversion and were afraid this entire scenario was an act to gain access to the inner circle of the church and kill even more people.

Eventually, he was taken in by Barnabas who sponsored Paul in a meeting with Peter and the other leaders of the church.

It appears Paul took up the work which Stephen had laid down at his death. He began preaching to the Greek-speaking Jews and quickly stirred up such opposition the apostles instructed him to leave the area and return to his hometown of Tarsus.

We are not sure how long he remained in Tarsus and we have no information concerning the events which would have taken place while he was there.

He would have been disinherited and ostracized by his family for his conversion to Christianity. They would not even have acknowledged his presence if he had attempted to attend any family gatherings.

He would be forced to take work as a tent maker in the marketplace of the city and make his own living.

This was probably a period of discouragement and difficulty for Paul. He knew he had been called and commissioned by God to preach the gospel.

Yet nothing seemed to be going as he thought it should. He was making no progress! No one seemed to listen to him when he preached! And no one wanted anything to do with him.

During his absence, the churches in Palestine and Syria had been growing rapidly. Barnabas had been sent to lead the church in Antioch of Syria.

This church was composed to a large extent by Greek-speaking Jews who had come to believe that Jesus was the Messiah. The work in the church was progressing so rapidly Barnabas felt he needed help. He knew just the man for the job! He set out to Tarsus to find Saul.

The word used to describe his search in the book of Acts indicates it was not easy for Barnabas to find this man. When he did finally locate him, he told him what was going on and asked him if he would come and help in the work at Antioch. Paul agreed and returned with Barnabas, the first man who had really believed in him, and began to work with the church in Antioch.

We are told, "So for a whole year Barnabas and Saul met with the church and taught great numbers of people. The disciples were called Christians first in Antioch."

Do you like to wait?

How hard do you think it was for Paul to wait?

If you were more like Barnabas, how might people respond to you differently from the way they do now?

The First Missionary Journey — Acts 13, 14

After working in Antioch for approximately two years God began to move again in the life of this man named Paul. He had been commissioned by God to carry the gospel to the Gentiles.

In Acts 13:2 we read, *"While they were worshiping the Lord and fasting, the Holy Spirit said, 'Set apart for me Barnabas and Saul for the work to which I have called them.'"*

The church fasted and prayed and laid hands on these two men and sent them out to change the world. I am sure no one had any idea of the monumental events which were about to take place in the expansion of Christianity.

From Syrian Antioch they went to the island of Cyprus. They had a young man traveling with them whose name was John Mark. They landed on the East coast of the island and moved across by land to the west side of the island.

Here they had the opportunity to preach to the proconsul of the island, Sergius Paulus. He was greatly impressed with the message delivered by Paul, but we are not told if he became a believer.

We are informed of an unusual event which took place during Paul's testimony to this man. There was a sorcerer present whose name was Bar-Jesus; this man was apparently an advisor to the proconsul. He attempted to interrupt the message and finally Paul turned and rebuked him, causing him to be blind.

This seems to be a turning point in the missionary ministry of the apostle Paul. Up until this point Barnabas had been the leader in the journey, but from now on Paul seems to be the one in charge and the one with the drive and vision to continue moving on.

From Cyprus they sailed north to the southern coast of Asia Minor. John Mark seems to have disagreed with this move and he returned home. Maybe he was upset his uncle Barnabas was no longer in charge.

Paul and Barnabas arrived at the coastal town of Perga and traveled north through the Tarsus mountain range into the southern part of the Roman province of Galatia.

Their first preaching station was in Antioch of Pisidia. It seems Paul became ill after their journey and they were forced to spend time in the city allowing him to recover.

He preached in the synagogue in Antioch and we have one of his longest recorded sermons (13:11-41) given at the synagogue in this city.

Paul's message was accepted by the Gentiles and a great multitude came to hear him. The Jews became jealous, raised opposition, and ran Paul and Barnabas out of the city.

The two missionaries continued the road through southern Galatia preaching in the cities of Iconium, Lystra, and Derbe.
Luke records one major event in this narrative which took place in the city of Lystra. Here Paul healed a crippled man who had been lame from birth.

Paul knew when someone needed to be healed and what people needed to hear; why was he so perceptive?

It was in this town Timothy was saved.

He will become a traveling companion of Paul and someone Paul considered his own son in the ministry.

Paul and Barnabas returned to Syrian Antioch and gave their reports concerning the salvation of the Gentiles throughout the area of southern Galatia.

Sometime later some "representatives" from the church in Jerusalem arrived in the city and began raising questions about the salvation of Gentiles.

These men taught "*Unless you are circumcised, according to the custom taught by Moses, you cannot be saved.*"

This created a great division in the church. Paul and Barnabas opposed this teaching and eventually were sent to Jerusalem to get a hearing with the apostles and decide this issue before it created more division.

Most of those who heard of the work among the Gentiles by Paul and Barnabas praised God and gave thanks the gospel was being spread throughout the Empire.

However, there clearly had developed in the early church a group of Jewish believers who felt Gentiles must abide by the Jewish law of circumcision and accept Jesus as Messiah in order to be saved.

The apostles and elders met in Jerusalem to consider this new development and what should be done to maintain the unity of the early church. There was a great deal of discussion.

Peter was the first to speak and he reminded those in the meeting of the events at Caesarea and the salvation of Cornelius and his family, all of whom were Gentiles. He concluded his discussion by saying Gentiles aren't saved through Judaism, but through faith and the Jews must be saved the same way.

Barnabas and Paul began to tell the miraculous signs and wonders God had done among the Gentiles through them. They told of the joy and the obedience of the new converts.

The largest portion of this chapter is devoted to the response by James. He was the pastor of the church in Jerusalem and the half-brother of Jesus.

He supports the salvation of the Gentiles by quoting Amos 9:11. He then concluded all attempts to impose circumcision and legalism on the Gentile converts should be refused.

In response to the problem of working out the differences between Jews and Gentiles, James and the church asked the Gentile converts to be sensitive to the beliefs of the Jews and observe some basic guidelines. These four items were requested: avoid food associated with idols, abstain from sexual immorality, do not eat meat of strangled animals, and do not consume blood. These may seem strange to us, but they were common practice in the pagan religions of the Roman Empire, and they were in direct violation of the Jewish practice of separation.

The entire church agreed with James' proposal and drafted a letter to return to the city of Antioch in Syria. Two men were chosen to accompany Paul and Barnabas and deliver the letter. One of these men, Silas, will become Paul's traveling companion on his next mission trip. This was the first major test of the gospel as it was being preached to the Gentiles. Satan had attempted to confuse the issue by adding works to grace.

But the Holy Spirit had guided the deliberations and salvation by grace was preserved.

What is the best way to solve disagreements among Christians?

How would you handle a difficult problem with another Christian?

Second Missionary Journey — Acts 15-18

Our narrative takes a very surprising turn at this point. After some time in Antioch Paul and Barnabas decided it was time to return to the cities they had visited and see how their new converts were doing.

Barnabas suggested they take John Mark with them and Paul absolutely refused, probably because he considered him a "quitter." The dispute became so pointed that the two men separated.

Barnabas took Mark and traveled to the island of Cyprus. Paul took Silas and began an entirely new missionary experience by returning to the cities he had visited in southern Galatia.

When they arrived in Lystra, Paul decided to add Timothy to the traveling group.

As they visited each church, they left copies of the letter from Jerusalem and the churches were strengthened and encouraged.

After visiting these churches Paul wanted to continue to preach the gospel in the Roman province of Asia. He made several attempts to begin new works in this area and was unsuccessful.

Finally, God led him to the port city of Troas. It was in this city Luke was added to the traveling group as well.

Here Paul had a dream in which he saw a man from Macedonia asking him to come over into that area and preach the gospel.

Following the vision Paul and his companions traveled across the Aegean Sea and arrived at Philippi. They had moved from the continent of Asia to the continent of Europe.

The gospel had just taken a major step west into Europe.

With the addition of Luke to the traveling team we began to read more specific events of what took place in this new European ministry. Churches are established in Philippi, Thessalonica, and Berea. The results were very similar to those in Asia Minor: Paul was accepted by the Gentiles and opposed by the Jews.

Eventually, for his safety and the safety of the new believers, he had to leave town and move on to another preaching place. From Berea Paul traveled to Athens where he encountered the Epicureans and the Stoics and delivered his sermon on Mars Hill.

From Athens Paul went to Corinth, were he began a ministry which lasted over three years and established one of the most important churches in the Roman Empire. Corinth was a city which was a crossroads for trade and travel in the Roman Empire. People from all over the Empire regularly moved through the city. It was a great commercial city and the capital of the Roman province of Achaia.

Paul devoted the next five years of his life to establishing two major churches on opposite sides of the Aegean Sea. Corinth is west of the Aegean and Ephesus is on the east of the Aegean.

How can you make the message of Christ clear to your non-Christian friends and coworkers?

What does the example of Paul and his companions teach us about obedience to God?

With whom has God led you to share the gospel?

Third Missionary Journey

Acts18-21

After returning and spending some time in Antioch, Paul traveled from place to place across the region of Galatia visiting the churches which had been started on his earlier visits.

There is an impression of haste in these verses; a journey of some 1500 miles is described. Finally, Paul arrived in the city of Ephesus. Ephesus was the chief city of the Roman province of Asia and probably had been where Paul was seeking to go when he wanted to preach in Asia on his second journey.

Ephesus was as much an international city as was Corinth. It was called the "Light of Asia." It had a busy seaport and was the center of trade moving from Asia to Rome and from Egypt to Rome. The great Temple of Artemis or Diana was in the center of the city. This Temple was one of the seven wonders of the ancient world. Legend says the original Temple mysteriously burned on the night of Alexander the Great's birth.

The new Temple was rebuilt larger and more magnificent. It was 425' x 225' with 127 columns 60 feet in height. It housed a huge image of the goddess Diana made from a black meteorite stone which, according to legend, had fallen from heaven years before.

The Temple was the center of economics for the entire city. It was a banking house. The priests loaned money and charged interest and sold idols of Diana to the visitors who came. The entire month of May was dedicated to the worship of Diana. People made pilgrimages from all over the Empire.

Following his usual custom Paul began by preaching in the synagogue and after three months he was forced out. He began using a lecture hall to preach and teach Jesus Christ in the afternoon. He continued his work in the city for two and a half years. His fellow travelers were sent out of the city and founded the churches throughout the Lycus Valley. These churches would have included all the churches mentioned in Revelation 2 and 3.

As a way of authenticating his preaching message God gave him the power to cast out demons and heal people. He made such an impact on the city that those selling the small idols of Diana began to feel the impact and their revenues began to decline.

A great revival is described with many of the citizens of Ephesus giving up their black magic and false religion. The silversmiths felt the economic impact of Paul's preaching created an uproar and managed to charge Paul with disturbing the peace and defaming the name of the goddess Diana.

There was a protest rally against Paul in the great stadium of Ephesus. Archaeology tells us this Temple had a seating capacity of over 25,000 people. The protesters were accusing Paul with blaspheming Diana. Finally, the town clerk arrived and managed to get things under control. He used an argument very similar to the argument Gideon's father used in the book of Judges.

Paul was forced to leave the city and he traveled to Philippi, visited the churches in Macedonia, stopped briefly in Corinth and returned to Antioch in Syria.

The gospel was now firmly established in Europe!

How long did it take you to become a Christian?

Who helped you understand God's plan of salvation?

When did you realize that the Holy Spirit was at work in your life?

Rome and Beyond

Acts 22-28

At the conclusion of Paul's third missionary journey he returned to Jerusalem to give his report to the church. When he arrived, he found the city was crowded with thousands of visitors to attend the feast of Pentecost.

Paul was still being accused of preaching against the Jewish law and so James and the elders of the church suggested he take part in a Jewish vow at the Temple to show he was not preaching and acting against the law of God.

Paul agreed and made this attempt during one of his visits to the Temple area. In the process of completing the vow he was accused of bringing Gentiles into the Temple court. This was absolutely forbidden and was viewed as blaspheming.

The Jews created a riot and Roman soldiers had to arrest Paul and take him into the fortress of Antonia to save his life. He would have been beaten to death if they had not come into the court of the Temple and saved him.
The Roman judicial system was not able to deal with the Jews and with all the chaos and so he was transferred to Caesarea to await a hearing by the governor.

This hearing was stretched out to involve three separate governmental officials. Paul was left in prison for over two years. The Roman officials were hoping for a bribe.

Finally, Paul was put on a ship headed for Rome. Luke probably traveled with him on this journey and we receive great detail concerning the shipwreck which Paul and his companions survived.

After being hailed as a god for surviving a snake bite while building a fire after the shipwreck, Paul was invited to the governor's home where he healed the governor's father.

Everyone was well treated and in the spring of the year they were sent on their way toward Rome on a different ship.

When they arrived in Italy, Paul and his traveling companions were met by many Christians as they traveled the Appian Way on their journey to Rome.

Paul was given reasonable liberty in Rome. He was allowed a private home and people were allowed to visit him. He was able to preach to many people including many Roman soldiers.

Finally, after two years when no one from Jerusalem had come to Rome to bring charges, he was released, and the book of Acts ends on a triumphal note.

From his later epistles we can put together some of Paul's final travels. It seems he did realize his goal of being able to travel to Spain and preach. He then returned and visited many of his churches around the Aegean Sea.

It is during this final period of travels he writes what we know as the pastoral epistles of I, II Timothy and Titus.

Why was Paul's teaching hard for some followers of Judaism to accept?

Why was the attitude of the Jewish leaders in Rome less hostile than that of the Jews in Jerusalem?

Paul wrote approximately half of the New Testament. We cannot conclude our study without examining each one of these letters briefly.

These letters were written over approximately 20 years, from the beginning of his missionary work to the conclusion of his life.

In many cases we can arrive at an accurate date for when the letter was written, in other cases there is a great deal of guesswork involved.

Our coverage will consist basically of discussing each one of these letters from three points of view

- The occasion: what events caused the writing of the letter?
  - The purpose: what did Paul intend to accomplish by writing a letter?
  - The characteristics: what is unique about this letter?

We will examine these letters as nearly as possible in the order in which they were written. **Galatians** Paul and Barnabas founded these churches on their first missionary journey. Paul visited Galatia again with Silas on his second journey. On the third missionary journey Timothy was added to the traveling group.

During Paul's absence from the area, teachers from Palestine had moved in and begun to strongly oppose the teaching of Paul. These false teachers even went so far as to deny Paul had the authority of an apostle and they repudiated the doctrine of salvation by grace.
Paul wrote this letter to correct the error because he could not immediately return to the area. **The Purpose**

- The first purpose of this letter is to vindicate the authority of Paul as one who is sent by God to preach the gospel.
- The second purpose is to give a detailed explanation of the doctrine of justification by faith.
- The final purpose of the letter is a reminder that Christian liberty does not give a license to sin and ask for forgiveness later.

This short letter gives us a great deal of information about Paul. It shows his courage, his tenderness, his earnestness, and sincerity as he tries to deal with these new converts.

We should also note this is a "harsh" letter; there is not one word of praise for his readers. He seems to be angry at their denial of the faith and how quickly it has taken place. One of the unique things about this letter is it was personally handwritten by the apostle himself.

"See what large letters I use as I write to you with my own hand!" Galatians 6:11

This verse is the reason many people believe Paul's thorn in the flesh was a problem with his vision.

Why do you think Paul was so angry at these people?

What do you do when you are angry with someone?

The tone of Paul's letter is serious and abrupt; why did he write this way?

Why was it important that Paul establish his credentials?

Why do some Christians base their identity on things other than Christ?

Having experienced the hatred of the Thessalonian Jews even at Berea, Paul was concerned about the welfare of the Thessalonian believers. Paul's concern was relieved by the return of Timothy and his report. Since it was impossible for him to revisit Thessalonica, he resorted to letter writing.

When Paul received Timothy's report, he wrote this letter out of the gratitude of his heart. This letter reveals the appreciative nature of his heart and his close friendship with his converts.

He expressed his joy and appreciation that his converts had remained true to the gospel under severe testing. He had warned them before of persecution to come; he was relieved to know they had not failed.

Along with the good news from Thessalonica, Timothy had information about certain lies being circulated about Paul. Paul, therefore, found it necessary to defend himself from these charges.

Along with these things Paul also encouraged his converts to be free from the immoral practices of the heathen. Paul wanted to correct a trend of spiritual defiance; he told them to respect their leaders.

There are two major areas here: doctrinal and the value of the early witness to the teaching of the second coming.

The doctrine of the second coming is preeminent in this epistle, each chapter ends on this note. 1:10; 2:19; 3:13; 4:16-17; 5:23. The clear revelation of the Lord coming for His church is important.

II Thessalonians

The nature of further information received by Paul gave rise to this letter. We do not know who the bearer of the first letter was, but whoever he was he must have stayed at Thessalonica long enough to see the results of the first epistle. He then returned to Paul with more information. The Thessalonians made progress in their faith and love. They stood firm in persecution.

But there was a problem concerning the second coming of Christ. Thus, this epistle is designed to answer the problems caused by the erroneous views about Christ's return.

Corrections of two dangerous doctrines.

Doctrinal – "The day of the Lord is already here." 2:2

Practical – Some members had given up their jobs. They were convinced Christ was coming. The result was idleness. Paul rebukes this (3:6-15).

Some unique characteristics

Contents – Of Paul's nine letters to churches this is the shortest. Only Titus and Philemon are shorter. Yet there are four prayers for his readers.

Prophecy – 2:1-12 is one of the most distinctive passages in Pauline writings. Nowhere else is there such a detailed prophecy of end time events.

How do you react when you hear predictions about the end of the world?

If you could ask God any three questions about how to live your life, what would you ask?

How can you remain joyful when things go badly?

The Corinthian Letters

These letters are two of the most important letters which Paul wrote. We have already discussed his work in this city and shown how he intended to make Corinth and Ephesus the two main centers for Christianity in the Roman world. The occasion for the writing of these letters was not a single event but a series of events which occurred while Paul was in Ephesus. During that time, he stayed in contact with Corinth by sending people back and forth carrying letters.

I Corinthians

Paul primarily wrote this letter to correct disorders which existed in the church. He also answered questions he had received by letter from the people arriving from Corinth. He adopted an interesting method as he replied to their questions. He alternated between the faults of the church and the replies to the questions.

Only Romans is longer than I Corinthians. A great variety of subjects are discussed, most questions and answers he gives are given an entire chapter of discussion. There are doctrinal discussions of the Lord's supper (11) the church is the body of Christ (12), and the greatest chapter on the resurrection (15) contained in the Bible. One writer has called this letter "the simplest and most direct of all of Paul's epistles."

II Corinthians

Finally, Titus arrived with his report. It was generally favorable. But there was a small minority of opposition lead by some Judaizers. This statement of affairs furnished the immediate occasion for II Corinthians. The predominant purpose of Paul in writing this epistle is to fully re-establish his apostolic authority.

Paul did not want to do this. However, it was made necessary by the development of opposition at Corinth. The opponents were Judaizers from Palestine who attacked his person, his teaching, and his character.

He also used this letter as an opportunity to express his great joy over the triumph of the gospel in the face of opposition. He offered the church some instruction regarding the repenting offender. He dealt with the collection for Jerusalem as well.

The language of the epistle reveals it was written during a time of great emotional stress. It is marked with boundless variety, yet it is intensely Pauline. Its content shifts from one topic to another rapidly. The epistle reflects the various stations in Paul's journey and his emotion at each place. This epistle gives us some interesting information about Paul that would have otherwise been lost.

- 11:32-33 - The Jews enlisted the help of the Ethnarch of Damascus.
- 12:1-4 -Paul being caught up into Paradise.
- 12:7-9 -The account of his thorn in the flesh.
- 11:23-28 - Reveals clearly how much there was in Paul's life that remains entirely unknown to us.

Important doctrinal teaching in II Corinthians

2:12-6:10 -The nature of the Christian ministry
3:4-18 - The contrast of the two covenants
4:3-6 - The blindness of the world to the glory of the gospel
5:1-9 - The hope of the beyond
5:18-20 - The message of reconciliation
5:21 - The substitutionary work of Christ
6:14-7:1 - The nature of the world and the duty of the believer to separate from it

What can you do to make sure you are ready for Christ's return each day?

What hope can you share with someone who is convinced that death is the end of our existence?

The occasion becomes clear as the letter is read. It is not due to any internal conditions in the Roman church. It is due to the development of Paul's own plans. He has finished his labors in the eastern provinces (Rom. 15:23), and now he feels free to begin his labors in the west (Acts 19:21). As soon as he has taken the collection to Jerusalem, he plans to stop at Rome. Then he plans to go on to Spain (Rom. 15:24).

Although the immediate occasion for the writing of this epistle is obvious, it is difficult to determine the reason why Paul wrote the kind of letter he did. Paul must have had several purposes in writing.

Missionary plans
Paul wrote to enlist the cooperation and assistance of the church at Rome in his missionary program in the west. Romans 15:24 indicates Paul expected the church in Rome to support his work in Spain.

Center for Pauline Gospel
Paul wanted to win the church at Rome as a basis for his world-wide gospel outreach. Paul is seeking to bring about a union of Jew and Gentile in the church.

- He fully presents the doctrine of salvation through faith (Ch. 1-8).
- Then he deals with the relation of the Jews to their Salvation (Ch 9-11).

He is also seeking prayer support for his trip to Jerusalem (15:30-33). He was worried about this mission.
Theological Statement
This letter is a clear and comprehensive presentation of the doctrine of salvation by faith. It gives the heart of the Gospel.

Character and style

- The most formal of Paul's writings
- The outstanding characteristic of Romans is the universalism
- It shows that in all times and in all nations, men are sinners
- The gospel is offered to everyone
- The epistle is characterized by the systematic and logical arrangement of its contents
- It is one of the finest pieces of logic ever penned

Contents: It is an explanation of salvation by grace through faith. It is not a systematic theology

- Person of Christ not developed as in the "Prison Epistles"
- The resurrection is assumed not argued as in I Corinthians 15
- Eschatology is not as prominent as in Thessalonians

It is a comprehensive statement of the doctrine of salvation by faith

- Ch. 1-8 Doctrine presented
- Ch. 9-11 Relation of the Jew to this salvation
- Ch. 12-16 Practical application

Its influence
This letter has been called the masterpiece of the apostle Paul. Another writer called it, "The most profound book in existence."

With whom could you share God's unfolding plan of salvation for the whole world?

How would you explain God's plan of salvation to a friend?

What does our level of generosity reveal about our understanding of God?

These epistles were written by the apostle Paul while he was under house arrest in Rome. This is the situation described in Acts 28. We will examine all four of these letters. The first two we will look at are Colossians and Philemon.

Philemon

This short letter was written by Paul to assure Philemon of his high esteem for both the master (Philemon) and the slave (Onesimus). Onesimus had robbed Philemon and run away to Rome. In Rome he had encountered Paul and had become a Christian. Now in order to do what is correct he wanted to return to his owner and make things right. Paul wrote this letter basically to persuade Philemon to forgive, forget, and accept his new Christian brother. It is interesting to see Paul's skill in dealing with such a difficult matter. He uses the Spirit of love and kindness which Christianity gives. This spirit will ultimately spell the death of this institution of slavery. The way Paul treats Onesimus indicates the way in which Christians should approach the evils of human society.

The letter contains no specific doctrinal instruction, but it is full of practical application and information

- Personal value — Throws light on the character of Paul
- Ethical value — Shows what is right
- Providential Value — God is behind and above all events
- Practical value — Application of highest principles to commonest affairs
- Evangelical value — Encouragement to select and save the lowest
- Social value — The relationship of Christianity to slavery and all unchristian institutions

Colossians

Since Colossae was the major city in the area where Philemon lived, Paul used the opportunity to write this letter and send it along with his letter to Philemon. The churches in the area had begun to develop several problems and Paul used this opportunity to confront those problems.

His goal was to stabilize the churches and to disprove the heresy which was being taught. We are unsure of what group was teaching the false doctrine.

Paul's method of refuting the error is worth remark

- He does not consume a lot of time denouncing the false teacher
- He does not expound the heretical views
- He shows the root of the error lies in an erroneous view of the person and work of Christ

The outstanding trait of this epistle is its Christology

He is the image of the invisible God, the firstborn over all creation. For by him all things were created: things in heaven and on earth, visible and invisible, whether thrones or powers or rulers or authorities; all things were created by him and for him. He is before all things, and in him all things hold together. And he is the head of the body, the church; he is the beginning and the firstborn from among the dead, so that in everything he might have the supremacy. For God was pleased to have all his fullness dwell in him, and through him to reconcile to himself all things, whether things on earth or things in heaven, by making peace through his blood, shed on the cross. Once you were alienated from God and were enemies in your minds because of your evil behavior. But now he has reconciled you by Christ's physical body through death to present you holy in his sight, without blemish and free from accusation. Col 1:15-22

What missionaries can you pray for on a regular basis over the next month?

To whom can you write an encouraging letter sometime during the next week?

Why do you think the letter to Philemon related to a specific relationship problem is included in the Bible?

Ephesians
Unlike most other Pauline epistles, the contents of Ephesians offer no indication as to the occasion for its composition. It does not appear to have been written to meet any crisis. It does not mention any false teachers. It appears the conflict which caused the writing of Colossians encouraged Paul to write this letter to the Ephesians as a preventative. Paul takes this opportunity to explain Christ and His relationship to the church.

The purpose is not specifically indicated in the epistle. It seems while the theme of Colossians was still fresh in his mind, Paul decided to write this epistle in which he set forth the positive significance of the negative truths expressed in Colossians. Colossians is a corrective epistle; Ephesians is meant to prevent the introduction of any such error. The richness of thought in the Epistle is shown in its vocabulary. The letter contains 42 words which occur nowhere else in the New Testament. It is usually conceded Ephesians is the "deepest" book in the New Testament. Its vision stretches from eternity to eternity. The theme is the church as the body of Christ.

There is a unique relationship between Ephesians and Colossians
Paul wrote both epistles at the same time and used the same person to deliver them. A unique factor in similarity is 78 of 155 verses have much the same phraseology. The main theme of each letter is that the relationship between Christ and His church is dominant.

Philippians
The immediate occasion for the writing of this letter is the return of Epaphroditus to Philippi. He had come to Rome to bring Paul a gift from the church at Philippi and during his visit he became ill and nearly died. He is now well enough to return to his home church.

Paul took this occasion to write a letter of appreciation, friendship, and love to this church which had become so dear to him. He used the opportunity to provide the Philippian church information about his circumstances. He is hopeful and confident. He also used this letter to provide a warning against some of the same dangers he had seen cause problems in the churches around Ephesus. He warns his friends because he wants them to avoid the problems and concerns which come from false teaching.

This letter has all the marks of a free and spontaneous letter to a close friend. Paul mentions himself more than in any other epistle. He uses the first-person singular pronoun, either alone or with the verb 120 times.

Nowhere else does he use such warm expressions of personal affection

- "brethren" six times
- "beloved" three times

The words "joy" or "rejoice" occur 16 times in the Greek. Remember this epistle was written in prison.

How can you say thank you to God this week for what He has done for you?

What do you need to do differently to live for the praise of God's glory this week?

"Christian joy is more and better than happiness, because it does not depend on what happens."

When was a time you felt contentment in the middle of problems or uncertainty?

How could Paul be so flexible in his approach to life's circumstances?

I Timothy
Paul had found Ephesus to be a storm center of false teaching, just as he had predicted in Acts 20:29-30. Paul was now in Macedonia. He wrote to Timothy to encourage and authorize him to proceed. He was to supervise the organization, worship, and life of the various churches in Asia as Paul's representative.

Personal – to aid Timothy in his difficult task
Paul evidently felt Timothy would need some special authority. Paul also instructs him:

- To deal with false teachers (1:3-7; 18-20; 6:3).
- To engage in positive teaching (4:11, 16; 1:2b).

This letter is less concerned with doctrine than with the application of sound doctrine to outward conduct.
Some Distinctive Passages

- 2:1-4 Nature, scope and effect of prayer
- 3:16 A summary of the work of Christ from the incarnation to His final glory
- 2:5 One mediator
- 4:1-3 Coming apostasy
- 6:6-10, 17-19 Christian and material wealth

Chapter 3 is the most detailed list of qualifications for the office of bishops and deacons in the Bible.

Titus
The immediate occasion for the writing of Titus seems to have been the coming visit of Apollos and Zenas to Crete (3:13). Paul was prompted to write because of his personal observation of conditions on Crete and his realization Titus would need the encouragement and authority which the letter would give him. Paul wrote to provide Titus with specific instructions concerning his work in the churches. The letter told Titus that Paul was planning to send either Artemias or Tychicus to replace him and he wished for Titus to join him at Nicopolis.

II Timothy
Paul knew of Timothy's need of encouragement. Thus, Paul wrote him, knowing Timothy felt alone and would need all the encouragement he could offer. These are Paul's final words to Timothy; his son in the ministry.

Three Important Passages
All Scripture is God-breathed and is useful for teaching, rebuking, correcting, and training in righteousness, so that the man of God may be thoroughly equipped for every good work. 2 Timothy 3:16, 17
Do your best to present yourself to God as one approved, a workman who does not need to be ashamed and who correctly handles the word of truth. 2 Timothy 2:15
Nevertheless, God's solid foundation stands firm, sealed with this inscription: "The Lord knows those who are his," and, "Everyone who confesses the name of the Lord must turn away from wickedness." 2 Timothy 2:19

Seven-fold picture of the believer in Chapter 2

- A child (1)
- A soldier (3,4)
- An athlete (5)
- A husbandman, farmer (6)
- A workman (15)
- A vessel (20, 21)
- A servant (24)

What "trustworthy saying" did Paul leave with Timothy to encourage him? Why is it important for us to do what is good?

His name is derived from the Roman goddess Aphrodite or Venus. Most dictionaries give the meaning of his name as "lovely."

He lived in Philippi and was sent by the Philippian church to Rome to see the apostle Paul.

When we consider the amount of material available relating to Epaphroditus we are at the extreme opposite of the spectrum from the apostle Paul. Epaphroditus is mentioned only twice in the Bible. Both of these references occur in Philippians (2:25, 4:18).

Epaphroditus was entrusted with the mission of delivering the gifts of support to Paul from the church at Philippi. This man is an excellent example of the way communication was achieved between churches and individual Christians throughout the Roman Empire.

The message, which was to be delivered, whether money, food, or information was hand carried and delivered personally.

By sending a messenger two things were accomplished: delivery to the correct recipient was assured, and the verbal communication between the recipient and the messenger insured the communication was understood and properly received.

This was necessary during this stage of the development of the early church because there was no written Scripture to give direction as each church began to develop. Paul's concern with the unity of the church is obvious in all of his letters.

Epaphroditus apparently spent several weeks or months with Paul and they became very close fellow workers. Paul even called him a "fellow soldier."

Sometime after Epaphroditus arrived in Rome he became very ill and nearly died. This illness apparently lasted for an extended period of time. Paul gives an insight into the burden of illness in the first century with his remarks.

He praises God for having mercy on his fellow servant. We can gain some insight into Paul's personal struggles and difficulties from his comment on the illness of Epaphroditus. He says "*Indeed he was ill and almost died. But God had mercy on him, and not on him only but also on me, to spare me sorrow upon sorrow.*"
I think sometimes we are prone to believe men like Paul never struggled with anxiety or cares about the world or the people they loved. Epaphroditus shows us Paul felt all the human emotions, anxieties, and difficulties each one of us experiences in our daily lives.

In a tremendous compliment to this otherwise unknown Christian, Paul called him my brother, fellow worker, and fellow soldier. He compliments him on his dedication by saying he risked his life to bring your gift to me.

Why could Paul count on Timothy and Epaphroditus?

In what ways have you proved to be a reliable servant of God?

In what ways can you be God's "courier" to others?

Timothy — Acts 14, I Timothy 3-4, II Timothy 1-2

His name means "honored by God." He was born in Lystra, a city in Asia Minor. Timothy was the son of a marriage between a Jewish woman and a Greek man. The name of his father is not known. Some believe his father was a man of influence in the city of Lystra. Since there is no mention of Timothy's father most people assume, he passed away while Timothy was very small. Timothy was raised by his mother and grandmother in the Jewish faith. This provides an interesting set of circumstances for this young man. He was raised in a thoroughly Jewish atmosphere at home and yet he lived in a very non-Jewish atmosphere. Lystra was a Roman colony and probably the home of a military garrison.

This type of a city gave Timothy a unique perspective on life. His mother and grandmother taught him Jewish practices and the Jewish law. He was daily exposed to all the common practices of the Roman and Greek world. Timothy probably came to accept Jesus as the Messiah as a result of Paul's preaching on the first missionary journey. He knew the Jewish promises of a Messiah. Timothy is not mentioned until the second missionary journey. During the time between the two missionary journeys of Paul into the area, Timothy had, no doubt, been instructed and mentored by the leaders of the church in Lystra.

Timothy became a traveling companion and assistant to the apostle Paul early on the second missionary journey. He was one of his constant companions as the apostle Paul began establishing churches.

Timothy was very involved with the churches at Thessalonica, Corinth, Philippi, Berea, and Ephesus. The epistles of 1 and 2 Timothy were written by Paul to encourage and direct Timothy as he was pastoring in the city of Ephesus.

This young man became an apprentice and learned to serve God at the side of the apostle Paul. What a privilege and responsibility!

The two epistles written by Paul to Timothy were written to encourage and instruct the young man on how to carry out the duties of a pastor. Paul tells him several things that are important for each one of us.

- Stir up your gift (1 Timothy 4:14-15)
- Be a good soldier (2 Timothy 2:3)
- Watch your own life (1 Timothy 4:16)
- Be gentle (2 Timothy 2:24-25)
- Be impartial (1 Timothy 5:21)
- Flee from sin (2 Timothy 2:22)
- Give prominence to the word of God (2 Timothy 2:15)

When has the Lord delivered you from a hostile situation?

To what fellow Christian can you show support this week? How?

What comfort or encouragement can you provide to a person who is battling for the faith in a hostile setting?

Study to show thyself approved unto God,
a workman that does not to be ashamed,
rightly dividing the word of truth.

Philemon was a wealthy Roman slave owner, probably born in the city of Colossae. This short letter was written by the apostle Paul during his first Roman imprisonment.
Philemon was a member of the church of Colossae. Based on verse 19 we are able to conclude he owed his salvation to the apostle Paul, "*You owe me your very self.*"

Philemon's character is described in this letter as of great nobility. The apostle praises his faith and love. He mentions his benevolence and hospitality.

Paul wrote the short letter to Philemon as an appeal for the freedom of Onesimus, who was a runaway slave. Evidently this runaway slave had come to Rome hoping to become lost in the large city.

It is worthy to note at this point we can run away from human distress and circumstances, but we can never run away and hide from God.

God's providential control somehow brought Onesimus into contact with Paul while Paul was under arrest in Rome. Paul was able to lead Onesimus to salvation through Jesus Christ.

Paul was now sending Onesimus back to Philemon with a request that he be received as a Christian brother. Paul exhorts Philemon, *"I appeal to you for my son Onesimus, who became my son while I was in chains."*

Paul goes on to tell Philemon that Onesimus was no longer a slave, he was a brother. He told Philemon he believed God's hand was in these events from the very beginning and with God's orchestration everyone had benefited from these events.

- Onesimus had been saved
- Philemon had received a new brother in Christ
- Paul had been given the opportunity to lead Onesimus to Christ
- Paul had been benefited by the service of Onesimus

In this unique account there are several points worthy of observation.

Paul never condemned the Roman practice of slavery, but he never openly approved of it either. He made it his practice to make the gospel of Jesus Christ his priority in all situations.

We are enabled to see how the early church played no favorites. This is exactly what Paul was saying in Galatians 3:28, *"There is neither Jew nor Greek, slave nor free, male nor female, for you are all one in Christ Jesus."*

Early Christian tradition affirms that Philemon became pastor of the church in Colossae and later was venerated as the Bishop of that area. Tradition also tells us he was martyred because of his faithfulness and witness for Jesus Christ.

What role should we play in helping people be reconciled to people with whom they have had conflicts?

What do you think was Philemon's response when Onesimus returned to him? Why?

What broken relationship or promise from your earlier life are you willing to take steps to rectify?

Tradition tells us he was born in Syrian Antioch. We know nothing of when he was born, but he was a traveling companion of the apostle Paul.

Luke is an interesting person to study. He was a medical doctor. We have no knowledge of where or when he received his training. He was not a Jew.

Luke is almost universally regarded as the author of the gospel which bears his name and the book of Acts. Much of our information relating to his life is from the book of Acts. Based on the fact he is the author of the book of Acts, when the first-person plural pronoun "we" is used it is to be concluded Luke is traveling with Paul. There are nearly 40 of these uses. This is one of the reasons certain portions of the book of Acts are so much more detailed than others.

Luke was with Paul at the seaside city of Troas when Paul raised Eutychus after the young man fell from the second story window. It is the doctor himself who describes Eutychus as "dead." He then goes on to say, *"The people took the young man home alive and were greatly comforted."* Imagine events like this and the impact they would have on a trained physician.

From Acts 20 until the arrival of Paul and his company in Rome recorded in Acts 28 Luke is traveling with Paul.

Luke faithfully ministered to Paul during several of his imprisonments. He was with Paul in Caesarea during Paul's two-year imprisonment. He traveled with Paul from Caesarea to Rome. He endured the shipwreck and the storm described in Acts 27 and 28. Colossians and Philemon indicate Luke remained with Paul in Rome during this first imprisonment.

When Paul was arrested and imprisoned in Rome the second time, Luke came to minister to him. Paul writes to Timothy in 2 Timothy 4:11 praising Luke for his faithfulness. We know Luke was not killed when Paul was executed. His writings contain details which could not have been known if he had died with Paul.

Luke's two books are detailed treatments of the gospel of Jesus Christ and the expansion of the early church. They were written to help those in the Greek speaking Roman world to comprehend Christianity. These two works helped Greek speaking people realize this new religion, "Christianity," was not simply another kind of Judaism.

Imagine what it would have been like to be a witness to all the events Luke saw.

He gave us all the material we have relating to the development of the early church and yet he is only mentioned in Scripture in three places.

Luke is evidence you do not have to be prominent to make an impact for Jesus.

What did Luke hope would be the result of his writings in the life of Theophilus?

What does the phrase "*know the certainty of the things you have been taught*" mean?

What steps can you take to be involved in telling others about Christ?

Luke wrote; what can you do?

Titus Titus

The name Titus is a Greek form of the Latin name Titos. This was a very common name in the Roman world. There is no hint about the original meaning of the name.

Titus was a Greek who most likely was born in Syrian Antioch. Some historians believe he was a brother of Luke. He traveled with Paul and became one of his most trusted and faithful companions.

Titus is never mentioned by name in the book of Acts. This is one of the factors which has led many to believe he was the brother of Luke. Our only source of information relating to this man must be collected from what is said of him by the apostle Paul in several of his letters.

Titus is mentioned by Paul in 2 Corinthians, Galatians, 2 Timothy, and of course the letter Paul wrote to Titus. It is very probable the journey mentioned in Galatians 2 is the same trip recorded in Acts 15. If this is true Titus was very closely associated with Paul in the work in Antioch and he traveled with Barnabas and Paul to Jerusalem.

At Troas the apostle was disappointed Titus was not there to meet him (2 Corinthians 2:13). Titus had been sent on an assignment to Corinth. This assignment took longer than anticipated and Titus later joined Paul in Macedonia (7:6-7, 13-15). Titus was then sent back to Corinth with two other trustworthy Christians, conveying the second epistle to the Corinthians. This letter contained the request and instructions for Titus to direct the collection being taken for the poor Christians of Judea (8:6, 17). The "brethren" who took the first epistle to Corinth (1 Corinthians 16:11-12) were Titus and his companion, whose identity we do not know.

In the period between Paul's first and second imprisonment at Rome, Paul and Titus visited Crete (Titus 1:5). Titus remained in Crete as pastor. He later received the letter which bears his name. This letter was written to him to give instructions about how to proceed with the church in Crete. It is from this letter we learn Titus was converted through Paul's instrumentality (v. 4).

In Titus 1:5 we read, "*The reason I left you in Crete was that you might straighten out what was left unfinished and appoint elders in every town, as I directed you.*" The rest of the short letter consists of specific direction to help Titus as he pastored in a very difficult area.

In this letter Titus was instructed to do the following:

- Reprimand the apathetic life-style of the Cretans (Titus 1:10-13)
- Eliminate all heresy and forewarn the heretics (Titus 3:10)
- Preach complete and comprehensive doctrine (Titus 2:1)
- Avoid foolish philosophical speculations and arguments (Titus 3:9)
- Exhort with all your power and strength (Titus 2:15)
- Meet Paul at the city of Nicopolis (Titus 3:12)
- Help Zenas the lawyer and Apollos with their journey (Titus 33:13)

What leader has had the most influence on you? How?

How can you show support for your church leaders? When?

James is the Greek form of the Hebrew name Jacob, which means "supplanter."

James was the son of Mary and Joseph (Matthew 13:55; Mark 6:3). He was born in Nazareth and raised in that small town with Jesus and his brothers and sisters.

James was not one of the 12 apostles. He was not an early believer or follower of his half-brother (John 7:5).

According to 1 Corinthians 15:7, Jesus personally appeared to James after His resurrection and James was converted. In Acts 1:13-14 the Scriptures tell us, *When they arrived, they went upstairs to the room where they were staying. Those present were Peter, John, James and Andrew; Philip and Thomas, Bartholomew and Matthew; James son of Alphaeus and Simon the Zealot, and Judas son of James. They all joined together constantly in prayer, along with the women and Mary the mother of Jesus, and with his brothers.*

James became the first pastor of the church at Jerusalem. Three chapters in the book of Acts (12, 15, and 21) show us the position of leadership and authority he occupied in the early church. His faithfulness, prayer life, and leadership in the church quickly gained him the title of apostle. Paul referred to him that way in Galatians 1:19, "*I saw none of the other apostles– only James, the Lord's brother.*"

Tradition describes James as a Hebrew of the Hebrews, a man of the most rigid and ascetic morality, faithful in his observance of all the ritual regulations of the Jewish faith.

He is said to have spent so much time in prayer on his knees begging forgiveness for the people, his knees became hard like those of a camel in consequence of his constantly bending them in his worship of God and asking forgiveness for the people.

He was called "James the Just." Everyone had confidence in his sincerity and integrity, and many were persuaded by him to believe on the Christ. This Jew, faithful in the observance of all the Jews held sacred, and more devoted to the temple-worship than the most religious among the Jews in Jerusalem, was a good choice for the head of the Christian church.

He is the author of the epistle that bears his name. Any study of that short letter will reveal the reverence James had for the Old Testament. He clearly continued to practice the principles of the Old Testament and recognized his half-brother, Jesus Christ, as the Messiah sent from God.

Eusebius records James was thrown down from the highest point on the Temple and stoned as he lay dying. Ananus the high priest ordered his death. As a result of this action there was such an uproar that Ananus was deposed as high priest after only three months' rule.

James was known for practicing what he believed!

His letter places such an emphasis on doing what one says he believes it has often been misunderstood as downplaying faith.

He believed and taught, *"Faith without works is dead."*

His name means "the grace of God." Both he and his brother James were nicknamed "Boanerges" by Jesus. The nickname means "Sons of Thunder" (Mark 3:17).

He was born in Bethsaida, a fishing village in Galilee. John was probably the younger brother of James (Matthew 4:21).

The mention of the following implies a position of some influence and wealth:

- "hired servants" (Mark 1:20)
- "private means"
- women who supported Jesus, including Simone, John's mother (Luke 8:3)
- "his own household" (John 19:27)
- his contact with Caiaphas the high priest (John 18:15)

John was a disciple of John the Baptist when he first met Jesus (John 1). John never mentioned himself by name in the gospel he wrote, but there are many euphemisms used to describe his presence. Andrew was the other disciple who followed Jesus that day. Simon Peter, Philip and Nathaniel soon joined with the other two spending time with Jesus.

Later they returned to their occupations in Galilee. I am sure as Jesus taught and ministered in the communities near the Sea of Galilee, they had many opportunities to hear Him speak and teach. John, his brother James, Peter, and Andrew were called at the same time. They were called "fishers of men." John, with Peter and James, was notable above the other apostles, entering more fully into a relationship with Jesus.

Mention is made of John

- at the healing of Peter's mother-in-law (Mark 1)
- at the ordination of the twelve apostles (Mark 3)
- at the raising of Jairus's daughter (Mark 5)
- at the transfiguration (Matt. 17; Mark 9; Luke 9)
- rebuking one who cast out devils in the Lord's name (Luke 9)
- seeking to call down fire from heaven upon a village of the Samaritans (Luke 9)
- with his mother and James asking for the highest places in the kingdom (Matthew 20; Mark 10)
- with Jesus on the Mount of Olives when He foretold the destruction of Jerusalem (Mark 13)
- sent to prepare the Passover (Luke 22)
- asking Jesus who would betray Him (John 13)
- with Peter and James in Gethsemane (Mark 14)

John was the only disciple present at the crucifixion and was appointed by Jesus to care for Mary (John 19). We are told by tradition he left the city of Jerusalem before 70 A.D. and began a long ministry in the city of Ephesus.

John is the author of five books of the New Testament; The Gospel of John, I, II, III John and the book of Revelation.

Along with Paul, John had more influence on the growth of the early church than any of the other apostles.

The Gospel of John is probably the most widely read book in the world.

Resources

It would be impossible to list every source which has been consulted in the preparation of this book. I have used material drawn from many years of teaching and study but let me make a few recommendations and observations.

One of the finest sources on the study of Bible characters is the "All" series by Herbert Lockyer. There are also numerous individual volumes written on Bible characters. Charles Swindoll has several excellent volumes. Several different historical studies were used. One of my favorite volumes is "A Survey of Israel's History" written by Leon Wood. The Baker Encyclopedia of Bible People edited by Mark Water is another excellent volume.

There are many good Bible dictionaries and encyclopedias which offer individual articles on Bible characters. Probably my favorite one volume Bible dictionary is by Merrill Unger. For a multi volume encyclopedia I recommend the International Standard Bible Encyclopedia; an older very dependable work. Also, the individual volumes in the NIV Application Bible Commentary was valuable. Zondervan's Handbook of Biblical Archaeology by Randall Price was also consulted.

Another very helpful volume was Jesus Through Middle Eastern Eyes by Kenneth Bailey; a series of cultural studies by an author who has worked, taught and written in the Middle East for many years.

–HS

About the Author

Hunter Sherman and his wife, Louisa, live in Springfield, MO. Dr. Sherman began his Christian service in 1966, taught at Baptist Bible College, Springfield, MO; pastored Bellview Baptist Church from 1983 to 2012; served as professor for Rockbridge Seminary; currently pastoring Flat Creek Baptist Church, Cape Fair, MO, and also currently Vice President of Academics, Baptist Bible College Asia, Manila, PI.

Dr. Sherman's education includes a Bachelor of Arts - University of California at Long Beach; Master of Divinity - Talbot Theological Seminary, La Mirada, CA, where he was the recipient of the Audrey Talbot Award for Bible Interpretation, and Doctor of Philosophy - California Graduate School of Theology, Pasadena, CA.

Dr. Sherman writes an online daily devotional blog, The DailyVIEW.

Dr. Sherman and Louisa have two children, Whitnae and Garrett. They have the "two best granddaughters in the world" - Cara and Ashlynn.

Dr. Sherman can be contacted via email at docsherman@aol.com or through BBCA.org.

Made in the USA
Lexington, KY
16 September 2019